Aging, Health and Society

Aging, Health and Society

Cary S. Kart, Ph.D.
Eileen K. Metress, Ph.D.
Seamus P. Metress, Ph.D.
University of Toledo

Jones and Bartlett Publishers
Boston/Portola Valley

Editorial, Sales, and Customer Service Offices
Jones and Bartlett Publishers
20 Park Plaza
Boston, MA 02116

Printed in the United States of America
10 9 8 7 6 5 4 3 2 1

Library of Congress Cataloging-in-Publication Data
Kart, Cary Steven.
  Aging, health and society / by Cary S. Kart, Eileen K. Metress,
Seamus P. Metress.—2nd ed.
    p.   cm.
  Rev. ed. of: Aging and health. © 1978.
  Includes bibliographies and index.
  ISBN 0-86720-406-0
  1. Geriatrics.   2. Gerontology.   3. Aging.   4. Aged—Health and
hygiene.   I. Metress, Eileen K.   II. Metress, Seamus P.   III. Kart,
Cary Steven. Aging and health.   IV. Title.
  RC952.K37 1988
  362.1'9897—dc19   87-29740
                                                             CIP

ISBN 0-86720-406-0

Production: Hoyt Publishing Services
Interior Design: Stanley Rice
Illustrations: Judith L. Macdonald
Typesetting: Omegatype Typography

Contributing Authors

Ruth E. Dunkle, Ph.D.
Associate Professor of Social Work
University of Michigan

Gere B. Fulton, Ph.D., J.D.
Professor of Health Promotion and Human Performance
University of Toledo

Linda A. Hershey, M.D., Ph.D.
Associate Professor of Neurology
School of Medicine, State University of New York, Buffalo
Chief of Neurology Service
Buffalo Veterans Administration Medical Center

Christina M. Whitney, B.S.N., R.N.
Advanced Clinical Nurse, Department of Neurology
University Hospitals, Cleveland, Ohio

Preface

We published a book in 1978 entitled *Aging and Health: Biologic and Social Perspectives.* At the time, we described three consensus points or reasons for doing the book. Despite the passage of ten years, these three consensus points continue to justify our efforts and are reflected in this new book.

First, our classes are still eclectic. Whether in sociology, health education or anthropology (our respective fields), these classes often include graduate students as well as advanced undergraduates. These students identify themselves as nursing, premedical and predental students; students in health education, public health and health promotion, the allied health professions, anthropology, psychology, social work and sociology are also well represented. Compared with ten years ago, more students identify themselves as gerontology majors or even as business majors broadly interested in the administration of nursing homes, hospitals or health care in general.

Second, students still bring a high level of interest and enthusiasm to the courses we teach. The field of aging or gerontology continues to develop at a remarkable pace, and public attention is riveted on issues of health and aging. Most people born in the United States during the twentieth century have already achieved or will achieve old age.

How we deal with this phenomenon as individuals and how the society will deal with it remain important questions. For example, as of this writing, the Reagan Administration has put forth a proposal to expand Medicare and provide acute catastrophic health insurance for older Americans. Occupational opportunities for working with the elderly continue to increase, albeit not at the level they are needed.

Finally, there remain real problems in selecting text material for our courses. The choice seems to be between high-priced though narrowly-focused source books that are geared to advanced students and scholars, on the one hand, and encyclopedic works that are dry, uneven in appeal and very expensive, on the other.

We believe that this volume, not intended to be an encyclopedia of health and aging, effectively introduces students to the basic aging and health concerns of older people and to broader issues of aging, health and society. Most of the material presented here has been tested in our own classes, and the results continue to encourage us. Students seem to be more interested in gerontology when they leave these classes than they were when they began them.

The book is divided into three parts. Part I, The Basics of Aging (Chapters 1 through 5), includes five chapters dealing with the demography of aging; social, economic, and health characteristics of the aging population; biological theories of aging; and the social and psychological aspects of aging. Part II, Biomedical Aspects of Aging (Chapters 6 through 17), surveys the biomedical changes associated with the various body systems as they age. In addition, this part contains chapters on nutrition, drugs and aging, exercise, and sexuality in later life. Part III, Selected Issues in Health and Aging (Chapters 18 through 21), includes individual chapters on the patterns of health services utilization among the elderly, issues of institutionalization, alternatives to the provision of long-term care in institutions, and death and dying. A glossary and subject index are also provided.

Special acknowledgment goes to our contributing authors, Ruth E. Dunkle, Ph.D., Gere B. Fulton, Ph.D., J.D., Linda A. Hershey, M.D., Ph.D., and Christina M. Whitney, B.S.N., R.N. Without question, their efforts made this a stronger volume. We also thank Professors Ken Ferraro (Northern Illinois University) and Georgeanna Tryban (Indiana State University) and several anonymous reviewers who offered helpful substantive and stylistic comments on various parts of the manuscript. Dr. George Chengelis (Harvard Medical School) also deserves special thanks for his help with Chapters 13 and 14.

Kathy Annable deserves to be singled out for special acknowledgment. With grace and good humor, she has served as research assistant, word processor, proofreader, and all-round "gofer" on the creation of this book. Kathy, thank you!

Ten years ago, our editor was James Keating; our current editor at Jones and Bartlett is the same fellow. On both occasions, he provided all the rope and editorial assistance we required, for which we offer him our deepest thanks.

CSK
EKM
SPM

Contents

PART **I**

The Basics of Aging

CHAPTER **1**

The Demography of Aging

There are now more than 27 million people aged 65 years and older in the United States, and this group represents the fastest-growing American population. If the U.S. population of those 65 years and over were all grouped together, they would make up the most populous state in the nation, exceeding the population of California. Actually, there are more people aged 65 and older in the U.S. than the combined resident populations of New England (Maine, New Hampshire, Vermont, Massachusetts, Rhode Island and Connecticut) and the Mountain States (Montana, Idaho, Wyoming, Colorado, New Mexico, Arizona, Utah and Nevada).

Assessing the circumstances of old people in the United States, including their health status, needs and service utilization patterns, requires an understanding of how this group is currently composed, how population composition has changed from the past, and how composition of the elderly population may change in the future. Population attributes, such as *fertility, mortality and migration,* influence and are influenced by social and economic conditions. High birth rates (fertility) in the first decades of the twentieth century have yielded large numbers of elderly 65 to 75 years later. Progress in public health and medicine has reduced the rates of illness and mortality, especially among infants and the young, allowing more of the population to live to be old. Immigration to the United States has also had an impact on the growth of the elderly population in recent years. Migrants who were young adults at the time of their immigration before World War I increased the numbers of persons in their respective age groups, leading to large numbers of older people decades later.

This chapter presents a systematic study of aged population trends and phenomena in relation to their social setting (Petersen, 1975). Much of the available data in the United States define the elderly as those 65 years of age and older. Although 65 + is an imprecise identifier of the older population, it is a useful designation for gerontologists, and we follow it in this chapter. This definition is not universal, however. We all may recognize the differences between 20-year-old persons and 40-year-olds, but we often overlook the same 20-year difference between those who are 55 and those who are 75. Neugarten (1974) makes the distinction between the *young-old* (55 to 74 years of age) and the *old-old* (75 years of age and older). Recently, the National Institute on Aging has sought research proposals to study those individuals 85 years of age and older. This activity suggests the usefulness of further subdividing the old-old into those 75 to 84 years *(the elderly)* and those 85 years and over *(the very*

old). The young-old are healthier, wealthier and better educated than the old-old, and their family and career experiences and expectations are quite different.

NUMBER AND PROPORTION OF THE ELDERLY

The elderly population of the United States has grown consistently since the turn of the century, when about 3.1 million men and women were aged 65 and over. By 1990 this population is expected to increase to almost 31.8 million (see Table 1.1), a more than tenfold increase. This is much greater than the rate of increase for the total U.S. population, which is expected to increase little more than three times, from 76 to 250 million, in the same period.

As Table 1.1 shows, the absolute and proportional increases in the aged population are expected to continue into the twenty-first century, though at a slowed pace until the 2010–2020 decade. Between 1990 and 2000 the projected increase in the aged population is about 3.2 million, or a 10.2 percent decennial increase. This compares with the

TABLE 1.1 Total aged population and percentage of total population that is aged, 1950–2020

	1950	1960	1970	1980	Projections			
					1990	2000	2010	2020
65 years and older (thousands)	12,397	16,675	20,087	25,708	31,799	35,036	39,269	51,386
Percent of total population (%)	8.1	9.3	9.9	11.3	12.7	13.1	13.9	17.3
Increase in preceding decade (%)	—	34.5	20.5	28.0	23.7	10.2	12.1	30.9

Note: Based on Middle Series Census Bureau Projections. These projections are based on the following assumptions: (1) an average of 1.9 lifetime births per woman; (2) life expectancy in 2050 of 79.6; and (3) net immigration of 450,000.
Source: Tables 2.1 and 2.5 in J. S. Siegel and M. Davidson, *Demographic and Socioeconomic Aspects of Aging in the United States* (U.S. Department of Commerce, Bureau of the Census, CPR Special Studies Series P-23, No. 138, August, 1984.

6.1 million or 23.7 percent decennial increase projected between 1980 and 1990. This slowed growth rate in the elderly population is a reflection of the small cohorts caused by the low birth rate during the Great Depression and up to World War II. (All persons born during the same year who are analyzed as a unit throughout their lifetimes constitute a *cohort* (Petersen, 1975). The earliest of these small cohorts reach age 65 during the last decade of this century. When the postwar babies reach 65 shortly after the year 2010, the growth rate in the elderly population will again increase. Table 1.1 shows this; the projected increase in the elderly population between 2010 and 2020 is 30.9 percent. Later, this growth rate will most likely fall, reflecting a decline in birth rates that began in the 1960s.

Demographers have considerable confidence in these projections, because all those who will be elderly by the year 2050 have already been born. The accuracy of these projections will be determined ultimately by how accurately demographers predict mortality among these maturing individuals. This is not an easy task. For a time, demographers employed a single assumption of regular small declines in mortality rates among older adults. Census Bureau demographer Jacob S. Siegel (1979) indicates that this is no longer a safe course to follow. Death rates may decline at different rates in successive periods, or may even rise occasionally as they have in the last several decades. Crimmins (1980) suggests that we have entered a new era of mortality decline due primarily to reduced death rates from cardiovascular diseases and death at older ages. If this is so, there would be a substantial increase in the number of people over 65 in the population.

How accurate have past projections of the older population been? U.S. Census Bureau projections of the population 65 years of age and over for 1975 were published at various dates from August, 1953 to December, 1972 and varied from 20.7 million to 22.2 million. The current figure used is 22.4 million, 7.9 percent above the low estimate and 1.1 percent above the high estimate. As Siegel (1979) points out, the percentage deviation from the current figure declined as the publication date approached 1975. This is what might have been expected. After all, the first projections were made about a future that was 22 years away; but in December, 1972, this future was only three years ahead.

This phenomenon has already appeared in projections for the year 2000. Until 1975 estimates for the older population of 2000 were in the 28–29 million range. In 1975 the Census Bureau increased the estimate to about 30.5 million. The latest projection is 15 percent greater, or almost 35.1 million people aged 65 and over in the year 2000. According to Siegel, these newly revised estimates reflect lower-than-anticipated mortality in the 1972–1976 period and the use of more favorable mortality rates in making future estimates.

Death rates are expected to continue to decline, though at a less rapid rate than in the past two decades (Siegel and Davidson, 1984). Still, there is the possibility of marked future reductions in death rates at the older ages. Such changes in the trends could bring a somewhat larger elderly population and greater increases than are shown by the Census Bureau's middle series of population projections used in this text. As Table 1.1 indicates, the middle series of population projections used by the Census Bureau assumes mortality rates consistent with achieving an *average life expectancy at birth* of 79.6 years in the year 2050. Using the "highest" series of population projections, including the assumption that life expectancy in 2050 will be 83.3 years, the Census Bureau projects 36.6 million elderly in the year 2000 and 57 million by the year 2020. The "highest" series projects an aged population that is 1.6 million (or 4.5 percent larger than that projected by the "middle" series) for the year 2000 and 5.7 million (or 11 percent larger) for the year 2020.

What *proportion* of the total population older people will make up in the future will be determined in great part by fertility (birth rate) levels. The "middle" series of population projections used by the Census Bureau include an assumption of 1.9 lifetime births per woman. As Table 1.1 indicates, under this assumption, the elderly are expected to constitute about 17.3 percent of the total U.S. population by the year 2020. Using a "lowest" series projection, which assumes a fertility rate of 1.6, the Census Bureau estimates the elderly constituting 17.8 percent of the total U.S. population in 2020; with the "highest" series projection, which assumes a rate of 2.3 lifetime births per woman, the elderly would constitute 16.7 percent of the total population in the U.S. in 2020.

AGING OF THE OLDER POPULATION

Not only has the older population of the United States grown in size and proportion to the total population during this century, but it has also become more aged. Table 1.2 shows that the proportion of the aged who are 65 to 74 years of age has been getting smaller and will continue to do so until 2010; the proportion 75 and over has been getting larger, and this trend is expected to continue. In 1900 the proportion of those 65 and over who were 75 and over was 29 percent. By the year 2000 this figure will be about 50 percent. After the year 2010, the aging trend of the population 65 years and over should reverse itself as larger cohorts born in the post-World War II period enter the younger segment (65 to 74 years) of the elderly population. The median age of the total population is expected to rise from the present approximately 30 years to about 38 years by 2030.

TABLE 1.2 Percent distribution of the population 65 years and over, by age, 1950–2020

	1950	*1960*	*1970*	*1980*	*1990*	*2000*	*2010*	*2020*
65 years and over	100.0	100.0	100.0	100.0	100.0	100.0	100.0	100.0
65 to 69	40.7	37.7	35.0	34.2	31.5	26.0	29.8	32.3
70 to 74	27.8	28.6	27.2	26.6	25.3	24.5	21.9	25.6
75 to79	17.4	18.5	19.2	18.7	19.6	20.7	17.1	17.0
80 to 84	9.3	9.6	11.5	11.6	12.8	14.2	13.9	10.8
85 and over	4.8	5.6	7.1	8.8	10.9	14.7	17.4	14.3

Note: Based on Middle Series Census Bureau Projections. See Table 1.1 for explanation of assumptions.
Source: Siegel and Davidson, 1984, Table 2.6.

The aging of the older population expected to occur over the next two decades or so has important policy implications for local and state governments as well as for the federal government. Changes in the numbers and proportion of the elderly and very old should effect planning for the needs of the aged population. In brief, we should expect to see a relatively greater frequency of chronic debilitating conditions, accompanied by greater requirements for extended care among the oldest old (Siegel and Davidson, 1984).

THE DEPENDENCY RATIO

The growth of the elderly population has led gerontologists to look to the demographic relationship between it and the rest of the population. To the degree that the old are to be supported by the society to which they have contributed, this relationship may suggest the extent of social, economic, and political effort a society must make in supporting its elderly.

One measure used to summarize this relationship is known as the *dependency ratio.* Arithmetically, the ratio represents the number or proportion of individuals in the dependent segment of the population divided by the number or proportion of individuals in the supporting or working population. Although the dependent population has two components, the young and the old, students of gerontology have especially concerned themselves with the old-age dependency ratio. Definitions of *old* and *working* are "65 and over" and "18 to 64" years of age, respectively. Thus the old-age dependency ratio is, in simple demographic terms, $(65+)/(18–64)$. This does not mean that every person aged 65 and over is dependent or that every person in the 18-to-64 range is working. Still, we use these basic census categories to depict the relationship between these two segments of the society's population.

Table 1.3 shows old-age dependency ratios for the United States from 1930 to 2020. The

TABLE 1.3 Societal old-age dependency ratios: 1930–2020

Year	$Ratio = \dfrac{Population\ 65\ years\ and\ over}{Population\ 18\ to\ 64\ years} \times 100$
1930	9.1
1940	10.9
1950	13.4
1960	16.8
1970	17.6
1980	18.6
Projections	
1990	20.7
2000	21.2
2010	21.9
2020	28.7

Note: Based on Middle Series Census Bureau Projections. See Table 1.1 for an explanation of assumptions.
Source: Siegel and Davidson, 1984, Table 8.14.

ratio has increased in this century and is expected to continue to do so until the year 2020, when it is expected to increase dramatically. During the decade between 2010 and 2020, the baby-boom children of the late 1940s and 1950s will have reached retirement age, thus increasing the numerator; and a lowered birth rate, such as now exists, means a relatively smaller work force population (18 to 64), reducing the denominator (Cutler and Harootyan, 1975). The projected old-age dependency ratio of 28.7 in 2020 indicates that every 29 individuals 65 years of age or over will hypothetically be supported by 100 working persons between the ages of 18 and 64. This constitutes a ratio of between 1 to 3 and 1 to 4. In 1930, this ratio was about 1 to 11.

Some demographers have begun to distinguish between a *societal* old-age dependency ratio (discussed above) and a *familial* old-age dependency ratio. The familial old-age dependency ratio can be used to illustrate crudely the shifts in the ratio of elderly parents to the children who would support them. This ratio is also defined in simple demographic terms: (population 65–79)/(population 45–49). This does not mean that all persons aged 65 to 79 need support or even have children, or that every person in the 45 to 49 age range is willing or able to provide. Yet we use these age categories to depict the ratio of the number of elderly persons to the number of younger persons of the next generation.

Table 1.4 shows familial old-age dependency ratios for the United States from 1930 to 2020. The ratios increased from 1930 to 1980, and then are projected to decline until the year 2020, when a dramatic increase is expected. In 1930 there were 82 persons aged 65 to 79 for every 100 persons 45 to 49. This figure reached 185 in 1980, and a higher figure of 220 is projected for 2020. Changes in the familial old-age dependency ratio result mainly from past trends in fertility. For example, the high ratio in 1980 reflects the combination of high fertility (and immigra-

TABLE 1.4 Familial old-age dependency ratios: 1930–2020

Year	$Ratio = \dfrac{Population\ 65\ to\ 79\ years}{Population\ 45\ to\ 49\ years} \times 100$
1930	82
1940	95
1950	166
1960	129
1970	135
1980	185
Projections	
1990	174
2000	126
2010	126
2020	220

Note: Based on Middle Series Census Bureau Projections. See Table 1.1 for an explanation of assumptions.
Source: Siegel and Davidson, 1984, Table 7.9.

tion) in the early part of this century (population 65–79) and reduced birth rates during the 1930s (population 45–49). The high ratio expected in the year 2020 results from high fertility during the post-World War II baby-boom years and the lower birth rates of the early 1970s.

Shifts in the societal and familial old-age dependency ratios suggest that problems of familial and societal support of the aged have become increasingly problematic through most of this century and are likely to become quite serious after 2010. From this perspective it would seem that unless future aged are better able to support themselves than are the current cohorts of elderly, an increasing burden will fall on the working population, requiring government to play a larger part in providing health and other services to the aged.

Some would disagree, though. It may be argued that the dependency burden of the elderly should not be measured in a vacuum, and that the level of the child- or "young-age" dependency ratio should be taken into account, since it affects the share of society's support available for the elderly (Siegel and Davidson, 1984). Table 1.5 presents the old-

and young-age dependency ratios for the U.S. for 1970 and 1980 and projected through the year 2020. The child- or young-age dependency ratio, the number of children under age 18 per 100 persons 18 to 64 years, is expected to decline from 61 in 1970 to 37 in 2020. This results from a continued expectation of reduced fertility and implies a generally decreasing burden on the working population to provide support for the young. The combination of old- and young-age dependency ratios, representing an overall dependency burden on the working-age population, declined sharply between 1970 and 1980 and is expected to be relatively stable through the year 2020. The total dependency burden in 2020, projected to be 66, is almost precisely the figure (65) used to describe the total burden in 1980. Importantly, though, we can compute that between 1980 and 2020, the share of the total dependency burden accounted for by those under 18 years of age declines from 71 percent to 56 percent. Presumably, this decline should permit the conversion of some funds and other support resources from use by children to use by the elderly. Still, support costs for the elderly are generally thought to be

TABLE 1.5 Old- and young-age dependency ratios, 1970–2020

Year	$Ratio = \dfrac{Population\ 65\ and\ over}{Population\ 18\ to\ 64} \times 100$	$Ratio = \dfrac{Population\ under\ 18}{Population\ 18\ to\ 64} \times 100$	Total dependency burden
1970	18	61	78
1980	19	46	65
Projections			
1990	21	42	63
2000	21	41	62
2010	22	36	58
2020	29	37	66

Note: Based on Middle Series Census Bureau Projections. See Table 1.1 for an explanation of assumptions.
Source: Siegel and Davidson, 1984, p. 113.

greater than for the young and historically more likely to become a public responsibility. In America, support for children tends to be a private family responsibility (Clark and Spengler, 1978). As a result, the earlier statement that government may be expected to play a larger part in providing health and other support services to the aged would seem likely to hold up.

SEX, RACE AND ETHNIC COMPOSITION

Elderly women outnumber elderly men in virtually all settings within which aging takes place (Cowgill, 1972), despite the fact that the number of male births in a population always exceeds the number of female births (Matras, 1973, pp. 145–146). Typically, after the earliest ages, the male excess is reduced by higher male mortality; at the most advanced ages the number of females exceeds the number of males.

In the United States, the number of males for every 100 females—the *sex ratio*—in the over-65 population has been declining throughout this century. In 1900 the sex ratio was 102; by 1930 it had declined to 100.4. The sex ratio in these years, however, was still heavily influenced by the predominantly male immigration prior to the first World War. As Table 1.6 shows, the 1980 sex ratio in the older population was 67.5 (it was 94.8 for the total population) and is projected to decline further until about 2010. Principally, we continue to explain the sex ratio of the aged population in terms of the higher mortality of males, particularly at the ages below 65. This higher mortality among males reduces the relative number of survivors at the older ages.

The female population 65 and over has been growing much more rapidly than the male population in this age stratum (Siegel, 1975, p. 34). Siegel notes that between 1960 and 1970 the female population 65 and over

TABLE 1.6 Males per 100 females by age and race, 1950–2020

Age and race	1950	1960	1970	1980	1990	2000	2010	2020
All races								
All ages	99.3	97.0	94.8	94.8	94.7	94.7	94.8	94.6
65 years and over	89.5	82.6	72.0	67.5	66.1	64.5	65.2	69.1
75 years and over	82.6	75.0	63.3	55.2	53.5	52.5	51.2	53.3
White								
All ages	99.6	98.1	96.3	95.2	95.4	95.5	95.5	95.4
65 years and over	89.1	82.0	71.3	67.2	66.4	65.3	66.4	70.7
75 years and over	81.9	74.2	62.6	54.5	53.3	52.8	52.0	54.4
Black								
All ages	96.5	93.8	91.8	89.6	90.7	91.2	91.7	92.1
65 years and over	95.8	86.5	76.3	68.0	61.7	56.1	54.5	58.2
75 years and over	93.2	82.6	70.5	60.0	53.0	47.9	43.7	43.7

Note: Based on Middle Series Census Bureau Projections. See Table 1.1 for an explanation of assumptions.
Source: Siegel and Davidson, 1984; Table 3.1.

increased 28 percent, while the comparable male population increased by about 12 percent; between 1970 and 1980 the projected increase in the aged female population is about 25 percent, for the aged male population about 18 percent. This differential in growth rates, added to the continued excess of males among the newborns, yields a proportion of those 65 and over among females that is considerably above that for males. For 1980 aged females constitute about 13.0 percent of the total female population, and aged males constitute about 9.3 percent of the total male population. The sex ratio of the elderly population in 1980 corresponds to an excess of 5 million women, or about 19 percent of the total aged population. Twenty years earlier, in 1960, the excess was less than 1 million women (accounting for about 5 percent of the aged population). The latest Census Bureau estimates for the year 2000 project an excess of 7.6 million women, or about 2 percent of the total population 65 and over (Siegel and Davidson, 1984).

Because of enumeration problems, statistics on *minority elderly* should be viewed with some caution. Black elderly make up about 8.2 percent of the total elderly population, while 11.8 percent of the total U.S. population is black. In general, the U.S. black population is younger than the population of whites. The proportion of the black population that is 65 years of age and over is considerably smaller than that of the white population, for both males and females. Smaller proportions of blacks than whites survive to old age, though survival rates within old age are quite similar across the races. Siegel and Davidson (1984) point out that according to *life tables* for 1978, 77 percent of whites survive from birth to age 65, as compared with 65 percent for blacks. Yet the percentages converge, to 34 and 31 respectively, for survival from age 65 to 85.

The key factor in the relative youthfulness of the black population is the higher fertility among blacks. On average, black women have 3.1 children, compared to the 2.2 recorded for white women. This disparity in fertility rates contributes to the fact that, whereas approximately 39 percent of all blacks are under 22, only about 30 percent of all whites are in this age grouping. The median age of blacks is roughly 6 years less than that of whites. In 1981, black women had a median age of 26.5 years; the comparable figure for white women is 32.5 years.

Next to blacks, *Spanish-Americans* make up the largest minority in the United States, and this population is fast growing. In 1980 Spanish-Americans constituted 6.4 percent of the U.S. population, or over 14 million people. Officially, this population increased by 50 percent between 1970 and 1980. The actual rate of growth has probably been higher as a result of illegal immigration. Some experts forecast that before the year 2000 Spanish-Americans will become the nation's largest minority group (Farley, 1982).

The Spanish-American population is a heterogeneous group. About 60 percent are of Mexican origin. One in seven Spanish-Americans is of Puerto Rican background (14 percent), while 6 percent are Cuban and 21 percent are of other Spanish heritage. About one-half of the Spanish-American elderly are foreign-born. Cubans and Puerto Ricans are more recent immigrants than Mexican-Americans, many of whom are descendants of original settlers of territories annexed by the United States in the Mexican-American War. The Spanish-American population is even younger than the black population (43 percent under 20 years of age, versus 39 percent for blacks). High fertility and large family size, in addition to immigration of the young and repatriation of the middle-aged, contribute to the youthfulness of this group.

Many *ancestry groups* are represented within the United States population. Table 1.7 presents some data on single-ancestry groups, collected through the Ancestry and Language Survey conducted by the Census Bureau in late 1979. Though relatively small in numbers, those who identified themselves as singly of Russian ancestry had the largest proportion of elderly (27.4 percent), followed by the Polish (19.2 percent), English (17.9 percent), and Irish and Italian (16.3 percent). The relative "agedness" of those of Russian and Polish ancestry results from the considerable migration to the United States that occurred early in this century, mostly before 1924. This explanation may similarly work for the Italians. English and Irish migration largely took place in the nineteenth century. Thus the high proportion of elderly in these groups is likely a result of declining fertility in the subsequent years of the twentieth century.

Migration has had great impact on the age distribution of the foreign-born population in the United States. Before World War I, immigration was relatively unrestricted. After the war, changes in immigration policy brought a sharp curtailment to immigration. In 1970, a relatively high proportion of the elderly were themselves foreign-born—among those 65 years of age and older, 15.3 percent were born outside the United States. By 1979 this figure had dropped to 11.4 percent. We can expect the proportion of the elderly population that is foreign-born to continue to decline. In 1979, only 7.7 percent of those aged 55 to 64 years and 5.1 percent of those aged 45 to 54 years were themselves foreign-born.

GEOGRAPHIC DISTRIBUTION

The elderly population, like the total population, is not distributed equally across the

TABLE 1.7 Percent of the population 65 years and over, for specified ancestry groups, 1979 (single ancestry only)

Ancestry	Number, all ages (in thousands)	Percent 65 years and over
German	17,160	14.8
English	11,501	17.9
Irish	9,760	16.3
Afro-American, African	15,057	7.3
Italian	6,110	16.3
Polish	3,498	19.2
Spanish (including Latin America)	9,762	4.6
Russian	1,496	27.4
French	3,047	13.1
All others	19,105	15.6
Total	96,496	13.6

Source: U.S. Bureau of the Census, *Current Population Reports*, Series P-23, No. 116, March 1982.

United States. Generally, the elderly are most numerous in the states with the largest populations. New York and California have the largest elderly populations, with more than 2 million each. Pennsylvania, Illinois, Ohio, Florida and Texas each have over a million aged residents. Together, these seven states account for 45.4 percent of the entire 1980 United States population. Table 1.8 presents a listing of the states by percentage of population aged 65 and over for 1980.

In all states the aged population increased between 1970 and 1980, though at widely differing rates. Whereas in the District of Columbia the number of persons 65 and over grew slowly (4.9 percent), in Nevada the number of persons 65 and over grew by 112.3 percent. Florida showed the greatest absolute growth between 1970 and 1980— from 985,000 to 1.7 million.

Figure 1.1 shows the data on the geographical distribution of the 1980 aged population in a graphic fashion. In particular, the figure highlights the relatively higher proportion of aged in states in the Northeastern, Mideast-

ern and Midwestern regions of the U.S. and the relative scarcity of the aged in the Western region.

Residential Mobility

Some of the growth in state elderly populations is due to natural increase, but some is the result of interstate migration. Compared to younger persons, the elderly are much less likely to be residentially mobile. Whereas 40 percent of those aged four and over lived in a different household in 1979 from that in 1975, only 17.7 percent of those 65 to 74 years of age exhibited this residential mobility. Only 15.6 percent of those aged 75 and over lived in a different household in 1979 from that in 1975. In general, this pattern reflects movement to a different household in the same county. Less than 5 percent of the U.S. elderly population made an interstate move between 1975 and 1980, compared with 10 percent of the total U.S. population (Biggar, 1984).

Biggar (1984) points out that 12 states drew more than one-half of the nation's eld-

---

TABLE 1.8 States by percentage of population aged 65 and over, 1980

17.3	1	Florida
13.4–13.7	2	Arkansas, Rhode Island
12.4–13.3	9	Iowa, Kansas, Maine, Massachusetts, Missouri, Nebraska, Oklahoma, Pennsylvania, South Dakota
11.4–12.3	11	Connecticut, District of Columbia, Minnesota, Mississippi, New Jersey, New York, North Dakota, Oregon, Vermont, West Virginia, Wisconsin
11.3	3	Alabama, Arizona, Tennessee
10.3–11.2	7	Illinois, Indiana, Kentucky, Montana, New Hampshire, Ohio, Washington
9.4–10.2	10	California, Delaware, Georgia, Idaho, Louisiana, Maryland, Michigan, North Carolina, Texas, Virginia
8.4–9.3	3	Colorado, New Mexico, South Carolina
7.4–8.3	4	Hawaii, Nevada, Utah, Wyoming
2.9	1	Alaska
Total	51	

Source: C.M. Tauber. *America in Transition: An Aging Society,* U.S. Department of Commerce, Bureau of the Census, CPR Special Studies Series P-23, No. 128, Revised December 1983.

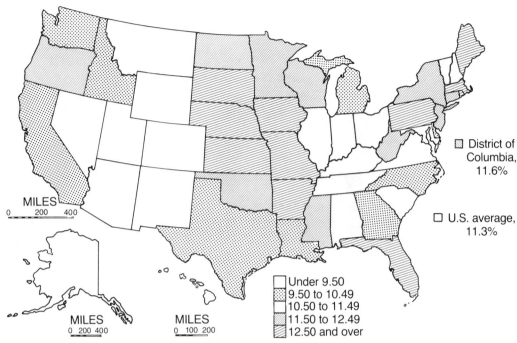

District of
Columbia,
11.6%

U.S. average,
11.3%

Under 9.50
9.50 to 10.49
10.50 to 11.49
11.50 to 12.49
12.50 and over

Figure 1.1   Percentage of the total population 65 years and over, for states, in 1980

erly migrants. Five *Sunbelt* states ranked among the top ten most popular destinations, and Florida, California, Arizona and Texas were ranked first through fourth, respectively. Florida alone attracted more than one-fourth of the entire nation's elderly migrants (Biggar, 1984). Elderly Sunbelt migrants seem to be younger, better educated, more financially secure, and more likely to be married than migrants to other states. This seems especially the case for Arizona and Florida. California appears to receive the greatest number of poorer migrants. According to Biggar (1984), in states such as Arizona and Florida, the "graying of the Sunbelt" brings increased demands for consumer goods as well as housing, recreational, health and protective services. For California, the elderly migration increases the demands placed on

state and local social and welfare service agencies for the aged.

Where do migrants to the Sunbelt come from? Several major "streams" from non-contiguous states provide a source of migrants to the Sunbelt. Between 1975 and 1980, major streams into Florida came from Connecticut, Indiana, Massachusetts, Michigan, New Jersey, New York, Ohio and Pennsylvania. From this list, only Michigan also provided a major stream of migrants to Arizona, which also drew from Illinois, Iowa, Minnesota, Washington and Wisconsin. Migrants to California were drawn from Illinois and Washington. In the central sunbelt, Texas has become a destination for streams of elderly migrants from Kansas and Missouri. Another newly emerging Sunbelt destination is North Carolina, drawing migrants from Maryland and New Jersey (Biggar, 1984).

Often, states with high in-migration rates also have high out-migration rates. This seems especially the case for California and Florida. Between 1975 and 1980, major streams of elderly migrants left Florida for Michigan, New York, Ohio and Pennsylvania. Longino (1979) has reported that one-third of the national interstate-migrating older population residing outside their state of birth in 1965 returned by 1970. Given that the states identified above all provide major streams of elderly migrants to Florida, Biggar (1984) hypothesizes that much of this out-migration involves "returning home" to be near family after a spouse dies or medical or financial problems develop.

California may represent a different case of "returning home." States receiving streams of outmigrants from California include Arkansas, Colorado, Idaho, Missouri, Oklahoma, Utah and Washington. Only Washington provided a sizable stream into California. Others on this list may represent states of birth for individuals who migrated to California in early adulthood. During the first half of the twentieth century, California was an important destination for migrants of all ages seeking a "land of opportunity."

Residential Concentration

Increasingly, the elderly have become an urbanized population, locating in central cities or in places that structurally and functionally are parts of larger metropolitan areas (Golant, 1975). In 1980 only one in four elderly whites and one in five elderly non-whites were located in rural areas. According to Golant (1972), the growth in the urban elderly population is largely the result of younger cohorts "aging in place" and of res-

idential relocations made earlier in the life span, rather than of relocation made after retirement. Still, we should remember that 21 states have at least 40 percent of their older population in rural areas; and in nine states (Alaska, Arkansas, Mississippi, North Carolina, North Dakota, South Carolina, South Dakota, Vermont and West Virginia), more than half of the older population is rural. Thirteen states have more than 10 percent of their older populations living on farms. (Here, for the moment, the elderly are defined as those 60 years of age and over.) This has important policy implications since so many government programs are designed to serve an urban population.

In 1980, 31 percent of all elderly in the United States were concentrated in central cities. Yet during the last decades suburbanization has proceeded rapidly, so that by 1980 the fastest growing site for the elderly population was the suburbs. In 1960 only about 17 percent of all elderly citizens were living in the fringe around central city areas; by 1980 this proportion exceeded 28 percent. This reflects less the migration of those 65 and over than the aging of suburban populations.

SUMMARY

The elderly population of the United States has been increasing since 1900. Changes in fertility, mortality, and migration have all contributed to this growth. The absolute number of the elderly and the proportion of the population they constitute are expected to increase further in this century, though at a slowed pace. In addition, the aged population is itself aging. By the year 2000, approximately 50 percent of the aged will be 75 years of age or over.

The old-age dependency ratio is a measure often used to summarize the demographic relationship between the elderly and the rest of the population. It is expected to increase in the coming years. Continued expectations for reduced fertility during this same period are projected to result in a decline in the young-age dependency ratio. Thus, the total dependency burden over the next 30 to 40 years should be relatively stable.

Elderly women outnumber elderly men, a difference that has been increasing for the past several decades. Because of enumeration problems, data on minority elderly must be evaluated cautiously. Blacks constitute the largest group of non-white elderly, although they represent a smaller proportion of the total elderly population than of the total general population. Some experts forecast that before the year 2000 Spanish-Americans will become the nation's largest minority group. This population, though, is even more youthful than the black population.

In general, the elderly population is concentrated in the largest states. Some growth in state populations of elderly is due to interstate migration. Sunbelt states rank among the most popular destinations for elderly migrants. "Streams" of elderly migrants seem to come to the Sunbelt principally from the Northeast and Midwest. Recently, gerontologists have identified streams of outmigrants returning home from the Sunbelt states. For individual elderly, this may be a consequence of widowhood or the onset of medical or financial problems.

Like the rest of the U.S. population, the elderly have become increasingly urbanized. Still, in nine states more than one-half of the older population is rural. These patterns reflect the "aging in place" of populations that may have relocated earlier in life, rather than migration of those over 60 years of age.

KEY TERMS

ancestry group
average life expectancy at birth
cohort
demography
family dependency ratio
fertility
life table
migration
mortality
old-age dependency ratio
old-old
sex ratio
very old
young-old

STUDY QUESTIONS

1. Discuss how three demographic factors, fertility, mortality and migration, have had significant impact on the growth of the aged population in the United States.
2. Should we have confidence in Census Bureau projections of the growth in numbers and proportion of the elderly population in the U.S. in the future? Why?
3. What is a dependency ratio? Distinguish between the *societal* old-age dependency ratio and the *familial* old-age dependency ratio. How is the "mix" of old-age and young-age dependency ratios expected to change in the future and what is the significance of this change?
4. Define *sex ratio*. Applying the concept to the elderly population, how has the sex ratio changed since the beginning of the twentieth century? Why has it changed?
5. Why is recognition of minority elderly issues likely to increase in the future? Why may the importance of ancestry groups diminish among the elderly in the future?
6. Describe the residential mobility patterns of the elderly in the contemporary United States. What role do the Sunbelt states play in elderly

migration? In this context, what do we mean by "returning home"?

7. How has the residential concentration of the elderly population changed in recent decades? Why?

BIBLIOGRAPHY

Biggar, J.C. 1984. *The Graying of the Sunbelt.* Washington, D.C.: Population Reference Bureau, Inc.

Clark, R.L. and Spengler, J.J. 1978. Changing dependency and dependency costs: The implications of future dependency ratios and their composition. In B. Herzog, ed., *Aging and Income: Programs and Prospects for the Elderly.* New York: Human Sciences Press.

Cowgill, D. 1972. A theory of aging in cross-cultural perspective. In D. Cowgill and L. Holmes, eds., *Aging and Modernization.* New York: Appleton-Century-Crofts.

Crimmins, E.M. 1980. Implications of recent mortality trends for the size and composition of the population over 65. Paper presented at the Annual Meeting of the Gerontological Society of America, November.

Cutler, N., and Harootyan, R. 1975. Demography of the aged. In D. Woodruff and J. Birren, eds., *Aging: Scientific Perspectives and Social Issues.* New York: Van Nostrand.

Farley, J.E. 1982. *Majority-Minority Relations.* Englewood Cliffs, N.J.: Prentice-Hall.

Golant, S.M. 1972. The residential location and spatial behavior of the elderly. Research Paper 143, University of Chicago, Department of Geography.

_____ . 1975. Residential concentrations of the future elderly. *Gerontologist 15:* 16–23.

Longino, C.F. 1979. Going home: Aged return migration in the United States 1965–70. *Journal of Gerontology 34* (5):736–745.

Matras, J. 1973. *Populations and Societies.* Englewood Cliffs, N.J.: Prentice-Hall.

Neugarten, B. 1974. Age groups in American society and the rise of the young-old. *Annals of the American Academy* (September): 187–198.

Petersen, W. 1975. *Population,* 3rd ed. New York: Macmillan.

Siegel, J.S. 1975. Some demographic aspects of aging in the United States. In A. Ostfeld and D. Gibson, eds., *Epidemiology of Aging.* Bethesda, Md.: National Institutes of Health.

_____ . 1979. *Perspective Trends in the Size and Structure of the Elderly Population, Impact of Mortality Trends and Some Implications.* Current Population Reports, Special Studies Series P-23, No. 78. Washington, D.C.: U.S. Department of Commerce, Bureau of the Census.

_____ , and Davidson, M. 1984. *Demographic and Socioeconomic Aspects of Aging in the United States.* Current Population Reports, Special Studies Series P-23, No. 138. Washington, D.C.: U.S. Department of Commerce, Bureau of the Census.

Tauber, C.M. 1983. *America in Transition: An Aging Society.* Current Population Reports, Special Studies Series P-23, No. 128. Washington, D.C.: U.S. Department of Commerce, Bureau of the Census.

CHAPTER **2**

Social and Economic Characteristics of the Aged

Each one of us is embedded in a network or system of social relationships. In recent years, numerous investigators have interested themselves in the role of this system of relationships, sometimes referred to as a *support system,* in the provision of health and social services to the aged. For example, it is commonly recognized now that most health care and social help provided to the elderly comes from such support systems through family, friends and neighbors (Shanas, 1979; Stoller and Earl, 1983). Some work has even tied participation (or non-participation) in such a support system to health status itself.

The parameters or dimensions of the systems of social relationships in which we are engaged are established by our social and economic characteristics. Such characteristics identify our family and marital status, living arrangements, employment status and economic situation.

In this chapter we describe some of the social and economic characteristics of the U.S. aged population. We hope to reveal important statistical dimensions of this elderly population, which may help us better understand the broader social context in which most older people live. In doing so, we hope to understand better the health problems of older people and the special difficulties they have in coping with those health problems.

One caveat is in order here. In describing the characteristics of a population, summary statistical measures are frequently used. These measures represent statistical generalizations. It is important to recognize that there is often variation within the population with regard to the measure in question. That is, although it may be reported that the median years of school completed by older people was 11.3 in 1985, you should remember that many older Americans—professors, doctors, attorneys and others—have completed 20 or more years of formal schooling. At the same time, too many Americans (of all ages) have completed less than 10 years of formal schooling.

THE FAMILY

The institution of the family is the one that is best known and that affects most people. Obviously, we feel the effects of other institutions—political, educational and economic—but it is the family that touches us more deeply and continuously than any other. Families help regulate sexual activity and provide the context within which children are conceived and raised. Families afford individuals protection, intimacy, affection and social identity (Federico, 1979).

Families change with time. The functions the family fulfills shift in importance, just as family structure and patterns of interrelationships change. Most family sociologists now use the concept of the *family life cycle* to characterize the changes families undergo. A well-known and frequently adopted staging of the family life cycle has been put forth by Duvall (1977):

Stage 1. Establishment (newly married, childless).

Stage 2. New parents (infant–three years).

Stage 3. Preschool family (child three to six years and possibly younger siblings).

Stage 4. School-age family (oldest child six to twelve years, possibly younger siblings).

Stage 5. Family with adolescent (oldest child 13 to 19 years, possibly younger siblings).

Stage 6. Family with young adult (oldest 20, until first child leaves home).

Stage 7. Family as launching center (from departure of first child to that of last child).

Stage 8. Postparental family (after all children have left home).

It is important to recognize that this sequence of stages is an ideal representation of the life of a couple that marries, has children and stays together through the course of the life cycle. Obviously, some people never marry, others marry and do not have children, and many who marry later divorce. Typical family life cycle stages may be measured in terms of the average or median ages at which critical events occur. Changes in timing of important life events may be observed when comparing individuals in different birth cohorts.

It should also be understood that the stages themselves are not stagnant. Significant changes in family structure and relationships may take place within each stage. For example, much literature suggests that the quality of the marriage relationship changes significantly in stage 2 with the onset of parenthood (for example, Rollins and Feldman, 1970). In addition, events that may occur during the last stage—birth of a grandchild, retirement, death of a spouse, remarriage—may clearly change the character of the older person's family life.

Table 2.1 shows the average age of selected critical life events in the early stages of the family life cycle of ever-married white mothers in five birth cohorts between 1900 and 1949. The mean age at marriage of the 1900–09 cohort is 1.5 years higher than that of the 1940–49 cohort. The average age of a mother at the time of the birth of a first child declined by 2.4 years across these five birth cohorts. These cohorts also completed their childbearing at very different ages. In part, this is explained by differences in the level of childbearing. However, the fact that these cohorts completed their childbearing in different historical periods cannot be overlooked. Women born between 1940 and 1949 finished childbearing in the 1970s and had, on average, 2.4 children; women born between 1900 and 1909 finished their childbearing in the Depression years and averaged 3.0 children.

Schoen and his colleagues (cited in Siegel and Davidson, 1984) have developed some measures of important events occurring in later segments of the family life cycle. Comparing cohorts born in 1908–12 and 1938–42, they observe a decline in the average duration of a first marriage that is slightly greater for men (28.7 years vs. 26.1 years) than for women (29.5 years vs. 27.4 years). This decline for men and women is clearly a function of an increase in the proportion of

first marriages ending in divorce. While 25 percent of men born between 1908 and 1912 had their first marriage end in divorce, almost 40 percent (39.4%) of those born between 1938 and 1942 had a first marriage end in that fashion.

The mean age at *widowhood* has increased more dramatically for men (64.5 vs. 68.4 years) than for women (64.7 vs. 66.1 years), while the average duration of widowhood has remained about the same (6.6 years for men and 14.3 years for women). In addition, to date, the percentage of first marriages ending in widowhood has declined. While 53 percent of women born in 1908–12 had their first marriages end in widowhood, 45.3 percent of women born in 1938–42 had their marriages end in a similar fashion.

Marital Status

Marital status is a simple, obvious criterion for distinguishing older people who are in families from those who are not. Table 2.2 presents a distribution of the population 65 years of age and over by marital status for both sexes for the years 1950 and 1981. The marital distribution of elderly men differs sharply from that of elderly women. In 1981 almost eight in ten elderly men (77 percent) were married and living with their wives; only

TABLE 2.1 Average age at which selected critical life events occurred for ever-married white mothers born between 1900 and 1949

Life cycle event	Birth Cohort				
	1940–49	1930–39	1920–29	1910–19	1900–1909
Age at first marriage	20.2	20.6	21.4	22.2	21.7
Age at birth of first child	21.8	22.3	23.6	24.6	24.2
Age at birth of last child	25.4	29.1	31.2	32.5	30.8
Mean number of children	2.4	3.4	3.3	3.0	3.0

Source: Spanier and Glick, 1980. Data from June 1975 Marital History Supplement of the Current Population Survey.

TABLE 2.2 Percent distribution of the population 65 years old and over by marital status, males and females, 1950 and 1981

	Males		Females	
	1950	1981	1950	1981
Single	8.0	4.5	8.0	5.7
Married	66.2	79.3	36.0	39.4
Spouse present	63.3	77.0	34.3	37.8
Spouse absent	2.9	2.3	1.7	1.6
Widowed	23.6	12.8	55.3	51.3
Divorced	2.2	3.4	0.7	3.6
Totals	100.0	100.0	100.0	100.0

Source: Siegel and Davidson, 1984; Siegel, 1976.

12.8 percent were widowed. Women 65 years of age and older are much more likely to be widowed than married. In 1981, 37.8 percent of aged women were married and living with their husbands; over one-half (51.3 percent) of all elderly women were widowed.

The changes in marital status from 1950 have been more substantial for men than for women. As the table indicates, the proportion of elderly men who are married has increased (66.2 to 79.3 percent), and the proportions of single (8.0 to 4.5 percent) and widowed (23.6 to 12.8 percent) have fallen significantly. While the pattern has been basically the same for elderly women, the proportional change has been rather modest in comparison with elderly males.

Two important factors contribute to the sharply different marital distributions of men and women. The first is the much higher mortality rates of married men than married women. In addition, husbands are typically older than their wives by a few years. Siegel (1976) indicates that life expectancy at age 65 of married women exceeds that of their husbands at age 70 by about 9 years. Thus,

not only do most married women outlive their husbands, but they tend to do so by many years.

A second factor accounting for the significantly higher proportion of widows than widowers is the higher remarriage rate of widowers. The marriage rate of elderly men is about seven times that of elderly women. The vast majority of these are remarriages (Siegel, 1976). Societal norms are much more supportive of an elderly man marrying a younger woman than of the opposite. Men also have a demographic advantage in finding a new spouse. As Table 2.2 shows, the proportion of unmarried women 65 years and over was almost three times as great as the proportion of unmarried men in this age group (60.6 vs. 20.7 percent in 1981).

Living Arrangements

Nearly all the elderly live in independent households, the majority with a spouse or other relatives. In 1981, 5.2 percent of the elderly were in institutions on any given day. Table 2.3 shows changes between 1970 and 1981 and projections to 1995 in the distribution of households, by type, for the aged. The percent of the non-institutionalized elderly residing in family households was 57.6 in 1970 and is expected to decline to 50 percent by 1995. At the same time, the proportion of elderly residing alone or with non-relatives is expected to reach 50 percent by 1995. Interestingly, as we approach the beginning of the twenty-first century, the proportion of the total elderly population made up by female householders living alone or with non-relatives (40.5 percent) is expected to approach the proportion of all elderly living in married couple family households (44.1 percent).

The proportion of the elderly living alone is increasing. This seems to be chiefly the result of the increasing number of widows among

TABLE 2.3 Percent distribution of households by type, for householders 65 years and over, 1970, 1981, 1995

Type of household	1970	1981	1995 (projection)
Family households	57.6	54.3	50.0
Married-couple family	46.0	45.2	44.1
Other family, female householder	9.0	7.3	4.7
Other family, male householder	2.6	1.8	1.2
Non-family households (living alone or with a non-relative)	42.4	45.7	50.0
Male householder	9.9	9.1	9.5
Female householder	32.5	36.6	40.5
All households	100.0	100.0	100.0

Source: Siegel and Davidson, 1984, Table 7.6.

the elderly, and the fact that more elderly people today can afford to live alone than in the past (Manard, Kart and van Gils, 1975). There are at least two factors that may determine the choice of a *shared household*, even one with non-family-members: poverty and physical illness or disability.

Soldo (1979) analyzed 1970 census data and found that older people living with relatives are twice as likely to have low incomes as are older people living independently. When the low income of the elderly person is pooled with that of the household in which he or she resides, a higher quality of living may be afforded all. Soldo found that 30 percent of elderly people living alone had incomes below the poverty level; among those living with younger relatives, only 8 percent of the household incomes were below the poverty level.

Data from the National Health Interview Survey (National Center for Health Statistics, 1974) shows the relationship between mobility or *activity limitations* and living arrangements. Living in the household of a non-relative or a relative other than a spouse implies greater limitations on mobility and

activity than living with a spouse or alone. About 9 percent of those elderly who live with a non-relative (9.4 percent) or a relative other than a spouse (9.5 percent) report "needing help getting around," while 7.7 percent of those living alone and 5.1 percent of those living with a spouse report needing similar help. Almost six in ten elderly living alone (58.3 percent) or with a spouse (57.8 percent) report no major activity limitations; comparable figures among those living with a relative who is not the spouse or with a non-relative are 52.0 and 49.9 percent. These differences, though not extraordinarily large, do suggest that a shared household may act as protection when circumstances preclude maintaining an independent household.

HOUSING

Most Americans live in single-family, owner-occupied homes. About 71 percent of the elderly live in their own homes, compared to 63 percent of the non-elderly (Allen and Brotman, 1981). Homes owned by the elderly are older than those owned by younger people. Data collected in 1976 on the characteristics of housing units occupied by the elderly shows that most elderly owner-occupants (59 percent) have lived in the same house since at least 1959, compared with only 19 percent of owner-occupants who are younger (Struyk and Soldo, 1980); almost one-half (46 percent) of all the homes occupied by the elderly had been built before 1940. Elderly renters also live in older homes, despite the fact that most elderly renters are not long-term occupants of these units.

The elderly tend to live in household units that are somewhat more modest than those of the non-elderly. Typically, elderly households are smaller by count of rooms and bathrooms, and are less likely than households headed by the non-elderly to have central heat. Struyk and Soldo (1980) used six indicators of deficiencies in their study of the quality of elderly housing. These indicators of *housing inadequacy* were related to plumbing, kitchen facilities, sewage, heat, maintenance, and public halls. For example, a housing unit would be declared deficient if it lacked a complete kitchen or the household had to share kitchen use, or if the heating system was completely unusable for six or more hours at least three times during the past winter. The elderly were found to have a higher incidence than the non-elderly of incomplete plumbing and kitchen facilities. Elderly and non-elderly households had a similar proportion of heating-system and sewage breakdowns, but elderly owners had slightly more maintenance deficiencies than their non-elderly counterparts, and elderly renters had fewer.

A principal problem for the elderly is that they have to pay too large a portion of their incomes to meet housing expenses. According to Struyk (1977), almost one in three (29 percent) of all elderly-headed households spend more than 30 percent of income on housing. Still, about 83 percent of elderly home owners have no mortgage debt on their property (Struyk and Soldo, 1980).

EDUCATION

The extent of formal education received by older persons is considerably less than that of the general population. It is important to remember that people who are 75 years of age and older today grew up at a time when one-half of the American population lived in rural areas, child labor was common, and few states had an adequate system of public high schools (Manard, Kart and van Gils, 1975). As Table 2.4 shows, in 1975 little more than one-third (35.2 percent) of the nation's elderly population had completed high school. This compared with almost two-thirds (62.5 percent) of the population 25 years of age and over. By the year 2000, this difference is projected to narrow considerably as current and future cohorts of individuals with the high school diploma arrive at old age. According to the Bureau of the Census, by the turn of the twenty-first century, individuals 65 years of age and over will have a median of 12.4 years of school completed, and 63.7 percent of this population will have graduated from high school.

LABOR FORCE PARTICIPATION

Labor force participation by elderly Americans has declined throughout the twentieth century. By 1940, the rate for elderly males had dipped below 50 percent. As Table 2.5 shows, by 1955 39.6 percent of all aged males were in the labor force; by 1985, less than one-fifth (17.5) were projected to be working. There is considerable difference by

TABLE 2.4 Educational attainment of the population 65 years and over and 25 years and over, by sex, 1975, 1985, 2000

Sex and year	Median school years completed		Percent high school graduates	
	65+	25+	65+	25+
Both sexes				
1975	9.0	12.3	35.2	62.5
1985	11.3	12.6	46.2	72.3
2000	12.4	12.8	63.7	80.4
Male				
1975	8.9	12.4	33.4	63.1
1985	11.0	12.7	45.0	73.2
2000	12.4	12.9	62.4	81.4
Female				
1975	9.3	12.3	36.5	62.1
1985	11.5	12.5	47.0	71.4
2000	12.4	12.7	64.6	79.4

Source: Siegel and Davidson, 1984.

age, though. Males 65 to 69 years of age are twice as likely as those 70 years and over to be working (25.9% vs. 12.3% in 1985). The percentage of women 65 years of age and over employed outside the home has not exceeded 11 percent in this century—despite the fact that the proportion of gainfully employed women of all ages has increased dramatically. Over 45 percent of all women were employed in the 1970s. Table 2.5 shows only one in ten (10.6 percent) elderly females as labor-force participants in 1955; 7.7 percent is the comparable figure projected for 1985.

Non-whites have had labor force experiences similar to those just described (see Table 2.5). The labor force participation rates of all non-white males has declined slightly, while that of elderly non-white males has fallen dramatically in this century. Almost 85 percent of aged black males were employed in 1900 (Achenbaum, 1978), 40 percent in 1955, 20.9 percent in 1975, and 16.2 percent for 1985. Aged black females have always had higher rates of employment than their white counterparts, although the difference in rates has narrowed. By 1985, about 9.7 percent of aged black females were employed—down from 12.1 percent in 1955.

What kinds of work do older workers do? Historically, most elderly men found work in farming—a lifelong occupation. Retirement on a farm was rare. An older worker physically unable to perform some duties could assume other—less demanding, though equally important—chores. This was especially true for white farmers. A greater proportion of blacks than whites were in farming, but whites were much more likely to be owners or managers. Thus they were in a position to remain in charge of planning and overseeing farm activities when they themselves were no longer able to carry out more physically demanding farm duties.

TABLE 2.5 Labor force participation rates, for the population 65 years and over, by age, race, and sex, 1955, 1975, 1985, 2000

Age, race and sex	1955	1975	1985	2000
All				
Males				
65 years and over	39.6	21.7	17.5	13.2
65 to 69 years	57.0	31.7	25.9	19.9
70 years and over	28.1	15.1	12.3	9.8
Females				
65 years and over	10.6	8.3	7.7	6.4
65 to 69 years	17.8	14.5	14.6	13.6
70 years and over	6.4	4.9	4.3	3.6
Blacks and other races				
Males				
65 years and over	40.0	20.9	16.2	11.2
65 to 69 years	—	—	24.2	17.2
70 years and over	—	—	11.1	7.6
Females				
65 years and over	12.1	10.5	9.7	8.2
65 to 69 years	—	—	17.1	16.1
70 years and over	—	—	5.2	4.2

Source: Siegel and Davidson, 1984, Table 8.1.
Figures for 1985 and 2000 are projections.

Obviously, farming has diminished in importance as a source of jobs—not just for older men but for younger men as well. Still, older workers are more likely to be found in farming than in the total population of employed persons. As can be seen from Table 2.6, elderly male workers are almost three times more likely to be found in farm work than are all male workers (11.3 vs. 4.3 percent), and elderly females in the labor force are about twice as likely to be in farm work as are female workers of all ages (1.8 vs. 1.0 percent).

Older workers are less likely than all workers to have *blue-collar jobs*. Many of these jobs are in industries where mandatory retirement has been the rule and where pension plans are prevalent. Moreover, many blue-collar jobs are physically arduous—

truck driving and construction work, for example. Many older workers are self-employed or work for small businesses. These include accountants, lawyers and tavern keepers, who simply continue at the same work beyond normal retirement age. Sales work and clerical work offer part-time employment and are thus amenable to elderly individuals attempting to supplement retirement income; over 40 percent (40.3%) of all elderly female workers were employed in these categories in 1980.

Elderly workers are more likely than all workers to be found in *service jobs:* gardeners, seamstresses, practical nurses, washroom attendants, night watchmen, ticket takers and domestics, for example. The 1980 census reports relatively large proportions of elderly people in each of these occupations.

TABLE 2.6 Occupational distribution of employed persons: The total population and the elderly population, 1980

	Total population		Population 65 +	
	Male (56,004,690)	Female (41,634,665)	Male (1,875,253)	Female (1,172,711)
White-collar	42.6%	67.0%	46.4%	58.3%
Managers and administrators	12.6	7.4	13.1	6.9
Professional and technical	11.0	14.1	11.3	11.1
Sales	9.1	11.2	14.2	15.0
Clerical and kindred	9.9	34.3	7.8	25.3
Blue-collar	43.9	14.0	26.7	10.9
Craftsmen and kindred	20.7	2.3	13.1	2.5
Operatives (except transpost)	9.7	8.8	5.0	6.5
Transport equipment workers	7.2	0.8	4.7	0.4
Helpers and laborers	6.3	2.1	3.9	1.5
Farm	4.3	1.0	11.3	1.8
Farm operators and managers	2.1	0.3	8.0	1.0
Other farm occupations	2.2	0.7	3.3	0.8
Service	9.2	17.9	15.0	29.0
Private household	—	1.4	0.2	7.4
Protective service occupations (e.g., police officer, firefighter)	2.3	0.4	4.0	0.4
Other service (e.g., health and personal service)	6.9	16.1	10.8	21.2

Source: U.S. Bureau of the Census, *Detailed Population Characteristics. United States Summary: 1980*, Table 280.

Although the twentieth century has brought with it increased life expectancy, an increase in the average number of years worked during a person's life (Fullerton, 1972), and increased expectation of retirement, it has also brought a significant decline in labor force participation rates among all elderly, with aged men particularly affected. How do we explain the declining employment level of older persons? What factors have become important in setting that employment level? Various explanations for the decline in labor force participation of older men have been put forth (Kart, 1982). A growing number of studies identify health

status and the development of pension systems (including Social Security) as the most significant factors influencing the labor supply of older workers. Research also shows changes in the population age structure, changes in labor force composition, and age discrimination in employment to be contributors to the declining employment rates of older workers.

ECONOMIC STATUS

The presence or absence of financial resources has considerable impact on a person's capacity to adjust to the aging process.

The older person with adequate financial resources can maintain some degree of control over his or her life, including making decisions about which leisure-time activities to pursue, how much to travel, what kind of diet to maintain, the amount of preventive medical care to seek, and so on. Older people without money can do none of these things.

Older Americans receive direct money income from a variety of sources. Some have earnings—salaries, wages or self-employment income; most have a retirement pension (including *Social Security)* of one kind or another. Direct money income can also come from welfare payments, dividends, interest, rents, alimony, unemployment, veterans' and workmen's compensation payments, and gifts from others. Figure 2.1 shows the sources of money income for the elderly. Clearly, Social Security is the major source (39 percent), although earnings (16 percent) and *asset income* (28 percent) contribute to the income position of many elderly. Not all elderly individuals receive income from all sources identified in the figure. Over 90 percent of the elderly receive some income from Social Security. Married elderly people are more likely than single elderly people to receive income from wages,

ᵃIncludes railroad retirement (1%).
ᵇIncludes public assistance (1%).

Figure 2.1   1984 sources of aged income. *Source:* S. Grad, *Income of the Population 55 and Over,* 1984. (Washington, D.C.: Social Security Administration, 1985).

savings, private pensions and government pensions. The unmarried aged are more likely to receive income from public assistance (Grad, 1985).

Just how much income do the elderly have? Table 2.7 shows the total money income of persons 65 and over, by marital status and sex, in 1984. The income of married couples in which at least one of the partners is aged (hereafter referred to as aged married couples) is substantially higher than the income received by the non-married aged (including widows, divorcées and the never-married). The median income of these married couples in 1984 was $17,250. The median income of non-married men was $7,490; that of non-married women was $6,500. Whereas 41.2 percent of aged married couples had income of $20,000 or more in 1984, only 12.2 percent of the non-married men and 9.0 percent of the non-married women 65 years and over were in this high-income group.

Another way to describe the income picture for the aged is in terms of family data. Table 2.8 provides the median incomes of all families in the United States in 1984, including the median income for families in which the head of household is 65 or over (hereafter referred to as aged families). The income of aged families is substantially higher than the income received by unrelated individuals, although it is still considerably below that of all families in the United States. The median income of aged families in the United States in 1984 was $18,215, $8,000 less than the median for all families.

Since 1965 the median income of aged families has increased more than five times, from $3,514 to $18,215. The relative income position of the aged has also improved over this period. For example, the ratio of median income of aged families to the median income of all families rose from 49.3 percent in 1965 to 68.9 percent in 1984. This improvement in relative income status sug-

TABLE 2.7 Total money income of persons 65 and over, by marital status and sex, 1984

Total money income	Percentage of married couples	Percentage of non-married	
		Men	Women
Less than $2,000	0.8	3.4	3.4
$2,000–3,999	1.1	11.7	13.6
$4,000–5,999	3.4	20.3	27.3
$6,000–7,999	6.3	18.1	17.3
$8,000–9,999	8.2	9.7	9.3
$10,000–14,999	22.1	16.0	13.0
$15,000–19,999	17.2	8.5	7.2
$20,000–24,999	11.9	4.1	3.6
$25,000 and over	29.3	8.1	5.4
Total*	100.3	99.9	100.1
Median income	$17,250	$7,490	$6,500

*Difference from 100.0 due to rounding.
Source: Grad, 1985, Table 12.

TABLE 2.8 Median total money income by age of head of family, 1984

	Median income
Families	
All ages	$26,433
Head 65 years and older	18,215
Unrelated individuals	
All ages	11,204
65 years and over	7,296

Source: U.S. Department of Commerce, Bureau of the Census, *Money Income of Households, Families, and Persons in the United States, 1984,* CPR, Series P-60, No. 151 (Washington, D.C.: U.S. Government Printing Office, 1986).

gests that elderly families have enjoyed growth rates in income in this period of time above the national average.

The aged are a heterogeneous group, and there is wide variation in income among them. We have already seen how income varies along the lines of sex and marital status. Two other factors associated with income variation among the elderly are retirement status and age. Not all older people are retired. As we have already seen, in 1985 17.5 percent of aged men and 7.7 percent of aged women were projected to be working. The income differences between those working and those not working are fairly substantial. Table 2.9 presents data on 1984 income from earnings of the aged by Social Security beneficiary status. Among those 65 years of age and older, non-beneficiaries have median dollar income from earnings that is five times as great as that for Social Security beneficiaries ($23,100 vs. $4,830). It is important to remember that beneficiaries may also be receiving retired worker benefits, dependents' or survivors' benefits, or disability benefits.

The elderly are not age-homogeneous. Chapter 1 distinguished between the "young-old" and the very old, or "old-old." Most data on the income of the aged group all persons 65 and over together. Only recently have some income data become available distinguishing age groups among the elderly. Although Table 2.10 does not make age distinctions consistent with the age groupings commonly employed to separate young-old from old-old, it does demonstrate income differences among age groups of elderly people. Median income declines with age, with a steeper slope of decline for married couples than for non-married persons. Some of the income differential may be a function of current work experience, with the youngest elderly more likely to be participating in the labor force (even if only part-time). In addition, many of the old-old began their work careers before Social Security or private pension plans became commonplace.

Twenty-eight percent of all income to the elderly in this country comes from financial assets (see Figure 2.1). These assets—sometimes referred to as *liquid assets* because of their easy conversion to goods, services, or money—generally take the form of bank deposits and corporate stocks and bonds. This income is not distributed equitably across the elderly population. According to Riley and Foner (1968), assets tend to be cor-

TABLE 2.9 Income from earnings by age and Social Security beneficiary status, 1984

	Median income
Beneficiaries	
62–64	$8,030
65 and older	4,830
Non-beneficiaries	
62–64	22,860
65 and older	23,100

Source: Grad, 1985, Table 29.

TABLE 2.10 Money income of married couples and non-married persons 65 and over, 1984

			Married couples			
Age	Median income	Less than $5,000	$5,000– 9,999	$10,000– 14,999	$15,000– 19,999	$20,000 or more	Total percent
65–69	$19,500	3.1%	11.3%	18.7%	18.7%	48.4%	100.2%
70–74	17,480	2.0	17.4	21.4	17.6	41.5	99.9
75–79	15,100	2.9	20.2	26.9	15.6	34.4	100.0
80 and older	13,190	4.8	27.2	27.3	14.2	26.6	100.1

			Non-married persons			
Age	Median income	Less than $5,000	$5,000– 9,999	$10,000– 14,999	$15,000– 19,999	$20,000 or more	Total percent
65–69	$ 7,510	27.3%	36.4%	14.9%	9.7%	11.5%	99.8%
70–74	7,100	27.3	39.0	16.2	8.0	9.3	99.8
75–79	6,660	29.3	40.3	12.9	7.8	9.7	100.0
80 and older	5,940	36.8	39.2	10.9	4.8	8.3	100.0

Source: Grad, 1985, Table 12.

related with income: Those families with the highest incomes are most likely to have substantial assets; those with the lowest incomes are least likely to have any assets.

Some assets have less liquidity because they require more time for conversion to money. These *non-liquid assets* include equity in housing or a business and possessions such as automobiles. Homes are the most common asset (liquid or non-liquid) of older people. About 70 percent of elderly households reside in an owned home. Four-fifths of these home owners own their homes free of any mortgage.

The elderly receive indirect or *in-kind income* in the form of goods and services they obtain free or at a reduced cost. There are currently more than 40 major federal programs benefiting the elderly, over and above those providing direct income. Perhaps the largest government program providing indirect income to the elderly is *Medicare*—federal health insurance for the aged, established in 1965. Other examples of programs providing in-kind income include housing subsidy programs run by the Department of Housing and Urban Development and the food stamp program. It is difficult to say how much in income these programs are worth to the individual aged person. Information on the value of comparable services available in the marketplace is sometimes difficult to obtain. In addition, the value recipients place on in-kind services may differ sharply from the market value (Schmundt, Smolensky, and Stiefel, 1975).

Is the income of aged people adequate to their needs? The most frequently used measure of income adequacy is the *poverty index* developed by the Social Security Administration, based on the amount of money needed to purchase a *minimum adequate diet* as determined by the Department of Agriculture. The poverty line is then calculated at three times the food budget (slightly smaller proportions for one- and two-person families), on the assumption—derived from studies of consumers—that a family that has spent a larger proportion of its income on food will be living at a very inadequate level

(U.S. House Committee on Ways and Means, 1967). The food budgets and the derivative poverty income cutoff points are estimated in detail for families of differing size and composition, with a farm/nonfarm differential for each type. In 1982 the poverty index level for a two-person family with an aged head was approximately $5,836; the comparable level for a single person was about $4,626.

Table 2.11 shows that in general poverty has been declining among older people during the period from 1959 to 1984, although about one in eight older persons is still "officially" impoverished. Poverty varies among subgroups of the elderly. Aged whites are less likely to live in poverty than is anyone in the total U.S. population, with 10.7 percent living below the poverty level, but 31.7 percent of aged non-whites are living in poverty.

Critics of the poverty index argue that it is set too low. The index is calculated at three times the minimum adequate food budget; this 3:1 ratio was established as a result of surveys made in 1955 and 1960–61 of the ratio of food consumption to other expenditures for *all* families in the United States. A recent congressional report indicates that, based on Consumer Expenditure Surveys of

1972–73, the current ratio exceeds 5:1 (Poverty Studies Task Force, 1976). In testimony before the U.S. House Select Committee on Aging, one student of aging in the United States suggested that shifting to more realistic levels of what constitutes poverty would more than double the number of aged poor, so that the number of either poor or near poor would include approximately 40 percent of the aged (Orshansky, 1978). Also, the index is not applied to the *hidden poor*—those who are institutionalized or living with relatives (Orshansky, 1978). Thus even the current figures on poverty status exclude millions of elderly people who are unable to live independently.

SUMMARY

The elderly are a heterogeneous group. Among themselves, they differ across a broad array of social and economic characteristics. These characteristics, described in this chapter, structure the lives of elderly people and affect their capacity to adjust to aging.

The institution of the family is the one that is best known and affects most people. The

TABLE 2.11 Poverty rates: 1959, 1968, 1977, 1984

	1959	1968	1977	1984
Total population	22%	13%	12%	14.4%
Total aged population	35	25	14	12.4
Whites	33	23	12	10.7
Non-whites	61	47	35	31.7

Source: Based on data in U.S. Bureau of the Census, *Consumer Income*, CPR, Series P-60, No. 116 (Washington, D.C.: U.S. Government Printing Office, 1978); and U.S. Department of Commerce, Bureau of the Census, *Money Income and Poverty Status of Families and Persons in the United States: 1982*. CPR, Series P-60, No. 140 (Washington, D.C.: U.S. Government Printing Office, 1983); U.S. Department of Commerce, Bureau of the Census, *Statistical Abstract of the United States, 1986* (Washington, D.C.: U.S. Government Printing Office, 1986).

concept of the *family life cycle* describes how an ideal typical family may undergo changes in structure and function over time. The latter stages of the family life cycle—the family as launching center and the postparental family—are of particular interest to us here. For example, the marital distribution of elderly men differs sharply from that of elderly women; 77 percent of elderly males are married and living with their wives, while 51 percent of all elderly females are widowed.

Nearly all the elderly live in independent households; most live with a spouse or other relative. Only 5 percent are in institutions on any given day. The proportion of the elderly living alone is increasing. This is due to the high rate of widowhood among the elderly and the fact that more elderly people today can afford to live alone. In addition to income status, physical illness or disability is an important determinant of an older person's living arrangement.

Most elderly Americans own their homes. In general, these homes are older and more modest than those of the non-elderly. The principal housing problem for many elderly is that they pay a large portion of their incomes (30 percent or more) to meet housing expenses.

People who are 75 years of age and older today grew up at a time when most Americans lived in rural areas and child labor was still common. Many systems of public education were inadequate. As a result, little more than one-third of the nation's current elderly population has completed high school. By the year 2000 this figure is expected to increase such that almost two of three elderly will have graduated from high school.

Prior to 1940, a majority of elderly males were still in the labor force; by 1985 less than one-fifth (17.5%) were working. Older workers are still more likely than the total population to be in farm work and less likely to have blue-collar jobs. Many older workers are self-employed, work for small businesses, or are in non-union industries.

The economic status of the elderly has improved greatly in recent decades. Whereas 35 percent of the elderly were officially impoverished in 1959, only 12 percent are so designated today. Older Americans receive direct money income from a variety of sources, with retirement pension of one kind or another playing a prominent role; Social Security accounts for about 40 percent of all money income of elderly Americans. In-kind income, through programs such as Medicare/Medicaid, food stamps, and housing subsidies, makes a major contribution to the economic situation of many middle- and low-income elderly. Still, critics argue that incomes above the official poverty line, especially among the near poor, are inadequate. Also, the near poor are arbitrarily excluded from access to in-kind sources of goods and services.

KEY TERMS

activity limitations
aged families
asset income
family life cycle
hidden poor
housing inadequacy
in-kind income
liquid assets
Medicare
minimum adequate diet
non-liquid assets
poverty index
shared household
Social Security
support system
widowhood

STUDY QUESTIONS

1. Identify some important life events in the family life cycle. How has the timing of some of these events changed during the twentieth century? Speculate on the impact of these changes on older people.
2. Explain the changes in the marital distribution of elderly men that has occurred in the past 25 or 30 years. Identify two factors that contribute to the different marital distribution between elderly men and women.
3. Discuss the living arrangements of the elderly in contemporary society. What is the impact of sex and marital status on those arrangements? How do income status (poverty) and physical disability affect the living arrangements of the elderly?
4. How does the housing of the elderly homeowner differ from that of the non-elderly with regard to quality and cost?
5. In what types of jobs are older workers likely to be employed? How has the occupational distribution of the elderly work force changed during the twentieth century?
6. Discuss the economic position of American elderly with regard to variation by sex, marital status, age, race and retirement status.
7. Define the poverty index and explain how it is used to determine the adequacy of elderly people's income. What are the problems inherent in using this measure of income adequacy?

BIBLIOGRAPHY

Achenbaum, W.A. 1978. *Old Age in the New Land*. Baltimore, Md.: Johns Hopkins University Press.

Allen, C., and Brotman, H. 1981. *Chartbook on Aging*. Washington, D.C.: Administration on Aging.

Duvall, E. 1977. *Marriage and Family Development*, 5th ed. Philadelphia: Lippincott.

Federico, R. 1979. *Sociology*, 2nd ed. Reading, Mass.: Addison-Wesley.

Fullerton, H. 1972. A new type of working life table for men. *Monthly Labor Review* (July): 20–27.

Grad, S. 1985. *Income of the Population 55 and Over, 1984*. Washington, D.C.: Social Security Administration.

Kart, C.S. 1982. Explaining changes in labor force participation rates of aged men. *Journal of Applied Gerontology 1:* 34–44.

Manard, B., Kart, C.S. and van Gils, D. 1975. *Old Age Institutions*. Lexington, Mass.: D.C. Heath.

National Center for Health Statistics. 1974. *Limitations of Activity Due to Chronic Conditions—United States, 1972*. Series 10, No. 96. Rockville, Md.: U.S. Department of Health, Education, and Welfare.

Orshansky, M. 1978. Testimony in U.S. House Select Committee on Aging. *Poverty among America's Aged*. Washington, D.C.: U.S. Government Printing Office.

Poverty Studies Task Force. 1976. *The Measure of Poverty*. Washington, D.C.: U.S. Department of Health, Education, and Welfare.

Riley, M.W., and Foner, A. 1968. *Aging and Society: An Inventory of Research Findings*. New York: Russell Sage Foundation.

Rollins, B., and Feldman, H. 1970. Marital satisfaction over the family life cycle. *Journal of Marriage and Family 32* (1): 20–28.

Schmundt, M., Smolensky, E., and Stiefel, L. 1975. The evaluation of recipients of in-kind transfers. In I. Laurie, ed., *Integrating Income Maintenance Programs*. New York: Academic Press.

Shanas, E. 1979. The family as a social support system in old age. *Gerontologist 19:* 169–174.

Siegel, J. 1976. *Demographic Aspects of Aging and the Older Population in the United States*. Current Population Reports, Special Studies Series P-23, No. 59. Washington, D.C.: U.S. Department of Commerce, Bureau of the Census.

—————, and Davidson, M. 1984. *Demographic and Socioeconomic Aspects of Aging in the United States*. Current Population Reports, Special Studies Series P-23, No. 138. Washington, D.C.: U.S. Department of Commerce, Bureau of the Census.

Soldo, B. 1979. The housing characteristics of independent elderly: A demographic overview. *Occasional Papers in Housing and*

Urban Development, No. 1. Washington, D.C.: U.S. Department of Housing and Urban Development.

Spanier, G.B., and Glick, P.C. 1980. The life cycles of American families: An expanded analysis. *Journal of Family History 5* (1): 98–111.

Stoller, E.P., and Earl, L.L. 1983. Help with activities of everyday life: Sources of support for the noninstitutionalized elderly. *Gerontologist 23* (1): 64–70.

Struyk, R. 1977. The housing expense burden of households headed by the elderly. *Gerontologist 17:* 447–452.

_____ , and Soldo, B. 1980. *Improving the Elderly's Housing.* Cambridge, Mass.: Ballinger.

U.S. House Committee on Ways and Means. 1967. *President's Proposals for Revision in the Social Security System: Hearings, part I.* Washington, D.C.: U.S. Government Printing Office.

CHAPTER **3**

Health Status of the Elderly

Gerontologists use the term *senescence* to describe all postmaturational changes and the increasing vulnerability individuals face as a result of these changes. Senescence describes the group of effects that lead to a decreasing expectation of life with increasing age (Comfort, 1979). Strehler (1962) distinguishes senescence from other biological processes in four ways : (1) its characteristics are universal; (2) the changes that constitute it come from within the individual; (3) the processes associated with senescence occur gradually; and (4) the changes that appear in senescence have a deleterious effect on the individual.

Is senescence a fundamental or inherent biological process? Comfort (1979) is doubtful. He believes that attempts to identify a sin-

gle underlying property that explains all instances of senescent change are misplaced. Yet, there does appear to be some pattern to our increased vulnerability through the course of life. Roughly speaking, it appears that the probability of dying doubles every eight years. This phenomenon has been recognized since 1825, when Benjamin Gompertz observed that an exponential increase in death rate occurred between the ages of 10 and 60. After plotting age-specific death rates on a logarithmic scale and finding an increase that was nearly linear, Gompertz suggested that human mortality was governed by an equation with two terms. The first accounted for chance deaths that would occur at any age; the second, characteristic of the species, represented the exponential increase with time. These observations, sometimes referred to as *Gompertz's law,* seem reasonably to describe human mortality in many human societies (Fries and Crapo, 1981). Still, while we can accept the principle that the probability of our dying increases with age, it is important to emphasize that the probabilities themselves differ— for males and females, and by race, among other variables—and change through time.

This chapter will begin with a discussion of current trends in *mortality* and *life expectancy;* special attention is given to variation along the lines of sex and race. Trends in morbidity and disability (including mental health status) are also reviewed. It is important to note that the relationship between *morbidity* and mortality is variable. As Chapman, LaPlante and Wilensky (1986) point out, in the past, when mortality was dominated by *acute illness,* increasing life expectancy implied fewer activity limitations and an increasing capacity to sustain a work career. Under a mortality structure dominated by *chronic illess,* however, increasing life expectancy may reflect an increased prevalence of morbidity and disability that results from postponement of death. In addition, many disease conditions do not cause death. Chapman, LaPlante and Wilensky (1986) calculate that only 36 to 41 percent of all disability is related to "fatal" disease. Also, mortality that results from suicide, homicide or accident is not related to any particular illness.

MORTALITY

During 1983 an estimated 2.0 million deaths occurred in the United States. The preliminary death rate for that year was 8.6 deaths per 1,000 population; the 1982 rate of 8.5 deaths per 1,000 population was the lowest annual rate ever recorded in this country. The majority of these deaths involved elderly people. Over 1.2 million (or about 60 percent) of the deaths occurred among individuals who had passed their 65th birthday.

The leading cause of death among the elderly is heart disease, which accounts for about 44 percent of all deaths in old age. Malignant neoplasms (cancer) account for another 18 percent of the deaths (19 percent for men, 16 percent for women); and cerebrovascular diseases account for 13 percent of deaths among the elderly. Together, these three account for 75 percent of all deaths of elderly people and over 50 percent of the deaths of those under 65 in the United States. Obviously, the high proportion of the deaths of elderly people due to these three causes is an expression of vulnerability to these afflictions, which begins earlier in the life cycle.

Figure 3.1 shows the pattern of death rates for five leading causes of death among the elderly between 1950 and 1979. Death rates for the elderly have declined overall since 1950, although most of the decline has been since about 1968. The age-adjusted death rate for the population 65 years of age and over fell by 27 percent since 1950, and the decline for females was twice as great as that for males. The death rate for elderly men was considerably higher than that for elderly women (almost 70% in 1975), though this continues a long-term trend. The sex differential in death rates was 34 percent higher for elderly men in 1950.

As the figure indicates, the death rates for two of the three leading causes of death, heart disease and stroke (cerebrovascular disease), have declined significantly between 1950 and 1979. The death rate for cancer,

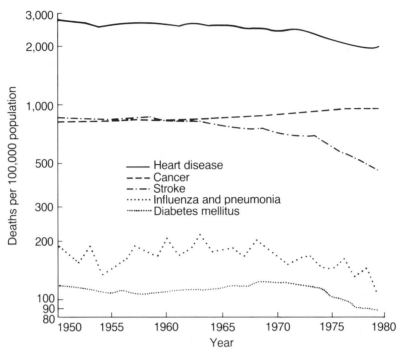

Figure 3.1   Age-adjusted death rates for persons 65 years of age and over, according to leading causes of death, United States, 1950–1979. Source: National Center for Health Statistics; computed by the Division of Analysis from data compiled by the Division of Vital Statistics. (Note: Causes of death are assigned according to the International List of Causes of Death. Because of the decennial revisions and changes in rules for cause-of-death selection, there may be some lack of comparability from one revision to the next. The beginning dates of the revisions are 1949, 1958, 1968 and 1979.)

the second leading cause of death in 1979, has increased slowly over the years (13 percent in the 1950–1979 period). Sex differences are quite pronounced for cancer—especially lung cancer, for which male mortality is about four times greater than female mortality. However, since 1960, there have been large annual increases in lung cancer mortality for older women, associated with cigarette smoking. The percent change from 1960 to 1982 in mortality rates from lung cancer among women aged 65–74 is 390.2. This compares with a 15.3 percent increase

in mortality rates from breast cancer for comparably aged women over the same time period. In 1982, for women aged 65–74, the death rate from lung cancer was higher than that from breast cancer (Metropolitan Life Insurance Company, 1985).

Most elderly people die as a result of some long-standing chronic condition, which is sometimes related to personal habits (e.g., smoking, drinking, poor eating habits) or environmental conditions (e.g., harsh work environments, air pollution) that go back many years. Preventing illness and death from these conditions must begin before old age. Some deaths, such as those from accidents, have declined significantly. The death rate from accidents (and violence) for white males 65 years and over in 1982 was 32 percent lower than that in 1960; the comparable decline for aged white females during this period was 47 percent.

Sex Differences in Mortality

As can be seen from Table 3.1, comparisons by race show that men have higher death rates than women in every age category. Some of this difference is almost certainly attributable to biological factors. For exam-

ple, the larger proportion of males who die in infancy is apparently not explainable by any systematic variation in physical or social environmental factors. For most adults, however, it may be difficult to distinguish between biological and environmental contributors to death. Male-female differences in mortality may be due, in part, to sex differences in the use of physician services. Typically, women report using health services more frequently than men do. This may result in earlier and more effective treatment of their illnesses and may contribute to lower death rates relative to men (Marcus and Siegel, 1982). The childbearing experience of females and the over-

TABLE 3.1 Age-specific death rates, by race and sex, 1980

| | Deaths per 1,000 | | | |
| | White | | Black | |
Age	Male	Female	Male	Female
All ages	9.8	8.1	10.3	7.3
Age-adjusted	7.5	4.1	11.1	6.3
Under 1	12.3	9.6	25.9	21.2
1–4	0.7	0.5	1.1	0.8
5–9	0.3	0.2	0.5	0.3
10–14	0.4	0.2	0.5	0.3
15–19	1.4	0.5	1.4	0.5
20–24	1.9	0.6	2.9	0.9
25–29	1.7	0.6	3.7	1.3
30–34	1.7	0.7	4.6	1.7
35–39	2.1	1.1	5.9	2.5
40–44	3.2	1.7	8.1	4.1
45–49	5.2	2.8	12.0	6.3
50–54	8.7	4.5	17.6	9.1
55–59	13.8	7.0	24.6	13.1
60–64	21.4	10.8	33.8	18.6
65–69	33.1	16.4	44.8	25.4
70–74	50.2	25.9	60.5	37.6
75–79	74.7	41.9	80.9	52.4
80–84	112.7	72.4	115.5	80.3
85 +	191.0	149.8	161.0	123.7

Source: National Center for Health Statistics, Advance Report of Final Mortality Statistics, 1980, *Monthly Vital Statistics Report,* vol. 32, no. 4 (1983), Tables 1 and 9.

representation of males in dangerous occupations are two additional factors that make it difficult to determine the relative effect on mortality of biological and environmental or sociocultural factors.

Madigan (1957) attempted to differentiate between biological and environmental factors in mortality. His classic study compared the mortality experience of Catholic brothers and nuns who were members of teaching communities. Madigan argued that the life patterns of these two groups are quite similar and that, over time, brothers and nuns are subjected to the same sociocultural stresses. Of particular importance here is the absence of sex-linked activities, which are relevant to mortality—namely, childbearing for females and participation in dangerous occupations for males. Madigan found that the difference in death rates between brothers and nuns was greater than between males and females in the population as a whole and that this difference had been increasing during the decades under study. From this he argued that biological factors are more important than sociocultural ones. Further, he hypothesized that the death rate advantage enjoyed by women was related to their greater constitutional resistance to the degenerative diseases (Madigan, 1957).

Such a hypothesis is difficult to test empirically. Table 3.2 presents ratios of male to female death rates for the population 65 years of age and over, by age and race, from 1940 to 1980. In general, the table shows increasing male-female mortality differences throughout this period, though there are still important differences in these ratios by age. Whereas among people aged 65–69 the male death rate is about twice that of females, the death rate of men in the 85 years

and older is still only 27 percent higher than that of women.

The general increase in mortality differences between the sexes very likely reflects a major shift in the causal-pattern of mortality. During the twentieth century, the contribution of infectious and parasitic diseases and maternal mortality to overall mortality rates has diminished relative to that of the chronic degenerative diseases such as diseases of the heart, malignant neoplasms and cerebrovascular diseases (Siegel, 1979). However, changes in recent decades in the male-female mortality ratio appear to be more associated with social and environmental factors than biological ones. For example, according to Petersen (1975), the age-adjusted death rate from cancers was 65 percent higher for females than males in 1900, about equal between the sexes in 1947, and 20 percent higher for males by 1963. This changing pattern would seem to have more to do with technological advancements than with innate biological factors. The diagnosis and cure of the cancers most frequent among females (breast and uterine) has improved at a more rapid rate than that of the cancers most frequent among males (those of the lung and digestive system.)

Can the pattern of increasing male-to-female death rate ratios among the elderly continue? Among those of all races and whites aged 65–69, ratios actually fell between 1970 and 1980. According to Zopf (1986), this deceleration suggests that the death rate differential between older men and women will not increase in the future as it has in the past. This is especially the case for the young-old, though increases in the mortality differential by sex are likely to continue for the old-old and for blacks.

Race Differentials in Mortality

The large race differential in mortality rates does not often receive the attention it deserves, because it is a hidden factor. If we return to Table 3.1 and look across the first row, "All ages," we observe that the death rate for black males is slightly higher than that for white males (10.3 vs. 9.8), while the death rate for black females is *slightly lower* than that for white females (7.3 vs. 8.1). However, because of higher birth rates, blacks have a younger age structure, and this tends to mask true mortality. If we examine mortality across the second row, "Age-adjusted," and in individual age groups, the full impact of race emerges. For example, infant mortality in the U.S. in 1980 was 121 percent higher among black than white females (21.2 vs. 9.6) and 111 percent higher among black than white males (25.9 vs. 12.3). Death rates among young adults 25–29 years of age are 118 percent greater for black males and 117 percent greater for black females. It is only at age 85 that the race differential in death rates tends to disappear. According to the demographer Donald Bogue (1969:595–596), "throughout almost all of the ages when great progress in death control has been accomplished,

TABLE 3.2 Male to female death rate ratios among the elderly, by age and race, 1940–1980

	Death rate ratio, by age				
Race and year	65–69	70–74	75–79	80–84	85 +
All races					
1940	1.34	1.25	1.20	1.15	1.08
1950	1.58	1.40	1.29	1.21	1.13
1960	1.83	1.62	1.42	1.26	1.11
1970	2.02	1.82	1.61	1.41	1.15
1980	1.98	1.90	1.76	1.55	1.27
White					
1940	1.36	1.26	1.19	1.14	1.07
1950	1.62	1.42	1.29	1.20	1.12
1960	1.88	1.65	1.43	1.27	1.12
1970	2.10	1.86	1.62	1.42	1.16
1980	2.02	1.94	1.78	1.56	1.27
Other races					
1940	1.20	1.20	1.28	1.33	1.25
1950	1.28	1.23	1.28	1.30	1.20
1960	1.47	1.37	1.30	1.30	1.18
1970	1.52	1.46	1.47	1.33	1.12
1980	1.74	1.58	1.53	1.45	1.32

Sources: Robert D. Grove and Alice M. Hetzel, *Vital Statistics Rates in the United States, 1940–1960* (Washington, D.C.: National Center for Health Statistics, 1968), Table 55; National Center for Health Statistics, *Vital Statistics of the United States, 1970,* vol. 2, *Mortality,* Part A (1974), Table 1-8; Advance Report of Final Mortality Statistics, 1980, *Monthly Vital Statistics Report,* vol. 32, no. 4 (1983), Table 1.

death rates for blacks are about double those of whites.''

While there has been some long-term progress in reducing the race differential in mortality, this has slowed to a standstill recently. In 1960 the age-adjusted death rate for blacks was 32 percent higher than the comparable figure for whites. For 1970 this differential was 35 percent, and by 1980 it was 33 percent.

The race differential in mortality is greater for females than for males. As Table 3.1 shows, in 1980 black males had an age-adjusted death rate that was 48 percent higher than the rate for white males in 1980 (11.1 vs. 7.5); this differential for females was 54 percent (6.3 vs. 4.1). Also, the sex differential in mortality is smaller for blacks on a proportional basis than for the white population. Among whites, males have an age-adjusted death rate that is 83 percent higher than that among females; among blacks this difference is 76 percent. It appears that black women have not been able to achieve as large a share of the available advancements in death control as have black men (Bogue, 1969:596–597).

Two additional points need be stressed with regard to race differentials in mortality. First, there is no reason to believe that blacks in particular or non-whites in general are biologically less fit than whites in their capacity to survive. What this point emphasizes is that race differentials in mortality reflect unnecessarily high mortality among non-whites. Second, other factors, not the least of which is socioeconomic status, confound mortality data. Kitagawa and Hauser (1973) have shown the age-adjusted mortality rates for Japanese-Americans to be about one-third the corresponding rates for whites and one-

half the rate for blacks. Their analysis of median family income among these groups suggests that socioeconomic status may account for a considerable proportion of the race differentials in mortality.

How does low socioeconomic status contribute to the higher mortality rates prevalent among blacks? Their lack of access to high-quality medical care is one reason. According to the U.S. Office of Health Resources (1979), black people receive considerably fewer preventive health services, on the average, than do white people. Also, medical treatment of blacks is often delayed until the onset of later stages of disease (Gonnella, Louis and McCord, 1976).

While we are unable to say precisely whether biological or social factors are more important contributors to mortality differentials among different population groups in our society, we recognize that aging, even biological aging, does not occur in a social vacuum. Age-adjusted death rates in our total population are, for example, only about one-third what they were at the beginning of this century. Additionally, even when considering those who as a group are already chronologically old, there has been a significant decline in death rates since 1960. For males aged 65–74 years, for example, the reduction from 1960 to 1983 is 20 percent; for comparably aged females, the reduction is 27 percent. These reductions in the death rates of our population reflect at least four factors, all of which involve attempts begun in the nineteenth century to increase control over the environment (Dorn, 1959): (1) increased food supply; (2) development of commerce and transportation; (3) changes in technology and industry; and (4) increased control over infectious disease.

LIFE EXPECTANCY

Progress in the reduction of mortality is also reflected in figures for average life expectancy at birth. Average life expectancy at birth (defined as the average number of years a person born today can expect to live under current mortality conditions) has shown great improvement since 1900. It rose from 49.2 years in 1900–02 to 73.9 years in 1980–81 (Table 3.3). This change constitutes a 50 percent increase in life expectancy at birth, or an average annual gain of more than 0.3 years in this period. Still, just as there are significant sex and race differentials in mortality, there are similar differentials in life expectancy. As Table 3.3 shows, the population group with the highest life expectancy at birth in 1980–81 is white female (78.4 years); non-white males have the lowest life expectancy (65.7 years). All groups have substantially increased life expectancies since 1900. Better sanitary conditions, the development of effective public health programs and rises in the standard of living are three additional factors often cited to explain increased life expectancy in this century.

Life expectancy at birth is a function of death rates at all ages. Thus the statistic does not tell us at what specific ages improvement has occurred. We are particularly interested in judging progress in *survivorship* for those 65 and over. One technique for judging such progress is to look at actual survivorship rates. For example, in 1900–02, 40.9 percent of newborn babies could be expected to reach age 65; by 1983 the figure had almost doubled, to 78.4 percent. The proportion of persons surviving from age 65 to age 85 more than doubled between 1900 and 1984. In 1900–02, 14.8 percent of those aged 65 could expect to survive to age 85; in 1984 this figure was 37.4 percent, though 46.1 percent of women aged 65 could expect to survive to age 85 (Metropolitan Life Insurance Company, 1985, 1987).

TABLE 3.3 Years of life expectancy at birth, by race and sex, 1900–02 to 1980–81

Years	All groups	White		Other races	
		Male	Female	Male	Female
1900–02[a]	49.2	48.2	51.1	32.5	35.0
1909–11[a]	51.6	50.3	53.7	34.2	37.7
1919–21[a]	56.5	56.6	58.6	47.2	47.0
1929–31	59.3	59.2	62.8	47.5	49.5
1939–41	63.8	63.3	67.2	52.4	55.4
1949–51	68.2	66.4	72.2	59.1	63.0
1959–61	68.9	67.6	74.2	61.5	66.5
1969–71	70.7	67.9	75.5	61.0	69.1
1980–81	73.9	70.8	78.4	65.7	74.8

Sources: National Center for Health Statistics, *Vital Statistics of the United States, 1978,* vol. 2, sec. 5, *Life Tables* (1980), Tables 5-A and 5-5; Annual Summary of Births, Deaths, Marriages, and Divorces: United States, 1981, *Monthly Vital Statistics Report,* vol. 30, no. 13 (1982), pp. 3–4 and 15.
[a]Death-registration states only.

A second technique for measuring changes in survivorship involves looking at changes in age-specific life expectancy. Table 3.4 presents life expectancies at various elderly ages, by sex and race, in the United States for 1900–02 and 1980. Life expectancy at age 65 has moved ahead more slowly than has life expectancy at birth since 1900 (4.8 vs. 24.7 years). The small increase of "expectation" values for those 65 and over between 1900–02 and 1980 is in part a function of the relative lack of success the health sciences have had in reducing adult deaths caused by heart disease, cancer and cerebrovascular diseases. These have been the leading causes of death among persons 65 years and over since 1950. While some modest progress in reducing death rates due to heart disease and cerebrovascular diseases has been made in the last quarter of a century, the death rate from malignant neoplasms (cancer) has increased by about 13 percent since 1950.

MORBIDITY AND DISABILITY

There has been a reduction in the incidence of infectious diseases in the United States and an increase in the importance of chronic conditions. Today, chronic conditions represent the key health problems affecting middle-aged and older adults. These conditions are long-lasting, and their progress generally causes irreversible pathology. Data recently made available by the National Center for Health Statistics shows that 25.9 percent of all office visits to physicians made by aged individuals were related to conditions of the circulatory system, including heart conditions. Another 9.4 percent of the office visits

TABLE 3.4 Years of life expectancy at various elderly ages, 1900–02 and 1980

	White		Black	
Year and age	Male	Female	Male	Female
1900–02[a]				
65	11.5	12.2	10.4	11.4
70	9.0	9.6	8.3	9.6
75	6.8	7.3	6.6	7.9
80	5.1	5.5	5.1	6.5
85	3.8	4.1	4.0	5.1
1980				
65	14.2	18.5	13.5	17.3
70	11.3	14.8	11.1	14.2
75	8.8	11.5	8.9	11.4
80	6.7	8.6	6.9	9.0
85	5.0	6.3	5.3	7.0

Sources: National Center for Health Statistics, *Vital Statistics of the United States, 1978*, vol. 2, sec. 5, *Life Tables* (1980), Table 5-4; Advance Report of Final Mortality Statistics, 1980, *Monthly Vital Statistics Report*, vol. 32, no. 4 (1983), Table 2.
[a]Death-registration states only.

made by those 65 years and over involved a diagnosis of disease of the nervous system or sense organs, including hearing and vision impairments; 9.3 percent of office visits involved diseases of musculoskeletal system and connective systems, a category that includes arthritis and rheumatism. Thus three disease categories dominated by chronic conditions accounted for 44.6 percent of all physician office visits by older people in 1975.

Table 3.5 presents data on chronic conditions among three age groups of people, according to type of conditions, sex and family income. The age groups include individuals 17 to 44, 45 to 64 and 65 years and over. The prevalence of chronic conditions among the elderly is higher than among younger persons. The reported prevalence rates among the elderly for arthritis, heart condition, hypertension, and vision and hearing impairments show the most substantial differences when compared with the prevalence rates of chronic conditions among those 17 to 44 years and 45 to 64 years. One exception is the category including impairments of the back or spine—those over 65 have a slightly lower prevalence rate for these orthopedic conditions than do those 45 to 64 years of age (67.1 vs. 68.2 per 1,000 population).

Among the elderly, women appear to be more likely to be troubled by arthritis, diabetes, hypertension, orthopedic ailments and vision impairments. Men are more troubled by respiratory ailments and hearing impairments. Heart conditions show almost no sex differentiation in prevalence rates. Women live longer than men, on the average, so they are more likely to suffer from a variety of chronic (and disabling) diseases. It should also be pointed out, though, that sex-role typing may make older women more ready to report chronic illness during the household interviews used to collect the data reported in Table 3.5.

The relationship between family income and the prevalence of chronic conditions is less than clear-cut. Only for arthritis does there appear to be a linear relationship between income and prevalence; the higher the family income, the lower the prevalence rate of arthritis (Table 3.5). Still, for each type of chronic condition, those elderly who have family income of less than $5,000 show a prevalence rate that is higher than that for the total population 65 years and over, while those elderly who have family income of $15,000 or more show a prevalence rate below that for the total elderly population. Most older people with low incomes had lower incomes before old age. Thus their access to medical care and their capacity to generate a favorable living environment have likely been reduced for a long period of time. This may result in higher rates of disease, as well as in earlier death. Also, some people suffer reduced incomes because of illness and disability.

The actual presence of a chronic condition is often not as important to people as the impact the condition has on their ability to carry out usual activities. Chronic illness can be burdensome, as Figure 3.2 shows, in terms of bed days, hospital days and doctor visits for selected conditions. Arthritis and rheumatism are particularly interesting examples in this regard. While accounting for relatively few hospital days, these conditions account for 16 percent of days spent in bed by older people (nearly as much as for heart disease) and 6 percent of doctor visits (more than for cancer). Yet, just as the prevalence rates for chronic conditions increase with age, so does limitation of activity. Almost 46

TABLE 3.5 Chronic conditions among persons 17 years of age and over, according to type of condition, age, sex, and family income, United States

Type of chronic condition and year: Prevalence per 1,000 population

Age, sex, and family income	Arthritis, 1969	Asthma, 1970	Chronic bronchitis, 1970	Diabetes, 1973	Heart conditions, 1972	Hypertensive disease,[a] 1972	Impairments of back or spine (except paralysis), 1971	Hearing impairments, 1971	Vision impairments, 1971
17–44 YEARS									
Total	40.3	26.2	23.2	8.9	24.6	37.8	49.0	42.4	31.9
Sex									
Male	28.0	24.6	16.7	6.9	19.5	36.4	51.9	51.4	44.7
Female	51.3	27.6	29.1	10.8	29.3	39.1	46.4	34.2	20.3
Family Income[b]									
Less than $5,000	46.9	34.1	28.4	11.4	32.5	48.9	59.4	55.4	43.2
$5,000–$9,999	40.5	23.6	22.3	9.1	23.3	40.8	50.5	44.0	31.7
$10,000–$14,999	38.7	24.4	21.8	8.4	22.5	35.9	47.4	39.3	28.7
$15,000 or more	35.9	26.8	23.7	8.0	24.3	29.8	42.4	35.8	30.9
45–64 YEARS									
Total	204.2	33.1	35.4	42.6	88.8	126.7	68.2	114.1	63.0
Sex									
Male	148.0	29.3	28.5	40.6	97.4	101.3	68.2	140.2	73.6
Female	255.3	36.7	41.6	44.4	81.0	149.6	68.2	90.5	53.4
Family income[b]									
Less than $5,000	297.8	53.5	44.2	74.1	139.3	172.7	102.8	158.9	114.1
$5,000–$9,999	200.3	33.5	38.7	43.8	92.5	125.4	67.2	118.1	57.4
$10,000–$14,999	163.7	23.7	29.0	37.8	74.3	121.3	62.3	107.3	45.9
$15,000 or more	159.8	22.7	30.3	30.5	66.6	105.3	52.2	85.9	48.9
65 YEARS AND OVER									
Total	380.3	35.8	41.2	78.5	198.7	199.4	67.1	294.3	204.6
Sex									
Male	287.0	42.3	47.3	60.3	199.3	141.2	54.6	338.2	183.1
Female	450.1	31.1	36.6	91.3	198.3	240.9	76.3	262.1	220.4
Family income[b]									
Less than $5,000	411.7	41.4	45.4	82.0	219.0	216.1	78.7	232.0	232.0
$5,000–$9,999	353.3	32.6	37.2	76.1	190.0	179.5	57.3	271.6	163.2
$10,000–$14,999	310.9	*	27.4	81.1	158.9	192.6	39.3	247.3	181.3
$15,000 or more	300.8	*	40.7	62.7	174.8	161.4	48.5	259.2	169.2

[a] Without heart involvement.
[b] Excludes unknown family income.
Data based on household interviews of samples of the civilian noninstitutionalized population.
Source: Division on Health Interview Statistics, National Center for Health Statistics. Selected reports from the Health Interview Survey, 1969–1973, Vital and Health Statistics, Series 10, and unpublished data from the Health Interview Survey.

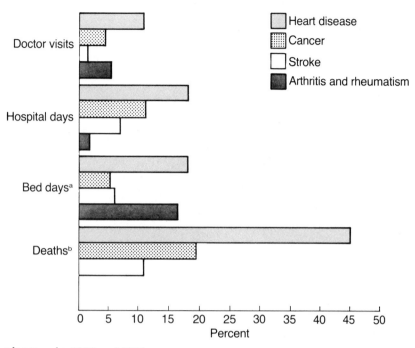

^aAverage for 1979 and 1980.
^bProvisional data.

Figure 3.2   Burden of illness for persons 65 years of age and over, according to selected conditions, United States, 1980. Source: National Center for Health Statistics: Division of Health Care Statistics, Division of Health Interview Statistics, and Division of Vital Statistics.

percent of all those 65 years of age and over report some limitation of activity; 17.1 percent report being unable to work or keep house (USDHEW, 1976).

Table 3.6 presents data on the number of restricted-activity days per person, by chronic activity limitation status, for those 45 to 64 years of age and those 65 years and over in the United States in 1979. In general, females show a higher number of restricted-activity days than do males. This is consistent with the generally higher rates of chronic illness they report. What is particularly interesting about this table is the favorable comparison it provides between those aged 65 years and over and those aged 45–64

years. For example, among males with limitation of activity, the number of restricted-activity days per person 65 years and over in each chronic activity limitation status is actually less than the comparable number for the 45–64 years group. This data seems supportive of Manton's (1982) argument that, primarily due to effective medical management, the rate of progression of many diseases has slowed. Presumably, as a result, an aged person with a limitation in activity can expect to suffer the same or a similar number of restricted-activity days in a year as a comparably limited person aged 45–64 years.

Some data are available for making cross-national comparisons on activity limitations

TABLE 3.6 Number of restricted activity days per person per year, by chronic activity limitation status, sex and age, 1979

Sex and age	Total population	With no limitation of activity	With limitation of activity			
			Total	Limited but not major activity[a]	Limited in amount or kind of major activity[a]	Unable to carry on major activity[a]
Total						
All ages	19.0	10.5	69.1	33.9	63.8	115.4
45–64 years	26.0	10.4	75.3	34.0	69.3	121.3
65 years and over	41.9	12.4	76.4	37.1	64.6	108.0
Male						
All ages	16.9	9.3	60.6	25.8	42.0	101.7
45–64 years	24.0	9.0	68.5	27.2	48.8	105.3
65 years and over	38.2	9.8	67.5	26.1	31.9	94.0
Female						
All ages	21.1	11.6	77.1	41.2	76.5	153.2
45–64 years	27.8	11.6	82.1	39.9	80.7	184.9
65 years and over	44.5	14.0	83.4	42.1	77.4	140.4

[a]Major activity refers to ability to work, keep house, or engage in school or preschool activities.
Source: National Center for Health Statistics, *Health, United States, 1985,* U.S. Department of Health and Human Services, Public Health Service, No. 86-1232 (Washington, D.C.: U.S. Government Printing Office, 1986).

among the aged of comparably developed countries. Table 3.7 presents data on the proportion of aged who are bedfast, housebound, and ambulatory with difficulty in Denmark, Britain, Israel, Poland, Yugoslavia, Japan and the United States. Combining the bedfast and housebound categories, only Yugoslavia has a lower proportion of its aged citizens so limited in activity than does the United States. Two important factors must be considered when observing this data. First, cultural considerations may be at work in the reporting. Shanas and her colleagues (1968), for example, suggest that "old people in the U.S., more than old people in Europe, seem to feel that to admit incapacity is somehow psychologically wrong." Palmore (1975) points out that the high proportion of Japanese aged who are housebound (16 percent)

may simply reflect their greater willingness to report being housebound. Finally, these data compare *only* the most disabled portion of the aged population of the selected countries; it does not compare the health of the great majority of aged persons in these seven lands.

MENTAL HEALTH

According to Pfeiffer (1977), approximately 15 percent of the elderly population in the United States suffer from significant, substantial or at least moderate psychopathological conditions. Whanger (1973) estimates that between 70 percent and 80 percent of aged nursing-home patients suffer from moderately severe or severe mental disorders. Among the specified diagnoses, *organic brain syndromes,* depressive disorders, schizophrenia and alcohol disorders accounted for the highest rates of patient care episodes in outpatient psychiatric services for old people in the United States in 1971. The same list obtains for inpatient facilities. Over 600,000 nursing-home residents in the United States in 1973–74 were diagnosed as senile.

Such figures must always be viewed with some caution. The epidemiology of psychopathological conditions is beset by conceptual and methodological difficulties. Even under careful conditions of assessment, diagnosing schizophrenia or depression is often difficult. The fact that doctors use different definitions and criteria, and vary widely in their competence as well as in their understanding of aging processes, should make one suspicious of the adequacy of their diagnoses. In addition, as Libow (1973) points out, much of the early mental change shown by elderly persons can be explained by changes in the environment. A National Institute of Mental Health study of healthy male volunteers, whose average age was 70 at the start of the study and who were followed for 11 years, found a strong relationship between survival and the organization of a subject's daily behavior (Bartko and Patterson, 1971). The greater the complexity and variability of a day's behavior, the greater the likelihood of survival.

Despite the conceptual and methodological difficulties involved in determining the degree and extent to which psychopathological conditions are distributed among the elderly, it is quite clear that some older people do have mental health problems. These problems are often categorized according to the degree of actual impairment in brain functioning.

Depression appears to be the most common of the functional psychiatric disorders in the later years, yet it is not often recognized in older people (Kermis, 1986). Depression can vary in duration and degree; it may be triggered by loss of a loved one or by the onset of a physical disease. A depressed individual may show any combination of psycho-

TABLE 3.7 Proportion of population aged 65 and over, bedfast, housebound, and ambulatory with difficulty, in seven countries

Country	Percentage bedfast	Percentage housebound	Percentage ambulatory with difficulty
Denmark	2	8	14
Britain	3	11	8
United States	2	6	6
Israel	2	13	n.a.
Poland	4	6	16
Yugoslavia	3	4	20
Japan	4	16	n.a.

Source: E. Palmore, *The Honorable Elders* (Durham, N.C.: Duke University Press, 1975). E. Shanas, P. Townsend, D. Wedderburn, H. Friis, P. Milhøj and J. Stehouver, *Older People in Three Industrial Societies.* (New York: Atherton Press, 1968).

logical and physiological manifestations. Kermis (1986) lists some atypical clinical features that further confuse diagnosis, including pseudodementia (apathy and slowness of cognition resembling dementia) and somatic complaints without obvious mood changes. Drug therapies are popular for treatment. Other modalities are available, although, as Butler and Lewis (1977) indicate, many professionals view the elderly as "poor candidates" for the psychotherapies.

Suicidal thoughts often accompany depression. Gardner, Bahn and Mack (1963) found in their research that the majority of older persons committing suicide have been depressed. According to the U.S. Center for Health Statistics, the suicide rate among the elderly in 1982 was 50 percent higher than that among the total population. This statistic may present a conservative picture. Many doctors do not report suicides because they think it stigmatizes the surviving family members; family members themselves often hide or destroy suicide notes—usually unnecessarily—to try to ensure payments by life insurance companies.

Table 3.8 presents suicide rates by sex, race and age group for 1982. Aged white males show the highest suicide rate of any group. Their rate is more than three times that of aged black males, more than five times that of aged white females, and about 22 times that of aged black females. Aged females in the United States have one of the lowest suicide rates in the world. Aged American males fall in the middle of the range represented by selected countries. Male elderly have higher suicide rates in Austria, Denmark, France and West Germany; countries in which the elderly have lower suicide rates than is the case in the U.S. include Ireland, England, Israel and Norway, among others (U.S. Bureau of the Census, 1982: Table 123).

Two additional common functional psychiatric disorders in the later years are *paranoia* and *hypochondriasis*. Paranoia is a delusional state that is usually persecutory in nature. It often involves attributing motivations to other people that they simply do not have. Paranoia is more common in individuals suffering from sensory deficits such as

TABLE 3.8 Suicide rates (per 100,000 population) by sex, race, and age group, 1982

	Males		*Females*	
	White	*Black*	*White*	*Black*
All ages	20.7	10.1	6.1	2.1
5–14 years	0.9	0.8	0.3	0.1
15–24 years	21.2	11.0	4.5	3.7
25–34 years	26.1	20.3	7.5	3.7
35–44 years	23.6	15.6	9.2	4.0
45–54 years	25.8	11.8	10.4	3.1
55–64 years	27.9	11.9	9.5	3.2
65 and over	38.9	12.4	6.6	1.8

Source: U.S. Bureau of the Census, *Statistical Abstract of the U.S.,* 1986 (Washington, D.C.: U.S. Government Printing Office, 1985), Table 122.

hearing loss (Post, 1980). Some paranoia may be caused by changes in life situation, such as relocation or other stresses. Kermis (1986) describes a 72-year-old woman hospitalized while recovering from major heart surgery. She had a persistent delusion that CIA agents were spying on her. She recorded these occurrences and reported them to the staff, who discovered that her CIA visits corresponded to security guards' checks of the floor. Characteristically, the initial premise of the paranoid is irrational, although the rest of the delusional system often follows logically. As Kermis (1986) notes, if the paranoid's basic premise is accepted, the rest of the delusion often makes sense. Most paranoids have a fairly focused problem and are not impaired in their daily functioning. If the disorder remains chronic, however, social and marital function may be negatively affected (American Psychiatric Association, 1980).

Hypochondriasis is an overconcern for one's health, usually accompanied by delusions about physical dysfunction and/or disease. The conventional wisdom is that hypochondriacs displace their psychological distress onto the body. A number of observers have emphasized the utility of the condition—after all, it is far more acceptable in this society to be physically ill than it is to be emotionally or mentally disabled (Pfeiffer and Busse, 1973). Hypochondriacs will diligently seek medical help, yet treatment of the disorder is difficult because they are not predisposed to psychological explanations of their condition.

The 1980 edition of the American Psychiatric Association's *Diagnostic and Statistical Manual of Mental Disorders* (DSM-III) makes the distinction between *organic brain syndromes* (OBS) and *organic mental disorders* (OMD). "Organic brain syndrome" is used to refer to a group of psychological or behavioral signs and symptoms without reference to etiology; "organic mental disorder" designates a particular OBS in which the etiology is known or presumed (APA, 1980). OBS can be grouped into six categories, the most common of which are Delirium, Dementia, and Intoxication and Withdrawal. Perhaps as many as one-half of the aged population with mental disorders have OBS (Kramer, Taube and Redick, 1973; Redick, Kramer and Taube, 1973); the prevalence rate of OBS appears to increase with age (Kramer, Taube and Redick, 1973), although onset usually occurs in the seventh to ninth decades and is more common in women than men (Fann, Wheless and Richman, 1976).

Primary Degenerative Dementia of the Alzheimer type may be the single most common OBS. According to the DSM-III, between 2 and 4 percent of the entire population over the age of 65 may have this dementia. *Alzheimer's disease* has an "insidious onset and gradually progressive course" (APA, 1980). It brings a multifaceted loss of intellectual abilities, including memory, judgment, and abstract thought, as well as changes in personality and behavior. The clinical picture may also be clouded by the presence of depression, delusions or, more rarely, Delirium.

Initially, the Alzheimer's victim experiences minor symptoms that may be attributed to stress or physical illness. With time, however, the person becomes more forgetful. Things get misplaced, routine chores take longer and already answered questions are repeated. As the disease progresses, memory loss as well as confusion, irritability, restlessness and agitation are likely to appear. Judgment, concentration, orientation, writing, reading, speech, motor behavior and naming of objects may also be affected. Even when a loving and supportive family is available, the Alzheimer's victim may ultimately require institutional care (USDHHS, 1984).

At the present time, there is no cure for Alzheimer's disease. What are the possible causes of this debilitating disease? Since the 1970s, research scientists have been studying the evidence of a significant and progressive decrease in the activity of the enzyme choline acetyltransferase (ChAT) in the brain tissue of Alzheimer's patients. ChAT is an important ingredient in neurotransmissions involved with learning and memory. There appears to be a link between change in this neurochemical activity and changes in cognition and the physical appearance of the brains of Alzheimer's patients (USDHHS, 1984). Additional research is needed to determine whether accumulations of trace metals in the brain (such as aluminum) are a primary cause of Alzheimer's disease or if other factors like slow-acting transmissible viruses might combine with environmental factors to trigger the onset of the disease (USDHHS, 1984).

Do social or psychological experiences contribute to the cause or development of Alzheimer's disease? Too little research has addressed this question. For the most part, social and behavioral scientists have focused on the development of diagnostic tests, the changes in language use that results from brain dysfunction, and the need for special support for the families of disease victims (USDHHS, 1984).

The descriptions of the organic brain syndromes presented in DSM-III are clear and straightforward; this gives the impression that their recognition and diagnosis are equally so. This is not the case, though. Not every

patient with the symptoms described in DSM-III has OBS (Wells, 1978). There is some reliable evidence to demonstrate that OBS is overdiagnosed (Clark, 1980; Fox, Topel and Huckman, 1975; Glassman, 1980; Kaercher, 1980; Marsden and Harrison, 1972; Seltzer and Sherwin, 1978; Wells, 1978). For example, Duckworth and Ross (1975) compared psychiatric diagnoses given to patients over age 65 in Toronto, New York and London. They found that organic brain disorders were diagnosed with more than 50 percent greater frequency in New York than in either Toronto or London. Though variation in patient populations may account for some of this difference, Wells (1978) suggests that in Toronto and London a greater emphasis is placed on recognizing functional disorders in the aged— thus elderly patients are more likely to be labeled correctly.

Libow (1973) has used the term *pseudo-senility* to refer to conditions that may manifest themselves as senility and thus cause misdiagnosis or mislabeling of OBS. Causes of pseudosenility include drug interactions, malnutrition and fever. When these conditions are treated, the senility often goes away. While admittedly there are no definitive studies identifying the frequency of pseudosenility, a task force sponsored by the National Institute on Aging suggests that 10 to 20 percent of all older people diagnosed with mental impairments have these reversible conditions (NIA, 1980).

The importance of organic brain syndromes, in both numerical and personal terms, is being increasingly recognized. This is reflected in gerontological and popular literature pointing out that many curable physical and psychological disorders in the elderly produce intellectual impairments that may be difficult to distinguish from OBS. More importantly, this growing body of literature states clearly, if not emphatically, that normal aging does not include the symptoms of OBS; these are diseases, not inevitable accompaniments of aging.

SELF-ASSESSMENT OF HEALTH

The prevalence of chronic conditions, including psychopathological conditions, and the relatively high levels of limitation of activity may give the impression that elderly people view themselves as being in poor health and unable to function. This is not the case. According to data collected by the National Center for Health Statistics, the majority of older people (68.9 percent) assess themselves as being in excellent or good health when compared to other people their own age. Table 3.9 presents data on the self-assessment of health according to age, sex and family income. Poor health was a somewhat more common assessment among older men than women (9.4 percent vs. 8.0 percent), although the difference is quite small.

TABLE 3.9 Self-assessment of health, according to age, sex, and family income: United States, 1975

Age, sex, and family income	All levels[a]	Level of health, percent distribution			
		Excellent	Good	Fair	Poor
ALL AGES					
Total	100.0	48.6	38.4	9.7	2.8
Sex					
Male	100.0	51.7	36.5	8.5	2.8
Female	100.0	45.7	40.1	10.8	2.8
Family income[b]					
Less than $5,000	100.0	31.9	41.7	17.9	7.8
$5,000–$9,999	100.0	40.9	42.8	12.3	3.4
$10,000–$14,000	100.0	51.9	38.1	8.0	1.5
$15,000 or more	100.0	60.3	33.3	5.0	1.0
65 YEARS AND OVER					
Total	100.0	28.6	40.3	21.5	8.6
Sex					
Male	100.0	28.1	40.0	21.4	9.4
Female	100.0	28.9	40.6	21.6	8.0
Family income[b]					
Less than $5,000	100.0	23.3	38.7	24.9	12.2
$5,000–$9,999	100.0	29.8	41.3	21.4	6.8
$10,000–$14,999	100.0	31.6	42.7	19.9	5.1
$15,000 or more	100.0	38.7	40.3	13.9	5.8

[a]Includes unknown level of health.
[b]Excludes unknown family income.
Data based on household interviews of a sample of civilian non-institutionalized population.
Source: Division of Health Interview Statistics, National Center for Health Statistics; data from the Health Interview Survey.

The proportion of the elderly who reported poor health increased as family income diminished. Less than 6 percent (5.8) of aged individuals with family incomes of $15,000 or more assessed their health as poor; 12.2 percent was the comparable figure among those with incomes of less than $15,000.

Self-assessment of health may be as important as actual medical status in predicting general emotional state and behavior (Maddox and Douglas, 1973). Self-assessed health status also correlates with other measures of health status and health behavior. For example, people who rate their health as poorer than others are more likely to utilize medical services than people who rate their health as better than others (Kovar and Wilson, 1975).

SUMMARY

Senescence refers to the effects that lead to the increasing vulnerability individuals face with increasing age. Is senescence an inherent biological process? That may be difficult to say, yet as long ago as 1825 Gompertz identified a pattern to our increased vulnerability through the course of life.

The leading cause of death among the elderly is heart disease, followed by cancer and stroke. Death rates differ significantly by sex and race. Average life expectancy at birth has increased about 50 percent since the turn of the century, and survivorship rates to old age have improved even more dramatically. In 1983, the proportion of newborn babies expected to reach age 65 was 78.4 percent, almost twice the figure in 1900–02. Age-specific life expectancy at 65 years has moved ahead more slowly than has life expectancy at birth during the twentieth century.

Chronic conditions (including psychopathological conditions) and their accompanying disabilities represent the key health problems affecting middle-aged and older adults. The prevalence of chronic conditions varies by age, sex, race and family income. Yet the majority of older people assess themselves as being in excellent or good health when compared to other people their own age.

Depression is the most common of the functional psychiatric disorders in the later years. Paranoia and hypochondriasis are also commonly experienced disorders of later life. In 1982, the suicide rate among the elderly was 50 percent higher than that for the total population. The single most common organic brain syndrome is Primary Degenerative Dementia of the Alzheimer type. Alzheimer's disease has a gradually progressive course and brings loss of cognitive function as well as changes in personality and behavior. Diagnosis is difficult, and there is some reliable evidence that the disease is overdiagnosed. While research continues, there is currently no cure for Alzheimer's disease.

KEY TERMS

acute illness
age-specific life expectancy
Alzheimer's disease
chronic illness
depression
hypochondriasis
life expectancy at birth
morbidity
mortality
organic brain syndrome

organic mental disorder
paranoia
pseudosenility
senescence

STUDY QUESTIONS

1. Define *senescence*. How is senescence distinguished from other biological processes?
2. What is the relationship between mortality and morbidity? Taking biological and social factors into consideration, explain the impact of sex on mortality rates. What role does socioeconomic status play in explaining racial differences in mortality in the U.S. today?
3. Distinguish improvement in this century that has come in life expectancy at birth from that which is reflected in survivorship for those 65 years and over. Explain the relatively small increase since 1900 in age-specific life expectancy at 65 years.
4. How have morbidity patterns in the U.S. changed in the twentieth century? To what extent do chronic conditions interfere with the activity levels of aging men and women?
5. Distinguish between organic brain syndrome and organic mental disorder. Identify and describe three common functional psychiatric disorders of the later years.
6. What is Alzheimer's disease? Describe its progressive course. What are the suspected causes? What are the diagnostic problems in determining the prevalence rate of this and other mental disorders afflicting the elderly?
7. What is the relationship between self-assessment of health and actual medical status? What factors influence the way older people assess their own health status? Describe the patterns of influence of these factors.

BIBLIOGRAPHY

American Psychiatric Association. 1980. *Diagnostic and Statistical Manual of Disorders*, 3rd ed. Washington, D.C.: author.

Bartko, J., and Patterson, R. 1971. Survival among healthy old men: A multivariate analysis. In S. Grancik and R. Patterson, eds., *Human Aging II: An 11-Year Follow-up.* Washington, D.C.: U.S. Government Printing Office.

Bogue, D. 1969. *Principles of Demography.* New York: Wiley.

Butler, R., and Lewis, M. 1977. *Aging and Mental Health*, 2nd ed. St. Louis, Mo.: Mosby.

Chapman, S.H., LaPlante, M.P., and Wilensky, G. 1986. Life expectancy and health status of the aged. *Social Security Bulletin* 49(10): 24–48.

Clark, M. 1980. The scourge of senility. *Newsweek*, September 15: 85–86.

Comfort, A. 1979. *The Biology of Senescence,* 3rd ed. New York: New American Library.

Duckworth, G.S., and Ross, H. 1975. Diagnostic differences in psychogeriatric patients in Toronto, New York and London, England. *Canadian Medical Association Journal 112:* 847–851.

Fann, W., Wheless, J.C., and Richman, B.W. 1976. Treating the aged with psychotropic drugs. *Gerontologist 16:* 322–328.

Fox, J.H., Topel, J.L., and Huckman, M.S. 1975. Dementia in the elderly—A search for treatable illnesses. *Journal of Gerontology 10:* 557–574.

Fries, J.F., and Crapo, L.M. 1981. *Vitality and Aging.* San Francisco: W.H. Freeman.

Gardner, E., Bahn, A., and Mack, M. 1964. Suicide and psychiatric care in the aging. *Archives of General Psychiatry 10:* 547–553.

Glassman, M. 1980. Misdiagnosis of senile dementia: Denial of care to the elderly. *Social Work 25:* 288–292.

Gonnella, J.S., Louis, D.Z., and McCord, J.J. 1976. The stage concept: An approach to the assessment of outcome of ambulatory care. *Medical Care 14:* 13–21.

Kaercher, D. 1980. Senility: A misdiagnosis. *Better Homes and Gardens,* November: 27–32, 34–37.

Kermis, M. 1986. *Mental Health in Late Life: The Adaptive Process.* Boston: Jones and Bartlett.

Kitagawa, E. and Hauser, P.M. 1973. *Differential Mortality in the United States: A Study in*

Socioeconomic Epidemiology. Cambridge, Mass.: Harvard University Press.

Kovar, M., and Wilson, R. 1975. Perceived health status—How good is proxy reporting? *Proceedings of the American Statistical Assn., Social Statistics Sect.,* pp. 495–500.

Kramer, M., Taube, C.A., and Redick, R.W. 1973. Patterns of use of psychiatric facilities by the aged: Past, present and future. In C. Eisdorfer and M. Lawton, eds., *The Psychology of Adult Development and Aging.* Washington, D.C.: American Psychological Association.

Libow, L. 1973. Pseudo-senility: Acute and reversible organic brain syndrome. *Journal of the American Geriatrics Society 21:* 112–120.

Maddox, G., and Douglas E. 1973. Self-assessment of health, a longitudinal study of elderly subjects. *Journal of Health and Social Behavior 14:* 87–92.

Madigan, F. 1957. Are sex mortality differentials biologically caused? *Milbank Memorial Fund Quarterly* 35(2): 202–223.

Manton, K. 1982. Changing concepts of morbidity and mortality in the elderly population. *Milbank Memorial Fund Quarterly* 60(2): 183–244.

Marcus, A.C., and Siegel, J.M. 1982. Sex differences in the use of physician services: A preliminary test of the fixed role hypothesis. *Journal of Health and Social Behavior 23:* 186–196.

Marsden, C.D., and Harrison, M.J.G. 1972. Outcome of investigation of patients with presenile dementia. *British Medical Journal 2:* 249–252.

Metropolitan Life Insurance Company. 1985. Slight gains in U.S. longevity. *Statistical Bulletin* 66(3): 20–23.

_____ . 1987. Trends in longevity after age 65. *Statistical Bulletin* 68(1): 10–17.

National Institute on Aging. 1980. Treatment possibilities for mental impairment in the elderly. *Journal of the American Medical Association 244:* 259–263.

Palmore, E. 1975. *The Honorable Elders.* Durham, N.C.: Duke University Press.

Pfeiffer, E. 1977. Psychopathy and social pathology. In J. Birren and K. Schaie, eds., *Handbook of the Psychology of Aging.* New York: Van Nostrand Reinhold.

_____ , and Busse, E. 1973. Mental disorders in later life: Affective disorder, paranoid, neurotic and situational reactions. In E. Busse and E. Pfeiffer, eds., *Mental Illness in Later Life.* Washington, D.C.: American Psychiatric Association.

Post, F. 1980. Paranoid, schizophrenic-like and schizophrenic states in the aged. In J. Birren and A. Sloane, eds., *Handbook of Mental Health and Aging.* Washington, D.C.: American Psychiatric Association.

Redick, R., Kramer, M., and Taube, C. 1973. Epidemiology of mental illness and utilization of psychiatric facilities among older persons. In E. Busse and E. Pfeiffer, eds., *Mental Illness in Later Life.* Washington, D.C.: American Psychiatric Association.

Seltzer, B., and Sherwin, I. 1978. Organic brain syndromes: An empirical study and critical review. *American Journal of Psychiatry 135:* 13–21.

Shanas, E., Townsend, P., Wedderburn, D., Friis, H., Milhhoj, P., and Stehouver, J. 1968. *Old People in Three Industrial Societies.* New York: Atherton Press.

Siegel, J.S. 1979. *Prospective Trends in the Size and Structure of the Elderly Population, Impact of Mortality Trends, and Some Implications.* Current Population Reports, Special Studies Series P-23, No. 78. Washington, D.C.: U.S. Department of Commerce, Bureau of the Census.

Strehler, B. 1962. *Time, Cells and Aging.* New York: Academic Press.

U.S. Bureau of the Census. 1982. *Statistical Abstract of the United States, 1982–83.* Washington, D.C.: U.S. Government Printing Office.

U.S. Department of Health, Education, and Welfare. 1976. *Health Characteristics of Persons with Chronic Activity Limitation: United States — 1974.* DHEW Publication No. (HRA) 77-1539. Rockville, Md.: National Center for Health Statistics.

U.S. Department of Health and Human Services. 1984. *Progress Report on Alzheimer's Disease,* vol. II. National Institutes of Health

Publication No. 84-2500. Washington, D.C.: U.S. Government Printing Office.

U.S. Office of Health Resources. 1979. *Health Status of Minorities and Low-income Groups.* DHEW Publication No. (HRA) 79-627, Health Resources Administration. Washington, D.C.: U.S. Government Printing Office.

Wells, C.E. 1978. Chronic brain disease: An overview. *American Journal of Psychiatry 135*: 1–12.

Whanger, A. 1973. A study of institutionalized elderly in Durham County. Paper presented at annual meeting, Gerontological Society, Miami, Florida.

Zopf, P.E. 1986. *America's Older Population.* Houston, Tex.: Cap and Gown Press.

CHAPTER **4**

Biological Theories of Aging

Numerous theories have proposed to explain why we age. No single one serves to answer this age-old question definitively. After all, aging is a complex phenomenon. Different explanations may be required for different aspects of the aging process; diverse phenomena may act together to account for biological aging. In general, theories of biological aging can be described as focusing on one of two fundamental suppositions. One presupposes a genetic basis for the aging process; the other views *senescence* as a result of "wear and tear." Attempts to explain the actual mechanism of biological aging have focused upon (1) changes in the properties of replicating cells; (2) the loss of or injury to *post-mitotic cells;* and (3) primary changes in non-cellular materials of the body. A fourth approach locates a mechanism of aging in a regulatory program of the body, such as the hormonal system or the immune system.

Biologic aging is viewed as a progressive decline in the ability to respond to the stresses of a dynamic environment. The decline in the ability to maintain *homeostasis* leads to functional impairment and, ultimately, death. Although it is difficult to distinguish between normal aging and disease, aging per se is usually distinguished by four criteria (Strehler, 1982). The aging process must be deleterious to the organisms, reducing function. Second, it must be progressive, occurring gradually over time. Third, aging is intrinsic and therefore unrelated to modifiable environmental factors. Finally, it is universal, occurring in all members of the species.

Differentiating between normal aging and superimposed disease is vital to understanding the aging process. The ultimate cause of the majority of deaths in older adults is the physiologic decline that increases the risk of disease. Mortality usually ensues when the ability to withstand the challenge of disease is overwhelmed. For instance, the increased risk of death from pneumonia among older persons is associated with age-related declines in the body's immune defense and reduced pulmonary reserve and function (Rothschild, 1984).

Unlocking the mystery of aging and extending the human life span has been the dream of many. Efforts at prolonging life have been in the written and oral records of societies dating back many thousands of years. Research in biogerontology continues. There are no magic potions to "cure" aging, despite the fact that books on longevity and its promotion have appeared on best-seller lists in recent years. Creams, vitamins and nutrient supplements have been among the life-extending aids promoted. They represent the continuation of a "fountain" theme, based on the idea that there is some unusual substance that has the property of greatly increasing the length of life. The search for the fountain of youth in 1513 by Juan Ponce de Leon (who accidentally discovered Florida instead) is a good example of this rejuvenation theme. Clearly, the fountain theme still lives. Various so-called anti-aging cures were recently highlighted in a congressional hearing on medical quackery (House Select Committee on Aging, 1984).

What follows in this chapter is an overview of some of the important research in the biol-ogy of aging. The goal of such research is not to grant immortality but to understand the aging process and, perhaps, improve the quality of life for the growing numbers of us who are joining the ranks of the aged.

CELLULAR THEORIES OF AGING

In the early part of this century it was widely believed that cells in tissue culture could divide indefinitely. This belief was founded largely on the work of Alexis Carrel and his associates at Rockefeller University. Carrel kept a culture of chick-heart fibroblast cells (cells that give rise to connective tissue) continuously dividing for a period of 34 years until he retired and terminated the work. The period of cell division exceeded the life of a chicken and was considered evidence that tissue cells were potentially immortal. Carrel's work had a significant impact on the field of gerontology. During the first half of the twentieth century, aging was not considered a characteristic of cells (Cristofalo, 1985).

During the late 1950s, Leonard Hayflick and Paul Moorehead, then at the Wistar Institute, began studying the effects of cancer-causing viruses on normal cells in culture. In maintaining such cultures, they observed that cells undergo a limited number of divisions and then die. Across several experiments, Hayflick and Moorehead (1961) noted that human fetal fibroblastic cells underwent an average of 50 divisions in vitro, with a range of 40 to 60, before losing the ability to replicate themselves. Others before them had noted the finite capacity for cell division. Because of the esteem accorded Carrel's work, they had not had confidence in their own findings. Eventually, it was discovered that Carrel's cultures had been contaminated. During the maintenance of the growth medium, fresh chick-cells had been added to the cultures.

The findings of Hayflick and Moorehead continue to be confirmed. Fries and Crapo (1981) report that in 1962 Hayflick froze some vials of embryo cells that had completed several divisions. Each year since that time, some vials have been thawed and cultured; they consistently go on to complete about 50 divisions.

The work of Hayflick and Moorehead (1961) proposed that senescence is a cellular as well as an organismic phenomenon. Aging, they held, is intrinsic to the cell and is not solely dependent on outside influences. Later, Hayflick (1965) reported that fibroblasts isolated from human adult tissue undergo a finite and predictable number of divisions. He noted that unless a cancerous transformation takes place (wherein unrestrained cell division occurs), senescence and cell death ultimately result.

Hayflick argued that (1) the limited replicative capacity of cultured normal human cells is an expression of programmed genetic events, and (2) the limit on normal cell division *in vitro* is a function of the age of the donor. It is now held that there is an inverse relationship between donor age and the replicative capacity of cultured cells (Martin, Sprague and Epstein, 1970; Schneider and Mitsui, 1976). That is, the older the donor, the fewer the number of cell divisions. Furthermore, the proliferative capacity of cells is directly related to the *maximum lifespan* of the species from which they are derived (Rohm, 1981).

As previously noted, cancer cells are capable of unlimited division. A famous line of human cancer cells referred to as HeLa (after Henrietta Lacks, the woman from whom they

were taken in 1951) is still being cultured for use in standardized cancer cell studies (Gold, 1981). The continued study of cancer cells may yet reveal the attribute that limits the replicative capacity of normal cells.

Tissue culture studies have limitations, and it is almost certain that these experiments do not literally replicate the aging process. Though they may add to our knowledge of aging, they do not necessarily dictate that the human life span is limited by what happens to cultured cells (Cristofalo, 1985). That humans age simply because their cells have an intrinsically limited capacity to divide seems unlikely. Post-mitotic cells, such as nerve and muscle cells, do not divide during adult life, yet they do show deterioration with age.

Researchers continue to suggest that aging may be genetically programmed into cells. Bernard Strehler hypothesized that programmed loss of genetic material could result in "aging." As Strehler (1973) notes, most cells possess hundreds of repetitions of DNA (the molecule of heredity) for the known genes they contain. Simply stated, the cell does not have to rely on a single copy of its genetic blueprint for any one trait. It has been found that as cells age a considerable number of repetitions are lost (Johnson, Crisp and Strehler, 1972). This is especially the case for brain, heart and skeletal muscle cells. Although these post-mitotic cells do not divide, with age the blueprints dictating their functional capacity might be affected. Strehler suspects that cells may be programmed, at a fixed point in life, to commence manufacturing a substance that inhibits protein synthesis within a cell.

An old school of thought maintains that aging is the result of genetic mutations. There are many variations of this theme. Orgel

(1963; 1973) hypothesized that random errors or mutations progressively accumulated in transcriptions of DNA into RNA (ribonucleic acid, carrying instructions from DNA) or through errors in the translation of RNA into protein synthesis in the cell. Since the functional ability of a cell is dependent on the quality of protein production, random errors in synthesis could eventually impair function. Hence *error catastrophe* results in cellular deterioration. Cristofalo (1972) asserts that cells with such serious errors would be limited in their capacity to influence survival. DNA is continuously repaired by enzymes that strike against faulty information. Current variations of error theories presuppose that the expression of mutations in protein synthesis may be influenced by errors in genes that are responsible for the repair capacity of the cell.

Another explanation of aging maintains that *free radicals,* produced in the course of normal cellular metabolism, cause an accumulation of cellular waste and reduce cellular efficiency. Free radicals are numerous and, though short-lived, may serve as a source of cellular damage. Such damage could be reflected in the aging process.

It is speculated that the fatty "age-pigment," *lipofuscin,* which accumulates to an appreciable extent in nerve, cardiac and skeletal muscle cells, may be an end product of cellular membrane damage caused by free radicals. Current thinking, however, holds that lipofuscin is an indicator rather than a cause of aging.

In addition to being created as a part of normal metabolic/oxidative reactions, free radicals may also be produced by radiation. The classic work of Harman (1956) demonstrated that an excess of free radicals was produced in cells as a result of radiation exposure. Animals suffering radiation damage presented symptoms of aging and a decreased life expectancy.

Advocates of the free-radical theory of aging propose that certain chemicals, called *antioxidants,* combine with and "disarm" free radicals. A number of dietary antioxidants (a common one is BHT, the food preservative) have been administered to different organisms in an attempt to increase life expectancy. Length of life has been extended in numerous studies (Clapp, Satterfield and Bowles, 1979; Comfort, Youhotsky-Gore and Pathmanathan, 1971; Economos, Ballard, Miquel, Binnard and Philpott, 1982; Harman, 1961; Munres and Minssen, 1976; Oeriu and Vochitu, 1965). Harman reported that the inclusion of dietary antioxidants increased the average length of life of experimental animals by 15 to 30 percent. Animals receiving antioxidants showed lower weight, suggesting the possibility that dietary restriction may increase longevity and confound interpretation of such experiments. Another effect of adding antioxidants to the diet of experimental animals was a reduction in tumor production (Harman, 1968).

Vitamin and mineral supplements have been promoted with the hope of extending human life. Vitamins A, E and C and the mineral selenium have antioxidant properties and deserve further study regarding possible anti-aging and anti-neoplastic action. However, there is no current evidence to support such dietary supplementation among humans for the prevention of cancer or the extension of life (Ames, 1983; Schneider and Reed, 1985; Willet and MacMahon, 1984).

Higher organisms do possess sophisticated biochemical systems for scavenging free radicals. The enzyme *superoxide dismutase* is a part of such a system. A relationship has been noted between superoxide dismutase activity and life span in varying species and species strains (Bartosz, Leyko and Fried, 1979; Kellogg and Fridovich, 1976; Munkres, Rana and Goldstein, 1984; Tolmasoff, Ono and Cutler, 1980). It is possible that the regulation of superoxide dismutase is under the control of the same genes that dictate the life span of a particular species (Schneider and Reed, 1985). Superoxide dismutase tablets have been touted for their "anti-aging" effect. However, there is no evidence that oral administration of the enzyme prolongs life. In fact, one report demonstrates that blood and tissue levels of this enzyme are not affected by its ingestion (Zidenburg-Cherr, Keen, Lonnerdal and Hurley, 1983).

PHYSIOLOGIC THEORIES OF AGING

The above considered work is concerned with aging at the cellular or molecular level. It is quite a leap from studying the aging cell to studying aging of the organism. There are several physiologic theories that attempt to relate aging to the performance of the organism. Several of these theories deserve special mention.

One physiological theory of aging involves the body's system of immune defense. Normally, the immune system, through the action of special immune cells and the production of antibodies, protects us from material that the body regards as foreign, including cancer cells. With age, immune function declines. Also, increased levels of certain *autoantibodies* are found in the blood (Goidl, Thorbecke, and Weksler, 1980; Walford, 1982; Weksler, 1982). These substances are produced against host tissue.

Normally, the body's immune defense distinguishes between host body cells (or self) and foreign substances subject to attack.

The significance of age-associated increases in autoantibodies is not well understood. They may contribute to inefficiencies in physiologic functioning. Why they are produced is also not known. Perhaps, once-normal body cells begin to appear different to the immune system. Their change in character may result from accumulated damage resulting from mutation or free-radical activity. If immune cells undergo similar changes, it might cause the production of aberrant antibodies. Also, body constituents may break down from disease or other damage and present themselves as "new" substances that the body's immune defense will not tolerate. Potentially, all of these factors might interact to produce *autoimmunity.*

One of the best established age-related changes is diminished *immunocompetence.* Indeed, it has been suggested that the decline in immune function may have evolved as a protective mechanism against the ravages of autoimmunity (Schneider and Reed, 1985). A vigorous immune reaction might allow for an even greater production of autoantibodies.

A study of organismal aging dictates that attention be directed toward the immune system; the immune system is itself "organismal." It is in constant contact with virtually all body cells, tissues and organs. Kay and Baker (1979) and Kay and Makinodan (1982) point out that an alteration in the immune system could be expected to exert an effect on all other body systems. As immune competence decreases, the incidence of autoimmunity, infection and cancer increases (Good and Yunis, 1974; Gross,

1965; MacKay, 1972; MacKay, Whittington and Mathews, 1977).

Immune function begins to decline shortly after puberty with the beginning atrophy and involution of the *thymus gland.* The thymus, located in the chest, is perhaps the structure central to the aging of the immune system. Thymic hormone influences immune functioning. Its progressive age-related loss is associated with declines in the reactivity of certain immune cells. The percentage of immature immune cells increases in association with the lack of thymic hormone. Other substances, termed *lymphokines,* are also important in activating and maintaining the immune response. One lymphokine, *interleukin-2 (IL-2),* undergoes limited production with age (Thoman, 1985).

The immune status of a group of healthy *centenarians* was recently studied by Thompson and associates (1984). They selected such a study population because its members represented those who had withstood the high risk of cancer and various other disease for at least 100 years. Their immune status appeared similar to that of young-old individuals. Thymus-dependent functions were reduced in association with an apparent failure of certain immune cells to differentiate to functional maturity. The researchers noted that further work is needed to determine (1) when changes in immune cells of these centenarians commenced, (2) whether the changes represent irreversible programmed aging that began later in such a group, and (3) whether other factors are responsible for immune decline.

Collagen, an extracellular component of connective tissue, has also been implicated in age-related changes in physiological functions. Collagen, widely scattered throughout the body, is included in the skin, blood vessels, bone, cartilage, tendons and other body organs. With age, connective tissue shows a reduction in its elastic properties as well as an increase in *cross-linkages.* Cross-linkage is a process whereby proteins in the body (including collagen) bind to each other.

The cross-linkage theory of aging postulates that aging results from increased cross-linking and that associated changes in collagen play a significant role in impairing functional capacities. Accumulated cross-linkages could theoretically be responsible for the deterioration of various organs. For instance, less elastic blood vessels may have altered permeability, affecting nutrient transport and waste removal. Likewise, connective tissue changes in small vessels may lead to reduced elasticity and increased blood flow pressure, leading to hypertension. Changes such as these could have far-reaching effects on all body organs.

Diabetics are susceptible to excessive cross-linking. They also undergo many complications, such as cataract formation and atherosclerosis, that are similar to age-related changes. Indeed, diabetes is often referred to as a model for studying the aging process. Elevated blood sugar levels promote cross-linkage formation (Cerami, 1985). It is presently believed that many of the long-term complications of diabetes are related to glucose-induced cross-linking, especially the cross-linking of collagen. Future work will likely provide greater insight into the possible role of glucose as a mediator of aging. Researchers at Rockefeller University are presently studying a drug that prevents blood sugar from promoting protein cross-linking. It is hoped that the drug can be used in the future treatment of diabetic complications. Perhaps its most provocative use in the distant future might be in the treatment of "aging" disorders in the non-diabetic (Wechsler, 1986).

Nathan Shock, noted gerontologist, has recently indicated that there is evidence suggesting that aging may emanate from impaired performance of endocrine and/or neural control mechanisms. Studies carried out by the National Institute of Health's Gerontology Research Center show that age-related declines in humans are greater for functions that require the coordinated activity of organ systems. Measurements of functions related to a single system, such as nerve conduction velocity, show considerably less age decrement than do functions that involve coordination between systems, such as maximum breathing capacity (which involves the nervous, respiratory and muscular systems) (Kart, 1985).

PROLONGEVITY

Can identification and understanding of the key biological mechanisms that contribute to the aging process help us extend the length of life? The information presented in Chapters 3 and 4 may lead readers to believe that the length of life has been increased and will continue to increase almost automatically as a by-product of scientific research and social changes. Whether or not this is really so is unclear. It is necessary to distinguish between the concepts *life expectancy* and *life span*. While *life expectancy* refers to the average length of life of persons, *life span* refers to the longevity of long-lived persons. Life span is the extreme limit of human longevity, the age beyond which no one can expect to live (Gruman, 1977:7). Currently, gerontologists

estimate the life span at about 110–120 years.

Is the human life span an absolute standard? Or can we expect a significant extension of the length of life? Proponents of *prolongevity,* defined as the significant extension of the length of life by human action (Gruman, 1977:6), share the view that human life should be lengthened indefinitely. Others believe that new treatments and technology as well as improved health habits may continue to increase life expectancy but that human life span is unlikely to increase.

Advocates of prolongevity often point to the "long-lived" peoples—in mountain regions of Ecuador (the Andean village of Vilacabamba), Pakistan (the Hunza people of Kashmir), and the Soviet Union (the Abkhasians in the Russian Caucasus)—as examples of populations that have already extended the human life span (Leaf, 1973). These groups purportedly show a statistically higher proportion of centenarians in the population, with many individuals reaching 120, 130, or even 150 and 160 years. Unfortunately, there are many reasons for doubting the validity of these claims (Kyncharyants, 1974; Mazess and Forman, 1979; Medvedev, 1974, 1975). The Russian gerontologist, Medvedev, says that none of these cases of superlongevity is scientifically valid. To exemplify his view, he offers the case of a man from Yakutia (in the Caucasus) who was found during the 1959 census to be 130 years of age. When his picture appeared in the central government newspaper, the puzzle was quickly solved. A letter was received from a group of Ukrainian villagers who recognized this centenarian as a fellow villager who deserted from the army during World War I and used his father's documents to escape remobilization. It was found that this man was really 78 years old (Medvedev, 1974).

The village of Vilcabamba (meaning "sacred valley") is about 5,000 feet up in the Andes mountains of Ecuador. It is quite isolated and has been described by one visitor as an "ecologist's dream," with clean air, water, and the like. Vilcabamba has a long and interesting history of factual and fictitious reports on its health conditions and on the longevity of its people. According to Holmes (1983), a Peruvian doctor, Miguel Salvador, took a medical team into Vilcabamba in 1969 to investigate the health and longevity claims. Physical exams were given to approximately 250 older people, and 9 centenarians were identified. If this is true, it represents a rate almost 200 times that of the representation of centenarians in the U.S. population. Salvador concluded that he had found "a natural island of immunity to the physical and psychological problems that shorten lives elsewhere."

A number of gerontologists have visited the Andes and returned with various speculations about the causes of this longevity. Contributing factors put forth include the constant physical exertion required to live in the mountainous terrain, the diet (which is low in fat and includes very little meat), and the isolated nature of the group. More recently, another explanation for this longevity has been put forth: Vilcabambans lie about their ages! Careful investigation of the records that were available led to the conclusion that systematic age exaggeration was rampant in the village, so that most of the reported centenarians were found to be in their 80s and 90s.

Despite the debunking of these tales of extreme longevity in faraway places, there is still considerable interest—even mass interest—in increasing human longevity. A good part of this interest originates in the *antediluvian* and *hyperborean* themes, found in tradition and folklore, that people lived much longer in the distant past and in remote, faraway places, respectively. Noah, after all, supposedly lived to be 950 years old.

What are the prospects for continued reduction in death rates and life extension? As we have already shown, death rates have declined and are likely to continue to do so. Additional improvements would seem to be attainable. According to Siegel (1975), if the lowest death rates for females in the countries of Europe are combined into a single table, the values for life expectancy at birth and at age 65 exceed those same values for the U.S. by 4.3 and 1.4 years, respectively. The nations of Canada, Denmark, France, the Netherlands, Sweden, Switzerland and Japan have life expectancies at birth for both males and females that exceed those of the United States.

Most elderly people die as a result of some long-standing chronic condition, which is sometimes related to personal habits (for example, smoking, drinking alcohol, poor eating habits) or environmental conditions (for example, harsh work environments or air pollution) that go back many years. Attempts to prevent illness and death from these conditions must begin before old age. But what if we could prevent death from these conditions? Table 4.1 gives a partial answer to this question. The elimination of all U.S. deaths caused by accidents, influenza and pneumonia, infective and parasitic diseases, diabetes mellitus and tuberculosis would increase life expectancy at birth by 2.2 years and at age 65 by 0.7 years. Even the elimination of can-

TABLE 4.1 Gain in life expectancy if various causes of death were eliminated

	Gain in years	
Various causes of death	*At birth*	*At age 65*
1. Major cardiovascular-renal diseases	11.8	11.4
2. Malignant neoplasms	2.5	1.4
3. Motor vehicle accidents	0.7	0.1
4. Influenza and pneumonia	0.5	0.2
5. Diabetes mellitus	0.2	0.2
6. Infective and parasitic diseases	0.2	0.1

Source: U.S. Public Health Service data of life tables by cause of death for 1969–71, U.S. Bureau of the Census, *Current Population Reports,* Series P-23, No. 59, January 1978 (revised).

cer as a cause of death would result in only a 2.5-year gain in life expectancy at birth and about half that at age 65. This is because cancer affects individuals in all age groups. If the major cardiovascular-renal diseases were eliminated, there would be an 11.8-year gain in life expectancy at birth, and even an 11.4-year gain in life expectancy at age 65. These diseases are not likely to be eliminated in the near future, although death rates as a result of them may be reduced.

Where there is substantial room for improvement in death rates and life expectancies in the United States is among men and non-whites. As noted in Chapter 3, the death rate for aged men is considerably higher than for aged women and, controlling for sex, the death rates for elderly blacks are higher than those for their white counterparts.

Much more discussion of biogerontological research on prolongevity is needed. Improving death rates and life expectancies in the U.S. would still not necessarily achieve an extension of the life span. Should people live to be 120 or 130 years of age? When thinking about your answer, assume first that this would involve more than a simple increase in time at the end of life. Imagine that research-

ers could alter the rate of aging in such a way as to give extra years to different stages of life. Under these conditions, extra years might be difficult to turn down. But what if a longer life meant a longer "old age?" How you think about old age may rule your answer to this question. If you think of this stage of life in terms of the continuation of productive possibilities, then you may very well accept these extra years however and whenever they come. If you believe old age to be a stage characterized by decrement and loss, your answer is likely to be quite different.

SUMMARY

Numerous theories have purported to explain why we age. No one of them serves to answer this question definitively. Biologic theories of aging are not mutually exclusive; aging is a complex process influenced by diverse phenomena. The many theories of aging focus on one of two fundamental proposals: one presupposes a genetic basis for the aging process; the other views senescence as a result of "wear and tear." Much of aging research has focused on changes at the cellular and molecular level. There has also been significant work on theories of aging that attempt to relate aging to the performance of the organism.

Finally, what will be the effect of a solution to the riddle of biological aging? Should we welcome prolongevity? Have we thought sufficiently about its potential impact on individuals as well as on society as a whole?

KEY TERMS

antediluvian theme
antioxidants
autoantibody
autoimmunity
centenarians
collagen
cross-linkages
error catastrophe
free radicals
homeostasis
hyperborean
immunocompetence
interleukin-2
in vitro
life span
lipofuscin
lymphokines
maximum life span
post-mitotic cells
prolongevity
senescence
superoxide dismutase
thymus gland

STUDY QUESTIONS

1. What are two fundamental suppositions inherent in most theories of aging?
2. Identify four approaches that have been taken in attempting to explain the mechanisms of aging.
3. How is biological aging defined? What are four criteria characteristic of aging per se?
4. How did the work of Hayflick and Moorehead influence the field of gerontology? How did their conclusions differ from those of Carrel and his colleagues?

5. Note some of the work that has focused on aging at the cellular level. Which cellular theories suggest that aging may be genetically programmed into cells? Which cellular theories of aging appear to implicate diet or nutrition in the aging process?
6. Note some of the work that has focused on aging at the physiological level. What is the significance of age-related decline in the immune system? What is the cross-linkage theory of aging?
7. Distinguish between life expectancy and life span. Define *prolongevity*. Do the Abkhasians of the Russian Caucasus and the Vilcabambans of the Ecuadorean Andes really live as long as they claim?
8. Extending life expectancy seems to be an inherently positive thing. Is the idea of extending the human life span equally as positive? Explain your answer.

BIBLIOGRAPHY

Ames, B. 1983. Dietary carcinogens and anticarcinogens: Oxygen radicals and degenerative disease. *Science 221*: 1256–1264.

Bartosz, G., Leyko, W., and Fried, R. 1979. Superoxide dismutase and life span of Drosophila melanogaster. *Experientia 35*: 1193.

Cerami, A. 1985. Hypothesis: Glucose as a mediator of aging. *Journal of the American Gerontological Society 33*: 626–634.

Clapp, N., Satterfield, L., and Bowles, N. 1979. Effects of the antioxidant butylated hydroxytoluene (BHT) on mortality in BALB/c mice. *Journal of Gerontology 34*: 497–501.

Comfort, A., Youhotsky-Gore, I., and Pathmanathan, K. 1971. Effect of ethoxyquin on the longevity of C3H mice. *Nature 229*: 254–255.

Cristofalo, V. 1972. Animal cell cultures as a modal system for the study of aging. In B. Strehler, ed., *Advances in Gerontological Research*. New York: Academic Press. Pp. 45–79.

_____. 1985. The destiny of cells: Mechanisms and implications of senescence. *Gerontologist 25*: 577–583.

Economos, A., Ballard, R., Miquel, J., Binnard, R., and Philpott, D. 1982. Accelerated aging of fasted Drosophila: Preservation of physiological function and cellular fine structure by thiazolidine carboxylic acid (TCA). *Exp. Gerontol. 17:* 105–114.

Fries, J., and Crapo, L. 1981. *Vitality and Aging.* San Francisco, Calif.: W.H. Freeman.

Goidl, E., Thorbecke, G., and Weksler, M. 1980. Production of auto-anti-idiotypic antibody during the normal immune response: Changes in the auto-anti-idiotypic antibody response and idiotype repertoire associated with aging. *Proceedings of the National Academy of Science 77:* 6788.

Gold, M. 1981. The cells that would not die. *Science 81* (2): 28–35.

Good, R., and Yunis, E. 1974. Association of autoimmunity, immunodeficiency and aging in man, rabbits and mice. *Federation Proceedings 33:* 2040–2050.

Gross, L. 1965. Immunologic defect in aged population and its relation to cancer. *Cancer 18:* 201–204.

Gruman, G. 1977. *A History of Ideas about the Prolongation of Life.* New York: Arno Press.

Harman, D. 1956. Aging: A theory based on free radical and radiation chemistry. *Journal of Gerontology 11:* 298–300.

————. 1961. Prolongation of the normal lifespan and inhibition of spontaneous cancer by antioxidants. *Journal of Gerontology 16:* 247–254.

————. 1968. Free radical theory of aging. *Journal of Gerontology 23:* 476–482.

Hayflick, L., 1965. The limited in vitro lifetime of human diploid cell strains. *Experimental Cell Research 37:* 614–636.

Hayflick, L. and Moorehead, M. 1961. The serial cultivation of human diploid cell strains. *Experimental Cell Research 25:* 585–621.

Holmes, L.D. 1983. *Other Cultures, Elderly Years.* Minneapolis, Minn.: Burgess.

House Select Committee on Aging, Subcommittee on Health and Long-Term Care. 1984. Anti-aging cures and quackery. In *Quackery: A $10 Billion Scandal.* Washington, D.C.: U.S. Government Printing Office.

Johnson, R., Crisp, C., and Strehler, B.. 1972. Selective loss of ribosomal RNA genes during the aging of post-mitotic tissues. *Mechanisms of Aging and Development 1.*

Kart, C. 1985. *The Realities of Aging,* 2nd ed. Boston: Allyn and Bacon.

Kay, M., and Baker, L. 1979. Cell changes associated with declining immune function: Physiology and cell biology of aging. In A. Cherkin, C. Finch, N. Kharasch, T. McKinodan, F. Scott and B. Strehler, eds., *Aging,* vol. 8. New York: Raven Press.

Kay, M., and Makinodan, T. 1982. The aging immune system. In A. Viidik, ed., *Lectures on Gerontology, vol. I: On Biology of Aging,* Part A. London: Academic Press.

Kellogg, E., and Fridovich, I. 1976. Superoxide dismutase in the rat and mouse as a function of age and longevity. *Journal of Gerontology 31:* 405–408.

Kyncharyants, V. 1974. Will the human life-span reach one hundred? *Gerontologist 14:* 377–380.

Leaf, A. 1973. Getting old. *Scientific American 299* (3): 44–52.

MacKay, I. 1972. Aging and immunological function in man. *Gerontologia 18:* 285–304.

MacKay, I., Whittington, S., and Mathews, J. 1977. The immunoepidemiology of aging. In T. MaKinodan and E. Yunis, eds., *Immunity and Aging.* New York: Plenum Press, Pp. 35–49.

Martin, G., Sprague, C., and Epstein, C. 1970. Replicative lifespan of cultivated human cells: Effects of donor age, tissue and genotype. *Laboratory Investigation 23:* 86–92.

Mazess, R., and Forman, S. 1979. Longevity and age exaggeration in Vilcabamba, Ecuador. *Journal of Gerontology 34:* 94–98.

Medvedev, Z.A. 1974. Caucasus and Altay Longevity: A biological or social problem? *Gerontologist 14:* 381–387.

————. 1975. Aging and longevity: New approaches and new perspectives. *Gerontologist 15:* 196–210.

Munkres, K., and Minssen, M. 1976. Aging of Neurospora crassa I: Evidence for the free radical theory of aging from studies of a natural-death mutant. *Mech. Aging Dev. 5:* 79–98.

Munkres, K., Rana, R. and Goldstein, E. 1984. Genetically determined conidial longevity is positively correlated with superoxide dismutase, catalase, gluthathione peroxidase, cytochrome c peroxidase and ascorbate free radical reductase activities in Neurospora crassa. *Mech. Aging Dev. 24:* 83–100.

Oeriu, S., and Vochitu, E. 1965. The effect of the administration of compounds which contain sulfhydryl groups on the survivial of mice, rats and guinea pigs. *Journal of Gerontology 20:* 417–419.

Orgel, L. 1963. The maintenance of the accuracy of protein synthesis and its relevance to aging. *Proceedings of the National Academy of Science 49:* 517.

——————— . 1973. The maintenance of the accuracy of protein synthesis and its relevance to aging. *Proceedings of the National Academy of Science 67:* 1496.

Rohme, D. 1981. Evidence for a relationship between longevity of mammalian species and lifespans of normal fibroblasts in vitro and erythrocytes in vivo. *Proceedings of the National Academy of Science 78:* 3584–3588.

Rothschild, H. 1984. The biology of aging. In H. Rothschild, ed., *Risk Factors for Senility.* New York: Oxford University Press.

Schneider, E., and Mitsui, Y. 1976. The relationship between *in vitro* cellular aging and *in vivo* human age. *Proceedings of the National Academy of Science 73:* 3584–3588.

Schneider, E., and Reed, J. 1985. Life extension. *New England Journal of Medicine 312:* 1159–1168.

Siegel, J. S. 1975. Some demographic aspects of aging in the United States. In A. Ostfeld and D. Gibson, eds., *Epidemiology of Aging.* Bethesda, Md.: National Institutes of Health.

Strehler, B. 1973. A new age for aging. *Natural History 2:* 8–18, 82–85.

——————— . 1982. Aging: Concepts and theories. In A. Viidik, ed., *Lectures on Gerontology. volume I: On Biology of Aging,* Part A. London: Academic Press. Pp. 1–57.

Thoman, M. 1985. Role of interleukin-2 in the age-related impairment of immune function. *Journal of the American Geriatric Society 33:* 781–787.

Thompson, J., Wekstein, D., Rhoades, J., Kirkpatrick, C., Brown, S., Roszman, T., Straus, R., and Tietz, N. 1984. The immune status of healthy centenarians. *Journal of the American Geriatric Society 32:* 274–281.

Tolmasoff, J., Ono, T., and Cutler, R. 1980. Superoxide dismutase: Correlation with lifespan and specific metabolic rate in primate species. *Proceedings of the National Academy of Science 77:* 2777–2781.

Walford, R. 1982. Studies in immunogerontology. *Journal of the American Geriatric Society 30:* 617.

Wechsler, R. 1986. Unshackled from diabetes. *Discover 7:* 77–85.

Weksler, M. 1982. Age-associated changes in the immune response. *Journal of the American Geriatric Society 30:* 718.

Willet, W., and MacMahon, B. 1984. Diet and cancer—an overview. *New England Journal of Medicine 310:* 633–638, 697–703.

Zidenberg-Cherr, S., Keen,C., Lonnerdal, B., and Hurley, L. 1983. Dietary superoxide dismutase does not affect tissue levels. *American Journal of Clinical Nutrition 37:* 5–7.

CHAPTER **5**

Social and Psychological Aspects of Aging

As Chapter 4 indicated, there are many answers to the question "Why do we become old?" These answers reflect the commitment of biogerontologists to research on aging. Clearly, such commitment is needed; aging is a complex phenomenon. Moreover, even answers to the riddle of biological aging are not likely to be sufficient to explain the great variation in human aging. A variety of factors influence the time when we become old and, in particular, the time when we show the kind of vulnerability to aging processes that results in illness and death. These include social and psychological factors that may limit the expression of biological potential.

This chapter presents material on the social and psychological aspects of aging. We begin with the big picture and identify three attempts to explain the relationship between society and its older members: modernization theory, the age stratification approach, and the political economy perspective. How do individuals adjust to their own aging? Answers to this question are organized into two groupings: those that emanate from sociological thinking and emphasize the social adjustment of individuals; and those that emphasize the life cycle and personality perspectives in psychology. Finally, we discuss age-related psychological changes, including sensory processes and psychomotor responses, the relationship between age and intellectual functioning, and memory and learning.

AGING AND SOCIETY

Modernization Theory

In their book, *Aging and Modernization,* Cowgill and Holmes (1972) developed a theory of aging in cross-cultural perspective. As the theory emerged and was subsequently revised (Cowgill, 1974), it described the relationship between *societal modernization* and the changes in role and status of older people. Stated tersely, the theory held that with increasing modernization the status of older people declines. This declining status is reflected in reduction in leadership roles, power, and influence, as well as increased disengagement of older people from community life.

Four subsidiary aspects of modernization were identified as salient to the conditions of older people in a society: (1) scientific technology as applied in economic production and distribution; (2) urbanization; (3) literacy and mass education; and (4) health technology. Each of these aspects of modernization helps produce the decline in status of older people in society (Cowgill, 1974).

Figure 5.1 presents, in schematic form, the modernization theory as revised by Cowgill. Briefly, the causal sequences depicted in the figure can be described as follows:

1. The application of health technology, including public health measures, nutrition and all aspects of curative and surgical medicine, dramatically affect the age structure of a society so that there is an aging of the population. This comes about through a prolon-

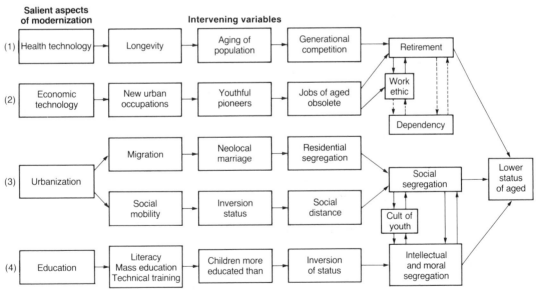

Figure 5.1   Aging and modernization. (Source: D. Cowgill, "Aging and modernization: A revision of the theory," in J. Gubrium, ed., *Late Life: Communities and Environmental Policies,* 1974. Courtesy of Charles C. Thomas, Publisher, Springfield, Illinois.)

gation of adult life as well as a decline in the birth rate. In an industrialized society with emphasis on youth and new occupations, the extension of adult life leads to an intergenerational competition for jobs. Older people are forced out of the labor market; they retire. This denies them participation in the work ethic, causes reductions in monetary income, prestige, and honor, and thus decrement in status.

2. The application of economic and industrial technology leads to new occupations that are located increasingly in an urban setting. Geographically and socially mobile youth migrate to these jobs. Older people are left in positions that are less prestigious and often obsolete. Lack of opportunities for retraining (especially in rural areas) leads to early retirement. Such retirement, accompanied by loss of income, brings a reversal of traditional family and community roles. Formerly, the young were dependent on the old; now the old suffer dependency.

3. Urbanization, including the separation of work from home and the geographical separation of youthful urban migrants from their parental homes, profoundly changes the nature of intergenerational relations. Residential segregation of the generations changes the bonds of familial association, increases social distance between generations and, with upward mobility among the young, leads to a reduced status of the aged. This effect is compounded by retirement and dependency.

4. Promotion of literacy and education (almost always targeted at the young in modernization efforts) generates a situation in which children are more literate and have greater skill than their parents. This has the effect of inverting roles in the traditional society: The child's generation has higher status than the parents'; children occupy positions in the community formerly held by their parents. The social change that modernization brings increases the gap between generations. This causes an intellectual and moral segregation of the generations. Youth comes to symbolize progress, and the society directs its resources toward the young and away from the old, accentuating the decline in status of the aged.

The work of Erdman Palmore has generally supported the modernization theory. Palmore and Whittington (1971) found that the status of the aged was lower than that of the younger population on a series of socioeconomic measures and had declined significantly from 1940 to 1969. More recently, Palmore and Manton (1974) explored the relationship between modernization and the economic status of the aged in 31 countries. Indicators of modernization included the gross national product per capita, the percent of the labor force engaged in agriculture, change in the proportion of the labor force engaged in agriculture, percent of adults who are literate, percent of people aged 5 to 19 who are in schools, and percent of the population who are in higher education.

The relative status of the aged was measured by indexes that compared the differences in employment and occupation of the older population (65 and over) with those age 25 through 64. In general, correlations between the indicators of modernization and measures of the status of the aged supported the theory. The relative status of older people was lower in the more modernized nations. Interestingly, Palmore and Manton discovered some patterns within their data that imply that the status of the aged decreases in the early stages of modernization (exemplified by nations such as Iran, El Salvador and the Philippines), but that after a period of modernization status may level off and even rise some (exemplified by New Zealand, Canada and the United States).

Finally, Palmore (1975) has used the case of Japan to show how culture may mitigate the impact of modernization on the status of the aged. According to Palmore, the social and ethnic homogeneity of the Japanese population, the attitude of the Japanese toward time, the tradition of respect for the aged reflected in filial piety, and the prominence of ancestor worship have all helped maintain the relatively high status and integration of older Japanese. Palmore quotes from Japan's 1963 National Law for the Welfare of the Elders, a law comparable to The Older Americans' Act in the United States: "The elders shall be loved and respected as those who have for many years contributed toward the development of society, and a wholesome and peaceful life shall be guaranteed to them." The Older Americans' Act makes no mention of love and respect for the aged, nor does it *guarantee* a wholesome and peaceful life.

Age Stratification

Age stratification is a conceptual framework for viewing societal processes and changes that affect aging and the state of being old (Riley, 1971, 1977; Riley, Johnson and Foner, 1972; Foner, 1975). Accordingly, society is divided into strata not only by social class but also by age. Members of the age strata differ in the social roles they are expected to play and in the rights and privileges accorded them by society. This is similarly the case for members of different social classes, who also have different societal expectations for behavior as well as varying access to rewards granted by society. Age stratification and class stratification approaches have much in common. In fact, Riley (1971) argues that two concepts central to class stratification theory, *social class* and *social mobility,* are analogous to two concepts central to age stratification, *age strata* and *aging.* She suggests that sociologists of age stratification use those questions that are important to class stratification theorists to stimulate thinking about age strata and aging. Four of these questions are reproduced below.

First, how does an individual's location in the class structure channel his attitudes and the way he behaves?

Second, how do individuals relate to one another within and between classes?

Third, what difficulties beset the upwardly (or downwardly) mobile individual, and what strains does his mobility impose upon the group (such as his parents of one class) whom he leaves behind and upon the new group (such as his wife's parents of a different class) who must now absorb him?

Fourth, to the extent that answers can be found to these three sets of questions, what is the impact of the observed findings upon the society as a whole? [Riley, 1971]

In age stratification terms, the first question becomes: How does an individual's location within the age structure of a society influence his or her behavior and attitudes? Research shows that age strata differ in political and social attitudes, world outlook, style of life, organizational attachments, happiness and so on (Riley and Foner, 1968). How do age stratification theorists explain these differences in behavior and attitudes among people of different age strata and the similarities among people within a stratum?

Riley (1971) suggests that two coordinates or dimensions useful for locating an individual in the age structure of a society are the *life course dimension* and the *historical dimension*. The first of these reflects chronological age, itself a rough indicator of biological, psychological and social experience. This is only to say that individuals of the same age have much in common. They are alike in biological development as well as in the kinds of social roles they have experienced (worker, spouse, parent). The second dimension refers to the period of history in which a person lives. People born at the same time share a common history. Those born at different times have lived through different historical periods. Even when people born at different times "share" an historical event, they are likely to experience it differently. For example, persons born in 1920 and 1950 were likely to "experience" the Vietnam War quite differently. Riley uses the term *cohort-centric* to describe the view of the world that develops from a particular intersection of the life course and historical dimensions. People in the same place on the life course dimension (in the same age stratum) experience historical events similarly and, as a result, may come to see the world in a like fashion. The "cohort-centricity" of different age strata explains the different behaviors and attitudes associated with those age strata.

The second question becomes: How do individuals relate to one another within (and between) age strata? This question stimulates thinking about the nature of social relationships within age strata and the nature of intergenerational relations. From the age stratification perspective, solidarity and consciousness within the age stratum are predictable. The shared experience of cohort members is a powerful force in this direction. Yet the continuous flow of cohorts in and out of an age stratum weakens identification with a particular stratum. As Foner (1975) points out, this is quite different from class strata, members of which share common experiences and often have a lifetime to reinforce identification with the group.

Relations among age strata reflect many factors, not the least of which is the distribution of power and wealth in a society. But what of intergenerational relations within the family? Are they sequential or reciprocal? Foner (cited in Riley, 1971) asked parents of high school students what they would do with money unexpectedly received. Two percent said they would use it to help their aged parents; most indicated a willingness to use the money to help the children get started in life. Furthermore, she reports that the aged generation concurs with this decision. This suggests agreement among generations about the flow of material support—sequential, not reciprocal, with each generation attempting to aid the younger generation.

The third set of questions deals with age mobility. When aging is viewed as mobility through the age strata, it is revealed as a process that brings many of the same strains and stresses as does class mobility. Still, age mobility is different. In the first place, social mobility affects only a few; age mobility affects everyone. Though individuals age in different ways and at different rates, no one can achieve downward age mobility. Second, each cohort, because of its special relationship to historical events, experiences age mobility differently. For example, successive cohorts in our own society in this century have experienced increased longevity and formal education. Both these facts have dramatically changed how successive cohorts have aged.

Finally, the fourth set of questions reminds us that age stratification cannot be viewed in isolation. The system of age stratification in society influences and is influenced by the changing social-political-economic fabric of society. Sometimes, social changes may directly reflect "innovations" emanating from one or more cohorts (Riley, 1971). Thus, for example, the large proportion of "early" retirements from the labor force in recent cohorts of those aged 55 to 65 has already had enormous impact throughout the society—on the financing of Social Security and other pension plans, housing, leisure, and so on—and will continue in the future.

Political Economy

The political economy perspective on aging requires that we view the problems of aging in social-structural rather than individual terms. According to Estes, Swan and Gerard (1984), this perspective "starts with the proposition that the status and resources of the elderly and even the trajectory of the aging process itself are conditioned by one's location in the social structure and the economic and social factors that affect it." Clearly, the political economy perspective is not concerned with old age as a biological or psychological problem. It is interested in old age as a problem for societies characterized by major inequalities in the distribution of power, income and property. Implicit in this approach is the question of whether the logic of capitalism as a productive social system is reconcilable with the needs of elderly people.

Radical political economists of aging answer that capitalism is irreconcilable with meeting the needs of the elderly. Phillipson (1982) offers four arguments. (1) Whenever capitalism is in crisis — as in the 1930s and in the early 1980s—it attempts to solve its problems through cuts in the living standards of working people. (2) Capitalism has a distinct set of priorities, which almost always subordinates social and individual needs to the search for profits. (3) Because of the cyclical nature of the capitalist economies, elderly people often find themselves caught between their own need for better services and the steady decline of facilities within their neighborhoods. (4) In capitalist economies, a ruling class still appropriates and controls the wealth produced by the working class.

Navarro (1984) has analyzed the health care problems of older Americans, using a political economy approach. He concludes that the misery and impoverishment many elderly suffer today is a function of the dominance of the capitalist class over U.S. political, economic, and social institutions. From his view, defense of capitalist class interests has required shifting government resources from social and health expenditures, which benefit the majority of the U.S. population, to military expenditures, which benefit the few. Interestingly, Navarro remains optimistic enough to suggest that the interest-group mentality prevalent in the United States be replaced by an appreciation among the majority of Americans (whites, blacks, Latinos, females, young and old people) for their shared working-class status and hence for their collective power.

Political economy of aging is not a theory in the strictest sense. It is not presented in the form of a set of systematically organized statements. Rather, political economy is an orientation or perspective, which at this relatively early stage in its development may provide a useful guide for aging policy and research. Estes, Gerard and Minkler (1984) employ the perspective to frame four important questions about aging policy. They believe that the answers to these questions speak to the heart of the relationship between this society and its aged constituents: (1) To what extent will aging interest groups ally themselves with a broader base and expand their concerns to encompass generic issues rather than those identified as aging issues only? (2) To what extent will state and local officials continue to accept the federal retrenchment and shift of governmental responsibility to state and local government? (3) Will the interests of the wealthy and the middle class continue to dominate public policy for the aging? (4) To what extent will the organizations serving the aging, as well as professionals and individuals, involve themselves in attempting to set the agenda for future public policy?

AGING AND THE INDIVIDUAL

How do individuals adjust to their own aging? A number of answers to this important question have been put forth by social theorists. Some of these answers show considerable overlap and differ only in emphasis. We present four of these answers below: role theory, activity theory, disengagement theory, and symbolic interactionist theory. No one of these answers represents the absolute truth about individual aging. As additional research is carried out, we may discover that one or all of these answers may accurately apply to some segment of the aging population.

Role Theory

The earliest attempt in social gerontology to understand the adjustment of the aged individual was placed within a role theory framework (Cottrell, 1942). Generally speaking, research done within this framework was concerned with the consequences of *role loss* among older people. Old age, characterized by some researchers as a "roleless role," was seen as a period of life in which feelings of dissatisfaction and low morale prevailed (Cavan, Burgess, Havighurst and Goldhammer, 1949; Cottrell, 1942). More recently, role theorists have concentrated on researching the adjustment to role change among the elderly.

The changes individuals undergo in the aging process fall into two categories: the giving up of social relationships and roles typical of adulthood; and their replacement by retirement and the acceptance of social relationships typical of the later years, such as dependency on offspring (Cavan, Burgess, Havighurst and Goldhammer, 1949). Phillips (1957) has shown the relationship between role loss and adjustment to old age. In his study of almost 1,000 aged individuals 60 and over—the retired when compared to the employed, the widowed when compared to the married, and people over 70 when compared to those aged 60 to 69—all showed significantly more *maladjustment* to old age. Maladjustment is measured by self-reports on the amount of time spent daydreaming about the past, thinking about death, and being absent-minded.

Another important variable that Phillips uses is labeled "identification as old." This item is a measure of self-image and simply asks, "How do you think of yourself as far as age goes—middle-aged, elderly, old?" Individuals who perceive themselves as elderly or old were significantly more maladjusted than those who perceive themselves as middle-aged. In addition, age identification appears to reverse the relationship between role loss and maladjustment. Thus, for example, those who are employed but identify themselves as old are more likely to be maladjusted than those who are retired but identify with middle age. How and why it is that some elderly individuals, even those who have suffered role loss, identify with middle age is still open to empirical investigation.

Activity Theory

One theory of aging that is related to role theory has appeared implicitly in much gerontological research. This theory, referred to here as *activity theory* but often called the *implicit theory of aging,* states that there is a positive relationship between activity and life satisfaction. The perspective of this theory is that while aging individuals face inevitable changes related to physiology, anatomy and health status, psychological and social needs remain essentially the same. Those who adopt this view recognize that the social world may withdraw from aging individuals, making it more difficult for them to fulfill these needs. Yet the older person who ages optimally is the one who stays active and manages to resist the withdrawal of the social world (Havighurst, 1968). According to this theory, the individual who is able to maintain the activities of the middle years for as long as possible will be well-adjusted and satisfied with life in the later years. Such an individual will find an avocation to substitute for work and will replace the old friends and loved ones lost to death with new ones.

Lemon and his colleagues (1972) attempted a formal and explicit test of the activity theory. Using a sample of potential in-movers to a Southern California retirement community, and distinguishing among informal activity (with friends, relatives, and neighbors), formal activity (participation in voluntary organizations), and solitary activity (e.g., maintenance of household), they found that only social activity with friends was significantly related to life satisfaction.

Recently, Longino and Kart (1982) reported on the results of a formal replication of the work on activity theory carried out by Lemon and his team. Using probability samples from three distinct types of retirement communities, they found support for the positive contribution made by informal activity to the life satisfaction of respondents. Interestingly, they observed formal activity to have a *negative* effect on life satisfaction. Longino and Kart speculated that participation in formal activities may damage self-concept and lower morale through the development of status systems that tend to emerge in formal activity settings. Invidious comparisons that can lead to dissatisfaction are less likely to operate in primary relationships with family and friends than in secondary ones limited to formal organizational settings.

Activity theory is often presented in juxtaposition with the disengagement theory of aging (discussed at some length below). Such presentation leads to comparison of the theories and often causes students to overlook problems that may be internal to the theory. Several theoretical problems inherent in the activity approach deserve some mention here.

First, the activity perspective assumes that individuals have a great deal of control over their social situations. It assumes that people have the capacity to reconstruct their lives by substituting new roles for lost ones. Clearly, this may be the case for the upper-middle-class individual whose locus of control has always been internal and whose social and economic resources allow for such reconstruction. But the retired individual who suffers a dramatic decline in income, or the widow who faces an equally dramatic decline in her social relationships, may find it difficult, even with sufficient motivation, to substitute an avocation for work or to replace old friends and loved ones lost to death.

Second, the activity perspective emphasizes the stability of psychological and social needs through the adult phase of the life cycle. This makes considerable sense if one thinks of these needs as developing in a stable social and physical environment. But what of the person whose environment changes at a particular age when he or she retires, is deprived of status, is widowed, and so on? Might this individual's social and psychological needs change in the face of the substantial change in environment?

Finally, an important problem in activity theory is the expectation that activities *of any kind* can substitute for lost involvement in work, marriage, parenting and so on. Weiss (1969), in his study of the Parents Without Partners (PWP) organization, dubbed this the *"fund of sociability" hypothesis.* According to this idea, there is a certain *quantity* of interaction with others that people require and that they may achieve in a variety of ways—through one or two intense relationships or perhaps through a larger number of lesser relationships. Weiss was not able to substantiate this hypothesis. He found that the "sociability" that accrued to a person participating in the PWP organization did not necessarily compensate for the marital loss. This suggests that substitutability for different losses may be governed by different considerations or may not be possible at all.

Disengagement Theory

Disengagement theory, put forth by Cumming and Henry (1961), stands in some contrast to the role theory and activity theory approaches. Using data based on 275 respondents ranging in age from 50 to 90, all of whom resided in Kansas City and were physically and financially self-sufficient, these authors characterized the decreasing social interaction they observed to come with old age as a *mutual withdrawal* between the aging individual and others in the social system to which he or she belongs. Under the terms of the disengagement theory, the aging individual is acceptant, perhaps even desirous, of the decreased interaction. In addition, the theory argues that gradual disengagement is functional for society, which would otherwise be faced with disruption by the sudden withdrawal of its members. As Cumming (1963) has stated it:

> The disengagement theory postulates that society withdraws from the aging person to the same extent as the person withdraws from society. This is, of course, just another way of saying that the process is normatively governed and in a sense agreed upon by all concerned.

In its original form, the disengagement theory was concerned with the modal case in America. Important disengagements included the departure of children from families and retirement for men or widowhood for women. It was not concerned with nonmodal cases—early widowhood or late retirement—nor was it concerned with the special effects of poverty or illness.

In summarizing the disengagement theory it is useful to point out that in the initial presentation of the theory Cumming and Henry argued that the process of disengagement was both *inevitable* and *universal*. All social systems, if they were to maintain successful equilibrium, would necessarily disengage from the elderly. Disengagement was seen as a prerequisite to social stability. "When a middle-aged, fully engaged person dies, he leaves many broken ties, and disrupted situations. Disengagement thus frees the old to die without disrupting vital affairs" (Cumming, 1963:384–385).

The disengagement theory has generated much critical discussion. Many have found the theory wanting and indefensible, yet others defend it quite strenuously. Through the 1960s and 1970s, most research efforts were unable to offer empirical support to the theory. Youmans (1967) found that a sample of the rural aged did not in general experience disengagement. Palmore (1968) interviewed 127 individuals who were an average age of 78. He found little to support the notion that disengagement necessarily increases with age. The research of others has suggested possible modifications on the disengagement theme. For example, Tallmer and Kutner (1970) found that physical and social stress, rather than aging per se, often produces disengagement. Atchley's (1971) study of emeritus professors showed that individuals could disengage socially without psychological disengagement.

Hochschild (1975) has examined the theory and found three problems that she believes continue to fire the controversy. First, Hochschild argues that the disengagement theory allows no possibility for counterevidence. She points out that in their original work Cumming and Henry offered four types of "back door" explanations to handle cases that did not fit the theory. These types included "unsuccessful" disengagers, those whose disengagement was "off schedule,"

exceptional individuals who had re-engaged, and those who were offered as examples of "variation in the form" of disengagement.

Second, the major variables in the theory (age and disengagement) turn out to be "umbrella" variables that are divisible into numerous other promising variables. Reference was made above to one study that distinguished between social and psychological disengagement. Carp (1969) distinguishes among types of social disengagement, including disengagement from family, friends, social activities, and material possessions. Similarly, in discussing psychological disengagement, one could differentiate among personal adjustment, "ego" energy, "affect intensity," mastery, and so on. As Hochschild points out, one consequence of this continual fission is that theoretical propositions that once appeared quite simple grow much more complex.

Third, the disengagement theory essentially ignores the aging person's own view of aging and disengagement. This simply means that behavior that looks like disengagement to the observer may have a completely different meaning for the aging person. Based on his exploratory study of retirement among 99 English couples, Crawford (1971) advances three types of meaning that men attribute to retirement: retiring back to something, retiring from something, and retiring for something. In the first and third types, men view their retirement in terms of continued engagement with new involvements—in the latter case, discarding past obligations to work and building a new social life outside of work; in the former, giving up work and returning to the family. Despite the "objective" disengagement (i.e., retirement), the men attribute different meanings to the event.

Aging and Symbolic Interactionism

According to Herbert Blumer (1969), the theoretical framework known as *symbolic interactionism* is based on the premise that people behave toward objects (including other people) according to perceptions and meanings developed through social interaction. From this perspective, individuals are seen as conscious actors in the world who adapt to situations and events on the basis of the perceptions and meanings they have constructed for these situations and events. It is important to note that perceptions and meanings are not constructed in a vacuum. Rather, they arise out of social interaction with others.

> Human beings in interacting with one another have to take account of what each is doing or is about to do; they are forced to direct their own conduct or handle their situations in terms of what they take into account . . . One has to *fit* one's own line of activity in some manner to the actions of others. [Blumer, 1969:8]

The importance of social interaction cannot be exaggerated for the symbolic interactionist. The emphasis in this theoretical perspective is on the human capacity for *socially* constructing reality.

In recent years, symbolic interactionism has been seen as having important implications for the study of aging. At one level, it may provide a basis for understanding how older people perceive and assign meaning to the experience of "old age" in American society. Ward (1979), for example, sees the symbolic interactionist perspective as essential to recognizing the importance of change in the social and symbolic worlds of the aging. He argues that role losses, residential mobility, health problems, and other age-related changes pull the elderly from familiar groups and situations. Thus they may become alienated from past worlds and identities and, at the same time, gain the potential for new worlds and new identities. This creates the possibility of satisfying personal change and growth but also may result in stress, marginality and unhappiness (Ward, 1979:504).

Marshall (1979) has applied the symbolic interactionist perspective to aging through his use of the concept of *status passage*. To speak of aging as a status passage is to suggest the image of an individual negotiating a passage from one age-based status to another (and, perhaps, to others), finally coming to the end of the passage through life, at death. A status passage may have both an objective and a subjective reality. Objectively, any status passage can be defined in terms of physical or social time and space, duration, the extent to which it is desirable or undesirable, inevitable or optional, voluntary or involuntary, among a series of dimensions. Subjectively, as Marshall indicates, awareness of any of the above properties of the passage can vary. Thus people may differ in their degree of awareness that they are even undergoing a passage. For the symbolic interactionist, the objective and subjective dimensions of the status passage set the parameters within which the lives of aging individuals will be shaped by themselves. The degree of control over the passage becomes of central importance for aging persons. This is particularly the case for this status passage because, unlike others, there is no exit from the passage except through death. Other passages in life involve preparation for something to come. Here, however, the passage is all there is. As Marshall indicates, "No future lies beyond the passage, only the passage and its termination become relevant. . . ."

One theme of this status passage, according to Marshall, is that preparation for death involves the attempt to make sense of death itself and to make sense of one's life. This theme appears in psychoanalytic theory and in Butler's concept of *life review*. An important difference for symbolic interactionists is their recognition that control over one's own biography involves reconstruction of the past through reminiscence. Marshall (1979) argues that this process is most successful when it is conducted socially. Unfortunately, as Marshall sees it, "socializing agents," such as institutional settings (including nursing homes and retirement communities), may severely threaten an aged person's ability to maintain control of the status passage. Too often, status passage control becomes a dilemma for aging individuals, who must choose between allowing others to shape their passages and isolation. This decision is most obvious in cases where others employ criteria for desired behavior that contradict the attempts of the aging person to maintain personal control (Marshall, 1979).

Much more empirical research must be done to determine the utility of the symbolic interactionist paradigm in social gerontology. Still, we can be optimistic about any framework that suggests that older people retain the human capacity to construct and share meanings, and the tendency of humans to attempt control over their own lives.

THE PSYCHOLOGY OF THE LIFE CYCLE

Only recently have mature adulthood and old age been placed within a developmental framework. This is different from the cases of childhood and adolescence, in which the developmental perspective has helped identify principles that affect us all as we pass through these life stages. The different rates of development of child psychology and psychology of adulthood are a function of several factors. There are conceptual and methodological difficulties involved in studying whole lives, not the least of which involves the fact that concepts and measures used by a researcher in a longitudinal study may be relevant at one age ("young adulthood") but not at a later age ("old age"). This has resulted in a relative scarcity of empirical research on the psychology of middle and later adulthood. Also, the work of Sigmund Freud has influenced and continues to influence the development of a psychology of adulthood. Freud generated a theory of personality that emphasized how development in the early years significantly influenced one's later life. He regarded adulthood as a theater in which the dramas of unconscious childhood conflicts are acted (and reenacted) out—adulthood itself was not for further development!

Still, several prominent theories of life cycle development have been put forth, and a number of them include a personality dimension. It may be useful to consider these theories and see how they conceptualize the relationships among life-cycle development, personality and aging.

Conceptions of the Life Cycle

An early pioneer of life-span developmental psychology was Charlotte Buhler. She was the head of the Vienna Research Center in Child Psychology, and her main interest was the psychology of childhood and adolescence. In the early 1930s she extended this work to include the rest of the life span. Buhler's (1933) early work is as interesting for its methodology as it is for its conceptualization of the course of the life span. Rather than limiting her analysis to specific segments of the life span, Buhler attempted to interpret the whole course of life through analyses of 250 individual lives; 50 of these were gathered in retrospective fashion from aged people, while the rest were taken from biographies and autobiographies. She suggests that there are five major phases or periods that can be identified, and that the psychological curve of life parallels the biological curve of rise and decline, ascent and decline, although these curves do not necessarily proceed in synchrony. The phases are as follows (Frenkel-Brunswick, 1963):

1. The first is the one in which the child lives at home, and in which his or her life centers around family and school.

2. The second begins at about age 15 and is characterized by entrance into independent activity. This period lasts until the latter half of the third decade. Often, the turning point for this phase can be placed at the time the young person leaves the home of his or her family.

3. The third phase begins between the 26 and the 30th years of life. It is representative of the most fruitful and creative aspects of life. Definitive career choices are made; marriage and the establishment of home and family are other likely accomplishments.

4. Decreases in the amount of activities as well as "negative dimensions" characterize the fourth and fifth phases (which begin at about age 50). Illness, loss of associates, death of relatives and friends, and reduction in social activities are more noteworthy in phase 4. Psychological crises, discontent and unrest are often evident in this phase.

5. The fifth period is often introduced by complete retirement from work (at about age 65). There is an obvious further decrease in social activities; retrospection and life review

is very characteristic of this period. Sickness and death are preeminent in these years.

While Buhler has attempted to identify and determine the regularity with which the various phases of life succeed one another, not all of the experiences mentioned above are expected to be present in every individual. For example, some people may not experience the reduction in physical and social activities that accompanies movement from phase 3 to phase 4 as negative. They may not seek their measure in "physical efficiency" but rather in a continued mental vitality, which brings new interests and attitudes.

The psychoanalytic theorists have dealt most explicitly with the personality dimension as it relates to age. Yet, as we have indicated above, much of this work involves developmental theories of childhood and adolescence. Stated tersely, the psychoanalytic theories regard adult personality as stable (Neugarten, 1977). Jung (1933) is an exception. He begins his discussion of the stages of life with youth—a period extending from after puberty to about age 35. In general this period involves giving up childhood and widening the scope of one's life. The next stage begins at about age 35 and continues to old age. He characterizes this stage as follows:

> Often it is something like a slow change in a person's character; in another case certain traits may come to light which had disappeared since childhood; or again, one's previous inclinations and interests begin to weaken and others take their place. Conversely—and this happens very frequently—one's cherished convictions and principles, especially the moral ones, begin to harden and to grow increasingly rigid until, somewhere around the age of fifty, a period of intolerance and fanaticism is reached. [Jung, 1971]

Jung sees significant changes in the personality in old age. The individual's attention may turn inward in an attempt to find meaning in life. Often, he says, individuals will change into their opposites: "We cannot live the afternoon of life according to the programme of life's morning; for what was great in the morning will be little at evening and what in the morning was true will at evening have become a lie" (Jung, 1971).

The most important exception to the general thrust of psychoanalytic theory has been the work of Erik Erikson (1950, 1963, 1968). Erikson outlines eight ages of man stretching from birth to death, each representing a choice or a crisis. If decisions are made well during one age, then successful adaptation can be made in the subsequent age. The first five ages rely heavily on the work of Freud and deal largely with childhood development. The last three ages focus on adult development. Theses ages are: in early adulthood, the development of *intimacy* (including more than simply sexual intimacy) vs. a sense of ego isolation; in middle adulthood, the development of *generativity* (achieving a sense of productivity and creativity) vs. ego stagnation; and in late adulthood, a sense of *ego integrity* (including a basic acceptance of one's life as having been appropriate and meaningful) versus a sense of despair.

The sense of ego integration generated in late adulthood is very much a function of what has taken place in the previous ages. Erikson contends that good adjustment in this age comes only when important matters have been placed in proper perspective and when the successes and failures of life have been seen as inevitable. A lack in this accumulated ego integration is often characterized by a failure to accept one's life and ultimately by fear of death.

Not all agree with Erikson. Butler (1975), for one, finds the idea that we are in old age a function of what we were before to be potentially regressive. He argues that although it is important to recognize the basic foundation of one's identity, it is equally important to know there can be continuing possibilities.

Still, Butler (1963) has provided us with the concept of *life review,* which seems integral to carrying out the tasks of Erikson's eighth age. All people reminisce. Yet, according to Butler, this is not an idle process. Rather, life review occurs naturally so that unresolved conflicts may be given attention and resolved. Old age (and perhaps impending death) highlights this process. If conflicts are not resolved, there may be a failure in adjustment, resulting in what Erikson describes as "despair."

Peck (1955) has attempted to refine Erikson's theory, paying special attention to the crucial issues of middle and old age. He sees three issues as central to old age. First, the individual must establish a wide range of activities so that adjustment to loss of accustomed roles such as those of worker or parent is minimized. Second, because nearly all elderly individuals suffer physical decline and/or illness, activities in the later years should allow them to transcend their physical limitations. Finally, although death is inevitable, individuals may in various ways make contributions that extend beyond their own lifetimes; this may provide meaning for life and overcome despair that one's life was meaningless or should have been other than it was.

More recently, Levinson and his colleagues (1978), based on their research on men aged 35 to 45 years, have come to view the life cycle as evolving through a sequence of *eras,* each lasting approximately 20 to 25 years. In the broadest sense, each era is a "time of life" with its own distinctive quali-ties. Apparently, there are personal crises and developmental tasks that are character-istic of each era. A primary developmental task of late adulthood (which begins at about age 60) is to find a new balance between involvement with society and with the self. It is during this era (according to Levinson) that Erikson's final age (ego integrity vs. despair) occurs.

Personality Theory

While most psychologists of the life cycle have dealt more or less implicitly with the relationship between personality and aging, there is no theory useful to gerontologists that conceptualizes this relationship specifi-cally. Havighurst (1968) suggests that what we need is a theory of the relationship between personality and successful aging.

Some research has already moved in this direction, though much of it is "trait-cen-tered" (Thomae, 1980). Reichard and asso-ciates (1962) studied 87 elderly working men in the San Francisco area, 42 retired and 45 not retired. They rated these respondents on 115 personality variables and, after a "cluster analysis," identified five types of "agers." Three of these types were judged on the basis of additional analysis to be well-adjusted to the aging process; two types were rated as low on the adjustment to aging measures. Those elderly men judged as suc-cessful in aging were labeled the "mature," "rocking-chair," and "armored," respec-tively; those judged unsuccessful were the "angry" and the "self-haters."

The mature group took a constructive view of life, while the rocking chair groups were more dependent. The armored men did not accept dependency; many of them protected themselves from it by avoiding retirement.

The angry men directed hostility at the world, which they blamed for all that was wrong in their lives. The self-haters blamed them-selves for their difficulties. As Havighurst (1968) has pointed out, these men were making quite different behavioral adjust-ments to aging. What is more interesting is that some achieved successful aging through activity, and others achieved it through disengagement.

Havighurst (1968) and his colleagues car-ried on the search for a personality theory of successful aging by studying women and men. The Kansas City Study of Adult Life rated 159 healthy middle- and working-class individuals on 45 personality dimensions. The researchers used a factor analysis to extract eight personality types, as follows:

1. Reorganized
2. Focused
3. Successfully disengaged
4. Holding-on
5. Constricted
6. Succorance-seeking
7. Apathetic
8. Disorganized

Group 1 people reorganize their lives by substituting new activities for lost ones. Group 2, the focused, are more selective about their activities. They focus time and energy on gaining satisfaction from one or two roles. Group 3 individuals have low lev-els of activity yet are highly satisfied. They have accepted withdrawal from social inter-action and are content. Group 4 shows a holding-on pattern. As long as they are able to continue the activities of middle age, they are satisfied with life. Group 5, like the focused, reduce their activity levels. They dif-fer from the focused in being much more defensive about their aging. Group 6, the succorance-seeking, are dependent on others for support. To the extent that they are successful in obtaining this support, they are satisfied with the level of activity they are able to maintain. Group 7 people are apathetic and have a low level of participation in activities; life satisfaction for this group is not high. Group 8, the disorganized, have difficulty in maintaining themselves in the community. Intellectual functioning has declined, and group members generally show reduced control over their lives.

According to Havighurst (1968), these eight personality types are probably established by middle age. It should be remembered, though, that a person's personality often develops along the lines of the demand for adaptation he or she receives from the social environment. Changes in the social environment may require changes in personality. In this regard, personality should not be seen as a fixed system that is completed in early childhood. Personality and personality changes in adults should be looked at in terms of long-range developmental changes in, among other things, motivations, intellectual functioning and the social environment.

One personality study, carried out by Douglas and Arenberg (1978), attempted to measure such changes with longitudinal and cross-sectional research designs. Over 300 males (N = 336) from the highly select group of participants in the Baltimore Longitudinal Study (Stone and Norris, 1966), ranging in age from 20 to 81, were tested with the Guilford-Zimmerman Temperament Survey (GZTS), then retested an average of seven years later. The GZTS provides an assessment of ten personality traits. Five of the scales showed significant change between the first and second testing, but only two

scales were interpreted as showing age effects: (1) Beginning at age 50, preference for rapidly paced activity declined, and (2) at all ages, men declined in masculine interests. The three other scales showing declines attributed to sociocultural changes include friendliness, thoughtfulness and personal relations.

These findings are supportive of earlier work carried out by Neugarten (1968) and others. Based on extensive interviews with middle-aged and aging persons in the 1950s and 1960s, Neugarten (1968) described an age-related move inward toward more preoccupation with satisfying personal needs. She referred to this as an increased *interiority of the personality.* "It is in this period of the life line that introspection seems to increase noticeably and contemplation and reflection and self-evaluation become characteristic forms of mental life" (Neugarten, 1968:140). Such changes seem equally characteristic of men and women. Neugarten and Gutmann (1968) have also noted that with age some women tend to have less inhibitions about expressing their aggressive feelings. This finding has led some to believe that women become more "masculine" after the menopause (Freiberg, 1983).

Schaie and Parham (1976) also carried out a test-retest study of 19 personality traits over a seven-year period. They concluded that "stability of personality traits is the rule rather than the exception." Still, they point out that such stability cannot be equated with lack of change after adolescence, as many personality theorists believe. Rather, it is likely that much change does in fact take place. The direction it takes may be a function of early socialization experiences, cohort differences and social change (Schaie and Parham, 1976).

AGE-RELATED PSYCHOLOGICAL CHANGES

Below we discuss age-related changes in psychomotor response, as well as the relationship between age and intelligence, and memory and learning. Age-related changes in the sensory processes are discussed in Chapter 8, while the more common forms of psychopathology observed in later life are presented in Chapter 3.

Psychomotor Responses

Psychomotor response is more complex than simple sensation or perception. If the concept of psychomotor response could be diagrammatically presented, it would show the organism taking in sensory input (or information), giving meaning to this new information through perceptual and integrative processes, determining whether or not this new information calls for any action, sending instructions to the appropriate activity center (a muscle, for example) and activating the appropriate response. Psychomotor performance may be limited by a weakness at any point in this chain of events. It may be limited by changes in the sensory threshold, the processes dealing with perception, the translation from perception to action, the strength of the sensory signal, and muscular output.

Psychomotor performance changes as an individual ages. *Reaction time* increases with age. This relationship is complicated by any number of factors. The nature of the stimulus and the complexity of the response appear to affect reaction time. When tasks are simple and little decision is required, the increase in reaction time observed in the elderly is slight. When choice is required, the task becomes more complex, and reaction time slows. The

particular motor skills involved and the familiarity of the task also make assessments of the relationship between reaction time and age difficult. Botwinick (1973) points out that practice at a task and exercise may reduce the effects of a slowing in reaction time. It should be remembered also that psychosocial variables such as motivation affect reaction time.

Older people show slower speed of movement when compared to the young. Precision of response also declines with age. Some research suggests that older individuals are willing to sacrifice speed for accuracy (Botwinick, 1967; Welford, 1959). This seems to indicate that if there are no pressures of time, older people are as capable of performance as their younger counterparts.

Age decrements in performance seem to relate to cerebral cortex functioning rather than to any loss of ability to move. Circulatory deterioration, reduced cerebral metabolism, and/or suppressed brain rhythms tend to produce slower reaction times (Hendricks and Hendricks, 1977). Botwinick and Storandt (1974) point out that cardiovascular problems may also serve to depress reaction time in a way that cannot be overcome by exercise.

The impact of an age-related decline in psychomotor performance on social functioning should be obvious. In general, such decline, especially in combination with sensory and perceptual decline, reduces the aged individual's ability to exert control over his or her environment. Tasks that were formerly routine, such as driving a car or using a sewing machine, may become problematic with advancing age. Activities directly related to health maintenance and care may also become more difficult to carry out. Also, as Atchley indicates (1977:49), the nature of the decline in psychomotor performance is such that it is difficult to offset mechanically in the way glasses or hearing aids can be used to offset decline in sensory processes.

Intellectual Functioning

The conventional view is that aging brings with it a decline in intelligence. Most researchers today agree that there are a great many problems associated with this assumption. Botwinick (1977) identifies five areas of concern that must be dealt with in evaluating the conventional view that age brings intellectual decline: (1) what age period we are looking at; (2) what tests we use; (3) how we define intelligence; (4) what sampling techniques are employed; and (5) what problems are associated with specific research methods.

Intelligence can only be surmised from performance scores; problems of measurement and testing affect outcomes. The most popular tool used to study age-related changes in intelligence is the Wechsler Adult Intelligence Scale (WAIS). Age is a central component in determining intelligence; there is an age factor built into the WAIS intelligence score in order to make the performance of young and old comparable. Interestingly, the age correction factor built into the WAIS assumes that it is "normal" for old people to perform less well than young people on the test. Thus, in the Wechsler scoring system, if a 25-year-old man and a 75-year-old man each make the same score, the actual performance of the older man is poorer than that of the younger man (Botwinick, 1973). Most studies do show older people performing less well than the young.

Critics of the WAIS argue that in addition to assuming performance decline with age,

the test measures mental skills and abilities that are currently being emphasized by the educational system. In general, WAIS questions are geared to predict success in learning various academic subjects. This may make it a more appropriate tool for determining the intelligence of younger people (Atchley, 1977; Hendricks and Hendricks, 1977), who are better educated and more test-wise than their elders. These critics and others argue that testing procedures that reflect the intellectual functioning required in everyday life should be used to test the relationship between age and intelligence; after all, intelligence is only one of the important ingredients necessary in carrying out successful behavior. This has been done to a limited extent. Demming and Pressey (1957) measured intellectual functioning in three task-related ways. They asked if respondents could (1) use the telephone directory, (2) understand some common legal terms, and (3) secure social services that might be required. Middle-aged and older adults scored higher as a group on these performance measures than younger respondents. Fisher (1973) suggests that the concepts of social competence and effectiveness be used in place of intellectual functioning when evaluating the aged.

Baltes and Labouvie (1973) argue that intelligence is not a single factor but consists of many abilities. In an extensive literature review, they report on many studies that conceptualize intelligence as a complex of mental abilities. The relationship between age and intelligence presented in these studies varies depending on which mental abilities are stressed.

Even the WAIS itself is divided into a Verbal scale, consisting of six subtests, and a Performance scale, consisting of five subtests.

The higher Verbal than Performance scores among elder subjects has been called a "classic aging pattern" because it has been demonstrated so many times (Botwinick, 1977). Eisdorfer, Busse, and Cohen (1959) reported the "classic aging pattern" to hold for men and women, whites and blacks, and those in different socioeconomic groups.

Research design appears to strongly influence the results of studies of age and intelligence. By and large, cross-sectional studies show early intelligence decrements, whereas longitudinal studies show stability of intelligence into late adulthood. *Cross-sectional research* is conducted at one point in time; the effect of age is determined by comparing people of different ages at the time the research is carried out. *Longitudinal research* involves observing the same people over an extended period of time. Because cross-sectional studies sample respondents from different age cohorts or generations and longitudinal studies sample respondents from a single cohort or generation, comparable outcomes should not be expected. Different generations differ as to their genetic potential and experiential backgrounds (Baltes and Labouvie, 1973). Many people who are old today did not have the advantage of long years of formal education. This may be especially the case for women. This intellectual underdevelopment is sometimes confused with a lack of intelligence. Schaie (1965) and Baltes (1968) propose the use of both cross-sectional and longitudinal studies to attempt to disentangle these genetic and experiential components.

Another factor that must be considered in the relationship between age and intelligence is health status. Birren (1968) argues that the average person growing older in our society need not expect to show a typical deteriora-

tion of mental functioning in the later years. Rather, "limitation of mental functioning occurs precipitously in individuals over the age of 65 or 70 and is closely related to health status" (Birren, 1968). Particularly problematic are vascular diseases, which affect the cerebral cortex and probably influence the brain's capacity to store information. Related to this are the results of several studies that show a relationship between intelligence decline and survival among elderly subjects. Five years after an initial survey of elderly subjects in good health, Birren (1968) compared survivors and non-survivors with respect to their WAIS scores. It was primarily the verbal skills tests that distinguished them; non-survivors had significantly lower verbal scores at the time of initial survey. Eleven years after the initial survey, Granick (1971) reported both low verbal *and* low performance scores to be associated with early death.

Health practitioners and others should be aware that intelligence differences among individuals are great enough that the use of conventional ideas in this area is problematic. Although aging influences intellectual functioning to some extent, careful observation and evaluation of each elderly person is in order before conclusions can be drawn. An individual should not be underestimated in these matters simply because he or she is old. Intellectual decline before the late 50s is probably pathological rather than normal. From the early 60s on there is decline in some but not all abilities, for some but not all individuals.

As we point out again in later chapters on old age institutions and alternatives to institutionalization, the impact of the environment (psychosocial and physical) in which the elderly person resides also deserves careful evaluation. The possibility that environmental considerations are constraining intellectual functioning in some of the aged should not be ignored. Finally, the pace of sociocultural change has been rapid. As a result, many older people (including the "young-old") suffer from what can only be described as "obsolescence" effects and compare poorly with younger peers, even though they may function as well as they ever have (Schaie, 1980).

Memory and Learning

Memory and learning are functions of the central nervous system. In general, age-related changes in learning ability appear to be small, even after the keenness of the senses has begun to decline. When there is impairment in learning, this is often due to an associated condition—some prior incapacity or a debilitating change in the individual. Arteriosclerosis and senile brain changes in old age have been linked to the dulling of memory and learning disability. In the presence of dulled memory or impaired learning, it should not be assumed that some typical process of normal aging is at work.

Age appears to involve a greater loss in recent memory than in old memory. Also, as age increases, the retention of things heard becomes increasingly superior to the retention of things seen (Atchley, 1977). Some suggest that new learning interferes with recall of old material. Although this is much discussed, there seems to be little support for either this proposition or the proposition that old memory interferes with new learning.

Attitudes toward learning may change with age as well. The older individual may be less ready to learn than was the case in youth. Aged individuals may be more likely to attempt to solve problems on the basis of what they already know, rather than learn new solutions.

SUMMARY

Social and psychological factors help explain the great variation that results from human biological aging. The relationship between a society and its older constituents can be complex. Modernization theory, the age stratification approach, and the political economy perspective represent three attempts to understand this complex relationship. How do individuals manage their own aging? Sociological answers to this question, including the role, activity, and disengagement theories and the symbolic interactionist perspective, emphasize the social adjustment of individuals. Psychological answers emphasize life span and personality perspectives. Is stability of personality traits in middle and old age the rule or the exception?

Psychomotor response changes as an individual ages. Speed and precision of response appear to decline with age, although some of this decrement may be disease-related, not age-related.

The relationship between intelligence and aging is a complex one, although a "classic aging pattern" appears to exist. Verbal skills hold up better than performance scores, across the life cycle. Health status is an important intervening variable. Still, whether health status affects intelligence functioning or whether intellectual decline is a precursor of ill health or even mortality is subject to debate.

Learning capacity per se appears to be relatively unaffected by age. Attitude toward learning may change more significantly with age. This is the case as well with old memory; recent memory shows greater loss with age.

KEY TERMS

age strata
age stratification
cohort-centric
cross-sectional research
disengagement theory
ego integrity
fund of sociability hypothesis
interiority of the personality
life review
longitudinal research
maladjustment
reaction time
role loss
societal modernization
status passage
symbolic interactionism

STUDY QUESTIONS

1. Four aspects of modernization have been identified as relevant to the conditions of older people in society. List them and explain how each affects the status of the elderly.
2. Explain how questions of social stratification can be adapted to a conceptual framework of age stratification.
3. Discuss the role theory in relation to adjustment in old age. What are the major changes individuals experience during the aging process according to this theory?
4. Compare and contrast disengagement theory and activity theory.
5. Explain how the theory of symbolic interactionism can be used to provide a basis for understanding how older people perceive and assign meaning to things, events and people in their lives.
6. Describe Jung's psychoanalytic theory of the life cycle. Explain how this interpretation of the adult stages of life differs from the traditional psychoanalytical wisdom.
7. List Erikson's eight ages of man. Briefly define the refinements suggested by Peck and Butler.
8. List and explain each of the five types of "agers" identified by Reichard and associates in their study of working men in San Francisco.
9. What changes in psychomotor response occur in old age? Explain how such changes can interfere with social functioning among the aged.
10. Discuss the weaknesses and strengths of intelligence testing with the elderly. What factors should be considered when administering and evaluating intelligence tests in this age group?
11. To what extent does the aging process influence memory? Learning?

BIBLIOGRAPHY

Atchley, R. 1977. *Social Forces in Later Life,* 2nd ed. Belmont, Calif.: Wadsworth.

_____ . 1971. Disengagement among professors. *Journal of Gerontology 26:* 476–480.

Baltes, P. 1968. Longitudinal and cross-sectional sequences in the study of age and generation effects. *Human Development 11:* 145–171.

_____ , and Labouvie, G. 1973. Adult development of intellectual performance: Description, explanation and modification. In C. Eisdorfer and M.P. Lawton, eds., *The Psychology of Adult Development and Aging.* Washington, D.C.: American Psychological Association.

Birren, J. 1968. Increment and decrement in the intellectual status of the aged. *Psychiatric Research Reports 23:* 207–214.

Blumer, H. 1969. *Symbolic Interactionism.* Englewood Cliffs, N.J.: Prentice-Hall.

Botwinick, J. 1967. *Cognitive Processes in Maturity and Old Age.* New York: Springer.

_____ . 1973. *Aging and Behavior.* New York: Springer.

_____ . 1977. Intellectual abilities. In J. Birren and K. Schaie, eds., *Handbook of the Psychology of Aging.* New York: Van Nostrand Reinhold.

_____ , and Storandt, M. 1974. Cardiovascular status, depressive effect and other factors in reaction time. *Journal of Gerontology 29(5):* 543–548.

Buhler, C. 1933. *Der Menschliche Lebenslauf als Psychologisches Problem.* Leipzig: Hirzel.

Butler, R. 1963. The life review: An interpretation of reminiscence in the aged. *Psychiatry 26:* 65–76.

_____ . 1975. *Why Survive? Being Old in America.* New York: Harper and Row.

Carp, F. 1969. Compound criteria in gerontological research. *Journal of Gerontology 24:* 341–347.

Cavan, R., Burgess, E., Havighurst, R., and Goldhammer, H. 1949. *Personal Adjustment in Old Age.* Chicago: Science Research Associates.

Cottrell, L. 1942. The adjustment of the individual to his age and sex roles. *American Sociological Review 7:* 617–620.

Cowgill, D. 1974. Aging and modernization: A revision of the theory. In J. Gubrium, ed., *Late Life: Communities and Environmental Policy.* Springfield, Ill.: Charles C. Thomas.

_____ , and Holmes, L. 1972. *Aging and Modernization.* New York: Appleton-Century-Crofts.

Crawford, M.P. 1971. Retirement and disengagement. *Human Relations 24:* 255–278.

Cumming, E. 1963. Further thoughts on the theory of disengagement. *International Social Science Journal 15*(3): 377–393.

_____ , and Henry, W. 1961. *Growing Old: The Process of Disengagement.* New York: Basic Books.

Demming, J., and Pressey, S. 1957. Tests "indigenous" to the adult and older years. *Journal of Counseling Psychology 2:* 144–148.

Douglas, K., and Arenberg, D. 1978. Age changes, cohort differences, and cultural change on the Guilford-Zimmerman Temperament Survey. *Journal of Gerontology 33*(5): 737–747.

Eisdorfer, C., Busse, E. W., and Cohen, L. 1959. The WAIS performance of an aged sample: The relationship between verbal and performance I.Q.'s. *Journal of Gerontology 14:* 197–201.

Erikson, E. 1950. *Childhood and Society.* New York: W.W. Norton.

_____ . 1963. *Childhood and Society,* 2nd ed. New York: W.W. Norton.

_____ . 1968. *Identity: Youth and Crisis.* New York: W.W. Norton.

Estes, C.L., Gerard, L.E., and Minkler, M. 1984. Reassessing the future of aging policy and politics. In M. Minkler and C.L. Estes, eds., *Readings in the Political Economy of Aging.* Farmingdale, N.Y.: Baywood Publishing.

Estes, C., Swan, J.H., and Gerard, L.E. 1984. Dominant and competing paradigms in gerontology: Towards a political economy of aging. In M. Minkler and C.L. Estes, eds., *Readings in the Political Economy of Aging.* Farmingdale, N.Y.: Baywood Publishing.

Fisher, J. 1973. Competence, effectiveness, intellectual functioning and aging. *Gerontologist 13:* 62–68.

Foner, A. 1975. Age in society: Structures and change. *American Behavioral Scientist 19*(2): 289–312.

Freiberg, K. 1987. *Human Development: A Life-Span Approach.* Boston: Jones and Bartlett.

Frenkel-Brunswick, E. 1963. Adjustments and reorientation in the course of the life-span. In R. Kuhler and G. Thompson, eds., *Psychological Studies of Human Development,* rev. ed. New York: Appleton-Century-Crofts.

Granick, S. 1971. Psychological test functioning. In S. Granick and R. Patterson, eds., *Human Aging II: An Eleven-Year Followup Biomedical and Behavioral Study.* Washington, D.C: U.S. Government Printing Office.

Havighurst, R. 1968. Personality and patterns of aging. *Gerontologist 8:* 20–23.

Hendricks, J., and Hendricks, C.D. 1977. *Aging in Mass Society: Myths and Realities.* Cambridge, Mass.: Winthrop.

Hochschild, A. 1975. Disengagement theory: A critique and proposal. *American Sociological Review 40:* 553–569.

Jung, C. 1933. *Modern Man in Search of a Soul.* New York: Harcourt, Brace & World.

_____ . 1971. The stages of life. In J. Campbell, ed., *The Portable Jung.* New York: Viking Press.

Lemon, B., Bengston, V., and Peterson, J. 1972. Activity types and life satisfaction in a retirement community. *Journal of Gerontology 27:* 511–523.

Levinson, D.J., Darrow, C.N., Klein, E.B., Levinson, M.H., and McKee, B. 1978. *The Seasons of a Man's Choice.* New York: Knopf.

Longino, C., and Kart, C.S. 1982. Explicating activity theory: a formal replication. *Journal of Gerontology 17*(6): 713–722.

Marshall, V. 1979. No exit: A symbolic interactionist perspective on aging. *International Journal of Aging and Human Development 9:* 345–358.

Navarro, V. 1984. The political economy of government cuts for the elderly. In M. Minkler and C.L. Estes, eds., *Readings in the Political Economy of Aging*. Farmingdale, N.Y.: Baywood Publishing.

Neugarten, B. 1977. Personality and aging. In J. Birren and K. Schaie, eds., *Handbook of the Psychology of Aging*. New York: Van Nostrand Reinhold.

——————— . 1968. The awareness of middle age. In B. Neugarten, ed., *Middle Age and Aging*. Chicago: University of Chicago Press.

——————— , and Gutmann, D. 1968. Age-sex roles and personality in middle age: A thematic apperception study. In B. Neugarten, ed., *Middle Age and Aging*. Chicago: University of Chicago Press.

Palmore, E. 1968. The effects of aging on activities and attitudes. *Gerontologist 8:* 259–263.

——————— . 1975. *The Honorable Elders: A Cross-Cultural Analysis of Aging in Japan*. Durham, N.C.: Duke University Press.

——————— , and Manton, K. 1974. Modernization and status of the aged. *Journal of Gerontology 29*(2): 205–210.

——————— , and Whittington, F. 1971. Trends in the relative status of the aged. *Social Forces 50:* 84–90.

Peck, R. 1955. Psychological developments in the second half of life. In J. Anderson, ed., *Psychological Aspects of Aging*. Washington, D.C.: American Psychological Association.

Phillips, B. 1957. A role theory approach to adjustment in old age. *American Sociological Review 22:* 212–217.

Phillipson, C. 1982. *Capitalism and the Construction of Old Age*. London: Macmillan.

Reichard, S., Livson, F., and Peterson, P. 1962. *Aging and Personality*. New York: Wiley.

Riley, M.W. 1971. Social gerontology and the age stratification of society. *Gerontologist 11:* 79–87.

——————— . 1977. Age strata in social systems. In R. Binstock and E. Shanas, eds., *Handbook of Aging and the Social Sciences*. New York: Van Nostrand Reinhold.

——————— , and Foner, A. 1968. *Aging and Society: An Inventory of Research Findings*. New York: Russell Sage Foundation.

——————— , Johnson, M., and Foner, A. 1972. *Aging and Society: A Sociology of Age Stratification*. New York: Russell Sage Foundation.

Schaie, K.W. 1965. A general model for the study of developmental problems. *Psychological Bulletin 64:* 92–107.

——————— . 1980. Intelligence and problem solving. In J.E. Birren and R.B. Sloane, eds., *Handbook of Mental Health and Aging*. Englewood Cliffs, N.J.: Prentice-Hall.

——————— , and Parham, I.A. 1976. Stability of adult personality traits: Fact or fable? *Journal of Personality and Social Psychology 34*(1): 146–158.

Stone, J.L., and Norris, A.H. 1966. Activities and attitudes of participants in the Baltimore Longitudinal Study. *Journal of Gerontology 21:* 575–580.

Tallmer, M., and Kutner, B. 1970. Disengagement and morale. *Gerontologist 10* (Winter): 317–320.

Thomae, H. 1980. Personality and adjustment to aging. In J.E. Birren and R.B. Sloane, eds., *Handbook of Mental Health and Aging*. Englewood Cliffs, N.J.: Prentice-Hall.

Ward, R.A. 1979. *The Aging Experience*. New York: J.B. Lippincott.

Weiss, R. 1969. The fund of sociability. *Transaction 6:* 26–43.

Youmans, E.G. 1967. Disengagement among older rural and urban men. In E.G. Youmans, ed., *Older Rural Americans*. Lexington, Ky.: University of Kentucky Press.

Welford, A. 1959. Psychomotor performance. In J. Birren, ed., *Handbook of Aging and the Individual*. Chicago: University of Chicago Press.

PART

Biomedical Aspects of Aging

CHAPTER **6**

The Aging Skin

The skin is a marvelous organ whose elegant simplicity belies its structural and functional complexity. The skin's diverse, specialized cells and zones protect the trillions of cells within the body against physical and chemical injury, solar radiation, pathogenic microbes and excessive temperature changes. As a sensory device it affords an evaluation of our physical surroundings and the satisfaction of a loving touch. Through paling, blushing and the movement of its underlying musculature, the skin also provides a way of expressing human emotion.

Life-long service to its owner subjects the skin to repeated insults. As a buffer zone between humans and their environment it undergoes frequent and cumulative injury. As a vehicle of emotion the face becomes etched with lines typical of its expression. In general, the skin becomes unevenly pigmented, dry, wrinkled and loose. The hair grows thin and becomes less dense; nails, especially those on the feet, thicken. By displaying its own time-imposed changes, this outermost organ and its appendages have also come to serve as a classic index of age.

GENERAL CHANGES

The largest and most thinly spread human organ consists of an outer zone, the *epidermis,* and an underlying area of vasculated connective tissue, the *dermis* (see Figure 6.1). With age the normally undulated border between the two, marked by the *basal membrane,* flattens. This change in the epi-

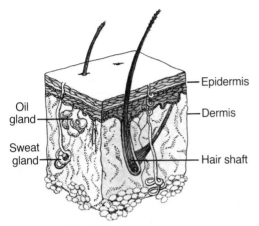

Figure 6.1   Skin cross section

dermal-dermal margin reduces surface contact and the nutrient transfer and waste clearance provided through diffusion from the dermal capillary beds below.

The epidermis, thanks to the living and dead cells comprising it, provides the body with a protective shield against an array of potentially hazardous and irritating substances. *Basal cells,* resting just above the basement membrane, divide regularly and produce the protein *keratin.* These cells die and eventually move to the body surface, where they form a protective layer of entirely dead cells that are continuously flaked off into the environment. The outer layer of cells consists mainly of keratin, which is largely responsible for the skin's ability to keep various microbes and chemicals from penetrating. Keratin also helps maintain the moisture of underlying tissues. Normally, epidermal cell formation and death occur at a steady rate, except during wound healing, when production must temporarily exceed cell death, or when a cancerous transformation causes basal cells to proliferate.

There is an age-related decrease in epidermal turnover rate and a reduction in the barrier function of the epidermis (Leyden, McGinley and Grove, 1978). Hence older skin becomes more susceptible to chemical irritants and allergens at the same time that the rate of skin repair declines. These functional changes are related not only to epidermal activity but also to reduced tissue perfusion, which can allow insulting substances to accumulate and slow down delivery of the body's protective components.

Pigment-producing cells, known as *melanocytes,* are scattered within the epidermis. They become less active with age (Gilchrest, 1982). The *melanin* these cells manufacture is responsible for an individual's skin color and for the degree of protection offered against the sun's ultraviolet rays. Almost as if to compensate for age-related reduction in activity, some melanocytes will produce substantial pigment. Variations in activity of aging melanocytes account for the blotchy pigmentation seen in older skin.

Graying of the hair is due to a total loss of functioning melanocytes from the hair bulbs. Losses here occur earlier than in the skin, probably because of the tremendous demands the rate of hair growth places upon these cells. The rate of hair and nail growth declines with age; hair distribution becomes less dense as the number of hair follicles declines. Sweat- and oil-producing glands also become smaller, less numerous and less active with age. Atrophy of hair bulbs and epidermal glands may be related to reduced blood flow.

Changes in sweat production, along with decreased dermal vascularity, reduced dilation and constriction of dermal vessels, and a loss of *subcutaneous fat* weaken *thermoreg-*

ulation in the older adult. Sweat production and blood flow work together to guard against excessive internal temperature. If the internal temperature increases, even slightly, the brain is stimulated to send impulses to dilate the small blood vessels of the dermis and activate sweat production. As the sweat evaporates, it cools the surface temperature of the skin and the blood within the dermis. Cooled blood then flows to the rest of the body. In cases where the internal temperature drops, the brain sends impulses constricting dermal vessels. Reduced blood flow to the skin follows, allowing the body to remain warmer. Subcutaneous fat insulates the body; as it is lost, greater amounts of body heat escape.

Compromised thermoregulation makes the older person more susceptible to heat exhaustion and *hypothermia*. Elderly persons should avoid hot, stuffy rooms, excessive sun exposure on warm days, and overexertion. Likewise, care should be taken to avoid excessive chilling. Older persons often complain of being cold when others around them are comfortable. Warm clothing and well-heated houses provide more than comfort; hypothermia can be life-threatening. Public policy programs at the state and local levels to provide temporary cool shelter during times of intense heat and economic assistance for fuel bills during winter months have been motivated not only by financial concerns but by physical needs of the elderly as well.

Besides undergoing a decline in vascularity, the dermis grows thinner with age, which explains the almost transparent quality of older skin. Additionally, dermal tissue becomes progressively cross-linked, accounting for the skin's looseness and loss of elasticity.

Wrinkling is the most obvious age-associated skin change. Wrinkling, which begins during the 20s and continues throughout life, is influenced by several factors: loss of skin elasticity, loss of subcutaneous fat and the repetitive nature of facial expression. The human face, because of its musculature, is capable of tremendous movement and range of expression. Indeed, facial expressions represent an extremely important component of human communication. Smiles, laughter, frowns, disappointment and anger are all recorded. The hand of time captures the lines typical of our expressions. Lines begin to form in areas of greatest movement, proliferate and become deeper as the years pass by. By the age of 40, most of us bear the lines typical of our expressions.

Fingernails and toenails become brittle and less translucent and develop longitudinal ridges and loosening of the nail bed. Toenails tend to become thickened and eventually deformed due to repeated microtrauma, circulatory impairment and associated faulty nutrition of the tissues. Debris may build up beneath the toenail, causing pressure and discomfort. It may also provide a site for bacterial and fungal infection. Corns and calluses form due to rubbing and weight-bearing pressure. Under these conditions the epidermis thickens, reflecting an increased number of cells stimulated by friction.

AGE-ASSOCIATED SKIN CONDITIONS

Dryness and Itching

Older skin has a tendency to become dry and scaly due to a less well-hydrated epidermis. Decreased perspiration may lead to the inefficient distribution of *sebum*, resulting in accelerated evaporation of skin moisture. The degree of dryness present, or *xerosis*, may depend on the time of year. It is generally most prevalent and severe during the winter months, when low humidity, central heating and drying winds hasten the evaporation of moisture from the skin.

Itching commonly associated with the dryness of older skin is referred to as *senile pruritis*. It may be aggravated in the individual who focuses on the problem, and it tends to be more pronounced at night. Contact dermatitis or drug reactions can lead to pruritis. Prolonged and generalized itching can be a warning sign of internal disease such as diabetes, circulatory dysfunction or malignancy and should not be dismissed.

Senile pruritis can be relieved by the application of emollients. Special care should be taken with creams and lotions purchased over the counter. Alcohol and perfume are common ingredients in these products and serve to dry the skin further. Superfatted soaps may be beneficial in maintaining moisture, as soap itself can be drying. If bath oil is used, it should be applied to the body after a bath; it can form a slippery coating on the tub, posing a special danger for the elderly. Fewer tub baths and more sponge baths are often recommended for the elderly. Protective clothing should be worn during the winter months to shield the skin from drying winds. However, rough woolens can irritate cracked skin.

Benign and Malignant Skin Tumors

Cutaneous tumors can originate from various cell types in the skin, such as epidermal cells or melanocytes. Many are benign, some malignant. That they arise so frequently in the elderly suggests that an age-related inability to regulate skin cell growth may be more striking a characteristic than is the

decline in skin cell turnover rate (Gilchrest, 1982).

Seborrheic keratosis is the most common of benign skin growths affecting the older adult. Lesions are derived from epidermal cells, but the cause of their appearance is unknown. It is a small, demarcated yellow-brown growth that appears glued to the skin; it is barely elevated and is covered with a greasy, textured scale. Lesions most commonly appear on the trunk, face, scalp and upper extremities.

These lesions are not considered premalignant but may be removed for cosmetic purposes since they can be unsightly. They may be subjected to frequent trauma by a belt, bra strap or comb. In such cases their removal can make life more comfortable and decrease the chance of infection.

Actinic keratosis is a localized thickening of skin. It most often occurs on sun-exposed areas of the body, especially the face, the back of the hands and the forearms, but also on the neck, ears, and bald scalp. Initially, the thickening is a well-defined, reddish colored, slightly raised, sandpaper-like patch. When peeled off, the scaley surface soon reappears. An actinic keratosis is considered to be a premalignant growth that can develop into a *skin cancer* known as *squamous cell carcinoma*. After removal of an actinic keratosis, future prolonged exposure to sunlight should be avoided. Sunscreens should be used to protect against harmful solar rays. Actinic keratoses appear most frequently in men who are beyond middle age. This higher incidence in men has been related to their over-representation in occupations associated with greater exposure to sunlight.

Excessive exposure to the sun's ultraviolet rays is a significant risk factor for all major forms of *skin cancer*. Epidermal cells and melanocytes can be transformed into perpetually dividing units by the sun's damaging rays. Skin cancer is the most common form of human cancer. It is most prevalent on exposed parts of the skin and in people who spend considerable time in the sun, either as outdoor workers or as dedicated sunbathers.

Tanning is a protective mechanism wherein melanocytes, stimulated by the sun's rays, produce melanin and disperse it to epidermal cells. Pigment actually enters epidermal cells, absorbing solar rays and reducing penetration of the epidermal nuclei. Individuals of all races undergo a deeper pigmentation as a result of prolonged exposure to sunlight. Skin cancer is most common among those who are fair-complected. The disease is relatively unimportant among blacks, whose melanocytes synthesize greater amounts of protective pigment.

The word *cancer* is extremely frightening to most people. Its diagnosis can have a tremendous psychological impact. Cancer of the skin, however, is not usually life-threatening, and this fact should be communicated to persons displaying cancerous skin changes. The devastating effects of cancer are largely due to its ability to metastasize. *Basal cell carcinoma,* the most frequent malignant tumor of the skin, rarely metastasizes and is relatively harmless if detected and treated early. The same is true for squamous cell carcinoma. *Melanoma* is potentially far more serious and does metastasize.

The visibility of skin can lead to early detection, treatment, and a good prognosis. Warning signs include an unusual change in the skin, especially a change in the color or size of a preexisting mole or pigmented spot.

Lesions and their surgical removal can be somewhat disfiguring, particularly since they often appear in the facial/head area. Scars become less obvious with time, and cosmetics and clothing can serve to conceal them. It should be acknowledged that concerns about appearance are not limited to the young. Older people also have vanity; concerns they express about appearance should not be ignored because of their age.

Basal cell carcinoma most often occurs on the face, head and neck. It usually presents itself as a small, smooth, translucent, pearly lesion. Lesions are slow-growing and locally invasive, extending down into the dermis. Ulceration frequently occurs with a crust forming on the surface. It is fortunate that this most frequent form of skin cancer rarely spreads. Treatment is important because the condition can be highly destructive, with major disfigurement or infection resulting. With prompt attention, the cure of basal cell carcinoma is almost assured.

The cure for squamous cell carcinoma is equally good with early diagnosis and treatment. Older, fair-skinned persons are more commonly victims of this rarely metastasizing form of cancer, which originates in epidermal cells. Lesions usually occur on areas of skin which have previously been sun-damaged or exposed to certain established environmental carcinogens. The lesions frequently appear as firm, slightly red or pearly nodules or plaques. The red, scaly, sharply outlined actinic keratosis may evolve into a squamous cell carcinoma.

Melanoma springs from the uncontrolled growth of pigment-producing cells and is the most dangerous form of skin cancer. Cancerous melanocytes, unlike other such transformed cells in the epidermis, are noted for their metastasizing nature. Although housed within the outer layer of skin, melanocytes originate in tissue near the spinal cord and spread within the fetus to their permanent home in the epidermis, where they normally remain (Singer and Hilgard, 1978). If transformed, they once again spread through the body but only to do damage as they divide at the expense of other body tissues.

Malignant melanomas generally begin as small mole-like growths, as illustrated in Figure 6.2. They change color, enlarge and bleed easily from minor trauma. Lesions may include flat or slightly raised areas, with irregular margins expressing obvious pigmentation. Melanomas are generally dark brown to black in color.

In an attempt to prevent skin cancer, it is best to avoid prolonged exposure to sunlight, especially during the time when ultraviolet rays are the strongest—from midmorning to midafternoon. Protective clothing and sunscreens, especially those containing para-aminobenzoic acid, should be worn.

Primary malignancies elsewhere in the body can spread to the skin, resulting in secondary skin cancer. Dispersal occurs by way of the lymph or blood vessels or through the direct expansion of an underlying tumor, although the latter is not considered a true metastasis. Metastatic skin lesions most commonly occur in persons between 50 and 70 years of age. Any new growth characterized as diffuse nodules, slightly marginated plaques or purplish hemorrhagic nodules should be investigated. Lesions tend to be diffuse in nature because the density of the dermis serves to restrict the infiltration and growth of large single tumors (Klaus and Kierland, 1976).

Metastatic skin lesions may appear before or after the primary cancer has been recognized. Less than 1 percent of all internal malignancies present themselves as pure skin metastases. Tumors with the greatest tendency to do so include those of the kidney, lung, ovary and pancreas. However, cancer of the breast and oral cavity often spread by direct extension to overlying skin, most often after the primary site is recognized (White, 1985). Secondary skin cancer may be the first indication of an internal malignancy in an otherwise asymptomatic individual. It may also be a sign that treatment of a known tumor was not successful in eradicating all malignant cells.

Pressure Sores

Several years ago an issue of *Medical World News* reported the case of an 85-year-old woman who attempted suicide by taking an overdose of sleeping pills. The major consequence of her unsuccessful act was the development of *pressure sores* over the heels of

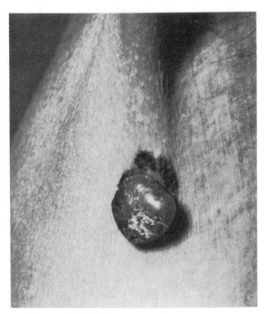

Figure 6.2 Malignant melanomas on posterior axillary fold. (From *Manual of Skin Diseases*, 4th Ed., by G. Sauer. Philadelphia: J.B. Lippincott, 1980. Reprinted by permission.

both feet. Having swallowed the pills, she had crawled into bed, where she remained flat on her back in a comatose state for six hours. During that time the pressure exerted on the woman's heels had denied them an adequate supply of blood. As a result, tissue in those areas died.

Not all pressure sores have so dramatic an onset. Lesions caused by unrelieved pressure to an area can occur in individuals who are debilitated in any number of ways, usually as a result of illness or injury. Victims may have altered mental status, are frequently incontinent, and are uniformly unable to walk without assistance, often being bed- or wheelchair-bound. Elderly patients are at special risk. Two-thirds of all inpatients in geriatric wards or nursing homes demonstrate one or more conditions that increase their susceptibility to the development of these lesions (Seiler and Stahelin, 1985).

Pressure sores are often called *decubitus ulcers* or bed sores, both of which are misnomers. The former term comes from the Latin root *decub* meaning ''a lying down.'' Confinement to bed is not the only way in which they develop. A large percentage of these sores result from unrelieved pressure exerted in a sitting position, often while in a wheelchair. Certain areas of the body are more likely to be involved than others, as illustrated in Figure 6.3. Those parts of the body where little tissue exists between bone and skin are most subject to a deprivation of normal blood flow in the face of unrelieved pressure. The vast majority of pressure sores are located in the lower part of the body. The following areas represent the most common sites of sore formation:

1. For a recumbent patient—the shoulder, lower back and heels.

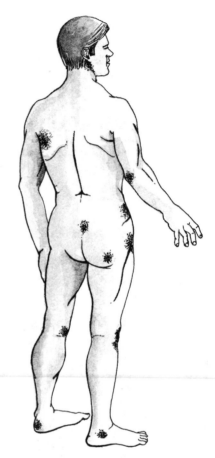

Figure 6.3   Common sites of pressure sore formation

2. For a patient lying on his or her abdomen—the knee, shin and pelvis.
3. For a patient lying on his or her side—the hip.
4. For a sitting patient—the buttocks.

The persistence of localized pressure is inversely related to an individual's ability to move. During sleep a person will normally change positions and restore circulation to a localized pressure spot. However, an individual who is heavily sedated, severely confused or even partially or totally paralyzed will not experience, or may remain oblivious to, signs of unrelieved pressure that are obvious in others.

Gilchrest (1982) reports three factors that may contribute to the development of pressure sores in the elderly. First, loose skin can fold over, compressing dermal vessels and superficial capillaries and compromising blood flow. Second, reduced subcutaneous fat may result in greater pressure over bony prominences. Third, blood flow to the skin may already be reduced by the presence of disorders common in advanced age, such as atherosclerosis or congestive heart failure.

In some instances, the ulceration that develops may be shallow, not involving full skin thickness. In such superficial cases, if the source of pressure is eliminated, healing may occur relatively quickly. The deeper the sore penetrates, though, the slower the healing process and the more dismal the prognosis. Deep ulceration can suddenly present itself. A reddened area of skin may erupt into a profound lesion without any further warning. Underlying fat, muscle and even bone may be involved. The large, deep-seated sore presents infection. Systemic disease may involve one or more organ systems. Multiple, and often life-threatening, complications can accompany pressure sores.

Treatment of pressure sores is costly in every way. For the patient, severe pain and discomfort must be borne. Deep pressure sores may be green in color and filled with the stringy debris of dead tissue. A foul odor may permeate the surrounding air. Patients may be stigmatized in the eyes of family, friends and others, including staff members at health care facilities.

Healing can take weeks to months. The care provided during this time is economically costly. Special materials to clean and dress the wound, long-term antibiotic therapy to counteract infection, and chemical or surgical procedures to remove dead tissue must be employed. Special attention to nutrition is necessary to aid the body's defenses and the healing of the wound. Nursing staff and time involved in attending to these measures must also be considered. Perhaps for no other condition is the adage "An ounce of prevention is worth a pound of cure" so appropriate.

Prevention of pressure sores must involve the relief of pressure. Bed-bound persons should be turned at two-hour intervals. They should be lifted rather than "dragged." Dragging contributes to a shearing force, which can also cause pressure and skin irritation. Care should be taken to guard against keeping the skin too dry or too moist. Broken skin adjacent to or overlying an at-risk area only increases the chance of a deeper opening and associated complications such as infection. Proper nutrition enhances the skin's integrity.

Patients newly admitted to a long-term care facility should be evaluated for risk of developing a pressure sore. Nutritional status, overall physical condition, degree of mobility, activity patterns, level of consciousness (including medication status) and ability to control bowel or bladder should be charted and considered in a care plan aimed at the prevention of this unnecessary and potentially devastating problem. Prevention may be difficult in high-risk groups such as the immobile and bed-ridden, but it is not as difficult as treatment and cure.

Educating the patient and family is important in prevention of pressure sores. This is especially the case given the importance of home health care of the elderly. Patients and home care providers should understand what the condition is and how it can be prevented. Even within an institution, informed family members can assist in repositioning loved ones in order to relieve pressure.

Herpes zoster

Herpes zoster, commonly referred to as *shingles,* is characterized by localized skin eruption and pain. Its incidence is highest among the elderly, for whom it represents the recurrence of the *varicella-zoster virus* (VZV) after a period of latency. Initial introduction to the virus results in the childhood disease chickenpox.

After initial activity the virus of chickenpox remains dormant in the *dorsal root ganglia.* As antibody levels wane with time, the virus becomes active again, spreading down nerve fibers to invade the skin. The manifestations of this viral attack are those of herpes zoster. Zoster can be elicited in response to other trigger factors associated with an altered immune response, including cancer, especially lymphoma, and the use of immunosuppressant drugs and X-ray therapy.

Before it was known that one virus was the cause of two clinically distinct diseases, chickenpox was said to be the result of a varicella virus infection. Shingles was linked with herpes zoster. After Weller and Coons (1954) established that these two agents were really one, the virus was renamed varicella-zoster virus (VZV). Reactivation of the virus, harbored within certain nerve cell bodies, occurs when immunologic capabilities can no longer contain the replicative efforts of the agent.

Onset of symptoms can be sudden, ranging from localized tingling, itching, and burning to pain. Eventually, an eruption appears along areas of supplied skin. Sometimes pain is present several days before skin lesions erupt. The localized pain of the preeruptive phase may be so intense that it is confused with gallstones, appendicitis, heart attack, pleurisy or acute glaucoma, depending on the skin field supplied by affected nerve roots (Harnisch, 1984).

After the lesions heal, *post-herpetic neuralgia* may persist for months in some people. This condition is characterized by localized pain that can last for four to eight weeks or more after the skin lesions have disappeared (Harnisch, 1984; Tenser, 1984). Persistent pain and attempts to manage it can be very frustrating for the victim of herpes zoster. Such patients need caring, sensitive reassurance that the pain will eventually disappear.

There has been speculation about the risk of cancer after herpes zoster because of the associated immune decline. A recent study (Ragozzino, Melton, Kurland, Chu and Perry, 1982) followed 590 patients diagnosed with zoster and concluded that the cancer risk was not significant for this group.

SUMMARY

The skin's lifelong service to its owner subjects it to repeated insults. As a buffer zone between humans and their environment, the skin undergoes frequent and cumulative injury. With age, epidermal cell turnover rate decreases, and the barrier function of the outermost layer of the epidermis is reduced. A decrease in the density of active melanocytes has also been noted. Coupled with an almost compensatory hyperactivity of some pigment-producing cells, this accounts for the blotchy pigmentation of aged skin. A total loss of functioning melanocytes from the hair bulbs results in graying hair. Sweat-and oil-producing glands become smaller, less numerous and less active. Along with changes in sweat production, decreased dermal vascularity and a loss of subcutaneous fat contribute to weakened thermoregulation in the older adult.

A flattened epidermal-dermal margin results in less nutrient transfer and waste clearance via diffusion from underlying dermal capillary beds. The dermis becomes thinner, giving the skin a transparent quality. The looseness and inelasticity of older skin results from the progressive cross-linkage of dermal tissue.

Nails on the fingers and toes represent appendages of the skin. They become brittle with age and longitudinally ridged. Toenails are more likely to thicken due to repeated microtrauma and circulatory decline. Corns and calluses may form, reflecting epidermal thickening that results from long-term rubbing and weight-bearing.

Certain skin conditions become significant for the older adult. These include dry, scaly skin, proliferative skin lesions, various types of skin cancer, pressure sores and the skin involvement of herpes zoster.

KEY TERMS

actinic keratosis
basal cell
basal cell carcinoma
basal membrane
cutaneous tumors
decubitus ulcer
dermis
dorsal root ganglia
epidermis

herpes zoster
hypothermia
keratin
melanin
melanocyte
melanoma
pressure sore
post-herpetic neuralgia
seborrheic keratosis
sebum
senile puritis
shingles
skin cancer
squamous cell carcinoma
subcutaneous fat
thermoregulation
varicella-zoster virus
xerosis

STUDY QUESTIONS

1. Differentiate the epidermis from the dermis. What types of age-related changes in structure and function take place in these two areas of skin?
2. Describe xerosis and senile pruritis. What factors are associated with the development and alleviation of these conditions?
3. Differentiate seborrheic keratosis from actinic keratosis.
4. How are exposure to sunlight and melanocyte activity related to skin cancer? Identify and differentiate the three major forms of skin cancer. Of what significance is secondary skin cancer to the older adult?
5. What are pressure sores? Identify some factors related to their development and prevention. What are some consequences of the development of pressure sores?
6. What is herpes zoster? How is it related to chickenpox?

BIBLIOGRAPHY

Fowler, E. 1983. Pressure sores. *Long-Term Care Currents 6*: 15–18.

Gilchrest, B. 1982. Skin. In J. Rowe and R. Besdine, eds., *Health and Disease in Old Age.* Boston: Little, Brown.

Harnisch, J. 1984. Zoster in the elderly: Clinical, immunologic and therapeutic considerations. *Journal of the American Geriatrics Society 32:* 789–793.

Klaus, S., and Kierland, R. 1976. When primary cancer spreads to the skin. *Geriatrics 31:* 39–43.

Leyden, J., McGinley, K., and Grove, G. 1978. Age related differences in the rate of desquamation of skin surface cells. In R. Adelman, J. Roberts and V. Cristofalo, eds., *Pharmacological Intervention in the Aging Process.* New York: Plenum Press.

Ragozzino, M., Melton, J., Kurland, L., Chu, P., and Perry, H. 1982. Risk of cancer after herpes zoster: A population-based study. *New England Journal of Medicine 307:* 393–396.

Seiler, W., and Stahelin, H. 1985. Decubitus ulcers: Preventive techniques for the elderly patient. *Geriatrics, 40*(7): 53–60.

Singer, S., and Hilgard, H. 1978. *The Biology of People.* San Francisco: W. H. Freeman.

Tenser, R. 1984. Herpes simplex and Herpes zoster. *Neurologic Clinics 2:* 215–240.

Weller, T., and Coons, A. 1954. Fluorescent antibody studies with agents of varicella and herpes zoster propagated in vitro. *Proceedings, Society of Experimental Biology and Medicine 86:* 789.

White, J. 1985. Evaluating cancer metastatic to the skin. *Geriatrics 40:* 67–73.

CHAPTER **7**

The Aging Skeletal System

Together our bones and muscles protect vital organs, give stability to the body, preserve its shape and allow the freedom of movement and locomotion. Additionally, the skeletal system acts as a metabolic reservoir. Through the continuing process of bone remodeling, calcium enters and leaves the bones. Most of us take these provisions of the skeletomuscular system very much for granted.

Joint changes, along with diminished bone and muscle mass, can lead to increased fractures and falls, stooped posture and shortened stature, loss of muscle power, misshapen joints, pain, stiffness and limited mobility. Arthritis and allied bone and muscular conditions are among the most common of all disorders affecting people over 65

years of age. In fact, joint and muscular aches, pains and stiffness are often expected in old age. Frequently, all such symptoms are lumped together as discomforts of arthritis or "rheumatism." Such a classification can be dangerous. For instance, pain associated with bone cancer or another disease may be dismissed and needed medical attention delayed. Chronic, recurrent muscular and bone pain is not natural. In response to such symptoms, people of all ages should seek prompt medical attention.

Skeletomuscular changes are significant in that they can greatly alter an individual's lifestyle by making the activities of daily living more difficult. Even though certain changes occur, they need not be disabling if proper diagnosis and treatment are given. Age-related changes or disease states of the skeletomuscular system rarely shorten the life span directly. Nevertheless, if one is immobilized or bedridden as a result of pain, stiffness, a fall or fracture, complications can lead to death.

A recognition of potential problems should not be used to paint a dismal picture for older people. Although the prevalence and disabling effects of certain skeletomuscular conditions increase with age, most older persons are not severely limited by changes or disease within this system. For certain disorders an increasing emphasis is being placed upon prevention. Primary prevention of arthritis may not be possible, but secondary and tertiary steps can be taken to retard serious effects and to increase the potential for independent living. It may be possible to prevent, or at least delay, the serious effects of bone loss by attention to modifiable lifestyle factors. This chapter will focus upon selected skeletomuscular conditions that may be encountered by the older adult, including several forms of arthritis, osteoporosis and Paget's disease.

ARTHRITIS

Arthritis is a major source of discomfort and disability for many older persons. It is one of the oldest known diseases. The cartoon image of a Neanderthal as a stooped brute with a bent-knee gait is in fact a caricature of an arthritic relative who lived over 40,000 years ago. The condition is still very much with us; it constitutes the number one crippler across all ages in the United States.

Arthritis is a generic term that literally means inflammation of a joint. There are over 100 different kinds of arthritis; each is not necessarily accompanied by inflammation. However, all forms of arthritis do signify some type of joint involvement.

The numerous types of arthritis vary in their causation, symptomatology, and degree of joint inflammation and damage. Some forms of arthritis may first present themselves in middle or old age. Others may have developed decades earlier. *Osteoarthritis, rheumatoid arthritis,* and *gout* will be discussed here, as conditions affecting the older adult.

To comprehend what arthritis is and the changes that accompany it, it is useful to understand the anatomy of joints or articulations. Where bones come together there exist articulating surfaces so that various body movements can be accomplished. The adjacent ends of bones are covered with *articular cartilage* and are encircled by a strong fibrous articular capsule. The *synovial membrane* lines the capsule and produces a lubricant for smooth articulation (Figure 7.1). The articular cartilage and synovial fluid allow for smooth, lubricated movement. The joint capsule and associated tendons and ligaments play an important part in lending stability to the joint.

Osteoarthritis

Osteoarthritis (OA), the most common joint disease, is usually encountered in persons older than 50 years. It is a defect of articular cartilage, characterized by the gradual loss of this cushioning substance. It is also referred to as *degenerative joint disease;* it used to be assumed that such deterioration resulted from the mechanical wear and tear of aging. Simply stated, it was held that the use of a joint over the years eventually eroded the articular surface and led to possible joint failure. Today, this explanation is considered simplistic and inexact. Certain joints that

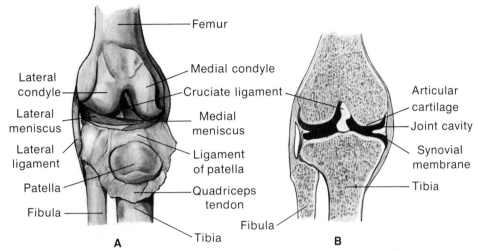

Figure 7.1   Knee joint. A. Dissected from the front, with patella hanging down onto the tibia. B. Section of the knee, revealing the joint cavity. (From P. Anderson, *Basic Human Anatomy and Physiology,* 1986. Courtesy of Jones and Bartlett Publishers.)

receive considerable use, such as the knee, are frequently involved; others subject to the lifelong stress of frequent movement, such as the knuckles, are rarely involved. Though poorly understood, when joint failure occurs it appears to be the culmination of numerous pathologic events. Biochemical, hereditary, inflammatory and mechanical factors possibly influence the degree and rate of cartilage thinning (Kaye, 1984).

As cartilage is lost the resultant exposure of rough underlying bone ends can cause pain and joint stiffness. Bony growths or spurs known as *osteophytes* may appear at the articular margin or at sites of ligament and tendon attachment, producing a characteristic "lipping." These bony spurs account for much of the associated joint enlargement. As the condition continues, low-grade inflammation of the synovial membrane develops. Thus inflammation is a secondary effect rather than the initial lesion of OA. Inflammation is often mild and unnoticed—in contrast to rheumatoid arthritis, the archetypal inflammatory joint disease (Altman and Gray, 1985).

In time, the joint capsule may become thickened, leading to restricted movement. Long-standing OA can result in joint instability and deformity. Occasionally, osteophytes may grow from both bone ends, causing the joint to meet and fuse. The joint becomes locked and incapable of movement (Figure 7.2).

Degeneration that occurs in the absence of a known cause is referred to as *primary* or *idiopathic OA. Secondary OA* occurs in conjunction with previous joint damage or disease. For instance, joint injury resulting from an accident or infection may lead to OA. The effect of running on joint degeneration is a present-day concern. Though much more research is needed, some studies indicate that running does not necessarily predispose to OA (Lane, Block, Jones, Marshall, Wood and Fries, 1986; Panush, Schmidt, Caldwell,

Edwards, Longley, Yonker, Webster, Stork and Petersson, 1986). In 1984, the Stanford Arthritis Center in California launched a prospective 5-year longitudinal study on the effect of running on osteoarthritic development. Running and control subjects range in age from 50 to 72 years. It is hoped that the results of this investigation will shed more light on this important question.

Weight-bearing joints, including the lumbar spine, knees and hips, are commonly affected by osteoarthritis (Brandt and Fife, 1983). However, weight-bearing does not necessarily indicate risk of OA. The condition is often asymmetric, with one knee or hip showing damage. Likewise, the ankle, although subject to such life-long stress, is rarely affected by primary disease.

The cervical spine, *metatarsophalangeal joint* of the great toe, first *carpometacarpal joint* and distal and proximal *interphalangeal joints* may also be affected. The familiar nodules known as *Heberden's nodes* may appear on the last joints of the fingers. *Bouchard's nodes* are the same phenomenon at the prox-

imal interphalangeal joints (Figure 7.3). Such cartilaginous/bony enlargements are seen in women more often than in men. Though disfiguring, they usually develop gradually and cause little pain. They are occasionally accompanied by swelling, pain and a burning/tingling sensation at the end of the fingers.

Primary OA rarely involves the wrist or knuckles, which are the joints stressed by frequent, repetitive movement. Likewise, the elbow and shoulder are rarely involved except as a result of previous trauma. Thus it is suggested that factors other than simple weight-bearing and joint use are involved in the development of the disease.

Osteoarthritis does not cause symptoms prior to radiographic change, although such change is not necessarily accompanied by symptoms. By the age of 75 years, 85 percent of individuals demonstrate radiographic evidence of OA in weight-bearing joints. Only 30 percent of these persons are symptomatic (Giansiracusa and Kantrowitz, 1982). It has been emphasized that OA is

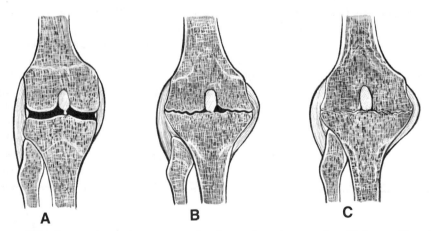

A   **B**   **C**

Figure 7.2   Osteoarthritis: degeneration developing from A, normal, to C, fusion. Note the increased joint width after fusion. (From P. Anderson, *Basic Human Anatomy and Physiology,* 1986. Courtesy of Jones and Bartlett, Publishers.)

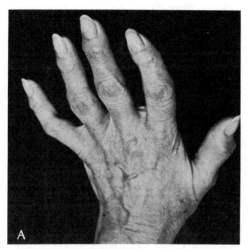
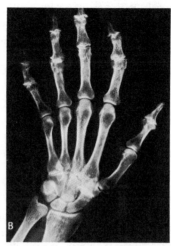

Figure 7.3   Osteoarthritis of the hand. A. Proximal interphalangeal involvement (Bouchard's nodes), along with some distal interphalangeal involvement (Heberden's nodes). B. X ray of the same hand. (From *Arthritis,* 8th ed., by J.L. Hollander. Lea & Febiger, 1976. Reprinted with permission.)

often overdiagnosed on the basis of radiographic evidence. Joint symptoms with X-ray changes may be due to conditions other than OA (Brandt and Fife, 1983). It is also possible for symptomatic OA to overlap with another disease, such as gout.

Symptomatic OA is generally characterized by pain upon movement of the affected joint. As the condition progresses, pain may occur at rest as well. The pain is frequently poorly localized. For instance, hip involvement may be associated with groin, thigh, buttocks and lower back discomfort. Stiffness on awakening or movement may also be present. Known as *gelling* or *gel phenomenon,* the stiffness is of relatively short duration. It usually subsides within a few minutes after movement, in contrast to that experienced by rheumatoid arthritis victims, among whom it may persist for hours. Over time a progressive loss of range of motion occurs. The joint may become unstable and deformed.

There is no cure for osteoarthritis. Symptomatic relief includes rest balanced with exercise, physical therapy, moist heat, and drugs (analgesics and anti-inflammatory agents). Aspirin is one of several nonsteroidal anti-inflammatory drugs that provide pain relief. It has been a mainstay of arthritis therapy. Though it is a highly effective product, certain side effects of long term aspirin use must be noted. *Tinnitus* and hearing loss are eventually inescapable and may be cause for a switch in medication. Gastrointestinal irritation as a part of long-term therapy may be minimized by taking the drug with food or through the use of a buffered or enteric-coated product. Bleeding is yet another side effect to be considered. The individualized needs of a patient must dictate whether aspirin or another drug should be administered. The decision must weigh patient tolerance, cost and the potential side effects of the given drug. Surgical intervention may be used to relieve pain and correct joint deformity.

Osteoarthritis patients need proper treatment and care. They, as well as many victims of other forms of arthritis, are easy prey for quackery. The Arthritis Foundation estimates that several hundred million dollars are spent annually on worthless gimmicks and so-called cure-alls. Medications, special devices, clinics, diets and dietary supplements have been falsely presented as remedies for a disease that orthodox medicine cannot cure.

Rheumatoid Arthritis

Joint involvement in rheumatoid arthritis (RA) begins with an inflamed synovial membrane. The normally thin lining swells, thickens and begins to override the articular cartilage. Eventually, the cartilage is softened as chemical reactions occur. Erosion of cartilage continues as fibrous connective tissue forms. In time, the joint can undergo extensive damage, with the capsule and ligaments inflamed, stretched and destroyed. Tendons may drift out of their normal position, shorten and produce deformity as the joint undergoes complete disorganization. Twisted, drawn fingers of the hand attacked by RA provide an example of joint distortion as a result of inflammation. Sometimes fibrous tissue formation can lead to joint fusion.

Rheumatoid arthritis is a chronic, systemic disease. It is not confined to joints; rather, it attacks connective tissue throughout the body. Symptoms of RA include general malaise, fatigue, weight loss, fever, anemia and nodules that develop on soft tissues. The associated arthritis tends to be symmetric and *polyarticular*. Hands and feet are commonly affected. The knee, hip, ankle, shoulder and elbow may also be involved. Red, swollen joints and gelling are characteristic of the disease.

The cause of RA is not fully known. It is recognized as an immunologic disturbance triggered by hereditary factors and most probably exposure to a commonly encountered virus. A self-perpetuating inflammatory response ensues; if left unchecked, it can lead to destruction of the joints. Rheumatoid arthritis is an autoimmune disease wherein antibodies launch an attack detrimental to the person's own tissues.

Rheumatoid arthritis can be diagnosed by a laboratory technique that demonstrates an elevated *erythrocyte sedimentation* rate, although a positive result can be indicative of disorders other than RA. Tests for *rheumatoid factor*, an abnormal antibody, are positive in 85 percent of RA patients. Radiographs and synovial membrane tests, along with a symptomatic history, are also a part of diagnostic review.

There are many drugs available to treat RA, including aspirin and other nonsteroidal anti-inflammatory drugs (NSAIDS). Serious consideration must be given to the use of various other agents when the disease cannot be controlled by the above measures. Balanced rest and exercise are important in the care of arthritis. Although rest is appropriate, prolonged rest can lead to stiffness, muscle weakness and "frozen joints." "Exercise" does not mean strenuous activity or athletics; it refers to prescribed activities that put joints through their full range of motion. Rheumatoid arthritis is a progressive disease, but with early diagnosis and treatment the majority of persons can maintain good control of the disorder. Surgical techniques, though not routine, have been developed to remove damaged tissue and to correct deformity.

Rheumatoid arthritis presents itself most commonly between the ages of 20 and 60. Thus the elderly RA patient has usually carried the disease into old age. In the older adult with advanced disease, other skeleto-muscular problems may cause the disorder to worsen. The crippling effects of arthritis may become more pronounced with age.

Spontaneous remission of RA can occur, but it is rare—the usual rate is 5 to 10 percent (Kaye, 1984; Giansiracusa and Kantrowitz, 1982). Progression of the disease is characterized by periods of symptomatic exacerbation and subsidence known as *flares* and *remissions*. Temporary periods of remission or control of the disease through treatment are not to be confused with spontaneous remission or disappearance of the disease.

Approximately 10 percent of patients undergo disease onset after the age of 60 (Giansiracusa and Kantrowitz, 1982). Sometimes the pattern of late-onset disease differs from that seen in younger patients. Some reports have shown men equally affected as women, which is a deviation from the normal profile of occurrence. Also, a high frequency of remission has been observed within the first year (Ehrlich, Katz and Cohen, 1970; Giansiracusa and Kantrowitz, 1982). In a group of 110 persons with late-onset disease, 74 percent had RA identical to that occurring in younger patients, while 26 percent experienced remission (Corrigan, Robinson, Terenty, Dick-Smith and Walters, 1974).

Gout

Gout is a metabolic disease that causes an acutely painful form of arthritis. It is frequently due to an inherited defect in *purine* metabolism, which results in excess blood levels of *uric acid*. Proteins in the body break down into purines. Uric acid is an end product of purine metabolism and is normally excreted through the kidneys. Heightened levels of the substance are caused by increased production or faulty elimination.

Uric acid excesses can precipitate out to the joints to form sharp crystals, thus initiating an attack of gouty arthritis. This acute condition is characterized by sudden, intermittent episodes of joint inflammation. The affected joint is painful, hot, swollen and tender. Crystal deposits may develop in almost any part of the body, but in the vast majority of cases the great toe is the initial site of attack.

Gout episodes generally subside after a few days. Symptoms usually begin to manifest themselves between the ages of 40 and 55 years and tend to become more apparent with advancing age. As the condition progresses, discomfort can become more prolonged. Anti-inflammatory drugs are called for during the acute stages of gout so that joint symptoms may be relieved. Drugs that lower blood levels of uric acid are used between attacks and aid in preventing recurrences.

Since gout represents disordered purine metabolism, foods high in purines should be restricted. Such foods include gravy, broth, boullion, consommé, meat (particularly organ meat), anchovies, mackerel, herring, sardines, scallops, mussels and sweetbreads. A restricted purine diet does not guarantee decreased uric acid blood levels. Purines can be manufactured by the body from simple metabolites. Hence uric acid levels can increase even though outside purine sources are controlled by dietary restriction.

Some general dietary recommendations are in order for gout sufferers. Fats, protein and carbohydrates are all necessary in a balanced diet. Excessive amounts of fat should be avoided, since they can serve to prevent uric acid excretion. Protein intake should not be excessive. A substantial proportion of calories should be derived from carbohydrates because of their association with increased uric acid elimination. During acute stages of gout, purine intake should be severely restricted. Fluid consumption can aid in the elimination of uric acid. Those with gout should never go on a diet for rapid weight loss. Fasting may cause precipitation of uric acid. It is important that weight loss be gradual and that a weight-loss diet not be initiated during an acute attack.

Gouty arthritis does not always arise from an inherited defect in purine metabolism. Secondary gout may be associated with a number of causes. Diuretic medications given to lower blood pressure and rid the body of excess fluid may be related to a gout attack. Secondary gout may also develop in association with other drugs as well as in certain medical conditions, such as leukemia or cirrhosis (Kaye, 1984).

OSTEOPOROSIS

The majority of the 15 to 20 million cases of osteoporosis in the United States occur in women. This condition, wherein bone loss is accelerated to a symptomatic level, is the major cause of skeletal fractures in post-menopausal women and older persons in general. Women are more prone to the disease because they have less bone mass to begin with and because changes during menopause lower calcium and estrogen levels, thereby accelerating loss of bone tissue.

Bone loss occurs in all humans as they age, regardless of gender, race, ethnic group or physical condition. Such normal age-associated loss of bone is termed *senile osteopenia*. For many persons, adult bone loss continues

to be asymptomatic. When it advances to the pathologic state known as osteoporosis, the structural integrity of bone tissue is so compromised that bones are more susceptible to fracture. Osteoporosis can result in diminished height, stooped posture, pain and tooth loss.

Certain non-modifiable factors have been identified as increasing the risk of osteoporosis. They include sex, race, heredity and body frame. As noted earlier, women are at higher risk than men. Men can develop osteoporosis but do so in fewer numbers and generally at a later age. White and Asian women are at higher risk than black women, who tend to have greater bone density. A family history of osteoporosis also increases the risk of the disorder, as does a slight frame. Thin, small-boned women are more susceptible than large-framed women. Although these factors cannot be controlled, there are modifiable lifestyle factors that may influence the integrity of bone and the bone-thinning process. Proper nutrition and regular exercise are among the lifestyle factors that will be presented in this chapter. However, a basic understanding of bone as living tissue is important to a full appreciation of preventive strategies in the development of osteoporosis.

Bone is dynamic tissue that is in a constant state of change. It consists of calcium and phosphorus in a protein matrix. Various other materials, such as fluoride and magnesium, lend support to the calcium and phosphorus crystals. Calcium is critical to the structural integrity of bone. Approximately 99 percent of the body's calcium is stored in bones (and teeth), giving them strength and rigidity. In turn, the skeleton serves as a "calcium bank" for the body.

Calcium concentrations in serum and body fluids must be maintained to allow for various vital activities such as blood clotting, enzyme activation and inhibition, muscle contraction, nerve conduction and regulation of heartbeat. If serum calcium levels are not adequate, hormones assist in releasing calcium from bone, thus making it available for such functions. If calcium levels rise above normal, another hormone shuts down its release. Calcium is also added to skeletal tissue. Thus bones are constantly being broken down and reformed.

The turnover of bone is a lifelong process known as *remodeling*. During *bone resorption, parathyroid hormone* (PTH) stimulates bone-destroying cells called *osteoclasts* to release calcium from skeletal tissue. *Bone formation,* wherein calcium enters the skeleton, is mediated by bone-forming *osteoblasts*. The rates of bone resorption and formation vary over the life cycle. During adolescence, when bones are growing and height is increasing, formation exceeds resorption. After growth is completed, bones continue to add mass. They reach their maximum strength and density sometime during early to middle adulthood, depending upon the bone. For instance, vertebrae peak in strength and density during the mid-20s, while the long bones of the arms and legs do so at about age 40 (Peck, 1985). During this period, formation and resorption equal one another. After a plateau is reached, the rate of bone resorption exceeds that of formation, initiating a period of progressive bone loss (Giansircusa and Kantowitz, 1982; Meunier, 1973). From middle adulthood, bones begin a gradual and silent decline in mass and strength. If bone volume reaches a low enough level, osteoporosis is the end result.

Although all bones lose mass with age, some are more critically affected than others. This situation exists because of the distribution of two basic types of bone. Located within skeletal tissue is porous, *trabecular bone*. Although hard, it looks like a sponge or honeycomb in cross-section. *Cortical bone,* in contrast, surrounds it (being located on the outside) and is very dense and solid. Trabecular bone loss begins at an earlier age, resulting in a relative increase in the ratio of cortical to trabecular bone. During the teen years, the ratio is 55:45. By age 85 it is approximately 70:30 (Giansircusa and Kantowitz, 1982). Those bones with the greatest amount of trabecular area will thus undergo a greater decline of their mass. Indeed, the vertebrae, wrist and hips, all high in trabecular bone, are the most common fracture sites.

Vertebral and wrist fractures are seen predominantly in women 10 to 15 years after menopause. They are associated with *Type I osteoporosis,* which is attributed to trabecular as opposed to cortical bone loss (Riggs and Melton, 1983). Their occurrence is a function not only of the trabecular area involved, but is related to the post-menopausal drop in estrogen levels as well. Estrogen deficiency makes bone more sensitive to PTH, which stimulates bone resorption (Berlyne, Ben-Ari and Kushelvesky, 1975; Gallagher, Riggs, Eisman, Hamstra and Arnaud, 1979; Slovik, Adams, Neer, Holick and Potts, 1981). It is also believed to lead to reduced intestinal absorption of calcium (Aloia, Cohn, Vaswani, Yeh, Yuen and Ellis, 1985). Estrogen loss is an established risk factor for osteoporosis (Lindsay, Hart, Purdre, Gerguson, Clark and Kraszewski, 1982; Meema, Bunkler and Meema, 1975; Nordin et al., 1981). The maintenance of testosterone levels in men appears to exert somewhat of a protective effect on bone mass (Orimo and Shiraki, 1979; Horsman, Marshall, Nordin, Crilly and Simpson, 1981).

Since vertebrae consist largely of trabecular bone, osteoporosis typically occurs first in the spine. Vertebral compression or *crush fractures* can occur spontaneously or from the stress of activities such as bending or lifting. Compressed vertebrae may lead to a loss of height and curvature of the thoracic spine (commonly known as *dowager's hump.*) Both of these changes are irreversible. In severe cases of *dorsal kyphosis*, the lower ribs may come to rest on the *iliac crests* of the pelvis. A horizontal band of thickened skin across the abdominal area may result, as well as intestinal distention and constipation. Chest wall mechanics may also be impaired, affecting respiratory ventilation.

Osteoporosis is a common cause of backache in elderly women. It can range from mild to severe and be localized or radiated toward the abdomen and into the pelvis or legs. Coughing, sneezing and straining at the stool may exacerbate the problem. Vertebral osteoporosis is frequently episodic. One or more crush fractures can produce severe pain that can last for several weeks. For some, backache may become chronic; for others it disappears. Recurrent incidents of vertebral compression fractures result in progressive loss of height and increasing deformity.

Wrist fractures called *Colles fractures* often result from minimal trauma in the osteoporotic individual. They typically involve the distal radius and usually occur when the arm is extended to break a fall. They are the least severe fracture associated with osteoporosis but may represent a warning of significant

bone loss. Bone loss in the jaw can contribute to tooth loss and *edentulism*. It can also make it difficult to construct and tolerate well-fitting dentures (Renner, Boucher and Kaufman, 1984).

Hip fracture is the greatest hazard associated with osteoporosis. It occurs later in life, usually in a person's 70s or 80s, when a significant amount of cortical bone has been lost. Due to the loss of cortical bone, it is regarded as *Type II osteoporosis*. Hip fractures are a significant cause of morbidity and mortality, costing the United States $800 million annually in acute care expenses alone (Owen, Melton and Gallagher, 1980). Fatal complications such as pneumonia and pulmonary embolism generally result from imposed immobility. Between 12 and 20 percent of elderly hip-fracture victims die within six months (Jensen and Tondevold, 1979).

Both elderly men and women are affected by Type II osteoporosis (Riggs and Melton, 1983). It is suspected that 33 percent of women and half as many men in the older age group sustain hip fractures (Owen et al., 1980). Type II osteoporosis is a function of cumulative loss of bone and age-related impaired calcium absorption. That twice as many females suffer hip fractures as men has been related to their greater longevity as well as to initially lower peak bone mass.

There are certain basic differences in the pattern of fractures in the young and old. In young adults it takes a considerable amount of force to break a bone. Among the elderly a fracture can result from minor trauma—even bearing weight. For instance, it is likely that many of the falls and associated hip fractures of old age actually represent an osteoporotic femoral neck that breaks under the stress of weight-bearing, resulting in a fall. Another difference in fracture pattern involves location. The shaft of a long bone is a common fracture site among the young, while a site adjacent to a joint is more typically involved in the older adult. The number of hip (actually femoral neck) and distal radius fractures testify to this fact. Finally, the fracture rate among young adults is higher for men; this is largely related to occupational factors and potential accident situations.

There is an emphasis today on prevention of osteoporosis. Ideally, such measures should start as early as possible. Maximizing bone construction during adolescence and early adulthood gives one a greater calcium reserve to carry into old age. The more calcium deposited in the "bone bank" when one is young, the more there will be to draw upon later. Prevention is not a goal reserved for the young. It is a lifelong aim. Although osteoporosis is an irreversible and progressive disease, there are measures which may slow further loss of bone tissue even among the osteoporotic patient. Consideration of preventive and treatment modalities is in order.

Diet is one of the major modifiable lifestyle factors that may affect progression of bone loss. The established RDA for calcium is 800 mg. Many consider the present RDA too low to maintain calcium balance, especially in post-menopausal women (Avioli, 1984; Heaney, Gallagher, Johnston, Neer, Parfitt and Whedon, 1982; National Institutes of Health, 1984). A calcium intake of 1000 mg/day has been suggested for pre-menopausal and estrogen-treated women and 1500 mg/day for post-menopausal women not on *estrogen-replacement therapy.* A National Institutes of Health (NIH) panel submitted that such recommended intakes might serve to

prevent fractures or to reduce their incidence after menopause (National Institutes of Health, 1984). Twenty-five percent of American women consume less than 300 mg per day; the median calcium intake for females approximates 500 mg.

Some researchers are presently questioning whether dietary calcium in adulthood plays a role in osteoporosis prevention (Kolata, 1986). One study involving 107 women ranging in age from 23 to 88 years found no correlation between calcium intake and bone loss (Riggs and Melton, 1986). The women, who were studied for an average of four years, had a wide range of calcium intake (from 269 to 2000 mg/day), with each subject's intake relatively steady throughout the period of investigation. When women consuming more than 1400 mg/day were compared with those whose intake was less than 500, the rate of bone loss was found to be essentially the same.

Various researchers are quoted from a 1986 meeting of the American Society for Bone and Mineral Research as questioning the 1984 dietary recommendations of the NIH panel on osteoporosis (Kolata, 1986). Some maintain that the advice was based on tenuous evidence. Due to uncertainties regarding the long-term efficacy of calcium in preventing osteoporosis, a number of researchers would not advise calcium supplementation. Riggs cautions that despite the "enormous media hype," the answers are not yet certain regarding osteoporosis prevention. Although he does not recommend calcium pills, Riggs does advise patients to consume 1000 mg/day from dietary sources.

The best sources of calcium are dairy products. Because of concern for calories, fat and cholesterol, low-fat dairy products are recommended. Sometimes "weight-watching" or *lactose intolerance* causes avoidance of dairy products. Leafy green vegetables such as collard, turnip and mustard greens and broccoli are also good calcium sources. Some green vegetables such as spinach contain *oxalates,* which bind the calcium they contain and prevent its absorption (Allen, 1984). Sardines and salmon provide calcium—if the bones are consumed. Legumes are also a source of calcium.

Various other dietary factors have been associated with calcium levels. High-protein/meat diets have been said to enhance bone loss and increase urinary calcium excretion. Presently, there is conflicting data on this matter (Margen, Chu, Kaufmann and Calloway, 1974; Spencer, Kramer, DeBartolo, Norris and Osis, 1983; Spencer and Kramer, 1986; Wachman and Bernstein, 1968). Soft-drink consumption and related high dietary phosphorus have caused concern that calcium absorption might be impaired, but this belief is being questioned (Allen, 1984). There is speculation that a high-calcium, high-phosphorus diet may help to prevent bone loss (Liebman, 1985). Data also suggest that bone loss might be increased by "heavy" caffeine consumption.

Alcoholics frequently show evidence of bone loss, probably due to impaired calcium absorption (Allen, 1984) and intestinal and liver problems (Baran, Teitelbaum and Bergefeld, 1980). Likewise, heavy drinkers frequently have poor diets and do not consume much calcium. Alcohol intake is recognized as a risk factor for osteoporosis; among males it increases the risk by 2.4 (Seeman, Melton, O'Fallon and Riggs, 1983).

A decreased ability to absorb calcium appears in both men and women during their 60s. Among women, an especially acute drop occurs at menopause. Most elderly women excrete approximately 60 mg more calcium per day than they eat (Allen, 1984).

Vitamin D is also important in preventing osteoporosis, because it is a major regulator of calcium absorption in the intestine. Vitamin D levels are dependent on dietary intake and upon exposure to sunlight, which initiates synthesis of a form of vitamin D in the skin.

Concern about osteoporosis has focused much attention on the use of calcium supplements. While such supplementation may be appropriate, there are several factors to consider. Although many forms of calcium are available, calcium carbonate tablets are most frequently recommended. They contain a higher percentage of elemental calcium, so fewer tablets are needed. This preparation may cause constipation, while calcium lactate and gluconate are less likely to do so. Supplements containing dolomite or bone meal should be avoided, because they may contain toxic contaminants, including lead. As previously indicated, various researchers would not recommend supplementation because its long-term safety and efficacy are not presently known.

Supplements are available with added vitamin D. For older women, who tend to get less exposure to sunlight (and who are less efficient at endogenously manufacturing vitamin D), this addition may be very appropriate. However, younger women may be getting enough in their diet and via sunlight. Too much vitamin D can be toxic (Hausman, 1985).

Daily calcium intake from diet and supplements should not exceed 1500 mg per day. Calcium excesses can lead to calcification of soft tissue. Individuals who are prone to or have a strong family history of kidneystones should take supplemental calcium only under the direction of a physician.

The role of physical activity in preventing bone loss has yet to be clearly defined. Research suggests that regular exercise, in conjunction with the dietary aspects of bone maintenance, is important in promoting bone formation and reducing skeletal losses (Goodman, 1985). While definitive data do not exist to prove that exercise will prevent the disorder, it is known that a lack of physical activity hastens bone loss (Donaldson, Hulley and Vogel, 1970;, Mack, LaChance and Vose, 1967; Rambaut, Dietlein and Vogel, 1972; Smith, 1982). Inactivity resulting in bone loss may be induced by immobilization, loss of muscle function or the weightlessness demonstrated in space flight.

Regular exercise that works muscles against gravity, such as walking, seems to maintain and strengthen bone (Aloia et al., 1978; Huddleston et al., 1980). Muscular activity has been found to increase bone mass in elderly as well as young persons (Smith, Reddan and Smith, 1981). Aloia, Cohn, Ostuni, Cane and Ellis (1978) reported that bone loss in younger women can be prevented by physical activity. It is possible that daily weight-bearing exercise may be the single most important external factor affecting bone formation.

Smoking is a risk factor for osteoporosis (Daniel, 1976). Although the reason for this association is not known, it may be related to an earlier onset of menopause in women who smoke (Lindquist and Bengtsson, 1979; Lindquist, Bengtsson and Hanson, 1979). Men who smoke are also at increased risk (Seeman et al., 1983). In one study it was found that 52 percent of osteoporotic smokers required dentures after age 50, compared to 26 percent for osteoporotic non-smokers, and 8 percent for non-osteoporotic non-smokers (Daniell, 1983).

A simple low-cost test for osteoporosis is a present-day goal. Such a test would be helpful in detecting bone thinning before it had progressed to a clinically significant point. For many people the first sign of the loss of bone that has been taking place is a fracture. Sometimes osteoporosis is detected inadvertently by an Xray taken for another problem. An Xray can detect bone loss, but only after a significant amount of tissue is gone. There are various bone density tests for detecting the disorder. However, because of cost and accessibility they are not now routinely used (Lane, Virginia and Falls, 1984).

Estrogen replacement therapy (ERT) is the most significant form of treatment currently used to slow bone loss after menopause. Evidence indicates that fracture risk is significantly reduced with estrogen therapy (Henneman and Wallach, 1957; Nachtigall, Nachtigall and Beckman, 1979; Weiss, Ure, Ballard, Williams and Daling, 1980). It is given shortly after menopause and seems to be most effective at reducing bone loss during the eight-to-ten year period following its onset. Not all women are candidates for ERT. It has been the subject of controversy and should be used only with close medical supervision. Use of estrogen has been linked with endometrial cancer, but the risk is negated when estrogen is given in conjunction with the hormone progesterone (Judd, Cleary, Creasman, Figge, Kase, Rosenwaks and Tagatz, 1981; Weiss and Scyvetz, 1980).

PAGET'S DISEASE

Paget's disease is a chronic, localized bone disease of unknown cause, occurring primarily in geriatric patients. It begins slowly and may progress to cause skeletal deformity. This condition, which was first described and labeled *osteitis deformans* in the late nineteenth century by Paget, affects approximately 3 percent of the population over 45 years of age. Men and women are equally affected.

Paget's disease is characterized by excessive bone resorption followed by accelerated formation of abnormal bone. Radiography will display porotic areas of bone surrounded by areas of sclerosis and bone "repair." The sites most commonly affected are the vertebral column and sacrum, femur, skull and pelvis. Single or multiple bone involvement may be expressed, the latter being most common.

SUMMARY

Although the prevalence and disabling effects of certain skeletomuscular conditions increase with age, most older persons are not severely limited by changes or disease within this system. Arthritis is a major source of discomfort for many older persons. It is a generic term that literally means joint inflammation. There are numerous types of arthritis, including osteoarthritis (OA), rheumatoid arthritis (RA) and gout.

Osteoarthritis is a defect of articular cartilage, and its causes are poorly understood. It is accompanied by pain, stiffness and joint enlargement. Inflammation of the synovial membrane may be present, though it is often mild compared to that of RA. Long-standing OA can lead to joint deformity. Osteoarthritis may be of primary or secondary nature; certain joints are commonly or rarely involved in primary OA.

There is no cure for OA. Symptomatic relief includes rest balanced with exercise,

physical therapy, moist heat and drugs. Surgical intervention is sometimes employed.

Joint involvement in RA begins with an inflamed synovial membrane. In time, the entire joint may be involved, and joint destruction can result. Rheumatoid arthritis is a systemic disease, not confined to joints. It attacks connective tissue throughout the body. Associated arthritis tends to be symmetric and polyarticular. The cause of RA is not fully understood. It is recognized as an autoimmune disease that might be triggered by hereditary factors and exposure to a microorganism. Rheumatoid arthritis cannot be cured but can be treated with various drugs, physical therapy and sometimes surgery.

Gout is a metabolic disease that causes an acutely painful form of arthritis. Uric acid crystals precipitate out to the joints, causing sudden, intermittent episodes of joint inflammation. Anti-inflammatory drugs are used during attacks. Other drugs aimed at lowering uric acid levels are used to prevent or postpone recurrences. Dietary recommendations are a part of maintaining the gout patient.

Osteoporosis is the major cause of skeletal fractures in post-menopausal women and older persons in general. Non-modifiable and modifiable risk factors have been identified for this condition, which is characterized by loss of bone density to a symptomatic level. Although all bones lose mass with age, some are more critically involved than others. This situation exists because of the distribution of two basic types of skeletal tissue, trabecular and cortical bone.

Osteoporosis is characterized as either Type I or II, depending upon fracture site and certain other associated factors. The vertebrae, wrist and hip are the most common fracture sites. Hip fractures are the most serious hazard related to osteoporosis; they represent a significant cause of morbidity and mortality.

Paget's disease is a chronic, localized bone disease of unknown cause, occurring primarily in geriatric patients. It is characterized by excessive bone resorption followed by accelerated formation of abnormal bone. The condition, affecting approximately 3 percent of the population over 45 years of age, may progress to cause skeletal deformity.

KEY TERMS

arthritis
articular cartilage
Bouchard's nodes
bone formation
bone remodeling
bone resorption
carpometacarpal joint
Colles fractures
cortical bone
crush fractures
degenerative joint disease
dorsal kyphosis
dowager's hump
erythrocyte sedimentation rate
estrogen-replacement therapy
gelling or gel phenomenon
gout
Heberden's nodes
iliac crests
interphalangeal joints
lactose intolerance
metacarpophalangeal joint
metatarsophalangeal joint
osteoarthritis
osteoblasts
osteoclasts
osteophytes
oxalates
Paget's disease
parathyroid hormone
polyarticular
primary or idiopathic OA
purine

rheumatoid arthritis
rheumatoid factor
secondary OA
senile osteopenia
synovial membrane
tinnitus
trabecular bone
Type I osteoporosis
Type II osteoporosis
uric acid

STUDY QUESTIONS

1. How significant are skeletal changes among the elderly?
2. What is arthritis? How do various types of arthritis differ?
3. Briefly outline the anatomy of a joint.
4. Distinguish osteoarthritis from rheumatoid arthritis—including cause, changes, diagnosis, age of onset, degree of disfigurement, symptoms, and treatment.
5. What is gout? Note its cause, symptoms and methods of treatment and management.
6. Differentiate senile osteopenia from osteoporosis.
7. With respect to osteoporosis, review:
   a. Risk factors
   b. Bone remodeling
   c. Bones most critically affected
   d. Type I and Type II osteoporosis
   e. Diagnosis
   f. Treatment
8. Discuss how osteoporosis might be prevented.
9. Note three differences between fracture patterns in the old and the young.
10. What is Paget's disease?

BIBLIOGRAPHY

Allen, L. 1984. Calcium absorption and requirements during the life span. *Nutrition News 47:* 1–3.

Altman, R., and Gray, R. 1985. Inflammation in osteoarthritis. *Clinics in Rheumatic Diseases 11:* 353–365.

Aloia, J., Cohn, S., Ostuni, J., Cane, R., and Ellis, K. 1978. Prevention of involutional bone loss by exercise. *Annals of Internal Medicine 89:* 356–358.

Aloia, J., Cohn, S., Vaswani, A., Yeh, J., Yuen, K., and Ellis, K. 1985. Risk factors for postmenopausal osteoporosis. *American Journal of Medicine 78:* 95–100.

Avioli, L. 1984. Calcium and osteoporosis. *Annual Review of Nutrition 4:* 471–491.

Baran, D., Teitelbaum, S., and Bergefeld, M. 1980. Effect of alcohol ingestion on bone and mineral metabolism in rats. *American Journal of Physiology 238:* E507.

Berlyne, G., Ben-Ari, J., and Kushelvesky, A. 1975. The aetiology of senile osteoporosis: Secondary hyperparathyroidism due to renal failure. *Quarterly Journal of Medicine 44:* 505–521.

Brandt, K., and Fife, R. 1983. The diagnosis of osteoarthritis. *Medical Student 9:* 4–7.

Corrigan, A., Robinson, R.G., Terenty, T.R., Dick-Smith, J.B., and Walters, D. 1974. Benign rheumatoid arthritis of the aged. *British Medical Journal 1:* 444–445.

Daniell, H. 1976. Osteoporosis of the slender smoker. *Archives of Internal Medicine 136:* 298–304.

———. 1983. Postmenopausal tooth loss: Contributions to edentulism by osteoporosis and cigarette smoking. *Archives of Internal Medicine l43:* 1678–1682.

Donaldson, C., Hulley, S., and Vogel, J. 1970. Effect of prolonged bed rest on bone mineral. *Metabolism 19:* 1071–1084.

Ehrlich, G., Katz, W., and Cohen, S. 1970. Rheumatoid arthritis in the elderly. *Geriatrics 25:* 103.

Gallagher, J., Riggs, B., Eisman, J., Hamstra, A., and Arnaud, S. 1979. Intestinal calcium absorption and serum vitamin D metabolites in normal subjects and osteoporotic patients. *Journal of Clinical Investigation 64:* 729–736.

Giansiracusa, D., and Kantrowitz, F. 1982. Rheumatic Disease. In J. Rowe and R. Besdine, eds., *Health and Disease in Old Age.* Boston: Little, Brown. Pp. 267–296.

Goodman, C. 1985. Osteoporosis: protective measures of nutrition and exercise. *Geriatrics 40:* 59–60, 65–67, 70.

Hausman, P. 1985. *The Calcium Bible.* New York: Warner Books.

Heaney, R., Gallagher, J., Johnston, C., Neer, R., Parfitt, A., and Whedon, G. 1982. Calcium nutrition and bone health in the elderly. *American Journal of Clinical Nutrition 36:* 986–1013.

Henneman, P., and Wallach, S. 1957. A review of the prolonged use of estrogens and androgens in postmenopausal and senile osteoporosis. *Archives of Internal Medicine 100:* 715.

Horsman, A., Marshall, D.H., Nordin, B.E., Crilly, R.G., and Simpson, M. 1981. The relation between bone loss and calcium balance in women. *Clinical Science 59:* 137–142.

Huddleston, A., Rockwell, D., Kulund, D., and Harrison, B. 1980. Bone mass in lifetime tennis athletes. *Journal of the American Medical Association 244:* 1107–1109.

Jensen, J., and Tondevold, E. 1979. Mortality after hip fracture. *Acta Orthopedica Scandinavia 50:* 161.

Judd, H., Cleary, R., Creasman, W., Figge, D., Kase, N., Rosenwaks, Z., and Tagatz, G. 1981. Estrogen replacement therapy. *Obstetrics and Gynecology 58:* 267–275.

Kaye, R. 1984. A clinical perspective on rheumatoid arthritis, osteoarthritis and gout. *American Pharmacy N.S.24* (7): 474–477.

Kolata, G. 1986. How important is dietary calcium in preventing osteoporosis? *Science 233:* 519–520.

Lane, J., Vigorita, V., and Falls, M. 1984. Osteoporosis: Current diagnosis and treatment. *Geriatrics 39:* 40–47.

Lane, N., Block, D.A., Jones, H.H., Marshall, W.H. Jr., Wood, D.D., and Fries, J.F. 1986. Long distance running, bone density, and osteoarthritis. *Journal of the American Medical Association 255:* 1147–1151.

Liebman, B. 1985. Losers weepers: Is your body absorbing all the calcium you consume? *Nutrition Action 12:* 9, 14.

Lindquist, O., and Bengtsson, C. 1979. The effect of smoking on menopausal age. *Maturitas 1:* 141.

Lindquist, O., Bengtsson, C., and Hanson, T. 1979. Age at menopause and its relation to osteoporosis. *Maturitas 1:* 175.

Lindsay, R., Hart, D., Purdre, D., Gerguson, M., Clark, A., and Kraszewski, A. 1982. Comparative effects of oestrogen and progestogen on bone loss in postmenopausal and osteoporotic women. *American Journal of Physiology 242:* 82–86.

Mack, P., LaChance, P., and Vose, G. 1967. Bone demineralization of foot and hand of Gemini-Titan IV, V and VII astronauts during orbital flight. *American Journal of Roentgenology 100:* 503–511.

Margen, S., Chu, J., Kaufmann, N., and Calloway, D. 1974. Studies in calcium metabolism. 1. The calciuretic effect of dietary protein. *American Journal of Clinical Nutrition 27:* 584–589.

Meema, S., Bunkler, M., and Meema, H. 1975. Preventive effect of estrogen on postmenopausal bone loss. *Archives of Internal Medicine 135:* 1436–1440.

Meunier, P. 1973. Physiological senile involution and pathological rarefaction of bone. *Clinical Endocrine Metabolism 2:* 239.

Nachtigall, L., Nachtigall, R., and Beckman, E. 1979. Estrogen replacement therapy I: A 10-year prospective study in the relationship to osteoporosis. *Obstetrics and Gynecology 53:* 277.

National Institutes of Health. 1984. *NIH Consensus Development Conference Statement on Osteoporosis*. Bethesda, Md.: author.

Nordin, B., and associates. 1981. Summation of risk factors in osteoporosis. In H. Deluca, H. Frost, W. Jee, C. Johnston, and A. Parfitt, eds., *Osteoporosis: Recent Advances in Pathogenesis and Treatment*. Baltimore, Md.: University Park Press.

Orimo, H., and Shiraki, M. 1979. Role of calcium regulating hormones in the pathogenesis of senile osteoporosis. *Endocrinology Review 1:* 1–6.

Owen, R., Melton, L., and Gallagher, J. 1980. The national cost of acute care of hip fractures associated with osteoporosis. *Clinical Orthopedics Rel. Research 150:* 172.

Panush, R.S., Schmidt, C., Caldwell, J.R., Edwards, N.L., Longley, S., Yonker, R., Webster, E., Stork, J., and Pettersson, H. 1986. Is running associated with degenerative joint disease? *Journal of the American Medical Association 255:* 1152–1154.

Peck, W. 1985. Brittle bones. *Nutrition Action 12:* 4–8.

Rambaut, P., Dietlein, L., and Vogel, J. 1972. Comparative study of two direct methods of bone mineral measurement. *Aerospace Medicine 43:* 646–650.

Renner, R., Boucher, L., and Kaufman, H. 1984. Osteoporosis in postmenopausal women. *Journal of Prosthetic Dentistry 52:* 581–588.

Riggs, B., and Melton, L. 1983. Evidence for two distinct syndromes of involutional osteoporosis. *American Journal of Medicine 75:* 899–901.

——————. 1986. Involutional osteoporosis. *New England Journal of Medicine 314:* 1676.

Seeman, E., Melton, L., O'Fallon, W., and Riggs, B. 1983. Risk factors for spinal osteoporosis in men. *American Journal of Medicine 75:* 977–983.

Slovik, D., Adams, J., Neer, R., Holick, M., and Potts, J. Jr. 1981. Deficient production of 1,25-dihydroxy vitamin D in elderly osteoporotic patients. *New England Journal of Medicine 305:* 372–374.

Smith, E. 1982. Exercise for prevention of osteoporosis: A review. *The Physician and Sports Medicine 10:* 72–83.

——————, Reddan, W., and Smith, P. 1981. Physical activity and calcium modalities for bone mineral increase in aged women. *Medicine and Science in Sports and Exercise 13:* 60–64.

Spencer, H., and Kramer, L. 1986. Does a high protein (meat) intake affect calcium metabolism in men? *Food and Nutrition News 58:* 11–13.

Spencer, H., Kramer, L., DeBartolo, M., Norris, C., and Osis, D. 1983. Further studies on the effect of a high protein diet and meat on calcium metabolism. *American Journal of Clinical Nutrition 37:* 924–929.

Wachman, A., and Bernstein, D. 1968. Diet and osteoporosis. *Lancet 1:* 958–959.

Weiss, N., and Scyvetz, T. 1980. Incidence of endometrial cancer in relation to the use of oral contraceptives. *New England Journal of Medicine 302:* 551.

Weiss, N., Ure, C., Ballard, J., Williams, A., and Daling, J. 1980. Decreased risk of fractures of the hip and lower forearm with postmenopausal use of estrogen. *New England Journal of Medicine 303:* 1193.

CHAPTER **8**

Age-Associated Changes in the Neurosensory System

The human nervous system coordinates and interprets the interactions of the individual and his or her environment. The senses provide a link with the outside world. Neurosensory changes that can influence functioning, activities, response to stimuli and perception of the world do occur with age. The world's perception of an individual may be influenced by neurosensory changes that he or she has undergone. The older person with impaired vision or hearing may be unfairly labeled as stubborn, eccentric or senile. The sane victim of *Parkinson's disease* may be viewed as demented because of the neuromuscular symptoms displayed.

This chapter is concerned with selected age-associated changes of a neurosensory

and neurological nature. Changes in the special senses of vision and hearing, as well as the implications of those changes, will be investigated. Parkinson's disease, a central nervous system disorder that remains primarily a disease of the geriatric age group, will be examined. Organic brain syndromes are considered in Chapter 5. Because the primary lesion of stroke is vascular, this condition is discussed in Chapter 12.

GENERAL CHANGES

With age, nerve conduction velocity decreases, voluntary motor movements slow down, and the reflex time for skeletal muscle is increased. Changes in muscle, peripheral nerves and the spinal cord result in decreased agility and strength. Brain weight begins to decline around the age of 25. By the age of 80 brain weight has decreased by approximately 16 to 17 percent (Jervis, 1971). Nerve cells shrink and are lost while stored lipofuscin and senile plaques are present (Caplan, 1982). These changes can be considered normal aspects of aging and have little influence on brain function. Likewise, the minor changes in cerebral blood flow do not produce symptoms. Degenerative changes and disease states involving the sense organs can alter vision and hearing.

VISION

Many persons maintain near-normal sight well into old age. Nevertheless, the aged eye is subject to various changes and disabilities. With *presbyopia*, an age-associated change occurs in the *lens* of the eye, leading to relative inflexibility and a tendency toward farsightedness. Its effects may become noticeable during middle age when glasses become necessary to do close work.

The lens of the eye also has a tendency to yellow. This change is significant because it results in difficulty discerning certain color intensities, especially the cool colors. Blue, green and violet are filtered out and may be difficult to differentiate. Warm colors, including red, yellow and orange, are generally more easily seen, which makes it advisable to mark objects such as steps and handrails with the colors that tend to stand out.

Three disorders—*cataracts, glaucoma* and *senile macular degeneration*—represent the most common visual problems of the elderly. Each can be responsible for serious loss of vision. With proper recognition, attention and treatment, these conditions need not

spell disaster. Although irreparable damage associated with them cannot be repaired, further losses can be prevented and an individual's functional ability maintained or improved. In the diabetic, *diabetic retinopathy* may also be a significant cause of visual loss.

Presbyopia

Presbyopia is not a disease but a degenerative change that occurs in the aging eye, in which the lens (Figure 8.1) loses its ability to focus upon near objects. *Visual accommodation* or focusing is normally permitted by the ability of the lens to change shape, thus adjusting for near and distant vision. The lens is flexible because of its elastic nature, but in the aging person, old lens fibers become compacted toward the center of the lens. This reduces its elasticity and, coupled with a weakening of the eye muscles, does not allow the lens to contract to a sufficiently convex form to focus on near objects.

Changes in the lens lead to farsightedness, so there is a marked tendency for older persons to hold things at a distance in order to see them. A newspaper or recipe card may be held at arm's length because the print cannot be discriminated at closer range. Because of presbyopia, the majority of individuals need reading glasses or bifocals by the time they are in their 40s or 50s. The glasses compensate mechanically for the loss of visual accommodation. Except for people who cannot afford to buy glasses, presbyopia does not pose any serious problems.

Reading glasses allow the individual to discern objects that are in the field of near vision. Bifocals may be called for, depending on the individual's overall visual ability. Bifocals consist of two parts, one for near and one for distance vision. Adjusting vision from one

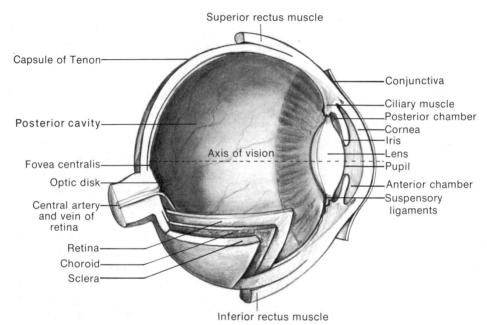

Figure 8.1   Structure of the eye, transverse section. (From P. Anderson, *Basic Human Anatomy and Physiology,* 1986. Courtesy of Jones and Bartlett, Publishers.)

area of the spectacle to another while viewing things at varying distances may not be easy. Adjustment problems may require much patience on the part of the wearer.

Senile Cataracts

Cataracts are the most common disability of the aged eye. A cataract involves an opacity of the normally transparent lens. The opacity may be focal or diffuse and is accompanied by reduced visual acuity. The crystalline lens focuses incoming light onto the photoreceptors of the *retina,* just as a camera's lens allows incoming light to be focused onto film. As the lens loses its transparency, there is interference with the passage of light. By definition a cataract involves an associated reduction in vision.

There are various types of cataracts, including the congenital, genetic, metabolic, traumatic, toxic and senile forms. Senile cataract, although the most common, is among the least understood. Its diagnosis involves lens opacity in those over 45 years of age, after other causes of cataract have been eliminated (Leske and Sperduto, 1983).

There is a strong relationship between increasing age and the development of senile cataract. However, its formation appears to be a complex process that is possibly affected by genetic and environmental factors as well. There is a great need for research to determine what factors might be associated with an increased risk of its development. Present data suggest that geographic locale, familial factors, exposure to various forms of radiation and to certain drugs, high blood pressure and the existence of diabetes in those under 65 years of age warrant further study as possible risk factors.

Depending on the degree of cataract development, an individual will suffer dimmed and blurred or "misty" vision. The person may need brighter light in which to read and may increasingly complain of glare. Objects may need to be held extremely close in order to be seen. As the cataract advances, useful sight is lost.

Treatment consists of surgical removal of the opaque lens. Surgery is indicated when vision loss interferes with the performance of activities (Straatsma, Foos and Horwitz, 1985). To compensate for the loss of the lens, eyeglasses, contact lenses or intraocular lens implants are used.

Glaucoma

Glaucoma is the second leading cause of blindness in adults in the United States and the first cause among blacks (Leske, 1983). It represents a group of diseases resulting, with few exceptions, from an obstruction in the normal escape route of the nutrient fluid that bathes the *anterior chamber* of the eye (the space between the *cornea* and *iris*) depicted in Figure 8.2. This clear fluid, known as *aqueous humor,* normally exits the anterior chamber into the *canal of Schlemm,* where it is eventually conducted through numerous small channels into the venous circulation. If the fluid is formed faster than it can be eliminated, an increase in *eye* pressure results. Pressure is transferred to the *optic nerve,* leading to irreparable damage. If intraocular pressure continues to exceed the tolerance of the affected eye, total blindness can result.

Glaucoma can be of a primary or secondary nature. *Primary glaucoma* is of unknown origin. It develops in the absence of previous eye disease or injury. It occurs most frequently in persons with a family history of the disease. It is suspected that there is a tendency to inherit the factors that might predispose one to the condition. *Secondary glaucoma* follows some eye disease or injury.

Primary glaucoma may be designated as *closed angle* or *open angle.* Closed-angle

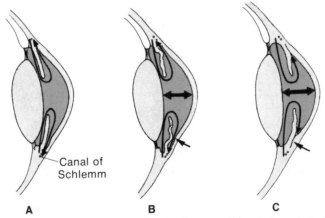

Figure 8.2   Glaucoma. A. Normal aqueous humor drainage through the canal of Schlemm. B. Open-angle glaucoma, showing a chronic condition treated by drugs. C. Closed-angle glaucoma, requiring surgery (iridectomy) for correction. (From P. Anderson, *Basic Human Anatomy and Physiology,* 1986. Courtesy of Jones and Bartlett, Publishers.)

glaucoma accounts for less than 5 percent of glaucoma cases (Jindra, 1984). In order to understand this form of disease it is necessary to review the production of aqueous humor and its passage to the anterior eye chamber. Aqueous humor is produced in a structure just behind the root of the iris and is secreted into a space bounded by the posterior surface of the iris and the anterior surface of the lens. The fluid circulates through the pupil into the anterior chamber.

There is some resistance to the flow of aqueous humor into the anterior compartment. If an individual has a narrow anterior chamber, the resulting pressure can lead to the root of the iris closing off the exit of fluid in this area. Production of the fluid continues, intraocular pressure increases rather rapidly and closed-angle glaucoma develops.

Primary closed-angle glaucoma is an acute glaucoma that appears suddenly and runs a short course. Its victim suffers nausea, vomiting, eye pain and redness, along with clouded vision. Prompt medical attention is imperative if severe vision loss or blindness is to be prevented.

Ninety percent of all primary glaucoma is of the open-angle type (Jindra, 1983; Leske and Rosenthal, 1979). In open-angle glaucoma the outflow of aqueous humor is obstructed by degenerative changes in the network that normally allows for its escape. This chronic type of glaucoma develops slowly and is often referred to as the "sneak thief of vision." The initial manifestations of the disease are so subtle that much damage may be done before medical attention is sought.

A gradual loss of *peripheral vision* is one of the earliest indications of glaucoma. This loss of side vision may cause its victim to bump into things or fail to see passing cars in the next highway lane. In time so much of the normal range of vision becomes eliminated that the victim is said to suffer from "tunnel vision." If the condition is left untreated, the nerve centers allowing for central vision are also damaged, and the individual loses all sight.

Persons over 40 years of age should have periodic eye examinations that include glaucoma testing. The irreparable damage it causes makes its prompt diagnosis and management imperative. There is no cure for glaucoma, but there are techniques for reducing the intraocular pressure or keeping it at a safe level. In severe cases surgery can be performed to provide a permanent filtration pathway for the aqueous humor. An opening for drainage can be made in the iris or the *sclera* (the outer, white part of the eyeball). Such surgery is delicate and is often avoided for as long as possible. There are drugs and eyedrops that can indirectly control the pressure within the eye.

In the past, diagnosis of glaucoma was made on the basis of intraocular pressure alone. Such a practice is no longer valid, since optic nerve damage can occur at any pressure level. Of persons with high pressure, 90 to 95 percent do not suffer optic nerve damage (Spaeth, 1984). They are considered to be at risk of developing a visual defect, but the risk is low and most never develop damage. Because prediction of defects in such persons is uncertain, some patients diagnosed on the basis of pressure level will be treated. Other physicians will monitor the patient until some evidence of optic nerve damage has occurred. Thus there is variation in the diagnostic criteria regarding glaucoma (Leske, 1983).

Since optic nerve damage can occur at any pressure level, tests to measure loss of vision field (rather than just intraocular pressure) are important. Visual field defects can be objectively determined, though there is some variation in defining and assessing them.

When optic damage occurs in the absence of elevated pressure, *low-tension glaucoma* is said to exist. It is estimated that one-third to one-half of persons with glaucoma damage have eye pressure below the characteristic diagnostic level when first detected (Bengtsson, 1981; Leske, 1983). Some such cases will later manifest a pressure increase, and some will continue as low-tension glaucoma.

Despite the variation in pressure levels and optic nerve damage, lowering pressure via surgery or drugs remains the method of treatment. In the same way that glaucoma definitions have de-emphasized specific numerical pressure values, treatment has come to concern itself with lowering pressure to the point where nerve damage is halted. Rather than reducing intraocular pressure to a specific, universal numerical level, the goal is to lower it to a point tolerated by the affected eye.

Senile Macular Degeneration

Senile macular degeneration (SMD) is the leading cause of registered blindness among adults in the United States, but it remains a poorly understood disease. Damage is done to the *macula*, the key focusing area of the retina. As a result there is a decline in central visual acuity, which makes it difficult to impossible to perform tasks dependent upon the discrimination of detail, such as driving or reading.

For many with SMD, *central vision* is maintained for years. In such cases an individual is said to manifest "dry" or *atrophic* SMD, a slow version of the disorder. The majority of patients who are legally blind due to SMD have undergone a *neovascular* or *exudative*

form of disease. In the latter condition, abnormal blood vessels form within the retina, with resultant hemorrhaging and destruction of vision (Ferris, Fine and Hyman, 1984).

Increasing age has the strongest association with SMD of all risk factors examined to date. Research suggests that familial/genetic factors are also important. Of the possible risk factors examined in one study, family history and blue- or medium-pigmented eyes were the characteristics most strongly associated with SMD (Hyman, Lilienfeld, Ferris and Fine, 1983). It has been suggested that as our population continues to age, blindness as a result of macular disease will increase unless appropriate preventive and treatment modalities are introduced (Ferris, 1983). A type of laser therapy, known as *argon laser photocoagulation*, seeks to seal off or destroy the abnormal blood vessels. It has been helpful for some patients with exudative SMD (Macular Photocoagulation Study Group, 1982). Perhaps, as treatment advances, cases of blindness associated with the disorder will be reduced. At present, not all persons with SMD are treatable.

Diabetic Retinopathy

Laser therapy is also proving beneficial in the treatment of diabetic retinopathy (Early Treatment Diabetic Retinopathy Study Research Group, 1985). This condition is a complication of diabetes that affects the capillaries and arterioles of the retina. A ballooning of these tiny vessels can eventually give way to hemorrhaging, neovascular growth, scarring and blindness.

Vascular changes of diabetic retinopathy occur in and around the macula, leading to macular edema. The retina swells, absorbing the fluid from leaking vessels. It eventually loses its shape, so that the image that it receives is distorted. A leading researcher at the National Eye Institute has likened it to having wrinkled film in a camera (Ferris, 1985).

The Visually Impaired Older Adult

Over a lifetime an individual becomes dependent upon vision for functioning in the surrounding world. For most people, carrying out daily living activities involves a dependency on visual acuity. Sewing on a button, setting the oven temperature, stirring the sauce, matching the same color socks, balancing the checkbook or receiving a visitor at the front door are all tasks that utilize eyesight.

Persons blind since birth have had a lifetime to adjust to living in a world that assumes everyone can see. Adjustment can be very difficult for those who suffer visual impairment after having been dependent on their sight. Family members, friends and health care workers can help to make the adjustment less difficult. An understanding of the kind and amount of visual loss is imperative. Losses may be minor or severe; they may involve central vision, peripheral vision or the entire visual field.

A thickened, yellowed lens may necessitate brighter light for performing tasks such as reading or sewing. For the cataract victim, light that is too bright can produce glare. Determine what degree of illumination is best for an individual and help to provide it. An individual who has lost peripheral vision may see only a limited area to the front. When talking with someone who has peripheral loss, be certain to position yourself in the person's visual field. If an object or task is being demonstrated, make certain it is done within the person's line of sight.

Vision loss can lead to problems in social interaction with others, especially if losses are undiagnosed or poorly understood. Family members may be suspicious of Aunt Mary's claims of poor vision when she is quite capable of detecting a spot directly in front of her that someone left while cleaning the window. While Aunt Mary's peripheral vision may have diminished, she still sees details within her central visual field.

Adapting to the dark requires a longer time because of age-related changes. Entering a dimly lit restaurant or theatre can be made easier by allowing time for adjustment. Night lights can help to prevent accidents when rising from bed in the middle of the night to answer the telephone or go to the bathroom.

Coding schemes can be employed in the home setting to facilitate independent living. Fluorescent tape around electric outlets, light switches, thermostats and keyholes can make chores easier. Coding can also make it easier to differentiate one bottle of pills from another. This might be achieved by taping different-colored pieces of paper to various medicine vials. For those not able to distinguish colors, other methods can be employed. The medicine with sandpaper glued to the cap can be identified as the pain reliever, and the one with the felt cap might be the antihypertensive. Large-print instructions from the pharmacy can help the older person to comply with doctor's orders.

A person who has suddenly suffered visual losses may need extra care and patience. Such an individual may be understandably fearful and distrustful. Relatives, friends, and health workers should take the person's anxieties into consideration and be thoughtful in their actions—for example, by announcing themselves when approaching the person.

Special consideration should be given those who have age-related vision defects and are placed in an unfamiliar environment such as a nursing home. Call switches and items on a bedside table should be placed where they can easily be located. Caregivers may need to be especially sensitive and patient when teaching self-care tasks to the visually impaired individual. Such an individual may feel self-conscious, slow and awkward. Caregivers should take time with the task and be willing to give praise for continuing efforts as well as for success.

HEARING

Impaired hearing is common among older persons. It is estimated that 30 to 60 percent of those over 65 and 90 percent of elderly nursing home residents suffer hearing loss (Libow and Sherman, 1981; Mader, 1984). Some loss is due to age-related physiological change in the auditory system, and some is due to disease and superimposed environmental insults. There is considerable variability in the gradual decline of hearing with advanced age.

There are three major types of hearing loss: *conductive, sensorineural* and mixed. Conductive losses involve the outer and middle ear; sensorineural losses involve the inner ear. An elderly person may manifest both conductive and sensorineural changes, resulting in a mixed loss.

Conductive Hearing Loss

Hearing loss can result from the interrupted conduction of sound waves. Normally these waves enter the external ear to be channeled to the *tympanic membrane* (eardrum), which marks entry to the middle ear (Figure 8.3). Here vibrations are established and transmitted mechanically by a series of three delicate bones or *ossicles* (known as the malleus,

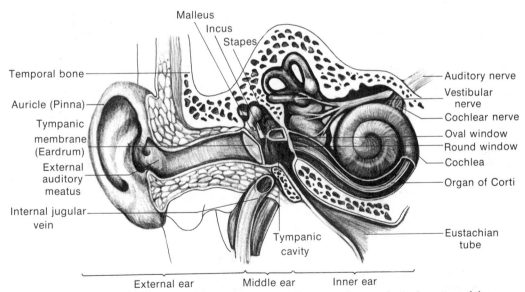

Figure 8.3 Frontal diagram of the outer ear, middle ear, and internal ear. A section of the cochlear duct has been cut away to show the position of the organ of Corti. (From P. Anderson, *Basic Human Anatomy and Physiology,* 1986. Courtesy of Jones and Bartlett, Publishers.)

incus and stapes). Sound transmission defects involving any one of these structures can lead to hearing loss.

Fortunately, the most common cause of conductive impairment in the older adult is reversible. It occurs when excessive ear wax or *cerumen* blocks the external ear canal. Older persons should be checked for a buildup of cerumen, which can be removed by irrigating the canal with a wax-dissolving solution.

Hardening of middle ear bone can impede the transmission of sound waves. This condition, known as *otosclerosis,* actually begins during youth but may not become evident until later life. It is the most frequent cause of conductive deafness in adults (Libow and Sherman, 1981). Though its cause is not fully understood, it can sometimes be corrected by surgery and a special hearing aid.

Paget's disease, a bone condition of unknown causation, may also cause conductive hearing loss due to closure of the external ear canal or ossicle involvement. *Otitis media,* a middle ear infection, is not a major cause of hearing loss in the elderly.

Sensorineural Hearing Loss

Sensorineural hearing loss is related to disorders of the inner ear, where conducted sound vibrations are transformed into electrical impulses by the *cochlea.* This auditory receptor organ has been dubbed the most complex mechanical apparatus in the human body (Hudspeth, 1985). A fluid-filled spiral cavity, the cochlea houses the *organ of Corti,* which has several rows of delicate, specialized *hair cells.* Sound waves transferred to the inner ear generate fluid movement in the cochlea and the undulation of hair cells. Hair cell stimulation produces nerve impulses that are carried by the auditory or *eighth cranial nerve* to the hearing center of the brain, where they are perceived as sound. Sensorineural hearing loss in older adults may be due to presbycusis, environmental/occupational noise, drug toxicity or disease.

Presbycusis is the most common cause of bilateral, sensorineural hearing deficit in older adults (Olsen, 1984). It is related to permanent loss of the ability to detect high-frequency tones. Presbycusis is due to various poorly understood senescent changes, which may include atrophy of the organ of Corti as well as hair cell decline.

At first, the loss of the ability to perceive higher frequencies does not involve normal speech patterns; but as the condition progresses, conversation becomes affected. Because consonant sounds are in the higher frequencies and vowel sounds in the lower frequencies, speech discrimination becomes poor. Speech can be heard, but words cannot be detected. The victim may hear an unintelligible collection of vowel sounds. As the condition advances, middle and lower tones may also be lost.

There is variability in the progression of presbycusis, and it can coexist with other factors that impede hearing acuity. It is estimated that an infant is born with up to 20,000 hair cells in each ear. Aging itself, combined with exposure to loud noise, certain drugs and disease, can rob the cochlea of functioning hair cells. Dennis Drescher, an auditory biochemist at Wayne State University, quoted in *Science News,* estimates that if human life expectancy could be greatly increased—say to 140 years—it would probably mean living without hair cells (Franklin, 1984).

Noise-induced hearing loss, known as *acoustic trauma,* is recognized as the second most common cause of irreversible hearing decline in older persons (Darbyshire, 1984; Surjan, Devald and Palfalvi, 1973). Exposure to excessive noise induces hair cell loss and sensorineural hearing deficit. The fact that older men have tended to exhibit slightly more hearing loss than older women may be related to workplace noise. Perhaps, as noise exposure becomes more uniform, we will see less gender-based difference in hearing decline.

Presbycusis and noise-induced loss are coexistent in many instances. Some studies have attempted to measure hearing loss in populations subjected to little noise pollution, in order to see if their profile of loss differs from that of the industrialized world. One such study reported little age-associated decline among a Sudanese tribe (Rosen, Bergman and Plester, 1962). However, this work has been criticized on methodological grounds (Mader, 1984). Distinguishing between normal, age-related physiologic decline in hearing and that due to environmental or other secondary causes is an important area of gerontologic research.

Medications that can compromise hearing are known as *ototoxic drugs*. Since elderly people often take several different drugs, their hearing should be monitored. Likewise, because elderly patients may already have some degree of hearing loss, known ototoxic drugs should be used with caution. It is sometimes possible to reverse the toxic effects of certain medications if early intervention takes place.

Underlying disease can sometimes result in sensorineural losses. Certain primary and metastatic tumors may result in unilateral hearing decline in the elderly. There is controversy regarding the association between atherosclerosis and hypertension and progressive hearing loss with age. The inner ear is dependent on a single end artery for its blood supply. Sudden and total deafness results if this artery is occluded (Libow and Sherman, 1981). Some type of auditory deficit occurs in 30 to 50 percent of persons with skull involvement in Paget's disease (Giansiracusa and Kantrowitz, 1982; Sparrow and Duvall, 1967). Associated conductive loss has been previously noted. When the temporal bone is affected, the cochlea (which rests within this bone) may be disrupted, causing a sensorineural hearing loss. Compression of the eighth cranial nerve is rare.

The Hearing-Impaired Older Adult

Hearing impairment can lead to social isolation, fear, frustration, embarrassment, low self-esteem and anxiety for its elderly victim. Depression is twice as common in this group (Herbst and Humphrey, 1980). It was conclusively demonstrated in a 1976 study that deafness can predispose to paranoid behavior (Cooper, Garside and Kay, 1976). Blindness in the elderly does not seem to be as closely associated with paranoia (Charatan, 1984). Sensitivity to these possibilities is extremely important; hearing-disabled individuals do not seem to be given the same consideration and understanding as those with other types of impairment (McCartney and Nadler, 1979).

An elderly individual with a permanent hearing loss should be evaluated for amplification via a hearing aid and have the benefit of aural rehabilitation. Of the approximately 1 million hearing aids sold in the United States in 1983, it is estimated that 56 percent were purchased by those age 65 and over (Cranmer, 1983; Mahon, 1983). About 500,000 hearing aids are sold annually to persons whose hearing deficit is at least partially attributed to presbycusis (Olsen, 1984).

Hearing aids are not a perfect substitute for normal hearing. They cannot restore the full frequency range of more severe losses; sounds are made louder, not necessarily clearer. Hearing aids pose adjustment problems, and many new users claim that the aids seem unnatural. For many persons who have lost their hearing over a long period of time, the new sounds delivered by the hearing aid surely seem unnatural. Hearing aids amplify all sounds, not just those of speech. The new hearing aid user may have a difficult time divorcing restaurant noises, car horns or television sounds from conversational patterns. Hearing aid users and their families need to be counseled appropriately.

There are some helpful principles and common courtesies for communicating with the hearing-impaired. In general, shouting should be avoided. It does nothing to aid in the delivery of lost frequencies and results in a booming sensation and distortion of intelligible sounds. Speech should be in a normal tone of voice, no more than a little louder than usual. Shouting often conveys the impression that the speaker is annoyed, and this can lead to defensive or withdrawn behavior.

Also, a speaker should talk slowly. It is much easier for all of us to understand someone if the message is delivered at a slower pace. Besides, talking rapidly can create an impression of being in a hurry, which can disturb a hard-of-hearing person and make him or her feel like a burdensome person who is taking too much of the speaker's time.

If a message is not understood the first time, finding other words to say the same thing may also be helpful. It not only gives the hard-of-hearing person an additional set of sounds from which to understand a message, but it also gives more context from which meaning can be derived. Often, hearing one word can make the meaning of a whole sentence clear.

A speaker should also be aware of the power of non-verbal communication. Facial expressions serve to convey moods, feelings, negatives, positives, excitement and disapproval, among other emotional states. They enhance the comprehension of the spoken words and let the hearing-impaired person share in the lives of those around him or her.

With or without a hearing aid, lip reading can help with communication. Another complicating factor is that some people do not form words normally when speaking to a hearing-impaired person; exaggeration can confuse the lip reader. The speaker can help the lip reader by facing him or her, by letting the light fall on the speaker's face, and by not exaggerating lip movements. For people who also have impaired vision, the task may be more difficult.

Patient compliance can be greatly affected by hearing loss. Health care institutions are complex facilities. A stay in one of them brings an individual into contact with a number of workers, many of whom have directions to give and important information to impart. Unfortunately, such information may not be heard or understood by the patient who is hard of hearing. Health workers may perceive a patient's limited reaction as apparent disinterest or evidence of little gratitude for the information they have attempted to deliver. Health workers may not be aware of a patient's hearing loss, not having known the person before admission to the health care facility. Too often confusion associated with hearing loss may be falsely attributed to senility in the older patient.

When planning for discharge from an institution, the hearing loss must be kept in mind so that instructions about the use of mechanical devices or drug therapy are understood. A failure to digest such instructions may mean delayed recovery or even tragedy in the home situation. Instructions could be written down for the patient in a clear and simple fashion. Keep in mind that the person may also have suffered visual losses. Write the instructions in large print. Also, a health worker or family member could ask the patient to repeat the instructions to make certain that they have been properly understood.

Hearing aids are most useful when background noise is at a minimum, as in a quiet theatre or lecture hall, or in private conversation in person or over the telephone. In noisy gatherings the wearer may do better by switching off the aid. Individual adjustments dictate the most appropriate behavior. Some persons may be initially annoyed by background noise but later learn to "tune it out."

Problems associated with a new hearing aid may be caused by an improperly fitted earmold. In order to serve the wearer, the earmold must closely fit the anatomic structure of the individual's ear canal. Prolonged complaints about a hearing aid should be investigated; the difficulty may be due to more than just a long adjustment period.

Only about 30 percent of the elderly who need hearing aids actually have them. This situation may be related to a number of factors. The older person may perceive that a hearing loss is an irreparable and normal part of getting old. Some researchers suggest that physicians, too, regard hearing loss as normal aging and intervention as futile (Humphrey, Herbst and Faurqui, 1981). The individual may not want to admit that a hearing loss exists. Likewise, the hearing aid may be rejected for cosmetic purposes and the social stigma associated with it. Also, hearing aids are expensive; neither routine hearing exams nor hearing aids are reimbursed under Medicare.

As losses advance, hearing aid amplification may become less useful (Hayes and Jerger, 1979). *Cochlear implants* are being tested and refined in order to bypass the cochlea and its faulty hair cells so that the auditory nerve can be directly stimulated. A cochlear implant is an electronic prosthetic device that utilizes electrodes that are microsurgically implanted into or near the cochlea to stimulate the nerve. They are intended for those with profound sensorineural hearing loss. To date, approximately 400 patients have received implants of this kind (Facer, 1985).

SENSORY DEPRIVATION

The need for sensory stimulation cannot be overemphasized. Vision and hearing are two very important links with the outside world; if these links are broken and no effective steps to reinstate them are taken, an individual may retreat into his or her own world. A false label of senility may be given such victims.

The term *sensory deprivation* first came into use in the 1950s. During that time it was demonstrated that subjects reacted with increased suggestibility after a few days of visual, auditory and tactile deprivation (Solomon, 1961). It is known that sensory deprivation results in impaired concentration, tension, anxiety, physical complaints and hallucinations.

Sundowner syndrome refers to a behavioral pattern often exhibited at night, when sensory stimulation is reduced. When the lights go out and quiet descends on the home or extended care facility, confusion and anxiety may lead to aggressive behavior. For a person whose sensory contact is already compromised, further reductions can lead to hallucinations. A night light can help to reduce confusion and its resultant symptoms (Charatan, 1984).

PARKINSON'S DISEASE

Parkinsonism or *Parkinson's syndrome* is a clinical condition characterized by muscular rigidity and a rhythmic tremor. The majority of cases are termed *idiopathic Parkinson's disease,* a chronic, progressive condition of the central nervous system that occurs primarily in the elderly. Two other variants of the disorder have been recognized. Post-encephalitic parkinsonism was postulated to result from a type of encephalitis that peaked in occurrence from 1919 to the early 1930s (Poskanzer and Schwab, 1963). Drug-induced parkinsonism is known to occur in some patients receiving large doses of certain drugs over time for the treatment of psychiatric disorders. The latter condition is often reversible if early diagnosis is followed by cessation of the drug therapy.

Symptoms of parkinsonism stem from a biochemical imbalance between the neurochemicals *acetylcholine* and *dopamine.* Normally, these *neurotransmitters* work to balance nervous excitation and inhibition, allowing for smooth motor function. This function is disrupted as dopamine-producing cells in the brain are lost. There is a direct relationship between the degree of dopamine deficiency and the severity of parkinsonism symptoms.

Muscular rigidity may involve one or both sides of the body and is responsible for decreased strength and speed of movement. Initiation of new movement is difficult. These symptoms can be very disabling. Postural problems lead to a forward-slanting, shuffling gait. The tremor, which occurs at rest, is an involuntary movement that can be socially embarrassing. Deliberate activity generally halts the tremor. The hands frequently show *pill-tolling tremor,* a rhythmic movement involving the thumb and first two fingers. Tremor may be worse when the individual is tired or emotionally distressed (Price and Wilson, 1982).

An expressionless, mask-like face is associated with the condition. The voice volume may be reduced and the speech pattern slow and monotonous. Handwriting deteriorates, becoming abnormally small and trailing off so that it cannot be deciphered. Many of these symptoms take a long time to develop.

It has been noted that some degree of impaired intellectual functioning, usually in the form of memory loss or decreased ability to internalize new concepts, occurs in some patients (Loranger, 1972). The older the patient is at the onset of Parkinson's disease, the more rapid is the progression of dementia (Lieberman, Dziatolowski and Kupersmith, 1979). Diagnosed dementia in association with Parkinson's disease is ten times more common than it is in age-matched controls (Fonda, 1985).

Attempting to restore the balance in neurotransmission by medication has been the mainstay therapy for Parkinson's disease. Various drugs are used, although the most effective therapy continues to be *levodopa* (L-dopa). Unfortunately, though L-dopa has done much to extend and maintain the functional capacity of the patient, its prolonged use can produce eventually disabling side effects (Greer, 1985). Drugs do not cure Parkinson's disease; it continues to progress despite their use.

The cause of the disease (first described by James Parkinson in 1917) remains unknown. However, some important features of the disorder, which affects approximately 400,000 Americans (Bower, 1985), have been recognized. Dopamine deficiency has been correlated with a localized loss of cells in a part of the brain known as the *substantia nigra*. As dopamine-producing cells are lost in this area, so too is the ability to carry out purposeful, coordinated and controlled movements. What remains elusive is why these cells are lost.

Recent investigations have led to the theory that Parkinson's disease may result from the combined effect of aging and environmental insult. With aging, cells in the substantia nigra are lost and dopamine levels decline. However, the majority of people who age do not develop Parkinson's disease. The 70-percent depletion in dopamine levels necessary for symptom onset may occur only among those who have suffered previous, subclinical damage (Calne, Langston, Martin, Stoessl, Ruth, Adam, Pate and Schulzer, 1985; Lewin, 1985a). Exposure to environmental toxins, including certain pesticides, various industrial chemicals, and food ingredients, might cause early, limited destruction of dopamine-producing cells (Snyder and D'Amato, 1985). Subsequent age-related losses then sufficiently compromise dopamine-producing capabilities to the extent that symptoms result.

Though controversial, this theory has been bolstered by studies linking a chemical by-product in synthetic heroin to the development of parkinsonian symptoms in humans and animals (Langston, Ballard, Tetrud and Irwin, 1983; Lewin, 1985b). There is no recognized association between symptoms and narcotic use unless the drug is contaminated with a substance known as MPTP (N-methyl-4-phenyltetrahydropyridine), which is actually converted to a *neurotoxin*. Animals and humans who have been exposed to the cell-damaging substance have demonstrated destruction of cells in the substantia nigra as well as symptoms of parkinsonism. Recent evidence suggests that synthetic heroin use can result in the loss of dopamine neurons in symptomless subjects as well (Calne et al., 1985). Young people using the drug for two years have begun to show symptoms of early parkinsonism. The chief of California's Division of Drug Programs in Sacramento reported that an epidemic of Parkinson's disease may be facing young adult users of synthetic heroin (Bower, 1985).

SUMMARY

Neurosensory changes occur with age and can influence functioning, activities, response to stimuli, and perception of the world. Degenerative changes and disease states involving the sense organs can alter vision and hearing.

Presbyopia is an age-associated change characterized by inflexibility of the lens and a resultant tendency toward farsightedness. Cataracts, glaucoma and senile macular degeneration are the most common visual disorders of the aged eye; they can cause serious loss of vision. Prompt diagnosis and treatment, although incapable of restoring the irreparable damage with which these visual disorders are associated, are important in the prevention of further loss and in the maintenance or improvement of the person's functional ability. In the adult-onset diabetic, vascular disease may lead to diabetic retinopathy, which can cause significant visual loss.

Impaired hearing is common among older persons. Some loss is due to age-related changes in the auditory system, while some is due to pathology and superimposed environmental insults. Considerable variability exists in the gradual decline in hearing with advanced age. The elderly person may present conductive, sensorineural or mixed hearing loss. Presbycusis is the most common cause of bilateral sensorineural hearing deficit in older adults.

Parkinson's disease is a chronic, progressive condition of the central nervous system that occurs primarily in the elderly. It is associated with a depletion of dopamine-producing cells in the brain and a resultant biochemical imbalance. The severity of symptoms is directly related to the degree of dopamine deficiency. The cause of Parkinson's disease remains unknown. Recent investigations have led to the theory that it may result from the combined effect of aging and environmental insult.

KEY TERMS

acetylcholine
acoustic trauma
argon laser photocoagulation therapy
atrophic senile macular degeneration
cataract
central vision
cerumen
cochlea
cochlear implant
conductive hearing loss
diabetic retinopathy
dopamine
eighth cranial nerve
exudative
glaucoma
hair cell
lens
levodopa (L-dopa)
low-tension glaucoma

macula
neovascular
neurotoxin
neurotransmitter
organ of Corti
ossicles
otitis media
otosclerosis
ototoxic drugs
Paget's disease
Parkinson's disease
peripheral vision
presbycusis
presbyopia
sclera
senile macular degeneration
sensorineural hearing loss
sensory deprivation
substantia nigra
sundowner syndrome
tympanic membrane

STUDY QUESTIONS

1. What is presbyopia? What is its significance for the older adult?
2. What are cataracts? How common are they? Can they be treated?
3. What is glaucoma? Differentiate primary and secondary glaucoma and closed-angle and open-angle glaucoma. What are the effects of glaucoma? How is it diagnosed and treated? What is low-tension glaucoma?
4. Identify the various types of senile macular degeneration, their significance and treatment possibilities.
5. What is diabetic retinopathy?
6. Briefly discuss some problems of and approaches to helping the visually impaired older adult.
7. Differentiate conductive from sensorineural hearing loss.
8. What is presbycusis? State its significance for the older adult.
9. Briefly discuss some problems of and approaches to helping the hearing-impaired older adult.
10. What are some significant consequences of sensory deprivation?

11. With regard to Parkinson's disease, describe:
    a. Major variants of the condition
    b. Symptoms
    c. Brain changes
    d. Treatment-cure
    e. Possible cause(s)

BIBLIOGRAPHY

Bengtsson, B. 1981. The prevalence of glaucoma. *British Journal of Ophthalmology 65:* 46–49.

Bower, B. 1985. Tracking the roots of Parkinson's disease. *Science News 128:* 212.

Calne, D., Langston, J., Martin, W., Stoessl, A., Ruth, T., Adam, M., Pate, B., and Schulzer, M. 1985. Position emission topography after MPTP: Observations relating to the cause of Parkinson's disease. *Nature 317:* 246–248.

Caplan, L. 1982. Neurology. In J. Rowe and R. Besdine, eds., *Health and Disease in Old Age.* Boston: Little, Brown.

Charatan, F. 1984. Mental stimulation and deprivation as risk factors in senility. In H. Rothschild, ed., *Risk Factors for Senility.* New York: Oxford University Press.

Cooper, A., Garside, R., and Kay, D. 1976. A comparison of deaf and non-deaf patients with paranoid and affective psychoses. *British Journal of Psychiatry 129:* 532.

Cranmer, K. 1983. Hearing aid dispensing—1983. *Hearing Instruments 34:*9–12.

Darbyshire, J. 1984. The hearing loss epidemic: A challenge to gerontology. *Research on Aging 6:* 384–394.

Early Treatment Diabetic Retinopathy Study Research Group. 1985. Photocoagulation for diabetic macular edema: Early treatment diabetic retinopathy study report number 1. *Archives of Ophthalmology 103:* 1796–1806.

Facer, G. 1985. Cochlea impact: Clinical status, 1985. *Mayo Clinic Procedings 60:* 137–138.

Ferris, F. III. 1983. Senile macular degeneration: Review of epidemiologic features. *American Journal of Epidemiology 118:* 132–151.

————. 1985. New laser role for diabetes eyed. *Science News 128:* 377.

Ferris, F., Fine, S., and Hyman, L. 1984. Age-related macular degeneration and blindness due to neovascular maculopathy. *Archives of Ophthalmology 102:* 1640–1642.

Fonda, D. 1985. Parkinson's disease in the elderly: Psychiatric manifestations. *Geriatrics 40:* 109–114.

Franklin, D. 1984. Crafting sound from silence. *Science News 126:* 252–254.

Giansiracusa, D., and Kantrowitz, F. 1982. Metabolic bone disease. In J. Rowe and R. Besdine, eds., *Health and Disease in Old Age.* Boston: Little, Brown.

Greer, M. 1985. Recent developments in the treatment of Parkinson's disease. *Geriatrics 140:* 34–41.

Hayes, D., and Jerger, J. 1979. Aging and the use of hearing aids. *Scandinavian Audiology 8:* 33–40.

Herbst, K., and Humphrey, C. 1980. Hearing impairment and mental state in the elderly living at home. *British Medical Journal 281:* 903.

Hudspeth, A. 1985. The cellular basis of hearing: The biophysics of hair cells. *Science 230:* 745–752.

Humphrey, C., Herbst, K., and Faurqui, S. 1981. Some characteristics of the hearing-impaired elderly who do not present themselves for rehabilitation. *British Journal of Audiology 15:* 25–30.

Hyman, L, Lilienfeld, A., Ferris, F., and Fine, S. 1983. Senile macular degeneration: A case-control study. *American Journal of Epidemiology 118:* 213–227.

Jervis, G. 1971. Senile dementia in pathology of the nervous system. In J. Minckler, ed., *Pathology of the Nervous System.* New York: McGraw-Hill.

Jindra, L. 1983. Open-angle glaucoma: Diagnosis and management. *Hospital Practice 18:* 114c–114p.

————. 1984. Closed-angle glaucoma: Diagnosis and management. *Hospital Practice 19:* 114–119.

Langston, J., Ballard, P., Tetrud, J., and Irwin, I. 1983. Chronic parkinsonism in humans due to a product of meperidine-analog synthesis. *Science 219:* 970–980.

Leske, M.C., 1983. The epidemiology of open-angle glaucoma: A review. *American Journal of Epidemiology 118:* 166–191.

Leske, M.C., and Rosenthal, J. 1979. Epidemiologic aspects of open-angle glaucoma. *American Journal of Epidemiology 109:* 250–272.

Leske, M.C., and Sperduto, R. 1983. The epidemiology of senile cataracts: A review. *American Journal of Epidemiology 118:* 152–165.

Lewin, R. 1985a. Clinical trial for Parkinson's disease. *Science 230:* 527–528.

_____ . 1985b. Parkinson's disease: An environmental cause? *Science 229:* 257–258.

Libow, L., and Sherman, F. 1981. *The Core of Geriatric Medicine.* St. Louis, Mo.: Mosby.

Lieberman, A., Dziatolowski, M., and Kupersmith, M. 1979. Parkinson's disease, dementia and Alzheimer's disease: Clinicopathological correlations. *Annals of Neurology 6:* 355–359.

Loranger, A. 1972. Intellectual impairment in Parkinson's syndrome. *Brain 95:* 405–412.

Macular Photocoagulation Study Group. 1982. Argon laser photocoagulation for senile macular degeneration. *Archives of Ophthalmology 100:* 912–918.

Mader, S. 1984. Hearing impairment in elderly persons. *Journal of the American Geriatrics Society 32:* 548–553.

Mahon, W. 1983. The million unit year: 1983 hearing aid sales and statistical summary. *Hearing Journal 1983:* 9–16

McCartney, J., and Nadler, G. 1979. How to help your patient cope with hearing loss. *Geriatrics 34:* 69.

Olsen, W. 1984. When hearing wanes, is amplification the answer? *Postgraduate Medicine 76:* 189–198.

Poskanzer, D., and Schwab, R. 1963. Cohort analysis of Parkinson's syndrome: Evidence for a single etiology related to sub-clinical infection about 1920. *Journal of Chronic Disease 16:* 961–973.

Price, S., and Wilson, L. 1982. *Pathophysiology.* New York: McGraw-Hill.

Rosen, S., Bergman, M., and Plester, D. 1962. Presbycusis study of a relatively noise free population in the Sudan. *Annals Otolaringology, Rhinology, Laryngology 71:* 727.

Snyder, S., and D'Amato, R. 1985. Predicting Parkinson's disease. *Nature 317:* 198–199.

Solomon, P. 1961. *Sensory Deprivation.* Cambridge, Mass.: Harvard University Press.

Spaeth, G. 1984. From eye pressure to nerve damage. *Science News 127:* 351.

Sparrow, N., and Duvall, A. 1967. Hearing loss and Paget's disease. *Journal of Laryngology 81:* 601.

Straatsma, B., Foos, R., and Horwitz, J. 1985. Aging-related cataract: Laboratory investigation and clinical management. *Annals of Internal Medicine 102:* 82–92.

Surjan, L., Devald, J., and Palfalvi, J. 1973. Epidemiology of hearing loss. *Audiology 12:* 396–410.

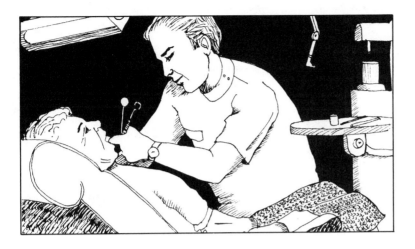

CHAPTER **9**

The Aging Process and the Gastrointestinal System

The human gastrointestinal tract is the product of four million years of biocultural evolution. Our species evolved from primate ancestors who were primarily vegetarian but were capable of omnivorous *alimentation*. The omnivorous nature of our species helped it to expand and evolve to fit a wide variety of ecological conditions. Judging from the development of a great variety of cultural traditions with dissimilar eating customs, it seems that our gastrointestinal system has served the species well.

All members of our species are subject to the aging process, which brings both general and specific changes in the gastrointestinal tract. These include *atrophy* of the secretion

mechanisms, decreasing motility of the gut, loss of strength and tone of the muscular tissue and its supporting structures, changes in neurosensory feedback on such things as enzyme and hormone release, innervation of the tract, and diminished response to pain and internal sensations. Although indisputable evidence for the relationship between these changes and aging is not abundant, there is certainly enough circumstantial evidence to suggest specific possibilities. It remains for further research to determine the magnitude of the changes and identify the possible preventive, rehabilitative, and supportive measures to effectively deal with them. Holt (1983) recently commented that the major extent of clinical digestive problems that affect the elderly in the United States is unknown because of lack of research.

Gastrointestinal symptoms such as indigestion, heartburn and epigastric discomfort increase with age, and the identification and evaluation of these symptoms are difficult. Many symptoms are caused by normal functional changes in the tract, but with increasing age, they are often associated with serious pathologic conditions such as cancer. Gastrointestinal symptoms are a matter of great concern to many people. The threat or fear of cancer often associated with such symptoms can exert a great deal of psychological pressure on an individual. Stress of this type not only affects the mental health of the individual but can also affect other body systems, causing or complicating problems such as *hypertension* and chronic respiratory disease.

Health professionals who deal with gastrointestinal disorders of the aged must be flexible in their approach. Every disorder should be carefully evaluated before it is dismissed as simply a functional manifestation. If further evaluation indicates a functional disorder, an effort should be made to explain the nature of the problem to the patient in clear, concise, jargon-free terms. A sympathetic attitude and face-to-face discussion of the situation may sometimes do more for an individual than explicit medical intervention.

The signs and symptoms that individuals often associate with one part of the gastrointestinal tract may in reality be associated with another part of the tract. This is caused both by the phenomenon of referral and the fact that the organs are part of an integrated system and thus interrelated; for example, discomfort perceived as originating in one's stomach may actually be coming from lower in the gastrointestinal tract. With this in mind and for the sake of convenience, simplicity and better organization, we now embark upon an organ-based survey of the gastrointestinal tract and its problems.

THE MOUTH

Older people often have poor oral hygiene and seem to lose sensitivity to irritations of the mouth. The former may result from the loss of positive self-image, irregular visits to a dentist or physical disabilities that hinder proper care of the mouth and teeth. Loss of sensitivity has serious implications for the health of the elderly person. Many irritations go unnoticed, and there is a tendency to think that all sores are canker sores and will heal. This often results in a delay in the inspection of sores that may be malignant.

Any sore that does not disappear in at least two weeks should be evaluated by a physician. Regular visits to a dentist who practices preventive dentistry would help in detection; unfortunately, regular dental visits are often a luxury for those on limited income (Medicare does not provide reimbursement for dental services to the elderly). Malignancies may occur where irritations are produced by broken and jagged teeth or around the periphery of an ill-fitting denture. Pain is usually not characteristic of the early stages of malignancy, but any slightly raised ulcers with raised edges that are painful to touch should be suspect. Treatment for a diagnosed malignancy will depend on the age and condition of the patient and on the nature and extent of the lesion.

Loss of taste is a common complaint among the elderly. This can be caused by atrophy of the taste buds, which comes with age, as well as lesions of the facial nerve and the medulla, *thalamus,* and temporal lobe of the brain. Hughes (1969) has suggested that taste, smell and hearing changes can be caused by cellular degeneration of the parietal lobe at the foot of the *postcentral gyrus.*

Some researchers have suggested that a person has 70 percent fewer taste buds at age 70 than at age 30. Arey, Tremaine and Monzingo (1935) observed an 80 percent reduction in taste function in a group of 74- to 80-year-olds. Rollin (1973) suggests that the number of taste bud nerve endings decreases with age, especially after age 60. This may be related to changes in the fifth and seventh cranial nerves (Harris, 1952). Changes in salivary flow, smoking and diseases such as *multiple sclerosis,* cancer, diabetes mellitus and hypertension all contribute to the alteration of taste and smell (Dye, 1984). Drugs taken to control diseases can also affect taste and smell (Schiffman, 1983). It has been suggested that zinc deficiency may contribute to reduced taste acuity. However, one double-blind study of institutionalized patients failed to show any significant improvement after 95 days of zinc supplementation (Gregor and Geissler, 1978). Henkin, Schechter and Raff (1974), however, suggest that zinc is only one among many substances that cause changes in taste acuity.

Age-related changes in the sense of smell may also contribute to the decline of *gustatory* sensation. Stevens, Cain and Plantinger (1982) note that older people (ages 65–83) rate odors as being only half as intense as do young adults (ages 18-25). The same researchers noted individual variation among older subjects, although this may be related to interaction of the aging process with existing pathological conditions. Changes in smell with age are less well-documented than changes in taste, but since smell contributes to perception of taste, we need more basic research on smell in order to understand declining taste acuity more completely.

Of the four basic tastes, sweet, bitter and sour decline in sensitivity, but salty taste does not appear to be affected by age (Hermel, Schonwetter and Samueloff, 1970). Balogh and Lelkes (1961) found that older adults were most sensitive to bitter tastes. The researchers suspect that this may be due to age-induced increases in the size and prominence of *papillae* sensitive to bitter tastes on the back of the tongue.

Thresholds for each taste are not as affected as is the ability to perceive subtle differences within each taste category. Reduced tactile thresholds in the oral mucosa and reduction in the sensitivity of the olfactory nerves also affect taste perception. Changes in taste perception may lead to increased use of spices, seasonings and flavoring by some older persons.

Loss of taste can affect appetite and thus indirectly affect nutritional status. Declining nutritional status can further affect a person's ability to cope with certain stresses and situations that affect health status. Loss of taste coupled with those social psychological changes that are often associated with aging, certainly does not stimulate a person to organize and prepare a meal, even if food is available. Still, for many elderly people there is nothing more enjoyable than preparing and eating a good meal.

Taste sensitivity and preference are affected greatly by lifelong consumption patterns. A study of laborers in India indicated that their ratings for the pleasantness of sour and bitter tastes differed significantly from Westerners (Moskowitz, 1975). The Indians repeatedly rated higher concentrations of quinine and citric acid as pleasant. The obvious explanation for this lies in the lifelong consumption of large amounts of sour foods by Indians.

A number of mucosal changes that occur in the elderly are worthy of note here. *Sublingual spider nevi* have been found in about half of some aged populations but are not associated with vitamin C deficiency (as suggested by some researchers) (Exton-Smith and Scott 1968). The appearance of the nevi is considered to be a normal aspect of the aging vascular system. *Leukoplakias,* which are small elevated white patches, were found in 21 percent of an elderly population; 12 percent of these were found to be premalignant (Bhaskar 1968). Dryness of the mouth, a common complaint, may be caused in part by mouth breathing, thicker mucus, decreased production of saliva, and/or an earlier bout with dehydration. A dry mouth can lead to the selection of self-lubricating foods such as custard and JellO, which may lack fiber or bulk and thus contribute to chronic constipation. Many drugs are known to affect the amount and consistency of saliva (Chauncey, Feldman and Wayler, 1983).

Dental changes such as missing teeth, attrition, weakening of tooth support and poorly functioning dentures affect oral function and can lead to dietary and cosmetic changes. Functionally, teeth serve to masticate food and initiate the process of digestion. They are important in proper speech, since certain sounds involve the contact of the tongue and the teeth. Socially, teeth function to some degree as symbols of sexuality, and their loss does affect facial appearance. Yet they are no longer essential to the survival of our species,

since cultural innovations can carry out most of their functions.

About 50 percent of all Americans have lost a majority of their teeth by age 65, and about 75 percent are totally edentulous by age 75. This is the result of neglect by both individuals and the dental profession. A number of factors lead people to neglect their teeth, including the expense of dental care, its low priority in the hierarchy of expenses, and the fact that little social stigma is attached to loss of teeth, especially in lower socioeconomic brackets. The loss of teeth generally does not itself pose a great health hazard. Finally, poor dental and nutritional education in the earlier years of the life cycle is associated with significant tooth loss in the later years.

Edentulousness is strongly correlated with low income and fewer than nine years of schooling, according to the National Center for Health Statistics. However, surveys indicate that edentulousness has decreased since 1960. During the decade 1960 to 1970, the proportion of edentulous males in the 65 to 74 age group dropped from 45 to 43.6 percent; edentulous females in the same ages dropped from 52.9 to 45 percent. These changes are more dramatic for aged black males, with a drop from 36 to 28 percent in ten years. It has been suggested that the greater availability and utilization of dental services may be responsible for these trends (Kiyak, 1984).

Since half the population of the United States has or needs dentures by age 65 and because about 75 percent of those over 65 have complete dentures, it should be apparent that denture problems are a major concern for the elderly. Well-fitting dentures probably do not exist; fit is a subjective category that depends largely upon the individual's capacity to adapt to dentures. Many people do well with dentures that are far from a perfect fit, yet others with dentures that meet all the criteria for a physically good fit complain incessantly about their performance. It is easier to fit and satisfy a younger patient in her fifties or sixties than the advanced elderly. The dentist of the geriatric patient should be cautioned that in long-time denture wearers, radical changes should not be made just to fit textbook theory.

Maxillary dentures are usually the best fitting and most functional. The broad-based structure of the maxilla allows for better construction and easier tolerance. The *mandible* has a number of characteristics that hinder the development of a truly effective plate. The mandible's narrow horseshoe shape is more difficult to fit. In addition, the greater mobility of the mandible causes the peripheral muccobuccal fold to be more active and thus have a tendency to dislodge the plate. The lower lip, tongue and sublingual muscles may tend to dislodge the denture during speaking or swallowing. For these reasons, healthy mandibular teeth should be preserved as long as possible to act as anchors for partial dentures. Friedman (1968) has suggested that the cuspids are excellent as anchors because their long roots make them less susceptible to loss.

Full dentures tend to be a last resort after attempts with partial plates have failed. They are also used in cases of serious *periodontal disease,* which necessitates the complete removal of all teeth. About every five years the dentures must be relined or replaced because of changes in the supportive tissues. After tooth loss there is a tendency for *resorption* of the alveolar bone forming the supporting ridges, thus leaving flat ridges that limit stabilization of the dentures.

Denture wearers typically complain of sore mouths, poor chewing capacity and the constant fear of losing their teeth at embarrassing moments. Widely advertised dental adhesives are distasteful and generally of limited effectiveness. The elderly denture wearer must be educated that the devices are a useful but inefficient compromise for lost teeth.

Dental Caries

Pathologic dental conditions in the aged present a somewhat different pattern than in younger groups. Dental caries, or tooth decay, is the greatest cause of tooth loss up to age 35; periodontal disease subsequently becomes the greatest source of tooth loss. Dental decay continues to occur in older people, however, and the effects of earlier dental caries persist in the form of missing teeth and the use of dental plates in later years. There is strong research and clinical evidence that indicates increased rates of root caries in the elderly. For example, Baum (1981) found that persons over age 60 had four times more root caries than those under 40.

Three factors are present in caries production: (1) A more or less susceptible tooth; (2) Bacterial plaque on the surface of the tooth and (3) A dietary substrate such as carbohydrates. A variety of oral bacteria is capable of causing tooth decay, but the major culprit appears to be *streptococcus mutans,* which readily ferments monosaccharides and disaccharides to lactic acid.

The process of tooth decay starts with the formation of a sticky, viscous film called plaque, in which bacteria grow, multiply, metabolize food debris, and convert carbohydrates to organic acids. The plaque protects the decay bacteria from normal oral cleansing. Organic acids, such as lactic acid, make contact with the tooth enamel and demineralize tooth hydroxyapatite. This, in turn, allows the bacterial proteolysis of tooth collagen, creating cavities. The amount of decalcification and decay seems to be related to the length of time that caries-causing bacteria are in contact with the tooth.

Sucrose is prominent in the decay process in three ways. It is easily converted by bacterial enzymes to dextrans and levans, which form the structural basis of plaque; in the plaque itself, it serves as a reserve food supply for bacteria, remaining available even after all traces of a meal have disappeared from the oral cavity; and it is readily converted to lactic acid by bacterial action.

The role of saliva in the process of tooth decay is still unclear. It has been suggested that it helps clear food residues and neutralizes the acid medium that is essential for decay. Urea in the saliva may be converted to ammonia by *ureolytic* microbes in the plaque, resulting in a higher pH. Others have suggested that saliva may serve as an ionic source of fluorine, calcium and phosphorus, all of which are incorporated into the tooth's surface structures.

It is difficult to determine the effects of specific nutrients on caries development. Tooth resistance is a developmental phenomenon, so an earlier nutrient imbalance may affect resistance to decay later in life. A number of nutrients have been implicated in the process of tooth decay, including protein, fat, phosphate, a variety of trace elements and simple carbohydrates. Protein may protect against tooth decay by increasing the salivary *urea* and ammonia levels to neutralize the pH, thus promoting an immune response that may inhibit bacterial colonization and generally assuring the integrity of body tissues. Fat seems to have cariostatic effects, such as increasing antimicrobial activity, reducing

the time and quantity of food that is retained on teeth, increasing the flow of saliva, and aiding the production of a protective film on the teeth (DePaola and Alfano, 1977).

It is possible that phosphates cleanse the teeth and aid in remineralization of tooth surfaces. The calcium-to-phosphorus ratio may also be related to caries development. Mann (1962) found a calcium-phosphorus ratio of .55 to be associated with few or no caries. A number of other trace elements—molybdenum, strontium, vanadium, lithium, barium, and boron—are described as cariostatic, while lead and selenium have been associated with cariogenesis (Glass, 1973). The systematic effects of most of these trace elements on tooth resistance are still unclear.

Fluorine has been shown to influence caries development through a variety of mechanisms that are still not fully understood. Its ingestion during tooth development can reduce caries by 60 percent, while topical applications after eruption can lead to reductions of 20 percent (DePaola and Alfano, 1977). Stam and Banting (1980) found increased rates of root caries with age but the older residents of a non-fluoridated community had twice as many untreated and filled root surface lesions. In one way, fluorine's effectiveness appears to be related to the formation of a stabilized enamel *apatite* that resists dissolution by organic acids. In another way, fluorine's effects may be related to the promotion of recrystallization of carious teeth. Some fluorine ions seem to replace hydroxide ions in the apatite (fluoroxyapatite), forming an acid-insoluble matrix that is fixed for the life of the tooth. It may also affect the efficiency of plaque formation or the capacity of some microbes to break down sugars to acids.

Dietary supplements in the form of fluoride tablets are apparently not practical, as they are rapidly cleared from the body, and it is hard to deliver the exact amounts needed physiologically. Fluorine added to salt at the level of 90 mg of fluorine per kilogram of salt can result in a 30 to 40 percent reduction in decay. At present, fluoride is added to water supplies throughout the United States and is most effective at levels of 0.7–1.2 parts per million (ppm) of drinking water. Levels of about 1.5 ppm can result in discolored or mottled teeth.

Although fluorine and phosphorus appear to be cariostatic, selenium, magnesium, calcium, lead, silicon and platinum have been reported as caries-promoting. Also, deficiencies of vitamin C, zinc and protein may increase the pathologic potential of oral bacteria by allowing easier penetration of the teeth by bacterial toxins.

Simple carbohydrates have been strongly implicated in the promotion of tooth decay. The form of the sugar and the length of retention in the mouth appear to be more important than the amount. The physical consistency of a food is related to retention and hence cariogenic potential; solid foods are worse than liquids, and sticky foods such as caramel, sweet pastry, ice cream and syrups are the most troublesome. The circumstances surrounding consumption also play an important role. For example, sugar at mealtime or with liquids is less cariogenic than between meals. It has also been suggested that sugary foods containing phosphates are less of a threat because of the cariostatic influence of phosphates.

General advice concerning diet and dental decay should include the elimination or reduced use of cariogenic foods and the addition of potentially caries-protective foods such as fats and proteins, and the inclusions of foods that require strong mastication.

Although caries constitute a less serious problem in later years, prevention of the condition should be a significant part of health maintenance among the aging. Previous caries experience determines the number and quality of teeth carried into old age, and the maintenance of healthy teeth should continue. The number and condition of the teeth affect the efficiency of the digestive process and can influence dietary intake. Also, the presence of healthy teeth is important for the anchorage of a partial dental plate, which is functionally preferable to a full plate.

Periodontal Disease

Periodontal disease is the leading cause of tooth loss after age 35. After reviewing data from two nationwide studies, Douglas and associates (1983) report that about 60 percent (58.9%) of the men aged 65 to 74 years and 43 percent of the women in the same age group were affected by periodontal disease.

When only the gums and soft tissues are involved, the periodontal condition is referred to as *gingivitis*. When bone is also affected, it is called *periodontitis*. Systematic factors involving hormones and nutrition as well as plaque formation are important in its etiology (Bahn, 1970). The process of periodontal deterioration is initiated by bacterial action in the gingival crevices. It appears that older people develop a greater susceptibility to microbial plaque with severe periodontal involvement (Holm-Pederson, Agerback, and Theilade 1975). Plaque develops, causing one of the most concentrated bacterial populations known to affect human beings. The gum margins fall away from contact with the teeth, and the process invades the bone, eventually affecting the periodontal ligament, which can lead to tooth loss. Chronic infection associated with this process can also lead to tooth loss.

Nutritional status affects an individual's susceptibility to periodontal disease. It may exert its influence by promoting an immune response, enhancing tissue integrity, and affecting the production of saliva and gingival fluid. Tough, fibrous foods may be effective in removing plaque. Tough foods also help minimize gland atrophy and encourage increased saliva flow with a higher protein content (Alfano, 1976), although there is little conclusive evidence at this time that saliva actively deters periodontal disease.

As with caries development, soft and sticky carbohydrate foods are an effective medium for bacterial growth, especially beneath the gum margin. Calculus or tartar, a hard deposit of calcium salts, mucin and bacteria, is also associated with periodontal disease. The cause of tartar formation is obscure, although it may simply be an advanced form of plaque. It appears that the massaging effect of rough food prevents its formation.

Lutwak (1976) has suggested that periodontal disease may partly be a form of nutritional osteoporosis, the dietary factor being a chronic dietary deficiency of calcium in association with excess dietary phosphorus. American diets are notably high in phosphorus due to the large amounts of meat, poultry, fish, milk, and flour consumed. Milk consumption has generally been declining in the American diet, often replaced by soft drinks that are notably unbalanced in their calcium-phosphorus ratios. As evidence, Lutwak (1976) cites retrospective studies that link the appearance of vertebral osteoporosis and periodontal disease, and severity of axial osteoporosis and edentulousness.

Clinical evidence that calcium supplementation can do more than halt the progress of osteoporosis has not been produced, but from a preventive point of view, proper calcium-phosphorus ratio should be stressed for dietary intake during the earlier adult decades.

ESOPHAGUS

We are generally taught that the esophagus is a part of the gastrointestinal tract that simply acts as a tube to connect the oral cavity with the stomach. Most people are barely aware of its existence and even less worried about its malfunctioning. During the aging process, however, this part of the tract may become a cause of great concern for many.

A number of symptoms associated with the esophagus become more common with advancing age. Among these are difficulty in swallowing (dysphagia), substernal pain, heartburn, belching and general epigastric discomfort. Any of these conditions can be a sign of great danger. Difficulty in swallowing can be related to stroke, Parkinson's disease, *diabetes mellitus,* pseudobulbar palsy, bronchial tumors, carcinoma of the esophagus or, more often, the general loss of motility that comes with advancing age. Heartburn, belching, substernal pain and epigastric discomfort can be related to aberrant peristalsis or defects in sphincter relaxation that may be related to age changes in the nerve tissue that stimulates these actions.

Esophageal pain can be readily confused with cardiac-related pain. More often these pains are caused by gastric reflux, *esophagitis* and/or diffuse muscular spasms of the sphincters. In general, esophageal pain can be distinguished from cardiac pain by its response to antacids and *anticholinergics* and by its characteristic burning sensation rather than suffocating pressure. Esophageal pain is most often brought on by changes in posture (such as stooping, lying down, or straining) as well as through the ingestion of too much food. Much relief can be obtained by avoiding postural stresses and by eating smaller and more frequent meals. More recently the role of hiatus hernia in reflux has been reevaluated by some researchers, who feel that a competent lower esophageal sphincter is the most important antireflux barrier (Castell, 1975).

Hiatus hernia can lead to a number of esophageal symptoms or complicate other existing conditions. There are two basic types of hiatus hernia: the common sliding type (Figure 9.1) and the paraesophageal type. In the common sliding type, the junction of the esophagus and the cardiac portion of the stomach move above the normal position at the diaphragm and lead to gastric reflux. In the paraesophageal type, a portion of the cardiac end of the stomach herniates through the diaphragm hiatus alongside the esophagus.

Hiatus hernia appears to be increasing in incidence, and the majority of affected individuals are over 50 years old; women appear to be affected more than men. In an early

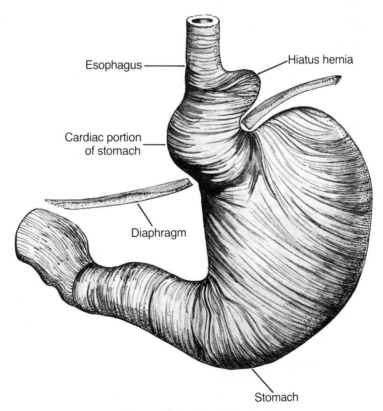

Esophagus

Hiatus hernia

Cardiac portion of stomach

Diaphragm

Stomach

Figure 9.1   Hiatus hernia.

study, Brick and Amory (1950) observed it in only 18 percent of their subjects below the age of 50 but in 28 percent of those over age 70. McGinty (1971) noted that hiatus hernia occurs in as many as 65 percent of those over 60, and most often in obese women.

Hiatus hernia can occasionally lead to such complications as esophagitis and ulceration stricture of the esophagus; surgical correction is rarely recommended and usually has a slim chance of success. Medical management such as weight reduction, changes in the size and frequency of meals, medication, and sometimes sleeping with the head of the bed elevated six inches can bring relief.

Although most disorders of the esophagus are not terminal, there is a steady rise in the incidence of carcinoma of the esophagus with age (Langman, 1971). The average age at diagnosis is 60. *Squamous carcinoma* accounts for 5 to 7 percent of all forms of malignancy (McKeown 1965) and about 20 percent of these cases occur in those over 70. Most tumors are located in the distal portion and are prevalent in men. The greater number of tumors in the distal portion may be a statistical artifact of the inclusion of cardio-esophageal junction tumors in this category.

The carcinoma can be the cause of great suffering in an elderly patient. The two most common symptoms are chronic difficulty in swallowing and esophageal spasms of long duration. Excessive salivation, which is often related to an obstruction or irritation of the esophagus such as that produced by malignancy, may accompany these conditions. Thirst, hiccups, bleeding and anemia are also common with these conditions. The causes of esophageal carcinoma are unclear, but some researchers have suggested relationships to smoking, alcoholism, *achalasia*, and dietary practices. Treatment with an esopha-

gectomy has a mortality rate of 20 percent and a 5-year survival rate of 5 percent. Many patients are not physically up to surgery anyway. In general, most treatment is *palliative,* including radiation therapy, and the prognosis is grave.

STOMACH

Although little absorption of nutrients takes place in the stomach, the digestive process (except for the minor action of *ptyalin* in the mouth) starts in this organ. Basically, gastric juice contains hydrochloric acid, pepsin, *lipase* and mucin, which initiate the digestion of proteins and some fats. It seems that a number of alterations of the stomach occur with advancing age, but researchers disagree on how much change occurs and the rate of such change. One thing upon which most researchers agree is that hyperacidity becomes rare, but hypoacidity and *achlorhydria* increase in incidence.

According to Fikry and Aboul-Wafa (1965), atrophic changes in the gastric mucosa initially affect acidity and fat digestion; later, the production of *pepsinogen,* needed in protein digestion, is affected; and finally the production of mucin is affected. (Mucin protects the stomach from its own juices.) These changes are caused by the active role of the normal gastric mucosa in the production of stomach acid, lipase, pepsinogen and mucin. Bertolini (1969) has suggested that the change from acid to alkaline pH affects the intestinal floral growth of older people. This can lead to some nutritional deficiencies because the intestinal flora are active in both the use and synthesis of essential nutrients.

The three most common categories of stomach disorder are *gastritis, peptic ulcer* and *gastric carcinoma. Gastritis,* which can be acute, is usually caused by some type of injury to the gastric mucosa, such as that associated with drugs, alcohol or some bacterial toxins. Chronic gastritis, on the other hand, can be of two types, chronic hypertrophic gastritis and chronic atrophic gastritis. The former is characterized by burning, gnawing pains and indigestion and must be diagnosed by a gastroscope, since barium radiographs give the appearance of normality. There does not appear to be much of a change in the gastric acid, but the gastroscopic examination reveals prominent and inflamed *rugae.* Atrophic gastritis is used to categorize a wide variety of gastric inflammations that show a range of symptoms from very vague epigastric discomfort to very painful, acute flare-ups. The disorder is asso-

ciated with reduced acid secretion, mucosal atrophy, chronic *pancreatitis* and alcoholism. Dietary and medical management is the most common approach to these disorders.

Ulcers (Figure 9.2) do not change in old age, although the symptoms may be atypical. Many cases are asymptomatic. Weight loss, anemia and painless vomiting (sometimes with blood) are common signs in the elderly, but perforation is rare, and great pain may be absent. A number of peptic ulcers in the elderly probably represent chronic ulcers acquired in middle age, when they are far more prevalent. First-time cases do occur in old age, and the prognosis for recovery is good. Peptic ulcers at advanced ages are more common and have a poor prognosis, with more than two-thirds of ulcer deaths being caused by peptic or gastric ulcers.

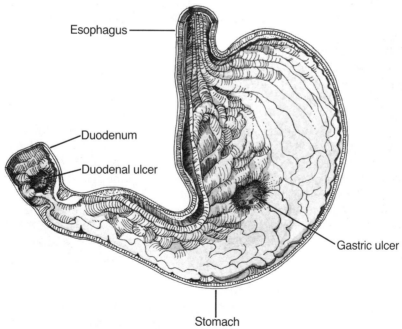

Figure 9.2 Gastric and duodenal ulcers.

Deaths from peptic ulcers are increasing at a time when deaths from stomach cancer are decreasing. Since many of the aged take a great number of medications for multiple problems, drug-induced ulcers are not uncommon. Drugs can increase gastric secretions and lower the resistance of the gastric mucosa, thus leading to ulcer development. Aspirin, phenylbutazone and corticosteroids are examples of drugs associated with ulcer development.

Preferred treatment for peptic ulcers should be conservative. Bed rest, an important part of ulcer therapy in younger patients, is not recommended for older people because some problems associated with immobilization (embolism, for example) are more serious than the ulcer. Ulcer diets have proved to be of little value in older people. Failure to heal within six weeks points toward a malignancy and possible surgery, although this is generally reserved for special cases such as pyloric obstruction. In England, McKeown (1965) observed that gastric ulcers make up 10 percent of all the ulcers in those over age 60; a third of all ulcer deaths were in the 60+ age group.

Recently, for unknown reasons, the incidence of stomach cancer has been declining, but it still remains a common tumor with an unfavorable prognosis. It is more common in men, people over 60 years of age, and those with type A blood. Stomach cancer reaches its peak incidence in the eighth and ninth decades of life. There are a few hints that it may be familial. Those with *pernicious anemia* and atrophy of gastric mucosa seem to have a higher probability of being affected. The most common sites are in the *pylorus* and *antrum*, but any portion of the organ can be affected.

Often symptoms are nonspecific and may involve weight loss, loss of appetite, malaise and anemia, with some epigastric discomfort possible. This situation can lead to self-medication with antacids and thus delay proper diagnosis. The more classic signs of nausea, indigestion, difficulty in swallowing, bloody vomit, and tarry stools will manifest themselves in many cases. Differentiating gastric ulcers and carcinoma by symptoms is very difficult. The early symptoms and initial response to the treatment of symptoms is often similar, but persistent weight loss, bleeding and anemia are suggestive of cancer. The size and location of lesions are poor indicators for differential diagnosis, but a lesion plus achlorhydria also suggests cancer.

Diagnosis can be best accomplished by gastroscopy, since a cytologic sample can give an accuracy of 85 to 95 percent. Radical surgery is often contraindicated in the elderly because of its high risk. Those experiencing such surgery show a 5-year survival rate of only 5 to 10 percent. Radiotherapy and chemotherapy are also of little help.

SMALL INTESTINE

Few changes occur in the small intestine, since cell renewal continues in this organ well into old age. Malignant tumors of the small intestine are rare, although changes in other organs such as the liver, gallbladder, pancreas and kidney can alter the functioning of the small intestine. A great deal of medical information is lacking on the aging of the small intestine. Testing and research procedures are complex and make excessive demands on both the elderly patient and the researcher.

In the *duodenum* there are two major problems associated with old age: *diverticula* and peptic ulcers. Duodenal diverticula were thought to be rare, but Bockus (1966:28) estimates that 10 percent of those over 55 years of age have them and that they increase in number with age. Diverticula are strongly associated with complications such as osteomalacia, iron deficiency anemia, and B12 and folate deficiency as well as general intestinal malabsorption. Thus in elderly persons, a vitamin deficiency or intestinal malabsorption might lead one to suspect duodenal diverticula as the basis. Surgery is rarely indicated. Patients seem to respond well to antibiotic therapy using septrin and lincomycin.

Duodenal ulcers are more frequent than gastric ulcers, and the risk is no greater in the elderly. Symptoms may present themselves differently because of diminished pain sensation in the elderly; surgery is usually not recommended because of its high risk. The main part of the therapy includes antacids and often anticholinergics; both precipitate diarrhea, constipation and urinary retention. A switch to a greater number of smaller meals (for example, six) of non-irritating foods will help keep the stomach from being empty and may act to neutralize stomach acid. Many researchers believe that the conventional bland diet does not promote ulcer healing and is too difficult for the patient to follow. The stress involved in strictly adhering to a special diet may counteract any positive effects. A common-sense approach to diet that considers the individual patient's needs, abilities and attitudes is important.

Upper gastrointestinal bleeding in the elderly should be evaluated to determine its origin. It can come from a variety of sources such as peptic ulcers. Persons affected by cirrhosis will bleed not only from the varices but also from gastritis, ulcers and gastric erosion, which is often associated with cirrhosis. The incidence of such bleeding ranges from about 15 to 40 percent of the cases. Gastric erosion from heavy aspirin use can lead to bleeding.

Ischemia, *polyps, fibromas, lipomas* and *lymphomas* can also lead to upper gastrointestinal bleeding.

Tarry blood in the stool usually indicates an upper gastrointestinal source, whereas bright red blood indicates a large bowel disorder. Sometimes a sluggish large bowel can lead to tarry stools, and a rapid transit time from the upper tract can result in bright red blood in the stool. Whatever the cause, bleeding from the upper tract should not be summarily dismissed by a simple diagnosis.

Malignant tumors of the small intestine are rare but are more frequent in men. They tend to affect the distal section more than the proximal. The appendix is the most common site, but it does not metastasize readily. The *ileum* is the next most common site, but here it is usually more malignant and frequently multiple.

Intestinal obstruction is one of the more common problems of the aging tract, usually falling into two classes, mechanical and paralytic. Table 9.1 compares the two conditions as to causes, symptoms and diagnosis. Mechanical obstructions are usually treated by surgery and paralytic obstructions by medical treatment such as antibiotic therapy and fluid replacement.

Appendicitis in the aged has a higher mortality rate than in the rest of the population (7 to 1 percent). This may be the result of a number of factors: (1) the misconception that appendicitis is rare in the elderly; (2) delayed diagnosis and treatment; (3) early perforation; (4) mildness of the symptoms; and (5) greater incidence of preexisting disease associated with it (Rossman 1986). In other words, it is often undiagnosed because it is not expected and the symptoms are atypical of *appendicitis*. Appendectomy appears desirable unless perforation with abscess has occurred; then drainage would be the wisest

TABLE 9.1 Obstructions of the small intestines[a]

	Mechanical	Paralytic
Causes	Adhesions, volvulus, worms, diverticulitis, hernias, tumors, gallstones, fecoliths	Pneumonia, pancreatitis, biliary colic, ureteral calculus, myocardial infarction, septicemia, hematoma, hypopotassemia, thrombus of mesentery, peritonitis
Symptoms	Cramped severe pain, vomiting, distension, constipation, borborygmi present (gas)	Absent or mild pain, vomiting, distension, constipation, borborygmi absent (gas)
Diagnosis	Plain radiograph shows fluid levels in distended loops; barium enema shows obstruction	Plain radiograph same as mechanical; barium enema shows no point of obstruction

[a]Adapted from Rossman, I., ed. 1986. *Clinical Geriatrics*. Philadelphia: J. B. Lippincott Co.

course, followed by surgery later if necessary. There is a strong correlation between delay in presentation of symptoms and perforation. Non-operative management, which might be necessary in some high-risk elderly, calls for bowel rest and antibiotic therapy followed by a carefully planned appendectomy at a later date.

A number of rare but serious conditions also occur in the small bowel, such as potassium deficiency related to thiazide use by heart patients and abdominal angina. The reader is referred to more detailed texts in geriatric medicine and gastroenterology for a more complete description and inventory of these disorders (for example, Brocklehurst, 1973).

The small intestine is the most important portion of the gastrointestinal tract with respect to both digestion and absorption of food. It is supplied with enzymes from the pancreas, bile from the *hepatobiliary* system and enzymes from its own intestinal mucosa. Its absorptive surface is increased many times by the fingerlike projections known as villi. Still, it is the portion of the gastrointes-

tinal tract about which the least is known with respect to the effects of aging.

A number of age-related changes have been identified, but researchers are not in agreement about them. It appears that a decrease in the size and the permeability of the capillary bed is a very important change. At the same time other changes diminish the elasticity of the blood vessels and the lungs. These changes have important implications for the effectiveness of nutrient absorption and the possibility of blood vessel blockage or obstruction. Delay in peripheral nerve transmission and vasomotor response is important, since the operation of the gastrointestinal system is under neurohormonal control.

Beginning at about age 40, there is a diminution of pancreatic enzymes, which are secreted into the small intestine. Few hard data exist that indicate age-related changes in the intestinal glands. A change in the composition of the bacterial flora of the intestine has been documented. These changes in the ecology of the gut can be detrimental. Reduction of gastric acidity and enzymes can lead to rapid growth of organisms such as the streptococci at the expense of the normal organisms of the gut. The replacement of these normal organisms results in a loss of many of the vitamins they synthesize. The overgrowth of ecologically foreign organisms can lead to lowered resistance of the tract as well as to an irritated and inflamed mucosal lining.

Abnormal bacterial growth can bind vitamin B12 and affect its systemic availability. Some bacteria deconjugate bile salts; this depletes the pool of bile salts available for fat metabolism. By-products of deconjugation may actually be toxic to the gut as well as carcinogenic. Species belonging to *Clostridia, Bacteroides* and *Veillonella* that are not usually found in the small bowel may invade from the large bowel and cause physical damage and imbalances in the small-intestine environment. Treatment in the short term usually involves antibiotic therapy plus the administration of vitamins. In chronic cases, intermittent antibiotic administration over a long period may be necessary.

In considering the changing absorptive characteristics of the small intestine, one must be aware that the situation in the bowel is complicated by changes occurring elsewhere in the gut. These interrelationships may alter any tests to determine functional changes. It appears that fat and carbohydrate absorption are somewhat curtailed but still remain adequate for normal nutrition. Protein absorption caused by slight enzymatic changes may be impaired to some small degree, especially with changes in the initial stages of protein digestion. This may be related to the reduced *trypsin* activity of the pancreas.

Fat digestion can be impaired by associated hepatobiliary disease (Figure 9.3). After age 20 lipolytic activity seems to be reduced

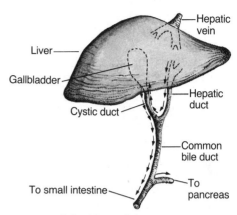

Figure 9.3   Hepatobiliary system.

by 20 percent, but apparently without an appreciable effect on fat digestion. Becker and colleagues (1950) observed that aged individuals absorb a high-fat meal in about twice the time it takes for a young adult.

Malabsorption and maldigestion in elderly people are common, and thus it is impossible to deal individually with all the causes or factors that contribute to a *malabsorption* or *maldigestion syndrome.* Some of the conditions that can lead to malabsorption are (Balachi and Dobbins, 1974):

1. Surgical alterations such as esophagectomy, gastrectomy and small bowel resections.
2. Pancreatic insufficiency caused by pancreatitis or a tumor.
3. Hepatobiliary insufficiency caused by such conditions as *decreased bile-acid synthesis, gallstones,* and *hepatitis.*
4. Stasis and bacterial overgrowth.
5. Drug-induced changes caused by alcohol, *anticonvulsants,* cathartics, diuretics, colchicine and antibiotics.

6. Cardiovascular abnormalities such as congestive heart failure, constrictive pericarditis, arteriosclerosis and intestinal angina.
7. Radiation injury caused by accidental, occupational or therapeutic exposures.
8. Endocrinopathy such as diabetes, Addison's disease and thyroid disease.
9. Paget's disease.
10. Collagen vascular disease.
11. *Amyloidosis.*
12. Celiac sprue.
13. Neoplastic disease.
14. Paraproteinemia such as *multiple myeloma.*

Malabsorption syndromes are difficult to manage because the small bowel mucosa are diseased. The syndromes are best treated by parenteral administration of vitamins and minerals or the oral administration of pharmacologic doses rather than physiologic doses of these nutrients. Correction of the underlying cause should be the clinical goal, but often this is either impossible, because its cause is not known, or impractical, because medical means are not available. Hence in most cases of malabsorption, nutritional management is the only way of sustaining the patient. The plan for management must fit the individual case or circumstances.

GALLBLADDER

Gallbladder problems are a major source of concern and stress for many elderly people. The incidence of most gallbladder problems increases markedly after age 65. The most consistent age-related changes are in the ability to empty the gallbladder and in the physical composition of bile. Bertolini (1969) found that bile tends to be thicker, richer in cholesterol and reduced in volume in the elderly. Statistics indicate an increase in the incidence of *gallstones* with age. Between 35 and 40 percent of those over 70 years of age, compared to 10 to 20 percent of those between 55 and 65 years, are afflicted by gallstones. Ponka, Welborn and Brush (1963) found that 55 out of 200 aged patients with abdominal pain had gallstones *(cholelithiasis).* Stones are more common in elderly women than men, except after age 70, when gender differences are insignificant. Those with diabetes, on estrogen therapy, and with bile-absorption problems have a high risk of developing gallstones.

Most cases of gallstones in the elderly appear to be asymptomatic. The most common manifestations are indigestion, nausea, vomiting, fat intolerance, obstructive *jaundice* and episodes of *cholecystitis.* The pain associated with gallstones is generally in the upper right quadrant just below the rib cage or in the right shoulder. The risk of obstruction of the common or cystic ducts is a real threat that can lead to inflammation, infection and *stasis* proximal to the stone. This can lead to complications such as pancreatitis, liver problems and retrograde cholecystitis. The lack of bile in the small intestine can lead to deficiencies of the fat-soluble vitamins. As a precaution, vitamin K should be supplemented when preparing such persons for surgery.

The course of treatment for gallstones is at issue among surgeons. Some prefer to perform surgery in an effort to forestall complications, even if the person is asymptomatic. The operation involves some added risks for the elderly, since the mortality for those over 70 is 7 percent compared to 1 percent for those below age 60 (Hyams 1973). Others believe that the best course of action is a more conservative approach with emphasis on medical management. The latter attitude is based on the increased risks of surgery, the fact that the incidence of carcinoma of the gallbladder is low, the possibility that other diseases or conditions may be causing the symptoms, and the general mental stress imposed by surgery.

Medical treatment usually consists of a program of weight reduction, avoidance of fatty foods and the use of antacids. Hospitalization is based on the severity of symptoms, the condition of the patient and an assessment of the overall risks associated with ambulatory or home treatment. Of course, surgical removal (cholecystectomy) is generally supported in acute situations such as obstruction, *cholangitis,* and other possible life-threatening situations.

Carcinoma of the gallbladder is a very rare condition but occurs more often in women than men; it is three times more common in those over age 70. Its diagnosis is very difficult, since it is often confused with liver carcinoma or mistaken as a manifestation of liver metastasis from more common cancer sites such as the stomach. It is often associated with chronic calculous cholecystitis. Treatment is not promising. Prognosis is very poor with an average life expectancy of six months.

THE LIVER

The liver is the largest gland and one of the most important of the body's organs. It metabolizes and stores carbohydrates, fats, proteins, minerals and vitamins and acts as a detoxifying and bactericidal agent. It also controls the production and secretion of bile. The liver does not decrease in size with age, and its percentage of body weight, 2.5 per-

cent, remains the same until about age 70, when it starts to decline until it reaches about 1.6 percent of body weight by the tenth decade (Morgan and Feldman, 1967). Haberman (1962) estimated that three-fourths of the aged have one or more functional abnormalities of the liver.

There is little evidence for cell loss with age, so it is likely that liver abnormalities are caused by changes in cell function such as slight anatomic changes or the changing interaction between spatially related cells (Shock 1964). Tauchi and Sato (1968) noted a reduction in the number of mitochondria in aging liver cells. This phenomenon is not accompanied by decline of liver function. It may be caused by the increased size of aging cells, which produce more enzyme, or by the oxidative capacity of older cells.

Certain enzymes capable of catabolizing proteins increase their production with age. This leads to a slightly reduced capability of the aging liver to synthesize protein. Thompson and Williams (1965) found a linearly decreased storage capacity with age, although the secretory transport maximum was not altered. Calloway and Merrill (1965) affirmed these observations in their research. It is possible that synthesis of certain enzyme systems can be maintained while general synthetic activity of the organ is decreasing. Despite obvious anatomic and physiologic changes, the functional capacity of the aged liver remains within the range of normal variation, but the elderly are common recipients of hepatotoxic drugs and combinations of chemical agents that could interfere with liver clearance.

Jaundice is a common manifestation of liver disease and can be associated with cirrhosis, drug effects and hepatitis. It appears that about half the cases of jaundice are caused by the benign disorders just mentioned, and the other half are caused by carcinoma of the pancreas or hepatobiliary tract. One must go through a four-to-six week observation period in cases of undetermined jaundice to allow for subsidence, which may make surgery unnecessary (Rossman, 1986).

Cirrhosis of the liver is the most serious or final stage of liver injury and degeneration. The liver is contracted and loses most of its ability to function, and once a fibrous connective tissue replaces the liver cells, the condition is irreversible. Cirrhosis is the fifth most common cause of death in the United States today. It is positively associated with chronic alcoholism, which itself is an important disorder in the elderly.

The nature of the relationship between cirrhosis and alcoholism is still being debated. One current view holds that cirrhosis is a result of the interaction of chronic alcoholism and long-term nutritional deficiencies, from which most alcoholics suffer. Such deficiencies can lead to fatty liver and eventual fibrosis of the liver. The liver is more susceptible to damage from toxic agents and infectious organisms when a nutritional deficiency exists.

Diet is an important aspect in the treatment of cirrhosis. It seems that the best regime for maximum recovery is a diet high in calories from carbohydrates and proteins with moderate amounts of fats and provision of vitamins. This allows for the repair of hepatic cells and supports hepatic function. Vitamin supplements and liver extract are often recommended. Protein should be rich in lipotrophic factors, which mobilize liver fat and thus act to prevent fatty infiltration and degeneration of the liver cells. Since the appetite is often poor, six to eight small meals a day would be most effective.

Viral hepatitis is an infectious disease of the liver that is becoming more common in older people, although it is still primarily a disease of the young. In the young it is usually rather mild, but in the elderly it can be quite serious, resulting in a progressive liver disease such as cirrhosis. Complete bed rest is mandatory with an accompanying diet high in carbohydrates and protein supplemented with B complex vitamins (Brewer's yeast) and vitamin K. Fat need not be restricted, as once thought, but alcohol is totally forbidden. Serum hepatitis is similar in causes and symptoms but is transferred by injection from a carrier to a victim. It is a more serious condition, although treatment is basically the same, with some persons requiring hospitalization. The elderly may contract it through transfusions and the use of poorly sterilized medical equipment and needles for drugs. It is more common in older men who take drugs or sell their blood for an alcohol stake.

PANCREAS

The pancreas is an important component of both the gastrointestinal and endocrine systems. Under both hormonal and neurologic control, it is thus subject to the effects of age changes in those systems. The specific changes in the pancreas are both enzymatic and structural. The organ pancreas exhibits an age-related reduction of the pancreatic proteolytic enzyme activity from age 40 onward. Trypsin is one of the most important proteolytic enzymes; it splits the larger protein molecules (polypeptides) into smaller ones (peptides), which the intestinal enzymes reduce further. Without trypsin, protein digestion could be seriously impaired, although the evidence for impairment is conflicting. Bartos and Groh (1969) stimulated the pancreas by single doses of *pancreozymins* and secretin and induced similar volumes of pancreatic juice in subjects of various ages. They also observed that with repeated stimulation, the volume of pancreatic juices decreases with increasing age.

Structurally, the major changes in the pancreas are reduced alveolar cell generation, *adipose* and *amyloid infiltration* and the obstruction of the pancreatic ducts. These conditions are major causes of pancreatitis.

The symptoms of pancreatic disease, except for acute pancreatitis, are vague. Pain is the most common symptom, although, Rittenbury (1961) observed that 12 percent of his patients over 60 did not exhibit pain. Acute pancreatitis can be confused with gallstones or other diseases of the hepatobiliary tract. Nausea and vomiting are usually associated with acute pancreatitis rather than with carcinoma. Loss of appetite, weight loss, general weakness, and epigastric pain radiating into the back and abdomen as well as tenderness and rigidity of the abdomen are usual symptoms of acute pancreatitis. Acute pancreatitis presents a picture of a critically ill patient who may be unconscious, hallucinating, severely disoriented and in a state of severe pain. Immediate hospitalization and application of intensive care are required.

Chronic pancreatitis is associated with loss of appetite, loss of weight, general weakness, jaundice and constipation, but less diarrhea than one finds in younger age groups. It can usually be managed at home with the use of anticholinergics and dietary restrictions.

Patients may experience persistent pain that requires consideration and understanding.

Carcinoma of the pancreas is a rare malignancy in those over 60, although more common in men. It is, however, increasing steadily and has become the fourth most common death-causing cancer in the United States. The sixth decade is the period of peak incidence while the male-female ratio is 3:1. It is very difficult to diagnose early and is often confused with peptic ulcer, chronic pancreatitis or liver disease. In 60 percent of the cases, it involves the head of the pancreas; it most often metastasizes to the liver, lungs, and bones. The general symptoms— loss of appetite, wasting weakness and weight loss—are similar to those of chronic pancreatitis, but with carcinoma there is epigastric pain that radiates to the back and is relieved by bending forward. Indigestion characterized by belching, heartburn and nausea are common, along with constipation and diarrhea. Persistent painless development of obstructive jaundice usually is indicative of carcinoma.

Blood may be present in the stools, but anemia is rare. Diabetics have a higher incidence of pancreatic carcinoma, and in possibly a third of the cases it can result in diabetes because of the destruction of the *islets of Langerhans*. Diagnosis may involve utilizing radioactive protoscan, pancreatic angiography, and serologic analysis of serum lipase, *amylase* and alkaline phosphatase levels.

Emotional disturbances in the form of depression occur in about three-fourths of the cases. Psychiatric and general supportive assistance are often necessary. Treatment is merely palliative to relieve pain and discomfort. The effectiveness of both surgery and chemotherapy is poor, and the prognosis is very poor.

LARGE INTESTINE

The picture of clinical problems in the large bowel is almost exclusive to the elderly. It also presents a complex of possibly interrelated syndromes that are amenable to preventive medicine.

Little attention has been paid to age-related anatomic and physiologic changes in the large bowel. The anatomic changes that may be of significance are atrophy of the mucosa and of the connective tissue, morphologic abnormalities in cell structure and arteriosclerosis, which generally affects the celiac axis and *mesenteric* vessels. Physiologically, the large bowel is not a digestive organ but a storage organ for waste and a major site for water absorption.

Because of its transitory storage function, large bowel motility is important and has been the subject of much research. Studies have attempted to measure motility by the use of balloons and open-ended tubes inserted into the rectum, but measuring pressure is difficult since the colon itself is an open-ended tube. Also, the contraction and inflation of the lower bowel presents a different picture of intrabowel pressure.

Measuring colonic activity is also problematic because colonic motility is unpredictable and shows significant variation over time within the individual. Motility increases during and after food intake, although this is not usually associated with propulsive activity unless the person is physically active (Holdstock 1970). Diarrhea and some drugs can cause hypermotility; other drugs, such as morphine, can lead to hypomotility.

Duthie and Bennett (1963) investigated sensation in the anal canal and noted a mechanism for recognizing the bolus contained in the rectum by sphincter sensation. This produces the ability to distinguish between feces, fluid and gas within the rectum, and it is possible that incontinent older people may have an impaired mechanism.

Some research has noted that bearing down and attempted forced defecation can diminish the tone of the external sphincter. In straining, too, the anterior rectal wall tends to descend following the stool, and it is possible that this can lead to prolapse in the elderly patient with a weak pelvic floor.

Many elderly people worry about constipation, but there is no evidence that it is an inevitable outcome of aging. These worries are often symptomatic of a lack of other interests. Concern about constipation may also be a holdover from an era of medicine when irregularity was thought to carry the risk of autointoxication. Many of the elderly today were raised during a time when a daily bowel movement was considered to be essential for good health. Perhaps this fixation on regularity will disappear as the younger generation becomes older, although the pharmaceutical and advertising industries keep the myth alive today. Of those elderly who claim to be constipated, 25 percent have normal transit time (Eastwood, 1972).

Careful evaluation of constipation in the elderly is important, since it is a possible symptom of underlying disease. The various causes of constipation are as follows:

1. Lesions of the gut (obstruction, idiopathic megacolon, and aganglionosis)
2. Neurologic trauma or damage
3. Metabolic causes (hypercalcemia, *porphyria* and drugs such as laxatives)

4. Endocrine system *(hypothyroidism)*
5. Psychological causes (depression and stress)
6. General immobility

Lack of exercise or unbalanced diets lacking bulk may also be implicated in cases of constipation.

In treating constipation an individual approach is most efficient. After the possibility of disease or obstruction has been ruled out, a therapeutic regimen consisting of dietary modification and increased physical activity should be worked out. Laxative dependence may be difficult to eliminate, but an intermediate compromise may be generated. Dietary changes are difficult to implement, since longstanding food habits often hold great emotional significance. Changes in physical activity may be impossible in many cases.

If fecal impactions form, manual removal may be necessary. Enemas may work, but care must be taken to avoid large volume, since sudden distension of the colon could rupture it or an existent diverticula. There is also the possibility of inducing shock in an elderly person.

Fecal incontinence is another serious problem in some older persons. It is not a threat to survival but rather to self-image. An alert person can be thoroughly embarrassed and very depressed by the onset of this condition, which rivals urinary incontinence as one of the major problems in the care of the elderly. Fecal incontinence is less frequent than its urinary counterpart and more readily managed, but it is far more unpleasant for patients, medical staff and family. Studies in England point out that fecal incontinence is a major problem in long-term-care patients. Watkins (1971), for instance, found an incidence of 60 percent in his study of geriatric wards, and Brocklehurst (1951) found 75 percent incontinent in a Glasgow long-term care facility.

The causes of fecal incontinence are diverse and include carcinoma of the colon or rectum, diverticular disease, ischemic colitis, protocolitis, diabetic neuropathy and the side effects of drug usage. It may also result from hemorrhoidal surgery, which disrupts the anal sphincter. Fecal impaction can be associated with a spurious diarrhea that can be carried around the impacted area. A variety of studies also point to a neurogenic basis for some cases of fecal incontinence in older persons.

Most fecal incontinence is preventable. The basic approach toward prevention involves treating the local causes of fecal impaction by treating the constipation. Treatment of neurogenic-based incontinence involves habit training similar to the potty training of a child. The induction of constipation followed by planned evacuation can make the process predictable and manageable, especially in an institutional setting. For management in the home, an enema followed by a bisacodyl suppository left in the rectum should complete the process within an hour and a half. By these means, the elderly person may be spared any embarrassment.

Carcinoma of the large bowel is the most common malignancy in those over 70 and second only to lung cancer as a killer among the cancers (McKeown 1965). Late diagnosis remains a distressing problem despite the fact that more than half the carcinomas are within range of the examining finger and about three-fourths are within range of the proctoscope. Five-year survival rates for early presymptomatic cases are 50 percent or higher, and the mortality rates associated with the surgery are low.

Cancer of the colon is more common in women, whereas rectal cancer is more common in men. The percentage involvement by site in the large bowel is shown in Table 9.2. The signs and symptoms vary with the section of the bowel affected. Any sign of change in bowel habits along with loss of appetite, weakness, weight loss and anemia should be thoroughly investigated. Sometimes colon cancer can be confused with fecal impaction of the rectosigmoid presenting a hard mass, although a carcinoma is usually fixed (Figure 9.4). Treatment generally involves resection of the bowel, and it has the best prognosis of all gastrointestinal carcinomas.

Benign polyps of the bowel, familial polyposis coli and ulcerative colitis are associated in half the cases and are thought to be possible precursors (Morson, 1971). Cancer of this region is geographically most closely related to economic development, with traditional or underdeveloped communities exhibiting very low incidence levels. Burkitt (1971) and others have proposed that the high incidence of colon cancer in the West is caused by a low-residue, highly refined diet that results in slower transit time of food through the tract. Presumably, intestinal carcinogens have prolonged contact with the

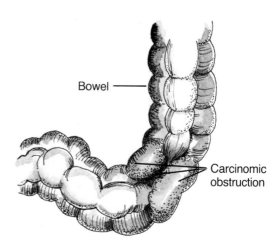

Figure 9.4   Carcinomic obstruction of the bowel.

bowel wall and a greater chance of inducing cancer.

Hemorrhoids are present in most people over 50 years of age. They consist of ruptured blood vessels that are located around the anal sphincter (Figure 9.5). They can be either external or internal, and they can be asymptomatic or very painful with bleeding that necessitates surgery. Some of the major causes in the elderly are constipation, prolonged use of cathartics or enemas, and straining at the stool. Dietary treatment can promote healing and make a bowel movement comfortable. In general, eight to ten glasses of water a day and a diet that is balanced but bulk producing can reduce or prevent hemorrhoids. One should also avoid the use of harsh laxatives and try to regularize the time of bowel movement each day. The increased incidence of hemorrhoids in the Western world has also been related to a low-fiber diet.

Polyps and benign tumors of the colon are often common in the rectosigmoid area. They can produce bleeding but probably do

TABLE 9.2   Differential occurrence of bowel cancer[a,b]

Rectum	55%
Sigmoid colon	16% to 20%
Right colon	15%
Left colon	10%
Transverse colon	5%

[a]Based on information in Rossman, I., ed., 1986. *Clinical Geriatrics.* Philadelphia: J.B. Lippincott Co.
[b]Categories are not mutually exclusive.

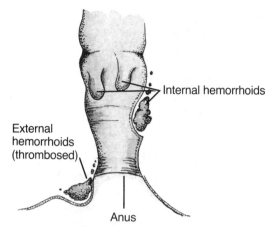

Figure 9.5 Internal and external hemorrhoids.

not cause cancer and are generally treated by simple excision. Familial *adenomatous coli polyps* have a high association with cancer and are treated by a complete colostomy. It is a hereditary disorder, and thus it would be wise to screen an afflicted person's relatives for the condition. Ulcerative colitis also has some pseudopolyps, which have a very high carcinogenic potential. Ulcerative colitis exhibits a second peak in those over 60. It makes a more rapid appearance with less systemic involvement and smaller relapse rate in the elderly.

Ischemic colitis is rarely diagnosed in the elderly. It is usually the result of an occlusion of the mesenteric arteries because of arteriosclerosis, most often at the splenic flexure, which is the most critical point in the circulation of blood to the bowel. The most common symptoms are abdominal pain and loose stools with red blood or clots. The onset can be sudden and accompanied by intramural gas in the bowel, the result of a bacterial invasion of the bowel wall. Congestive heart failure seems to be an important

precipitating factor. Any fear of eating in the elderly should merit consideration of this disorder. Treatment may involve surgical removal of the bowel, especially if stricture is present. The prognosis is poor after surgery, but most cases are transitory.

Diverticular disease of the colon tends to be a disease of the later decades of life, increasing from age 40 onward. By one estimate, it occurs in 18 percent of those aged 40 to 59, 19 percent of those 60 to 79 and 42 percent of those over 80 years of age (Minaker and Rowe, 1982). It appears to be increasing in incidence, especially in industrial nations. Women are affected more often than men, and the overall number of diverticula increase with age. The most common site is the sigmoid colon. McKeown (1965) found the incidence with symptoms to be about 7 percent in those over 70, but symptoms can range from none at all to *peritonitis*.

Diverticula are actually tiny herniations of the mucous and submucous layers through the muscle layer. They form a pocket or balloon-like structure that projects from the bowel about 1 to 2 cm. Fecal matter can collect at the opening of a diverticulum and form fecoliths; these ulcerate the mucosa and promote infection. The symptoms of diverticulitis are abdominal pain, diarrhea, constipation or alternating bouts of each, and bleeding. Complications are rare, but on occasion they can perforate and give rise to pericolic abscess, peritonitis, or *fistula* of the bladder, vagina or other parts of the gut. These conditions call for immediate surgery.

In general, medical management consists of a high-residue diet and antibiotic therapy. The use of a high-residue diet is a complete therapeutic turnabout from the previous treatment, which called for a bland, low-residue diet. Painter and Burkitt (1971) showed that adding bran to the diet as a fiber supplement gave good results in treating diverticular disease.

In 1900 diverticular disease was practically unknown in the Western world. In the past 75 years it has become the most common affliction of the colon. It may affect more than a third of the population over the age of 50 in industrial countries, but it is unknown or rare in most developing countries. Burkitt (1971) has proposed that diverticular disease, along with gallstones, hiatus hernia, adenomatous polyps of the large bowel, varicose veins, appendicitis, carcinoma of the large bowel, ischemic heart disease and even obesity can be associated with a highly refined diet that is low in dietary fiber.

Indigenous African populations eating higher-fiber diets have a rapid transit time for food passage through the gastrointestinal tract and large, soft stools. In industrial societies this is not so; transit times are three to seven days, compared to a little over 30 hours in Africa, and stool weight averages 100 grams a day as compared to 300 grams in Africans. Burkitt believes that viscid feces are more difficult to propel, thus raising the pressure within the lumen of the intestine, forcing the pouches of the intestine out through weak spots in the muscle layer to form diverticula. At this point the weight of the evidence supports the Burkitt hypothesis, but fiber diets are not a miracle cure-all. It is most likely that diet is but *one* of a complex of factors involved in the causes of the disorders cited by Burkitt.

OVER-THE-COUNTER PREPARATIONS FOR GASTROINTESTINAL RELIEF

Since gastrointestinal disturbances are of great concern to many people, over-the-counter remedies are very popular. The remedies most often purchased generally deal with indigestion, constipation, diarrhea and hemorrhoids. Some of these remedies are simply a waste of money, but the use or misuse of many of them can lead to serious health problems.

Antacids

Antacids, used to treat indigestion, are varied in composition and side effects. Sodium bicarbonate is a basic element in such products as Alka-Seltzer, Bromo-Seltzer, Brioschi, Eno and Fizrin. Sodium bicarbonate is a patent antacid but the least desirable for regular use. The major problems associated with sodium bicarbonate use are alkalinization of the body fluids, which can lead to kidney stone formation, and recurrent urinary infections. Sodium bicarbonate use can also result in diminished kidney function and be harmful to those with hypertension or congestive heart failure.

Any antacid that has more than 115 mg of sodium per maximum daily dose is unsuitable for those on a low-sodium diet. Since many people have undetected kidney and heart disease, they must consider the sodium content of any antacid. Kidney and heart disease tend to increase with age. No one over 60 should take more than 2300 mg of sodium antacid tablets a day. For example, a heart patient on a 1000 to 2000 mg sodium diet could upset the dietary balance with a single dose of many of the sodium bicarbonate antacids. A single dose of Alka-Seltzer contains 1040 mg of sodium, and a single dose of Bromo-Seltzer contains more than 1496 mg. Each can add significantly to a person's sodium intake if used regularly.

Alka-Seltzer also contains aspirin, which is a stomach irritant and problematic for an ulcer patient. Bromo-Seltzer contains phenacetin and caffeine. The former has been implicated in kidney disease, and the latter stimulates acid secretion in the stomach; both ingredients are unnecessary in antacids. Fizrin contains sodium carbonate, which is obsolete as an antacid and is a highly alkaline irritant that is also possibly corrosive. Brioschi and Eno contain only sodium bicarbonate.

Another major group of antacids contains calcium carbonate as its major ingredient. Calcium carbonate is rapid-acting and has a high neutralizing capacity. Tums and Pepto Bismol tablets are the major brands of this type. Calcium carbonate antacids cause constipation and raise calcium levels to an undesirable state, which can lead to impaired kidney function and possibly kidney stones. It is recommended that the maximum dosage be 8 gm per day for a maximum duration of two weeks. Tums at .5 g per tablet could accomplish this with 16 tablets, and there are indications that some people approach this level of use. Calcium carbonates cause acid rebound, and as little as .5 g can increase gastric acid production; thus the remedy may be self-defeating.

Pepto Bismol tablets contain calcium carbonate plus glycocoll, whereas Pepto Bismol liquid contains no antacids, only bismuth subsalicylate. It can lead to blackened stools, which could possibly mask gastrointestinal symptoms of pathologic conditions.

Two of the safest antacids are aluminum hydroxide and magnesium hydroxide. Aluminum hydroxide has no dosage limits; it is slow in its action but generally gives prolonged relief. Some have suggested that it decreases phosphate absorption, thus helping kidney patients with high phosphate levels. Its major side effect is severe constipation. Amphogel is a well-known antacid of this type. Rolaids combines aluminum hydroxide with sodium bicarbonate, but the 53 mg per tablet of sodium is high for those on low-sodium diets.

Magnesium hydroxide is good except for those with chronic kidney disorders. Those with kidney problems should take no more than three teaspoons or four tablets a day. Milk of magnesia is an example of this type; it is effective and safe but has a laxative effect.

An alternative approach has been to combine the aluminum and magnesium compounds into one type. This allows the constipating and laxative tendencies to cancel each other out, thus eliminating any side effects. Maalox and Digel use aluminum and magnesium hydroxide, but Digel also contains simethicone, which is an unproved gas-control agent. Gelusel contains aluminum hydroxide and another magnesium compound, magnesium trisilicate. Magnesium hydroxide is faster acting and somewhat more effective than the trisilicate. Some remedies such as Mucotin and Magnatril contain all three compounds.

Constipation Remedies

Constipation remedies are also an important consideration, since the elderly purchase them in attempts to achieve regularity. It is estimated that 40 to 60 percent of the elderly use laxatives regularly. Advertising techniques tend to heavily exploit the elderly population with strong emotional pitches that are often family or nostalgia oriented. More than 700 over-the-counter constipation remedies exist; this is strong testimony to their marketability. Despite the advertising and testimonials, none are perfect or harmless. Laxatives are no different from cathartics—simply milder. There is a general belief among gastroenterologists that regular use of cathartics does more harm than good. Actually, they can be the cause rather than the cure of constipation in many cases. Laxatives can also decrease absorption of certain vitamins and possibly upset the body's electrolyte balances.

Diarrhea is another common occurrence in the elderly. It is generally self-limiting but can be a symptom of serious pathologic conditions. Most over-the-counter antidiarrheal agents are mixtures of kaolin and *pectin*, and their efficacy is questionable. Some prescription antidiarrheal drugs containing codeine, opium and paregoric are very effective and not habit-forming in the quantities prescribed.

Hemorrhoidal Remedies

Hemorrhoids are often the result of straining associated with constipation. Many preparations exist that purport to relieve pain and itching, shrink swollen tissues and promote healing. There is much evidence that most of these products do not accomplish what they advertise. Hemorrhoid preparations come as suppositories or topical ointments. The suppositories usually contain mixtures of bismuth salts, topical anesthetics such as Benzocaine, vasoconstrictors such as ephedrine, and antiseptics. Ointments contain the same substances and might be more useful, since contact with the affected area is direct. The suppositories often move up the rectum after insertion, away from the problem area. More effective in treating hemorrhoid problems than any combination of pharmaceuticals, would be hot sitz baths for 15 minutes three or four times a day and a dietary changes to produce a softer, bulkier stool. The real dangers in using these self-treatment preparations is the delay in having the symptoms checked by a physician for links with more serious conditions. Rectal problems of this sort can be associated with serious gastrointestinal disease higher in the tract or with minor bacterial or fungus infections around the anal opening.

Mouthwashes

Mouthwashes used in an effort to counteract bad breath may also be used quite often by the socially conscious older person. Most mouth odors do not originate in the mouth but further down the gastrointestinal tract, and there is no evidence that mouthwashes do anything to eliminate such odors. At most, the effect is temporary or psychological because the individual perceives a fresher mouth. Mouthwashes can contribute to the drying of the mucous membranes or aggravate preexisting inflammation or infection, since most of them contain alcohol. This effect can complicate the dry mouth complaints of the elderly, which are related to mouth breathing, decreased salivation and a tendency toward dehydration.

SUMMARY

The gastrointestinal system is of much interest to the elderly. Symptoms related to this system are often a source of fear and anxiety. Age-related changes of the gastrointestinal tract can often affect nutritional intake, digestion and the absorption of nutrients. A number of major pathologic conditions in this system can threaten life as well as effective functioning. Some of the most significant pathological conditions are hiatus hernia, stomach cancer, stomach ulcers, duodenal ulcers, periodontal disease, gallstones, gastritis, cirrhosis of the liver, diverticulitis and colon cancer. Although these conditions occur at all ages, they take on special significance for the elderly when superimposed on chronic conditions and the normal changes that accompany aging.

The symptoms of many gastrointestinal disorders are often non-specific. The system is readily affected by psychosocial stress. These characteristics can make an exact diagnosis and treatment difficult. Many individuals treat gastrointestinal disorders initially by the use of over-the-counter drugs. However, this course of action sometimes produces unwanted side effects and delays the application of necessary therapy of proven efficacy.

KEY TERMS

achalasia
achlorhydria
adenomatous coli polyps
adipose
alimentation
amylase
amyloid infiltration
amyloidosis
anticholinergics
anticonvulsants
antrum
apatite
appendicitis
atrophy
attrition
cholangitis
cholecystitis
cholelithiasis
colostomy
diabetes mellitus
diverticula
duodenum
esophagitis
fibromas
fistula
gallstones
gastritis
gingivitis

gustatory
hepatitis
hepatobiliary
hypertension
hypotension
hypothyroidism
ileum
islets of Langerhans
jaundice
Leukoplakias
lipase
lipomas
lymphomas
mandible
mandibular dentures
maxillary dentures
mesenteric
multiple myeloma
multiple sclerosis
palliative
pancreatitis
pancreozymins
papillae
pectin
pepsinogen
peptic ulcer
periodontal disease
periodontitis
peritonitis
pernicious anemia
polyps
porphyria
postcentral gyrus
ptyalin
pylorus
resorption
rugae
squamous carcinoma
stasis
Streptococcus mutans
sublingual spider nevi
thalamus
trypsin
urea
ureolytic

STUDY QUESTIONS

1. What is the significance of gastrointestinal symptoms to the elderly?

2. Describe some general changes that take place in the mouth and comment on the following:
   a. Significance of sores in the mouth
   b. Loss of taste and its influence on eating patterns
   c. Changes in smell
   d. The loss of teeth and eating habits
   e. Denture problems
3. What factors interact in the production of dental caries? How does the caries experience differ for the elderly? What is the possible role of nutrition in tooth decay?
4. What is the significance of periodontal disease to the elderly? Identify the factors that lead to the development of periodontal disease.
5. What are some esophageal symptoms that are significant for the aged? Identify hiatus hernia and its importance for the elderly.
6. What are the major age-related changes in the stomach? What are the major disorders of the stomach and their significance for the elderly? Identify the two major problems of the duodenum. Compare the incidence and significance of ulcers in the stomach and duodenum.
7. Discuss the possible changes in the small intestine related to the digestion and absorption of food. What is the possible significance of change in the ecology of the bacterial flora of the intestine? What are some of the conditions that can lead to malabsorption?
8. Why is the gallbladder a major source of concern for the elderly? Identify the changes in the liver with age. What are some of the major disorders of the liver that are important for the elderly?
9. Identify some age-related changes in the pancreas. What are some of the major disorders of the pancreas?
10. How does the large bowel present a clinical picture with an almost exclusive set of problems for the elderly? Identify some of the age-related changes in the large bowel. Discuss the origins and significance of constipation in the elderly. What is the importance of fecal incontinence?
11. In what ways may cancer of the colon, hemorrhoids and diverticular disease be related to diet?

12. Discuss the problems associated with the over-the-counter use of:
    a. Antacids
    b. Constipation remedies
    c. Hemorrhoid remedies
    d. Mouthwashes

BIBLIOGRAPHY

Alfano, M.C. 1976. Controversies, perspectives, and clinical implications of nutrition in periodontal disease. *Dental Clinics of North America 20*(3): 519–548.

Arey, L.B., Tremaine, M.J., and Monzingo, F.L. 1935. The numerical and topographical relation of taste buds to human circumvallate papillae throughout the life span. *Anat. Rec. 64:* 9–25.

Balachi, J.A., and Dobbins, W.V. 1974. Maldigestion and malabsorption: Making up for lost nutrients. *Geriatrics 29:* 157–166.

Bahn, A.N. 1970. Microbial potential in the etiology of periodontal disease. *Journal of Periodontology 41:* 603–610.

Balogh, K., and Lelkes, K. 1961. The tongue in old age. *Gerontol. Clin. 3*(suppl.): 38–54.

Bartos, V., and Groh, J. 1969. The effect of repeated stimulation of the pancreas on the pancreatic secretion in young and old men. *Gerontol. Clin. 17:* 56–62.

Baum, B.J. 1981. Characteristics of participants in the oral physiology component of the Baltimore longitudinal study of aging. *Comm. Dent. Oral Epidemiol. 9:* 128–134.

Becker, G.H., Meyer, J., and Necheles, H. 1950. Fat absorption in young and old age. *Gastroenterology 14:* 80–92.

Bertolini, A.M. 1969. *Gerontologic Metabolism.* Springield, Ill.: Charles C. Thomas.

Bhaskar, S.N. 1968. Oral lesions in the aged population. *Geriatrics 28:* 137–149.

Bockus, H.L. 1966. *Gastroenterology.* Philadelphia: W.B. Saunders.

Brick, I.B., and Amory, H.I. 1950. Incidence of hiatus hernia in patients without symptoms. *Archives of Surgery 60:* 1045.

Brocklehurst, J.C. 1951. *Incontinence in Old People.* Edinburgh, U.K.: Churchill Livingstone.

Burkitt, D.M. 1971. Epidemiology of cancer of the colon and rectum. *Cancer 28:* 3.

Burkitt, D.M. 1971. Possible relationship between bowel cancer and dietary habits. *Proceedings of the Royal Society of Medicine 64:* 964.

Calloway, N.O., and Merrill, R.S. 1965. The aging adult liver. *Journal of the American Geriatric Society 13:* 594–598.

Castell, D.O. 1975. The lower esophageal sphincter: Physiologic and clinical aspects. *Annals of Internal Medicine 83:* 390–401.

Chauncey, H.H., Feldman, R.S., and Wayler, S.H. 1983. Oral aspects of aging. *American Family Physician 28:* 147–152.

De Paola, D.P., and Alfano, M.C. 1977. Diet and oral health. *Nutrition Today 12*(3): 6–11.

Douglas, C.W., Gillings, D., Sollecito, W., and Gammon, M. 1983. National trends in the prevalence and severity of periodontal diseases. *Journal of American Dental Association 107:* 403–412.

Dye, C. 1984. Age related changes in taste and smell that affect nutritional adequacy. In H.J. Armbrecht, J.M. Prendergrast, and R.M. Coe, eds., *Nutrition Interventions in the Aging Process.* New York: Springer-Verlag.

Duthie, H.L., and Bennett, R.C. 1963. The relation of sensation in the anal canal to the functional anal sphincter: A possible factor in anal incontinence. *Gut 4:* 179–182.

Eastwood, H.D.H. 1972. Bowel transit studies in the elderly. *Gerontology Clinician 14:* 154–160.

Exton-Smith, A.N., and Scott, D.L. (eds.) 1968. *Vitamins in the Elderly.* Bristol, U.K.: Wright and Sons.

Fikry, M.E., and Aboul-Wafa, M.H. 1965. Intestinal absorption in the old. *Gerontology Clinician 7:* 171–178.

Friedman, J.W. 1968. Dentistry in the geriatric patient. *Geriatrics 23:* 98–107.

Glass, R.L. 1973. Prevalence of human dental caries and waterborn trace metals. *Archives of Oral Biology 18:* 1099–1104.

Gregor, J.L., and Geissler, A.H. 1978. Effect of zinc supplementation on the taste activity of the aged. *American Journal of Clinical Nutrition 31:* 633–637.

Haberman, J.L. 1962. Liver function studies in the aged. What are normal values? *Northwestern Medicine 61:* 1038–1040.

Harris, W. 1952. Fifth and seventh cranial nerves in relation to the nervous mechanism of taste sensation: A new approach. *Butler Journal of Medicine 1:* 831–836.

Henkin, R.I., Schechter, P.J., and Raff, M.S. 1974. Zinc and taste activity. In W.J. Pories et al. eds., *Clinical Applications of Zinc Metabolism.* Springfield, Ill.: Charles C. Thomas.

Hermel, J., Schonwetter, S., and Samueloff, S. 1970. Taste sensation and age in man. *Journal of Oral Medicine 25:* 39–42.

Holdstock, D.J. 1970. Propulsion in the human colon and its relationship to meals and somatic activity. *Gut 11:* 91.

Holm-Pederson, P., Agerback, N.M., and Theilade, E. 1975. Experimental gingivitis in young and elderly individuals. *Journal of Clinical Periodontology 2:* 14–24.

Holt, P.R. 1983. Digestive disease and aging: Past neglect and future promise. *Gastroenterology 85:* 1434–1436.

Hughes, G. 1969. Changes in taste sensitivity with advancing age. *Gerontol. Clin. 11:* 224.

Hyams, D.E. 1973. The liver and biliary system. In J.C. Brocklehurst, ed., *Textbook of Geriatric Medicine and Gerontology.* Edinburgh, U.K.: Churchill Livingstone.

Kiyak, H.A. 1984. Utilization of dental services by the elderly. *Gerodontology 3:* 17–26.

Langman, M.J. 1971. Eppidemiology of cancer of esophagus and stomach. *British Journal of Surgery 58:* 792–793.

Lutwak, L. 1976. *Periodontal Disease.* In M. Winick, ed., *Nutrition and Aging.* New York: Wiley.

Mann, G.V. 1962. The health and nutrition states of Eskimos. *American Journal of Clinical Nutrition 11:* 31–76.

McGinty, M.D. 1971. Hiatal hernia. *Hospital Medicine 7:* 133–143.

McKeown, F. 1965. *Pathology of the Aged.* London: Butterworth.

Minaker, K.L., and Rowe, J.W. 1982. Gastrointestinal system. In J.W. Rowe and R.W. Besdine, eds., *Health and Disease in Old Age.* Boston: Little, Brown.

Morgan, Z., and Feldman, M. 1967. The liver, biliary tract and pancreas in the aged. *Journal of American Geriatrics 5:* 59–69.

Morson, B.C. 1971. Precancerous conditions of the large bowel. *Proceedings of the Royal Society of Medicine 64:* 959.

Moskowitz, H.R. 1975. Cross-cultural differences

in simple taste preferences. *Science 190:* 1217–1218.

Painter, N.S., and Burkitt, D.P. 1971. Diverticular disease of the colon: A deficiency disease of Western civilization. *British Journal of Medicine 2:* 450–454.

Ponka, J.L., Welborn, J.K., and Brush, B.E. 1963. Acute abdominal pain in aged patients: An analysis 200 cases. *Journal of the American Geriatric Society 11:* 993–1007.

Rittenbury, M. 1961. Pancreatitis in the elderly patient. *American Surgeon 27:* 475–495.

Rollin, H. 1973. Elektrische Geschmacksschwellen der Zunge und des weichen Gaumens. *Arch. Klin. Exp. Ohr. Nas. Kehlk. Heilk. 204:* 81–88.

Rossman, I., ed. 1986. *Clinical Geriatrics,* 3rd ed. Philadelphia: Lippincott.

Schiffman, S.S. 1983. Taste and smell in disease. Part I. *New England Journal of Medicine 308:* 1275–1279.

Shock, N.W. 1964. Intrinsic factors in aging. In J.F. Hansen, ed., *Age with a Future.* Copenhagen: Munksgaard.

Stam, J.W., and Banting, D.W. 1980. Comparison of root caries prevalence in adults with life-long residence in flouridated and non-flouridated communities. Paper presented at Annual Meeting International Association for Dental Research, Los Angeles.

Stevens, J.C., Cain, W.S., and Plantinger, A. 1982. Reduction of odor and nasal pungency associated with aging. *Neurobiology of Aging 3:* 125–132.

Tauchi, H., and Sato, T. 1968. Age change in size and number of mitochondria of human hepatic cells. *Journal of Gerontology 23:* 454–461.

Thompson, E.N., and Williams, R. 1965. Effect of age on liver function with particular reference to bromusulphalein excretion. *Gut 6:* 266–269.

Watkins, J.S. 1971. Personal communication cited in Brocklehurst, J.C. The large bowel. In J.C. Brocklehurst ed., *Textbook of Geriatric Medicine and Gerontology.* Edinburgh, U.K.: Churchill Livingstone.

CHAPTER **10**

Nutrition and Aging

Human aging is a complex process caused by a number of mechanisms that operate simultaneously. Several of the major theories of biological aging include nutritional components. In general, it appears that nutrition plays a dual role in the aging process. First, nutritional components are probably involved in the physiological and anatomical changes that cause cell destruction and limit cell regeneration. Second, diet plays an important part in the course of degenerative diseases that often accompany aging.

Diet plays a role in *protein synthesis* by supplying the nutrients necessary for normal enzyme activity and production. One theory of biological aging postulates that aging is caused by flaws in the mechanism of protein synthesis. For instance, alteration of enzymes may result in defects in one or more of the steps in protein synthesis. Such changes in process could result in the synthesis of abnormal proteins.

The immunologic theory suggests that aging is caused by the gradual breakdown in the immunological process in the body. Antibody synthesis may become defective and produce antibodies that attack the body itself. Antibodies are proteins and thus need amino acids for their synthesis; it is possible that certain dietary amounts of protein are required for normal antibody production.

Another theory proposes that molecular fragments called *free radicals* may react with *polyunsaturated fatty acids* in the cell membranes to form *peroxidation products.* These products may hinder the flow of nutrients in and out of the cell, thus enhancing cell death. Vitamin E may play a leading role in protecting the excessive *oxidation* of cellular *lipids* through inhibition of the *peroxidation reaction.* Vitamin C may also be important because it acts as a synergist in vitamin E activity and as a trap for free radicals.

The etiology of many degenerative diseases includes a nutritional component. Adequate lifelong consumption of fluorine may not only help prevent caries in the young but also may be related to a decreased risk of osteoporosis. British researchers are convinced that adequate fiber in the diet can prevent diverticulosis, large bowel cancer and a variety of other degenerative diseases. Excessive sodium intake is related to the course of congestive heart disease, hypertension, cirrhosis of the liver and retention of fluids in body tissues. Arteriosclerosis seems to be related to intake of saturated fat and cholesterol. Many researchers now believe that refined sugars may be the major culprit in heart disease, in addition to playing a role in the development of dental caries and diabetes mellitus.

Little has been done in the past to research the use of proper nutrition and diet supplementation to ward off the effects of the aging process. Despite the examples cited above, nutritional components in the diseases of the elderly have only recently begun to be studied. Unfortunately, many elderly persons have become converts to expensive food fads at the same time that the scientific community has been underactive in the field of geriatric nutrition. In the face of inaction by nutritional scientists, food faddists give the elderly some hope in their battle against advancing age.

In this chapter, we describe the basic nutritional requirements of the elderly. Chapter 11 includes discussion of the social and cultural aspects of geriatric nutrition.

NUTRITIONAL NEEDS OF THE ELDERLY

There is no evidence that requirements for nutrients decrease with age. Suggested decreases in food quantity relative to metabolic changes and decreased activity mean that the nutritional quality of the food must be higher than at earlier ages. Recommended dietary allowances for the aged should not be followed rigidly but should be used as a guide in planning individual diets. Placing people into broad categories is always dangerous—it ignores *biochemical individuality.* This concept is most relevant for the elderly, since so many have one or more chronic disorders that interact with their nutritional status.

Nutrients are chemical constituents of food that are necessary for proper body functioning, supplying us with energy, aiding in the growth and repair of body tissues and helping in the regulation of body processes. Some nutrients perform all three functions.

Presently, there are six major accepted categories of nutrients: carbohydrates, fats, proteins, vitamins, minerals and water. Although all types of dietary fiber (except lignin) are recognized as carbohydrates, fiber is not yet recognized as an essential nutrient. However, fiber should not be ignored in a consideration of the food constituents essential to proper body functioning. This nondigestible portion of plant food adds bulk to the diet and is important in maintaining intestinal motility. Some epidemiological data indicate that it may be an important variable in the prevention of such disorders as colon cancer and cardiovascular disease.

Although these categories of nutrients are well recognized, the specific amounts of each nutrient needed for optimal functioning is a matter of much controversy. Scientists are debating how much of a particular nutrient is needed on a daily basis to assure the body's efficient performance. Part of the reason for confusion in this area may be because the field of nutritional science is relatively young. Nutrition did not become officially identified as a separate discipline of study until the founding of the American Institute of Nutrition in 1934. Atwater, Rose, Lusk, McCallum and others pioneered the study of nutritional science, especially in the area of energy balance and vitamin deficiency. Since then, much more has been learned about animal nutrition than human nutrition, as research priorities have focused on such issues as the cost-benefit concerns of raising livestock for a profit. However, our knowledge is increasing and, we hope, will continue to do so as more research on human nutrition is undertaken.

Dietary Standards

Two kinds of "standards" are involved in a consideration of the nutritional requirements of the elderly (and everyone else, for that matter). Intake at levels of *minimal requirements* of certain nutrients prevents the development of overt symptoms of nutritional deficiency disease. *Optimal requirement* intake provides nutrients at levels that should assure the maintenance of optimal health in most individuals. Nutritional scientists generally agree on the minimal requirements, but the optimal requirements sometimes are subject to controversy. Much of this contro-

versy surrounds the concept of *Recommended Dietary Allowances* (RDAs), which originated from human population surveys used to determine health status in relation to nutrient intake, controlled human-feeding experiments and animal studies on metabolism. The RDAs, as shown in Table 10.1, do not represent minimal or optimal requirements but are intended as reference points for planning diets for all groups of people to provide the greatest health benefits. The RDAs are continually being researched, and revisions are made approximately every five years.

Previously, it was believed that the nutritional requirements of the elderly were quite similar to those of other age groups. New data have helped change this belief. For example, it is now clear that the progressive physical changes associated with aging are capable of affecting nutritional requirements. Changes in digestive functions, enzyme-producing organs, intestinal mucosa and kidney functioning influence the speed and efficiency with which food is digested, nutrients are absorbed, and the residual matter excreted (Brocklehurst, 1979). Age-related changes in blood vessels influence their ability to nourish body tissues at the levels they once did. Diseases associated with age may also directly or indirectly modify nutrient needs. More research is needed in this area to achieve a better understanding of how the progress of different diseases interacts with age-related changes to modify nutrient needs. It is already known that in many instances drugs used to treat disease can also affect nutritional status. However, all of these factors exhibit a great deal of variability in individuals of particular ages.

Social factors associated with aging may also affect the nutritional requirements of

TABLE 10.1 Recommended dietary allowances (RDAs) 1980, for individuals aged 51–75

	Males	Females
Fat-soluble vitamins		
A	1,000 μg R.E.[1]	800 μg R.E.[1]
D Cholecalciferal	5 μg	5 μg
E	10 T.E.[2]	8 T.E.[2]
K	70–140 μg	70–140 μg
Water-soluble vitamins		
C	60 mg	60 mg
Thiamin	1.2 mg	1.0 mg
Riboflavin	1.4 mg	1.2 mg
Niacin	16 mg	13 mg
B6	2.2 mg	2.0 mg
Folic Acid	400 μg	400 μg
B12	3.0 μg	3.0 μg
Pantothenic Acid	4–7 mg	4–7 mg
Biotin	100–200 μg	100–200 μg
Energy		
Age 51–75	2400[3] Calories	1800[4] Calories
Over 75	2050[3] Calories	1600[4] Calories
Protein	56 grams	44 grams

[1]R.E. = Retino Equivalents
[2]T.E. = Tocopherol Equivalents
[3]For men average height 70 inches, 154 pounds
[4]For women average height 64 inches, 120 pounds
Source: National Research Council, Food and Nutrition Board, 1980.
Recommended Dietary Allowances, Revised 1980. (Washington, D.C.: National Research Council, National Academy of Sciences).

older people. For example, older people may be more vulnerable to protein deficiency as sociocultural and physical stresses contribute to the excretion of nitrogen, an important constituent of protein. This deficiency may be exacerbated by low consumption of protein and the presence of absorption problems.

As we have already seen, assessing nutritional adequacy in the elderly is not simple. Yet it is an essential stage in formulating sound ideas on the possibility of variable nutritional needs of the elderly. The major assessment problems for clinicians, planners and researchers may be characterized as follows:

1. Many of the changes associated with the aging process often overlap or imitate the signs of a nutritional deficiency. For example, vascular "spiders" under the tongue are often noted as a sign of vitamin C deficiency. In most cases, however, they are simply a sign of the increased capillary fragility associated with aging.

2. Some nutrient deficiencies have nonspecific symptoms, and some of these may be due to deficiencies of one or more nutrients.

3. Chronic disease or other disorders may alter the nutritional requirements for an affected individual.

4. Diseases with a related nutritional component (such as osteoporosis or periodontal disease) may be associated with a poor dietary history. What we eat throughout life influences our nutritional status in later years.

5. The use of vitamin supplements is believed to be widespread among the elderly. Such use might not be accounted for in surveys of dietary adequacy. Vitamin supplementation may possibly upset dynamic balances among nutrients, thus altering the "normal" requirements of a given nutrient or nutrients.

6. The impact of age is variable among individuals—each individual is a unique sum of life experiences, diseases, and the aging process. However, most changes are more marked and possibly more uniform after age 75, although the aged are far more heterogeneous as a group than are other population groups.

National surveys carried out in the last 20 years indicate that a substantial proportion of the U.S. aged population is nutritionally vulnerable. Many elderly people have diets that are insufficient in calories and deficient in the nutrients necessary to maintain physical health and well-being. The low-income aged and those who are sick or disabled would seem to be particularly vulnerable. Although these surveys generally exclude the institutionalized and do not evaluate the general health status of respondents, it is well known that disease significantly undermines adequate nutritional status. The national surveys also show that many aged have diets that are wholly inappropriate for complementing therapeutic regimens to manage acute or chronic diseases. Data from a wide array of local and regional studies (see Kart and Metress, 1984, for a review of some of these

studies) further emphasize the complexity of factors that may interact to affect the food intake and nutritional status of the aged. These include socioeconomic considerations such as income and education, gender, living arrangements and the availability of meal programs to supplement dietary intake.

Recognizing the nutritional vulnerability of the aged requires understanding the nutritional needs of older people. What are these nutritional needs?

Calories

Most nutritionists agree that there is a strong case for recommending a reduced intake of calories for the elderly. Calories represent measures of food energy and are derived from three nutrients: carbohydrates, fats and protein. In general, the energy needs of the elderly decline due to a reduction of activity and a slowing of the *basal metabolism rate* (BMR), although the former may decline more drastically than the latter. The BMR refers to the amount of energy that the lean body mass needs to carry out its basic functions. With age, there is a decline in the ratio of lean body mass to fat. This results in a lower BMR, since the metabolic needs of fat tissue are less than those of lean. Even for those who exercise regularly, fewer Calories need to be consumed.

According to the National Research Council (1980), the rate of reduction of caloric needs varies by individual but may approximate 5 percent per decade between ages 55 and 75 and seven percent per decade after the age of 75. The amount of reduction in energy needs also varies with an individual's size and level of physical activity. Disease and disability complicate the situation in two ways. They can contribute to inactivity and decreased energy needs, or they can lead to increased energy demands for the performance of certain tasks, because of various kinds of increased stress and strain.

Reduced activity itself may be related to changes in motivational state, social conditions (e.g., the advent of retirement) or the presence of chronic disease. Activity is valuable for the health and well-being of the elderly individual for a variety of reasons, including the following:

1. It requires energy expenditure, thus helping to maintain an energy balance and aiding in the avoidance of obesity.
2. It leads to greater activity and increases work capacity, both of which lead to greater consumption of Calories. Failure to consume adequate Calories can contribute to fatigue and lassitude.
3. It prevents or slows the *atrophy* associated with chronic disease and inactivity by maintaining good muscle tone.
4. It lowers blood-sugar levels, often improving glucose tolerance and lowering insulin-dosage level in diabetics.
5. It is stimulating and may serve to lift an individual's spirits.

Although caloric needs are reduced in later life, the need for specific nutrients does not decrease. Quantitative and qualitative variety must be included in the diet in order to provide the necessary amounts of all essential nutrients. However, it must be emphasized that adequate Calorie consumption is necessary to allow for a sufficient intake of the essential nutrients.

Carbohydrate Needs

Carbohydrates constitute a major portion of most diets. Over the years, they have developed an undeserved reputation as the cause of weight gain. Certainly this energy-yielding nutrient can contribute to excess weight if included in a dietary plan that totals too many Calories. For instance, many of the so-called snack and junk foods are high in Calories, refined carbohydrates and fats, and low in other nutrients. However, cookies, crackers, pastries and doughnuts are not the only foods in the carbohydrate category, which also includes the complex carbohydrates found in fruits, vegetables, cereals and breads. These foods are also rich in protective nutrients such as vitamins and minerals. Carbohydrates are the main sources of dietary fiber. It is recommended that the majority of Calories consumed consist of complex carbohydrates in the form of the above-mentioned foods. Foods high in refined sugars, although a source of pleasure to many, should be eaten in moderation; this avoids unnecessary increments in energy intake. Such advice regarding carbohydrate consumption applies to persons in all age categories.

Protein Needs

Apparently protein needs are similar for both the young and the old. However, important physical and social factors must be considered for older adults that may increase the likelihood of marginal protein status. Poor chewing ability and the expense of protein-rich foods may limit protein intake. The substitution of dairy products or eggs for harder-to-chew meats may pose other difficulties. These products are expensive, and milk may not be tolerated due to a lactase deficiency or merely because the adult has not included it in a regular diet since youth. Transporting heavy cartons of milk may also be difficult, especially for the socially isolated individual who has no assistance in shopping.

Some adults may be advised by a physician to curtail the intake of red meat and unskimmed dairy products because of their high cholesterol and saturated fat content. Fish, poultry and combinations of plant foods can supply the necessary protein in the diet. Animal products are known as complete proteins, which means that they supply all of the eight essential amino acids, or building blocks, for protein. In general, plant foods contain smaller amounts of proteins and, in most cases, are lower in one or more of the essential amino acids. Proteins without the proper balance of essential amino acids are known as incomplete proteins. A better protein balance can be obtained by combining plant foods. For example, casseroles containing beans and rice are complete in amino acids and are an easy-to-chew, less-expensive "steak substitute."

It has been noted that increased stress leads to higher rates of nitrogen excretion, which may result in a negative nitrogen balance (Young et al., 1976; Young, 1978). The elderly are potentially subject to multiple stress factors, including role changes, increased risk of illness, and multiple disease states, thus "normal" protein intake may be insufficient for optimal health. Age-induced changes in the digestive system may lead to decreased ability to absorb nutrients, affecting protein balance. Evidence is presently inconclusive to support the contention that the elderly have increased needs for the amino acids lysine and methionine (Young et al., 1976).

It has also been suggested that protein needs may be reduced in old age. Such suggestions are related to observations that body protein mass declines with age (Forbes and Reina, 1970) and that the rate of protein synthesis decreases (Winterer, Steffer, Per-

era, Uauy, Scrimshaw and Young, 1976). Declining renal function may also make it difficult to handle high concentrations of protein waste.

Fat Needs

Age does not alter an individual's need for fat. Fats should be limited to less than 25–30 percent of total Caloric intake at all ages. Reducing fat consumption is an easy way to reduce the total intake of calories. Although the data are conflicting, the relation of fat consumption to cardiovascular disease must be considered in dietary planning even though there is no conclusive evidence to indicate that modifying fat intake in older persons will lessen the risk of heart attack or stroke.

Restricting fat intake too drastically may interfere with absorption of fat-soluble vitamins. Besides serving as carriers of certain vitamins and linolec acid, an essential fatty acid, fats are important in the diet for flavor and satiety. A completely fat-free diet would be monotonous, tasteless and counter-productive to good eating habits. Furthermore, we must consider that fat absorption often decreases as one ages, and that absorption time is consequently lengthened. This situation involves several factors, including a decreased production of pancreatic lipase (a fat-splitting enzyme), gallbladder and liver disorders that decrease fat *emulsification,* and structural changes in the intestinal mucosa that interfere with fat absorption.

Vitamin Needs

Nutrition-conscious people seem to be showing particular attentiveness to vitamin intake. Table 10.2 describes the many dietary sources of essential vitamins. Many people, unsure of the status of their vitamin intake,

TABLE 10.2 Major dietary sources of essential vitamins

Fat-soluble vitamins	Foods
A	Milk, butter, cheese, liver, and fortified margarine (retinol)
	Green and yellow vegetables and fruits (carotene)
D	Cod liver oil, fortified milk and margarine, liver, fatty fish, eggs
E	Seeds; nuts; green, leafy vegetables; corn oil margarines; oils such as corn, safflower
K	Green, leafy vegetables; liver

Water-soluble vitamins	Foods
Thiamin	Pork, organ meats, whole grains, legumes
Riboflavin	Milk, eggs, cheese, meats, green vegetables, legumes
Niacin	Liver, lean meats, whole grains, legumes
B6	Whole grains, meat, vegetables, bananas, legumes
Pantothenic Acid	Organ meats, eggs, legumes, whole grains
Folacin	Legumes, whole wheat, green vegetables
B12*	Organ meats, muscle meats, eggs, shellfish, liver, dairy products
C	Citrus fruit; tomatoes; green peppers; cabbage; potatoes; other fruit (melon, strawberries); other dark green, leafy vegetables

*No known plant source

seek insurance, or "super-effects," by turning to the use of vitamin supplements. The elderly are no exception. Although some evidence of vitamin deficiencies among the aged exists, there seems to be little justification for wholesale vitamin supplementation by older people. However, it might be useful to supplement "at risk" groups such as elderly men living alone, those with physical disorders or sensory impairment and those suffering from depression, including the recently bereaved.

Vitamin supplementation is not without problems. Vitamin absorption or storage may be affected by organs that are no longer functioning optimally due to age-related changes in organ structure and function. A field study by Baker and his colleagues (1980) demonstrated that because of vitamin malabsorption in the elderly, intramuscular vitamin injections may be necessary to maintain adequate blood levels of certain vitamins. A few vitamins pose the threat of toxic effects in those engaged in overzealous consumption.

Furthermore, vitamin supplementation can disturb the dynamic interrelationships among certain nutrients. With these points in mind, let us examine specific vitamin needs of later years.

Fat-soluble vitamins. The fat-soluble vitamins are A, D, E and K. These are absorbed in the small intestine and carried by digested dietary fats. These vitamins are stored mostly in the liver. Toxic symptoms may result from the storage of excess levels of vitamins A and D.

Vitamin A promotes healthy epithelial tissues, tooth growth and tooth enamel development in children, and the ability to see in dim light. It has also been shown to have a role in carbohydrate metabolism and may serve in an anti-infective capacity through its role in normal mucus formation. Healthy mucous membranes that are bathed in their secretions provide a more effective barrier to the invasion of various pathogenic microorganisms. Some investigators have also reported a correlation between a low intake of vitamin A and a susceptibility to chemical carcinogens that affect the respiratory system, colon and urinary bladder (Wald, Idle, Boreham and Bailey; 1980).

Vitamin A deficiencies can result from poor intake, poor intestinal absorption or from diseases that affect the utilization of vitamin A. In the elderly, vitamin A deficiency is most likely to become a problem due to impaired absorption or disease rather than because of underconsumption. A variety of factors can lead to poor absorption, including reduced availability of bile (important in the emulsification of fats), overuse of laxatives, antibiotic therapy, and cirrhosis of the liver. Increasing dysfunction of the gallbladder and liver are often associated with aging and can lead to reduced availability of bile because of physical obstruction or inadequate production by the liver. Low levels of bile disrupt fat digestion and absorption as well as absorption of the fat-soluble vitamins. Laxative use, which is high in the elderly, may serve to flush this vitamin out of the body. Oil-based laxatives (such as mineral oil) act as carriers of vitamin A and are especially significant in the disruption of vitamin A absorption.

Antibiotic therapy may both introduce disruptive ecological changes in the digestive tract and result in altered absorption of nutrients. Cirrhosis of the liver, common in elderly alcoholics, affects the ability of the liver to metabolize and store vitamin A.

The primary function of vitamin D appears to be in aiding the absorption of calcium for maintenance of healthy bone tissue. It contributes to this function by increasing the absorption of calcium from the small intestine and increasing the rate of bone mineralization. Common factors associated with a deficiency of this nutrient in the elderly are malabsorption syndromes and limited exposure to the sun. Sunlight converts a biologically inactive substance in the skin, 7-dehydrocholesterol, to vitamin D. Available information on vitamin D metabolism and the elderly is limited. Osteomalacia, the adult counterpart of rickets, has been observed in the elderly living alone. This condition is probably the result of a complex set of factors including reduced outdoor activity (which reduces exposure to sunlight), malabsorption, declining renal function (which influences calcium resorption) and inadequate intake of vitamin D. A deficiency of vitamin D and calcium can be most severe in its effects on skeletal integrity.

Vitamin E has been championed by faddists as a panacea for a variety of ailments and conditions (Roberts, 1981), ranging from heart disease to a poor-quality sex life. The alleged benefits have great appeal to many of the elderly. In fact, the *antioxidant* qualities of the vitamin are presumed by some to fight or retard the aging process itself (Roberts, 1981). Few of vitamin E's suggested benefits have been confirmed by well controlled scientific research, although some evidence does suggest a higher requirement needed for older populations (Machlin and Brin, 1980).

Vitamin E is necessary for the integrity of the red blood cell and for the proper metabolism of polyunsaturated fats. Its supplementation has improved a painful leg condition known as *claudication*. Deficiency of vitamin E has rarely been observed except in premature infants and has proven exceptionally hard to induce in control populations (Horwitt, 1976).

Vitamin K is essential for the formation of *prothrombin* in the liver and thus is necessary for proper blood clotting. Deficiency of this vitamin has never been reported in healthy adults. However, low levels of vitamin K may be related to bleeding tendencies often associated with biliary disease and surgery. Likewise, availability of this vitamin may be affected by antibiotic therapy that disrupts the vitamin K–producing *intestinal flora* and by diseases such as colitis that affect the absorptive mucosa of the small intestine.

Vitamin K deficiency is not a major problem among the elderly. However, blood levels of this vitamin should be checked and possibly supplemented because of its importance in proper blood clotting when preparing elderly persons for surgery.

Water-soluble vitamins. The water-soluble vitamins include the B-complex vitamins and vitamin C. Sometimes termed labile, water-soluble vitamins taken in excess of daily needs are excreted in the urine. They differ from the fat-soluble vitamins in that they normally do not accumulate in toxic quantities, although symptomatic changes have been observed in those who take megadoses of some B vitamins. However, excessive amounts of water-soluble vitamins may alter the dynamic balance among other nutrients or increase the need for others. More studies are needed to determine the risk of kidney damage as a result of consistent and excessive ingestion of the water-soluble vitamins. Many of these are subject to destruction as a result of food preparation and cooking practices, especially when large amounts of water are involved.

B-complex vitamins include thiamin (B1), riboflavin (B2), niacin, vitamin B6 (pyridoxine), folacin (folic acid), vitamin B12, biotin, and pantothenic acid. These vitamins differ chemically, but their functions are interrelated.

Thiamin has an important role in the process that changes glucose to energy. It functions as part of a *coenzyme* that is indispensable in carbohydrate metabolism, providing a supply of energy to the nerves and brain. Because of this relationship, thiamin deficiency usually involves neurological manifestations and mood changes. Thiamin also appears to be essential for fat and protein metabolism. Poorly balanced or highly refined diets, stress, alcoholism and impaired intestinal absorption are most often the precipitating factors in thiamin deficiency.

Serum levels of thiamin are often reported to be low in surveys of older populations. Frequent use of diuretics can contribute to a deficiency as a result of increased excretion. The high carbohydrate diets often consumed by the elderly on marginal or fixed incomes can disturb the thiamin-carbohydrate balance, leading to a deficiency because of thiamin's role in the proper utilization of carbohydrates (Wilson, Fisher and Fuqua, 1975; Brin and Bauernfeind, 1978). Compared to the young, the elderly may need more thiamin because of age-associated health conditions. Common among these are elevated temperature, malignancy, *parenteral* administration of glucose without thiamin, *hemodialysis* (which removes thiamin), the stress of surgery, and alcoholism.

Whanger (1973) has suggested that thiamin may be inactivated in older people due to both a lack of hydrochloric acid in gastric secretions and altered intestinal flora that bind ingested thiamin. Cheraskin and his colleagues (1967) suggested a relationship might exist between low thiamin intake and greater frequency of cardiovascular complaints in older people. Thiamin intake and status should be regularly monitored in the elderly.

Riboflavin is essential for normal tissue maintenance, tear production and corneal integrity. It is also a constituent of enzymes that are important in energy metabolism. Deficiencies are often associated with high carbohydrate diets lacking in animal protein, milk and vegetables. Visual impairments, such as sensitivity to bright light, and skin problems, such as epithelial lesions, are common signs of a deficiency. Deficiencies of riboflavin have been reported with some regularity in the elderly. Some researchers have suggested that it might be the most common subclinical deficiency among the elderly poor whose diets are notoriously low in meats and vegetables (for example, see Exton-Smith and Scott, 1968).

Niacin is a functional component of coenzymes that are essential for the release of energy from carbohydrates, fats and proteins. It also plays a significant role in the synthesis of fats and protein. Niacin can be *endogenously* manufactured rather inefficiently from the amino acid tryptophan (60 mg tryptophan yields 1 mg niacin). Niacin deficiency is associated with narrow, maize-dominated diets or highly refined diets limited in animal protein. Alcoholics, food faddists and those with malabsorption problems may also suffer from niacin deficiency.

The deficiency is rarely reported among the elderly, however, with the exception of elderly alcoholics. Those on heavy aspirin therapy for conditions such as arthritis are at risk since aspirin may interfere with the passage of niacin from plasma to tissue. Some personality changes observed in the elderly that are usually attributed to the aging process, such as mental confusion and depression, may be due to deficiencies of niacin and other B-complex vitamins (Exton-Smith and Scott, 1968).

The vitamin B6 group includes three closely related components that serve as coenzymes for biological functions involving amino-acid metabolism and protein synthesis. The B6 group seems to be poorly absorbed by individuals with liver disease and is commonly deficient in persons with uremia and gastrointestinal disease. Since these conditions are often present in the elderly, these relationships bear watching.

The drug dihydroxphenylalanine (L-dopa), a neurotransmitter, is used in treatment of Parkinson's disease. The B6 vitamin, pyridoxin, enhances the conversion of L-dopa to *dopamine*. Since dopamine cannot cross the blood-brain barrier, conversion may result in nullification of the therapeutic effects of the drug. Therefore persons on L-dopa therapy should avoid taking vitamin supplements containing vitamin B6.

Folic acid (or folacin) is important in the metabolism of a number of amino and nucleic acids, and especially in hemoglobin synthesis. This vitamin's activities are interrelated with those of vitamin B12. Folacin intake is frequently reported as low among the elderly, and may be the most common deficiency in the older adult (Girdwood, Thompson and Williamson, 1967). Herbert (1967) suggests it is the most common overall nutritional deficiency. A number of conditions often associated with old age affect folic acid availability. Stomach and small intestine surgery are associated with decreased absorption of the vitamin. Leukemia, Hodgkin's disease, Crohn's disease, collagen disease, tuberculosis and malignancies appear to increase the demand for folacin (Exton-Smith and Scott, 1968).

Anticonvulsant drugs frequently used by the elderly are antagonistic to folacin. Research indicates that possibly 90 percent of all alcoholics are deficient in folic acid (Leevy and Kurnan, 1975; Halsted, 1980). This deficiency may result from liver damage or damage to the intestinal mucosa. Folacin is vital to the production of red blood cells, and without proper levels, *macrocytic anemia* occurs, a condition in which the red blood cells are larger and fewer in number than normal. Organic brain syndrome (OBS) has also been associated with low folacin intake (Batata *et al.,* 1967). However, the nature of the relationship between the two is not clear. It is not known if the disorder leads to decreased dietary intake and a consequent folacin deficiency or if such a deficiency results in the impaired mental ability associated with OBS (Sneath *et al.,* 1973).

Vitamin B12 is a compound that contains cobalt as a central part of its organic molecule. The exact functions of this vitamin are not completely understood. It appears to be necessary for cellular formation and functioning, especially in the bone marrow and digestive tract, and to maintain the integrity of the nervous system. It is chemically interrelated with the vitamin folacin and is stored in the liver and absorbed very slowly from the small intestine.

An intrinsic factor produced by the stomach is necessary for B12 absorption. If absorption does not take place, *pernicious anemia* results with its concomitant production of characteristically large, immature red blood cells. As with folacin, vitamin B12 is needed for the maturation of red blood cells. When it is unavailable, these cells are pale, irregularly shaped and reduced in number. Vitamin B12 absorption seems to decrease with age. This may result from a decrease in the *intrinsic factor* produced by the gastric mucosa. Antibodies against the gastric

mucosa have been found in the blood of some patients, suggesting an autoimmune condition that may be responsible for disruption of the absorption of this particular vitamin (Davidson *et al.,* 1975). Changes in gastric acidity, a malabsorption syndrome associated with partial or total removal of the stomach or ileum, and the taking of certain drugs can also interfere with the uptake of vitamin B12. Deficiencies in the elderly are rarely due to low dietary intake, but when B12 cannot be properly absorbed, it may be administered by injection.

A B12 deficiency may be associated with a folacin deficiency. In fact, suspected folacin problems should not be treated without first investigating vitamin B12 status. Folacin therapy can mask the earliest symptoms of B12 deficiency, delaying detection until irreparable nerve damage has been done. There is a possibility that some elderly labeled "senile" or arteriosclerotic may have a B12 deficiency and suffer consequent alterations in brain functioning. Fleck (1976) has reported that some elderly persons who demonstrate confusion and disorientation show an alleviation of these symptoms when B12 is administered.

Pantothenic acid, as a component of coenzyme A, is necessary to change fats and sugar into energy and to form adrenal and other hormones that also change proteins to fat and sugar. Some investigators (for example, Baker *et al.,* 1968) have suggested that it plays an undetermined role in *hypoglycemia.* The vitamin is widely distributed in foods and no deficiency has been reported in human beings. Thus the elderly do not appear to suffer any special risk of a deficiency.

Vitamin C (ascorbic acid) is the only water-soluble vitamin not part of the B-complex group. Most species of animals are able to synthesize it from simple sugars, but man and his primate relations must include an external source of vitamin C in their diet. Although vitamin C was the first vitamin synthesized in the laboratory, we still know very little about its specific chemical activity. Recently, vitamin C has been promoted as a cure or preventative for a wide range of conditions from the common cold to cancer. These claims have not been confirmed by carefully controlled scientific studies.

Vitamin C plays an important role in cellular metabolism but the mechanisms involved are poorly understood. Its most important function is in the formation and maintenance of collagen, which forms the organic matrix of the connective tissue found in skin, bones, teeth and muscle. The vitamin also plays an important role in wound healing and promotes elasticity and strength of capillary walls.

Vitamin C is important in folic-acid metabolism as part of the reaction that converts folic acid to its active form, folinic acid. It also prevents the oxidation of folates, thus assuring their physiological activity. Vitamin C plays an important part in the absorption of iron from the intestine by reducing ferric iron to the more efficiently absorbed ferrous iron. Its role as an antioxidant in the utilization of vitamin B12 and in the body's *detoxification process* is not yet fully understood. The possible role of vitamin C in cholesterol metabolism and atherosclerosis must be investigated as well. Its role in the prevention of cancer has recently been challenged by a well-designed, carefully controlled double-blind study by Creagen and his associates (1979). These researchers found that the administration of 10 grams of vitamin C per

day to cancer patients did not improve immune response or survival time.

The use of vitamin C to prevent the common cold has been the subject of controversy among researchers. Anderson, Reid, and Beaton (1972), in one of the best known and carefully conducted double-blind studies, concluded that vitamin C reduced the severity and frequency of colds, but cautioned that the observed reduction might result from a pharmacological rather than a nutritional effect (Anderson, Reid and Beaton, 1972). To some researchers, it appears that vitamin C reduces the symptoms of a cold by an *antihistamine* effect, while at the same time leaving an individual's ability to transmit the disease unaffected. Contradictory studies in this area necessitate more research and possibly better criteria for determining the presence or absence of "colds."

The role of vitamin C in the aging process may involve its relationship with vitamin E. It has been suggested that vitamin C synergistically aids vitamin E in *antiperoxidative activities* (Weg, 1978). At this time, there is little evidence to support this hypothesis. *Megadoses* of vitamin C may simply be a waste of money unless one is biochemically deficient in this vitamin. Toxicity from larger doses of vitamin C has not been a major problem, but side effects such as urinary tract stones (Stein, Hasan and Fox, 1976) inactivation of vitamin B12 (Herbert and Jacobs, 1974) and dependency deficiency have been reported (Rhead and Schrauger, 1971).

Vitamin C intake has been reported to be low in elderly populations, especially among those living alone or those who have disabilities that hinder shopping. Low serum ascorbic-acid levels are not a normal accompaniment of biological aging, and the fact that older persons respond to supplementation seems to support this observation. The multiple stresses associated with aging, as well as some drugs, may depress vitamin C levels (Baker, 1967). Vitamin C is readily destroyed in food preparation and cooking and thus a marginal diet leaves little room for error. There is no reason to recommend an increase in vitamin C intake for the average older adult, unless future research supports higher RDAs of this vitamin for all age groups. This increase has been suggested by Linus Pauling and his supporters, but rejected by most orthodox nutritionists.

Minerals

Minerals are homogeneous inorganic substances that are necessary for the proper functioning of the body. Some are referred to as *macronutrients* because they are needed in relatively large amounts (over 100 mg per day). Others, needed in very small amounts, are termed *micronutrients*. Table 10.3 contains the 1980 RDAs and major dietary sources for minerals. The amount of a particular mineral needed in the body is not necessarily related to its relative biological importance. Each of these essential nutrients serves the body in one or more of five different ways: as a structural component of the skeleton; in the maintenance and regulation of the body's *colloidal systems;* in the maintenance of the *acid-base equilibrium;* as a component or activator of *enzyme systems;* and as a component or activator in other biological units or systems. Minerals are often interrelated in function, so a deficiency of one may affect the functioning of others. For example, copper is necessary for the proper utilization of iron.

The degree of solubility of a mineral is generally related to its use in the body. Insoluble minerals are found in the teeth, bones, nails and hair, while the more reactive minerals, such as the *electrolytes,* are found in the blood.

Inefficient mineral absorption occurs easily. A number of dietary, morphological and physiological factors add to decreased absorption, including the following:

1. Chemical compounds, such as *phytic acid* and *oxalic acid,* found in some foods (for example, spinach and oatmeal), combine with some nutrients (such as calcium and iron) to form insoluble compounds, which are excreted.
2. High cellulose diets reduce the availability of absorption time by inducing hypermotility.
3. Laxatives and diarrhea can also produce hypermotility.
4. A deficiency or excess of one nutrient can reduce the absorption of another.
5. Hypogastric activity due to antacid use or old age can reduce the solubility of all minerals.

In the elderly, mineral malnutrition may be related to decreased absorptive ability that comes with age, and marginal diets and to the effects of stress and immobilization on mineral balance. The major minerals that may be of significance to the elderly will be surveyed next.

Calcium.   Calcium is necessary for the proper mineralization of bone. It is important in the growth and maintenance of the skeleton, blood clotting, cell wall permeability, muscle contractability, neuromuscular transmission and cardiac function. The function of calcium is closely related to that of phosphorus and vitamin D. The ratio of calcium to

TABLE 10.3 RDAs and major dietary sources for minerals

	Males	*Females*
Macronutrients		
Calcium (Ca)	800 mg	800 mg
Magnesium (Mg)	305 mg	300 mg
*Sodium (Na)	1,100–3,300 mg	1,100–3,300 mg
*Potassium (K)	1,875–5,625 mg	1,875–5,625 mg
Phosphorus (P)	800 mg	800 mg
*Chlorine (Cl)	1,700–5,100 mg	1,700–5,100 mg
Sulfur (S)	No RDAs at this time	
Micronutrients (trace elements)		
*Manganese (Mn)	2.5–5 mg	2.5–5 mg
Iron (Fe)	10 mg	10 mg
Copper (Cu)	2–3 mg	2–3 mg
Iodine (I)	150 μg	150 μg
Zinc (Zn)	15 mg	15 mg
*Fluorine (F)	1.5–4 mg	1.5–4 mg
*Molybdenum (Mo)	.15–0.5 mg	.15–0.5 mg
*Selenium (Se)	.05–0.2 mg	.05–0.2 mg
*Chromium (Cr)	.05–0.2 mg	.05–0.2 mg
Vanadium (V)		
Cobalt (Co)		
Tin (Sn)	No RDAS at this time	
Nickel (Ni)		
Silicon (SI)		

Minerals	*Foods*
Ca	Milk; cheese; dark green, leafy vegetables; legumes
P	Milk, cheese, meat, poultry, grains
K	Fruits, meat, milk, potato
Cl	Salt
Na	Salt, meat, cheese, processed food
Mg	Whole grains; green, leafy vegetables
Fe	Eggs; meat; legumes; green, leafy vegetables
F	Drinking water, tea, seafood
Zn	Meat, shellfish, nuts
Cu	Meats, drinking water
I	Iodized salt, marine products
Mn	Legumes, cereals, nuts
Mo	Legumes, meats
Cr	Vegetables, whole grains

*Less information is available so the ranges are less precise and not as well graded by age.
Source: National Research Council, Food and Nutrition Board, 1980, *Recommended Dietary Allowances, Revised 1980*. Washington, D.C.: National Research Council, National Academy of Sciences.

phosphorus in the diet, which should be 1:1 and certainly not greater than 1:2, is crucial in determining the balance of calcium metabolism. If phosphorus levels become too high, calcium is withdrawn from the bones to restore a proper equilibrium. Over the long term, this process can result in a gradual reduction of bone density.

Vitamin D aids calcium metabolism by enhancing transport of the mineral across the intestinal wall. Deficiency of this vitamin can result in disturbances of calcium metabolism known as rickets in the young and osteomalacia in the older adult. The body may be able to adapt to low intakes of calcium without immediate ill effects, but there is evidence that long-term low intake is undesirable since the amount of bone present in old age may be directly related to the integrity of the skeletal mass at maturity (Garn, 1975). Chronic nutritional imbalance during the 20s and 30s may affect the health of the skeleton in old age.

When a deficiency of calcium occurs, it is often accompanied by overly sensitive motor nerves, loss of muscle tone and occasional decalcification of the bones. *Osteoporosis,* a decrease in total bone mass, is common in the elderly, especially females. Its cause has been attributed to the aging process, changes in hormone balance, long-term dietary practices and physical inactivity. In the opinion of some researchers, the condition does not respond to calcium supplements (for example, Garn, 1975). However, calcium supplementation may still prove helpful in preventing further progression of the condition and in bone resorption (Albanese, 1979). Poor calcium intake may also be a significant factor in the origin and progression of periodontal disease, some evidence also suggests that periodontal disease can be reversed by adequate calcium intakes (Lutwak, 1976).

There is no direct evidence of the necessity for increased calcium intake among the elderly. However, calcium intake can become deficient or imbalanced in older people due to chronic illness, malabsorption syndrome, increased lactase deficiency and economic limitations. Chronic illness and malabsorption reduce the bioavailability of the mineral. The stress associated with both chronic illness and diminished psychosocial status also can lead to increased calcium excretion as well as decreased appetite (Albanese, 1979; Watkin, 1979).

Phosphorus. Phosphorus is important in bone formation, metabolism and the transport of fatty acids. Phosphorus intake is frequently excessive among Americans who consume large quantities of meat and carbonated soft drinks while reducing their intake of dairy products. Excessive levels of phosphates in the blood are a threat to those of the elderly experiencing decreased renal function, and can be controlled by a diet high in carbohydrates and low in protein and phosphorus, or by use of an *aluminum hydroxide gel* to bind phosphorus in foods and the intestinal fluid (Watkin, 1979).

Magnesium. Magnesium plays an important part in cell respiration and in the metabolism of fats, proteins and carbohydrates. It is involved in the following functions: bone and tooth formation; muscle and nerve irritability; delay in the formation of *fibrin* (necessary in blood clotting); and prevention of kidney stone formation.

Magnesium may lower cholesterol and retard lipid deposition in the aorta. A deficiency of magnesium is generally rare. Calcium/magnesium ratios may be more significant than the total level of magnesium. Reduced serum calcium levels are often present with magnesium depletion. Several complicating conditions common in the elderly can contribute to the production of a deficiency characterized by depression, muscular weakness and convulsions (Shils, 1969). These conditions include chronic alcoholism, acute or chronic renal disease with defective renal tubular reabsorption, excessive use of diuretics, impaired gastrointestinal absorption, the use of certain antibiotics and excessive use of enemas.

Potassium. Potassium is necessary for the maintenance of the body's acid-base and water balances as well as for proper neuromuscular function. Potassium deficiency can be a significant problem for the elderly. It is characterized by muscular weakness, disorientation, depression and irritability. This deficiency becomes more common with age, especially among those on diuretics or with prolonged diarrhea. Low potassium levels have been correlated with muscular weakness, and some researchers suggest potassium supplementation as a course of treatment (MacLeod *et al.,* 1975; MacLeod, 1975). Reestablishing a balance by dietary means can be difficult due to the frequently noted reluctance of the elderly to eat citrus fruits and milk. Bananas and apple juice seem to be more readily accepted and are good sources of potassium.

Sodium. Sodium, like potassium, is essential for water balance, acid-base equilibrium and proper nerve function. A dietary deficiency of sodium is virtually unheard of in healthy adults, but can result from sodium-restricted diets or diuretic therapy. A sodium deficiency can cause muscle cramps, mental apathy and reduced appetite. For most Americans, sodium deficiency is of less concern than excess sodium intake.

Iron. Iron is needed for the formation of hemoglobin, and a deficiency of this mineral produces anemia. Iron deficiency anemia can cause fatigue, weakness and listlessness, adding to the variety of factors reducing the quality of life for many of the elderly. To maintain an iron balance, an individual must absorb at least 1 mg of iron per day to compensate for daily losses in the shedding of cells, even though the body recycles much of the heme from these shed cells.

Iron is converted to a more absorbable form by the activity of hydrochloric acid in the stomach. Many older individuals have a reduced secretion of hydrochloric acid and a consequently reduced availability of dietary iron. Elderly people suffering from ulcers, malignancies and hemorrhoids lose blood into the intestine and may thus develop an iron deficiency. Furthermore, many elderly people take aspirin or *phenylbutazone,* which may cause internal blood loss.

Iron deficiency is difficult to treat by increased iron intake alone. Only an average of 10 percent of dietary iron is absorbed, and the absorptive potential varies from food to food. Meat consumption generally enhances iron absorption. Vitamin C and copper are necessary for the proper utilization of iron. Supplementation with ferrous iron may be necessary to meet the suggested daily intake of 10 mg. For the elderly on a low income, the daily intake of iron may be rather low, given the expense of meat. In addition, fruits, which are a vital source of vitamin C, may similarly be avoided because of their high cost.

Zinc. Zinc is a component of several enzyme systems. It plays an important role in the synthesis of proteins and *nucleic acids* and is involved in insulin production. Deficiency in adults can result in poor appetite, an impaired ability for wound healing and a diminished sense of taste and smell. Marginal zinc deficiency can be a problem in the elderly.

A number of conditions not uncommon in the elderly such as cirrhosis, kidney disease, malabsorption syndrome, malignancy and alcoholism can promote a zinc deficiency. Some studies have suggested that healing and taste acuity improved after zinc supplementation, although significant change has been difficult to demonstrate (Nordstrom, 1982). Since a relationship exists between zinc/copper ratios and *hypercholesteremia,* zinc supplementation must include a careful consideration of copper intake as well. It would, therefore, be wise for individuals of any age to avoid megadoses of zinc.

Iodine. Iodine is essential for proper thyroid function. Deficiencies do not appear to be a significant nutritional problem in the elderly. However, if an individual must go on a salt-free diet, alternative sources of iodine might be necessary. Many researchers believe that use of iodine in food processing has greatly increased the amounts supplied in North American diets (Mertz, 1981).

Fluorine. Fluorine has been linked to the prevention and treatment of osteoporosis (Nordstrom, 1982). Its preventive role is probably established in early adulthood. Fluorine salts used in the treatment of osteoporosis can approach toxic levels and their administration should therefore be carefully monitored.

Chromium. Chromium is essential for the maintenance of normal *glucose tolerance* (Gurson, 1977), and it may function as an *insulin cofactor* that serves to potentiate insulin by binding it to the cell membranes (Mertz, 1967, 1981). Chromium levels in the blood decline with age along with glucose tolerance. Some researchers have reported that chromium supplements for adult-onset diabetes improve glucose tolerance (Levine *et al.,* 1968). Chromium may also be involved in controlling the level of blood lipids and the rate that lipid deposits accumulate in the aorta (Nordstrom, 1982). Chromium supplements have been used successfully in older people to treat hypercholesteremia (Schroeder, 1976).

Selenium. Selenium is utilized by enzyme systems that are essential to the integrity of cell membranes. Selenium and selenium-containing amino acids may aid in preserving the stability of the membranes of such subcellular structures as the mitochrondia, microsomes and lysosomes. Selenium appears to inhibit peroxidation, which can result in cell damage. It might also work with vitamin E or at least serve to spare vitamin E in its antioxidant capacity (Li and Vallee, 1973). Thus a potential relationship between selenium and biological aging exists.

Table 10.4 summarizes the possible functions of eight additional trace-mineral nutrients that are significant in the overall consideration of an individual's nutritional requirements.

Water

Water is one of the most significant components of a balanced diet at any age, although the elderly can be particularly vulnerable to water balance disturbances. All metabolic

TABLE 10.4 Additional essential minerals

Mineral	Function
Copper	Enzyme component
	Essential for iron metabolism
Manganese	Energy use (thiamine utilization)
	Exotropic actions
Cobalt	Constituent of vitamin B12 (dietary sources may be
	unnecessary since B12 is an essential nutrient)
Vanadium	Mineralization of teeth and bones
	Inhibition of a cholesterol synthesis
	May also have a toxic effect
Nickel	Health of epithelial tissue
Molybdenum	Prevent dental cavities
	Iron metabolism
Sulfur	Part of cell protein, cartilage and tendons
	Detoxification process
	Constituent of many proteins via S-containing amino acids
Chlorine	Acid-base balance
	Formation of gastric juice

reactions require water, and sometimes even small changes in water balance can lead to metabolic irregularities.

Water is essential in a number of physiological functions. It aids the processes of swallowing, digestion and transport of ingested food, and is an important medium for waste elimination. It also functions in the regulation of body temperature through sweating and may aid in reducing the osmotic load on the kidney. In some geographic areas characterized by hard water, it can contribute to mineral nutrition by adding zinc, fluorine and copper to the diet.

Dehydration is not an infrequent occurrence in some elderly people. The condition may result from disease and be exacerbated by minimal water intake. Dehydration can affect both fluid and electrolyte balance. The relationship of water intake to constipation and urinary problems have been discussed in Chapter 9.

Symptoms of water imbalance that are simply accepted as characteristic of old age can sometimes be controlled by carefully monitoring water intake. Water imbalances may result in such symptoms as apathy, body weakness, depression, mental confusion and difficulty in swallowing. In order to maintain a proper balance of body fluid, water intake should be of sufficient quantity to produce a quart or more of urine per day. Nutritionists and physicians suggest the equivalent of approximately six to seven glasses of water per day to ensure a proper water balance.

NUTRITION AND DRUGS

Nutrients and drugs interact in two major ways. First, drugs may have an effect on nutrient absorption and metabolism. For example, certain antibiotics lead to malabsorption of nutrients and a decrease in appetite. Second, the nutritional and health status of the host may affect drug metabolism. An example is the relationship between adequate protein intake and the potentiation of L-dopa in Parkinson's disease. These two types of interactions must be viewed against the declining ability of the aging organism to deal with the effects of some drug therapies.

Pharmacokinetics and pharmacodynamics provide specific information that is useful when considering interactions between nutrients and drugs. *Pharmacokinetics* concerns itself with how much, how long, when, how, if and where a drug will be absorbed, transported, used, metabolized and excreted (Poe and Holloway, 1980). *Pharmacodynamics* is the study of the biochemical and physiological effects of drugs and their mechanisms of action (Comfort, 1977). The study of pharmacokinetics and pharmacodynamics indicates that changes in drug utilization occur due to age-dependent factors.

Cardiovascular output decreases as one ages and thus can affect the distribution of pharmacological agents throughout the body. Gastrointestinal changes can reduce the absorption of drugs, and altered renal capacity affects their excretion. These observations necessitate the consideration of altered dosages, alternative drug choices and efforts to reduce multiple-drug usage.

Roe (1976) has reviewed the evidence for nutritional deficiencies during prolonged drug therapy. Elderly individuals and their health-care providers should be aware of the negative effects of uncompensated drug therapy and the impact of certain foods on the effectiveness of certain drugs. It should be remembered that the elderly, compared to the general population, take more drugs and are more likely to take multiple drugs and be chronic users of drugs (Lamy, 1980, 1981). They are therefore especially susceptible to drug-nutrient interactions. The problems, prospects and theoretical models of drug nutrient interaction are complex and varied. An outline of the most important drug/nutrient interactions affecting the elderly is presented in Table 10.5. Additional material on drugs and the elderly is presented in Chapter 15.

SUMMARY

National surveys seem to indicate that large numbers of the elderly population are nutritionally vulnerable. The low-income elderly and the sick and disabled may be particularly susceptible. In fact, the nutritional status of the elderly seems more tied to income and health status than to age itself.

The six major nutritional constituents found in food sources are carbohydrates, fat, protein, vitamins, minerals, and water. These nutrients supply us with energy, aid in the growth and repair of body tissues, and help regulate body processes. Nutritionists continue to debate the specific amounts of each nutrient needed for optimal functioning in old age. This discussion includes the concept of recommended dietary allowances (RDAs). Intended as reference points in planning diets to provide the greatest possible health benefits, RDAs are revised approximately every five years.

The elderly have different nutritional requirements than do other age groups. Changes in digestive secretions, enzyme-producing organs, intestinal mucosa and kidney functioning are examples of age-related physiological changes that affect how food is digested and how nutrients are absorbed and excreted. Changes associated with aging often imitate the signs of nutritional deficiency. Many symptoms of nutritional defi-

TABLE 10.5 Nutrient/drug interactions to be aware of in elderly persons

Drug	Nutritional Effects
Alcohol	Can lead to deficiencies in all nutrients, especially B vitamins Can replace eating
Aminopterin Methotrexate (used to treat leukemia)	Inhibits folate utilizations. However, if folate is supplemented, drug may not be as effective.
Antacids	Magnesium salts can cause diarrhea, limiting absorption of all nutrients. Protein absorption may be adversely affected when stomach acidity is reduced. Aluminum hydroxide binds phosphates.
Antibiotics	1. Tetracycline can bind iron, magnesium and calcium salts. 2. Many antibiotics are antagonistic to folic acid and can result in deficiencies of other nutrients. 3. Can lead to malabsorption. 4. Neomycin binds bile acids and affects fat-soluble vitamin absorption. 5. Neomycin causes intestinal structural changes that result in malabsorption of N, Na, K, Ca, lactose.
Anticoagulants	Can cause vitamin K deficiency
Anticonvulsants	Primadone, phenobarbitol induce folate deficiency and vitamin D deficiency.
Antidepressants	Some cause accelerated breakdown of vitamin D. If the monamine oxidase (MAO) inhibitor-type is used, patients become intolerant to foods containing tyramine, such as aged cheese, red wine, beer, dry salami and chocolate. These foods can precipitate hypertensive crisis when MAO inhibitors are being used.
Aspirin and other anti-inflammatory drugs	1. Many cause gastrointestinal bleeding; arthritic patients who ingest large quantities may develop iron-deficiency anemia secondary to blood loss. 2. Aspirin usage can affect folic-acid status. 3. Aspirin and indomethacin can increase need for vitamin C by impairing its effectiveness.
Barbituates	1. Some cause breakdown of vitamin D 2. Excessive sedation of nursing home patients for behavior control can result in missed meals. 3. Folic acid is malabsorbed.
Cathartics	Reduce intestinal transit time necessary for proper absorption of some nutrients
Cholesterol-lowering drugs such as chlofibrate	Any drug-altering blood lipids can affect absorption of fat-soluble vitamins. Vitamin K deficiencies can be produced.
Colchicine, used in gout	Causes malabsorption of fat, carotene, sodium, potassium, vitamin B12, folic acid and lactose
Diuretics	Most diuretics cause potassium to be lost in urine. Blood levels of potassium must be monitored, since mental confusion can result from low levels of potassium. Dietary sources of potassium should be consumed. (Magnesium may be deficient in long-term diuretics.)
Glucocorticoids, used in allergy and collagen disease	Impair calcium transport across mucosa

TABLE 10.5 *continued*

Drug	Nutritional Effects
Hormones	1. ACTH and cortisone therapy increases excretion of sodium, potassium and calcium, and may contribute to the development of diabetes, hypertension, obesity and water retention. Calcium and potassium supplements may be needed, as well as special diet prescriptions if hypertension and diabetes develop. 2. Calcitonin treatment: Decreases serum calcium levels as calcium is deposited into bone. Tetany may develop without oral calcium supplements. 3. Estrogen therapy: Over an extended period, may result in deficiencies of folic acid and vitamin B6. Patient should not receive folic acid supplements until vitamin B12 status is confirmed to be satisfactory. 4. Hormone therapy can cause peptic ulcers, which require dietary management. 5. Prednisone causes malabsorption of calcium.
Isoniazid (INH) (a drug used to treat tuberculosis)	Causes B6 deficiency in some persons because it is an antagonist to the vitamin
Laxatives	Harsh laxatives may cause diarrhealike effects: Food passes through the GI tract too fast to be absorbed. Mineral oil absorbs vitamins A and D, preventing them from being absorbed.
Licorice candy	Limits potassium absorption
Metformin and Phenformin Hypoglycemic agents used in diabetics	Competitively inhibit vitamin B12 absorption
Para-amino salicylic acid, used to treat tuberculosis	Can cause malabsorption of fat and folic acid; blocks absorption of vitamin B12
Potassium chloride, used to replenish potassium lost due to diuretic use	Depresses absorption of vitamin B12

ciency lack nutrient specificity. Diseases also alter the nutritional requirements of an affected individual.

Drugs and nutrients may interact in two important ways. First, the nutritional (and health) status of the individual may affect drug metabolism. Second, drugs themselves may have an effect on the way nutrients are absorbed and metabolized.

KEY TERMS

aluminum hydroxide gel
anemia
anticonvulsant drugs
antihistamine
antioxidant
antiperoxidative activities
atrophy
basal metabolism rate (BMR)
biochemical individuality
claudication
coenzyme
detoxification process
dopamine
emulsification
endogenously
fat-soluble vitamins
free radicals
glucose tolerance
hemodialysis
hypoglycemia
intestinal flora

intrinsic factor
L-dopa
lipids
macrocytic anemia
macronutrients
megadoses
micronutrients
neurotransmitter
nucleic acids
oxalic acid
oxidation
parenteral
pernicious anemia
peroxidation reaction
pharmacodynamics
pharmacokinetics
phenylbutazone
phytic acid
polyunsaturated fatty acids
prothrombin
water-soluble vitamins

STUDY QUESTIONS

1. Differentiate between minimal and optimal nutritional requirements, and indicate how they are related to the RDA concept.
2. In what ways can physical activity contribute to nutritional balance in elderly individuals?
3. What are the major problems associated with carbohydrate, protein and fat consumption among the elderly?
4. Discuss the pros and cons of vitamin supplementation for the elderly.
5. Identify the roles of the following substances and indicate some of the major problems they might cause among the elderly:
   a. Fat-soluble vitamins
   b. B-complex vitamins
   c. Vitamin C
6. What are the major functions of the essential mineral nutrients? Differentiate between macro- and micronutrients. Why is the absorption of most minerals inefficient? Is this particularly significant for the elderly?
7. Identify the roles of each of the following and indicate the most significant problems they present to the elderly:

calcium	zinc	potassium	selenium
phosphorus	iodine	chromium	iron
magnesium	fluorine	sodium	

8. Discuss the role of water in the physiological functions of the elderly. What are the major problems associated with water imbalance among the aged.
9. Differentiate between pharmacokinetics and pharmacodynamics. What age-dependent factors influence drug utilization? Identify several drug-nutrient interactions among the elderly to which health care professionals need to be sensitive.

BIBLIOGRAPHY

Albanese, A.A. 1979. Calcium nutrition in the elderly. *Nutrition and the M.D.* 5(12): 1–2.

Anderson, T.W., Reid, D.B., and Beaton, G.H. 1972. Vitamin C and the common cold: A double blind trial. *Canadian Medical Association Journal 107:* 503–508.

Baker, E.M. 1967. Vitamin C requirements and stress. *American Journal of Clinical Nutrition 20:* 583–590.

Baker, H., Frank, O., and Jaslow, S.P. 1980. Oral versus intramuscular vitamin supplementation for hypovitaminosis in the elderly. *Journal of American Geriatrics Society 28*(1): 42–45.

Batata, M., Spray, G.H., Bolton, F.G., Higgins, G., and Woolner, L. 1967. Blood and bone marrow changes in elderly patients with special reference to folic acid, vitamin B12, iron and ascorbic acid. *British Medical Journal 2:* 667–669.

Brin, M., and Bauernfeind, J.C. 1978. Vitamin needs of the elderly. *Postgraduate Medicine 63*(3): 155–163.

Brocklehurst, J.C., ed. 1979. *Textbook of Geriatric Medicine and Gerontology.* Edinburgh, U.K.: Churchill Livingstone.

Cheraskin, E., Ringsdorfer, W.M., and Hicks, B.S. 1967. Thiamin-carbohydrate consumption and cardiovascular complaints. *Internationale Zeitschrift Fuer Vitamin Forschune 37:* 449–455.

Comfort, A. 1977. Geriatrics: A British view. *New England Journal of Medicine 297:* 624.

Creagen, E.T., Moertel, C.G., O'Fallon, J.R., Schutt, A.J., O'Connell, M.J., Rubin, J., and Frytak, S. 1979. Failure of dose vitamin C therapy to benefit patients with advanced cancer. *New England Journal of Medicine 301*: 687–690.

Davidson, S., Passmore, R., Brock, J.F., and Truswell, A.S. 1975. *Human Nutrition and Dietetics*. London: Churchill Livingstone.

Exton-Smith, A.N., and Scott, D.L. 1968. *Vitamins in the Elderly*. Bristol, U.K.: Wright and Sons.

Fleck, H. 1976. *Introduction to Nutrition*. New York: Macmillan.

Forbes, G.B., and Reina, J.C. 1970. Adult lean body mass declines with age: Some longitudinal observations. *Metabolism 19*(9): 653–663.

Garn, S. 1975. Bone loss and aging. In R. Goldman, and M. Rockstein, eds., *The Psychology and Pathology of Human Aging*. New York: Academic Press.

Girdwood, R.H., Thompson, A.D., and Williamson, J. 1967. Folate status in the elderly. *British Medical Journal 2*: 670–672.

Gurson, C.T. 1977. The metabolic significance of diet. In Draper, H.H., ed., *Advances in Nutrition Research*. New York: Plenum.

Halsted, C.H. 1980. Folate deficiency in alcoholism. *American Journal of Clinical Nutrition 33*: 2736–2740.

Herbert, V. 1967. Biochemical and hematologic lesions in folic acid deficiency. *American Journal of Clinical Nutrition 20*: 562–672.

——————— , and Jacobs, E. 1974. Destruction of vitamin B12 by ascorbic acid. *Journal of the American Medical Association 230*: 241–242.

Horwitt, M.K. 1976. Vitamin E: A re-examination. *American Journal of Clinical Nutrition 29*: 569–578.

Kart, C.S., and Metress, S.P. 1984. *Nutrition, the Aged, and Society*. Englewood Cliffs, N.J.: Prentice-Hall.

Lamy, P.P. 1980. Drug interactions and the elderly—A new perspective. *Drug Intelligence and Clinical Pharmacy 14*: 513–515.

——————— . 1981. Nutrition and the elderly. *Drug Intelligence and Clinical Pharmacy 15*: 887–891.

Leevy, C.M., and Kurnan, T. 1975. Nutritional factors and liver disease. *Modern Trends in Gastroenterology 5*: 250–261.

Levine, R.H., Streetan, D.P., and Doisy, R. 1968. Effects of oral chromium supplementation on the glucose tolerance of elderly human subjects. *Metabolism 17*(2): 114–125.

Li, T.K., and Vallee, B. 1973. Biochemical and nutritional role of trace elements. In R.S. Goodhart and M.E. Shils, eds., *Modern Nutrition in Health and Disease*. Philadelphia: Lea and Febiger.

Lutwak, L. 1976. Periodontal disease. In M. Winick, ed., *Nutrition and Aging*. New York: Wiley.

Machlin, L.J., and Brin, M. 1980. Vitamin E. In R.B. Alfin-Slater and D. Kritchevsky, eds., *Nutrition and the Adult Micronutrients*. New York: Plenum.

MacLeod, C.C., Judge, T.G., and Caird, F.I. 1975. Nutrition of the elderly at home, III: Intakes of minerals. *Age and Aging 4*(1): 49–57.

MacLeod, S.M. 1975. The rational use of potassium supplements. *Postgraduate Medicine 57*(2): 123–128.

Mertz, W. 1967. The biological role of chromium. *Federation Proceedings 26*: 186–193.

——————— . 1981. The essential trace elements. *Science 213*: 1332–1338.

National Research Council, Food and Nutrition Board. 1980. *Recommended Dietary Allowances, Revised*. Washington, D.C.: National Research Council, National Academy of Sciences.

Nordstrom, J.W. 1982. Trace mineral nutrition in the elderly. *American Journal of Clinical Nutrition 36*: 788–795.

Poe, W.D., and Holloway, D.A. 1980. *Drugs and the Aged*. New York: McGraw-Hill.

Rhead, W.J., and Schrauger, G.N. 1971. Risks of long-term ascorbic acid overdosage. *Nutrition Reviews 29*: 262–263.

Roberts, H.J. 1981. Perspectives on vitamin E as therapy. *Journal of American Medical Association 240*(2): 129–131.

Roe, D. 1976. *Drug-induced Nutritional Deficiencies*. Westport, Conn.: Avi Publishing.

Schroeder, H.A. 1976. Nutrition. In E.V. Cowdry and F.U. Steinberg, eds., *The Care of the Geriatric Patient*. St. Louis, Mo.: Mosby.

Shils, M.E. 1969. Experimental production of magnesium deficiency in man. *Annals of the New York Academy of Science. 162*(2): 847–855.

Sneath, P., Chanarin, I., Hodkinson, H.M.,

McPherson, C.K., and Reynolds, E.H. 1973. Folate status on a geriatric population and its relationship to dementia. *Age and Aging 2:* 177–182.

Stein, H.B., Hasan, A., and Fox, I.H. 1976. Ascorbic acid-induced uricosuria: A consequence of megavitamin therapy. *Annals of Internal Medicine. 84:* 385–388.

Wald, N., Idle, M., Boreham, J., and Bailey, A. 1980. Low serum vitamin A and subsequent risk of cancer. *Lancet 2:* 813.

Watkin, D.M. 1979. Nutrition, health and aging. In M. Rechcigal, ed., *Nutrition and the World Food Problems.* Basel, Switzerland: S. Karger.

Weg, R. 1978. *Nutrition and Later Years.* Los Angeles: University of Southern California Press.

Whanger, A.D. 1973. Vitamins and vigor at sixty-five plus. *Postgraduate Medicine 53*(2): 167–172.

Wilson, E.D., Fisher, K.H., and Fuqua, M.E. 1975. *Principles of Human Nutrition.* New York: Wiley.

Winterer, J.C., Steffer, W.P., Perera, W.D., Uauy, R., Scrimshaw, N.S., and Young, V.R. 1976. Whole body protein turnover in aging man. *Experimental Gerontology 11:* 78–87.

Young, V.R., Perera, W.D., Winterer, J.C., and Scrimshaw, N.S. 1976. Protein and amino acid requirements of the elderly. In M. Winick, ed., *Nutrition and Aging.* New York: Wiley.

_____ . 1978. Diet and nutrient needs in old age. In J.A. Behnke, C.E. Finch, and G.B. Moment, eds., *Biology of Aging.* New York: Plenum.

CHAPTER **11**

The Biocultural Basis of Geriatric Nutrition

Aging is a *biocultural* process. Biology determines the potential duration of life, the relative length of the various phases of the life cycle, the physical signs associated with aging, and the nature and development of chronic and degenerative disease. Culture enables us to extend life expectancy through the development and application of science and technology. Culture also defines the stages of the life cycle and the ways in which people make the transition from one phase to another. Cultural stresses may even hasten the aging process.

There are two general but complementary approaches to a discussion of the biocultural basis of geriatric nutrition. The first explores the influence of nutrition on the biological aging process itself and its effect on the development of degenerative disease that often accompanies aging. A second approach, emphasized in this chapter, examines the factors that influence the eating patterns of the elderly.

SOCIOCULTURAL FUNCTIONS OF FOOD

Food is necessary for an organism to survive and prosper physiologically. In humans, food and eating behavior are embedded in a *sociocultural matrix:* In addition to biological nourishment, food serves many socially and culturally significant functions. These include the development of interpersonal relationships as well as feelings of security. Depending on the culture in question, food may also serve to express status, religious or ethnic identity, and feelings of pleasure and creativity.

Food influences behavior through *enculturation*, the process by which new generations come to adopt traditional ways of thinking and behaving (Harris, 1985). The process is based largely on the control that older generations exert over younger ones in terms of rewards and punishments. According to psychoanalyst Erik Erikson (1968), the first sustained human contact is the mother-infant relationship, in which infant trust of the mother is learned as a function of the interaction associated with the feeding process. For older children, rewards and punishments may also involve food; dessert may be offered or withheld in an attempt to influence behavior. For adults, certain types of food are used to gain social and economic advancement, to show conformity or rebelliousness and to recognize important achievements. In our society, births, confirmations and bar mitzvahs, weddings and even death may be "celebrated" with food.

Food is used to initiate and maintain a variety of interpersonal relationships. In most cultures, in fact, food is one of the most important means of fostering social relationships. Individuals can be held together or set apart by food and eating behaviors and relationships. Examples of this include coffee breaks and "brown bag" lunch groups at work or school, and community groups that share food and eat together at church or other gathering places. Generally, people share meals with friends, not strangers, although sitting down together for a meal is often symbolic of a truce between antagonists.

Food is important in the expression of group identity or solidarity. The former Catholic custom of abstaining from meat on Fri-

day served as a group identification for those who adhered to it in the face of societal pressure to ignore church doctrine. Religious or supernatural ideologies often influence, even dictate, eating patterns. Eating or not eating certain foods or combinations of foods can demonstrate one's faith or serve as a protective device. Specific foods may serve as commemorative symbols recalling significant past events (for example, Easter or Passover). Among Eastern Orthodox Christians, lentil soup with vinegar is often served on Good Friday. The lentils are symbolic of the tears of the Virgin Mary, while vinegar reminds the faithful of Christ on the cross, given vinegar instead of water to drink.

Ethnic or racial identity can be reaffirmed by the use of traditional foods. The popularity of "soul foods" (for example, collard greens and chitlins) among northern blacks is viewed by some as a return to cultural roots. The black Muslim views this phenomenon quite differently and rejects soul food as symbolic of slavery, poverty and degradation.

People also eat for sensory pleasure. Taste, texture, appearance, novelty and other organoleptic qualities may be the major reasons for eating or not eating certain foods. In the absence of other kinds of gratifications, special or forbidden foods may satisfy those who are generally deprived in other ways.

Finally, food may serve to express an individual's creativity. The preparation of good or exotic food may be an individual's only recognized achievement. In such a case, food is a very important source of attention, status and personal worth. Some individuals may exhibit creativity in food preparation in addition to other accomplishments. Such creativity may simply add to or enhance the individual's own perception of personal worth or increase his or her status in the eyes of others.

FACTORS AFFECTING NUTRITIONAL STATUS

The factors that affect the nutritional status of the elderly can be divided into two broad groups: (1) those that result from metabolic and physiological changes associated with aging, and (2) those that affect the amount and type of food eaten. The latter group includes sociocultural factors, which are probably the most important influences on eating habits at any age. The group also includes biological factors that can affect food selection and intake.

Effects on Metabolism and Physiology

It is generally recognized that caloric needs often decrease after age 55 (Winick, 1980). This results from decreased basal metabolism and a diminished activity pattern that is generally associated with aging. The slowing of basal metabolism is probably due to a loss of cell and tissue mass. Diminished activity may be a result of limitations brought on by chronic disease, lack of interest or social isolation, among many other reasons.

The ability of the human body to respond to chemical imbalances is lessened with age. For example, after ingesting a dose of sodium bicarbonate (baking soda), the body takes eight times longer at age 70 than at age 30 to reestablish normal sodium levels in the blood. There is some evidence of an age-associated decrease in the size and permeability of the capillary bed of the small intestine as well as a possible change in the permeability of the blood vessels as a result of collagenous changes. These alterations may diminish the capacity of blood vessels to take up and distribute nutrients (Exton-Smith, 1972).

Changes in digestive secretions may affect the digestion and absorption of food. Around age 60, the salivary glands begin to deteriorate. This factor as well as certain others, such as "mouth-breathing," tends to dry the mouth, possibly forcing the selection of soft, self-lubricating foods. This in turn reduces the range of foods chosen and can result in a fiber-deficient diet that leads to or aggravates chronic lower bowel problems such as constipation (Niessen, 1984). The secretion of the intrinsic factor of the gastric mucosa decreases, which may be related to an age-associated decrease in the production of hydrochloric acid. This is significant because decreased intrinsic factor lowers the absorption of vitamin B12, while reduced acidity affects iron and calcium absorption (Winick, 1980). A diminution of secreted pancreatic enzymes begins at about age 40, but there is little hard data to indicate that age-related changes occur in the enzymes of the intestinal mucosa.

Age-related changes in the composition of the bacterial flora of the intestine have been documented. These changes can be detrimental, and are probably related to reduced gastric acidity or enzymatic action that allows the rapid growth of other organisms, such as streptococci, at the expense of the normal flora. This condition can result in the loss of nutrients synthesized by the displaced organisms as well as lowered resistance of the tract to disease. It also results in an irritated and inflamed mucosal lining.

Abnormal bacterial growth in the intestine can bind vitamin B12 and affect its availability for the body's use. Fat metabolism can be affected due to a bile-salt depletion resulting from *bacterial deconjugation* of bile salts. Furthermore, some of the by-products of deconjugation may be toxic or carcinogenic to the gut. Occasionally, bacterial groups such as *Clostridia, Bacteroides* and *Veillonella* invade the small intestine from the large, causing physical damage and upsetting environmental balances. This condition may necessitate a short-term antibiotic therapy in conjunction with the administration of vitamins. In rare cases, when chronic conditions develop, intermittent long-term antibiotic therapy may be necessary.

Disorders of the hepatobiliary tract can also lead to fat maldigestion. This, in turn, can affect the body's utilization of the fat soluble vitamins A, D, E and K. There is some evidence of a 20 percent reduction in lipolytic activity in the elderly, but this has no appreciable affect on fat digestion. Becker and his associates (1950) observed that it took aged individuals about twice the time required by younger people to absorb high-fat meals.

Maldigestion and *malabsorption* are common conditions in the elderly, and the causal factors are numerous. These conditions, perhaps especially malabsorption, are responsible for many of the nutrient imbalances observed in the elderly. Balachi and Dobbins (1974) note some of the conditions that can lead to malabsorption. These include:

1. Surgical alterations (for example, esophagectomy, gastrectomy and small-bowel resections).
2. Pancreatic insufficiency caused by inflammation or tumor.
3. Hepatobiliary insufficiency caused by such conditions as gall stones and hepatitis.
4. Stasis and bacterial overgrowth.
5. Drug-induced changes caused by alcohol, anticonvulsants, cathartics, diuretics and antibiotics.

6. Cardiovascular abnormalities such as congestive heart failure, constrictive pericarditis, arteriosclerosis and abdominal angina.
7. Radiation injury caused by accidental, occupational or therapeutic exposures.
8. Endocrinopathy such as diabetes, Addison's disease and thyroid disease.
9. Paget's disease.
10. Collagen vascular disease.
11. Amyloidosis.
12. Celiac disease, sprue.
13. Neoplastic disease.
14. Paraproteinemia such as multiple myeloma.

Malabsorption syndromes are difficult to manage when the small-bowel mucosa are diseased. The syndromes can best be treated by parenteral administration of vitamins and minerals or the oral administration of pharmacologic rather than physiologic doses of these nutrients. Correction of the underlying condition should be the clinical goal, although this may be impossible in many cases because the cause of malabsorption is not known or the medical means to correct it are not available. In most cases of malabsorption, nutritional management is the only way to sustain the patient. Any plan for its management must fit the individual case or circumstances.

Large-bowel problems are common concerns for many of the elderly. In particular, constipation or the fear of constipation has long been a concern for many older people. Even the casual observer might note the frequency with which advertising campaigns for laxatives are directed toward the elderly. Judging from the popularity of books on high-fiber diets (for example, Fredericks,

1983; Reuben, 1976; Galton, 1976; Westland, 1982; Adams and Murray, 1986), there is continuing interest in the use of such diets. Recommendations for the use of high-fiber diets seem to be related to an effort to prevent bowel cancer as well as a variety of other conditions, including hemorrhoids, diverticulosis and diabetes. The clinical and epidemiological evidence to support the widespread health benefits of a high-fiber diet is controversial and incomplete (Kelsay, 1978). Despite these inconclusive findings, a great number of people have embarked upon preventive health programs based largely on increasing the amount of fiber in the diet.

Little evidence exists to suggest that significant amounts of essential nutrients are absorbed by the large intestine, but large-intestine distress, real or imagined, can greatly affect the variety and nature of individual dietary choice, thus creating problems of nutrient imbalance. Many of these problems seem to be readily amenable to treatment if techniques of preventive medicine are used. Diet plays a significant role in preventive medicine, although dietary changes may be difficult to implement because of long-standing habits. But the most efficient approach to most functional-bowel problems is a therapeutic regimen consisting of dietary modification and increased physical activity.

Factors Governing Food Intake

Those who work with the elderly often come to realize that metabolic and physiological barriers to proper nutrition may be minor compared to those factors that actually regulate food intake. Factors governing food intake determine the quantity, quality and combinations of foods eaten, and are intricately interwoven into the fabric of the elderly person's social life. Again, food can be as important among the elderly for social and psychological reasons as it is for physiological well-being.

Biophysical and sociocultural variables affect food intake. The interaction of these variables results in a systematic process that affects both the biological and sociocultural environment of an individual in the aging process. Such adaptation is truly biocultural in nature.

Biophysical changes that affect dietary intake include loss of teeth, reduced fine-motor coordination, diminished vision, reduced sense of taste and smell, physical discomfort associated with eating, chronic disease and decreased physical activity. These changes affect the efficiency of the alimentary tract, can alter dietary choice and are sometimes associated with changes in self-image as well as problems of isolation and depression. It is extremely important to remember that not all of these conditions are "natural" and inevitable outcomes of the aging process. Many can be corrected or alleviated. For example, cataracts are the most common disability of the aged eye. It has been said that all of us would develop them, even if only to a mild degree, if we lived long enough. Those who have cataracts develop an opacity and frequently a yellowing of the normally transparent lens of the eye. The opaqueness of the lens interferes with the passage of light rays to the retina. Depending on the extent of cataract development, an individual will suffer a certain degree of blurred and dimmed vision. An afflicted person may need brighter and brighter light for reading and may also need to hold objects extremely close in order to see them. Today, however, surgical removal provides safe and effective treatment for cataracts.

Loss of teeth or the existence of denture problems can lead to dietary modifications that stress foods that are softer and easier to chew. This can lead to reduced dietary bulk in the diet, further complicating any existing lower-bowel conditions. Chewing problems of a mechanical nature are real for many of the elderly. Some studies have noted decreased efficiency in mastication with the successive loss of teeth. For example, the loss of a first molar can reduce efficiency on one side of the mouth by as much as 33 percent (Neumann, 1970).

A denture wearer must chew food four times as long to reach the same level of mastication as a person with natural teeth. Half the population of the United States is in need of dentures by age 65 and about two-thirds are totally edentulous by age 75 (Busse, 1978). Well-fitting dentures do not exist, since "fit" is a subjective phenomenon that often depends on the adaptive qualities of the individual involved. It is easier to fit and satisfy the younger-old (those in their 50s or 60s) than the "old-old"—shrinkage of the gums and palate complicate the problems of fit for the very old.

Maxillary dentures usually fit better than *mandibular dentures* because of the broad-based structure of the maxilla. The greater mobility of the mandible and the tendency for the muscles and tongue to dislodge the denture during speech and swallowing make a comfortable fit less likely. Public dislodgement of dentures can be embarrassing for sensitive individuals. Fear of such embarrassment can result in the rejection of certain foods to the detriment of the individual's nutritional status.

The loss of neuromuscular coordination is a biophysical problem associated with aging. This condition can be further complicated by deteriorating vision, Parkinson's disease, stroke or chronic arthritis. Fine-motor coordination declines with age, but the existence of a chronic disease such as arthritis may greatly magnify the functional significance of any change. Neuromuscular problems may lead to an inability to handle certain utensils, appliances or foods. For those living alone, this inability can lead to the inefficient use of food resources. In the presence of others, both at home or in public, it is a source of embarrassment that can lead to a diminished use of important foods. The psychological effects of these reduced capacities and the situations they may precipitate can further diminish self-image and affect the social functions of eating. People who work with the elderly must be aware of these possibilities and try to suggest alternatives to ensure adequate nutrition while preserving personal dignity.

A declining number of taste buds as well as neurological problems can affect appetite. At age 70, there are only 30 percent of the number of taste buds present at age 30 (Arey, 1935), so loss of taste is a common complaint among the elderly (Schiffman, 1977). The ability to distinguish sweet, bitter and sour tastes declines with age, but the recognition of saltiness does not appear to be affected (Hermel, Schonwetler and Samueloff, 1970). Apparently thresholds for each taste are not as affected as the ability to perceive subtle differences within each taste category. This may be problematic in combination with sociocultural factors that tend to suppress appetite. A diminished sense of taste can lead to overseasoning of foods with consequent irritation of sensitive parts of the digestive tract. In the case of salt, overuse can contribute to hypertension, heart disease and kidney malfunction. No firm conclusion about the relationship between sensitivity to smell and aging can be drawn, although odor sensitivity seems to be stable over age (Enger, 1977).

Most gastrointestinal discomfort associated with food ingestion is psychologically based, although biophysical causes such as hiatus hernia do exist. Useful research on the effect of particular foods on the digestive tract is scarce. If eating certain foods seems to induce symptoms such as heartburn and distension, elderly individuals should be encouraged to avoid them. Care must be taken to replace the nutritional contribution of the eliminated foods with alternative foods that are adequate sources of the lost nutrients; this is vital if an eliminated food was a key dietary source of essential nutrients. For example, if citrus fruit juice is eliminated from the diet, care must be taken to assure proper vitamin-C intake through consumption of alternative sources such as tomatoes and potatoes.

Chronic diseases also may necessitate modified diets. Chronic illness affects motivation and can deplete the energy needed to perform certain daily routines. Modified diets are often expensive and can be difficult to follow, especially if the person does not fully understand either their necessity or the directions. Unfortunately, nutritional counseling is rarely available when this situation arises.

Elderly individuals can and must be made to realize the nature of their dietary problems. They should be educated to fully understand the regimen prescribed and the consequences of not following the regimen. An adequate counseling program does more

than provide information on special diets. Diets should be devised to allow individual choice—monotony can destroy even the most well-conceived diet.

Changes in the level of physical activity are also related to nutritional status. Exercise is needed to aid in the metabolism of foods. It is useful also in relieving tension and maintaining mental well-being and is necessary to maintain the strength and vigor to undertake everyday tasks. Lack of energy for shopping or meal preparation can lead to an undesirable emphasis on easily prepared, high-carbohydrate refined foods, such as bread, jelly, jam or ready-to-eat cereals and cakes. Many of these foods have an extremely high sugar content. Mental stress from depression (and related inactivity) can lead to a further reduction in physical activity and consequently decrease energy and motivation necessary to shop for and prepare food.

The sociocultural factors that affect food intake are more varied and have a greater impact on nutrients than the biophysical factors discussed above. Each elderly person is the product of years of experience in a sociocultural setting modified only by individual perception and choice. Dietary habits and ideas are likewise longstanding and difficult to change. People often seem to arbitrarily prefer or reject certain foods in the face of direct evidence that they are good or bad for them.

The tendency to establish an attachment to certain foods may represent an individual's desire for security at a time in life when his or her level of insecurity, due to changing roles and status, is quite high. Dietary habits are often associated with memories of youth, pleasant and unpleasant, and in this context take on increased significance. Elimination of preferred foods or the addition of objectionable ones should not be attempted unless there is a definite threat to health. The psychological stress of such impositions can negatively affect the value associated with the dietary change.

Income is a primary factor in determining diet at all ages. Many gerontologists believe that the major problems of geriatric nutrition are a function not of age, but rather of the socioeconomic status of the aged. A summary of the findings of recent national nutrition surveys would suggest they are right.

Retirement income, in comparison with pre-retirement earnings, is reduced for the great majority of older people. Poverty is a fact of life for many, especially the non-white aged. Housing, health care, transportation and other expenses compete with money needed for food. Figure 11.1 shows the percentage distribution of average expenditures for families whose head-of-household is under 65 years of age as well as for those with older heads-of-household. When compared with younger families, aged families spend a

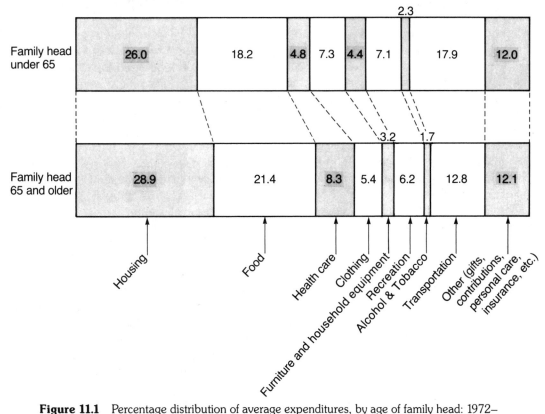

Figure 11.1   Percentage distribution of average expenditures, by age of family head: 1972–73. (Source: Herman B. Brotman, "The Aging of America: A Demographic Profile," in *The Economics of Aging, A National Journal Issues Book*. Washington, D.C.: Government Research Corporation, 1978, p. 38.)

greater proportion of their income on food, housing and health care.

Many elderly shoppers cannot buy food using the criteria of past eating habits or optimal nutrition because they lack purchasing power. They may develop a tendency to purchase cheaper foods that are high in refined carbohydrates, such as bread and cereals, rather than buying more expensive protective foods such as meat, fruit and vegetables. It is not the carbohydrates per se that are bad; rather, the lack of dietary variety fostered by such purchasing patterns often leads to reduced dietary quality and the risk of malnutrition.

The elderly, like the poor in general, are often forced to shop at more expensive stores due to the absence of chain stores in local neighborhoods or a lack of transportation to volume-sale stores with lower prices. Alternatively, the need to obtain credit to purchase food between retirement checks may arise. This necessitates the use of "Ma and Pa" grocery stores that give credit, but must charge higher prices and carry a smaller variety of products than do chain stores.

The elderly are often unable to take advantage of sales or quantity discounts because they lack proper storage facilities such as refrigeration and pest-free cupboards. Many people take for granted conveniences not always available to the poor or elderly. If money is not available for food at the time of the month when sales occur, the advertised bargains are unobtainable. Food activist groups have observed the deliberate price inflation of food products by food retailers at the time of the month when welfare and Social Security checks arrive. The poor certainly do pay more (Caplovitz, 1967), and a significant proportion of the elderly are poor.

Marketing techniques aimed at higher profits, such as end-of-aisle displays and multi-ple-item pricing, also affect young and old. But many elderly have less margin for error in budgeting their limited funds.

Modern marketing procedures are geared toward the younger consumer with a family. The elderly need smaller quantities of food, especially those who live alone or have storage problems. Small quantities are often unavailable or more expensive than the same foods bought in larger amounts. The current trend toward prepackaging perishables also creates problems for the elderly. The quantities prepackaged are aimed at families, not single consumers. This makes it necessary, yet often embarrassing, for the elderly shopper to ask for less, which necessitates repackaging of the product. Furthermore, the packaging of food itself is a challenge to open, even for the young. Elderly individuals with failing vision, waning strength and declining fine coordination may be frustrated by such packaging materials.

As we have emphasized, eating is a social-psychological activity (Pike, 1968), part of the complex arrangements of interpersonal interactions. As such, it has significant social and psychological impacts on the elderly. For them, food can be of great comfort during times of loss, such as the death of a spouse or companion or the loss of social involvements. Losses force the rearrangement of the individual's world and upset balances. However, reestablishment of an old balance or creation of a new one may be difficult. Foods associated with significant events and periods in the lives of old people and their loved ones may be helpful in readjusting the individual's world.

Dietary stress can follow the loss of a spouse. Widowers remarry at a substantially higher rate than widows, but those who do not remarry may have special difficulty in adjusting. Widowers are often unable to take care of their own basic needs, especially if they have been married since youth and were socialized to depend heavily upon their wives. Because of this, some of the worst nutritional problems often occur among elderly widowers.

Widows are often able to continue performing the domestic tasks they have performed throughout their lives, but they may find themselves in financial distress. If her spouse functioned as the money manager throughout the marriage, a new widow may be unable to cope with even simple household management problems. Even for women prepared to handle these aspects of a spouse's death, the going may be difficult. Loss of companionship can seriously affect an individual's motivation to shop, cook, eat, remain active or even go on living.

Loss of companionship may also reduce physical activity or social participation that previously diverted attention from many of the problems associated with old age. Emotional stress and depression are often associated with changing roles, isolation, chronic disease and disabilities, financial stress and, simply, the fear of getting old. Depression is found in 8 to 15 percent of those over 65 in the community and 50 percent of those over 65 in nursing homes (Garetz, 1976). It may be associated with both over- and undernutrition, either of which can lead to disability or death.

Emotional stress can cause a loss of appetite and the development of negative protein, calcium and magnesium balances because of the increased excretion often associated with stress (Altschule, 1978; Scrimshaw, 1964). Stress can also lead to compulsive eating and the onset of obesity, which may further complicate health problems. The elderly person who feels rejected or neglected by his or her family and friends may also use eating as an attention-getting device. Others may not listen to frequent complaints about arthritis, but if a person does not eat or eats too much, friends and relatives generally worry and pay more attention.

Isolation can affect motivation to eat, shop, prepare meals and maintain social relationships. Many people can adjust to isolation if it is self-imposed and some may even prefer it. They may handle isolation well even when it is not self-imposed, if there is some hope of an eventual positive change in the situation. But few persons can manage involuntarily imposed isolation that leaves them with no hope in sight.

Phillips (1957) has studied the relationship between losses, role changes and adjustment to old age. His study of almost 1,000 aged individuals 60 and over—the retired compared to the employed, the widowed compared to the married—showed significantly more maladjustment among retirees, widows and those with role losses. Maladjustment was measured by self-reports on the amount of time spent daydreaming about the past, thinking about death and being absent-minded. Phillips argued that individuals who spend considerable time in such activities have difficulty in fulfilling their needs, including the need for appropriate caloric intake and dietary balance. Interestingly, Phillips employed a research variable he referred to as "identification as old." The item is a measure of self-image and simply asks, "How do you think of yourself as far as age goes—middle-aged, elderly or old?" He found that individuals who perceive themselves as elderly or old are significantly more maladjusted than those who perceive themselves as middle-aged. In addition, age identification appears to *reverse* the relationship between role loss and maladjustment. Thus, for example, those who are employed but identify themselves as old are more likely to be mal-adjusted than those who are retired but iden-tify with middle age. How and why it is that some elderly individuals, even those who have suffered a role loss and are widowed, identify with middle age is still open to empir-ical investigation.

Finally, a number of basic logistical prob-lems affect the ability of the elderly to get enough to eat. Lack of adequate cooking facilities may be a problem for those living in low-cost housing such as rented rooms or single-room-occupancy hotels. The use of cooking facilities may be discouraged by the presence of appliances or utensils that are old or dangerous. Pots with loose or absent han-dles and dull can openers can cause painful burns or cuts for an elderly person with poor vision or coordination problems. One solu-tion to such minor environmental threats is avoidance, although losing the option to use such devices may seriously limit the range of possibilities for meal preparation and nutri-tional intake.

FOOD FADDISM

The dangers of *food faddism* are a subject that nutrition educators tend to overwork or exaggerate. The large majority of people who engage in food faddism—patronizing health food stores or stocking up on megavitam-ins—do not have their health threatened, but simply pay more for what they eat (Metress, 1980). It is often alleged that the elderly are particularly susceptible to the promises of food faddism (Davis and Davis, 1981). Although no empirical attempt has been made to ascertain whether the effects of food fads are positive or negative, most standard sources simply assume a negative impact. But recently a study of nearly 3200 elderly

participants in a health-screening program revealed that 46 percent of women and 34 percent of the men regularly used vitamin supplements (Hale, Stewart and Cerda, 1982).

If the elderly are indeed more susceptible to food faddism, what are the possible rea-sons, and what are the possible effects on health? The attitude of organized medicine toward aging and geriatric problems may play an important role in the popularity of geriatric food faddism. With minor excep-tions, modern medicine, which still empha-sizes acute, curative care, has shown little interest in geriatric medicine. For many phy-sicians, the problems of elderly patients are seen in terms of a negative prognosis. In this regard, physicians may mirror the values of our society as a whole with regard to aging.

Given this situation, it is not surprising that many elderly people turn to food fads. The fad gives the individual what appears to be some authoritative sanction for what are often false hopes. However, at least the indi-vidual can feel that he or she is actively doing something about his or her condition, and not just passively allowing it to deteriorate.

Poor nutrition education during younger years also affects an individual's ability to evaluate nutritional claims. Without accurate knowledge, the consumer (at any age) is easy prey for flashy, manipulative advertising pitches by both food faddists and corporate producers. According to Gussow (1978), the deficiencies in current nutrition education in the United States are due to poorly trained health educators, government neglect and corporate control. We have been socialized to "a quick-fix mentality" (Metress, 1980). Americans seem to be constantly searching for simplistic technological solutions to soci-etal problems of all types. Socially and psychologically, food fads are an example of a falsely simplistic solution to fears and doubts about health and aging.

Many basic-nutrition textbooks have made reference to the harmful effects of food faddism on the health of the elderly (for example, *hypervitaminosis*). Is there really a threat, and if so, is it of minor or major proportions? Certainly, a variety of harmful effects can occur. These include vitamin toxicity, complication of existing health conditions, delay in seeking needed treatment, undue expense, unbalanced diets and simple disappointment. But what are the realities of these threats to the well-being of the elderly?

Toxicity due to superintake of some nutrient is a common charge of critics of food faddism. A review of the literature, however, discloses no quantitative and little anecdotal evidence of toxicity from food fads among the elderly. Actually, the two best known threats of hypervitaminosis involve the fat-soluble vitamins A and D. Given the fat-malabsorption problems often associated with the aging gut, it seems unlikely that enough of either of these vitamins would be absorbed to lead to hypervitaminosis in most cases (Metress, 1980). However, the threat of complications in existing conditions is real. Occasionally, radical diets can aggravate a pathological state such as constipation or diabetes or cause gallbladder trouble. Most people have some awareness of the limitations imposed by their known medical problems. However, undiagnosed threats could pose a problem for the fad eater, although the necessary coincidence of pathology and fad is probably rare.

Self-treatment with fad diets could mean delays in securing necessary medical treatment, perhaps the most serious consequence of all self-care strategies. Most serious disorders, however, are of such a nature as to cause alarm in a person despite attempts to deal with it through self-care. The undue expense of adherence to self-treatment regimens has been advanced as another negative effect, especially for those on marginal incomes. The costs of the fad may divert needed money elsewhere—a real concern for many (Hale, Stewart and Cerda, 1982).

The threat that unbalanced fad diets might lead to covert or even overt malnutrition would not seem to be significant except for those on extreme dietary regimens. To date, there is no evidence that elderly people suffer from such dietary deficiencies due to this factor. Finally, the disappointment that false hope brings is most often short-lived and is certainly of no great long-term psychological significance for most people. The concept and consequence of false hopes is relative to a particular situation. A so-called false hope may lead to better adjustment to a condition for which little can be done anyway.

Are there benefits in the practice of food fads? If so, do they outweigh the possible threats? Empirically this is a difficult question to answer. Some food fads may actually have beneficial effects or at least lead to better eating habits. With regard to the recent revival of interest in fiber as an important constituent of the diet, it should be recalled that for years this nutrient was also promoted by food faddists.

Participation in faddism may result in a psychological lift related to the feeling that at least one is doing something about the "miseries" of old age. This kind of psychological uplift may motivate some elderly to resume activities that were given up or curtailed. Increased participation can lead to a renewed interest in life and the development of a more positive attitude toward the aged.

SUMMARY

Hanson (1978) has suggested that physicians could become more effective if they employed a concept of "social nutrition" in counseling elderly patients. This requires taking a detailed biocultural history in which the physician considers the various factors discussed in this chapter and how these factors interact to affect the health and nutritional status of the elderly. Hanson also suggests that given a more complete knowledge of geriatric nutrition, physicians could use their status to encourage the elderly to maintain a balanced diet. Furthermore, physicians should become advocates for social nutrition for the elderly by learning about potential community programs and resources (e.g., Meals on Wheels) and supporting the use and expansion of such programs.

Factors that affect the nutritional status of the elderly can be divided into two broad groups: (1) those that are the result of metabolic and physiological changes that accompany aging, and (2) those that affect the amount and type of foods eaten. The first group comprises factors that are principally biological and biophysical; the latter group includes sociocultural factors.

Sociocultural factors that affect food intake are more varied and have a greater impact on choice of nutrients than do biological and biophysical factors. Among these sociocultural factors are dietary habits associated with youth and security, income, place of residence, living arrangements and marital status.

KEY TERMS

bacterial deconjugation
Bacteroides
biocultural
Clostridia
enculturation
food faddism
hypervitaminosis
mandibular dentures
maxillary dentures
sociocultural matrix
Veillonella

STUDY QUESTIONS

1. Why is aging considered a biocultural process? What is the role of nutrition in this process?
2. What are the two general but complementary approaches to the discussion of the biocultural basis of geriatric nutrition?
3. What are the major sociocultural functions of food?
4. Discuss the effects of age-related changes in metabolism and physiology on the nutrition of the elderly. Identify the major age-related biophysical changes that affect the intake of food by the elderly.
5. Identify the major sociopsychological and socioeconomic changes that affect nutritional intake in the elderly.
6. Discuss the possible impact of food faddism on the elderly.
7. What are some of the major problems associated with nutrition education that can affect efforts to communicate with the aged consumer?

BIBLIOGRAPHY

Adams, R., and Murray, F. 1986. *A Healthier You with a High-Fiber Diet.* Atlanta, Ga.: Communications Channel.

Altschule, M. 1978. *Nutritional Factors in General Medicine.* Springfield, Ill.: Charles C. Thomas.

Arey, L.B. 1935. The numerical and topographical relation of taste buds to human circumvallate papillas throughout the life span. *Anatomical Records 64:* 9–25.

Balachi, J.A., and Dobbins, W.V. 1974. Maldigestion and malabsorption: Making up for lost nutrients. *Geriatrics 29:* 157–160.

Becker, G.H., Meyer, J., and Necheles, H. 1950. Fat absorption in young and old age. *Gastroenterology 14:* 80–92.

Brotman, H.B. 1978. The aging of America: A demographic profile. In *The Economics of Aging: A National Journal Issues Book.* Washington, D.C.: Government Research Corp.

Busse, E.W. 1978. How mind and body and environment influence nutrition in the elderly. *Postgraduate Medicine 63:* 118–125.

Caplovitz, D. 1967. *The Poor Pay More: Consumer Practices of Low-income Families.* New York: Free Press.

Davis, A.K., and Davis, R.I. 1981. Food facts, fads, fallacies and folklore of the elderly. In J. Hsu and R.L. Davis, eds., *Handbook of Geriatric Nutrition.* Park Ridge, N.J.: Noyes Publishing.

Enger, T. 1977. Taste and smell. In J. Birren and K. Schaie, eds., *Handbook of the Psychology of Aging,* New York: van Nostrand Reinhold.

Erikson, E. 1968. *Identity, Youth and Crises.* New York: Norton.

Exton-Smith, A. 1972. Psychological aspects of aging: Relationship to nutrition. *American Journal of Clinical Nutrition 25*(8): 853–859.

Exton-Smith, A.N. 1978. Nutrition in the elderly. In J.W.T. Dickerson, and H. Lee, eds., *Nutrition in the Clinical Management of Disease* Chicago: Year Book Medical Publishers.

Fredericks, C. 1983. *Carlton Fredericks' High-fiber Way to Total Health.* New York: Pocket Books.

Galton, L. 1976. *The Truth About Fiber in Your Food.* New York: Crown Books.

Garetz, F.K. 1976. Breaking the dangerous cycle of depression and faulty nutrition. *Geriatrics 31*(6): 73–75.

Gussow, J.D. 1978. Thinking about nutrition education: Or why it's harder to teach eating than reading. Paper presented at AAAS Meeting, Houston, Texas.

Hale, W.E., Stewart, R.G., and Cerda, J.J. 1982. Use of nutritional supplements in an ambulatory population. *Journal of the American Geriatric Society 30:* 401–409.

Hanson, R.G. 1978. Considering "social nutrition" in assessing geriatric nutrition. *Geriatrics 33:* 49–51.

Harris, M. 1985. *Culture, People and Nature: An Introduction to General Anthropology.* New York: Thomas Y. Crowell.

Hermel, J., Schonwetler, S., and Samueloff, S. 1970. Taste sensation identification and age in man. *Journal of Oral Medicine 25:* 39–42.

Kelsay, J.L. 1978. A review of research on effect of fiber intake in man. *American Journal of Clinical Nutrition 1:* 142–159.

Metress, S.P. 1980. Food fads and the elderly. *Journal of Nursing Care 13:* 10–13, 24.

Niessen, L.C. 1984. Oral changes in the elderly: Their relationship to nutrition. *Postgraduate Medicine 75*(5): 231–251.

Neumann, G. 1970. *Lectures in Bioanthropology.* Bloomington, Ind.: Indiana University Press.

Phillips, B. 1957. A role theory approach to adjustment in old age. *American Sociological Review 22:* 212–217.

Pike, M. 1968. *Food and Society.* London: John Murray.

Reuben, D. 1976. *The Save-Your-Life Diet.* New York: Ballantine.

Schiffman, S.S. 1977. Food recognition by the elderly. *Journal of Gerontology 32:* 586–592.

Scrimshaw, N. 1964. Ecological factors in nutritional disease. *American Journal of Clinical Nutrition 14:* 114–122.

Westland, P. 1982. *High-Fiber Cookbook: A Positive Health Guide.* New York: Arco.

Winick, M. 1980. *Nutrition in Health and Disease.* New York: Wiley.

CHAPTER **12**

The Cardiopulmonary System and Cerebrovascular Disease

Age-related changes in the heart and blood vessels are critical to the entire aging process. While current knowledge does not allow us to specify the rank order of various systems' effects on senescent decline, the cardiovascular system has been targeted as deserving considerable attention in evaluating such decline (Eisenberg, 1984).

It is well known that cardiovascular disease has tremendous impact on individual survival. It is a major contributer to morbidity and mortality in the elderly. Heart attack, high blood pressure, congestive heart failure and stroke afflict millions of Americans. The chances of experiencing any of these conditions increase with age. Heart disease is the

leading cause of death among older adults. Heart disease, stroke and related disorders kill almost as many Americans as all other causes of death combined (American Heart Association, 1985). The most important underlying factor in the incidence of these disorders is atherosclerosis, a condition characterized by a build-up of fatty deposits within the arterial wall.

Attempts are being made to reduce the risk of heart disease and stroke. The United States and a few other countries have witnessed a downward trend in cardiovascular mortality (Feinleib, 1983a; Havlik and Feinleib, 1979; Pyorala, Salonen and Valkonen, 1985). The rate of decline started in the

United States around 1970 and has been impressive for both coronary heart disease and stroke (Feinleib, 1983a; Gordon and Thom, 1975; Pyorala, Epstein and Kornitzer, 1985; Walker, 1974). It is estimated that during a ten-year period, 300,000 persons aged 35 to 64 were saved due to a reduction in coronary heart disease (Feinleib, 1983a). The reason for the decline in mortality is not fully understood, but it is believed that both primary and secondary prevention have contributed to this decline (Epstein, 1983).

This chapter will review the aging cardiovascular system. It will examine coronary heart disease, high blood pressure, congestive heart failure and stroke. Additionally, it will briefly consider pulmonary heart disease (cor pulmonale), the most common cause of which is chronic obstructive pulmonary disease (COPD).

The prevalence of COPD increases with age. Cigarette smoking is the single most important factor in the development of obstructive pulmonary disease and lung cancer. Both pulmonary diseases will be reviewed, as will upper- and lower-respiratory infections that are significant for older adults.

GENERAL CHANGES

Present knowledge of the heart and disease in old age does not always make it possible to distinguish between intrinsic age-related changes and those induced by either deconditioning or disease. The consensus is that the aging human heart gradually increases in size until approximately age 90. How much of this hypertrophy is true aging is unknown (Eisenberg, 1984). Animal studies demonstrate that the mammalian heart enlarges

with age as a result of increased size of heart muscle cells (LaKatta, 1979; LaKatta and Gerstenblith, 1982).

Cardiac enlargement may result from increased peripheral vascular resistance, which places a greater work load on the heart. It may also be related to the loss of elasticity of the aorta (Figure 12.1). This large artery receives blood freshly pumped from the left ventricular chamber, and its branches ultimately carry blood to all parts of the body. The aorta stiffens and dilates with age, and a greater work load is placed on the heart as it pumps against the resistance of an inelastic aorta.

Although it can be retarded by physical conditioning, there is an age-related decline in cardiac output. This decline cannot be totally explained by a sedentary lifestyle, since it is observed among the physically conditioned as well. Other factors influencing cardiovascular performance must be partly responsible for this age-associated decline (LaKatta and Gerstenblith, 1982).

The reduced cardiac output of the elderly need not be significant as long as the individual is not under stress. During the stress of exercise, the younger person's heart beats faster and undergoes an increase in the strength of muscular contractions, but the heart's ability to respond to stress declines with age.

Generally, the anatomic and physiologic changes that take place in the aging heart allow it to function adequately if the coronary artery system is not greatly damaged. However, because coronary artery disease is such a prevalent condition among older Americans, it is very difficult to determine to what extent the heart ages independently of the disease.

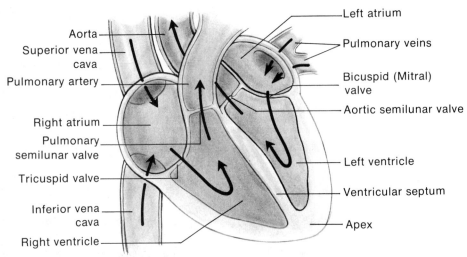

Figure 12.1   Diagram of the heart. Arrows indicate direction of blood flow. (From P. Anderson, *Basic Human Anatomy and Physiology,* 1986. Courtesy of Jones and Bartlett Publishers.)

CORONARY ARTERY DISEASE

Coronary artery disease increases in incidence with age and is the major cause of heart disease and death in older Americans. It occurs when arteries supplying heart tissue become narrowed, reducing blood flow to the heart. Tissue that is denied an adequate blood flow is called *ischemic*. Hence, coronary artery disease is also known as *ischemic heart disease* as well as coronary heart disease (CHD).

Factors responsible for the narrowed and constricted arteries are not fully understood. What is known is that an overwhelming number of persons develop a condition known as *atherosclerosis*. In atherosclerosis, the large arteries, in particular, undergo a narrowing of their *lumen* due to the build-up of *atherosclerotic plaque*. Plaque contains various substances including cholesterol crystals, calcium salts, and connective tissue. As plaque formation advances, a blood clot is likely to form, increasing the risk of blocking an already narrowed artery.

Plaque formation is a gradual process localized within the *intima* of the arterial wall (Figure 12.2). Lesions of atherosclerotic development are categorized as *fatty streaks, fibrous plaques* and *complicated lesions* (Ross, 1983). Autopsy data indicate that fatty streaks are the earliest detectable lesions or *atheromas*. Moon (1957) examined the coronary arteries in subjects ranging from fetuses to young adults. He found no evidence of fatty streaks or incipient plaque formation in the fetus but did note what he interpreted as beginning atheromas in infants three to four months of age. Studies by Holman and associates (1958) revealed evidence of fatty streaks in the aorta by three years of age. The fatty streak is randomly distributed in young persons and is clinically insignificant.

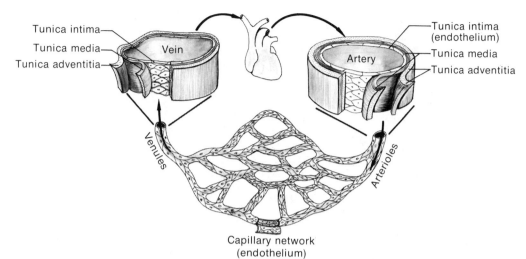

Figure 12.2   Blood vessels. Diagrammatic sketch showing the single-cell endothelium of all the vessels and the layered muscular coats of arteries and veins. (From P. Anderson, *Basic Human Anatomy and Physiology,* 1986. Courtesy of Jones and Bartlett Publishers.)

The appearance of fibrous plaque increases in occurrence from young adulthood into the later years. It is composed of a cap of fibrous connective tissue overlaying a lipid-containing region. Autopsy data on 200 Korean War battle casualties revealed a high incidence of these more advanced atheromas in young U.S. soldiers. The mean age of the soldiers examined was 22.1 years and 77.3 percent demonstrated extensive plaque formation (Enos, Holmes and Beyer, 1953, 1955). The fibrous plaque can progress to the complicated lesion characterized by calcification, ulceration, *thrombosis* and occlusive disease (Figure 12.3).

Although the mechanism behind plaque development is the subject of much study, a leading theory regarding its initiation is the *response to injury hypothesis* (Ross, 1986; Ross and Glomset, 1973). This poses that damage is done to the inner lining of the arterial wall, exposing it to blood flow. *Platelets,*

carried in the blood, can thus adhere to the exposed area and release growth-promoting substances that stimulate smooth-muscle-cell division. These cells, normally located in the middle layer of the arterial wall *(media),* proliferate, moving into the intima where they fill with lipids. The normally smooth arterial margin swells, becoming bumpy and irregular, narrowing the passageway. It is speculated that arterial injury could be triggered by numerous factors including cholesterol, cigarette smoke, high blood pressure and diabetes. Theoretically, if exposure to the damaging substance is repetitive, lesion formation will progress.

Another major theory regarding atherosclerotic development is the *monoclonal hypothesis,* which holds that plaques are essentially benign tumors that arise from single smooth-muscle cells. A monoclonal origin for atheromas does not negate the response to injury hypothesis. It maintains

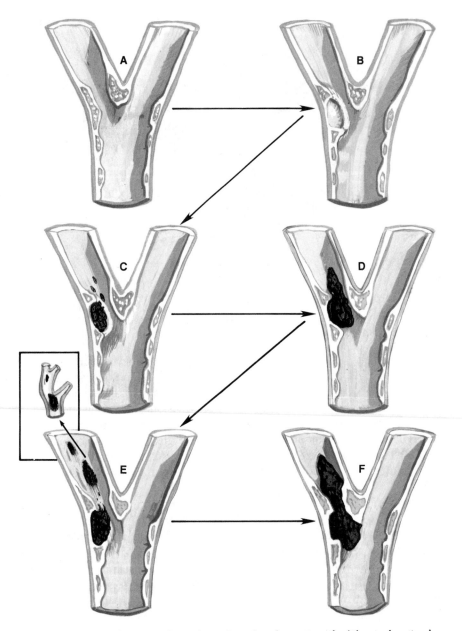

Figure 12.3 Atherosclerosis with resultant thrombus formation. **A,** Atherosclerotic plaque at arterial bifurcation. **B,** Loss of intimal continuity (ulcer formation). **C,** Aggregation of platelets and fibrin on roughened surface; fibrinoplatelet emboli may occur. **D,** Thrombus formation superimposed. **E,** Embolization of contents of plaque (cholesterol and/or calcium) and fragments of organized thrombus; occlusion of blood vessels distally in arterial tree. **F,** Thrombus causes total arterial occlusion. (From P. Anderson, *Basic Human Anatomy and Physiology,* 1986. Courtesy of Jones and Bartlett, Publishers.)

that at least some atherosclerosis is characterized by a cancer-like event whereby single smooth-muscle cells are transformed to proliferate. The role of serum cholesterol in this transformation is unknown.

Over the years plaque formation slowly and silently progresses. As reduced blood flow becomes significant, the syndrome of *angina pectoris* may be present. Angina is a recurring, dull pain emanating from behind the breastbone. It may be reported as burning, heaviness, tightness, pressure, severe pain or squeezing in the chest. It happens when the blood supply to the heart muscle is inadequate, and it may be triggered by physical activity or emotional upset. Symptoms are transitory and usually only last for a few minutes.

Coronary artery disease can lead to a *myocardial infarction* (MI) or heart attack. Although an MI can result from a sudden, abnormal heart rhythm, it generally occurs as a result of atherosclerosis. Indeed, ischemic heart disease accounts for 80 to 90 percent of all cardiac deaths (LaKatta and Gerstenblith, 1982). The extent of involved heart tissue determines the severity of the episode. If a small portion of heart muscle is affected, cardiac reserves allow the work of the heart to continue. Sometimes an individual's pattern of *collateral circulation* will be life-saving. This is a system of smaller blood vessels that helps to compensate for a main vessel blockage by supplying blood to the critical area. If it were not for these collateral vessels, death from heart attack would occur much earlier and much more frequently than it presently does. However, with age there may not be sufficient cardiac reserve to withstand the attack. Mortality associated with myocardial infarction for persons over 70 years of age is twice that of those under 70. It should be

emphasized that the effect of age itself is not known. Prognosis probably rests with the severity and duration of disease.

It is generally recognized that symptom presentation for myocardial infarction among the elderly is variable. Chest pain, though still common (Konu, 1977; MacDonald, Baillie and Williams, 1983; Tinker, 1981; Williams, Begg, Semple and McGuinness, 1976), becomes a less-frequent complaint with advancing age (Bayer, Chadha, Farag and Pathy, 1986; MacDonald, 1984). In extreme old age, shortness of breath or acute confusion are sometimes more prominent symptoms. One study concludes that in patients over 85, atypical symptom presentation becomes the rule (Bayer *et al.*, 1986). *Silent heart attack* may occur (Bayless, 1985), where pain and discomfort are absent. However, in some cases myocardial infarctions have been inappropriately termed silent (because of the absence of chest pain) in spite of the presentation of other symptoms (Marchand, 1955).

The reason for the possible absence of pain during myocardial infarction is not known. The silence of the episode may be due to an age-associated diminished sensitivity to ischemic pain. Desensitivity, confusion and failure to note such an event may also result from reduced blood flow to the brain, which is secondary to the related reduction in cardiac output.

Intermittent claudication is often a signal of widespread atherosclerotic involvement and a forerunner of impending heart attack (Kannel and McGee, 1985). It is characterized by pain as well as fatigue and weakness in legs affected by occlusive disease. The pain of *peripheral vascular disease* usually begins in the toes and may gradually involve the entire lower leg. Changes characteristic of poor nourishment of the lower limbs include thinning of skin, hair loss and toenail thickening. Ischemia may also result in decreased muscle mass contributing to limb weakness (Adelman, 1982). Gangrene and amputation may result, although the risk is low. This serious complication occurs predominantly among advanced diabetics who continue to smoke. Peripheral vascular disease is not an inevitable consequence of aging and should yield to the same preventive measures as cardiovascular disease.

Prevention of the morbidity and mortality associated with the atherosclerotic process must take into account certain important risk factors. Cigarette smoking, high blood pressure, elevated serum-cholesterol levels and diabetes are recognized as major risk factors that are subject to modification. Obesity, sedentary lifestyle and excessive stress are also contributing factors. Heredity, gender (male), race (black) and age are major risk factors that cannot be changed. The more risk factors present, however, the greater the chance of serious atherosclerotic lesions. Attention should be given to those factors that are under individual control as well as those that are modifiable under physician care.

Cigarette smokers have twice the rate of heart attack compared to non-smokers. Severity of risk is related to the number of cigarettes smoked per day. Smoking is the most powerful risk factor for peripheral vascular disease and the most prevalent risk factor for sudden death resulting from a heart attack. The American Heart Association (1985) reports that smokers experience two to four times the risk of sudden death (within an hour) after a heart attack compared to non-smokers. Of women dying suddenly from coronary heart disease, 62 percent

have been designated heavy smokers, defined as smoking more than 20 cigarettes per day (Spain, Siegel and Bradess, 1973).

Smoking cessation can reduce the risk of heart attack even among long-time smokers. Ten years after quitting, those who smoked a pack a day or less demonstrate a risk of death from coronary heart disease nearly the same as if they had never smoked. In general, persons who quit smoking reduce their risk to half that of those who continue to smoke (American Heart Association, 1985; Gordon, Kannel and McGee, 1974). One study suggests that women who stop smoking before the onset of heart attack experience no excess risk when compared with life-long abstainers (Willet, 1981).

Research suggests that smoking may affect the arterial lining, platelet adhesion, heart rhythm, oxygen utilization and transport, heart rate and blood pressure, and blood-cholesterol levels (American Heart Association, 1980). Smoking is significant as an independent factor but is especially harmful when other risk factors are present.

High blood pressure adds to the workload of the heart and is associated with an increased risk of CHD. Treatment of high blood pressure may reduce the risk of CHD and has been demonstrated as effective in reducing CHD mortality. Proper diet, exercise and medication are a part of blood-pressure control.

Serum cholesterol level is consistently correlated with CHD risk. Though controversial, studies relate the regular intake of large amounts of saturated fat and cholesterol as contributory to elevated blood-lipid levels. The American Heart Association has recommended a "prudent diet" in which 30 to 35 percent of total Caloric intake is derived from fats; less than one-third of these Calories should be derived from *saturated fats* while up to 10 percent can come from *polyunsaturated fats* and oils. To make up for lost Calories via fat restriction, *complex carbohydrate* consumption should be increased to allow for 50 percent of energy intake. Practically applied, these recommendations call for an increased intake of fruits, vegetables, legumes and whole grains, a reduced intake of high-fat red meat, pork and organ meat, and the use of unsaturated and polyunsaturated vegetable oils and margarine for table spreads, salad dressings, cooking and food preparation.

Vegetarians in the United States demonstrate below-average blood-lipid levels and a lower incidence of CHD (Taylor, 1976). Cholesterol itself is insoluble in aqueous solution, so it is transported throughout the body attached to fat and protein complexes known as *lipoproteins*. Four major groups of lipoproteins—chylomicrons, very low-density lipoproteins, low-density lipoproteins, and high-density lipoproteins—have been identified on the basis of their density. Density is said to increase with an increasing proportion of protein in the lipoprotein complex.

Approximately 80 percent of circulating cholesterol is carried in the form of *low-density lipoprotein* (LDL). LDLs transport cholesterol from the bloodstream to cells. They have been termed "bad cholesterol" because their increased levels are associated with an increased risk of coronary heart disease. Conversely, increased concentrations of *high-density lipoprotein* (HDL) seem to protect against coronary heart disease. HDLs transport cholesterol from cells to the liver and perhaps facilitate cholesterol excretion.

As noted earlier, dietary fat, particularly saturated fat, and cholesterol are proposed to be the major dietary factors influencing blood-lipid levels. HDL levels are also influenced by exercise, cigarette smoking, gender and age (Khan and Manejwala, 1981). Women usually have higher levels of HDL than men, and generally, among adults, the ratio of LDL:HDL increases with age (Gordon, Casteli, Hjortland, Kannel and Dawber, 1977). Research is now needed on age-related aspects of cholesterol metabolism in humans.

Most cases of diabetes occur during middle age and among people who are overweight, and significantly increases the risk of heart attack. Control of elevated blood-sugar levels alone does not seem to reduce atherosclerotic involvement characteristic of the large blood vessels in the diabetic. Attention to the various modifiable risk factors associated with CHD is imperative.

Obesity is related to CHD through its influence on serum cholesterol, high blood pressure and the development of adult-onset diabetes. Weight loss should be achieved by a proper diet and exercise. A program of regular physical activity should be encouraged as part of one's CHD prevention program. Exercise that may protect against disease or improve survival following a heart attack includes walking, running, cycling and swimming. Such activities should be engaged in from 15 to 30 minutes every other day. The functional capacity of the cardiovascular system increases and the myocardial oxygen demand decreases for any given level of physical activity with regular exercise of this nature.

Atherosclerosis is one form of *arteriosclerosis*. The latter is a generic term that refers to the loss of elasticity or hardening of the arteries. It can occur secondary to a disease state and as a result of aging. Unfortunately, these two terms are often used interchangeably, causing confusion regarding their distinction. Several years ago Kohn (1977:297) put the distinction in perspective by stating:

> It would be more useful to restrict the term arteriosclerosis to its original and literal meaning—hardening of the arteries—and to consider the other varieties of vascular changes as separate entities. While loss of distensibility is a general aging phenomenon, occurring in all populations and possibly developing at comparable rates, degree of atherosclerosis in individuals and populations is variable.

Age-related change in the arterial wall is not in itself atherogenic, but it can predispose the development of atherosclerosis. The normally thin intima thickens and lipid accumulation increases. Loss of elasticity raises peripheral resistance and limits the capacity for blood flow (Adelman, 1982).

HIGH BLOOD PRESSURE

Blood pressure represents the force exerted by blood flowing against vessel walls. The pumping action of the heart creates the force. An increase in blood pressure with age is not uncommon in Western societies; indeed, it has often come to be expected with advancing years. High blood pressure, also known as *hypertension*, should not be regarded as a benign or inevitable part of the process of aging (Borhani, 1986). Its presence is an especially serious risk factor for the elderly.

High blood pressure is dangerous because it indicates reduced blood flow to vital organs and increases the risk of heart attack, heart failure, stroke and renal failure. Kidney damage may be a cause of high blood pressure, although more often the kidney is the victim.

Hypertension associated with inelastic and occluded renal arteries leads to ischemic renal tissue. Poorly nourished kidneys cannot remove sufficient fluid from blood for urine output, and so a vicious cycle begins. The fluid volume of the blood increases, as do blood pressure and the workload placed upon the heart.

In 90 percent of the cases, high blood pressure is of unknown cause and is categorized as *essential, idiopathic* or *primary hypertension.* An underlying problem such as previous kidney disease, a congenital aortal defect or an endocrine disorder is responsible for 10 percent of the cases. When high blood pressure is related to such a definable cause, it is referred to as *secondary hypertension.*

Blood pressure readings are represented by two numbers as shown in Figure 12.4. The first is *systolic pressure,* which measures the force exerted when the heart beats and sends blood into the arteries. The second is *diastolic pressure* which denotes the pressure in the arteries when the heart rests between beats. High blood pressure may be defined as systolic/diastolic pressure equal to or greater than 160 mm Hg/95 mm Hg (Borhani, 1986). Cardiovascular risk is associated with both systolic and diastolic hypertension.

Among the elderly, high blood pressure is generally categorized as either *isolated systolic hypertension* (ISH) or *combined systolic-diastolic hypertension.* ISH exists when a systolic pressure level of 160 mm Hg or above occurs in the presence of a diastolic pressure of less than 90 mm Hg (Borhani, 1986; Hulley, Feigal, Ireland, Kuller and Smith, 1986). ISH is associated with a loss of arterial elasticity and a rigid aorta (Gifford, 1986). The impact of systolic blood pressure on mortality is independent of the corresponding level of diastolic pressure.

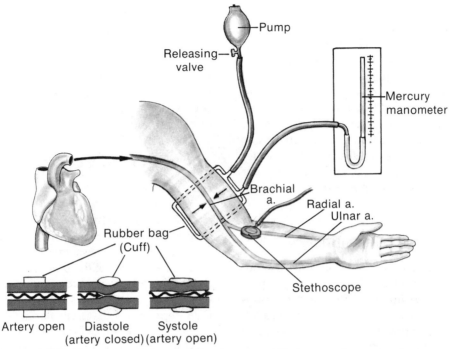

Figure 12.4   Measurement of arterial blood pressure. Application of an external pressure closes the brachial artery. As the external pressure is decreased, the manometer registers the first passage of blood through the constriction (systole). As the external pressure decreases further, the pulsation diminishes and disappears (diastole). (From P. Anderson, *Basic Human Anatomy and Physiology*, 1986. Courtesy of Jones and Bartlett, Publishers.)

Unlike systolic pressure, the diastolic measure is less likely to increase during old age (Gifford, 1986). It tends to peak during the mid-50s in men and the early 60s in women. Elevated diastolic pressure is a prevalent condition and a strong risk factor for cardiovascular disease. Treatment is important in lowering mortality.

Various medications are available to treat high blood pressure. Diuretics rid the body of excess fluid and sodium; vasodilators widen constricted or narrowed blood vessels; and other drugs attempt to prevent vascular constriction.

Although specific causes of high blood pressure are usually unknown, a number of predisposing factors have been identified. Black Americans are more likely to develop high blood pressure than are whites. Obesity and elevated blood lipids are implicated as is excessive alcohol consumption (Potter and Beevers, 1984; West, Maxwell and Nobel, 1984). Deficiency of potassium, calcium and magnesium may also contribute to high blood pressure (Kannel, 1986; Karanja and McCarron, 1986; Khaw and Thom, 1982; McCarron, Morris, Henry, and Stanton, 1984; McCarron and Morris, 1985).

Weight reduction with or without sodium restriction has been associated with lowering blood pressure (Koolen and Van Brumme-len, 1984; Maxwell, Kushiro and Dornfeld, 1984). Strong evidence exists that a reduced salt intake can lower high blood pressure among humans (MacGregor, Best, Cam, Markandu, Elder, Sagnella and Squires, 1982). There is less firm evidence that a low salt intake can prevent the condition. Vege-tarian diets have also been linked to lower blood pressure (Ophir, Peer and Gilad, 1983).

CONGESTIVE HEART FAILURE

Congestive heart failure is not a disease but rather a state of circulatory congestion pro-duced by the impaired pumping perform-ance of the heart. It generally involves left heart failure, known as *left ventricular hyper-trophy,* and is associated with atherosclero-sis, myocardial infarction, high blood pressure and impaired renal blood flow. Such conditions put additional strain on the heart forcing it to work harder. Heart enlarge-ment occurs as cardiac tissue responds to increased pumping demands. With time, overextended cardiac muscle fibers become greatly weakened. Right heart failure, as well as failure of both sides of the heart, can also occur.

Because the heart cannot pump efficiently, blood collects in tissues, producing symp-toms. *Edema* (a swelling) of the legs and ankles is common. When fluid backs up in the lungs, shortness of breath results. Con-gestive heart failure can be treated with drugs, diet and rest. If an underlying cause of congestive heart failure is recognized (such as high blood pressure) then that problem must be treated.

Congestive heart failure increases with age. Three-quarters of all ambulatory patients with the condition are over 60 years old (LaKatta and Gerstenblith, 1982). Heart failure does not mean that the heart has stopped beating. Though presentation occurs in an older person with superimposed disease(s), most cases respond to treatment.

CEREBROVASCULAR DISEASE

Atherosclerotic changes in blood vessels that serve brain tissue can reduce its nourishment and result in the malfunction or death of brain cells. Impaired brain tissue circulation is known as *cerebrovascular disease.*

When a portion of the brain is completely denied blood, a cerebrovascular accident (CVA), or stroke, results. The severity of a CVA depends on the particular area as well as the total amount of brain tissue involved. Thus a stroke may affect such a small brain area that it goes unnoticed or such a large area that it causes severe damage or death. Cerebrovascular accident represents the third leading cause of death among the eld-erly in the United States.

A number of specific events typically cause CVAs in older persons. Cerebral thrombosis is the main form of stroke among the elderly, occurring when a blood clot or *thrombus* forms in an artery supplying the brain. Often the artery is damaged by atherosclerosis and the thrombus becomes lodged in the nar-rowed channel. A cerebral embolism may also be responsible for a CVA. In this instance, a clot called an *embolus* forms else-where and travels to obstruct a brain artery. Emboli arising from the heart are well-known causes of stroke.

A *cerebral hemorrhage* is another form of stroke wherein a blood vessel bursts, depriving an area of the brain of its blood supply. Likewise, accumulated blood from the rupture may put pressure on surrounding brain tissue, further causing damage. Cerebral hemorrhage is more likely to cause death than are the other forms of stroke. A victim usually goes into a coma and dies within a few days.

Short-lived symptoms may precede a CVA. These episodic symptoms are known as little strokes or *transient ischemic attacks* (TIAs). Sudden motor weakness or numbness on one side of the body, speech disturbances, dimness or vision loss (especially in one eye), dizziness and sudden falls are among the transitory symptoms that might be present. TIAs are warning signs of a possible impending stroke. They often precede a major stroke by days, weeks or months. These transient ischemic attacks are sometimes labeled as *carotid artery syndrome* in reference to a transient occlusion of the major arteries supplying the brain. Because a narrowed carotid artery may eventually be the focus of a complete occlusion, an operation known as an *endarterectomy* is sometimes performed to clear the inner lining of the artery.

When a stroke occurs, varying degrees of damage may result. *Hemiplegia* (paralysis of one side of the body), *aphasia* (speech disorders) and sensory disturbances present special problems for the stroke victim. Rehabilitation efforts should begin immediately. Successful rehabilitation depends on the area and degree of brain damage, as well as on the supportive attitude and encouragement of the rehabilitation team, family and friends. Sudden neurologic and motor changes can greatly alter a person's perception of self and the world and can cause a person to withdraw. A stroke may occur during sleep. Imagine how traumatic it would be to awaken and be unable to move a body part and possibly be unable to speak or understand what is said.

Brain damage affects opposite sides of the body. Right-brain damage may result in left-side paralysis or weakness *(hemiparesis)*. It may be accompanied by memory deficits, spatial-perceptual deficits and an impulsive behavioral style. Left-brain damage may cause right-side hemiplegia or hemiparesis as well as speech-language deficits, memory deficits and a slow, cautious behavioral pattern. These noted deficits are typical for right-handed individuals. For left-handed persons the opposite may be true.

Aphasia may denote impaired ability to comprehend or express language. In *receptive aphasia* a person has difficulty processing external stimuli. Because of damage within the speech center of the brain, the individual may not understand others' speech or what is read. When a person understands what is said but cannot form the words or gestures to respond to stimuli, *expressive aphasia* has resulted. An aphasic patient may also suffer from a mixed condition.

Tragically, aphasia may be incorrectly associated with mental deterioration. Tactless statements may be made in the presence of a person who can understand what is going on but who cannot appropriately respond. Likewise, the patient may be infantilized and treated as a child while being fully aware of the indignity of such treatment.

Patients should be encouraged to speak and those around them should listen patiently. The patients should not be rushed or cut off in the middle of their attempts. Such behavior on the listener's part can cause the person to feel awkward and self-conscious.

The aphasic victim may thus become depressed and withdrawn.

Despite aphasiac involvement, some persons may be able to repeat words or phrases that are a part of what is known as primitive or automatic language. For instance, they may be able to count, to sing, to respond with "okay" and "goodbye" while not being able to construct sentences or express original ideas. It is easier for the bilingual person to regain command of his or her native language. This factor should be kept in mind when working with such persons.

Stroke patients may also suffer from defective vision or blindness in one-half of their visual field. This condition is known as *hemianopsia*. In stroke patients, such visual losses are often compensated for by head turning. Those who work with or care for stroke victims should be aware of such possible losses and attempt to aid the patients in their compensation. For example, an individual with hemianopsia may eat only the food that appears on half of the plate because the rest of it cannot be seen. Rotating the plate for the person can be most helpful.

As a result of hemianopsia, a stroke victim may not react to the appearance of someone in the doorway or may be startled as someone who has entered the room seems suddenly to come within view. This lack of awareness about a visitor's presence is related to the loss in visual field. Position yourself within the persons field of vision when approaching.

Care should be taken in positioning a hemianopsic patient within a room. For example, a person who has lost the right field of vision should not be placed with his/her left side to a wall. The person would not be able to see what was taking place within the room itself, but would have a clear view of the wall!

It is imperative that paralyzed patients be turned regularly to prevent pressure sores, exercised to prevent joint contractures and positioned so that they do not aspirate or choke on nasal-oral secretions. Rehabilitative efforts with them should also include understanding and patience. Useful gains may not be obvious for weeks or months after the initiation of a rehabilitation program.

Family members and health workers must be made aware that their attitudes toward the CVA victim and the recovery process can encourage the person to work harder or to give up. Short-term goals should be set, and small gains should be favorably praised. Above all, dignity and independence must be respected. The patient must be allowed to do as much for him- or herself as is possible. A paternalistic or overly helpful attitude, although well-intended, may slow recovery and make the patient feel helpless or useless. Gains in independent living can only enhance a person's sense of self-worth and dignity.

Of the approximately 300,000 persons who annually suffer their first stroke, the majority survive with residual neurologic deficits that can impair independence. For those with preexisting functional disability, stroke may impose additional impairment that serves to increase the risk of institutionalization. Proper care of the elderly stroke victim demands functionally directed clinical examinations and ongoing periodic functional evaluation (Kelly and Winograd, 1985).

Treatment for stroke may involve drugs, surgery (carotid endarterectomy) and rehabilitation. Anticoagulants including aspirin may be employed in an attempt to prevent clot formation. Attention to various types of heart disease that might promote the formation of a "wandering" clot is also important.

Diagnosis and treatment of TIAs may prevent a stroke. A number of factors increase the risk of a CVA. In general, risk of stroke is greater in men and among blacks. The high risk of stroke among blacks may be due to a greater prevalence of high blood pressure in this population. High blood pressure, especially diastolic hypertension, is one of the most significant risk factors for stroke. In 65- to 74-year olds with diastolic pressure less than 90 Hg, the incidence of CVA increases dramatically with incremental elevations in systolic blood pressure (Borhani, 1986). Heart disease, leading to pumping failure or serving as a source of emboli, increases the risk of stroke. Risk is also greater among diabetic individuals.

PULMONARY HEART DISEASE

There is a very precarious relationship between the heart and lungs. In fact, the cardiovascular and respiratory systems could be said to operate as a unit. Damage or disease in one of these organ systems is often secondarily reflected in the other. In pulmonary heart disease the right side of the heart enlarges in response to certain lung changes. This condition is known as *right ventricular hypertrophy* or *cor pulmonale*. Delicate capillary beds within the air sacs of the lungs allow for the gaseous exchange of carbon dioxide and oxygen. If a significant number of these beds become destroyed as a result of obstructive lung disease, blood begins to back up between the lungs and the right side of the heart from which it has been pumped. In an attempt to compensate for the undue strain placed upon it, the right side of the heart enlarges. Right-side heart failure can eventually result.

Symptoms associated with pulmonary heart disease are those of a respiratory and circulatory nature: cough, shortness of breath, bluish skin as a result of a short supply of oxygen, edema, chest pain and substernal discomfort. Treatment and management of pulmonary heart disease is closely associated with the treatment and management of the lung disorders that give rise to the condition.

THE PULMONARY SYSTEM

A number of age-related changes collectively exert an effect on the respiratory system. These changes, which reduce maximum breathing capacity, are significant in that they cause fatigue in an elderly person more easily than in a younger person. But these changes are not sufficient to cause apparent symptoms at a resting state. In the absence of disease they do not significantly affect the lifestyle of an older individual.

The efficiency of the respiratory system declines as evidenced by weakened *intercostal muscles*, decreased elasticity of the thoracic cage and chest wall, less efficient emptying of the lungs and increased rigidity of internal lung structures (Ostrow, 1984; Piscopo, 1981).

Respiratory diseases are more prevalent in older individuals than in the general population. The threat of serious respiratory infection increases with age, as do the threats of chronic obstructive pulmonary disease and lung cancer. The threat of respiratory infection is partially related to age-associated reductions in host resistance to infectious microorganisms. However, obstructive pulmonary conditions and lung cancer do not increase in incidence because of inherent aging factors. Environmental conditions such as exposure to cigarette smoke and polluted air play an important role in their development.

Respiratory Infection

Pneumonia and respiratory infections are one of the leading causes of death among the elderly. Pneumonia in the elderly may not present the typical symptoms of cough, sputum production or fever. Sometimes the older patient will demonstrate confusion, loss of appetite, weakness or a fall (Yoshikawa, Norman and Grahn, 1985). Thus the appearance of such non-specific symptoms should not be dismissed. Bacterial pneumonia among the aged is related to a more diverse array of microorganisms than those associated with lower-respiratory disease in younger adults (Andrew, Chandrasekeren and McSwiggan, 1984; Verghese and Berk, 1983; Yoshikawa, Norman and Grahn, 1985).

Pneumococcal infections, especially pneumococcal pneumonia, are a major cause of morbidity and mortality among the American elderly (Fedson, 1985; Goodman, Manton and Nolan, 1982). The economic toll for pneumococcal pneumonia is high. Hospital care accounts for 97 percent of medical costs for elderly patients with this condition (Office of Technology Assessment, 1979). The pneumococcal vaccine is recommended for adults over 65 years as protection against pneumococcal pneumonia (Centers for Disease Control, 1984), although it may not be as effective among elderly persons (Shapiro and Clemens, 1984). Immunization is especially important for the institutionalized elderly population.

The threat of aspiration pneumonia increases with age. This condition develops as a result of sucking foreign material or gastric contents into the lung tissue. Although everyone is at risk of having an accident of this nature, those older persons who may be confined to bed, suffering from esophageal disorders or from diminished levels of consciousness are at special risk. As Zavala (1977:46) notes, "In extended care facilities and hospitals, aspiration occurs all too frequently when a well-meaning attendant attempts to force-feed elderly stroke victims or senile, debilitated patients in an attempt to 'put meat on their bones.'"

The seriousness of the aspiration depends on the amount and the kind of material aspirated. The incident may result in serious lesions, minor irritation, debilitating pulmonary disease, or suffocation. Those who work with older patients should be aware of this risk and be careful not to rush them in swallowing their medication or in eating their food.

Influenza is a major cause of respiratory disease for older adults (Setia, Serventi and Lorenz, 1985). The Advisory Committee on Immunization Practices of the Centers for Disease Control recommends annual vaccination especially for elderly nursing home residents (Centers for Disease Control, 1985). Clinical attack rates of 25 to 60 percent have been reported in nursing homes with case-fatality rates as high as 30 percent (Barker and Mullooly, 1980a, 1980b).

Although tuberculosis has declined in incidence in the general population, data indicate that it is increasingly prevalent among the elderly (U.S. Public Health Service, 1982; Stead, 1981; Stead and Lofgren, 1983). Its significance in the elderly is related to its natural history and to the special medical conditions of aged persons. Initial exposure to *Mycobacterium tuberculosis*, the agent that causes the disease, may produce inactive infection (no discernible symptoms) and immunity. The bacteria generally remain dormant for many years but are capable of reactivating to produce lung changes and disease symptoms. Tuberculosis in the elderly is often of this reactivation type, in fact, the elderly who have survived long-standing inactive infection now represent the largest reservoir of potentially active tuberculosis (Nagami and Yoshikawa, 1983).

Besides having lived through a time period when the chance of exposure to M. tuberculosis was high, the elderly are also subject to special conditions that serve to increase the susceptibility of reactivation, including impaired cell-mediated immunity, malnutrition, alcoholism and various superimposed diseases.

Tuberculosis can be managed, but untreated it remains a fatal disease. Rudd (1985) warns that it is a problem for diagnosis and treatment among the geriatric population. Clinical presentation may be atypical and without fever, sweats, cough or blood-stained sputum. There may also be atypical radiographic findings (Nagami and Yoshikawa, 1984), and tuberculin tests may be false negative (Battershill, 1980). On the other hand, a chronic fever, unexplained anemia, unexplained weight loss or failure to thrive might indicate tuberculosis (Yoshikawa, Norman and Grahn, 1985). Physicians treating older patients should maintain an index of suspicion for this disease (Rudd, 1985). Delayed diagnosis and indifferent medical care have been cited as contributing to the extremely high rate of tuberculosis in today's elderly (Iseman, 1985).

Tuberculosis has resulted in severe outbreaks in nursing homes (Narain, Lofgren and Warren, 1985; Stead, 1981; Stead, Lofgren and Warren, 1985), where reactivation and primary-contact type disease must both be respected. Employees can transmit infection, emphasizing the significance of preemployment and annual screening for tuberculosis as well as work restriction for workers who are ill (Crossley, Irvine, Kaszar and Loewenson, 1985; Smith, 1985).

Chronic Obstructive Pulmonary Disease

Chronic obstructive pulmonary disease (COPD) includes *chronic bronchitis* and *emphysema*. Chronic bronchitis is defined on the basis of clinical symptoms and their duration. It is manifested as a chronic cough and sputum production for a minimum of three consecutive months for at least two consecutive years. Its prevalence increases with advancing age. Cigarette smoking is the single most important risk factor in the development of the condition. Atmospheric and industrial pollution is an additional but less significant risk factor.

Respiratory airways contain mucus-producing cells. Their secretions normally serve to trap various foreign invaders. Hairlike projections called *cilia* use whiplike motions to propel mucus toward the mouth where it is either expectorated or swallowed. Chronic irritation overwhelms the anatomic defenses of the respiratory tract. Cilia become paralyzed and eventually disappear. Mucus-producing cells enlarge. Hypersecretion of mucus along with mucosal swelling allows mucus plugs to become trapped in the airways. Persistent cough and expectoration develop as the body attempts to clear the airways. Oxygen intake is reduced. With widespread obstruction, carbon dioxide is retained. Eventually, greater demand is placed upon the heart.

As the condition continues, air becomes trapped beyond the mucus plugs and in time causes the *alveoli* of the lungs to remain inflated. Normally, the elastic alveoli inflate as they receive inhaled air. Oxygen thus comes into contact with the capillaries of the delicate walls of the air sacs. During the process of exhaling, stale air is removed from the air sacs, allowing space for a fresh supply of oxygen to make its way once again to lung tissue. When air sacs remain inflated by trapped air, the amount of space provided for gaseous exchange is reduced. Air sac walls may eventually rupture, irreversibly reducing the total amount of respiratory surface space.

When the air sacs become overinflated, the walls stretched and torn, and capillary beds destroyed, emphysema has made its appearance (Figure 12.5). The term *emphysema* actually refers to these anatomic changes. Shortness of breath becomes pronounced, and exhalation becomes prolonged and difficult.

Chronic obstructive lung disease develops slowly and insidiously. As symptoms begin to

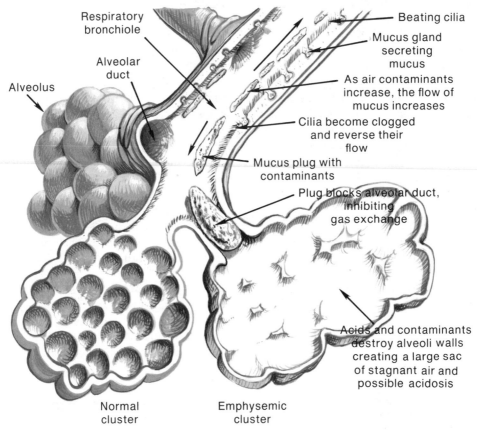

Figure 12.5 Diagrammatic representation of the development of emphysema. (From P. Anderson, *Basic Human Anatomy and Physiology,* 1986. Courtesy of Jones and Bartlett Publishers.)

unfold, they may be considered a part of old age. It should be emphasized that chronic cough, chronic expectoration, and shortness of breath are not signs of aging. Persons displaying these symptoms must be urged to visit their physicians.

Depending upon the degree of damage suffered, persons will be more or less limited in their activities. When symptoms first appear, the individual may experience fatigue after climbing stairs or walking down the street. As the disease progresses, exhaustion may result from buttoning a shirt. Shortness of breath, the chief symptom of emphysema, initially presents itself as exertion. Eventually, it is present even at rest.

Most persons dying from emphysema actually succumb to heart disease. The changes in the lungs lead to cor pulmonale and can result in congestive heart failure. Respiratory infections also become a special risk for these lung disease patients. The disease changes make them more susceptible to infection and complicate their recuperation.

LUNG CANCER

Diseases related to cigarette smoking may be considered as the United States' most preventable health problems. Such is the case for lung cancer, whose causal association with cigarette smoking has been outlined in a series of Surgeon General's Reports on Smoking and Health (U.S. Public Health Service, 1964, 1982; Wynder and Goodman, 1983). Internationally, cigarette smoking is the leading cause of premature death. The Insurance Court of Appeal in Sweden has awarded compensation to the family of a woman who died in 1982 from a type of lung cancer seen almost exclusively in smokers.

Ms. Palm was a non-smoker who had shared an office for 20 years with several colleagues who did smoke. The Swedish court designated Ms. Palm's lung cancer as an occupational injury due to passive smoking in the workplace.

In a 1986 U.S. report, the National Research Council of the National Academy of Sciences declared that non-smokers are imperiled by their exposure to tobacco smoke. The U.S. group found that exposure to smoke increases the incidence of lung cancer in non-smokers. The report noted several studies showing a 30 percent higher incidence of lung cancer in non-smoking spouses of smokers than in non-smoking couples.

To prevent primary lung cancer in mid-to-late adulthood, smoking should be avoided throughout life. If you smoke, stop! Unfortunately, the decline in risk for lung cancer with smoking cessation does not decrease as dramatically as that for heart attack and associated sudden death. For those who have smoked 20 years, it takes about three years for an alteration in the risk of lung cancer to be demonstrated. Slowly, the reduced risk will approach that of a non-smoker 10 to 15 years after smoking has ceased (Doll and Peto, 1976).

SUMMARY

Cardiovascular disease is a major contributer to morbidity and mortality in the elderly. Heart attack, high blood pressure, congestive heart failure and stroke afflict millions of Americans. Chances of experiencing any of these conditions increases with age. The most important factor associated with the incidence of these disorders is atherosclerosis. Coronary artery disease increases with age and is the major cause of heart disease and death in older Americans.

Prevention of the morbidity and mortality associated with atherosclerosis must take into account certain important risk factors. The major risk factors that are subject to individual control or are modifiable under physician care include cigarette smoking, high blood pressure, elevated serum cholesterol levels and diabetes.

High blood pressure is not uncommon with age in Western societies. Its presence is an especially serious risk factor in the elderly. It indicates reduced blood flow to vital organs and increases the risk of heart attack, heart failure, stroke and renal failure. Although the specific causes of essential hypertension are unknown, a number of predisposing factors have been identified.

Cerebrovascular accident, or stroke, represents the third leading cause of death among the elderly in the United States. Its severity depends on the particular area as well as the total amount of brain tissue involved. Short-lived symptoms known as transient ischemic attacks (TIAs) may precede a stroke.

Pneumonia and respiratory infections are one of the leading causes of death among the elderly. The threat of aspiration pneumonia increases with age, with the seriousness of the episode dependent upon the amount and kind of material aspirated. Influenza is also a major cause of respiratory disease in older adults. Although tuberculosis has declined in incidence in the general population, it is increasingly prevalent among the elderly.

The threats of chronic obstructive pulmonary disease (COPD) and lung cancer increase with age, although their appearance is not related to inherent aging factors. Cigarette smoking is the single most important risk factor associated with their appearance. To prevent primary lung cancer in mid-to-late adulthood, smoking should be avoided throughout life.

KEY TERMS

alveoli
angina pectoris
aphasia
arteriosclerosis
atheroma
atherosclerosis
atherosclerotic plaque
carotid artery syndrome
cerebral hemorrhage
cerebrovascular disease
chronic bronchitis
cilia
collateral circulation
combined systolic-diastolic hypertension
complex carbohydrate
complicated lesions
congestive heart failure
coronary artery disease
cor pulmonale
diastolic pressure
edema
embolus
emphysema
endarterectomy
essential hypertension
expressive aphasia
fatty streaks
fibrous plaques
hemianopsia
hemiparesis
hemiplegia
high-density lipoproteins
hyptertension
idiopathic hypertension
intercostal muscles
intermittent claudication
intima
ischemic heart disease
isolated systolic hypertension (ISH)
left ventricular hypertrophy
lipoproteins
low-density lipoproteins

lumen
media
monoclonal hypothesis
Mycobacterium tuberculosis
myocardial infarction (MI)
peripheral vascular disease
platelets
polyunsaturated fats
primary hypertension
receptive aphasia
response to injury hypothesis
right ventricular hypertrophy
saturated fats
secondary hypertension
silent heart attack
systolic pressure
thrombosis
thrombus
transient ischemic attacks (TIA)

STUDY QUESTIONS

1. How significant is cardiovascular disease among the elderly? List some general changes that occur in the aging heart.
2. Define the following terms: coronary artery disease; ischemic; ischemic heart disease; coronary heart disease; atherosclerosis; atherosclerotic plaque.
3. Identify the various lesions of atherosclerotic development.
4. Briefly explain the response to injury hypothesis; monoclonal hypothesis.
5. Identify each of the following: angina pectoris; myocardial infarction; collateral circulation; intermittent claudication; silent heart attack.
6. Identify and discuss risk factors associated with atherosclerosis and heart attack.
7. Differentiate atherosclerosis from arteriosclerosis; essential from secondary hypertension; systolic from diastolic pressure.
8. How is high blood pressure generally defined? Identify the two categories important among the elderly. What are some risk factors related to high blood pressure?
9. What is congestive heart failure?
10. What typically causes cerebrovascular accidents in older persons?

11. What is the significance of a TIA? Note some of the possible consequences of a stroke. Identify risk factors for cerebrovascular accident.
12. What is right ventricular hypertrophy or cor pulmonale?
13. How significant is pneumonia and respiratory disease, in general, for the older adult? Explain.
14. What is chronic obstructive pulmonary disease? Differentiate chronic bronchitis from emphysema.

BIBLIOGRAPHY

Adelman, B. 1982. Peripheral vascular disease. In J. Rowe and R. Besdine, eds., *Health and Disease in Old Age*. Boston: Little, Brown.

American Heart Association. 1980. *Risk Factors and Coronary Heart Disease: A Statement for Physicians*. Dallas, Tex.: National Office.

American Heart Association. 1985. *Heart Facts, 1985*. Dallas, Tex.: American Heart Association, National Center.

Andrew, J., Chandrasekeren, P., and McSwiggan, D. 1984. Lower respiratory infections in an acute geriatric male ward: A one-year prospective surveillance. *Gerontology 30:* 290.

Barker, W., and Mullooly, J. 1980a. Impact of epidemic type A influenza in a defined adult population. *American Journal of Epidemiology 112:* 799.

——————. 1980b. Influenza vaccination of elderly persons: Reduction in pneumonia and influenza hospitalizations and deaths. *Journal of American Medical Association 244:* 2547.

Battershill, J. 1980. Cutaneous testing in the elderly patient with tuberculosis. *Chest 77:* 188.

Bayer, A., Chadha, J., Farag, R., and Pathy, M. 1986. Changing presentation of myocardial infarction with increasing old age. *Journal of the Amererican Geriatrics Society 34:* 263–266.

Bayless, R. 1985. The silent coronary. *British Medical Journal 290:* 1093.

Borhani, N. 1986. Prevalence and prognostic significance of hypertension in the elderly. *Journal of the American Geriatrics Society 34:* 112–114.

Centers for Disease Control. 1984. Pneumococcal polysaccharide vaccine usage in the United States. *Morbidity and Mortality Weekly Report 33*: 273–281.

_____. 1985. Prevention and control of influenza. *MMWR 34*: 261–275.

Crossley, K., Irvine, P., Kaszar, D., and Loewenson, R. 1985. Infection control practices in Minnesota nursing homes. *Journal of the American Medical Association 254*: 2918–2921.

Doll, R., and Peto, R. 1976. Mortality in relation to smoking: 20 years observation on male British doctors. *British Medical Journal 2*: 1525–1536.

Eisenberg, S. 1984. Cardiovascular changes as risk factors for senility. In H. Rothschild and C. Chapman, eds. *Risk Factors for Senility.* New York: Oxford University Press.

Enos, W., Holmes, R., and Beyer, J. 1953. Coronary disease among United States soldiers killed in action in Korea. *Journal of the American Medical Association 152*: 1090–1093.

_____. 1955. Pathogenesis of coronary disease in American soldiers killed in Korea. *Journal of the American Medical Association 158*: 912.

Epstein, F. 1983. Coronary heart disease—geographical differences and time trends. *Atherosclerosis 6*: 723–732.

Fedson, D. 1985. Improving the use of pneumococcal vaccine through a strategy of hospital-based immunization: A review of its rationale and implications. *Journal of the American Geriatrics Society 33*: 142–150.

Feinleib, M. 1983a. The magnitude and nature of the decline in coronary heart disease mortality. In *The Decline in Coronary Heart Disease Mortality—The Role of Cholesterol Change?* Proceedings of the College of Physicians and Surgeons of Columbia University. Anaheim, Calif.: Nov. 1983., pp. 5–9.

_____. 1983b. Risk assessment, environmental factors and coronary heart disease. *Journal of the American College of Toxicology 2*: 91–104.

Gifford, R. 1986. Management of isolated systolic hypertension in the elderly. *Journal of the American Geriatrics Society 34*: 106–111.

Goodman, R., Manton, K., and Nolan, T. 1982. Mortality data analysis using a multiple-cause approach. *Journal of the American Medical Association 247*: 293.

Gordon, T., Casteli, W., Hjortland, M., Kannel, W., and Dawber, T. 1977. High density lipoprotein as a protective factor against coronary heart disease: The Framingham Study. *American Journal of Medicine 62*: 707–714.

Gordon, T., Kannel, W., and McGee, D. 1974. Death and coronary attacks in men after giving up cigarette smoking. *Lancet 2*: 1348.

Gordon, T., and Thom, T. 1975. The recent decrease in CHD mortality. *Preventive Medicine 4*: 115–125.

Havlik, R., and Feinleib, M. 1979. *Proceedings of the Conference on the Decline in Coronary Heart Disease Mortality.* U.S. Department of Health, Education and Welfare, Public Health Service. National Institutes of Health. Publ. No. 79–1610.

Holman, R., McGill, H.C., Jr., Strong, J.P., and Geer, J.C. 1958. The natural history of atherosclerosis: Early aortic lesions as seen in New Orleans in the middle of the 20th century. *American Journal of Pathology 34*: 209.

Hulley, S., Feigal, D., Ireland, C., Kuller, L., and Smith, W. 1986. Systolic hypertension in the elderly program (SHEP); The first three months. *Journal of the American Geriatrics Society 34*: 101–105.

Iseman, M. 1985. Tuberculosis in the elderly: The grey plague. *Journal of the American Geriatrics Society 33*: 517.

Kannel, W. 1986. Nutritional contributors to cardiovascular disease in the elderly. *Journal of the American Medical Association 34*: 27–36.

_____, and McGee, D. 1985. Update on some epidemiologic features of intermittent claudication: The Framingham Study. *Journal of the American Geriatrics Society 33*: 13–18.

Karanja, N., and McCarron, D. 1986. Calcium and hypertenison. *Annual Review of Nutrition 6*: 475–494.

Kelly, J., and Winograd, C. 1985. A functional approach to stroke management in elderly patients. *Journal of the American Geriatrics Society 33*: 48–60.

Khan, M., and Manejwala, A. 1981. Cholesterol metabolism and atherosclerosis in Aging. In J. Hsu and R. Davis, eds., *Handbook of Geriatric Nutrition*. Park Ridge, N.J.: Noyes Publications.

Khaw, K., and Thom, S. 1982. Tandomized double-blind cross-over trial of potassium on blood pressure in normal subjects. *Lancet 2:* 1127–1129.

Kohn, R. 1977. Heart and cardiovascular system. In C. Finch and L. Hayflick, eds., *Handbook of the Biology of Aging*. New York: Van Nostrand Reinhold.

Konu, V. 1977. Myocardial infarction in the elderly. *Acta Medica Scandinavia 604*(suppl): 9.

Koolen, M., and Van Brummelen, P. 1984. Sodium sensitivity in essential hypertension: Role of the renin-angiotension-aldosterone system and predictive value of an intravenous frusemide test. *Journal of Hypertension 2:* 55.

LaKatta, E. 1979. Alterations in the cardiovascular system that occur in advanced age. *Federal Proceedings 38:* 163.

LaKatta, E., and Gerstenblith, G. 1982. Cardiovascular system. In J. Rowe and R. Besdine, eds., *Health and Disease in Old Age*. Boston: Little, Brown.

MacDonald, J. 1984. Presentation of acute myocardial infarction in the elderly—a review. *Age and Aging 13:* 196.

MacDonald, J., Baillie, J., and Williams, B. 1983. Coronary care in the elderly. *Age and Aging 12:* 12.

MacGregor, G., Best, F.E., Cam, J.M., Markandu, N.D., Elder, D.M., Sagnella, G.A., and Squires, M. 1982. Double-blind randomized cross-over trial of moderate sodium restriction in essential hypertension. *Lancet 1:* 351–354.

McCarron, D.A., Morris, C.D., Henry, H.J., and Stanton, J.L. 1984. Blood pressure and nutrient intake in the U.S. *Science 29:* (224) 1392–1398.

McCarron, C.A., and Morris, C.D. 1985. Blood pressure response to oral calcium in persons with mild to moderate hypertension: A randomized, double-blind, placebo-controlled, crossover trial. *Annals of Internal Medicine 103* (6): 825–831.

Marchand, W. 1955. Occurrence of painless myocardial infarction in psychotic patients. *New England Journal of Medicine 253:* 51.

Maxwell, M., Kushiro, T., and Dornfeld, L. 1984. Blood pressure changes in obese hypertensive subjects during rapid loss: Comparison of restricted versus unchanged salt intake. *Archives of Internal Medicine 1144:* xx.

Moon, H. 1957. Coronary arteries in fetuses, infants and juveniles. *Circulation 15:* 366.

Nagami, P., and Yoshikawa, T. 1983. Tuberculosis in the geriatric patient. *Journal of the American Geriatrics Society 31:* 356.

———. 1984. Aging and tuberculosis. *Gerontology 30:* 308.

Narain, J., Lofgren, E., and Warren, E. 1985. Epidemic tuberculosis in a nursing home: A retrospective cohort study. *Journal of the American Geriatrics Society 33:* 258–263.

Office of Technology Assessment. 1979. *A Review of Selected Federal Vaccine and Immunization Policies*. Washington, D.C.: U.S. Government Printing Office.

Ophir, O., Peer, G., and Gilad, J. 1983. Low blood pressure in vegetarians: The possible role of potassium. *American Journal of Clinical Nutrition 37:* 755.

Ostrow, A. 1984. *Physical Activity and the Older Adult*. Princeton, N. J.: Princeton Book Co.

Piscopo, J. 1981. Aging and human performance. In E. Burke, ed., *Exercise, Science, and Fitness*. Ithaca, N.Y.: Mouvement Publications.

Potter, J., and Beevers, D. 1984. Pressor effect of alcohol in hypertension. *Lancet 1:* 119.

Pyorala, K., Epstein, F., and Kornitzer, M. 1985. Changing trends in coronary heart disease mortality; Possible explanations. *Cardiology 72:* 5–10.

Pyorala, K., Salonen, J., and Valkonen, T. 1985. Trends in coronary heart disease: Mortality and morbidity and related factors in Finland. *Cardiology 72:* 35–51.

Ross, R. 1983. Recent progress in understanding atherosclerosis. *Journal of the American Geriatrics Society 31:* 231–235.

———. 1986. The pathogenesis of atherosclerosis. *New England Journal of Medicine 314:* 488–500.

Ross, R., and Glomset, J. 1973. Atherosclerosis

and the arterial smooth muscle cell. *Science 180:* 1332.

Rudd, A. 1985. Tuberculosis in a geriatric unit. *Journal of the American Geriatrics Society 33:* 566–569.

Setia, U., Serventi, I., and Lorenz, P. 1985. Factors affecting the use of influenza vaccine in the institutionalized elderly. *Journal of the American Geriatrics Society 33:* 856–858.

Shapiro, E., and Clemens, J. 1984. A controlled evaluation of the protective efficacy of pneumococal vaccine for patients at high risk of serious pneumococcal infections. *Annals of Internal Medicine 101:* 325–330.

Smith, P. 1985. Infection control in nursing homes. *Journal of the American Medical Association 254:* 2951–2952.

Spain, D., Sidgel, H., and Bradess, V. 1973. Women smokers and sudden death: The relationship of cigarette smoking to coronary heart disease. *Journal of the American Medical Association 224:* 1005–1007.

Stead, W. 1981. Tuberculosis among elderly persons: An outbreak in a nursing home. *Annals of Internal Medicine 94:* 606.

Stead, W., and Lofgren, J. 1983. Does the risk of tuberculosis increase in the elderly? *Journal of Infectious Diseases 147:* 951.

Stead, W., Lofgren, J., and Warren, E. 1985. Tuberculosis as an epidemic and nosocomial infection among the elderly in nursing homes. *New England Journal of Medicine 312:* 1483–1487.

Taylor, C. 1976. Serum cholesterol levels of seventh-day adventists. *Paroi Arterielle/Arterial Wall 3:* 175.

Tinker, G. 1981. Clinical presentation of myocardial infarction in the elderly. *Age and Aging 10:* 237.

U.S. Public Health Service. 1964. *Smoking and Health: Report of the Advisory Committee to the Surgeon General of the Public Health Service.* U.S. Department HEW, PHS Publ. No. 1103.

――――――. 1982. *The Health Consequences of Smoking—Cancer: A Report of the Surgeon General.* U.S. Department HHS, PHS Publ. No. 82–50179.

――――――. 1982. *1982 Tuberculosis Statistics, States and Cities.* U.S. Department of Health and Human Services, Public Health Service. Atlanta, Ga.: Centers for Disease Control.

Verghese, A., and Berk, S. 1983. Bacterial pneumonia in the elderly. *Medicine 62:* 271.

Walker, W. 1974. Coronary mortality: What is going on? *Journal of the American Medical Association 227:* 1045–1046.

West, L, Maxwell, D., and Nobel, E. 1984. Alcoholism. *Annals of Internal Medicine 100:* 405.

Willet, W. 1981. Cigarette smoking and non-fatal myocardial infarction in women. *American Journal of Epidemiology 113:* 575–582.

Williams, B., Begg, T., Semple, T., and McGuinness, J.B. 1976. The elderly in a coronary unit. *British Medical Journal 2:* 451–453.

Wynder, E., and Goodman, M. 1983. Smoking and lung cancer: Some unresolved issues. *Epidemiologic Reviews 5:* 177–207.

Yoshikawa, T., Norman, D., and Grahn, D. 1985. Infections in the aging population. *Journal of the American Geriatrics Society 33:* 496–503.

Zavala, D. 1977. The threat of aspiration pneumonia in the aged. *Geriatrics 32:* 47–51.

CHAPTER **13**

Disorders of the Urinary System

Urinary disorders are significant causes of death and morbidity for the elderly. Only 3 percent of the elderly have histologically normal kidneys. Total renal function in an elderly individual may only be 50 percent of that of the young adult (Anderson and Williams, 1983). Urinary incontinence is a major problem in old age, and urinary tract infections are a common complaint. Renal complications accompany a variety of pathologic conditions that are common among the elderly. Prostate disease, a major etiologic factor in many bladder disorders, is a disease category often associated with death. Given this pattern, it is no wonder that the urinary tract's functional impairment is a matter of great practical concern for both the elderly and those who care for them.

SYMPTOMS OF URINARY TRACT DISTURBANCE

A number of common symptoms of dysfunction are important in considering the aging urinary tract. Although not diseases themselves, they are often indicative of existent disease or malfunction. These symptoms are polyuria, nocturia, frequent urination, urinary retention, blood in the urine, urinary incontinence, and uremia (Hodkinson, 1976).

Polyuria

Polyuria is a condition characterized by increased urine excretion (a daily urine volume greater than 2500 ml). Its cause can be excess intake of fluids such as coffee, tea or beer; use of diuretic substances such as ace-tazolamide (Diamox) for glaucoma; and altered renal function. Disorders such as *diabetes insipidus,* diabetes mellitus and hypocalcemia also are associated with increased excretion of urine. Diabetes insipidus is rare in the elderly, but diabetes mellitus and hypocalcemia are not uncommon. Polyuria can be a feature of early renal failure. It is important for individuals with polyuria to compensate for the fluid loss by increasing intake to prevent dehydration.

Nocturia

Nocturia is the need to get up to urinate during the night. It is estimated that almost two-thirds of the elderly awaken to urinate two or more times a night. This condition can be simply related to too much fluid intake during the late evening; reduced intake prior to bedtime can afford some relief from this condition, as can urinating before going to bed. However, nocturia can also be related to urinary infections such as cystitis and pyelonephritis, prostatic hypertrophy, certain medications and uninhibited neurogenic bladder. It may be a reflection of early renal disease but it is commonly associated with cardiac and hepatic failures. Frequent nighttime urination in the absence of high fluid intake should cause some concern.

Increased Frequency of Urination

Under normal conditions a person passes urine four to six times a day, a total volume of about 700–2000 ml per day. Persons with urinary frequency will pass urine every hour or two during the day and possibly three to four times each night. The most common cause of increased urination is infection of the bladder, kidneys or prostate. The condition also can be caused by polyuria, anxiety, a small bladder or irritative or obstructive lesions. Prostate hypertrophy and urinary infection can be differentiated by other symptoms, the latter usually being associated with scalding or burning dysuria, the former with hesitation, a poor stream and dribbling. The frequency of urination accompanying diabetes mellitus can be identified by its association with excessive thirst, hunger, weight loss and often a family history of diabetes.

Dysuria

Dysuria is a condition that varies in symptoms from a slight burning on urination to severe pain in the urethra and bladder neck. It is usually associated with increased frequency of urination and is often related to urinary infection, most commonly from bacteria. It is also associated with prostatic enlargement, bladder stones, urethritis and senile vaginitis. Persistent symptoms in the absence of infection require careful examination of the bladder and urethra.

Retention of Urine

The inability of elderly men to urinate is most often associated with prostate enlargement (Figure 13.1). It may come without warning or be associated with another illness such as a cold or influenza. There may be no pain even when the condition is acute, but restlessness or confusion may develop. It can also result from drugs, nervous disease or urinary tract obstructions. Large doses of medications for colds, ulcers or diarrhea, tranquilizers and anticholinergics may cause urinary retention. Frequent voiding of very small units of urine can be regarded as urinary retention. In women, fecal impaction and urethral stricture are among the most common causes of retention. Lesions of the frontal cortex of the brain and degenerative

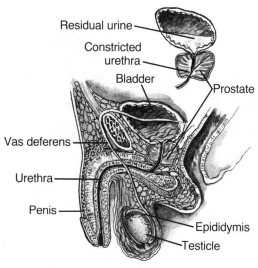

Figure 13.1   Prostate-urethra relationship.

changes of the bladder are causes of urine retention as well.

Hematuria

Blood in the urine may be detected by *urinalysis* or, in some cases, by a red to brown discoloration, depending on the amount of blood and the acidity of the urine. Slight hematuria may cause no discoloration and may only be detected by chemical or microscopic examination. Bloody urine associated with pain is most often caused by an infection or the presence of a stone. In the absence of pain, bloody urine may be the first sign of cancer of the bladder or kidney. Thus it is very important that hematuria be evaluated for its cause; this is usually done through pyelography and cystoscopy. When such an examination is to be done, it would be helpful for the physician to discuss the entire procedure in detail with the patient. If not, it can be very traumatic. *Hematuria* is also associated

with renal embolism, subacute bacterial endocarditis, diseases with abnormal bleeding tendencies such as thrombocytopenia, acute nephritis, and trauma such as catheter accidents or misuse.

Uremia

The accumulation of toxic materials in the blood—*uremia*—is an important condition associated with a number of renal disorders. Hodkinson (1981) identifies three types.

Prerenal uremia is caused by a fall in renal blood flow. This leads to a decline in the glomerular filtration rate, which in turn leads to nitrogen retention in the blood stream. The chief causes of prerenal uremia are dehydration due to vomiting, diarrhea, the use of diuretics and insufficient consumption of water. Cardiac output failure associated with hemorrhages, shock, acute myocardial infarction and heart failure may also be causative factors. Prompt recognition is important, since the condition is reversible if discovered early enough.

Postrenal uremia is a result of an obstruction of the urinary outflow from the kidneys with the development of a back-pressure effect. It is reversible, but sustained pressure can lead to irreversible damage. The major associated causes of obstruction are prostate problems and carcinoma of the bladder, which obstruct the bladder outlet and/or the ureters. Postrenal uremia is less prevalent than prerenal.

Renal uremia results from kidney disease. It is a progressive condition, irreversible in many cases.

Uremia is not specific to any disease but is a general result of renal failure and is due to a variety of causes. Early symptoms include fatigue, lack of vigor, weakness, weight loss and lack of mental alertness, which may gradually develop over a period of weeks or even years. Some neuromuscular manifestations such as muscle cramps, twitches and convulsions may occur along with gastrointestinal symptoms such as nausea, vomiting, diarrhea and loss of appetite. Malnutrition will sometimes develop, and hypertension and heart failure are common. Untreated, uremia will inevitably result in death. The prognosis for uremic patients is generally good for those in whom the precipitating factors (such as urinary obstructions) can be identified and treated. On the other hand, patients whose uremia is of unknown cause, or the result of a multitude of physiologic insults to the kidneys over a long period of time, have a very poor prognosis.

AGE CHANGES IN THE TRACT

Bladder and Urethra

The bladder of an elderly person has a capacity of less than half (250 ml) that of a young adult (600 ml) and often contains as much as 100 ml of *residual urine* (Figure 13.2). The onset of the desire to urinate also is delayed in older persons. Normally, the *micturition* reflex is activated when the bladder is half full, but in the elderly it often does not occur until the bladder is near capacity. The origin of this alteration of the micturition reflex is unclear, but it may be related to age changes in the frontal area of the cerebral cortex, or to damage associated with a cerebral infarction or tumor. Reduced bladder capacity coupled with a delayed micturition reflex can lead to problems of frequent urination and extreme urgency of urination. These conditions, even if they do not render the individual incontinent, are annoying. They often make the individual feel useless, so it is helpful if the

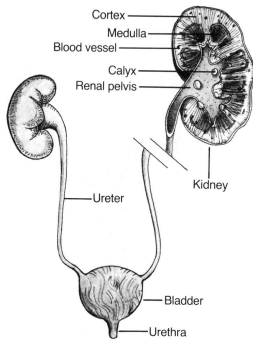

Figure 13.2   Urinary system.

physician explains the changes in an effort to negate these feelings.

The bladder outlet in aged women exhibits a high incidence of funneling, which may be the result of deterioration of the pelvic diaphragm. The *pelvic diaphragm* is a muscular mass that helps to maintain the tone of the bladder and contributes to proper closure of the bladder outlet. If the pelvic diaphragm is weak, it can contribute to imperfect closure of the bladder and leakage known as stress incontinence. Stress incontinence occurs when there is a sudden rise in intravesical pressure such as occurs in coughing or sneezing. Surveys among even young women indicate that stress incontinence can occur at any age. Muscular strengthening and retraining under the supervision of a physiotherapist can afford relief in many cases. Incontinent women often exhibit a mucosal prolapse of the external urethra. The specific causes and significance of prolapse of the urethra are uncertain, but it does not appear to be related to parity or urinary infections.

Bladder diverticula are common (25 to 30 percent) in elderly men and undoubtedly are related to bladder obstruction with raised pressures and hypertrophy of the bladder muscle (trabeculation). In women, bladder diverticula are rare but are sometimes found in women with bladder problems of neurologic origin. The importance of bladder diverticula in the development of bladder disorders is still unclear.

Urinary Incontinence

Urinary incontinence is a major problem of the elderly, especially those who are institutionalized. Surveys indicate that institutionalized persons have a greater incontinence rate than those living in the community. This difference in rates is probably due to the fact that a large number of the institutionalized are there because of incontinence. If one uses only severe incontinence as a category, approximately 7 percent of those over 65 years are incontinent, and the problem tends to become more prevalent with advancing age, peaking in the 80s (Yeates, 1976).

Urinary incontinence can be defined as the involuntary passing of urine in an undesirable place or situation (Yeates, 1976). Undesirability of place, however, may reflect personal or community norms. The condition is complicated and poorly understood. It is a matter of great concern for the elderly individual, family members, age mates and the geriatric personnel caring for the individual. Many times families give up trying to care for elderly members if they become incontinent. Shuttleworth (1970) estimated that more than 20 percent of the admissions to geriatric units are prompted by inability to deal with incontinence. Incontinent patients greatly increase the work load in geriatric units and can seriously test the morale of many geriatric staffs. However, patients feel depressed, helpless and useless. Group therapy with the family and the patient should be encouraged to help mutual understanding and lead to better communication on both sides. Possibly the patient will feel less ashamed and cause less anger in the family.

Incontinence may lead to an admission refusal by a residential home. It can also make one an unwelcome member of any social group or club. Psychologically, the depression, insecurity and apathy can be devastating to an individual and require great supportive care by a geriatric staff. The nurse or family member should retain a positive approach at all times. If the staff or family does everything for the patient, however, dependency will develop. Continence should be expected and the incontinent patient made to feel that continence and independence will return. If the staff has minimal expectations, the patient's performance will most likely be correspondingly low.

The actual prevalence of incontinence among the elderly is difficult to determine because of problems in defining the category and because of the self-report nature of many health inventories. Only skillful questioning may lead to identification of an incontinent person. The words urinary incontinence mean different things to different researchers, and so surveys are not universally comparable.

A number of factors have been studied in relation to incontinence. Among them are sex, age, infection, physical activity, diseases of the central nervous system and the ability to care for oneself. A number of researchers have found little difference between the sexes, although Brocklehurst (1951) and Brocklehurst and associates (1968) found incontinence in twice as many women as men. He suggests that this difference might be related to the greater prevalence of dementia in women. Age differences are unimportant, and most researchers believe that infection does not play a significant role.

Incontinence is not as common in those who are physically active, or who are still able to dress, walk and feed themselves. However, studies of elderly persons who are confined to bed indicate that 25 percent are incontinent. Diseases of the central nervous system (such as stroke, upper motor neuron lesions and organic brain syndrome) are the most important predisposing factors. Prostatic hypertrophy and senile vaginitis may also be associated with incontinence.

According to Brocklehurst (1963), old-age urinary incontinence is usually the result of the interaction of predisposing and precipitating factors. The sequence of events is schematically outlined in Table 13.1.

Yeates (1976) has defined four categories of incontinence that are affected by mechanical changes: (a) passive (stress) incontinence, which is caused by a weakness in the bladder outlet and is sometimes traceable to the strain of childbirth; (b) active incontinence with emptying caused by overactivity of the whole bladder mechanism; (c) acute incontinence with residual urine, in which contractions occur but fail to empty the bladder; and (d) retention with overflow incontinence, in which the bladder is constantly distended and results in more or less continuous leakage. Knowledge of these mechanisms will be important in systematizing an approach to an individual patient's problem.

Psychological factors such as regression, feelings of helplessness, dependency, attention seeking, insecurity, rebellion, sensory deprivation and disturbed conditioned

TABLE 13.1 Urinary incontinence[a]

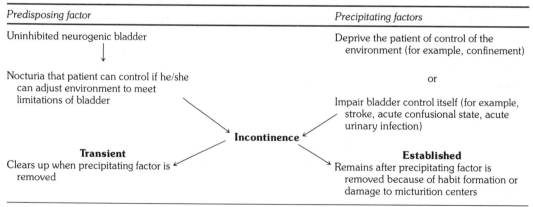

Predisposing factor	Precipitating factors
Uninhibited neurogenic bladder ↓	Deprive the patient of control of the environment (for example, confinement)
Nocturia that patient can control if he/she can adjust environment to meet limitations of bladder	or
	Impair bladder control itself (for example, stroke, acute confusional state, acute urinary infection)
	Incontinence
Transient Clears up when precipitating factor is removed	**Established** Remains after precipitating factor is removed because of habit formation or damage to micturition centers

[a]Information used for this table can be found in J.C. Brocklehurst, 1963. The aetiology of urinary incontinence in the elderly. In J.C. Brocklehurst, *Current Achievements in Geriatrics*. London: Anderson & Isaacs.

reflexes can all contribute to the development of incontinence. Continence depends on alertness; oversedation, drowsiness, stupor or coma can disrupt continence. Poor motivation can also play an important role. Confused, depressed and demoralized patients whose lifelong routine has been seriously disrupted may also deliberately violate social conventions regarding urination. Loss of home, youth, and life can cause an individual to give up and lose his or her psychological ability to cope.

Psychiatric problems such as a variety of dementias, schizophrenia, neuro confusional states and psychotic depression can also cause incontinence. Although neurologically caused incontinence may be uncommon, diseases such as multiple sclerosis, spinal cord lesions, acute spinal cord compression, vascular stroke, and Parkinson's disease may also be associated with incontinence. From the foregoing catalog of possible causative factors, it should be evident that no one approach to treatment is possible. Treatment and control must be individualized in each case.

Treatment of incontinence is complex and often time-consuming. At the most basic level, treatment should attempt to remove or overcome the precipitating factors. Reeducation in bladder function is important. This involves a positive attitude by the staff and the patient. Special exercise can diminish frequency of urination and nocturia (Shepherd, 1980). Drug therapy can follow several courses, including the pharmacologic blockage of the bladder reflex, the regulation of diuresis with powerful diuretics, the use of hormones such as estrogen to affect the trigone of the bladder and increase capacity, or the use of a variety of drugs to reduce bladder overactivity.

Physical therapy may help to restore muscles that play a part in incontinence or to enable the patient to retain muscles to perform their basic functions. Occupational therapy can distract the patient's attention from the condition and promote his or her general physical and mental well-being, thus possibly overcoming some psychological causes of incontinence.

Some groups of patients will never regain continence. For these one must consider the *catheter* and external appliances to control the condition. Catheters have been criticized because of the attendant risk of infection. However, this is often associated with the techniques of the caregivers who empty the appliance. The apparatus can become clogged by deposited sediments (sanding), especially from dehydrated patients who excrete concentrated urine or residual urine. The apparatus also can kink, thus interrupting flow. To avoid this, a careful record of output should be kept and recorded at about two-hour intervals. Older patients, especially those in confused states, will often pull out their catheters.

The indwelling catheter should not cause pain. Sometimes the bladder neck is constricted, and the catheter is too large. If a patient does complain of pain, assessment by a professional should be made. Placement in a room or ward with persons having similar problems can often help the patient to accept and deal with the problem more effectively. Social activity also can divert the patient's attention from the catheter. The risk from infection today is considerably reduced because of the advent of disposable plastic catheters. Despite the problems associated with catheters, they will probably remain an important method of dealing with incontinence.

External appliances have not been too successful for women, although the recent introduction of *marsupial pants* (Willington, 1972) has been of help to some. One problem with external appliances involves keeping the patient from his or her urine to keep them warm and comfortable. Consideration of social and ego needs is also important. The devices should not be degrading or socially offensive. The control of odors and stains also is esthetically and psychosocially important. Until recently, most external devices have been devised with staff convenience and routine in mind rather than the patient's condition and therapy.

The marsupial pants conduct fluid outward through a pad in the genital area that is external to the body of the pant. As long as this pad remains unsaturated, the patient remains warm and dry. Trials in England indicate that the pants not only work in practice but that patients previously considered hopeless have learned to become continent or have reduced their incontinence. The garment is intended for self-use and is psychologically and socially satisfying to most patients (Willington, 1973). This type of development clearly caters to the patient's recovery or successful adaptation rather than to the logistical needs of the staff or institution.

Prevention of incontinence has rarely been considered in the past. Isaacs (1976) suggests a number of strategies that can be taken to intervene at various points of vulnerability: strengthening weakened sphincter and muscles by exercises, faradism, surgery and external devices; taming the detrusor muscle mass; regulating fluid intake; or blocking hyperactivity with drugs. The signal to urinate can be amplified by diuretic drugs or by higher fluid intake; activity programs can be used to sublimate bladder anxieties. Finally, the hospital or institutional environment can be adapted to promote human dignity by allowing free and ready access to lavatory facilities and by encouraging the staff to become aware of opportunistic micturition.

The careful recording of incontinence helps to determine the extent of the individual's problem. The regimen of record keeping can serve to direct the staff's attention to the patient at regular intervals and lead to establishing routines to get the patient to the lavatory to empty the bladder. The staff can also reinforce the patient by a positive attitude that will meet psychological needs such as self-esteem and independence. These procedures can go a long way toward establishing a workable pattern of micturition.

Urinary Tract Infections

Urinary infections have been studied in three residence groupings of elderly patients: private homes, extended-care facilities, and hospitals. The highest incidence of infection occurs in hospitals, and the lowest is found among those living in private households. Rates for hospitalized patients were found to be 32 to 33 percent (Brocklehurst, Dillane and Griffiths, 1968; Gibson and Pritchard, 1965; and Walkey, 1967). Dontas and colleagues (1966) observed a rate of 25 percent for nursing home patients, and Sourander (1966) and Brocklehurst (1963) found rates of 20 percent for those in private households. Women over 65 living at home had an incidence of 20 percent, whereas men had low rates through the sixth decade and showed a gradual rise to 20 percent from the seventh decade on (Brocklehurst, Dillane and Griffiths, 1968). It is possible that the increase among men is related to prostate surgery, since some researchers believe that prostate fluid may have bactericidal or *bacteriostatic* properties.

Urinary infections are generally accompanied by burning sensations, painful urination, increased nocturnal frequency, precipitancy, suprapubic tenderness, flank pain and, sometimes, fever. In the elderly and in diabetics, a urinary infection may present only fever or clinical deterioration, such as confusion in the elderly and worsening glucose control in the diabetic. Infection is not related to incontinence, the other common urinary disorder of the elderly. The most common pathogen is the bacteria *E. coli.* Two categories of urinary infection have been identified, acute and chronic. The acute type is usually associated with precipitancy and incontinence and seems to localize in the lower urinary tract. It usually clears up if properly treated with antibiotics. The chronic type does not respond well to treatment. It is often associated with some kind of obstruction and affects both the kidney and lower urinary tract.

Bacteriuria is common in the elderly, and there is some debate about whether to treat it if it is asymptomatic, which is most often the case. Active cystitis may be encouraged by various neurogenic or mechanical factors that lead to urinary retention. It is often associated with such conditions as benign *prostatitis,* diverticula of the bladder, bladder stones, arteriosclerosis of the bladder and irritable bladder of senile dementia. *Cystitis* is common in women with a congenitally short urethra. Finally, clinical instrumentation for diagnostic or therapeutic purposes induces a surprising number of infections.

The differential prevalence among women of urinary infections could be related to a number of factors such as the tendency toward having a short urethra in close proximity to the rectal opening, dilation and slowed peristalsis of the urethra in pregnancy, urethral compression by an enlarging uterus in pregnancy, and the absence of prostatic fluid with its bacteriostatic qualities. Sociocultural factors such as the nature of sexual activity, personal hygiene practices, socioeconomic status and analgesic abuse may affect the incidence of urinary infections. Metabolic disturbances, too, such as diabetes, stones and gout appear to lower the system's resistance to infection.

Treatment of urinary infections should start with a thorough diagnosis to avoid unnecessary therapy and expense. Proper diagnosis in the beginning allows the correct choice of drugs and ensures the success of aggressive therapy. Adequate antimicrobial treatment is necessary to assure that infection is eradicated and to prevent its possible spread to other areas. Usually 10 to 14 days of drug therapy is recommended. The patient must be adequately instructed with respect to the importance of continuing the therapy prescribed even after early relief from symptoms. Therapeutic regimes are varied, ranging from antibiotic therapy to the use of ascorbic acid tablets.

Another aspect of infective care is high fluid intake. High fluid intake helps relieve symptoms by diluting the urine, increasing urine flow for a flushing effect, preventing dehydration because of fever or polyuria, and acidifying the urine. However, large amounts of fluid may lower the concentration of antibacterial drugs below their level of effectiveness and render antimicrobial therapy useless. Patients should be cautioned about folk medicine approaches that might interfere with the orthodox medical treatment for urinary tract infections.

Recurrent or stubborn infections should be checked for association with obstructions, metabolic disturbances or structural abnormalities. In some chronic patients the medical goal may be bacterial control, since eradication may be impossible or might require aggressive means that could lead to other problems.

Prostate Gland

The prostate gland is often implicated in a variety of disorders of the urinary tract. Two groups of changes in the gland have been identified by Moore (1952). Pre-senile changes occur between ages 40 and 60 and are characterized by irregular changes in the smooth muscle fibers and prostate tissue. Senile changes occur between ages 60 and 80 and develop more slowly and diffusely, exhibiting less variation from one part of the gland to another.

Prostate problems are a major concern to many elderly men, but many do not report their symptoms until a late stage (Anderson and Williams, 1983). There are three major causes of prostate troubles: *vesical* contracture of the neck, *nodular (benign) hyperplasia*, and carcinoma. Vesicular neck obstruction is usually characterized by slight urination hesitancy in early stages and by nocturia in its later stages. Slowing of the urinary system or complete retention usually indicate some lesion of the bladder neck. Some precipitating factors have been identified as acute illness, exposure to cold and excessive alcohol intake.

Nodular or benign hyperplasia is very common from age 50 on, with individuals in their 60s showing high rates of incidence. Most corrective operative procedures are carried out on individuals in these age cohorts. Hyperplasia is also an important cause of death. McKeown (1965) found that 8 percent of her patients exhibiting hyperplasia died from it or its complications. Men in their 70s and 80s show a decline in problems, and the gland is characterized by nodules within it. It is possible that an endocrine connection exists, since nodules do not develop unless the testes are operating. The inner and outer areas may be affected by different hormones. The symptoms associated with benign hyperplasia are increased frequency of urination, poor stream formation, dribbling, nocturia and retention with overflow. Occasionally hematuria results because of the rupture of veins in the prostate. Treatment may include prostatic removal. The most common type of surgery, retropubic prostatectomy, has a high level of safety.

Carcinoma of the prostate is the most frequent malignancy of elderly men (Hodkinson 1981), and all older men should have regular physical examinations to monitor the condition of their prostates. Carcinoma is rare before age 50 but present in possibly 95 percent of men in their eighth decade (Anderson and Williams, 1983). It may produce little or no obstruction, but when it does, the condition may be too far along to treat successfully. It commonly spreads to the pelvis and lumbar spine, where it is usually associated with great pain. Prostate removal does not rule out the development of cancer in the area. In those over 70, surgery is rarely recommended, since the individual's life expectancy is relatively unaffected by the condition. At advanced ages individuals often die of other causes before the carcinoma takes its toll. However, Klein (1979) reports 42,000 new cases each year in the United States with 17,000 deaths. Table 13.2 summarizes the developmental aspects of prostate carcinoma along with possible therapeutic approaches.

Many men are concerned about the effects of prostatic surgery or therapy on their sexual potency or masculinity. Some time should be devoted to explaining to the patient the real and imagined side effects associated with treatment of prostate disease. Possible adverse side effects should be weighed against the effects of non-treatment. In some cases the patient may choose non-treatment rather than risk a change in his real or perceived male image.

CHANGES AND DISEASES IN THE AGING KIDNEY

The aging kidney appears macroscopically normal in 50 percent of cases, but histologically only 3 percent are without some abnormality. Renal function declines with age, leading to decreases in glomerular filtration rate, effective plasma flow and tubular absorption and excretion. There appears to be a decrease in average renal function with age; this accelerates with advancing age (Lindeman, 1975). It has been suggested that this decline is related to loss of nephrons. At age 70 one has one-half to one-third fewer nephrons than at age 30 (McKeown 1965), and after age 40 there is an increasing inability to replace injured renal cells. With increasing age the kidneys themselves are found to be smaller—250 grams at age 40 but 200 grams at age 80 (Epstein, 1985)—and the nephrons themselves are smaller in size and fewer in number.

Despite these dramatic changes, loss of renal tissue is probably secondary in importance to the structural vascular changes that occur with age. The arterial tree atrophies, and a thickening of the intimal layer of the small arteries develops. This is caused by a proliferation of elastic tissue, which decreases the functional efficiency of the system. The large arteries often develop intimal

TABLE 13.2 Developmental stages of prostate carcinoma[a]

Stages	Treatment
1. Not suspected clinically Not palpable Discovered incidentally (as by surgery)	No treatment; careful observation
2. Hard and irregular but not too large Palpable prostatic nodules Confined to prostate	Radical prostatectomy if young enough and healthy
3. Obvious spread to adjacent pelvic tissues with fixation	Radiation therapy
4. Distant metastases	Hormonal treatment Radiation of painful metastastic sites

[a]Information used for this table can be found in Whitmore, W.F. 1956. Symposium on hormones and cancer therapy: hormone therapy in prostatic cancer. *American Journal of Medicine 21*: 697.

hyperplastic layers many times complicated by arteriosclerosis. Williams and Harrison (1937) observed that narrowing of the large arteries is usually due to aging, whereas the smaller arteries are influenced by both age and hypertension. Anatomic narrowing of the blood vessels and persistent vasoconstriction have a tendency to reduce flow through the system. It is estimated that the total renal blood flow declines 10 percent each decade (Epstein, 1985).

It appears, then, that vascular changes may be more significant in declining renal efficiency than renal tissue loss. Still, vascular changes may have secondary effects that contribute to the loss of nephrons. This is very significant when the kidney is seriously malfunctioning or when severe atherosclerosis is superimposed on the aging process. But in the absence of diagnosed renal insufficiency the age-related changes are significant enough to require adjustments in drug dosage (Epstein, 1985).

Pyelonephritis

Pyelonephritis, an inflammation of a part of the kidney, is the most common kidney disease at any age. The changes in the kidney that are the result of previous inflammations and past infections complicate this condition. This disease is more prevalent with advancing age, with the 80s being the period of highest prevalence. More than two-thirds of the observed cases are in those over 60 years of age. In observing a sample of 70-year-olds, McKeown (1965) found an incidence of 16 to 20 percent. The condition is prevalent much earlier in women. For organizational purposes we will now consider acute and chronic pyelonephritis as separate problems of the elderly.

Acute Pyelonephritis

Acute pyelonephritis is associated with bacterial infections such as *E. coli,* staphylococci, streptococci and Proteus, with *E. coli* being responsible in the majority of cases. There is some dispute about whether the pathway taken by the infecting microorganisms is through the bloodstream or by the ascension of the urinary tract. This condition is often associated with obstructions in the lower tract. The kidneys are often swollen and soft and generally unequal in size. A variety of forms of stasis related to prostate problems, *calculi,* neurologic disease, circulatory disorders, prolonged recumbency and tumors are associated with acute pyelonephritis. It is twice as frequent in diabetics, possibly because sugar in the urine may favor bacterial growth and because of the greater frequency of catheterization among these individuals. In younger age groups acute pyelonephritis is associated with or contributes to complications of hypertension.

Any form of urinary instrumentation carries with it the risk of infection. Indwelling catheters result in infections in about 90 percent of cases, although they may take a long time to develop. Cystitis associated with infections can result in a vesicoureteral reflux that can lead to pyelonephritis. Instrumentation apparently can either introduce bacteria to the tract or induce transient bacteremia through mechanical pressure. It is also possible that infection can be carried by the blood from another infective locus in the body.

In old age acute pyelonephritis can often lead to death through a combination of infection with uremia. In an old-age series, McKeown (1965) found 5 percent mortality from acute pyelonephritis; one-half of these deaths resulted from complications of prostatic disease. In the other half of this series death was associated with carcinoma, renal or vesical calculi or cerebral vascular accidents.

Chronic Pyelonephritis

Chronic pyelonephritis is the result of recurrent inflammatory episodes of the kidney in most cases. It is often, as its name implies, a progressive inflammatory process. It is also more common and more refractive to treatment than acute pyelonephritis, which responds to antibiotics. By the time it is detected in its chronic phase, its cause is obscure. Some experimental evidence indicates intrarenal scars of treated pyelonephritis may render the kidney more susceptible to reinfection. McKeown (1965) noted its occurrence in 11 percent of an old-age series and observed a slightly higher incidence in men with prostatic disease. Its prevalence increases with age, but overdiagnosis in autopsy must be considered a possibility. It is not often fatal, although occasionally it precipitates hypertensive heart failure or uremia.

The kidney is generally reduced in size and presents a deformed outline in chronic pyelonephritis. The scars are U-shaped as opposed to the V-shaped scars associated with vascular lesions. It is difficult to differentiate the scars of pyelonephritis from vascular scarring (which itself may predispose the kidney to local pyelonephritis infections). Both types of lesions occur together but are etiologically independent of each other. In the case of scarring, whatever the cause, damage to kidney tissues and blood vessels occurs and leads to reduced functional efficiency. Therapeutic measures for treatment

and management of these infections have been mentioned in the section on general urinary infections. Again, precautions are necessary in approaching infections of the urinary tract. Pyelonephritis-associated infections will be more difficult to treat than those in the lower tract.

Renal Calculi

Renal calculi (kidneystones) are clinically more common in the years from 30 to 60. On autopsy they tend to be high in the 50- to 70-year-old group (McKeown, 1965). Vesical calculi start in middle age, and increase to old age. More prevalent in men, they are often complications of urinary tract obstructions related to infection and prostate enlargement. Most calculi are asymptomatic, and new ones are rare in old age. Over three-quarters of all stones are passed spontaneously without medical assistance. People rarely die from them, but they are not as readily passed by older people and can present dangerous obstructions that should be diagnosed and treated. The causes of their formation are still rather obscure, and several theories exist. It has been noted that sterile urine usually is associated with stones composed of uric acid and oxalate, whereas infective urine is most often associated with stones of phosphate and carbonate composition, which are the most common. It has been suggested that a large daily fluid intake of more than two liters might significantly reduce the incidence of stone formation.

Glomerulonephritis

Inflammation of the glomeruli in both the acute and chronic forms is known as *glomerulonephritis*. Both conditions are generally rare in old age and an uncommon cause of renal failure. Few patients with chronic nephritis would survive beyond 70. The pathologic condition is the same at any age, but when present in the elderly it may be complicated by arteriosclerosis, hypertension and pyelonephritis. Acute glomerulonephritis may be so mild that it is asymptomatic, but in other cases it may proceed rapidly to uremia and death. It often presents itself nonspecifically with nausea, malaise, arthralgias and a tendency toward pulmonary infection (Morrin, Hinglais and Nabaira, 1978). In a majority of cases it has its origin in an untreated streptococcal infection of the respiratory system. It is probable that the renal damage is caused by an autoimmune response in the kidney of a susceptible individual. This response may promote a lingering inflammation after the infecting microbe is eradicated.

Treatment is based on responding to the individual symptoms of renal failure. Penicillin treatment for 10 days may be prescribed to eradicate the causative agent. Once the inflammation is established it can continue even without the presence of the streptococcus organism. Complete and usually uneventful recovery occurs in 95 percent of children. Adults have a more difficult time because coexistent conditions may lead to complications. Up to 50 percent of adults may show signs of the disease for more than a year, although complete healing usually occurs within six months.

Chronic glomerulonephritis occurs when the acute phase lasts beyond a year, although it may occur in patients with no evidence of an acute phase. After this time period it is unlikely that the condition will ever completely heal. A variable period of time may pass during which the only symptoms are proteinuria and abnormal urinary sediment.

This is called the latent phase. Eventually most patients will develop progressive renal failure with uremia and death. The psychologic aspects of patient care are extremely important in chronic glomerulonephritis. The patient must understand the variable nature of his or her ultimately grave prognosis. Many patients are able to continue work and social activity almost until the time of death.

Treatment involves medication to relieve symptoms or associated problems such as congestive heart failure. There is no evidence that restricted activity or bed rest is particularly beneficial. Some dietary modifications of salt and protein intake are often necessary. In general the best approach is to allow the patient to determine his or her physical limitations.

Nephrotic Syndrome

Nephrotic syndrome is associated with two primary features: great amounts of protein in the urine and lowered levels of blood protein. *Proteinuria* may exceed 3 to 4 g per 24 hours and is ultimately responsible for most of the clinical manifestations of the disease (Finkelstein and Hayslett, 1976). The other features associated with nephrotic syndrome are edema, hypercholesterolemia and fat in the urine. The causes of nephrotic syndrome are unknown in a majority of the cases. It is associated with two major groups of diseases. Primary renal diseases such as chronic glomerulonephritis, lipoid nephrosis, proliferative glomerulonephritis, and membranous *nephropathy* account for over 95 percent of the cases in children, but systemic diseases are more often indicated in the elderly. Systemic diseases such as malignancies, polyarteritis, lupus erythematosis, amyloidosis, syphilis, malaria, renal vein thrombosis and, especially, diabetes mellitus account for most cases in older people.

The basic mechanism involved is the enhancement of glomerular permeability, letting higher-molecular-weight material (protein) pass through into the urine. The nephrotic syndrome has been identified traditionally as a relatively common problem in the elderly, but Fawcett and associates (1971) found no impact of age on the condition. The prognosis in adults does become poorer with advancing age, and those afflicted will probably die from uremia. Temporary remission may occur.

Treatment for nephrotic syndrome involves supportive treatment to relieve or control symptoms, since in most cases the disease process involved cannot be controlled. Corticosteroids often cause a remission in a small percentage of adults, but they are much more effective in children. It is not known for sure how corticosteroids prevent the inevitable progression toward uremia, and steroid therapy is very controversial. Restriction of sodium intake is suggested to control edema, since the capacity to excrete sodium is reduced in nephrotic syndrome. Diuretics can be used if sodium continues to accumulate, but they should be started at low dosage to avoid depletion of intravascular volume. Elderly patients do not tolerate such sudden shifts because of waning homeostatic function, which could send them into shock. A high-protein diet of at least 90 to 100 g per day should help control proteinuria and avoid any possible undernutrition associated with the loss of protein.

Nephrosclerosis

Nephrosclerosis, which is a hardening and thickening of the kidney tissues, is due to the development of thickened and hardened arteriolar walls in most people affected by high blood pressure. There are no known cures, but antihypertensives used to lower the blood pressure can sometimes slow or stop the development of this condition. Before nephrosclerosis becomes medically important, a person so affected often dies from cardiac or cerebral complications. Death when associated with nephrosclerosis is most often due to uremia.

Diabetic Kidney Problems

Nephrosclerosis, nodular glomerulosclerosis (Kimmelstiel-Wilson lesion), pyelonephritis and nephrotic syndrome are all common in diabetics. Renal disease is the most common cause of death in diabetics when the disease is of more than 20 years in duration. Management of renal disease in diabetics presents many problems because of the need to concurrently treat and control diabetic changes as well as the renal disease symptoms. Much of the treatment involves a symptomatic approach: Renal dialysis and transplants are risky even in young diabetics, but because of individual variability, each case should be evaluated to determine appropriate treatment.

TUMORS OF THE TRACT

Tumors are relatively rare in the kidney, accounting for only 1 to 2 percent of all malignancies. Renal tumors are infrequent in the elderly and very rarely metastasize. Urethral tumors are also rare and difficult to diagnose, and usually inoperable by the time they are discovered. An intermittent small urine stream, along with blood in the urine, may suggest a tumor. Bladder tumors decrease in incidence from a peak in the 60s. Bladder cancer is usually contained within the organ and is thus operable. However, 80 percent of all masses are cysts.

A FINAL WORD ON URINARY DISORDERS

In the control of urinary disorders in the elderly, several diagnostic examinations are very important. The evaluation of urinary tract dysfunction should consist of the following steps: routine urinalysis, digital examination of the prostate, estimation of residual urine by catheterization and, finally, urography and cystography. The latter tests should not be applied routinely, since substantial risk and discomfort are involved. Urinary symptoms in any age group should be promptly and thoroughly investigated. Treatment should be prompt, as exact as possible, and as aggressive as warranted in order to prevent further or future damage to the urinary tract.

The urinary tract is a complex and poorly understood organ system. The more intricate aspects of its functioning are just beginning to be delineated. Recent advances in dialysis and kidney transplants have increased medical ability to deal with some of the more threatening problems, although these avenues are expensive and rather rare in their utilization, especially with respect to the elderly. Many people believe that transplantations and dialysis should not be considered for the very old. It would seem that the best approach to the problems of the urinary tract in old age is to encourage adequate care in the younger years.

SUMMARY

Urinary disorders are significant causes of death and morbidity among the aged.

Impairment of the functional efficiency of the urinary system is a matter of great concern for many elderly people and those who care for them. Renal disease alone is not a major cause of death, although renal complications occur in a variety of life-threatening conditions. Urinary incontinence, however, is a major cause of institutionalization, a situation not often welcomed by anyone.

The sociopsychological impact of urinary problems is perhaps greater than the physiological effects of overt pathology. Stress related to fears of institutionalization, loss of independence and diminished personal image can be significant. Prompt, decisive and understanding action can lessen unnecessary mental trauma. Early diagnosis and treatment can often prevent further physical damage and deterioration of the quality of an individual's life.

KEY TERMS

bacteriostatic
bacteriuria
calculi
catheter
cystitis
diabetes insipidus
dysuria
glomerulonephritis
hematuria
micturition
nephropathy
nephrosclerosis
nocturia
nodular (benign) hyperplasia
polyuria
prostatitis
proteinuria
pyelonephritis
renal calculi
residual urine
uremia
urinalysis
vesical

STUDY QUESTIONS

1. What are the general symptoms of urinary tract disturbance and their significance?
2. What are the significant changes that take place in the bladder and urethra with aging?
3. What are the causes of urinary incontinence? How prevalent is it among the elderly? What are some of the possible methods of treatment or management of urinary incontinence?
4. What is the prevalence of urinary tract infections in the elderly? What are some of the symptoms of tract infection?
5. Identify some factors that might help to precipitate urinary tract infections. Why do women have a higher prevalence of tract infections? Why is it important to treat such infections?
6. Identify the major changes associated with aging in the prostate gland. What is the prevalence and significance of prostate cancer in older men?
7. Identify some of the major age-related changes in the kidney.
8. Identify and note the significance of:
   a. Pyelonephritis
   b. Renal calculi
   c. Glomerulonephritis
   d. Nephrotic syndrome
   e. Nephrosclerosis
   f. Diabetic kidney
9. Why are urinary problems of special socio-psychological significance to elderly populations?
10. How can prompt identification and explanation of urinary symptoms by health workers serve the mental health and well-being of an affected individual?

BIBLIOGRAPHY

Anderson, F. and Williams, B. 1983. *Practical Management of the Elderly*, 4th ed. London: Blackwell.

Brocklehurst, J.C. 1951. *Incontinence in Old People*. Edinburgh, U.K.: Churchill Livingstone.

_____ . 1963. The aetiology of urinary incontinence in the elderly. In *Conference on Medical and Surgical Aspects of Aging*. Cur-

rent Achievements in Geriatrics. London: Cassell and Co.

_____ , Dillane, J.B., and Griffiths, L. 1968. The prevalence and symptomology of urinary infection in an aged population. *Gerontologica Clinica 10*: 242.

Dontas, A.S., Papanayiotou, P., and Marketos, S. 1966. Bacteriuria in old age. *Lancet 2*: 305.

Epstein, M. 1985. Aging and the kidney: Clinical implications. *American Family Practice 31*(4): 123–137.

Fawcett, I.W.P., Hon, H., and Jones, H.F. 1971. Nephrotic syndrome in the elderly. *British Medical Journal 2*: 387–390.

Finkelstein, F.O., and Hayslett, J.P. 1976. Nephrotic syndrome: etiology, diagnosis, and treatment. *Geriatrics 31*(8): 39–52.

Gibson, I.I.J., and Pritchard, J.G. 1965. Screening investigations in the elderly. *Gerontologica Clinica 7*: 330.

Hodkinson, H.M. 1981. *An Outline of Geriatrics*, 2nd ed. New York: Academic Press.

_____ . 1976. *Common Symptoms of Disease in the Elderly*. Oxford, U.K.: Blackwell.

Isaacs, S. 1976. The preservation of continence. In F.L. Willington, ed., *Incontinence in the Elderly*. New York: Academic Press.

Klein, L.A. 1979. Prostatic carcinoma. *New England Journal of Medicine 300*: 824–833.

Lindeman, R.D. 1975. Age changes in renal function. In R. Goldman and M. Rockstein, eds., *Physiology and Pathology of Human Aging*. New York: Academic Press.

McKeown, F. 1965. *Pathology of the Aged*. London: Butterworth.

Moore, R.A. 1952. Male secondary sexual organs. In A.L. Lansing, ed., *Cowdry's Problems of Aging*, 3rd ed. Baltimore, Md.: Williams and Wilkins.

Morrin, P.A., Hinglais, N., and Nabaira, B. 1978. Rapidly progressive glomerulonephritis. *American Journal of Medicine 65*: 446–456.

Shepherd, A.M. 1980. Re-education of the muscles of the pelvic floor. In D. Mandelstam, ed., *Incontinence and its Management*. London: Croon-Helm.

Shuttleworth, K.E. 1970. Incontinence. *British Medical Journal 4*: 727–729.

Sourander, L.B. 1966. Urinary tract infection in the aged: An epidemiological study. *Annals of Internal Medicine, Fenniae Supplement 55:* 45.

Walkey, F.A. 1967. Incidence of urinary infection in the elderly. *Scottish Medical Journal 12:* 411.

Whitmore, W.F. 1956. Symposium on hormones and cancer therapy: Hormone therapy in prostatic cancer. *American Journal of Medicine 21:* 697.

Williams, R.H., and Harrison, T.R. 1937. A study of renal arteries in relation to age and hypertension. *American Heart Journal 14:* 645–658.

Willington, F.L. 1972. Marsupial pants for urinary incontinence. *Nursing Mirror 135:* 40–41.

_____ . 1973. The marsupial principle in the management of urinary incontinence. *British Medical Journal 3:* 626–628.

Yeates, W.K. 1976. Normal and abnormal bladder function in incontinence of urine. In F.L. Willington, ed., *Incontinence in the Elderly.* New York: Academic Press.

CHAPTER **14**

The Endocrine System and Age

The endocrine system exhibits a variety of changes with aging, and many researchers look to this system with the hope of finding the key to the aging process. Some have suggested that changes in the pituitary, thyroid or adrenal glands may be related to the onset of senescence. As far back as 1889, Brown-Sequard in France suggested that some of the functional changes associated with aging could be reversed or prevented by hormone extracts or cell suspensions. Throughout the twentieth century a number of researchers have subscribed to *rejuvenation* procedures based on hormone replacement therapy (Hull, 1984). Little evidence from clinical observation or empirical research supports this kind of hypothesis. At this time there is a paucity of research data available on the significance of the biochemical and anatomic changes that occur in the endocrine glands with advancing age. Histologic changes do occur but none are unique, and we are unsure how they are related to function.

Disorders of the endocrine system are not frequent in old age, and when they do occur they are most often related to pathologic changes rather than age. In fact, most endocrine disorders exhibit their highest incidence in early and middle adulthood. Diabetes and thyroid disorders are the most important endocrine problems of the elderly that have a significant effect on health and function.

Because of the integrated nature of the endocrine system, in which each gland can affect the others as well as the central nervous system, it is difficult to isolate the factors that cause deviation in endocrine function. There seems to be a wide margin of compensation that buffers the system in the face of age-related atrophy of organs. Multiple health problems and the many drugs taken by the elderly also complicate diagnosis, treatment and research efforts with respect to the endocrines. Conflicting results make cross-checking, patience and aggressive diagnostic procedures important elements in the identification of an endocrine problem in the older person.

THYROID GLAND

With aging, the thyroid decreases in mass relative to a person's body weight, but related functional changes are difficult to substantiate. *Nodularity* increases with age and it is estimated that after the eighth decade the incidence of nodularity is 100 percent. Much of this is micronodularity and there are no good statistics on the incidence of palpable nodules in the elderly (Gilbert, 1981). Aging is also associated with an increase in *interfollicular* fibrous tissue (Gambert and Tsitouras, 1985). At the beginning of the twentieth century, the elderly were observed to have lower basal metabolism rate (BMR) than young persons, leading to the idea that hypothyroidism was associated with aging. However, Tzankoff and Norris (1977) (using a healthy, upper-middle class population from Baltimore) showed that the decline in BMR with age was due to an age-related decline in lean muscle mass, not an aging thyroid.

Thyrotoxicosis

Hyperthyroidism was once thought to be rare in elderly populations, but better diagnosis, more widespread testing, greater clinical awareness, and greater longevity have

changed this view. It is estimated that 25 to 30 percent of all *thyrotoxicosis* occurs in those over 65 (Gilbert, 1981). The disease apparently is often unnoticed because its symptoms may be atypical, not conforming to the textbook picture. As many as 25 percent of the cases in the elderly will present atypical symptoms.

The primary symptoms are cardiac failure, atrial fibrillation, tachycardia, angina pectoris, congestive heart failure, increased body temperature, higher blood pressure and apathy. It is often accompanied by a weight loss of as much as 20 pounds coupled with depression and mental confusion. Muscle-weakening tremors and fatigue often occur but are ignored because they tend to be so common in the elderly. *Exopthalmia,* so characteristic of younger age groups, and raised basal metabolism are often not present. The enlarged thyroid mass *(Grave's disease)* of younger ages is not observed in up to 20 percent of elderly thyroid patients (Ingbar, 1978). However, multinodular goiter *(Plummer's disease)* makes up as much as three-quarters of the goiter cases among the elderly.

Hyperkinesis is not as common as in the young, and anorexia is more common than increased appetite. Increased carbohydrate intake often associated with hyperthyroidism can lead to the development of *hyperglycemia* or loss of sugar control in a diabetic person. In fact, hyperglycemic irregularities may be the first clue toward hyperthyroidism in the elderly. Heat intolerance with continuous perspiration is often reported by the elderly.

The nature of the condition puts great stress on the heart, and cardiac symptoms and complications increase with the duration of illness and age. These complications often result in death, and preexisting heart disease results in a poor prognosis for those with thyrotoxicosis.

Thyrotoxicosis can often be managed by drug treatment alone, but *radioiodine* therapy may be necessary. This therapy is used most commonly in the elderly, since we do not have to worry about genetic effects or the induction of hyperthyroidism, as we do with younger groups. Hyperthyroidism in the elderly does require lifetime follow-up. Surgery is used only in unusual situations, when there is a question of malignancy or with large obstructive goiters.

Hypothyroidism or Myxedema

Myxedema or extreme *hypothyroidism* is purported to be a much less frequent thyroid disorder than thyrotoxicosis. It is caused by a deficiency of thyroid hormone due to: (1) Hashimoto's disease; (2) iodine deficiency; (3) hypothalamic or pituitary insufficiency; (4) surgical or chemical ablation of the thyroid, as in treatment of Grave's disease. However, after diabetes, it is the most common endocrine disorder of the elderly. About 4 percent of the hospitalized population over 65 are affected. Women have a five times greater incidence than men (Jeffreys, 1972). Obvious cases of hypothyroidism are generally recognized, but it has been suggested that less overt cases go unnoticed, since the signs are generally attributed to normal aging. The symptoms are basically the same in both the elderly and young and include puffy face, weakness, cold intolerance, croaky voice, thickened tongue, mental and physical sluggishness, perceptual deafness and constipation. Signs related to hair loss and skin changes are not too useful in the aged, but vague musculoskeletal symptoms such as stiffness and aching may be important. The mental changes are so important among the elderly that often the condition is confused with dementia or psychosis.

The full picture of myxedema develops only after a long period of hypothyroidism and thus is often clinically overlooked in its earlier stage. If adequately treated before related damage is done, the condition can be compatible with long life expectancy. However, severe changes are often accompanied by ischemic heart disease with its possibility of myocardial infarction; also, the associated dementia may not be totally reversible.

Treatment usually involves life-long hormone replacement therapy. *L-Thyroxine* is the simplest, safest drug of choice. Its dosage must be carefully monitored for individual variability, especially in cases with coexistent ischemic heart disease. The initial dosages should be small and gradually increased to a maintenance level of 0.2 to 0.3 mg per day. Sawin and colleagues (1983) have recently demonstrated that required dosage of thyroxine for those 60 years of age is considerably less than for younger groups. An electrocardiogram should be a requirement before initiating treatment, since thyroid treatment can precipitate a myocardial infarction in those with ischemic heart disease.

Thyroid Cancer

Thyroid cancer is infrequent, causing only 0.5 percent of all cancer deaths, with the peak between 40 and 60 years of age. Thyroid cancers are even less frequent with increasing age. Those that do occur may be more aggressive and carry a poor prognosis. Anaplastic carcinomas account for less than 10 percent of all thyroid malignancies and are rare malignancies at all ages. However, 50 percent of these carcinogens occur in those over 60 years of age, and they are almost uniformly fatal within six months (Gilbert 1981). Voice changes related to nodular presence deserve careful evaluation (Rowe and Besdine, 1982).

DIABETES AND THE ISLET OF LANGERHANS

Diabetes is an ancient disease. It was first described in the Egyptian Ebeas papyrus in 1500 B.C. It is a true disease of civilization—prevalence rates increase with urbanization, sedentary life styles, modern work patterns, and the dietary changes associated with modern life. Although diabetes was recognized very early, it was not until 1788 that Rollo proposed a sound dietary approach to its treatment.

Diabetes is the fifth most prominent cause of disease-related death in the United States. It is estimated that more than 10 million people in the United States are affected by diabetes, and its prevalence appears to be increasing at an annual rate of six percent for all sex and age groups. A 1977 estimate by the federal government suggests that this condition costs about 6 billion dollars annually in the form of medical expenses and lost productivity. In terms of individual affliction, diabetes can lead to blindness, kidney failure, stroke and gangrene in the extremities. Coronary heart disease, due to blood vessel degeneration, is twice as likely in victims of diabetes than in their unafflicted counterparts.

As a result of increasing life expectancy and effective management of the disease, diabetics generally live long lives. In fact, there is a growing number of older diabetics. Besides those who have had the disease since youth, older diabetics include those who have developed it in late middle age and those who first manifest it in later life. Individuals in the latter group often experience the mildest course of pathology and are easiest to manage.

However, many cases of diabetes go unnoticed, so the exact incidence among the elderly is unknown, although there appears to be a steady increase in its incidence from childhood to old age. It is estimated that 2 million Americans over 65 are diabetic and possibly an additional 2 million remain undiagnosed (Bennett, 1984). The rate peaks between the ages of 65 and 75 at 64.4/1,000 tested, and at age 75 drops to 57.9/1000 people tested. Approximately 20 percent of all diabetics are 60 years or over, and 5 percent of the entire population over 65 are diabetic (U.S. Public Health Service, 1978). The number of known diabetics in the United States over 65 has doubled in the last 20 years (Bennett, 1984). Older men are now exhibiting a higher prevalence of diabetes than older women (Palumbo, Elveback, Chu, Connally and Kurland, 1976) which is in sharp contrast to a decade ago, when the percentage of women was appreciably higher (U.S. Public Health Service, 1978). This change could be due to: (1) more men being diagnosed today; (2) lowered mortality of men with diabetes; and (3) an increased incidence in male diabetics due to changing lifestyle.

Diabetes is not a single-disease entity, and at least two major categories of the condition are recognized. Type I is known as *idiopathic insulin-dependent diabetes* (or juvenile diabetes), while Type II is called *idiopathic insulin-independent diabetes* (adult-onset). There is little evidence to suggest a nutritional component in the etiology of Type I, which is probably associated with an immunulogical disturbance possibly influenced by heredity or a viral infection. Type I, while primarily associated with children, has occasionally been known to develop at other ages. Type II, the most common diabetes, usually occurs after age 40 and is associated with obesity and possibly enkephalin sensitivity (Baird, 1981). Ketoacidosis does not develop in these patients but they may need insulin to control symptomatic hyperglycemia. However, some diabetes develops in association with other conditions such as pancreatic disease, Cushing's Syndrome, acromegaly drug damage, and insulin-receptor abnormalities.

The true incidence of diabetes in the elderly is unknown. The condition is easily missed because of at least three factors. First, the classical symptoms of thirst, increased urination, severe wasting or weakness, and elevated fasting blood glucose are rarely present. Second, hyperglycemia can occur without glycosuria. Finally, the condition's symptoms may be confused with those of other conditions common among the elderly, such as congestive heart failure, uremia and cholecystitis.

Overdiagnosis of diabetes occurs in some cases. This may occur if the diagnostician uses only the standard tests; glucose tolerance normally decreases with age, thus affecting norm interpretations. There is also much disagreement on the efficacy of diagnostic criteria that can be applied to older persons.

The detection of diabetes in older persons is usually incidental to such things as hospitalization, eye examinations, testing for other disorders and complications from other diseases. Blurred distance vision because of refractory changes produced by hyperglycemia is common in the elderly. *Pruritus vulvae* is a common symptom among elderly women. In screening procedures the most sensitive test is a blood glucose test two hours after a high-carbohydrate meal (100 g). If further testing is required, a glucose tolerance test is in order, but if it is not done properly the test is worthless. According to Moss (1976), the following procedural points are important to ensure a valid glucose tolerance test:

1. Use a high-carbohydrate diet (300 g) for three days.
2. Do not perform the test under the stresses of infection, surgery or emotional upset.
3. Suspend all medications that could affect the test results.
   a. Cortisone, estrogens, and nicotinic acid raise blood glucose.
   b. Aspirin, antihistamines, and antidepressants lower blood glucose.
4. Adjust the amount of glucose used for individual body weight and age.

Many cases in the elderly are associated with being overweight. In fact, some researchers believe that diabetes is the only significant pathologic condition related to obesity (Mann, 1971). The mortality rates for diabetics over age 60 are higher than for the general population, but only modestly so (Bennett, 1984). The onset of diabetes in the elderly is occasionally associated with the use of corticosteroids, thiazide diuretics and pancreatic disease. Often cases of secondary diabetes occur in which there is direct damage to the pancreas. This diabetic pattern is quite unstable and difficult to control as in juvenile diabetes.

The long-term complications of diabetes are numerous. Such complications as hypertension, coronary artery disease, cerebrovascular disease, peripheral vascular disease, retinopathy, glaucoma, neuropathies and a variety of renal disorders are important to consider when planning for the management of diabetes. Vascular disease is responsible for about 75 percent of the deaths from diabetes (Hirohata, 1967). Atherosclerosis progresses twice as fast in diabetics, and coronary heart disease is twice as common in diabetic men and five times as common in diabetic women. The characteristic pain of myocardial infarction is less severe in diabetics, but the mortality rate after heart attacks is higher.

Peripheral vascular disease is an important complication and can be associated with the development of gangrene. Amputation of the feet is 50 times more common in diabetic men and 80 times more common in diabetic women than in the normal population. The threat of eventual amputation can be very traumatic for the elderly diabetic who already fears confinement due to other factors.

Neuropathies associated with diabetes are varied, but the most common manifestations are associated with the lower extremities. Symptoms can vary from numbness, tingling and nocturnal burning to loss of the Achilles reflexes and loss of the ability to sense vibrations with the feet. These problems often can be greatly improved by control of diabetes. Because there is little or no feeling present in the lower extremities, one must avoid extremes of heat and cold and such traumatizing situations as tight shoes. Ulcerations can readily become infected with most serious results.

The upper extremities are also affected but not as frequently and with milder manifestations. Autonomic nervous system neuropathies can lead to impotence, urinary bladder distension, gastric dilation and orthostatic hypotension. The latter condition should alert diabetics about the necessity of getting out of bed carefully to avoid a possibly damaging fall.

Renal disorders are common in diabetics. In many diabetics, renal lesions appear within 10 years of onset of the disease. Pyelonephritis is common in the elderly. Progressive renal failure may result in heart failure, hypertension, uremic acidosis and eventually death. Low-salt and low-protein diets are prescribed in the latter stages of renal disease. There is no specific treatment for diabetic renal disease, and little evidence thus far supports the advantages of diabetic control in delaying the progression of nephropathy. A variety of factors such as infection and loss of sodium-retaining capabilities disturb renal function. The prognosis for a diabetic with renal problems is indeed grave.

Ocular disorders are frequent in older persons. The three most common are cataract, retinopathy and glaucoma. *Diabetic retinopathy* is the leading cause of blindness among persons subject to chronic disease. The prevalence in the United States is 16/100,000. Diabetics have a 13 times greater chance of becoming blind than do non-diabetics. Even if one is not totally blind, varying degrees of impaired vision are common in the older diabetic. Retinopathy can be slowed by blood glucose control, glaucoma responds to pressure-reducing drugs, and cataracts can be removed surgically. All diabetics should be examined by an opthalmologist yearly, and those showing proliferative changes even more often.

Skin problems are also associated with diabetes. Some skin lesions are probably associated with small blood vessel diseases in the skin structures. Skin infections are common, especially *moniliasis*. Care must be taken to keep skin lesions clean and free of infection. Warm, soapy water for cleansing and the application of antibiotics such as neomycin have proved helpful.

Diet and Diabetes

A simple cause-and-effect relationship between diet and diabetes does not exist, but the American Diabetes Association (1974) suggests that improved nutrition could reduce its incidence in the United States by 30 percent. Most researchers would probably agree that obesity is the one proven diabetogenic factor. In fact, some researchers believe that diabetes is the only significant pathological condition related to being overweight (Mann, 1971). Diabetes is rare in societies where obesity is uncommon. In the United States, approximately 75 percent of those with adult-onset diabetes are obese, and obese people are three times more likely to manifest diabetes than those of normal weight.

Baird (1981) found the incidence of obesity to be higher among diabetics in all social classes and in both sexes. She could not find any significant differences in the quality of food consumed by her general samples of obese and nonobese subjects. However, those with diabetes ate significantly more food than nondiabetics. It also is significant that weight loss does reverse some of the metabolic disturbances of diabetes. In an early piece of research, Newburgh and Conn (1939) showed that weight loss corrected abnormal glucose tolerance in 90 percent of a middle-aged population.

The search for qualitative nutritional factors that promote diabetogenesis is very controversial and plagued with contradictory results. Nutritional factors could be involved relative to damage to the pancreas, impaired glucose tolerance and impaired function of the beta cells. Little experimental data, however, are available to strongly support a nutritional basis for any of these mechanisms.

Epidemiological studies correlating diabetes with dietary variations are abundant, but the evidence presented is generally inconclusive for establishing cause and effect. Noting the fall in diabetic mortality during wartime, Himsworth (1949) proposed that a high-fat diet was diabetogenic since fat consumption noticeably dropped during wartime food shortages. But he failed to consider that sucrose consumption also dropped abruptly and significantly at the same time. Other data available at the time would also have pointed out that Eskimos have a diet very high in animal fat but exhibit a very low incidence of diabetes.

A number of researchers have sought a correlation between a high incidence of diabetes and consumption of sucrose, or refined sugar. Cohen (1961) noted that Yemenite Jews emigrating to Israel had a low incidence of diabetes. However, after a period of years in the country and adoption of a typical Israeli diet with 20 to 25 percent of total Calories coming from sucrose, prevalence rates of diabetes increased to approximately those of Western countries. Campbell (1963) arrived at conclusions similar to Cohen's while studying Asians and Africans in and around Durban, South Africa. Cleave and Campbell (1966) also found diabetes related to the increased use of refined sugar in the Natal area of India. Yudkin (1969) demonstrated a significant correlation between the amount of sugar consumed and mortality from diabetes in 22 countries.

A number of other epidemiologists found little data in their studies to support a sucrose-diabetes relationship. Baird (1972), in Scotland, found no relationship between sugar consumption and diabetes, while similar studies in England came to the same conclusion. Poon-King and associates (1968) studied five geographical districts in Trinidad and found the incidence of diabetes lowest in districts with the highest per capita consumption of sugar. In the South Pacific, Prior (1974) found variations in diabetes not accounted for by dietary consumption of sugar and suggested that other (as yet unidentified) environmental factors might be more important. Is it possible that some individuals, or even populations, may have a genetically based sensitivity to sucrose? If so, it might be possible to prevent diabetes in such populations by having them avoid high-sucrose stimulation (Cleave and Campbell, 1966).

Trowell (1975) and others have suggested a link between fiber-depleted diets and a high incidence of diabetes. He noted that mortality from diabetes fell in Britain during the world wars when a coarser, less refined flour was consumed. The same research (Trowell, 1978) suggested that the incorporation of fiber into the diet may lower blood insulin and blood glucose levels. Miranda and Horowitz (1978) support this contention. The specific effects of selected components of the dietary fiber complex are also being investigated in relation to lowering the incidence of diabetes. It must be remembered that when dietary fiber is increased, the protein, fat, vitamin and mineral content of the diet may be altered as well, and these factors must be considered in any explanation of observed effects. Some investigators have suggested a strong genetic component among various ethnic groups, especially blacks, American Indians and Mexicans.

In a study among Mexican Americans in Starr County, Texas, Harris and colleagues

(1983) found that 14.5 percent of those between ages 65 and 74 had diabetes, compared to an age-equivalent population of Anglos in Rancho Bernardino California that exhibited a rate of 5.9 percent (Barrett-Connor, 1980). Recently Gardner and colleagues (1984) suggested that the higher prevalence in Mexican-Americans may be a result of Amerindian admixture, among which extremely high prevalences are found (Knowler, Bennett, Hamman and Miller, 1978).

A recently published study tends to support the Indian admixture hypothesis (Gardner, Stern and Haffner, 1984). These investigators found that even when controls for increased obesity were taken into account, Mexican-Americans showed a two to four times greater incidence of diabetes than Anglos. This excess appears to be proportional to the amount of Amerindian admixture in the Mexican-American population. It would appear that ethnic or racial studies of genetic propensity for the development of adult onset diabetes could be useful in the early identification of individuals at risk. This kind of information could also be useful in health promotion or health counseling programs that emphasize a preventive approach to diabetes.

Treatment and Management

Mild late-onset diabetes can often be controlled by dietary restriction of carbohydrates to around 100 g per day. Some cases will require oral drug treatment with sulfonylureas such as tolbutamide (Orinase), chlorpropamide (Diabinese), acetohexamide (Dymelor) and tolazamide (Tolinase). Oral treatment should be used only in persons whose diet has failed to control hyperglycemia. The oral treatment may not be sufficient to control diabetes during severe stress, such as surgery or systemic infections. These drugs are not recommended for people with severe liver or kidney disease. The most common side effects of oral drugs are rashes, flushing, headaches, nausea, GI distress, tachycardia, hypoglycemia and hyponatremia.

Severe cases require insulin injections. Although the procedures are essentially the same for any age group, older people may have trouble administering insulin because of poor eyesight and manipulative ability. Testing their urine to monitor glucose levels may also be a chore under these conditions. Home-health-service visits may be required to keep severe diabetics in the community.

Diabetic coma and insulin shock are two important acute complications of diabetic management. *Diabetic acidosis* (coma) is the result of impaired glucose utilization that leads to high blood sugar. This is followed by increased utilization of fats, which produces an excess of *ketones,* causing ketosis. The diabetic may suffer rapid dehydration, circulatory collapse, rapid deep breathing, dulling of the senses and finally coma. This is a grave emergency, often requiring hospitalization. Insulin must be supplied and the water and electrolyte balance restored. This condition may be precipitated by infections, injuries, stress or negligence in insulin therapy.

A variant form of diabetic coma is *hyperosmotic non-ketotic coma.* It is a relatively frequent occurrence in the elderly, and mortality is very high, often due to thrombic incidents. It occurs most frequently in those over age 50 with mild or undiagnosed diabetes. Almost one-half the patients developing this kind of coma die. Treatment must include massive intravenous fluids to replace the substantial losses of water and insulin. In both

forms of diabetic coma, potassium deficiency must be remedied by potassium supplements after the patient's condition has been stabilized. Even with adequate treatment the mortality rate remains 40 to 70 percent (Arieff and Carroll, 1972).

Insulin shock or acute hypoglycemia can occur in connection with an overdose of insulin or oral hypoglycemics that lowers the blood glucose level below normal. It can also be precipitated by taking insulin or oral drugs without eating, and it can be caused by unusual exercise. Early symptoms are perspiration, pallor, numbness, tremors, confusion, gait instability, convulsions and loss of consciousness. It must be recognized quickly, since cerebral damage, myocardial infarction and death are possible complications.

Diabetics should carry a source of glucose at all times to counter the onset of insulin shock. Orange juice, carbonated beverages, candy, and other sources of sugar may be used in this situation. The diabetic should pay careful attention to insulin dose, avoid skipping meals and drinking alcohol, and carefully monitor urine glucose levels. In a person who is unable to swallow, forced feeding should be avoided; an injection of 1 mg glucagon will sufficiently raise the blood sugar. All individuals working with or related to diabetics should be aware of the distinction between diabetic coma and insulin shock. Mistaken action could result in death (Table 14.1). In diabetic coma the patient will exhibit the odor of acetone on the breath and have sugar and acetone in the urine, but in insulin shock these characteristics are absent.

In the past, two methods were used in the care of older diabetics. One stressed strict and rigorous diet control while the other allowed more freedom in selecting a diet and

TABLE 14.1 Differentiating ketosis and insulin shock

Ketosis	Insulin shock
Dry skin and tongue	Moist skin and tongue, sweating
Low blood pressure	Normal or raised blood pressure
Hyperventilation	Shallow or normal breathing
Diminished reflexes	Brisk reflexes
Plantar responses: usually flexion	Plantar responses: usually extension
Ketonuria	No ketonuria
Glycosuria	No glycosuria
Hyperglycemia	Hypoglycemia
Reduced plasma bicarbonate	Normal plasma bicarbonate
Several days of poor health common	Onset sudden, usually good health prior to attack
Recent infection or digestive disturbance common	Skipping a meal or unusual overexertion common

used insulin to control hyperglycemia. In the late 1950s the introduction of the oral hyperglycemic tablet led to the neglect of dietary therapy and promoted an overdependence on medication. The negative impact of this abuse has yet to be determined.

A balanced diet is the key to the management of diabetes. Remember that the lifelong food habits of an individual will be difficult to change. The less the diet is manipulated and modified to achieve balance, the greater the probability of adherence to the diet. A number of principles are important when developing the balanced diet.

1. It should be compatible with an individual's economic and social background.
2. It should be compatible with an individual's activity profile.
3. It should be made up of readily available, commonly used foods.
4. It should include three well-balanced, regularly spaced meals with small, nutritious snacks in-between.
5. Foods high in pure sugar must be eliminated.
6. The diet should contain a balance of carbohydrates, proteins and fats at approximately the following levels: 45 to 55 percent complex carbohydrates, 10 to 20 percent protein and 30 to 35 percent fat.
7. Adequate salt intake must be assured, and potassium should be watched; chromium supplements might be helpful to those who do not respond well to insulin.
8. A broad-spectrum multivitamin supplement might be helpful, since excretion of water-soluble vitamins is often excessive.
9. Large, heavy meals should be avoided, particularly before retiring for the night.
10. Midmorning and midafternoon snacks are a must for those taking insulin.

Recent dietary recommendations suggest lower amounts of fat, saturated fat and cholesterol, and higher amounts of complex carbohydrates than are typical of the North American diet. Gerald Reaven of Stanford University's School of Medicine, however, has recently cautioned about high-carbohydrate, low-fat diets because very low-fat diets can promote heart disease. A panel of the National Institutes of Health recently suggested a precaution that any diabetic who goes on a high-carbohydrate diet should be tested to prevent against adverse effects of high blood-lipid ratios (Kolata, 1987).

Exercise and Diabetes

Exercise promotes increased insulin secretion and better utilization of glucose by the body. The principal problem is that the elderly are less active because of declining physical status or lack of motivation. An exercise program should be related to an individual's functional capacity and need not be rigorous. Mild exercise performed in several sessions can be effective. Elderly persons should be encouraged to walk daily, since recent research indicates that the effects of exercise on diabetics are short-lived, disappearing in 72 hours (Kolata, 1987). Asking another person to take part in an exercise program can make it more interesting and more likely to be continued. The social aspect of the walk can satisfy certain interpersonal needs for the older person while at the same time answering the need for some physical activity.

Problems in Patient Education

Patient education is a part of complete diabetic therapy. The diabetic has a lifelong condition that he or she must learn to control and live with. If the diabetic is in possession of accurate, up-to-date medical information, the incidence of complications and hospital admissions can be reduced. People working with the elderly should be able to convey and clarify practical information about diabetic management.

The diabetic must become a careful observer of his or her own physical condition. Daily examination of the body, especially the feet, is a must. Each body part should be checked for any change in appearance such as swelling, redness, numbness and bleeding. Changes in vision, coordination and ability to walk should be noted. Changes of this sort should be reported to one's healthcare practitioner. The diabetic should avoid tight clothes or shoes and the use of any external medicine or application not recommended by one's practitioner.

Reduced blood supply and lessened peripheral nerve sensation make foot problems more serious in diabetics. Shoes that are too tight or poorly shaped can cause unnoticed trauma that might ulcerate, become infected and lead to the loss of foot or leg. The purchase of good-fitting shoes is important. It has been suggested that inspection of the feet be done in the evening or late afternoon to allow for expansion of the feet. Sores, cracks and other injuries should receive prompt attention to avoid complications. Bed rest is usually needed to heal them. Thick, tough toenails must be trimmed regularly but can present a problem that may require podiatric care.

According to Duncan (1976), 7 percent of diabetics are blind, and many more have partially impaired vision. This means that they will have total or partial problems seeing syringe calibrations and mechanations, traumatized parts and toenails. Depending on the circumstances, a home visitor may be required for maintenance care. Also, premeasured syringes, Braille devices and magnifying glasses will help in many instances.

The diabetic patient living at home should also be cognizant of environmental hazards that may lead to injury. Trauma from slippery floors, steep stairs and poorly lit areas is common. Care must be taken to eliminate or modify such hazards. Steep stairs should be replaced and slippery, bare wood floors carpeted. The diabetic at home should have easy access to a supply of quick sugar, glucagon and insulin. Relatives or people living with or visiting known diabetics should know the location of such supplies and be able to use them in emergencies.

With proper management, diabetics can live long, useful lives. They need not be embarrassed by overprotective family and friends concerned over the presence of sweets and sources of trauma. Diabetics need not be subjected to harassment by insurance companies who cancel their health insurance and double their life-insurance premiums. Employers need not feel that diabetics must be specially treated or eliminated. The diabetic is a person with a highly manageable pathologic condition; he or she is not an invalid or handicapped individual.

PARATHYROID

The parathyroid gland's importance in the regulation of calcium metabolism (and thus skeletal integrity) makes it of some interest to those who study aging. *Radioimmune assays* indicate an 80 percent increase in the circulation level of parathormone elements between age 30 and 80. More sensitive tests that only detect the intact hormone detect a 30 percent increase over the same period (Rowe and Besdine, 1982). This condition is possibly due to "mild hyperparathyroidism" associated with the age-related decrease in intestinal calcium absorption (Bullamore et al., 1970). Such a decrease results in lower levels of ionized calcium in the blood, which leads to parathormone release.

Hyperparathyroidism in the elderly differs from that of younger age groups by lower serum calcium threshold levels and altered mental status (Mannix, 1980). Mental status is altered by a state of *hypercalcemia,* which is thus an important treatable cause of mental failure in the elderly. Parathyroid surgery can produce dramatic results, and the elderly

seem to tolerate it well, except those with severe heart or respiration problems (Mannix, 1980). These patients can often be managed by more conservative drug therapy. The possible relationship of the parathyroid to some cases of osteoporosis is also of interest to those studying the aging process.

POSTERIOR PITUITARY GLAND

One of the most serious and least recognized electrolyte disorders of the elderly is the tendency toward water intoxication (hyponatremia). This condition can be associated with oversecretion of *antidiuretic hormone (ADH);* in the absence of renal failure, the condition can be relatively well-diagnosed clinically. The elderly appear prone to the development of ADH-induced water intoxication in a variety of stress states, including viral illness, after anesthesia and surgery, during some kinds of drug therapy and in concert with a variety of pulmonary and central nervous system disorders (Rowe and Besdine, 1982).

The symptoms of *hyponatremia* are anorexia, confusion, depression, lethargy and weakness. In more severe cases seizure and stupor may be present. Given the nature of these symptoms and their non-specificity, it might be valuable to check for this syndrome in those elderly who exhibit them following recent stress.

SUMMARY

The endocrine system has fascinated some students of aging since the nineteenth century, and some have hoped to find the key to the aging process in the endocrines. Little clinical or empirical evidence supports such a hypothesis, however.

The endocrines undergo a variety of age-related changes, but with the exception of estrogen secretion, old age does not result in the failure of any major endocrine function. Aging is characterized by possible decreased target receptiveness of some hormones (such as insulin) and some altered control of hormone secretion. Disorders of the endocrine system are not frequent in old age, and when they do occur they are most often associated with pathologic rather than age-related changes.

Most endocrine disorders exhibit their highest incidence in early and middle adulthood. Diabetes and thyroid disorders are the most important endocrine problems of the elderly that have a significant effect on their health and function.

Thyroid problems such as thyrotoxicosis and hypothyroid, while not massive problems in terms of sheer numbers, do affect a significant number of older people. Both conditions require some diagnostic skill to identify in the older patient but can often be effectively managed. Diabetes is a major problem in term of numbers as well as in qualitative damage among older populations. Diabetes is a major health threat and a significant socioeconomic drain on the elderly. Early diagnosis, careful monitoring, effective medical management and changes in life style can allow older diabetics to lead a normal life with full integration into their community.

KEY TERMS

antidiuretic hormone (ADH)
diabetic retinopathy
exopthalmia
glycosuria
Grave's disease
hypercalcemia
hyperglycemia
hyperkinesis
hyperthyroidism
hypoglycemia
hyponatremia
hypothyroidism
idiopathic
insulin shock
ketones
ketonuria
L-Thyroxine
moniliasis
myxedema
Plummer's disease
Pruritus vulvae
radioiodine
radioimmune assays
thyrotoxicosis

STUDY QUESTIONS

1. Why is a consideration of the endocrine system significant in the study of aging?
2. How does the thyroid gland change with age?
3. What is the significance of thyrotoxicosis in the aged? How does the symptomology of thyrotoxicosis differ in the elderly from that of earlier years?
4. How is thyrotoxicosis managed in the elderly? What is the importance of hypothyroidism among the elderly? Why do many cases go unnoticed?
5. What are the symptoms of hypothyroidism? Do the symptoms exhibit age-related differences?
6. What is the significance of diabetes as a health problem for the elderly? Why have we seen a higher prevalence of diabetes in older men in recent years? Why is the true incidence of diabetes in the elderly unknown?
7. Differentiate insulin-dependent and insulin-independent diabetes. Identify the problems associated with the diagnosis of diabetes in the elderly.
8. Identify the major long-term complications of diabetes and their significance. What is the possible association of diabetes with diet? What do cross-cultural studies indicate about the possible causes of diabetes?
9. What are the major methods for controlling late onset diabetes? Differentiate insulin shock from diabetic coma. How is each condition dealt with therapeutically? What are some major principles of diet management that are of importance to diabetics?

10. What is the role of exercise in diabetic management? Identify the major patient-education problems associated with diabetic management in the elderly. What are some of the sociopsychological aspects of living with diabetes?
11. What is the possible significance of hyperparathyroidism among the elderly?
12. How might pituitary disorders be of significance to the elderly?

BIBLIOGRAPHY

American Diabetes Association. 1974. *Annual Report.* New York: author.

Arieff, A.L., and Carroll, H.J. 1972. Non-ketotic hyperosmolar coma with hyperglycemia. *Medicine 51:* 73–94.

Baird, J.D. 1972. Diet and the development of clinical diabetes. *Acta Latina 19:* 621–637.

—————— . 1981. Diet and the development of clinical diabetes in man. *Proceedings of the Nutritional Society 40:* 213–217.

Barrett-Connor, E. 1980. The prevalence of diabetes mellitus in an adult community as determined by history or fasting hyperglycemia. *American Journal of Epidemiology 111:* 705–712.

Bennett, P.H. 1984. Diabetes in the elderly: Diagnosis and epidemiology. *Geriatrics 36*(5): 37–41.

Bullamore, J.R., Wilkinson, R., Gallagher, J.C., and Nordin, B.E.C. 1970. Effect of age on calcium absorption. *Lancet 2:* 535–540.

Campbell, C.D. 1963. Diabetes in Asians and Africans in and around Durban. *South African Medical Journal 37:* 1195–1208.

Cleave, T.L. 1974. *The Saccharine Disease.* Bristol, U.K.: Wright and Sons.

—————— , and Campbell, C.D. 1966. *Diabetes, Coronary Thrombosis and the Saccharine Disease.* Bristol, U.K.: Wright and Sons.

Cohen, A.M. 1961. Prevalence of diabetes among different ethnic Jewish groups. *Metabolism 10:* 50–58.

Duncan, T.G. 1976. Teaching common sense health habits to diabetic patients. *Geriatrics 31*(10): 93–96.

Gambert, S.R., and Tsitouras, P.D. 1985. Effect of age on thyroid hormone physiology and function. *Journal of the American Geriatrics Society 33*(5): 360–365.

Gardner, L.I., Stern, M.P., and Haffner, S.P. 1984. Prevalence of diabetes in Mexican-Americans: Relationship to the percent of gene pool derived from American Indians. *Diabetes 33:* 86–92.

Gilbert, P.D. 1981. Thyroid function and disease. In L.S. Libow and F.T. Sherman, eds., *The Core of Geriatric Medicine.* St. Louis, Mo.: Mosby. Pp. 246–274.

Harris, C.L., Ferrell, R.E., and Barton, J.S.A. 1983. Diabetes among Mexican-Americans in Starr County, Texas. *American Journal of Epidemiology 118:* 659–672.

Himsworth, H.P. 1949. The syndrome of diabetes and its causes. *Lancet 1:* 465–472.

Hirohata, T. 1967. The natural history of diabetes I mortality. *Diabetes 16:* 878–881.

Hull, D.A. 1984. *The Biomedical Basis of Gerontology.* London: Wright and Sons.

Jeffreys, P. 1972. The prevalence of thyroid disease in patients admitted to a geriatric department. *Age and Aging 1:* 33–40.

Ingbar, S.H. 1978. The influence of aging on human thyroid economy. *Geriatric Endocrinology 5:* 13–17.

Knowler, W.C., Bennett, P.H., Hamman, R.F., and Miller, M. 1978. Diabetes incidence and prevalence in Pima Indians: A 19-fold greater incidence than in Rochester, Minnesota. *American Journal of Epidemiology 108:* 497–505.

Kolata, G. 1987. Diabetics should lose weight and avoid diet fads. *Science 235:* 163–164.

Mann, G.V. 1971. The obesity spook. *American Journal of Public Health 61:* 1491–1498.

Mannix, H. 1980. Hyperparathyroidism in the elderly. *American Journal of Surgery 64:* 729–731.

Miranda, P.M., and Horowitz, D.L. 1978. High-fiber diets in the treatment of diabetes mellitus. *Annals of Internal Medicine 88:* 482–486.

Moss, J.M. 1976. Pitfalls to avoid in diagnosing diabetes in the elderly. *Geriatrics 31*(10): 52–55.

Newburgh, L.H., and Conn, J.W. 1939. A new interpretation of hyperglycemia in obese middle-aged persons. *Journal of the American Medical Association 112:* 7–11.

Palumbo, P.J., Elveback, L.R., Chu, C.P., Connally, D.C., and Kurland, L.T. 1976. Diabetes mellitus: Incidence, prevalence, survivorship and causes of death in Rochester, Minnesota, 1945–1970. *Diabetes 25:* 566–573.

Poon-King, T., Henry, M.V., and Rampersad, F. 1968. The prevalence and natural history of diabetes in Trinidad. *Lancet 1:* 155–160.

Prior, I.A.M. 1974. Diabetes in the South Pacific. In S.S. Hildebrand, ed., *Is the Risk of Becoming a Diabetic Affected by Sugar Consumption?* Bethesda, Md.: International Sugar Foundation. Pp. 4–13.

Rowe, J.W., and Besdine, R.W. 1982. Endocrine and metabolic systems. In J.W. Rowe and R.W. Besdine, eds., *Health and Disease in Old Age.* Boston: Little, Brown. Pp. 137–156.

Sawin, C.T., Herman, T., MoLitch, M.E., London, M.H., and Kramer, S.M. 1983. Aging and the thyroid: Decreased requirement for thyroid hormone in old hypothyroid patients. *American Journal of Medicine 75:* 206–209.

Trowell, H.C. 1975. Dietary-fiber hypothesis of the etiology of diabetes mellitus. *Diabetes 24:* 762–765.

_____ . 1978. Diabetes mellitus and dietary fiber of starchy foods. *American Journal of Clinical Nutrition 31:* 553–557.

Tzankoff, S.R., and Norris, A.H. 1977. Effect of muscle mass decrease in age-related BMR changes. *Journal of Applied Physiology 3:* 1001–1009.

U.S. Public Health Service. 1978. *Diabetes Data.* Bethesda, Md.: U.S. Department of Health, Education and Welfare.

Yudkin, J.M. 1969. Dietary fat and dietary sugar in relation to ischemic heart disease and diabetes. *Lancet 2:* 4–5.

_____ . 1978. *Pure, White and Deadly.* London: Davis-Poynter.

CHAPTER **15**

Drugs and the Elderly

Linda A. Hershey, M.D., Ph.D.
Christina M. Whitney, B.S.N., R.N.

Drugs account for 10 percent of the total per capita health care bill of those 65 years of age and over (Kovar, 1977). On average, most elderly patients take more than three therapeutic agents (a range of 3.8–7.2 drugs per patient), although care must be taken to identify the settings in which these patients are found before extrapolating these averages to the elderly population at large (Table 15.1).

This chapter will emphasize how demographic factors influence the results of studies of drug use in the elderly, how alcohol, over-the-counter agents and foods influence the body's handling of drugs; and how the disposition of drugs changes with increasing age. It will examine in detail two key problems associated with drug use in the elderly: adverse drug reactions and medication errors. Finally, it will spell out guidelines for how nurses, physicians and pharmacists can work together to maximize the benefits and minimize the risks of drug use in the elderly.

STUDYING DRUG USE AMONG THE ELDERLY: DEMOGRAPHIC VARIABLES

Demographic variables need to be clearly identified in any study of drug use in the eld-

TABLE 15.1 Effect of the population sample on patterns of drug use

Reference	N	Age	A/I	Drugs (#/pt)	% Drug type
Chien et al. (1978)	242	73	A	3.8	67% analgesics 33% card/vasc. 16% diuretics 4% antipsych.
Ingman et al. (1975)	131	?	I	4.6	45% analgesics 35% card/vasc. 33% antipsych. 32% diuretics
Guttmann (1978)	447	72	A	?	55% analgesics 39% card/vasc. 14% sed/tranq.
Brown et al. (1977)	188	?	I	5.8	————
Cooper et al. (1978)	142	78	I	7.2	37% analgesics 29% card/vasc. 23% diuretics 23% antipsych.

A = ambulatory
I = institutionalized
card/vasc. = cardiovascular
antipsych. = antipsychotic
sed/tranq. = sedative/tranquilizer

erly, since they often have a significant impact on the findings. Table 15.1 demonstrates how the results of various studies differ according to the size of the sample (N). Ingman and colleagues (1975) found that the most commonly prescribed classes of drugs in their study sample of 131 elderly were *analgesics, cardiovascular agents* and *antipsychotic agents*. Chien and associates (1978) and Guttmann (1978) studied larger populations (242 and 447 elderly, respectively) and found much lower rates of antipsychotic drug usage among the elderly. The latter studies did, however, support Ingman's observations about the widespread use of analgesics and cardiovascular agents among the elderly. It is possible that Ingman's observations about antipsychotic drug prescribing in the elderly were biased by his small sample

size and were therefore not representative of the elderly population as a whole.

The average age of study subjects may also influence the results, since the prevalence of chronic disease (and thus the necessity for chronic drug therapy) increases sharply with age. Knapp and associates (1984) found that the most frequently prescribed drugs for patients 85 years of age and older were for cardiovascular problems, consistent with the fact that the most frequent diagnoses in this age group were *hypertension, ischemic heart disease* and *heart failure*. Some drugs were actually used less frequently, as the patients' age increased. Central nervous system drugs, for example, are prescribed more frequently in the 25–64 age group than for the "old-old" (Knapp, Wiser, Michocki, Nuessle and Knapp, 1984).

Differences in living arrangements may explain variation in drug use among study populations of the elderly. Among persons 65 and older, 5 percent are found in old-age institutions on any given day; and among those 85 and older, 19 percent are institutionalized (Kovar, 1977). Table 15.1 shows data that support the hypothesis that institutionalized patients are more heavily medicated than non-institutionalized ambulatory patients (4.6–7.2 drugs per patient compared to 3.8 drugs per patient, respectively). This pattern follows for specific drugs classes. Table 15.1 suggests that differences in antipsychotic drug prescribing may be related to the different living environments of the study subjects. Antipsychotic drugs were prescribed for 23 to 33 percent of chronically institutionalized patients, while much smaller proportions of the noninstitutionalized ambulatory elderly received these agents (4 to 14 percent). It may be that a higher proportion of institutionalized patients have *dementing illnesses* or chronic *schizophrenia* and thus require antipsychotic agents.

Urban versus rural or solitary versus family living arrangements may influence the results of drug usage studies in the elderly. Brown and associates (1977) found that the average number of drugs prescribed per patient was higher in rural nursing homes (7.4 drugs per patient) than in urban homes (3.1 drugs per patient). Cooper and Bagwell (1978) also examined drug prescription in a rural nursing home and suggested that higher numbers of "as needed" *(p.r.n.)* drugs were used in rural homes (3.9–4.0 drugs per patient). Schwartz and colleagues (1962) studied elderly residents in New York City and found a higher rate of medication errors among those living alone than among those living with one or more other persons. On the other hand, stud-

ies of elderly residents in smaller cities or rural communities, found no influence of household composition on non-compliance (Neely and Patrick, 1968; Cooper, Love and Raffoul, 1982).

ALCOHOL AND OVER-THE-COUNTER DRUG USE

Alcohol abuse among the elderly may not be as prevalent as has been suspected in the past, at least according to self-reports by the elderly. Only 2 percent of the ambulatory elderly subjects reported on by Chien, Townsend and Townsend (1978) had social or medical problems associated with alcohol usage, even though 53 percent in the sample admitted to social drinking. In Guttmann's study of 447 ambulatory seniors (1978) the majority (56 percent) denied alcohol use altogether, while only 1 percent admitted to alcohol-related problems such as blackouts, accidents, absence from work or marital problems. Alcohol use correlated positively with income in Guttmann's study, and alcohol users considered themselves to be in better physical health than non-users.

Self-medication is the most prevalent form of medical care among the elderly (as it is for all age groups). Ostrom and associates (1985) found that 82 percent of their Seattle sample of elderly high-rise residents used *over-the-counter (OTC)* drugs regularly, while a slightly lower percentage (75 percent) reported regular use of prescription medications. These OTC usage figures were slightly higher than those reported by Guttmann (1978). He found that 69 percent of 447 elderly residents of Albany, New York, were regular users of OTC agents. The use of OTC drugs is appealing to elderly patients because they are easily available and less expensive than prescription medications. They are perceived as being safe, since they can be purchased without a prescription. Analgesics and vitamins are the most commonly used.

The dangers posed by self-medication include the risk of *adverse drug reactions (ADR)*, especially *drug-drug interactions*. For example, persons taking *anticoagulants* ("blood-thinners") are usually cautioned by their physicians not to take aspirin since this would increase their risk of bleeding. Most patients are unaware, however, that aspirin is contained in a wide variety of OTC preparations, including many cold remedies. Yet Schwartz and colleagues (1962) found that only 7 percent of all serious medication errors were associated with self-medication. It would be of interest to study this question again today, since many more OTC agents are now available.

ADVERSE DRUG REACTIONS

An adverse drug reaction is defined as any unintended or undesired effect of a drug. Borda, Slone and Jick (1968) described examples of the various types of ADRs. If a patient developed tinnitus (ringing in the ears) with 1,200 mg of aspirin four times a day, it would be considered an *overdosage* in spite of the fact that this dosage can be tolerated without symptoms by many. The bone-marrow depression (which produces a lowering of the white-blood-cell count) that is occasionally produced by the antibiotic chloramphenicol is considered an *idiosyncratic reaction* since it occurs rarely and unpredictably. Dose-related (and predictable) *excessive effects* include diarrhea with certain laxatives or hypoglycemia with antidiabetic agents. A *secondary side effect* is an indirect consequence of the drug's primary action. This type of ADR is also unavoidable, but usually predictable. An example of a secondary side effect would be the hypokalemia (lowering of blood potassium levels) that often develops with *diuretics*. A drug-drug interaction occurs when a second drug modifies the way the body handles or reacts to the first agent. The anticoagulant-aspirin interaction described above is a good example of this ADR; others are outlined in Table 15.2.

Adverse drug reactions lengthen the hospital stay for those admitted to inpatient medical services (Seidl, Thornton, Smith and Cluff, 1966) and chronic care facilities (Borda *et al.*, 1968). One study that involved 2,000 inpatients in 42 British geriatric units showed that about one in ten admissions was due solely or in part to an ADR (Williamson

TABLE 15.2 Drug interactions and their potential results

Drug a	Drug b	Potential results
Digoxin	Furosemide	Reduced potassium produced by *b* could increase risk of arrhythmia produced by *a*.
Warfarin	Aspirin	Protein displacement of *a* by *b* could increase risk of bleeding.
Tetracycline	Antacid	Absorption impairment of *a* by *b* could reduce the antibiotic efficacy of *a*.

and Chopin, 1980). Fatal or life-threatening reactions accounted for 7 percent of all ADRs reported by Seidl *et al.* (1966) and for 26 percent of those reported by Borda *et al.* (1968).

Demographic data and study design are as important to consider in evaluating ADR reports as they are in assessing other aspects of drug use in the elderly. For example, studies in which nurses and physicians report and verify ADRs are bound to have higher incidence figures (35 percent in Borda *et al.,* 1968) than those relying on self-reporting of symptoms (12 percent in Guttmann, 1978). These incidence figures are also influenced by the setting of the study. The 35 percent incidence of ADRs was found in a chronic hospital setting where the inpatient course is usually prolonged, multiple illnesses are common and more drugs are prescribed per patient. The 12 percent incidence reported by Guttman (1978) occurred in an ambulatory setting. This compares well with acute admissions to an English geriatric facility (15 percent in Williamson and Chopin, 1980) and on a general medical inpatient service (14 percent in Seidl *et al.,* 1966).

Striking differences in ADR incidence figures are found when cross-cultural comparisons are made. Lawson and Jick (1976) compared 721 Scottish inpatients on a general medical ward (mean age 56 years) to an age-matched group of 1,442 American inpatients. The frequencies with which ADRs developed from any given drug did not differ from one country to the next (15 percent of those treated with heparin, 12 percent with furosemide, 11 percent with digoxin, etc.). Nevertheless, the total incidence of ADRs in Americans was twice as high as that seen among the Scottish. This can be most easily

explained by the fact that American inpatients received twice as many drugs (9.1 per admission, compared to 4.6 per admission for the Scottish).

PHARMACOKINETICS AND PHARMACODYNAMICS

The observation that the risks of ADRs increase with age (Seidl *et al.,* 1966) can be largely explained by the changes in drug disposition that occur with advancing years (Greenblatt, Sellers and Shader, 1982). The *pharmacodynamic hypothesis* argues that a given concentration of drug produces more dramatic effects at receptor sites in elderly individuals than in younger patients. Minor tranquilizers, for example, produce greater central depression (sleepiness, inattentiveness) in the elderly at any given blood concentration than they do in the young. Anticoagulants produce more thinning of the blood (and more risk for bleeding) in the elderly than in the young. Phenothiazines and other major tranquilizers are more likely to produce abnormal involuntary movements (drug-induced parkinsonism and *tardive dyskinesia)* with chronic use in the elderly than in the young.

The *pharmacokinetic hypothesis* argues that a given dose of drug produces higher blood concentrations in elderly patients than in the young. At any given dose, *beta-blockers* produce more light-headedness, weakness and slowing of the heart rate in the elderly. This is because liver metabolism is slower and higher blood concentrations develop in the elderly than in the young (beta-blockers depend more on liver metabolism than on *renal excretion* for their clearance). The fact that blood flow through the liver falls with age further decreases the clearance of beta-blockers in the elderly. Digoxin is more likely to produce confusion, visual symptoms and slowing of the heart rate in the elderly at any given dose, since renal clearance falls with advancing age (and digoxin depends more on renal excretion than on liver metabolism for its clearance).

DRUG AND FOOD INTERACTIONS

A few drugs can be influenced by pharmacokinetic and pharmacodynamic interactions with certain foods. For example, levodopa (a treatment for *Parkinson's disease)* competes with *amino acids* (protein breakdown products) for its absorption into the blood from the gut and into the brain from the blood. A Parkinson's patient who takes a dose of levodopa following a large steak dinner (or any other high-protein meal) might notice little therapeutic benefit, since absorption of levodopa into the blood and brain is delayed and peak levels are reduced (Nutt, Woodward, Hammerstad, Carter and Anderson, 1984).

A group of antidepressant drugs called *monoamine oxidase inhibitors* (MAOIs) work by preventing the metabolism of monoamines *(neurotransmitters)* in the brain. Sudden increases in the concentrations of these transmitters are thought to cause malignant hypertension. Foods such as red wine, bleu cheese and pickled herring contain a "false" neurotransmitter (tyramine) that can produce malignant hypertension in patients taking MAOIs. Patients who cannot rigidly control their diet (as is typical of elderly residents of institutions) should not be treated with these agents. Fortunately, this ADR is now exceedingly rare since physicians and

pharmacists are being more cautious and advising patients of this important drug-food interaction.

MEDICATION ERRORS

Medication errors pose a significant problem for the elderly. They include taking medication that is not ordered by the physician (self-medication), not taking medication that is ordered (omission), taking medication in the wrong dosages (incorrect dosage), taking it at the wrong times (incorrect timing), or taking it with total lack of understanding about the condition for which the medication has been prescribed (inaccurate knowledge). Schwartz *et al.* (1962) studied 220 ambulatory elderly patients and found omission (15 percent) and inaccurate knowledge (11 percent) to be the factors most likely to lead to potentially serious medication errors. This was later confirmed by Neely and Patrick (1968), who also found the frequency of potentially serious errors to be highest for omissions (11 percent) and inaccurate knowledge (7 percent).

One study showed that the number of errors per patient did not increase linearly as a function of age, but actually peaked in the 75 to 79 year age group (Schwartz *et al.,* 1962). In fact, none of the patients who were 85 years or older made serious medication errors. Neither blindness, the inability to read English, nor the total number of drugs prescribed contributed to an increased risk of errors in this study. Neely and Patrick (1968), on the other hand, found that the number of serious errors did increase as a function of the total number of drugs prescribed.

Factors that Schwartz and colleagues (1962) found to increase the risk of medication errors in the elderly included marital status, living arrangements, educational background and number of clinical diagnoses. Single and married patients made *less* severe and *less* frequent errors than those who were widowed, divorced, or separated. The number and severity of errors was higher in those who lived alone than in those who lived with one or more other persons. Relatively uneducated patients (those with three years or less of formal education) were more likely to make serious errors than their better educated counterparts. Patients with four or less diagnoses made fewer errors (55 percent) than did those with five or more diagnoses (71 percent).

NURSING INTERVENTION

The nurse is the health-care professional whom elderly patients most frequently encounter, whether it be in the inpatient setting, the outpatient clinic or at home. Nurses are in an ideal position to educate elderly patients about their medications. A complete drug history is essential. As Todd (1981) explains, a good drug history includes more than simply reading the names of medications and their dosages from the bottles. It means taking a 24-hour drug history, beginning from the time of awakening until the time the patient retires at night. The drug history includes identifying medications (both prescription and OTC agents), the doses taken at each time interval, and the reasons why the medications are being taken. This information can be compared to the instructions on the bottles or the orders in the patient's chart so that the nurse can assess the patient's understanding of the treatment plan.

If omissions are detected in the drug history, the nurse should try to determine why they have occurred. Is the patient forgetful? Is the capsule difficult to swallow? Is the childproof bottle difficult to open? Can the patient afford the medication? Does the patient have difficulty finding transportation to the pharmacy for refills? Does the patient's family understand the treatment plan? Does the patient fear dependence on a particular medication? Some authors have found no benefit from memory aids, but Wandless and Davie (1977) studied inpatients in a rehabilitation unit and found that a tear-off calendar or a card detailing the medication regimen significantly improved compliance.

The community health nurse who visits the elderly patient in the home should ask to see all medications that are not currently in use. Ostrom, Hammarlund, Christensen, Plein and Kethley (1985) found that 78 percent of their ambulatory elderly sample stored non-current prescription drugs or non-current OTC medications in their homes. Schwartz *et al.* (1962) also noted that hoarding outdated medications was common among the elderly. This is a potentially serious practice, since drugs such as tetracycline can become toxic when kept beyond the expiration date. Nurses should also ask where drugs are stored, since some require protection from light and heat (such as nitroglycerin).

Teaching inpatients about medications should begin as soon as possible after admission. Teaching at the time of discharge is usually rushed and does not give the patient enough time to assimilate the information or to ask questions. The nurse should explain the purpose of each medication, how it is taken (on an empty stomach or with food), possible side-effects and contingency plans to follow in case an adverse drug reaction occurs. For example, a Parkinson's patient treated with an *anticholinergic agent* should be told to expect dry mouth and constipation, since they are common secondary side effects of these drugs. If the patient experiences urinary retention or blurred vision, however, the drug should be stopped and the physician contacted immediately. Listing a few of the most common and most dangerous side effects on the patient's drug chart prevents more needless anxiety than it creates.

PHYSICIAN INTERVENTION

A complete drug history is also important for the physician. This should not be considered a duplication of the nurse's effort, since patients often tell nurses things they do not tell their physicians (and vice versa). When taking an adverse drug reaction history, words should be used that are familiar to the patient such as "allergy" or "overdose." True allergies constitute a small percentage of ADRs in the elderly (14 percent), but this term is probably the most commonly used by patients. A patient with a true allergy could experience dangerous side effects if he were rechallenged with that medication. It is important to educate the elderly patient about which ADRs are the result of an excessive dose (where rechallenge with a lower dose poses no problem) and which ones are true allergic reactions (where rechallenge could be fatal).

The physician should explore the reasoning behind drug omissions and use the opportunity to educate patients about their disease, their drug requirements and the risks incurred if medications are discontinued. Fears of dependence on medication are widespread, but the consequences of drug omissions are occasionally fatal. For example, patients with angina (chest pain brought on by exertion) are often treated with beta-blockers. If angina patients suddenly discontinue their beta-blockers, they may experience worsening chest pain, heart attack or, in rare cases, death. Adults with seizure disorders *(epilepsy)* are usually treated with anticonvulsant agents. Epileptic patients who suddenly discontinue their anticonvulsants are at risk for developing *status epilepticus,* a medical emergency that carries with it a 10 percent mortality rate. Thus the physician's obligation extends beyond writing an accurate prescription; it includes an explanation of the consequences of sudden drug discontinuation.

The literature on ADRs and medication errors argues that physicians should work to minimize the total number of medications prescribed per patient, since there is a clear relationship between the incidence of these problems and the total number of prescribed medications (Seidl *et al.,* 1966; Borda *et al.,* 1968; Neely and Patrick, 1968; Lawson and Jick, 1976). The patient's drug profile should be reviewed periodically to identify potential drug interactions and to assess the need for continued drug therapy. This task may be difficult if multiple health-care providers are involved. Cooper and associates (1982) found that patients who are intentionally non-adherent to a physician's treatment plan are more likely to be using two or more physicians and two or more pharmacies.

PHARMACIST INTERVENTION

The dispensing pharmacist is a valuable ally in the prevention of ADRs and medication errors. The elderly patient often views the pharmacist as more accessible than the physician (the pharmacist's phone number is usually clearly displayed on every prescription bottle). The pharmacist can explain to the patient how to store the medication, what OTC drugs to avoid and what side effects to expect. Using modern computer record systems, many pharmacists can detect whether a patient is taking similar drugs prescribed by more than one physician.

Pharmacists in many community and hospital pharmacies have access to automated drug-interaction screening systems that detect potential drug interactions by examining patient-medication profiles. One such data base described in the literature contained 24,000 combinations of drugs that have been reported to cause drug interactions (Greenlaw and Zellers, 1978). Systems in current use are continually updated. In the 635-bed hospital where the above data-base system was first developed, the computer was able to detect potential drug interactions in about 9 percent of patients per day. Table 15.2 describes examples of drug interactions detectable by this type of screening system.

Consultant pharmacists play an increasingly important role in assuring optimal use of medications in chronically ill nursing home patients. Cooper and Bagwell (1978) began conducting daily pharmacy rounds with health-care students and the nursing supervisor in a rural skilled-nursing facility in 1976. They began contacting the attending physicians by phone if medication orders needed to be changed and developed protocols for *p.r.n.* drug orders. After one year, they saw a 19 percent reduction in the number of regularly prescribed medications (from 3.3 to 2.7 drug per patient) and a 46 percent reduction in the number of *p.r.n.* agents (from 3.9 to 2.1 drugs per patient). The overall reduction in prescribing (34 percent) was significant.

SUMMARY

Drug use patterns among the elderly are influenced by the sample size, age, living arrangements, and whether they are institutionalized or ambulatory and urban or rural.

The incidence of adverse drug reactions differs from one population to the next, depending upon the age of the patients, the acuteness of the illness, whether they are institutionalized or ambulatory, and whether ADRs are reported on the basis of self-reports or professional evaluations. Pharmacodynamic and pharmacokinetic factors are likely to contribute to the increasing incidence of ADRs with increasing age.

The likelihood of a medication error in an elderly patient depends most upon the patient's marital status, educational background and total number of clinical diagnoses. Surprisingly, neither increasing age nor the inability to read English enhances the chance for error. Various researchers have debated the influence of living arrangements and total number of medications on the incidence of medication errors.

Both physicians and nurses need to take careful and independent drug histories and compare notes with each other, since patients seem to have "differential recall," depending on the historian. Patients need to be questioned about why they omit certain medications and educated about the consequences of doing so. Pharmacists, physicians and nurses all need to remind patients about a drug's potential ADRs, the possibility for its interaction with other agents and the dangers associated with suddenly stopping it. It is of paramount importance to educate and encourage patients to be their own health advocates and to assume as much responsibility for their own medical care as possible.

KEY TERMS

adverse drug reaction (ADR)
amino acids
analgesics
anticholinergic agent
anticoagulants
antipsychotic agents
beta-blockers
cardiovascular agents
dementing illness
diuretics
drug-drug interaction
epilepsy
excessive effect
heart failure
hypertension
idiosyncratic reaction
ischemic heart disease
monoamine oxidase inhibitors (MAOIs)
neurotransmitters
overdosage
over-the-counter (OTC)
Parkinson's disease
pharmacodynamic hypothesis
pharmacokinetic hypothesis
p.r.n.
renal excretion
schizophrenia
secondary side effect
status epilepticus
tardive dyskinesia

STUDY QUESTIONS

1. In any descriptive study of drug use in the elderly, which demographic features of the study population need to be clearly identified? Why?
2. Describe five different types of adverse drug reactions (ADRs). How can demographic variables and study design influence ADR incidence figures? What accounts for the increased risk of ADRs with increasing age?
3. Describe five different types of medication errors. What is the social and medical profile of an elderly patient who is most likely to make medication errors?
4. What can the nurse do to minimize the chances that an elderly patient will develop adverse drug reactions? The physician? The pharmacist?

5. What can the physician do to prevent medication errors in the elderly? The nurse? The pharmacist?

BIBLIOGRAPHY

Borda, I.T., Slone, D., and Jick, H. 1968. Assessment of adverse reactions within a drug surveillance program. *Journal of the American Medical Association, 205:* 645–647.

Brown, M.M., Boosinger, J.K., Henderson, M., Rife, S.S., Rustia, J.K., Taylor, O., and Young, W.W. 1977. Drug-drug interactions among residents in homes for the elderly. *Nursing Research 26:* 47–52.

Chien, C.P., Townsend, E.J., and Townsend, A.R. 1978. Substance use and abuse among the community elderly: The medical aspect. *Addictive Diseases 3*(3): 357–372.

Cooper, J.K., Love, D.W., and Raffoul, P.R. 1982. Intentional prescription nonadherence (noncompliance) by the elderly. *Journal of the American Geriatrics Society 30:* 329–333.

Cooper, J.W., and Bagwell, C.G. 1978. Contribution of the consultant pharmacist to rational drug usage in the long-term care facility. *Journal of the American Geriatrics Society 26:* 513–520.

Greenblatt, D.J., Sellers, E.M., and Shader, R.I. 1982. Drug disposition in old age. *New England Journal of Medicine 306:* 1081–1088.

Greenlaw, C.W., and Zellers, D.D. 1978. Computerized drug-drug interaction screening system. *American Journal of Hospital Pharmacists 35:* 567–570.

Guttmann, D. 1978. Patterns of legal drug use by older Americans. *Addictive Diseases 3*(3): 337–356.

Ingman, S.R., Lawson, I.R., Pierpaoli, P.G., and Blake, P. 1975. A survey of the prescribing and administration of drugs in a long-term care institution for the elderly. *Journal of the American Geriatrics Society 23:* 309–316.

Knapp, D.A., Wiser, T.H., Michocki, R.J., Nuessle, S.J., and Knapp, W.K. 1984. Drug prescribing for ambulatory patients 85 years of age and older. *Journal of the American Geriatrics Society 32:* 138–143.

Kovar, M.G. 1977. Health of the elderly and use of health services. *Public Health Reports 92*(1): 9–19.

Lawson, D.H., and Jick, H. 1976. Drug prescribing in hospitals: An international comparison. *American Journal of Public Health 66:* 644–648.

Neely, E., and Patrick, M.L. 1968. Problems of aged persons taking medications at home. *Nursing Research 17:* 52–55.

Nutt, J.G., Woodward, W.R., Hammerstad, J.P., Carter, J.H., and Anderson, J.L. 1984. The "on-off" phenomenon in Parkinson's disease. *New England Journal of Medicine 310:* 483–488.

Ostrom, J.R., Hammarlund, E.R., Christensen, D.B., Plein, J.B., and Kethley, A.J. 1985. Medication usage in an elderly population. *Medical Care 23:* 157–164.

Schwartz, D., Wang, M., Zeitz, L., and Goss, M.E.W. 1962. Medication errors made by elderly, chronically ill patients. *American Journal of Public Health 52:* 2018–2029.

Seidl, L.G., Thornton, G.F., Smith, J.W., and Cluff, L.E. 1966. Studies on the epidemiology of adverse drug reactions. *Bulletin of Johns Hopkins Hospital 119:* 229–316.

Todd, B. 1981. Drugs and the elderly: What does a good drug history include? *Geriatric Nursing 2*(1): 63–64.

Wandless, I., and Davis, J. W. 1977. Can drug compliance in the elderly be improved? *British Medical Journal 1:* 359–361.

Williamson, J., and Chopin, J.M. 1980. Adverse reactions to prescribed drugs in the elderly: A multi-center investigation. *Age and Aging 9:* 73–80.

CHAPTER **16**

Sexuality in Later Life

Gere B. Fulton, Ph.D., J.D.

It seems quite common to regard sexuality in later life as amusing, at best, or as repugnant. Young people are as uncomfortable with the sexuality of their parents as the parents are by the sexuality of their adolescent children. Pocs and his colleagues (1977) reported that a majority of the 646 college students they surveyed believed that their parents (1) never had intercourse before they were married, (2) never had oral-genital sex and (3) had intercourse once a month or less. About one-fourth of the students, both men and women, believed their parents *never* had intercourse or had it less than once a year!

It was evident that some students felt it was wrong even to *think* about parental sexuality. Six percent refused to answer most of the items that dealt with premarital petting, premarital, marital and extramarital intercourse, and oral-genital sex. Nearly 20 percent ignored the questions about past and present parental masturbation. A few students expressed their feelings about the survey more bluntly: "This questionnaire stinks." "Whoever thinks about their parents' sexual relations, except perverts?"

While thinking about their parents engaging in sexual behavior was obviously problematic for many college students, what might the response have been had the survey focused on the sexuality, not of their parents, but of their grandparents? It is only too obvious that most of these students (and we, too) have been raised in a society that still retains certain Victorian standards regarding sexual expression by older persons.

There is some evidence that these repressive attitudes are becoming less common. In some cases the attitudes of staff who work with the institutionalized elderly may be more supportive concerning sexual expression of nursing home residents than the elderly themselves. The explanation for this may lie partially in the interplay of factors such as illness, dependency and isolation that lead the elderly to view themselves as unattractive and sexless. An alternative explanation might be that staff attitudes might be little more than an expression of the fashionable response and quite unrelated to behavior. One researcher (Kaas, 1978) has called for observational studies to determine if staff members do indeed behave consistently with how they respond in surveys. Other researchers of sexuality in nursing homes have concluded that:

> To be old is to be sexually oppressed. The old values inhibit, then the younger generations disapprove, and finally society sets up many formal barriers to accessibility of sexual partners. Sexual behavior for the aged, though not physiologically impossible nor affectionately dismissible, is culturally and psychologically restricted. The news should be spread around that sexuality for the aged is a good thing, for those who want it (Wasow and Loeb, 1979:79).

SEXUAL ACTIVITY AND THE AGED

Sexuality for the aged is a good thing for those who want it. Well, then, what kind of a problem are we talking about? Just how many of the elderly want to continue to engage in sexual behavior? Kinsey and his colleagues (1948, 1953) found that both male and female sexual activity declined with age, although the pattern of decline was less dramatic among the females. Male sexual activity began a steady decline after reaching a peak in the late teenage years or early 20s; female sexual activity was likely to peak later and decline less noticeably with aging.

Pfeiffer and his colleagues (1968, 1969a) came to a somewhat different conclusion concerning the differential effects of aging on the sexual attitudes and appetites of men and women. They reported that, among their subjects over the age of 60, men were far more likely than women to report both interest in and current participation in sexual intercourse. Among the subjects who had stopped having intercourse, women were more likely to attribute the cause to factors beyond their control; men who had ceased this form of sexual activity were more likely to attribute causation to themselves. In decreasing order of importance, women cited death of their spouse, husband's illness, and divorce or separation. A large number indicated that impotence or loss of interest in sex by the mate heralded the end of their sexual activity.

Men were less likely to accept celibacy as the inevitable outcome of the loss of a spouse. The most frequently cited reason for not engaging in sexual intercourse among older men was impotency (50 percent); smaller percentages identified either their illness or a loss of sexual interest. Nearly two-thirds of the women between the ages of 61 and 71 in this study *were not* participating in *coitus*, whereas nearly three-quarters of the comparably aged men *were*. One-third of the women stated that they had "no interest in sex''; only 6 percent of the males responded similarly.

This difference between the findings of Kinsey and associates and those of Pfeiffer and his co-workers may be the result of several factors, including data-collection techniques, the characteristics of the samples and differences in the time periods in which the data were collected.

SEXUAL ATTITUDES OF THE AGED

Much remains to be learned about sexuality and aging. Wasow and Loeb (1979:73) have noted that ''when we focus on elderly persons confined to nursing homes, the literature dealing directly with sexuality is almost nonexistent.'' Research in the area of sexuality, let alone geriatric sexuality, is not ''politically'' proper and recruitment of subjects can be difficult. Pfeiffer (1969b) has noted that relatives, too, can be a problem, especially when they insist that participants withdraw from ''such foolishness.''

Two recently reported studies have significantly furthered our understanding of sexuality and aging. In the first of these, Starr and Weiner (1981) collected data from 800 subjects between ages 60 and 91. Participation in the study was requested from those who attended a series of presentations on ''Love, Intimacy and Sex in the Later Years.'' The sample included only relatively healthy men and women who were living independently.

The picture that emerges from this study of the elderly is of a zest for life, including sex. Their findings, which the authors identify as ''surprising,'' reveal:

1. A strong continuing interest in sex;
2. the belief that sex is important for physical and mental well-being;
3. the perception of most of the respondents that sex is as good now as when they were younger;
4. that for a large number, both male and female, sex is *better* in the later years;
5. orgasm is considered an essential part of the sexual experience;
6. most of the women are orgasmic and always have been;
7. the orgasm for many is stronger now than when younger;
8. masturbation is an acceptable outlet for sexual needs;
9. for the majority, living together without marriage is acceptable;
10. an overwhelming number of respondents, including widows, widowers, divorcees and singles, are sexually active;
11. most are satisfied with their sex lives;
12. many vary their sexual practices to achieve satisfaction;
13. for some older people, oral sex is considered the most exciting sexual experience;
14. respondents typically show little embarrassment or anxiety about sex;
15. most enjoy nudity with their partners;
16. the ideal or fantasized lover for most, particularly women, is close to their own age;
17. most see their sex lives remaining pretty much the same as they grow even older.

The authors hasten to add, however, that this was not the case for all the elderly they interviewed.

Some who had cast themselves in society's mold of the older person, were living in a wasteland that senselessly denied them pleasure and fulfillment. And it was they, we felt, who could perhaps most benefit from what we were learning (Starr and Weiner, 1981:7).

Consumer's Union, the organization that publishes the magazine *Consumer Reports,* has released the results of their study of "Love, Sex, and Aging" (Brecher, 1984). Responding to an announcement in the November 1977 issue of the magazine more than 5,000 men and women, aged 50 and over, requested more than 10,000 questionnaires. Although the questionnaire was long, usable responses totaled 4,246; 1,844 were from women, 2,402 from men. Brecher and his colleagues (1984:15) acknowledge that there is a bias in the sample.

It is limited to those particular readers of *Consumer Reports* who filled out and returned the November 1977 coupon—and to their relatives and friends. It is also limited to those who, having received the questionnaire in the fall of 1978, answered the questions and mailed back their answers during the next few months. It is probable that sexually inactive women and men were less likely than the sexually active to mail back their questionnaires—though some did. No doubt those with little interest in sex, or with a dislike of sex, were also less likely to mail back the questionnaires—but some did.

The findings clearly cannot be extrapolated to the total U.S. population over 50, but they may apply to other groups that resemble the sample: those with higher-than-average socioeconomic status (as reflected by income and education), better-than-average health (as with the Starr-Weiner sample referred to above), greater interest in sex, and so on. This is clearly the largest study of sexuality and aging undertaken to date and, for that reason alone, the findings are compelling.

Some of the comparative generalizations that emerge are:

1. The sexual aspect of marriage is more important for the husbands than for the wives.

2. Unmarried women and men who remain sexually active after 50 (either with a partner or through masturbation) report higher levels of life enjoyment than those who do not engage in sex.
3. More husbands than wives have engaged in extramarital sex since age 50.
4. More men than women have engaged in homosexual activities since age 50. More women than men, however, have felt sexually attracted to a person of their own gender since 50.
5. Fewer women and men in their 80s are sexually active than are younger women and men; but some women and men in their 80s continue to engage in and enjoy a wide range of sexual activities.
6. Relatively few men engage in sex with prostitutes after 50. Some of those who do, however, report that their encounters with prostitutes contribute substantially to their enjoyment of life.
7. Post-menopausal women taking estrogen are more active sexually than post-menopausal women not taking estrogen.

The picture that emerges from these studies is that sexuality, in both men and women, endures a great deal better than many other functional systems. In the absence of disease, sexual desire and capacity are lifelong. Even when intercourse fails as a result of infirmity, need for other aspects of the sexual relationship persists, such as closeness, touching, caressing, sensuality and being valued. This is both contrary to folklore and to the preconceptions of some hospital and nursing-home administrators. It is even contrary to the beliefs of many of the elderly themselves. Many of the elderly have been, to use Alex Comfort's terminology, "hocussed out" of continuing sexual activity by a society that disallows it for the old, exactly as they have been "hocussed out" of so many other valuable activities of which they are fully capable (e.g., useful work or social involvement).

Still, as evidenced by the above-cited research, "hocussing" has not been totally successful. Many older people have simply gone on having sex without talking about it, unabashed by the accepted and destructive social image of the "dirty old man" and the asexual, undesirable older woman. Older people have not been asked about their sexual experiences because many physicians and researchers "knew" that they had none, and they were assumed to have none because few thought to ask. For some elderly, the fantasy of the celibate senior that they held when they were younger became a blueprint for their own aging, what Comfort refers to as a "classical case of bewitchment by expectation" (Comfort, 1976).

AGE-RELATED CHANGES IN SEXUAL FUNCTION

There are, to be sure, changes in sexual function that are related to the aging process. Often these changes are not understood and, consequently, are experienced with greater anxiety. The changes are far more subtle than those foretold by the ever-witty Tom Lehrer when he sings, "In all probability I'll lose my virility and you your fertility and desirability." Perhaps they are best understood when viewed in the context of the sexual response cycle, as first proposed by Masters and Johnson (1966).

Masters and Johnson arbitrarily divided the sexual response cycle into four phases, identified as (1) excitement, (2) plateau, (3) orgasm and (4) resolution. These phases are characterized in the sexually responsive female as follows.

Excitement Phase

In the sexually aroused female there is an engorgement of blood in all distensible body parts. This includes the breasts, the *labia* and the *clitoris*. This *vasocongestive response* is diminished in the post-menopausal female. The diminution seems linked to estrogen deficiency and may not be experienced among women on estrogen replacement therapy (ERT). *Myotonia,* or generalized muscle tension, decreases with age. The onset of vaginal lubrication, which may occur in younger women within seconds, may occur more slowly with the aging female.

Plateau Phase

Perhaps the most noticeable change that occurs during this phase of the sexual response cycle is a swelling in the outer or distal one-third of the vagina. This swelling narrows the *introitus* and increases the traction on the penis during coital thrusting. Masters and Johnson labeled this phenomenon the *orgasmic platform*. Although the intensity of the vasocongestion is somewhat reduced, the aged female develops an orgasmic platform much as her younger counterpart.

The "ballooning" of the inner two-thirds of the vagina, labeled the "tenting" phenomenon by Masters and Johnson, and the accompanying elevation of the uterus, may also be diminished by hormonal alterations associated with *menopause*. This loss of vaginal elasticity, along with the lessened lubrication, may be a source of discomfort during coital thrusting. There is the increased probability that sudden penile penetration or intercourse of long duration may create small fissures in the lining of the vagina. These changes, too, are less likely to be seen among women who receive exogenous estrogen. Water-soluble lubricants, such as K-Y Jelly, are also helpful in compensating for vaginal dryness.

Orgasmic Phase

The *orgasmic phase* is marked by contractions of the uterus, the paravaginal musculature and the muscles of the pelvic floor, including the rectal sphincter. Both the number and the intensity of these contractions may be reduced in the post-menopausal female. This is experienced as a change in the character of the orgasm. Masters and Johnson (1982:53) indicate that "although these involuntary physiologic alterations may be experienced, the subjectively appreciated levels of sensual pleasure derived from coital connection usually continue unabated."

Much less frequently encountered by the aging female, although associated with the aging process, are painful uterine spasms during orgasm. This problem, too, is prevented or abated by estrogen-replacement therapy.

Resolution Phase

During resolution the expanded inner two-thirds of the vagina shrinks back to a collapsed, unstimulated state with marked rapidity. This rapid vaginal collapse in older women, as opposed to younger women, may be the result of the increased rigidity and lack of elasticity in the senescent vaginal barrel.

ADDITIONAL AGE-RELATED SEXUAL CHANGES

Females

Some additional general changes in the aging female were also noted by Masters and Johnson (1966). After the ovaries reduce or cease estrogen production, the walls of the vagina begin to involute. They become very thin, lose the rough, corrugated appearance of the younger woman's vagina and change in color from a reddish-purple to a light pink. There is a shortening in vaginal length and a reduction in width that, in association with the loss of expansive ability described above, may make comfortable accommodation of the erect penis difficult. The resulting *dyspareunia* (pain with intercourse) may trigger the onset of *vaginismus* (involuntary contractions of the muscles surrounding the outer portion of the vagina) as a self-protective response to painful stimuli. Vaginismus should be suspected where there is a history of painful coitus or following a long period of incontinence in the aging female. The diagnosis can be clinically made by a pelvic examination. Masters and Johnson (1982:53) indicate that it is "probably the most frequently missed diagnosis in the field of gynecology." Once identified, it can be readily reversed with relaxation and muscle-retraining exercises.

Also linked to diminished lubrication is a burning on urination in the hours subsequent to intercourse. This discomfort develops as a result of coital thrusting that has caused mechanical irritation of the bladder and urethra. Symptoms of *dysuria* (pain with urination) and dyspareunia may last for 24 to 36 hours after intercourse.

Males

The changes in the aging male are not quite so detailed as the female and, consequently, do not lend themselves as nicely to explanation within each phase of the sexual response cycle. As the male ages, the major differences in sexual response relate to the duration of each of the phases in the cycle. The older man is slower to obtain an erection and the erect penis is likely to be less firm than during the younger years. He is less likely to experience an erection as a result of purely psychic stimuli requiring, instead, more direct stimulation either by himself or his partner. Along with this is an occasional reduction in or loss of ejaculatory demand. While the male continues to have a high level of interest in the sensual pleasure associated with coitus, the subjectively experienced demand to ejaculate may be reduced. Alex Comfort has described this reduced demand to ejaculate in the older male as follows: "It takes him a little longer to get an erection, but he can hold it just as well when he's got it, and he can have an awful lot more sex per orgasm" (Easton, 1977). In view of the fact that loss of ejaculatory control—premature ejaculation—is the most commonly experienced sexual dysfunction among young men, it would seem that this phase of sexual functioning, rather than deteriorating, improves considerably with age.

The aging male, with the sensation of ejaculatory imperativeness, has the psychosexual demand to ejaculate but may be subject to a loss of or inefficiency in neurophysiological control of the process. Ejaculation, which is a two-stage process in the younger male, is reduced to one stage in the older male. There is also a lessening of expulsive force propelling the seminal fluid. It has been suggested that these two factors combine to make coitus a less pleasurable physiological experience for him as compared to his younger days. *Penile detumesence* occurs immediately after ejaculation and the *refractory period* may last for a number of days, depending upon the individual.

There is no question that the human male's sexual responsiveness wanes as he ages. Not only does his coital activity typically decrease, but the incidence of masturbation and nocturnal emission also declines with advancing years. Compared to changes in other areas such as vital capacity, muscular strength, and flexibility, however, sexual changes are functionally minimal. Sexuality, in both sexes, endures a great deal better than many other functional systems.

The reasonably healthy aging male does not lose his facility for erection at any time; this is demonstrated by the occurrence of morning erections in men who think they are impotent. There is no physiological reason why an older man cannot achieve an erection for purposes of intercourse if he experiences erections during sleep or in the mornings. If the aging male avoids talking himself out of effective sexual functioning by worrying about the physiological factors in his sexual response cycle, if his peers do not destroy his sexual confidence, and if he and his partner maintain a reasonably good state of health, he certainly can and should continue unencumbered sexual functioning late in life.

Although a common cause of *erectile dysfunction* among older men—as is true for younger men—is performance anxiety, other causes in order of frequency are alcohol, medication, obesity and diabetes. Alcohol, which can interfere with erection in men of all ages, seems to inhibit sexual response in much smaller doses with the elderly. Erectile dysfunction is seen as both an acute and chronic effect of alcohol consumption, especially in cases of drug dependency or abusive drinking. Other drugs—both prescribed and over-the-counter varieties—may also be implicated in erectile failure. Prominent among this group are the anti-anxiety and anti-hypertensive medications. Obesity interferes with sexual functioning and may be esthetically displeasing to a partner. Diabetes probably interferes with potency in several ways; whether due to diabetic neuropathy or some specific effect of hyperglycemia on the complicated hydraulics in the penis, the effect on sexual function is well recognized.

On the other hand, since many diabetics know of this consequence of diabetes, there could even be some components of a self-ful-filling prophecy at work here.

Members of both sexes may find it difficult to resume sexual functioning following extended periods of abstinence. This problem is often described in women and men, respectively, as the Widow's and the Widower's Syndromes. Upon attempting a resumption of sexual activity, depending upon the person's age and the duration of sexual continence, the combination of heightened anxiety and lack of sexual activity may commonly result in failure. This seems to be a classic case of "Use it or lose it."

Despite the physiological changes associated with menopause, if the opportunity for regular coital expression is present or if there is opportunity for regular sexual activity, it will have a significant influence upon the sexual performance of the aged female. In Masters' and Johnson's (1966) study of the geriatric response cycle, some women over 60 were repeatedly observed to expand and lubricate the vagina effectively even with thinning vaginal walls and shrinking labia. The past history of these women revealed that they had maintained regular intercourse, once or twice a week, for their entire adult lives. It would seem that both the male and the female, in the absence of physical or mental infirmity, are capable of sexual performance throughout their lives.

AGING, SEX AND SOCIETY

As was mentioned earlier, Victorian influence upon our society has for years decreed that the aged possess little or no socially acceptable sexuality. What our prejudiced culture regards as virility at 25 becomes lechery at 65. Such attitudes are unfair. They create guilt, misunderstanding and undeserved condemnation. While many of the taboos concerning sexuality for adults, and even adolescents, have been re-examined and discarded, the taboos against sex in old age have been more durable.

The reasons for these attitudes are many. Traditionally, sexuality has been equated with youth and beauty. What is so often forgotten is that we are sexual beings all of our lives; we are libidinous from birth to death. Perhaps it is the loss of procreative ability and the fading of conventional sex appeal that stigmatize the desires and behavior of the aged.

Older people themselves may have many negative attitudes towards sexuality in the aged. They may suppress their sexual desires, regarding them as unnatural. This may be traced, in part, to the difficulties children have in imagining their parents or grandparents making love or even having sexual desires. They tend to reject sexuality for their elders and often discourage remarriage. As children they were cautioned about sex and taught to regard it as dirty; when they became parents they reversed the process and condemned sex in their elders. What must be remembered, however, is that we all have the same need for intimacy and touch regardless of age. Sex is often viewed, moreover, as an affirmation of life and a denial of death. Levitan (1973) has suggested that an active sex life may well be a significant deterrent to suicide. A sexual relationship in old age can be and often is a boost to the older person's psyche.

Physicians' attitudes toward sexuality among the aged are extremely important. Very often their response to a geriatric patient's sexual problem is, "Well . . . what do you expect at your age?" Most older people respect the opinions of their doctors. When physicians give the impression that they deem sex as unnecessary and something strictly for the young, they reinforce everything society has said about aged sexuality. Many times the physician has been poorly trained in the area of human sexuality, may be unsure of his or her own sexuality, or may have difficulty in his or her own mind with the idea that older people have sexual needs.

Occasionally an older man will discontinue sexual relations within marriage. Masters and Johnson (1966) have suggested several reasons why this might occur. Monotony is probably the most constant factor in the loss of an aging male's interest in sex with his spouse. He may simply be bored with his partner and chooses to abstain. Other variables include male concern with economic pursuit, which reduces the time and attention needed to maintain a good marriage and a happy sex life, physical or mental infirmities and the fear of impotence.

There is every reason to believe, however, that maintained regularity of sexual expression, coupled with adequate physical well-being and a healthy mental orientation to the aging process, will combine to provide a sexually stimulating climate within a marriage. This climate will provide a capacity for sexual performance that frequently may extend to and beyond the eighth and ninth decades of life.

Sex can and does play an important part in the lives of the aged. The most important factors contributing to the variation in sexual behavior appear to be past sexual experience, age and sex of the individual. Income and social class are also involved. Continuity of lifestyle seems to be instrumental in the sexual behavior of the aged. Those for whom sex was important early in life are more likely

to continue to be sexually active later in life; those for whom sex was of little importance early in life will be more likely to reach an early terminus of their sexual behavior in later life.

But what about the aged woman who is a widow? What opportunity does she have for sexual expression? Pfeiffer and colleagues (1969a) suggest that much of the decline in sexual interest in aging females is not physiological but a protective mechanism. It may well be adaptive to inhibit sexual desire when little opportunity for sexual fulfillment exists. Christenson and Gagnon (1965) found that widowed female subjects masturbated twice as much as their married counterparts. They also discovered that one factor in maintaining post-marital sexual activity was the woman's ability to experience orgasm fairly regularly. Once the capacity for sexual response is discovered by the female, it is clear that she is more likely to continue to have coitus post-maritally (Christenson and Gagnon, 1965). This study did not take into account the difficulties some women may have in accepting masturbation and the dearth of male sexual partners available. As noted by Pfeiffer and colleagues (1968), many women find masturbation unfulfilling and are unwilling to engage in post-marital sexual behavior. There seems to be no easy answer to the problem that aged females experience in finding adequate sexual outlets.

SEX, AGE AND THE HELPING PROFESSIONS

If there is to be any progress in the quest for acceptance of sexuality among the aged, the responsibility rests most heavily upon those in the health and helping professions. Support and encouragement of sexual behavior should be given without embarrassment or evangelization. Sexuality in old age is a different, perhaps quieter experience, but no less sexual and no less an experience than in youth.

In addition to establishing a climate in which the sexualtiy of the aged is acknowledged and valued, we need to address ourselves to four more specific concerns:

1. We need to ensure that sexual growth programs are available to habilitate and rehabilitate the sexually dysfunctional aged. In the case of the disabled, it has been traditional to suggest that reference to their sexual needs would embarrass them; in fact, however, when counseling and rehabilitation programs were offered they were enthusiastically embraced. It seems reasonable to suspect that the same would happen with the elderly (Comfort, 1974).

2. In old-age homes and mental institutions, a re-examination of policies that have led to the total segregation of the sexes and even the separation of husbands and wives should be undertaken, since such practices are now realized as contributing to failure in treatment. The institutionalized old should have the same right to *engage in or abstain from* sexual activity as the rest of us have, without interference.

3. In the health field, proper attention must be given to training medical personnel to give equal attention to the sexual needs of the aged in all aspects of medical practice. Physicians must realize that a negative attitude on their part can very often pronounce a death sentence upon the sexual life of older patients. As with younger persons, sexual

information should routinely be included when taking the histories of older persons who must, in turn, be encouraged to bring their sex-related problems to their physicians for treatment.

4. For our youth-oriented culture as a whole, an end is needed to the concept that debilities come with age and the belief that a person is "over the hill" at 60. There is one great problem with ageism. Think of the other prejudices: White racists do not turn black, and anti-Semites do not wake up to find they are Jewish. But we shall all, if we are lucky, get to be old. About the most unproductive prejudice there can be is one directed against a group that you are going to join! (Easton, 1977)

Comfort (1974) has suggested that old people often stop having sex for the same reasons that they stop riding bicycles—general infirmity, thinking it looks ridiculous, or having no bicycle. However, most people can and should expect to have sex long after they no longer wish to ride bicycles. Such people may well require fewer tranquilizers and less institutionalization and may expect to live richer lives. Certainly there will be fewer "obstreperous malcontents" among the old whom the society has heretofore worked so industriously to desexualize.

SUMMARY

Many young people are uncomfortable discussing or even thinking about the sexuality of their parents and grandparents. In part, this suggests that certain Victorian standards regarding sexual expression by older persons are still strong today.

In general, it seems that sexual activity declines with age. Kinsey and his colleagues reported that female sexual activity was likely to peak later and decline less noticeably with aging than was the case for males. In contrast, Pfeiffer and his associates found aged men more likely than women to show interest and participate in sex.

Recent studies of healthy aged individuals show positive attitudes toward sexuality and suggest that sexuality, in both males and females, may endure a great deal better than other functional systems in the body.

There are age-related changes in sexual function. In the aged female, these changes readily lend themselves to explanation of the sexual response cycle within Masters and Johnson's four phase description. As males age, major differences in sexual response relate more to the duration of each of the phases of the cycle. Despite age-related changes described in this chapter, both males and females are capable of sexual performance throughout their lives.

Continued progress in the quest for acceptance of sexuality among the aged rests heavily with those in the health and helping professions. These professionals must help in the development of a climate in which the sexuality of the aged is acknowledged and valued.

KEY TERMS

clitoris
coitus
dyspareunia
dysuria
erectile dysfunction
introitus
labia
menopause
myotonia
orgasmic phase
orgasmic platform
penile detumesence

refractory period
vaginismus
vasocongestive response

STUDY QUESTIONS

1. Compare the findings of Kinsey and co-workers with those of Pfeiffer and associates regarding sexual activity and age.
2. On the basis of studies concerning sexual attitudes of the aged, what, in general, can be concluded about "geriatric sexuality"?
3. Review the four phases of the sexual response cycle in the female, including changes noted in post-menopausal women.
4. Identify some general changes in the aging female that may influence symptoms experienced with or as a result of sexual intercourse.
5. Present an overview of changes in the aging male that may influence sexual response.
6. Review some factors that contribute to sexual behavior of the aged.
7. Discuss the responsibilities of the health and helping professions regarding sexuality and the aged.

BIBLIOGRAPHY

Brecher, E.M. 1984. *Love, Sex, and Aging*. A Consumer's Union Report. Boston: Little, Brown.

Comfort, A. 1976. *A Good Age*. New York: Crown.

_____ . 1974. Sexuality in old age. *Journal of the American Geriatrics Society 22*(10): 440–442.

_____ . 1970. Sexuality and aging. *SIECUS Report. IV*(6): 1ff.

Christenson, C.V., and Gagnon, J. 1965. Sexual behavior in a group of older women. *Journal of Gerontology 20*(3): 351–356.

Easton, D.M. 1977. Alex Comfort speaks on sex and aging. *Resource Guide*. San Francisco: Multi Media Resource Center.

Kaas, M.J. 1978. Sexual expression of the elderly in nursing homes. *Gerontologist 18*(4): 372–378.

Kinsey, A.C., Pomeroy, W.B., and Martin, C.E. 1948. *Sexual Behavior in the Human Male.* Philadelphia: Saunders.

——————. 1953. *Sexual Behavior in the Human Female.* Philadelphia: Saunders.

Levitan, D. 1973. The significance of sexuality as a deterrent to suicide among the aged. *Omega* 4(2): 163–174.

Masters, W.H., and Johnson, V.E. 1966. *Human Sexual Response.* Boston: Little, Brown.

——————. 1982. Sex and the aging process. *Medical Aspects of Human Sexualtiy* 16(6): 40ff.

Pfeiffer, E., Verwoerdt, A., and Wang, H.S. 1968. Sexual behavior in aged men and women. *Archives of General Psychiatry* 19: 753–758.

——————. 1969a. The natural history of sexual behavior in a biologically advantaged group of aged individuals. *Journal of Gerontology* 24: 193–198.

Pfeiffer, E. 1969b. Geriatric sexual behavior. *Medical Aspects of Human Sexuality* 3: 19ff.

Pocs, O., Godow, A., Tolone, W., and R.H. Walsh. 1977. Is there sex after 40? *Psychology Today* 6: 54–58.

Starr, B.D., and Weiner, M.B. 1981. *The Starr-Weiner Report on Sex and and Sexuality in the Mature Years.* New York: Stein and Day.

Wasow, M., and Loeb, M.B. 1979. Sexuality in nursing homes. *Journal of the American Geriatrics Society* 37(2): 73–79.

CHAPTER **17**

Exercise, Aging and Health

Recently a number of research reports have indicated that moderate exercise can retard the effects of aging (Ostrow, 1984; Thomas, 1981; Shephard, 1978). There also are some indications that exercise may be able to reverse some age-related effects (Ostrow, 1984). The role of physical activity in the aging process has interested humans since as early as 3,000 B.C.. In the Middle East and China, scholars attempted to explain how balanced physical and mental activity might influence longevity.

In ancient Greece, Hippocrates was the first to note that regular exercise might retard the aging process (Sager, 1983). Plato believed that moderate exercise could help preserve the body and mind by ordering "the particles and affections which are wandering about the body." Despite these early thoughts on the subject, throughout much of history the tendency has been to think that age-related changes were inevitable and uncontrollable.

In contemporary Western society, the relationship between aging and exercise is typically characterized as inverse. That is, with aging there is a tendency to do less exercise. This decline may be related to cultural values that urge us to "slow down," "act our age" and "take it easy." Until recently many people felt that this decline in activity was caused by biological changes associated with aging that naturally limited our ability to exercise. Bortz (1982), however, has called attention to the similarities between the physiological changes that occur with aging and the response that occurs in people of any age when they are subject to periods of prolonged inactivity.

It is perhaps more important today than ever before to distinguish the limitations on activity imposed by age from those that are the products of our individual and societal experiences. This approach may allow us to learn how to use fitness-promoting exercise to delay age-associated declines in body function. Yet efforts to study exercise and aging are beset by difficulties in interpretation. Longitudinal studies are scarce. Most research has been cross-sectional in nature, comparing different ages at one point in time. Such studies may be flawed if they fail to take into account cohort effects on health status.

The improved status of older cohorts may be due to the elimination of weaker individuals by death and disease and by the fact that usually the volunteers for fitness tests are healthier older people. This situation produces a homogeniety in older subjects that is not often found in other groups (Ostrow, 1984).

AGE-RELATED CHANGES: EXERCISE, WORK AND ACTIVITY PATTERNS

Cardiopulmonary Changes

The heart muscle decreases in mass and contractility with age. Cardiac mass, however, is directly related to heart strength. This reduction in strength influences three major processes: (1) the duration of systole, (2) the volume of blood expelled from the ventricles and (3) the blood pressure generated.

Decreased contractility of the heart muscle is probably due to infiltration by connective tissue as well as by the formation of small scars. Because of these changes, it takes longer to expel blood from the heart, while at the same time allowing less time for filling. This in turn contributes to a decline in maximum heart output.

The amount of blood expelled from the heart is known as stroke volume. *Stroke volume* declines with age, but in most individuals it is generally adequate for carrying out mild work. However, the maximum stroke volume necessary for heavier work declines by 15 to 20 percent from early adulthood to old age. At the same time that maximum stroke volume and maximum heart rate are declining, the resistance to the flow of blood through the arteries and arterioles is increasing. This increase in resistance is due to plaque formation in the vessels and the calcification of the medial layer of arterial vessels. The plaque provides physical resistance, while the changes in arterial structure limit expansion of the vessels during systole. This increased resistance to blood flow can raise the blood pressure 10 to 40 mm Hg at systole and 5 to 10 mm Hg at diastole.

The *vital capacity* of the lungs declines 40 to 50 percent as we age. This may be due to (1) lung tissue becoming less elastic, (2) the thoracic cage becoming stiffer, (3) decreased lung surface and (4) decline in alveolar function. The total surface area of the lung decreases from 80 to 60 square meters (Smith and Gilligan, 1984). Alveolar decline may be the result of loss of elasticity, which results in the closure of some air sacs and the reduction or cessation of capillary blood flow to some alveoli.

As a result of these pulmonary changes as well as the decreasing strength and efficiency of heart muscle, maximum consumption of oxygen at peak all-out effort declines with age. Bortz (1982) and Smith and Gilligan (1984) suggest a rate of decline of close to 10 percent per decade. Such a decline can lead to a dramatic change in the activity pattern of an older person.

Changes in Muscular Strength

Skeletal muscle mass also declines with age. Calloway and Zannie (1980) suggest that the rate of decline after age 25 is 2 to 3 percent per decade. Smith and Gilligan (1984) found a muscle mass decline of 20 to 25 percent with age that is accompanied by a parallel decline in strength. Muscle-mass declines include a reduction in both the number and size of muscle fibers.

Grip strength and grip-strength endurance have been extensively studied and show a decline with age after peaking between 20 and 24 years. The decline is most dramatic after age 60. Harris (1977) found the greatest loss of strength with age occurs in the leg and trunk muscles, an observation with significant implications for the mobility of elderly individuals.

Changes in Muscular Flexibility

A gradual loss in the range of joint motion has been observed with age. It may be due to shortening of muscles, calcification of cartilage, ligaments and tendons, and the prevalence of arthritic conditions. Joint flexibility is important for the efficient performance of ordinary, every-day activities. A joint may lose a considerable range of motion through inactivity or degenerative disease, although Adrian (1981) suggests that there is no evidence to show that biological aging causes decreased flexibility.

Changes in Neuromuscular Integrity

Aging brings a lengthening of rapid muscular reaction time. Nerve conduction velocity declines between 10 and 15 percent as we age and leads to increased reaction time for muscle contraction. This situation may reflect (1) chemical and structural change at the synapse, (2) change in the nerve fiber itself and (3)) changes in muscle fiber. It is also probable that the central nervous system contributes to the change in neuromuscular efficiency. Fast-twitch muscle fibers needed for quick all-out contractions show greater changes with age than do slow-twitch fibers. Slow-twitch fibers are significant for prolonged endurance activity. This differential change may be related to noticeable declines in quick reactions and the more gradual declines observed for muscular endurance. Neuromuscular efficiency and weakness may be more influenced by disease than by age.

Bone Strength and Integrity

Loss of bone mass is a universal characteristic of aging. It starts earlier in women—around 35—and progresses at a more rapid rate of 1 to 2 percent per year. Men are also affected, but the process starts at age 50 and proceeds at a rate of only .5 percent per year. The impact of bone mass loss is far greater in women, and by age 75 fractures related to osteoporosis are widespread in this group.

Fractures related to osteoporosis are significant for the elderly population in general. It is estimated that osteoporosis is responsible for 1.3 million fractures a year and the costs in health care are between 3 and 6 billion dollars per year. For 15 to 30 percent of those affected, the condition is fatal; others suffer pain and deformity as well as limitation of mobility, with a possible loss of independence.

THE EFFECTS OF EXERCISE ON THE ELDERLY

Cardiopulmonary Change

Most of the research on endurance-type training among the elderly suggests that regular participation improves cardiopulmonary efficiency (Sidney, 1981). The evidence for this generalization is based on epidemiological and experimental research. Devries (1970) found that regardless of prior habits of exercise, the maximum oxygen consumption (VO_2) increases 10 to 30 percent with a program of aerobic exercise. It has also been noted that aerobic exercise lowers the blood pressure 5 to 10 mm Hg, although it has been suggested that this decrease is due to reduction in anxiety experienced by participants in programmed exercise (Buccola and Stone, 1975).

Muscle Strength and Endurance

Moritani (1981) did experiments with the elderly that showed increases in strength and significant improvement in muscle function through training after a one-year aerobic program. Sidney, Shepherd and Hamson (1977) found a 10 percent increase in lean body mass and muscular strength. In another study, Sidney (1977) also observed that a one-year walking program led to a 17 percent decrease in skinfold fat.

With respect to muscular strength and endurance, the trainability of older people does not apparently differ from younger people, if the age groups are compared on a percentage of change basis (Moritani, 1981). Serfass (1980) found that by the sixth decade, strength gains through training are independent of sex.

Flexibility Change

Joint flexibility is modifiable through training across age groups. Munns (1981) at the Biogerontology Laboratory of the University of Wisconsin studied 40 participants age 65 to 88 who took part in an exercise dance program. She tested six body sites with a *Leighton flexometer* and noted a statistically significant change at all the sites.

In a study of 20 participants who averaged 72 years of age, Munns found an increased range of motion in all joints after a 12-week flexibility program. The percentage increases for each joint were: neck, 28 percent; wrists, 13 percent; shoulder, 8 percent; knees, 12 percent; ankles, 48 percent; and hips and back, 27 percent.

Neuromuscular Changes

After extensive studies on exercise and neuromuscular change, Spirduso (1980) proposed that exercise:

1. Aids in greater synchronization of motor units and reduces random firing of neurons;
2. Postpones structural changes in nerve cells and the loss of dendrites in the aging brain (enhances blood flow to various parts of the brain);
3. Maintains hormonal regulator systems that to some extent control the integrity of the nervous system;
4. Delays reductions with age of oxidative capacities of the brain and in neurotransmitter substances; and
5. Retards the age-related decline in fast-twitch muscle fiber.

Bone Loss and Exercise

When stress is placed on bone through weight-bearing exercise, calcium content and resistance to fracture are increased. In a three-year, low-intensity exercise program for the elderly, Smith and Redden (1976) noticed a 4.2 percent increase in bone mineral content among exercisers and an average 2.5 percent decrease in the non-exercising control group. Smith, Redden and Smith (1981) noticed some change even in the very old. They studied 12 female nursing home residents, all in their 80s. Chair exercises were provided for 30 minutes, three times a week for one year. The bone mineral content of the group increased 2.29 percent while members of the control group lost 3.28 percent.

Psychological Effects

The psychological evaluation of test groups is difficult among the elderly. This is because many of the participants desire to please the investigator, thus affecting reported or perceived gains. It is also possible that observed changes may be due to increased attention of a personal and medical nature rather than from exercise (Thomas, 1979).

Some investigators have reported that exercise reduces anxiety and relieves tension (Ostrow, 1984). Relief of stress could be the result of the fact that exercise does one of the following:

1. Retards possibly harmful chemicals released as part of the stress response;
2. Speeds up the metabolism of chemicals released as a stress response; or
3. Helps release chemicals that lift depression.

A recent Purdue study of men between 40 and 60 years of age indicates that those who jogged three times a week had less depression than a sedentary control group (Ostrow, 1984).

Regular exercise may also lead to improvements in body image as well as in attitude toward life. It is also possible that those who attempt an exercise program and fail may suffer negatively in terms of both body image and attitude. When exercise is done as part of a group, the social aspect of group activity may help overcome loneliness as well as give a sense of belonging and worth. Blumenthal and colleagues (1982) found improved mood and greater feelings of satisfaction in 40 to 50 percent of the elderly participants in an 11-week stationary-bicycle study. Buccola and Stone (1975) reported greater feelings of self-sufficiency after a 14-week program of walking and jogging.

EXERCISE PROGRAMS FOR THE ELDERLY

It would appear from the research evidence that exercise programs for the elderly can be useful in improving physical and psychological health. However, the perceptions that older people have about the role of physical activity may affect implementation of more widespread programs. Conrad (1976) found that older people held the following views about physical activity:

1. The need for physical activity decreases with age.
2. Exercise is dangerous for the elderly.
3. Light, sporadic exercise is beneficial to health.
4. Their own personal physical abilities are limited.

Those over age 60 tended to overestimate the time spent at heavy physical activity. Their perception at all levels of heart rate was two to three times higher than in younger people (Conrad, 1976). It also appears that physical training alters perceived exertion at any given work load. This perception phenomenon surely influences many older people who attempt to maintain an appropriate level of physical activity.

Medical Evaluation Prior to Exercise

It is wise to consult a physician before starting an exercise program. Radeheffer (1984) has estimated that by age 70, more than one-half of the men in the United States have some form of coronary artery disease, and the case for women is only a little less significant. It is estimated that about one in five of those screened for exercise programs are rejected for entry.

A medical evaluation should include a detailed medical history and a basic physical examination. Although a *stress test* is not mandatory, it is useful for detecting asymptomatic coronary artery disease. Studies indicate that the stress test is more valid in elderly groups than in younger ones (Morse and Smith, 1981). However, even if the medical indication clears an individual for exercise, knowledge of coronary artery disease symptoms would be helpful. Fair, Rosenaur and Thurston (1969) believe that the elderly should be made aware of such symptoms as a precautionary measure.

Aerobic Exercise

Aerobic exercise is that which strengthens the cardiopulmonary system. It includes jogging, cycling, skiing, swimming, brisk walking, dancing and circuit training. Aerobic exercise aims to place a moderate stress on the heart

in order to strengthen this muscle. As the heart becomes stronger the rest of the system will operate more efficiently.

In order for the stress on the heart to be beneficial, it should result in a heart rate that equals 60 to 90 percent of the maximum heart rate. In order to calculate the maximum heart rate for any individual's age the following formula is used:

$$220 - [\text{age} \times (90\%*)] = \text{target rate}$$
(in heart beats/minute)

For example, if one is 50 years of age, the target rate at the 60 percent level is 102 heart beats/minute ($220 - 50 \times .60$), and at the 90 percent level is 153 heart beats/minute ($220 - 50 \times .90$). It is suggested that 100 beats per minute be the lowest level targeted, since we have little research on the effects of a target rate under 100 bpm. It is important to remember that a 65-year-old requires less activity than a 40-year-old to reach a targeted maximum. (See Table 17.1.)

Previously sedentary individuals should move into an exercise program slowly. This will avoid physical injury to a muscle or joint and hopefully encourage continued participation. For a program to be helpful it should consist of three sessions per week for 15 to 60 minutes. The duration of a session is determined by the intensity of the activity. If one is operating at 60 percent of maximum, the duration should be for one hour, but if operation is 90 percent of maximum, then 15 minutes would suffice. Warm-up and cool-down periods of five minutes are also helpful in the avoidance of trauma. These sessions can consist of stretching, light calisthenics or slow walking.

*depending on what percentage of maximum heart rate it is desired to attain

TABLE 17.1 Target heart rate zones (all heart rates are for 1 minute)

Age	Level I (50–60% MHR)	Level II (60–70% MHR)	Level III (70–85% MHR)
20–29	102–120	120–150	150–168
30–39	96–114	114–144	144–162
40–49	90–108	108–138	138–156
50–59	86–102	102–126	126–144
60–69	78–96	96–120	120–132
70 and older	72–90	90–108	108–126

Beginners who have been inactive for some time can exercise at 50 to 60 percent of their maximum heart rate (MHR). Most people can tolerate this comfortably for 20 to 30 minutes. Beginners who have been active can exercise at 60 to 70 percent of their maximum heart rate.
If you're reasonably fit, exercise at 70 to 85 percent of your maximum heart rate.

Circuit Training as Aerobic Exercise

Weightlifting does not qualify as aerobic exercise due to the longer rests between exercise and the smaller number of repetitions. It simply does not maintain the heart beat at the targeted maximum long enough. However, circuit training, a modified form of light weightlifting, does qualify as aerobic.

Circuit training consists of 20 to 40 minutes of lifting relatively light weight for 10 to 20 repetitions per station or exercise. The rest between each exercise is about 15 seconds, so the heart beat does not fall below the targeted maximum. It is continuous exercise that is certainly less aerobic than jogging but can result in a VO_2 increase of 5 to 8 percent (Gettman and Pollack, 1981).

It can be used as a beneficial supplement to heavier aerobics or for those with locomotor problems. In addition to its aerobic benefits, circuit training helps with muscle strength and flexibility.

The Effects of Aerobics

Epidemiological and clinical evidence suggests that aerobics can inhibit the progression of coronary artery disease. Though the evidence for this is substantial, it is not absolute (Thomas, 1979). Exercise itself is valuable physiologically (see Table 17.2), but it also

TABLE 17.2 Effects of heavy exercise*

	Resting	Heavy exercise
Cardiac output	5 liters/min.	35 liters/min.
Heart rate	75 beats/min.	195 beats/min.
Ventilation	8 liters air/min.	16 liters air/min.
Oxygen utilization	.25 liter/min.	5 liters/min.
Systolic pressure	120 mm	180 mm
Diastolic pressure	80 mm	85 mm

*Running, jogging, rowing, skiing, cycling, brisk walking (4 mph)

TABLE 17.3 Approximate number of Calories burned per minute*

Activity	120 lbs	Weight 160 lbs	200 lbs
Canoeing	2.5	3	4
Cycling	5.5	7	9
Fishing	3.5	4.5	5.5
Hiking (no load)	6.5	8.5	11
Running (8 min./mi.)	11.5	15	18
Skiing, cross-country	7.5	10	12.5
Skiing, downhill	6	8	10
Snowshoeing	9	12.5	15
Swimming (crawl)	7	9	11.5
Walking	4	5.5	7
Weight training	10	13	16.5

*Adapted from Katch and McArdle, *Nutrition, Weight Control, and Exercise*, 1977, Appendix B.

TABLE 17.4 Myths about exercise and conditioning

Myth	Fact
Muscle will turn to fat if you stop exercising.	Muscle itself does not turn to fat, but if unused it atrophies. Many people who stop exercising gain weight.
Strenuous exercise is bad for your heart.	Exercised hearts grow more muscular and stronger, which makes them more efficient.
Avoid fluids when exercising.	Exercising causes sweating, and this lost water must be replaced to avoid dehydration.
Heavy sweating is a way to lose weight.	The loss is only temporary and should be replaced promptly to avoid harm.
The body needs extra protein to make muscle grow faster.	A normal, balanced diet is all that is needed for muscle growth and repair. The body does not store excess amino acids.
Women who exercise regularly lose femininity.	Women who exercise regularly may become slimmer and more graceful. Bulging, male-like muscles do not develop.
Eating a candy bar before exercise will give you extra energy.	The energy used in exercise is already stored in the muscles. The candy would not be digested, absorbed and assimilated fast enough to be used for exercise.
Exercise is dangerous for older people.	In the absence of severe pathology, exercise can improve the strength, flexibility and endurance of people at all ages.

affects other risk factors, such as weight and lipid level. Aerobic exercise also has the following possible benefits:

1. Lowered blood pressure in hypertensives
2. Weight reduction (see Table 17.3)
3. Improved glucose tolerance in diabetics
4. Increased levels of high-density lipoproteins (HDLCs)
5. Reduced blood-clotting tendencies
6. Encouragement of a more health-conscious lifestyle (Thomas, 1981)

Low-Intensity Exercises

Low-intensity exercises are those that have little effect on the cardiopulmonary system. They include light calisthenics, light walking, golfing, bowling, fishing and weightlifting. These kinds of exercise, however, help in weight control and bone demineralization as well as in muscle strength and flexibility.

Many myths surround the concepts of exercise and conditioning, eight of which are listed in Table 17.4. For the elderly, these myths can be a source of anxiety and can thus discourage the elderly from participating in an appropriate exercise program.

OBESITY AND WEIGHT CONTROL AMONG THE ELDERLY

Determining whether an individual is overweight or obese is more difficult than it would seem. By one definition, obesity is present when the accumulation of fat in body tissue is equal to or more than 20 percent of the body weight in males and 30 percent in females. However, one can be overweight without being fat, with the excess weight being muscle, as is seen, for example, in football players and weightlifters.

Diagnosing obesity poses at least as many problems as defining it. Appearance is often used, but does not differentiate between fat, muscle and water accumulation. Weight and height tables are difficult to use with the elderly because of their lessened physical stature. These tables have recently come under criticism for persons of all ages, since they tend to underestimate ideal weight by as much as 20 percent, even when body build is controlled for (Kart and Metress, 1984). X rays are hazardous and expensive, and flotation techniques are impractical for most people. An accurate approach in the determination of obesity involves the use of skinfold measurements, although the elderly present special problems for this technique due to age-related skin changes. Triceps-skinfold thickness is a measure of subcutaneous fat and is considered an index of the body's energy stores. Precision in measurement is absolutely necessary. In addition, as with weight in general, measurements must be evaluated in terms of actual age, height and even the theoretically correct weight for a given age.

Estimates of obesity in the general American population vary between 25 and 45 percent. Data on older adults is available from the Ten-State Nutrition Survey (U.S. Department of Health, Education and Welfare, 1975). Older black women had the highest prevalence of obesity—more than 45 percent of the 45- to 60-year-old group. More than one-third of all white women aged 55 to 65 years in the survey were defined as obese. Among the elderly, the lowest prevalence of obesity was found in black males. The HANES data show a similar pattern (National Center for Health Statistics, 1974). In both studies, low income was associated with a higher incidence of obesity.

Some obesity is juvenile in its onset. Over-eating in childhood may give rise to fat tissue containing large numbers of fat cells. One hypothesis is that an excess of fat cells makes it difficult to keep weight off because these cells have to be depleted before a normal weight can be reached. However, a number of researchers have challenged the method-ological basis of this hypothesis (Salans, Cushman and Weismann, 1973).

Another form of obesity is called adult-onset and appears in the middle years of adulthood. This obesity usually has its origin in overeating, ignorance of proper nutrition, and reduced activity. Metabolic problems probably account for only a small proportion (perhaps 2 percent) of all obesity in adulthood.

Obesity is reported as adversely affecting almost every system of the body. Life expec-tancy is lower and morbidity rates are higher. High blood pressure, gallbladder problems, coronary heart disease, diabetes, and post-surgical complications are more prevalent among the obese. However, Mann (1971) is not sure that obesity by itself is bad. Becom-ing obese through diminished activity and increased consumption of refined sugar and fats is another matter. He states that the effect of obesity alone as a predictor of heart dis-ease is very small and of borderline statistical significance. Recent research by Keys (1980a, 1980b) also tends to support a less negative approach to the effects of being overweight.

The elderly have a special problem of weight control. Busse (1978) estimates that basic metabolism declines 16 percent between 20 and 70 years of age, necessitat-ing a decrease in Caloric intake of approxi-mately one-third. Ahrens (1970) calculated a per-decade decline of 43 Calories/day in the requirements for males from age 25 on, and a per-decade decline of 27 Calories/day for females from age 25. It is likely that this change is due to alterations in basal metab-olism, body composition and activities related to aging per se. In addition to basic metabolic decline, many of the elderly are subject to additional stresses that contribute to obesity. These include grief, economic insecurity and social isolation, to name a few. In such cases, sociopsychological counsel-ing, support and contact with others may be more important in dealing with the problem of obesity than might nutrition education or medical aid.

Advertising encourages eating in general and heavily emphasizes sugar and snack foods that can contribute to Caloric imbal-ance. Affluence allows us to eat for entertain-ment and pleasure rather than just for subsistence. At the same time, we can afford labor-saving devices that reduce exertion of energy. Modern processing allows us to eat low-bulk foods that are sweet and highly refined simply for their great palatability. Par-adoxically, impoverished people may become obese because cost forces them to eat high-Calorie foods that are generally cheaper than protective foods.

What available weight-control methods are functional for the elderly? Logically, reduced intake of food along with increased activity go a long way in controlling weight. The elderly (like everybody else) must be educated to moderation in these matters. Realistic goals should be established, meals should not be skipped and plateaus in weight loss must be anticipated. It is also wise to avoid eating out, since little control over food preparation can be exerted and the social atmosphere is conducive to overeating. A reduction of about 500 Calories per day can

TABLE 17.5 Using calories

	Calorie content	Average time needed to burn calories by activity (minutes)*				
		Recline	Walk	Bicycle	Run	Swim
Apple, 1 lg	100	66	28	16	5	8
Bacon, 2 strips	96	64	27	16	5	8
Beer, 1 glass	115	76	32	19	6	9
Bread/butter	78	60	15	10	4	6
Cookie, plain	15	12	3	2	1	1
Doughnut, 1 med	125	96	24	15	4	8
Hamburger/bun	350	233	100	58	19	30
Orange juice	120	92	23	15	6	9
Potato chips, 10	115	76	32	19	6	9

Average time needed to burn Calories by activity (minutes)*

result in the loss of one pound per week. Some people have found a pattern of one day on diet and one day off diet to be successful, especially for weight maintenance.

Crash diets, including fasting and novelty diets, can be harmful and should be avoided. Real medical problems may be aggravated or potentiated by such diets. Dietary regulation with drugs should be approached with caution and medical supervision. Even under supervision, the usefulness of so-called diet pills is limited, and tolerance can develop, necessitating an increased dosage. Initial success in weight loss is often nullified by a "rebound effect" that finds the individual eating more than before to compensate for feelings of deprivation.

In the elderly, drugs present special problems for weight loss because of interaction with other medications and potential errors of dose and timing. Liquid protein formulations designed for the extremely obese (50 or more pounds overweight) should probably be avoided. Although reactions vary individually, these formulas can be extremely dangerous. More than 40 deaths, most often related to calcium and potassium imbalances, have been associated with their use

(Lantigua, Amatruda, Biddle, Forbes and Lockwood, 1980).

Increased activity, including exercise, should be a part of any dietary plan, although age and the existence of chronic disease or disability must be taken into account. Strenuous activity can burn Calories, decrease appetite, raise resting metabolism and increase muscular efficiency and tone. (See Table 17.5.) The psychological lift, sense of achievement, improved self-image and confidence that many of the elderly get from participation in activity and exercise programs cannot be overlooked. Positive aspects of exercise carry over into those daily activities related to psychosocial well-being, eating habits and overall health maintenance.

LIFELONG PHYSICAL ACTIVITY AND AGING

It is apparent that aerobic exercise can have both preventive and rehabilitative effects with respect to age-associated and degenerative changes. We are entering an era of research and knowledge that indicates we are far better off if we develop life-long programs of physical activity. The development of such programs must start in our school years and continue throughout life.

Recently, Paffenbarger and colleagues (1986) released the results of a large study of Harvard University alumni. They studied 16,936 males who graduated between 1916 and 1950, following this group up to 1978. Their findings have interesting implications for programs of lifelong physical activity. Among these findings were:

1. Men who walked nine miles per week had a 21 percent lower risk of mortality.
2. Men who exercised strenuously for six to eight hours per week (cycling) had a 50 percent lower mortality risk.
3. Extremists, those who used more than 3,500 calories per week at such things as full-court basketball and squash, had a higher mortality risk.

Among athletes, the researchers found that the risk was higher for those who were too active or those who completely ceased activity. They also found that those men who had gained 15 pounds since graduation lived longer than those who had lost considerable weight. In Paffenbarger's opinion, if we eliminated cancer, the years gained per person would be the same as those gained by lifelong exercise. He feels that a lifelong exercise program is comparable to a major medical breakthrough in preventing or curing disease.

SUMMARY

The relationship of exercise to longevity has long interested humans. In studying this relationship, research must differentiate those age-related physical changes that are due to life style and degenerative disease from those that are the result of the aging process itself. There are a great many cases in which changes are reversible or at least modifiable. The major age-related changes that affect work capacity and daily activity are related to: (1) cardiopulmonary function, (2) muscular strength and integrity (3) muscular flexibility, (4) neuromuscular integrity, (5) bone strength and integrity and (6) changes in metabolism.

Research indicates that exercise programs, especially those of an aerobic nature, have the potential to improve work capacity and daily functioning in all six of the above listed areas. Aerobic training programs for the elderly pose some special problems related to perceptions of the role of exercise by the elderly themselves and precautions that are necessary when dealing with older populations.

Lifelong exercise programs seem to show some promise for increasing the length and quality of life. Exercise can be helpful in changing a variety of life style risks, from obesity and high blood pressure to sound mental health and feelings of psychological well-being.

KEY TERMS

circuit training
Leighton flexometer
stress test
stroke volume
vital capacity

STUDY QUESTIONS

1. Identify the major age-related changes associated with the following:
   a. Cardiopulmonary function
   b. Muscular strength and endurance
   c. Muscular flexibility
   d. Neuromuscular integrity
   e. Bone strength and integrity

2. Identify the major biological and psychological effects that an exercise program can have on the elderly. How are individual perceptions of the role of exercise and exertion significant in the implementation of exercise programs for the elderly?
3. What is the nature and role of a medical examination and consultation prior to embarking upon an exercise program?
4. Differentiate aerobic and low-intensity exercise. What are some basic principles that are necessary to consider in the development of aerobic programs for the elderly? How do you calculate the maximum heart rate for reference in aerobic-training programs?
5. What is circuit training, and what is its significance for the elderly? What are some of the major effects of aerobic training on the individual?
6. In what ways are low-intensity exercises valuable to the individual?
7. Why is an accurate diagnosis of obesity so difficult? Differentiate juvenile from adult-onset obesity.
8. Why does Mann disagree with the idea that obesity in itself is bad? Is obesity a special problem for the elderly?
9. List some important principles of weight control for the elderly.
10. How does metabolism change with age? In what ways can strenuous activity affect metabolism?
11. What were some of the major results of Paffenbarger's work that are significant for exercise and longevity? According to Paffenbarger, what is the significance of a lifelong exercise program?

BIBLIOGRAPHY

Adrian, M.J. 1981. Flexibility in the aging adult. In E.L. Smith and R.C. Serfass, eds., *Exercise and Aging*. Hillside, N.J.: Enslow.

Ahrens, R.A. 1970. *Nutrition For Health*. Belmont, Calif.: Wadsworth.

Blumenthal, J.A., Schocken, D.D., Needels, T.L., and Hindle, P. 1982. Psychological and physiological effects of physical conditioning in the elderly. *Journal of Psychosomatic Research 26:* 505–510.

Bortz, W.M. 1982. Disuse and aging. *Journal of the American Medical Association 148:* 1203–1208.

Buccola, V.A., and Stone, W.J. 1975. Effect of jogging and cycling programs on physiological and personality variables in aged men. *The Research Quarterly 46:* 134–139.

Busse, E.W. 1978. How mind, body, and enviroment influence nutrition in the elderly. *Postgraduate Medicine 63:* 118–125.

Calloway, D.H., and Zannie, E. 1980. Energy requirements of elderly men. *American Journal of Clinical Nutrition 32:* 2088–2092.

Conrad, C.C. 1976. When you're young at heart. In *Aging*. Washington, D.C.: U.S. Department of Health, Education and Welfare, Administration on Aging.

Devries, H.A. 1970. Physiological effects of an exercise training regimen upon men aged 52 to 88. *Journal of Gerontology 25:* 325–336.

Fair, J., Rosenaur, J., and Thurston, E. 1969. Exercise management. *Nurse Practitioner 4:* 13–15, 17–18.

Gettman, L.R., and Pollack, M. 1981. Circuit weight training: A critical review of its physiological benefits. *The Physician and Sports Medicine 9:* 44–60.

Harris, R. 1977. Fitness and the aging process. In R. Harris and L.J. Finkel, eds., *Guide to Fitness After 50*. New York: Plenum.

Kart, C., and Metress, S. 1984. *Nutrition, the Aged and Society*. Englewood Cliffs, N.J.: Prentice-Hall.

Keys, A. 1980a. Overweight, obesity, coronary heart disease, and mortality. *Nutrition Today 15:* 4:16–22.

_____. 1980b. Alpha lipoprotein. *Lancet 2:* 603–606.

Lantigua, R., Amatruda, J.M., Biddle, T.L., Forbes, G.B., and Lockwood, D.H. 1980. Cardiac arrythmias associated with a liquid protein diet for the treatment of obesity. *New England Journal of Medicine 303:* 735–738.

Mann, G.V. 1971. The obesity spook. *American Journal of Public Health 61:* 1491–1498.

Moritani, T. 1981. Training adaptations in the muscles of older men. In E.L. Smith and R.S. Serfass, eds., *Exercise and Aging*. Hillside, N.J.: Enslow.

Morse, C.E., and Smith, E.L. 1981. Physical activity programming for the aged. In E.L. Smith and R.C. Serfass, eds., *Exercise and Aging*. Hillside, N.J.: Enslow.

Munns, K. 1981. Effects of exercise on the range of joint motion in elderly subjects. In E.L. Smith and R.C. Serfass, eds., *Exercise and Aging*. Hillside, N.J.: Enslow.

National Center for Health Statistics. 1974. *First Health and Nutrition Survey, U.S., 1971– 1972*. Washington, D.C.: U.S. Department of Health, Education and Welfare.

Ostrow, A.C. 1984. *Physical Activity and the Older Adult*. Princeton, N.J.: Princeton Book Co.

Paffenbarger, R.S., Hyde, R.T., Wing A.L., and Hsieh, C. 1986. Physical activity, all cause mortality and longevity of college alumni. *New England Journal of Medicine 314*(10): 605–613.

Radeheffer, R.J. 1984. Exercise cardiac is maintained with advancing age in healthy human subjects. *Circulation 69:* 203–213.

Sager, K. 1983. Senior fitness—For the health of it. *The Physician and Sports Medicine 11:* 3– 36.

Salans, L.B., Cushman, S.W., and Weismann, R.E. 1973. Studies of human adipose tissue: Adipose cell life and number in nonobese and obese patients. *Journal of Clinical Investigation 52:* 929–941.

Serfass, R.C. 1980. Physical exercise and the elderly. In G.A. Still, ed., *Encyclopedia of Physical Education, Fitness and Sports*. Salt Lake City, Utah: Brighton.

Shephard, R.J. 1978. *Physical Activity and Aging*. Chicago: Yearbook Publishers.

Sidney, K.H. 1981. Cardiovascular benefits of physical activity in the exercising aged. In E.L. Smith and R.C. Serfass, eds., *Exercise and Aging*. Hillside, N.J.: Enslow.

──────── . 1977. Activity patterns of elderly men and women. *Journal of Gerontology 32:* 25–32.

──────── , and Shepherd, R.J. 1977. Perceptions of exertion in the elderly, effects of aging, mode of exercise and physical training. *Perceptual Motor Skills 44:* 999.

──────── , and Hamson, J.E. 1977. Endurance, training and body composition in the elderly. *American Journal of Clinical Nutrition 30:* 326–333.

Smith, E.L., and Gilligan,G. 1984. Exercise sport and physical activity for the elderly: Principles and problems of programming. In B. McPherson, ed., *Sport and Aging*. Champaign, Ill.: Human Kinetics. Pp. 97–100.

Smith, E., and Redden, W. 1976. Physical activity: A modality for bone accretion in the aged. *American Journal of Roentgenology 126:* 1297.

──────── , and Smith, P. 1981. Physical activity and calcium modalities for bone mineral increases in aged women. *Medicine and Science in Sports and Exercise 13:* 80–84.

Spirduso, W.W. 1980. Physical fitness, aging and psychomotor speed: A review. *Journal of Gerontology 35:* 850–865.

Thomas, G.S. 1979. Physical activity and health: Epidemiologic and armed evidence and policy implications. *Preventive Medicine 8:* 89– 103.

──────── . 1981. *Exercise and Health: The Evidence and the Implications*. Cambridge, Mass.: Oegleshlager, Gunn and Hain.

U.S. Department of Health, Education and Welfare. 1975. *Ten-State Nutrition Survey, 1968– 70*. Washington, D.C.: Health Resources Administration.

PART

Selected Issues in Health and Aging

CHAPTER **18**

Health Services Utilization among the Aged

This chapter begins by identifying the patterns of utilization of health and medical services among the elderly. Of particular interest are physician visits and the use of non-physician professional and hospital inpatient services. Long-term care service use by elderly Americans is described in Chapter 19, "Institutionalization," and Chapter 20, "Alternatives to Institutionalization." In addition, we assess funding mechanisms available for the health and medical care of the elderly. The chapter concludes by placing health care in the broader perspective of the political economy of aging.

USE OF SERVICES

Table 18.1 presents data on physician visits per person per year by age for 1983. The

average number of physician contacts by persons 65 years and older was 7.6 visits. This compared with 5.0 visits for persons of all ages and as the data generally show, with the exception of children under six years of age, the average number of physician contacts per person increases with age. In 1983, the aged were more likely than the total population to receive care at the doctor's office (58.9 vs. 55.9 percent) and less likely than the total population to be treated in a hospital outpatient department (12.3 vs. 14.9 percent) or over the telephone (11.9 vs. 15.5 percent). Physician visits are up only slightly over the last 20 years. In 1964 the average number of physician contacts among those 65 years and over was 6.7.

This lack of substantial change in the indicator for the entire elderly population may

TABLE 18.1 Physician visits, according to source or place of care and age; United States, 1982 and 1983 (data are based on household interviews of a sample of the civilian non-institutionalized population)

Age	Physician visits (number per person)		Source or place of care (percent of visits[2])					
			Doctor's office		Hospital outpatient department[1]		Telephone	
	1982	1983	1982	1983	1982	1983	1982	1983
Total[3,4]	5.1	5.0	56.9	55.9	14.5	14.9	14.9	15.5
Under 17	4.2	4.4	55.7	55.0	13.8	13.7	17.6	19.3
Under 6	6.0	6.5	54.3	54.3	12.7	12.8	20.4	20.6
6–16	3.2	3.2	57.0	55.8	14.9	14.7	14.8	17.9
17–44	4.6	4.5	56.0	54.4	15.2	16.4	13.7	14.6
45–64	6.1	5.8	58.2	58.7	15.5	15.2	13.5	12.5
65 and over	7.7	7.6	61.4	58.9	11.7	12.3	12.9	11.9

[1]Includes hospital outpatient clinic, emergency room and other hospital visits.
[2]Includes source or place unknown.
[3]Age-adjusted.
[4]Includes all other races not shown separately.
Source: Division of Health Interview Statistics, National Center for Health Statistics; data from the National Health Interview Survey.

mask some changes that have taken place within the population. According to the U.S. Department of Health and Human Services, the number of physician contacts per person per year has *increased* for the elderly poor and *decreased* for the non-poor. This suggests that differences in the rate of physician utilization by the poor and non-poor elderly have been narrowed or eliminated in recent years. One problem with this suggestion is that it fails to distinguish the differential need for health and medical services in various income groups. The inference here is that six or seven physician contacts per year may be sufficient given the need for services of an average elderly individual with income at or above the median for the total population. However, six or seven office visits may not meet the needs of the average elderly individual whose income is at 125 percent or less of the poverty level. Aday (1975) has developed an index of use of services that takes into account need for care as measured by disability data. She reports that the poor continue to use fewer services relative to medical need than do those in higher socioeconomic circumstances.

Physician visits also vary by race and gender. Elderly whites report more physician visits per year than elderly non-whites; elderly women also report more physician visits than elderly men. Differences in health and medical service use by race are generally explained by racial differences in socioeconomic status. The gender differential in utilization of physician services exists in all age groups except for those ages when a mother usually makes the health-care decisions. The largest differential occurs between the ages of 15 and 44 when women are most likely to be making use of obstetrical and gynecological services.

Explanations for these gender differences in utilization of medical services (and in morbidity rates) have focused primarily on the social situation of women. Nathanson (1975) shows three categories of explanations: (1) Women report more illness and utilize medical services more frequently than men because it is culturally more acceptable for them to be ill; (2) a woman's role is relatively undemanding, thus reporting illness and visiting the doctor is more compatible with her other role responsibilities than is the case for men; (3) women's assigned social roles are, in fact, more stressful than those of men—consequently, they have more real illness and need more care. As Nathanson points out, insufficient data are available to evaluate the merits of these explanations.

According to the National Center for Health Services research, the elderly visit nurses, chiropractors, physical therapists and other such health workers more often than do other Americans. In 1977, 29.7 percent of the elderly had contacts with non-physician providers; this compared with 23.2 percent of the total population (Berk and Schur, 1985). "Non-physician" providers is a category that also includes optometrists, podiatrists and psychologists. Differences by age in the average number of non-physician contacts for those with at least one contact were substantial. For example, on average the aged had twice as many contacts per year (7.7 vs. 3.9) as did adults 19 to 24 (Berk and Schur, 1985).

Table 18.2 presents data on one aspect of medical care service utilization that gets looked at all too infrequently—utilization of dental services. Dental problems increase with age. More than one-fourth of persons aged 45 to 64 have lost all their teeth; almost 90 percent have diseases of the tissues sup-

TABLE 18.2 Dental visits and interval since last visit, according to age; United States, 1964, 1978 and 1983 (data are based on household interviews of a sample of the civilian non-institutionalized population)

Age	Dental visits (number per person)			Interval since last dental visit (percent of population[1])								
				Less than 1 year			2 years or more			Never visited dentist		
	1964	1978	1983	1964	1978	1983	1964	1978	1983	1964	1978	1983
Total[2,3]	1.6	1.6	1.8	42.0	49.9	51.8	28.1	25.1	23.7	15.6	10.5	10.8
Under 17	1.4	1.6	1.9	41.6	50.7	50.6	6.3	8.0	7.6	42.6	29.4	30.4
Under 6	0.5	0.6	0.5	16.5	21.2	23.1	0.6	0.9	1.0	80.4	74.3	70.5
6–16	2.0	2.1	2.6	56.9	64.2	66.1	9.8	11.2	11.3	19.6	9.1	7.8
17–44	1.9	1.6	1.8	50.0	54.3	56.6	27.8	25.1	24.9	3.2	1.9	1.6
45–64	1.7	1.7	2.0	38.4	48.8	51.9	45.5	37.0	34.3	1.3	0.6	0.6
65 and over	0.8	1.2	1.5	20.8	32.3	37.8	66.8	58.2	51.3	1.5	0.6	0.9

[1]Includes unknown interval since last dental visit.
[2]Age adjusted.
[3]Includes all other races not shown separately.
Source: Division of Health Interview Statistics, National Center for Health Statistics; data from the National Health Interview Survey.

porting or surrounding remaining teeth (Shanas and Maddox, 1977). Yet in 1983, elderly individuals averaged only 1.5 dental visits each year; this is up from 1.2 dental visits in 1978 and 0.8 visits in 1964. Unlike medical care, dental care is rarely financed by public programs or private health insurance. Thus financial barriers to dental care are still substantial. Data from the National Health Interview survey in 1975 reveal that an elderly individual with income of 15,000 dollars or more makes almost three times as many dental visits a year as the elderly individual with income below 5,000 dollars a year (2.0 vs. 0.7).

The lack of dental care among the elderly is serious. Fully 50 percent of the elderly have no natural teeth. Of those, 10 percent have no false teeth or an incomplete set. Even those with false teeth do not use them all the time; many elderly report that their dentures fit improperly. Increasing availability of dental services could improve the quality of life of many older people. Fear and embarrassment about socializing because of oral health problems has led many older people to iso-

lation. This could be overcome if dental care services were made available to more elderly. Nutritional status could also be improved by making it possible for those people who are edentulous or who have periodontal disease (and are thus restricted in diet) to eat a wider variety of foods.

Hospital utilization rates also vary according to age, gender, race, and family income. The elderly are the heaviest utilizers of hospital care; in 1977, on the average, every person 65 to 79 years of age spent almost 11 days in short-term, general non-federal hospitals; this compares with 8.4 days for those 40–64 years and 12.0 days for those 80 and older (Granick and Short, 1985). As data from the Hospital Cost and Utilization Project in Table 18.3 show, while more diagnoses are recorded for patients 65 and older, fewer surgical procedures are performed on this group.

Utilization of short-term hospitals has increased since *Medicare* was implemented in 1966. This increase was greatest among the elderly poor. According to Wilson and White (1977), discharge rates increased by

TABLE 18.3 Characteristics of patients in short-term, general, non-federal hospitals, by age group (HCUP Patient Sample, 1977[a])

	40–64 years (n = 104,584)	65–79 years (n = 64,603)	80 + years (n = 23,773)
Average length of stay (days)	8.4[b]	10.8[b]	12.0[b]
Average number of diagnoses	2.5[b]	3.1[b]	3.5[b]
Average number of surgical procedures	1.3[b]	1.2[b]	1.0[b]
Percent operated upon	52.2[b]	41.5[b]	30.2[b]
Percent discharged to another health facility	1.9[b]	6.3[b]	17.4[b]
Percent Medicare	8.1[b]	93.3[b]	95.7[b]
Percent female	54.2[b]	53.5[b]	62.3[b]

[a]Hospitalizations for conditions that would not occur in the elderly are excluded; these include the entire range of conditions associated with childbirth, complications of pregnancy and abortions.
[b]Indicates differences between age groups significant at the .05 level using a standard two-tailed *t*-test.
Source: National Center for Health Services Research and Health Care Technology Assessment; Hospital Studies Program; Hospital Cost and Utilization Project.

47 percent for the poor and 18 percent for the non-poor elderly between 1964 and 1975. Obviously some financial barriers to inpatient hospital care for the poor have been lifted by Medicare and *Medicaid,* although in light of their greater need for care, the poor, relative to the non-poor, are still undersubscribers to hospital care.

The elderly have lower rates of admission to inpatient psychiatric facilities than all other age groups except those under 18 years of age. Data for 1980 from the Veterans Administration Patient Treatment File and biennial inventories of mental health organizations show lower rates of admission for the aged for all diagnoses in an array of inpatient psychiatric organizations. In general, only for organic disorders do those 65 years and older have higher rates of admission to psychiatric facilities than the total population.

EXPLAINING USE OF HEALTH AND MEDICAL SERVICES

While we have concentrated on the impact of age (and sometimes gender, race and income) on utilization of medical services, other variables are at play also. Certainly, health beliefs or values and knowledge about health and the health care system are related to use of health services (Andersen and Newman, 1973). What Ward (1977) calls "community variables" also affect utilization. These include location of residence—central city, suburban or rural (Andersen, Greenley, Kravits and Anderson, 1972), density of age peers, availability of local transportation, and availability of neighborhood-based services and social supports (Cantor, 1975; Carp, 1975; Lopata, 1975).

Other writers and researchers have looked at how the health care delivery system itself affects patterns of utilization. Harris (1975)

and Hammerman (1975), for example, criticize the current system of service delivery as too fragmented and disorganized. Such critics emphasize the extent to which financing programs are predisposed to fund inpatient care at the expense of community-based or home care, and the way public-funding mechanisms discourage preventive care and mental health services.

Determining the conditions under which people use health care services is a difficult enterprise. The presence of an impairment or a self-assessment of poor health does not necessarily indicate a need for medical care. Even an objective indication of need for medical care may not be a foolproof predictor of whether an individual will use available health services.

A number of studies have implicated structural, social and psychological factors in utilization behavior. The costs of medical care (Berki and Ashcraft, 1979), gender (Verbrugge, 1976), level of psychological distress (Tessler, Mechanic and Dimond, 1976) and the availability of social support (Shuval, 1970) are among those variables that apparently have an effect on the utilization of health services among the population at large.

Andersen (1968) and colleagues (Andersen, Anderson and Smedby, 1968; Andersen and Newman, 1973) have generated a conceptual framework within which to sort factors that contribute to the use of health services. Three groups of variables are identified in this conceptual framework: *predisposing factors* are social structural variables (e.g. race, religion, ethnicity) as well as family attitudes and health beliefs that may affect the recognition that health services are needed; *enabling factors* include individual characteristics or circumstances, such as available family income and accessibility of service, that might hinder or accelerate use of a health service; and *need factors,* which include subjective perceptions and judgments about the seriousness of symptoms, the level of physical disability or psychological impairment and an individual's response to illness. Using this categorization schema in a Swedish study, Andersen and his colleagues (1968) found that the social class (a predisposing factor) and income (an enabling factor) of an individual were important predictors of the use of health services.

Well-designed and executed studies focusing specifically on the use of medical care by the elderly are not well represented in the literature. Roos and Shapiro (1981), using data from a sample of Manitoba (Canada) elderly, suggest that a relatively few elderly account for a disproportionate share of health service utilization. The majority of older people in their study use services at approximately the same rate as do younger people. Having advanced age, low self-perceived health status and several self-reported health problems seem to place individuals at a higher risk for the use of hospital services. Still, while the very old were at greater risk to be hospitalized, they used only slightly more physician services than did their younger counterparts. This finding is in opposition to a widely held belief that advancing age significantly increases the consumption of *all* types of health care (Roos and Shapiro, 1981).

Several studies have recently tried to identify additional sociodemographic determinants of medical care use among the elderly. Haug (1981) has found that older persons in general are more likely to get physical checkups and to overutilize the health care system for minor complaints than are younger persons. Yet they are little different from the younger in underutilization for conditions that should receive a doctor's attention. Interestingly, currently married elderly are more likely than younger marrieds to overutilize the health care system. As Haug points out, this may be due to what Eliot Freidson (1961) has described as the *lay-referral system:* A spouse is turned to first for advice when a person is ill; it appears that spouses are more likely to recommend contacting a physician when an older husband or wife has a complaint.

Wan (1982) has studied the use of health services among almost 2,000 elderly individuals residing in low-income areas of cities such as Atlanta, Georgia, Kansas City, Missouri and Boston among selected others. He describes the regular user of neighborhood health centers as black, with an income under $5,000 per year, relatively uneducated and on some form of public assistance. Persons using a hospital ambulatory clinic as a regular source of health care have a similar profile, although they seem more likely to be "younger" (65–69 years old), male and suffering from acute episodes of illness and chronic disability.

In a multivariate analysis of his data, Wan (1982) found that health status (as measured by number of acute illnesses experienced by an individual and level of chronic disability) accounted for more variation in physician contacts than did access to a regular source of medical care. Access to medical care (as measured by the availability of a usual source of care and insurance coverage) did correlate with more frequent visits to physicians. Those with a regular source of care were three times as frequent users of ambulatory care as those with no regular source.

Interestingly, Wan's analysis showed Medicaid recipients and those with access to neighborhood health centers to be the most frequent users of physician care. Blacks also had a greater number of physician contacts than whites. Previously, a number of studies had indicated that the poor have less accessibility to health care services. At least in the United States this was the case prior to the implementation of Medicare and Medicaid when, for example, the lowest socioeconomic groups had fewer physician visits than those with more income (Mechanic, 1978). According to Wan (1982:104), poor elderly blacks appear to have significantly benefited from the advent of Medicaid and other forms of public assistance. They have also taken advantage of various services provided by the neighborhood health center. Wan concludes,

> One inference that can be drawn is that the removal of financial barriers, coupled with a concerted effort toward making health services readily available to the medically needy, has greatly facilitated the use of ambulatory physician care.

Recently, Coulton and Frost (1982) have reported on a study of health service utilization by the elderly, using the conceptual framework put forth by Andersen and his colleagues (discussed above). The source of data was the *Study of Older People in Cleveland, Ohio, 1975, 1976*, conducted by the U.S. General Accounting Office. This data set includes more than 1,800 non-institutionalized elderly persons interviewed in 1975; approximately 1,500 were interviewed again a year later. Variation in use of medical care services among the elderly was largely attributable to need factors, including perceived need as well as evaluated need. Enabling and predisposing factors offered little additional help in explaining why some older people use medical care services and others do not. Having an established pattern of utilization and a medical-care provider with expectations for continued contact were additional determinants of health service utilization. This latter point is important. Some studies show that medical visits are often initiated by the medical care provider, so being affiliated with a source of care increases the likelihood of continued utilization. Finally, this study showed only weak effects of gender differences and psychological distress on utilization of health services among the elderly.

Wolinsky and his colleagues (1983) have studied the health services utilization patterns of the non-institutionalized elderly in St. Louis, also using Andersen's (1968) model (discussed above). They significantly distinguish between the "informal" and "formal" use of health services among the elderly. Informal use of health services occurs when an individual gives provisional validation to being ill and initiates some form of self-treatment. In this study, informal use of health services is measured by self-reports of restricted-activity and bed-disability days. Formal health service utilization is measured in more typical fashion and includes measures of physician and dental contact, emergency room visits and hospitalizations.

Four important trends are evident from this research. First, Andersen's model is more successful at explaining "informal" than "formal" utilization of health services. The level of dental contact evidenced by this population of elderly people is almost entirely explained by whether a regular source of dental care was available. Similarly, formal use of physician services was strongly influenced by the availability of a regular source of medical care.

Second, as is evident from previous studies (including Coulton and Frost, discussed above), the need characteristics are the most powerful predictors of the use of health services. Third, consistent with previous studies, predisposing factors show no significant effect on the use of health services except for the effect of need. Fourth, there are no significant effects of any enabling factors aside from those of having a regular source of care. Also, the effect of having a regular source of care does not contribute to explaining informal utilization or the three most policy-relevant formal measures of utilization—number of physician visits, number of emergency-room visits and hospitalizations.

PAYING FOR MEDICAL CARE

During the fiscal year 1974 the total cost of health care in America was more than $116 billion, an average of $522 per person. By 1984, these numbers had more than tripled. National health care expenditures were in excess of $387 billion with per-capita expenditures reaching approximately $1,580. Health expenditures were projected at almost 10.6 percent of the gross national product (GNP) in 1984. For that year, the annual percentage increase in health-care costs was 9.1, the lowest annual increase since the early 1970s. This is a radically different picture from 1965, when Congress passed the Medicare and Medicaid legislation. Total health-care expenditures in 1965 amounted to $42 billion, 6.1 percent of the GNP or $207 per person.

Health expenditures for the elderly have increased at a similar, if not a more rapid, pace. The amount of money expended on Medicare alone has increased more than eight times between 1970 and 1984 ($7.5 vs. $64.6 billion). In 1981, the average medical care bill for the aged was three times that for those aged 19 to 64 and seven times that for those below age 19. The source of funds to pay for health care of the elderly has also changed dramatically. During 1966, the year Medicare and Medicaid were implemented, only 30 percent of these funds were public; by fiscal 1981, 64 percent of the expenditures came from public funds.

The largest single item on the health-care bill of elderly individuals is hospital care. In 1981, this item cost $36.6 billion and accounted for 44 percent of all personal health-care expenditures for the aged. Public monies (including Medicare and Medicaid) paid for 85.5 percent of this bill. The 14.5 percent not covered by public funds must be paid by the individual or by some form of private health insurance.

Hospital care, nursing-home care and physicians' services combined account for $71.6 billion or about 86 percent of the $83.2 billion spent on health care for the elderly in fiscal 1981. Items such as drugs, dental services, eyeglasses and appliances constitute a very small part of the total bill as well as of the privately funded bill. Still, expenditures for these items may be low because elderly people are going without them. As costs continue to rise (over the last decade, medical care costs for the elderly have risen at an average annual rate of about 15 percent) and such services continue to remain outside the scope of most public funding mechanisms for health care of the elderly, we can expect continued low utilization. In 1981, private sources funded 82.3 percent of the costs of drugs and drug sundries for older people. How many older people go without needed drugs because public funding mechanisms do not generally underwrite the costs for drugs and personal funds are unavailable?

Payments for health care are made under a variety of public and private programs designed to provide care or access to care for specified population groups. The two largest programs are Medicare and Medicaid. They are the principal public funding mechanisms for health care of the elderly and deserve our special attention.

Medicare

In 1965, the *Social Security Act of 1935* was amended to provide health insurance for the elderly. This amendment, which became effective July 1, 1966, is known as Title XVIII or Medicare. It marked the inauguration in the United States of a national system of financing individual health services on a social insurance basis. It was not, however, the country's first attempt at establishing national health insurance. Such attempts and their failures date back to the beginning of the twentieth century. The historical record is worthy of a brief detour.*

During the years 1915–1918, a group of academics, lawyers and other professionals who were organized under the American Association for Labor Legislation attempted to push a "model" medical care insurance bill through several state legislatures. They had no success. The American Medical Association (AMA) opposed the bills as did the American Federation of Labor (AFL). The AFL feared that any form of compulsory

*Historical material on Medicare comes primarily from Marmor (1973) and Feingold (1966).

social insurance might lead to further government control of working people. It was not until the Great Depression that sustained interest in governmental health insurance reappeared.

In 1934 President Franklin D. Roosevelt created an advisory Committee on Economic Security. In the climate of destitution and poverty that accompanied the Great Depression, this committee was charged with drafting a social security bill providing a minimum income for the aged, the unemployed, the blind and the widowed and their children. The result was the Social Security Act of 1935. The act was originally intended to include health insurance provisions also. However, as Feingold points out, the extent of this intention was little more than one line in the original bill that suggested that the Social Security Board study the problem and report to Congress. When opposition to this line became so strong that it appeared to jeopardize the Social Security bill itself, the line was dropped.

Although advocates of compulsory health insurance proposed congressional bills annually from 1939 on, it was not until Truman's "Fair Deal" that the possibility of passing such a bill became strong. In the interim (1939–1949), private health insurance (endorsed by the AMA) through Blue Cross, Blue Shield and commercial insurance carriers became firmly established in America as a way of paying for medical expenses.

In 1949 President Truman requested congressional action on medical-care insurance. In order to placate the AMA and its allies, it was specified that doctors and hospitals would not have to join the plan. In addition, doctors would retain the right to refuse to serve patients whom they did not want. This was not enough. The AMA was adamantly opposed to "socialized medicine," and despite Truman's characterization of the AMA as "the public's worst enemy in the efforts to redistribute medical care more equitably," efforts at passing a national health insurance bill were defeated.

What were the major objections to these early national health insurance proposals? According to Marmor, they were as follows: (1) medical insurance was a "give-away" program that made no distinction between the deserving and undeserving poor; (2) too many well-off Americans who did not need financial assistance in meeting their health needs would be helped; (3) utilization of health-care services would increase dramatically and beyond their capacity; and (4) there would be excessive control of physicians, constituting a precedent for socialism in America.

Clearly another strategy was necessary. The one that developed turned away from the health problems of the general population to those of the aged. There was great appeal in focusing on the aged. As a group, they were needy yet deserving. Most had made a contribution to America. Still, through no fault of their own, many suffered reduced earning capacity and higher medical expenses. Proponents of this new strategy waged a public war of sympathy for the aged and a private war of pressure politics from 1952 until 1965. Not until then was the political climate ripe for amending the original Social Security Act to provide health insurance for the nation's aged (Medicare).

Medicare consists of two basic components. Part A is a compulsory hospital insurance (HI) plan that covers a bed patient in a hospital and, under certain conditions, in a skilled nursing facility or at home after having left the hospital. It is financed by employer–employee contributions and a tax on the self-employed. Most of the elderly are automatically eligible as a result of their own or a spouse's entitlement to Social Security. In 1983, almost 92 percent of those 65 years and over were covered by Medicare. If for any reason a person is not eligible for HI at age 65, it can be purchased on a voluntary basis. The monthly premium became $248 on January 1, 1987.

Part B represents a voluntary program of supplemental medical insurance (SMI) that helps pay doctor bills, outpatient hospital benefits, home health services and certain other medical services and supplies. Financing is achieved through monthly premiums paid by enrollees and matching funds by the federal government. As of January 1, 1987, the monthly premium was $17.90 or $214.80 for the year.

Hospital insurance (Part A) benefits are measured by periods of time known as *benefit periods*. Benefit periods begin when a patient enters the hospital and end when he or she has not been a hospital bed patient for 60 consecutive days. This concept is an important one to grasp since it determines how much care a Medicare beneficiary is entitled to at any particular point in time. Medicare will help to pay covered services for a patient for up to 90 days of in-hospital care, for up to 100 days of extended care in a skilled nursing facility and for posthospital home health care in each benefit period. If an individual runs out of covered days within a benefit period, he or she may draw upon a lifetime reserve of 60 additional hospital days. Use of these days within the lifetime reserve, however, permanently reduces the total number of reserve days left. For example, if a patient has been in the hospital for 90 days and needs 10 more days of hospital care, he or she may draw 10 days from the reserve of 60, leaving a reserve of 50 days.

Part A Medicare benefits will pay for such services as a semi-private room, including meals and special diets, regular nursing services, lab tests, drugs furnished by the hospital, and medical supplies and appliances furnished by the hospital. It will not pay for convenience items, a private room or private-duty nurses, for example.

A Medicare patient is financially responsible, through co-payments and deductibles, for various components of his or her hospital insurance plan. As a bed patient in a participating hospital, she is responsible for the first $520 of costs in each benefit period (1987 figure). After this, Part A pays for covered services for the first 60 days of hospital care. From day 61 through day 91 in a benefit period, hospital insurance pays for all covered service except for $130 a day. If more than 90 days of inpatient care is required reserve days may be used. The co-payment after 90 days of care is $260 a day. Beyond 150 days in a hospital, Medicare pays nothing.

Extended-care benefits provide for covered services for the first 20 days in a benefit period. After the first 20 days, the recipient must pay $65 (1987 figure) a day for up to 80 days in a benefit period. Home health care, from a home health agency participating in Medicare, covers part-time nursing care by a registered nurse or under her or his supervision, physical or speech therapy, and medical supplies and appliances. It does not cover services of part-time health aides at home.

The medical insurance program (Part B) of Medicare is a voluntary one, and an individual must pay a monthly premium in order to be eligible for coverage. In addition, the subscriber pays a deductible each year and 20 percent of the remainder. Although Part B pays for a broad array of outpatient hospital services, doctors' services, home health benefits and other medical supplies, it does *not* cover such things as routine physical examinations, regular eye or hearing examinations, eyeglasses or hearing aids, prescription drugs, false teeth or full-time nursing care.

Medicaid

Medicaid, or Title XIX of the Social Security Act, passed also in 1965, becoming effective in July 1966. According to Stevens and Stevens (1974), some observers at the time saw Title XIX as the "sleeper" of the 1965 legislation. After all, Medicare is limited in terms of who is covered (primarily the aged), the types of services covered (described above) and the presence of deductibles and co-payments. Medicaid was intended as a catchall program to handle the medical expenses not covered by Medicare as well as to provide medical assistance to needy groups other than the aged. The program is jointly funded by federal and state governments with the federal government contributing in excess of 50 percent in "poorer" states. Eligibility varies by state, although one requirement seems to be almost universal. Wherever an individual qualifies for Medicaid, "pauperization" has preceded qualification. All persons, including the elderly, may find themselves eligible for Medicaid only after they have drained their resources and qualified as a member of the poor.

IS THERE A CRISIS IN MEDICAL CARE FINANCING?

The Medicare program has made and continues to make various medical services available to many persons who would not receive them otherwise. There are older people living on low, relatively fixed incomes who might not be able to secure the services of a physician, a hospital, a skilled nursing home or a home health care program without Medicare. However, the Medicare program is riddled with various out-of-pocket deductibles and co-payments for its beneficiaries, not to mention limitations in services provided. Medicare now pays approximately 44 percent of the medical care expenditures of the elderly, leaving the rest to be paid for by Medicaid (17 percent). and by personal resources (39 percent).

A recent report by the U.S. Senate Special Committee on Aging (1978) indicates that many elderly Americans supplement their Medicare with some private health insurance plan. In 1975, almost 63 percent did so for hospital care and up to 55 percent had some form of private insurance coverage for physician's services. Such plans have little impact and are not heavily drawn upon. Only about 5 percent of the health care bill for older Americans is paid for by private health insurance coverage. Abuses are rampant. Senator Lawton Chiles of Florida reported on the case of an 87-year-old woman who had been sold 19 separate policies from nine different companies by six agents in just over a year. The woman was committed to insurance premium payments of almost $4,000 a year, most of the policies were worthless because of the duplication and overlap in coverage. Many elderly Americans fear health care costs beyond what Medicare will cover, but excess insurance premiums are clearly not a solution to limited coverage.

President Ronald Reagan has proposed an extension of Medicare to provide "catastrophic" health insurance coverage to older Americans. Under this proposal, a low monthly premium would protect an older person from being impoverished as a result of an acute illness; maximum out-of-pocket expenditures per year for the ill elderly would be about $2,000.

In addition to the problems of limited coverage, Medicare focuses too narrowly on providing acute care. The maintenance of chronic health conditions and quality of life issues do not receive adequate attention. Eye examinations for eyeglasses, hearing examinations for hearing aids, orthopedic shoes, and false teeth are all excluded from coverage. Under this system, Medicare patients could not take advantage of geriatric consultation clinics that are concerned with the prevention of illness and the maintenance of chronic conditions. Such clinics could only exist for private, paying patients. The Reagan administration proposal to offer catastrophic insurance coverage to older Americans continues the Medicare emphasis on acute care. This "extra" catastrophic insurance would not apply to long-term care needs of the elderly.

The language employed throughout the Medicare regulations refers to medical need, medical care and medical necessity. Health teaching, health maintenance, prevention of illness, aspects of rehabilitation and personal care are related to health care but not necessarily to medical care. The elderly are often in need of health care services in far greater proportion than medical care services (Schwab, 1977). If the health needs of the elderly population are to be served and if suitable health maintenance programs are to be developed, then a financing system must be initiated that allows for funding of services that prevent illness and maintain health.

Because Medicare and Medicaid result from legal entitlements to services, there has been some concern that expenditures from these programs are uncontrollable. The costs of providing medical care under these programs has increased at a rate exceeding the growth of the federal economy and the consumer price index. Frustration over apparently uncontrollable costs has led to major reform in Medicare and Medicaid. Starting in October 1983, a new system began that fixed Medicare hospital-payment rates in advance. Under this *prospective payment system,* hospitals know in advance what Medicare will pay them for treating a patient with a particular ailment. A fee is set for the treatment of 467 illnesses and injuries categorized into *Diagnosis-Related Groups* (DRGs). Fees vary by region, according to whether the hospital is in an urban or rural setting, and according to the prevailing wage rate in the area. Rates will probably be adjusted annually. Psychiatric care, long-term care, rehabilitation and children's hospitals were initially excluded from this prospective payment system.

The fixed fee will have to be accepted as payment in full for treatment of a Medicare patient who has been hospitalized. Those hospitals that can provide the care for less than the fixed payment rate will be allowed to keep the extra money. If hospitals are unable to provide the care for the fixed payment rate, they may charge patients only for the deductibles and co-payments that are already part of the Medicare payment system. Some argue that this prospective payment system provides incentives to hospitals to admit

patients at a later stage in the progression of illness and discharge them at an earlier stage of illness recovery. Only analysis of "hard" data will determine if such incentives are at work.

An additional important reform of Medicare is the payment for *hospice* care for the dying (see Chapter 21). Under new hospice provisions, the federal government will purchase a comprehensive package of services for those terminally ill who no longer receive curative medical care (Rabin, 1985). This package would include the cost of institutional as well as home care, drugs, counseling and other medical and social services. The Congressional Budget Office estimates that the availability of reimbursement for hospice care will reduce the time that patients would otherwise spend in hospitals and nursing homes, thus saving Medicare tens of millions of dollars annually.

Medicaid has also experienced reform. As Rabin (1985) reports, states have been given greater program autonomy over which services to provide. They may limit the freedom to select a medical care provider, develop new formulas for hospital reimbursement and emphasize community-based alternatives to institutional care. Furthermore, states are now in a position to negotiate with providers about the organization and price of health and medical care.

Despite these reforms, Medicare and Medicaid still represent legal entitlement to medical care. While the price of medical care is more regulated than in the past, costs continue to rise. It was expected that combined spending for Medicare and Medicaid spending in 1985 would exceed $100 billion. The Medicare Board of Trustees has reviewed the actuarial status of the Hospital Insurance (HI) and Supplementary Medical Insurance (SMI)

Trust Funds (Klees and Warfield, 1986). Using intermediate assumptions (somewhere between optimistic and pessimistic), the board found the present financing schedule for the HI program to be barely sufficient to ensure the payment of benefits through the late 1990s. The SMI program is actuarially sound, but the Board recommended that Congress take action to curtail the rapid growth in this part of Medicare (Klees and Warfield, 1986).

TOWARD A POLITICAL ECONOMY OF HEALTH AND AGING

In attempting to understand the relationships among aging, health and health-services utilization, students of aging in the United States have directed their analyses primarily at the individual older person. Resultant research has been concerned with biomedical, psychological and social-psychological models of aging. Much of the material presented in this text can be located in one or more of these models. Thus we ask, How do individuals adjust to the aging process? Why are certain aged persons healthier than others? Why do some elderly avail themselves of health services and others not?

As Estes and her colleagues (1984a, 1984b) point out, questions such as these make the economic and political structure of the society residual in explaining old age. These authors offer an alternative approach that "starts with the proposition that the status and resources of the elderly and even the trajectory of the aging process itself are conditioned by one's location in the social structure and the economic and social factors that affect it" (Estes, Swan and Gerard, 1984b).

From this *political economy* perspective, the structure and operation of the major societal institutions (including the family, the work place and the medical and welfare institutions) shape both the subjective experience and objective condition of the individual's aging. In the area of health and aging, the political economy perspective emphasizes:

1. The social determinants of health and illness
2. The social creation of dependency and the management of that dependency status through public policy and health services
3. Medical care as an ideology and as an industry in the control and management of the aging
4. The consequences of public policies for the elderly as a group and as individuals
5. The role and function of the state vis-a-vis aging and health
6. The social construction of reality about old age and health that both undergirds and reinforces the institutional arrangements and public policies concerning health and aging in the society (Estes, Gerard, Zones and Swan, 1984).

Political economy provides a critical approach to the study of aging that does *not* attempt to psychologize the health problems of the aging. An analysis of health and aging from a political economy perspective instead emphasizes the broad implications of economic life for the aged and for society's treatment of the aged and their health. This view also examines the special circumstances of different classes and subgroups of older persons. It is a systematic view based on the assumption that old age cannot be understood in isolation from other problems or issues raised by the larger social order.

From this perspective, the future seems grim for positive health policy initiatives for the elderly. Minkler (1984), for example, sees a continuation of victim-blaming and scapegoating of the elderly for economic problems and fiscal crises such as the federal budget deficit, although the character of victim-blaming is changing. She describes how earlier efforts at victim-blaming defined the elderly as a social problem, and consequently devised solutions for dealing with that problem. Medicare and Medicaid represent but two highly visible programs generated to deal with the problems of the aged. Now, victim-blaming in the 1980s defines these "solutions" as part of the problem. Not only are the elderly themselves seen as a problem, but programmatic efforts to address their needs are characterized as "budget busting" and in need of being either dismantled entirely or privatized.

The political economy perspective raises a whole new set of questions that need to be asked *and* answered as we proceed into the future. These questions and their answers will provide a significant opportunity for students of aging policy to rethink the relationship between society and its aged constitutents.

SUMMARY

The average number of physician visits per person increases with age. Yet the number of physician contacts per aged person per year has not changed dramatically in the last 20 years. While differences in the rate of physician utilization by the elderly poor and non-poor have been narrowed or eliminated in recent years, the poor likely continue to use fewer services relative to their needs than do those in higher socioeconomic circumstances.

There is a gender differential in the utilization of physician services in all adult age groups. Explanations have focused primarily on the social situation of women. In general, the utilization of dental services by older people is lower than among younger groups. This is despite the fact that dental problems increase with age. Hospitalization rates also vary according to age, gender, race, and family income.

Health care expenditures have increased rapidly in recent years. The amount of money expended on Medicare alone has increased more than eightfold between 1970 and 1984. The source of funds to pay for health care for the elderly has also changed. By fiscal 1981, two out of three health care dollars expended were public monies. The largest single item on the health care bill of elderly people is hospital care. Public monies, including Medicare and Medicaid, pay for about 85 percent of this bill.

The Medicare program for the elderly contains many out-of-pocket deductibles and co-payments, as well as limitations in services, and focuses too narrowly on acute care problems. The language employed throughout the Medicare regulations refers to medical need, medical care and medical necessity. The elderly are often in greater need of *health promotion* and illness prevention services than they are of medical care services. Some reforms of Medicare have recently been made. The most notable among these are the institution of a prospective payment system for hospitals and the payment for hospice care for the dying. In the future, we may see catastrophic health insurance for the aged. Despite these reforms, Medicare and Medicaid still represent legal entitlement to medical care, and costs continue to rise.

The political economy perspective is a newer, critical approach to understanding the relationships among aging, health and health services utilization. Rather than psychologizing the problems of health and aging, this perspective tries to place problems of health and aging in the broader context of the economic and political life of the society.

KEY TERMS

benefit periods
Diagnostic-Related Groups (DRGs)
enabling factors
hospice
lay-referral system
Medicaid
Medicare
need factors
political economy
predisposing factors
prospective payment system
Social Security Act of 1935

STUDY QUESTIONS

1. How does use of physician services vary by gender? What are some possible explanations for this difference in utilization of medical services between men and women?
2. What is the apparent relationship between age and dental problems? Dental visits? How do we explain the low rates of utilization of dental services among the aged?
3. Identify the three factors in Andersen's categorization schema that contribute to the use of health services. Give an example of each of these factors. How do the three factors rank in their ability to account for variation in health-care utilization by the elderly?

4. How have programs such as Medicare and Medicaid influenced the amount of physician contact among poor elderly blacks?
5. Distinguish between Medicare and Medicaid. What are the major gaps in these programs?
6. Is there a crisis in medical care financing? What reforms have been instituted to ensure the financial integrity of Medicare?
7. What is the value of the political economy perspective in understanding the relationships among aging, health and health services utilization?

BIBLIOGRAPHY

Aday, L. 1975. Economic and noneconomic barriers to the use of needed medical services. *Medical Care 13:* 447–456.

Andersen, R. 1968. *A Behavioral Model of Families' Use of Health Services.* Research Series 25. Chicago: Center for Health Administration Studies.

_____ , Anderson, O., and Smedby, B. 1968. Perceptions of and response to symptoms of illness in Sweden and the U.S. *Medical Care 6:* 18–30.

_____ , Greenley, R., Kravits, J., and Anderson, O. 1972. *Health Service Use: National Trends and Variations: 1953–71.* Chicago: Center for Health Administration Studies.

_____ , and Newman, J. 1973. Societal and individual determinants of medical care utilization in the U.S. *Milbank Memorial Fund Quarterly 51:* 95–124.

Berk, M.L., and Schur, C.L. 1985. *Nonphysician Health Care Providers: Use of Ambulatory Services, Expenditures, and Sources of Payment.* DHHS Pub. No. (PHS) 86–3394. Rockville, Md.: National Center for Health Services Research.

Berki, S.E., and Ashcraft, M. 1979. On the analysis of ambulatory utilization. *Medical Care 17:* 1163–79.

Cantor, M. 1975. Life space and the social support of the inner city elderly of New York. *Gerontologist 14:* 286–288.

Carp, F. 1975. Life-style and location within the city. *Gerontologist 15:* 27–34.

Coulton, C., and Frost, A.K. 1982. Use of social and health services by the elderly. *Journal of Health and Social Behavior* 23(40): 330–339.

Estes, C.L., Gerard, L.E., Zones, J.S., and Swan, J.H. 1984a. *Political Economy, Health, and Aging.* Boston: Little, Brown.

Estes, C.L., Swan, J.H., and Gerard, L.E. 1984b. Dominant and competing paradigms in gerontology: Towards a political economy of aging. In M. Minkler and C.L. Estes, eds., *Readings in the Political Economy of Aging.* Farmingdale, N.Y.: Baywood Publishing.

Feingold, E. 1966. *Medicare: Policy and Politics.* San Francisco: Chandler Publishing.

Freidson, E. 1961. *Patient Views of Medical Practice.* New York: Russell Sage Foundation.

Granick, D.W., and Short, T. 1985. *Utilization of Hospital Inpatient Services by Elderly Americans.* DHHS Pub. No. (PHS) 85–3351. Rockville, Md.: National Center for Health Services Research.

Hammerman, J. 1975. Health services: Their success and failure in reaching older adults. *American Journal of Public Health 64:* 253–256.

Harris, R. 1975. Breaking the barriers to better health-care delivery for the aged. *Gerontologist 15:* 52–56.

Haug, M. 1981. Age and medical care utilization patterns. *Journal of Gerontology 33:* 103–111.

Klees, B., and Warfield, C. 1986. Actuarial status of the HI and SMI Trust Funds. *Social Security Bulletin* 49(7): 10–17.

Lopata, H. 1975. Support system of elderly urbanites: Chicago of the 1970s. *Gerontologist 15:* 35–41.

Marmor, T. 1973. *The Politics of Medicare.* Chicago: Aldine Publishing.

Mechanic, D. 1978. *Medical Sociology,* 2nd ed. New York: The Free Press.

Minkler, M. 1984. Blaming the aged victim: The politics of retrenchment in times of fiscal conservatism. In M. Minkler and C.L. Estes, eds., *Readings in the Political Economy of Aging.* Farmingdale, N.Y.: Baywood Publishing.

Nathanson, C. 1975. Illness and the feminine role: A theoretical review. *Social Science and Medicine 9:* 57–62.

Rabin, D.L. 1985. Waxing of the gray, waning of the green. In Institute of Medicine/National Research Council, eds., *America's Aging: Health in an Older Society.* Washington, D.C.: National Academy Press.

Roos, N., and Shapiro, E. 1981. The Manitoba longitudinal study on aging: Preliminary findings on health care utilization by the elderly. *Medical Care 19:* 644–657.

Schwab, M. 1977. Implications for the aged of major national health care proposals. *Journal of Gerontological Nursing 3:* 33–36.

Shanas, E., and Maddox, G. 1977. Aging, health, and the organization of health resources. In R. Binstock and E. Shanas, eds., *Handbook of Aging and the Social Sciences.* New York: Van Nostrand Reinhold.

Shuval, J. 1970. *The Social Functions of Medical Practice.* San Francisco: Jossey-Bass.

Stevens, R., and Stevens R. 1974. *Welfare Medicine in America: A Case Study of Medicaid.* New York: The Free Press.

Tessler, R., Mechanic, D., and Dimond, M. 1976. The effect of psychological distress on physician utilization: A prospective study. *Journal of Health and Social Behavior 17:* 353–364.

U.S. Senate Special Committee on Aging. 1978. *Medi-gap: Private Health Insurance Supplement to Medicare.* Washington, D.C.: U.S. Government Printing Office.

Verbrugge, L. 1976. Sex differences in morbidity and mortality in the United States. *Social Biology 23:* 275–296.

Wan, T. 1982. Use of health service by the elderly in low income communities. *Milbank Memorial Fund Quarterly 60:* 82–107.

Ward, R. 1977. Services for older people: An integrated framework for research. *Journal of Health and Social Behavior 18:* 61–70.

Wilson, R., and White. 1977. Changes in morbidity, disability and utilization differentials between the poor and the nonpoor, data from the Health Interview Survey, 1964 and 1973. *Medical Care 15:* 636–646.

Wolinsky, F.D., Coe, R.M., Miller, D.K., Prendergast, J.M., Creel, M.J.M, and Chavez, M.N. 1983. Health services utilization among the noninstitutionalized elderly. *Journal of Health and Social Behavior* 24(4): 325–336.

CHAPTER **19**

Institutionalization

Long-term care entails "one or more services provided on a sustained basis to enable individuals whose functional capacities are chronically impaired to be maintained at their maximum levels of psychological, physical and social well-being. Those served can reside in their own homes or in some type of institutional facility" (Brody, 1984). Koff (1982) specifies long-term care services as designed to provide diagnostic, preventive, therapeutic, rehabilitative, supportive and maintenance care. According to the U.S. Senate Special Committee on Aging (1982), the goals of long-term care involve a three-pronged strategy: (1) to delay the onset of preventable disease in healthy adults; (2) to lengthen the period of functional independence in elderly people with chronic disease; and (3) to improve the quality of later life.

Traditionally, the phrase long-term care has been synonymous with institutionalization, mainly because few or no other options were available. With the aging of the U.S. population and the increasing proportion of persons with health problems in need of some care, various alternative non-institutional arrangements have evolved. In this chapter we equate the concept of long-term care with institutional care. In Chapter 20 the concept is extended to include the delivery of an array of services in non-institutional settings.

We begin this chapter with a discussion of the actual risks of an older person being institutionalized in the United States. In addition, we discuss the logic of long-term care and what effects institutionalization may have on the aged individual.

THE RISKS OF INSTITUTIONALIZATION

The 1980 census reports that approximately 5 percent of those 65 years and older, or 1.3 million elderly, are in old-age institutions. Using projected changes in the number of elderly with problems in carrying out activities of daily living, one researcher expects that those requiring long-term care will grow by 70 percent between 1980 and the end of the century (Hing, 1981). Fox and Clauser (1980), assuming current age-specific rates of institutionalization remain unchanged, estimate that about 650,000 additional elderly will be in nursing homes in the year 2000.

On the one hand, this represents a dramatically different picture than that at the turn of the century in the United States when only about 80,000 persons could be found in comparable institutional settings. On the other hand, estimating that 2 million elderly will be institutionalized on any given day in the year 2000 reflects a projected rate of institutionalization that approximates 6 percent—only 1 percent more than the current rate of institutionalization. Recognizing the enormous growth that has occurred in this century in this segment of the health care industry is important. Yet emphasizing the figures (current and future) of the institutionalized elderly may serve to diminish an array of issues surrounding the provision of long-term care. After all, the numbers cited above provide a picture of the institutional population at only one point in time. They are of *no value* in attempting to estimate the total or cumulative chance of an elderly person being institutionalized for some period of time during the years preceding death.

Kastenbaum and Candy (1973) were the first to point out the fallacy of assuming that the institutionalization rate for the elderly could be used as an estimate of their cumulative chances for institutionalization. They read all the obituaries reported in the *Detroit News* during 1971 and found 926 cases in which the age of the deceased individual was 65 years or older and the place of death was specified. Of these reported deaths, 13.3 percent occurred in nursing homes. This is almost three times the 4.8 percent rate of institutionalization reported by the Bureau of the Census and based on its 1970 count of persons in institutions. The fact that almost 22 percent of all the deaths of those aged 65 and over identified in the newspaper did not specify a place of death, and the fact that a substantial number of deaths may not have been reported in the form of an obituary, make it easy to see why the authors believed the 13.3 percent to be an underestimation of the rate of institutionalization in Detroit.

In a second study, Kastenbaum and Candy reviewed 20,234 death certificates for those aged 65 and older filed in the metropolitan Detroit area during the 1971 calendar year. They found that approximately 20 percent of all these deaths were reported in nursing homes, and approximately 24 percent were reported occurring in a larger category of institutions that included all identifiable extended-care facilities. The findings from this second study show five times as many elderly individuals dying in extended-care facilities in the Detroit metropolitan area than were assumed to be living in such facilities by the 1970 population count. Still, there is reason to believe that this is an underestimation; clearly, more people have lived in nursing homes and other extended-care facilities than have died there. Many an elderly person may sustain an injury in a nursing home, be transferred to a hospital for medical reasons and subsequently die in the hospital. Still others may recuperate from illness or injury in a nursing home and then be discharged to their homes. Kastenbaum and Candy were unable to determine the number of such cases they may have missed in their two studies.

If one looked at all these data from the perspective of an elderly individual, it might be assumed, using the 1980 Census report of persons in institutions, that the odds of such a person entering a nursing or rest home of some type were only about 1 in 20 (based on 5 percent). The findings of Kastenbaum and Candy offer a very different set of odds: a 1 in 4 chance of dying in an extended-care facility. Other researchers, using different populations and different methods, have substantiated these findings. Palmore (1976) reviewed the cases of 207 individuals from the Piedmont, North Carolina, area who were studied in the Duke First Longitudinal Study of Aging from 1955 until their deaths prior to the spring of 1976. He observed that 54 of the 207 persons, or 26 percent, had been institutionalized in some type of extended-care facility one or more times before death. On the basis of this and other findings, he concluded that "the total chance of institutionalization before death among normal aged persons living in the community would be about one in four."

Presenting a picture that shows that one in four elderly Americans can expect to be institutionalized in a nursing home or rest home makes it easier to understand why a major fear of many older persons is that they will become dependent and have to face institutionalization. Such figures also make it easier to begin to understand the potentially high financial and human costs of institutionaliza-tion and the tremendous strain this phenomenon may place on public and private resources in our society.

WHO GETS INSTITUTIONALIZED?

A number of factors seem to influence who among the elderly gets institutionalized. A U.S. Department of Health, Education and Welfare report (1977) describes the "typical" nursing home resident as white, female, widowed, age 79 and living in the facility for 2.6 years. Most of the residents lived in another institution prior to entering the nursing home. Almost 81 percent of nursing home residents were admitted primarily for physical reasons. The chronic conditions that are most prevalent in the elderly institutionalized population are stroke, heart disease, arthritis, and rheumatism.

More than 71 percent of elderly nursing home residents are female. The disproportionate number of elderly women in old-age institutions reflects their predominance in the elderly population and the fact that considerably more elderly women than men are older than 75. Non-whites constitute about 8 percent of the institutionalized elderly population. One explanation of the low utilization of nursing homes by non-whites is simply that elderly non-whites live in states (e.g., the Deep South) that are found to have low institutionalization rates in general (Manard, Kart and van Gils, 1975). Another explanation is that elderly non-whites are being denied access to nursing home care they may require or are being institutionalized in other types of facilities. Kart and Beckham (1976) report a great dissimilarity between the distribution of elderly whites and elderly blacks across various types of institutions in the

United States. They found elderly blacks to predominate in state mental hospitals and elderly whites to predominate in nonprofit and proprietary homes for the aged. The authors argued that socioeconomic factors, including the inability of many elderly blacks to afford the cost of care in proprietary homes for the aged, and racial discrimination against blacks by nonprofit and proprietary homes, were two reasons why elderly blacks and whites in America have very different institutionalization experiences.

More than four out of five (81.5 percent) elderly nursing home residents are 75 or older. One recent study found the age of an elderly population to be strongly associated with institutionalization. Manard and her colleagues (1975), using 1970 census data, found that those states with a high proportion of elderly who were 75 and above had a high rate of institutionalization. A factor that contributes to the relationship between age and institutionalization is that the chances of developing major health problems and of losing one's living companion (spouse, friend or sibling) increase with age.

More than 60 percent (62.3) of aged nursing-home residents are widowed; many of these people lived alone prior to institutionalization. Both widowhood and living alone appear to put some at risk for institutionalization. Generally speaking, people who grow old and sick will be less able to cope with the situation if they live alone. Still, almost 35 percent of nursing home residents in 1973–74 moved there from a general or short-stay hospital. To some degree, this reflects Medicare regulations that allow coverage for extended care (up to 100 days) only if the patient had recently been discharged from a hospital after a stay of three days or more.

THE LOGIC OF LONG-TERM CARE

In 1984, 32 billion dollars were spent on nursing-home care; this accounted for 8.3 percent of total national health expenditures for that year. Almost one-half (49 percent) of the bill for care in nursing homes was paid out of public funds (U.S. Bureau of the Census, 1985). The principal programs involved are Medicare and Medicaid, both of which began in 1966.

Medicare's Part A benefits for nursing homes are extremely limited. Only persons in Medicare-certified homes are eligible and benefits cover the first 100 days of care. (All charges are covered for the first 20 days of care. As of this writing, for days 21 to 100, the patient pays the first $61.50 per day with Medicare paying the difference between this amount and actual charges). Patients must have first been hospitalized, and only persons with conditions certified as requiring skilled nursing care may be covered, and that condition must be related to the illness that caused the initial hospitalization. Thus, no benefits are provided for so-called *intermediate nursing care* or for *custodial care*.

Part B of Medicare pays for such things as doctor's services, diagnostic tests and some drugs. As of January 1, 1987, the estimated monthly premium for Part B was $17.90, or $214.80 a year. In 1973, Medicare coverage was extended to those persons under 65 who required certain expensive medical procedures, such as renal dialysis.

Medicaid is a joint federal–state program established to pay for medical care for low-income Americans. As has been true of other categorical assistance programs, states set their own eligibility requirements. In general, persons who are eligible for state public assistance or for Supplemental Security Income (SSI) under the federal program for the aged, blind or disabled poor are automatically eligible for Medicaid. Other eligibility requirements and benefits are based upon personal income and assets, but vary significantly from state to state. Many formerly middle-income older people have come to rely on Medicaid after exhausting personal financial resources to pay nursing home costs. In effect, such people have become medically needy by "spending down," that is, by showing that their out-of-pocket medical costs have reduced their income and assets to the Medicaid eligibility level in their state.

Medicaid provides long-term, unlimited nursing-home care without requiring previous hospitalization. Not surprisingly, Medicaid has become the principal public mechanism for funding nursing-home care. In 1984, Medicaid accounted for 90 percent of government expenditures for nursing-home care and 45 percent of all costs for nursing homes in the United States; approximately 60 percent of nursing-home patients receive Medicaid payments.

The authors of the early Medicare and Medicaid legislation intended, among other things, to encourage the development of new types of facilities less expensive than hospitals for long-term care of the aged sick and to improve the quality of existing nursing homes.

Three types of facilities, *extended care facilities* (ECF), *skilled nursing facilities (SNF)*, and *intermediate care facilities (ICF)*, were initially defined in the federal legislation. Congress used the ECF label to describe facilities certified for Medicare participation, and standards for these facilities required extensive professional nursing and supportive staffs. The SNF category was devised to provide a somewhat lower level of care at lower costs for long-term convalescent and terminal patients. Both Medicare and Medicaid fund reimbursement programs for SNFs. As the cost from this legislation increased, it was asserted that many of the publicly supported patients in skilled nursing facilities required fewer professional services. Intermediate care facilities (ICFs) were designed as a less costly alternative for persons who required more than room and board but less than a full range of medical services—care limited to help with personal hygiene and administration of daily medication, for example. Medicaid covers all costs of intermediate nursing-home care.

Characteristics of Nursing Homes

Table 19.1 presents data on the selected characteristics of nursing homes in the United States, collected in the 1977 National Nursing Home Survey. The great majority of nursing homes are run for profit. These facilities, defined as *proprietary,* did not appear in significant numbers until the 1940s. In 1977, about 74 percent of all nursing homes were operated for profit. Proprietors include individuals, partnerships and corporations. Although the nonprofit and government nursing homes made up only about 26 percent of the facilities, their greater capacity (average size 97 beds vs. 68 beds for proprietary facilities) enable them to serve about one-third of all nursing-home residents.

Nursing homes may also be classified according to their certification status. About 75 percent of all nursing homes in 1977 were certified as SNF, ICF, or both. Intermediate care facilities constitute about 34 percent of all facilities and 45 percent of all certified facilities. Facilities certified as both SNF and ICF were larger (124 beds per facility) than

TABLE 19.1 Selected characteristics of nursing homes, United States, 1977

Nursing home characteristics	Nursing homes		Beds		Residents	
	Number	% Distribution	Number	% Distribution	Number	% Distribution
All nursing homes	18,300	100.0	1,383,600	100.0	1,287,400	100.0
Ownership:						
Proprietary	13,600	74.3	926,100	66.9	851,700	66.2
Non-profit and government	4,700	25.7	457,600	33.1	435,700	33.8
Certification:						
Skilled nursing facility	3,600	19.9	271,700	19.6	252,100	19.6
Skilled nursing and						
intermediate care facility	3,900	21.1	484,300	35.0	462,200	35.9
Intermediate care facility	6,200	33.7	455,700	32.9	414,300	32.2
Not certified	4,600	25.3	171,900	12.4	158,800	12.3
Number of Beds:						
Less than 50	7,800	42.5	205,700	14.9	193,500	15.0
50–99	5,200	28.5	376,600	27.2	353,000	27.4
100–199	4,600	24.9	590,600	42.7	547,400	42.5
200 or more	a	a	210,800	15.2	193,500	15.0
Geographic region:						
Northeast	4,300	23.4	302,100	21.8	274,600	21.3
North-central	5,800	31.8	472,300	34.1	446,700	34.7
South	4,200	22.9	404,000	29.2	377,800	29.3
West	4,000	21.9	205,300	14.8	188,300	14.6

Note: Figures may not add to totals due to rounding.
[a]Figure does not meet standards of reliability or precision.
Source: National Center for Health Statistics; "An overview of nursing home characteristics: Provisional data from the 1977 National Nursing Home Survey," *Advance Data,* no. 35, DHEW pub. no. (PHS) 78–1250 (Hyattsville, Md.: Public Health Service, September 6, 1978).

the other facilities, and thus accommodate almost 36 percent of all nursing-home residents.

Almost one-third of all nursing homes and more than one-third of all residents are located in the north-central region of the country. Facilities in the South are largest, averaging 96 beds (representing newer corporate-run facilities), while those in the West are smallest, averaging 51 beds.

During the 1960s all medical care prices rose much faster than prices in general. Hospital charges, for example, rose four times as fast as other items in the consumer price index (CPI). Between 1964 and 1969, the average monthly charge for care in nursing homes and rest homes of all kinds rose from $186 to $328, an increase of 76 percent. Such increases were sustained in the 1970s. By 1973–1974, average monthly costs in nursing homes had risen to $479 and between this time period and 1977 rose another 46 percent to $699. This compares with an approximate 36 percent increase in the CPI for the period. Through the 1980s to date, nursing-home charges have continued to rise at a faster pace than the CPI. According to a 1986 publication of the American Association of Retired Persons (AARP), nursing-home costs range as follows: For skilled nursing care, from $65 to about $140 a day; for intermediate nursing care, from $41 to

$70 a day; and, for custodial care, from $37 to $55 a day. These per diem charges vary as a function of ownership type, certification status, facility size and region of the country.

THE DECISION TO INSTITUTIONALIZE AN OLDER PERSON

American institutions for the elderly have an unfavorable reputation. Old-age institutions have been described as "dehumanizing" and "depersonalizing" (Townsend, 1962). Nursing-home critics describe many facilities as "human junkyards," and Frank Moss, former chairman of the U.S. Senate's Special Committee on Aging, has used the term "warehouse" to describe many nursing homes (Butler, 1975). Nursing homes have been the target of investigations of abuses in human caretaking institutions (Mendelson, 1974; Townsend, 1970). In a broad body of gerontological and popular literature, they have been accused of causing more incapacity than cure. Studies of old persons residing in a variety of institutional settings show they are more maladjusted, depressed and unhappy, have a lower range of interests and activity, and are likely to die sooner than aged persons living in the community (Lieberman, 1969).

Most elderly have a negative attitude toward life in an old-age institution. Twente (1970) studied the rural elderly and reported that of all the moves possible, the one most dreaded is that to an institution. The consensus among those studied was that what remained of freedom and independence was likely to vanish once a person was inside institutional walls.

On the basis of her national survey of the elderly, Ethel Shanas summarized the feelings about institutions as follows:

Almost all older people view the move to a home for the aged or to a nursing home with fear and hostility. . . . All old people—without exception—believe that the move to an institution is a decisive change in living arrangements, the last change he will experience before he dies. . . . Finally, no matter what the extenuating circumstances, the older person who has children interprets the move to an institution as rejection by his family. (Shanas, 1962:102–103)

Most of the old persons still living in the community, and interviewed by Tobin and Lieberman in their study of old-age institutions, anticipated that entering an institution would be a calamity. One respondent said:

Most of them go before they have to. Their children don't want them. They have no money. They're weaker. Their mates are dead. They have no choice. They play cards, look at TV, sit and look out of the window, read newspapers, listen to sermons, lecturers, debates. They have entertainment. I know everthing's regimented. You have to be up at a certain time. You have to have a bath at a certain time. Meals are at a certain time. Then there are times when you're free and you can go to the sun parlors and talk or laugh with your friends. I wouldn't like it. If I have to, because of deterioration, I would make up my mind that that's my fate. I think it's a place to die. (Tobin and Lieberman, 1976)

Despite the unfavorable reputation of old-age institutions and the negative attitudes of elderly citizens toward them, many elderly individuals need institutional care. Usually this need is apparent to family members or is based on a physician's recommendation. In fact, in cases involving illness or physical debility, the need may be apparent to the elderly patient as well. Under such conditions, wherever possible, the older person should participate in all decisions, including those of institutionalization. However, the availability and applicability of home support services should be seriously discussed and considered before a final decision on institutionalization is made.

The availability of adequate and applicable *home-care services* can prevent the institutionalization of many elderly patients. Individuals who have inconsequential lapses of memory, or who are mildly confused as a result of chronic brain syndrome, diabetes, cardiovascular disease, terminal malignancy or recent head injury, should be treated at home if adequate social-support services are available (Butler and Lewis, 1977). Individuals who need only adequate living accommodations with economic and other social-support services should not be institutionalized if it can be avoided. A distinction also needs to be made between medical hospitalization and institutionalization in a nursing home or a home for the aged, and between long-term and short-term care. Individuals with syndromes symptomatic of grave physical illness and those who are comatose, for example, are much more likely to require long-term medical hospitalization than nursing-home care.

Family members are often very much involved in decisions concerning the institutionalization of an elderly person. Many family members are extremely ambivalent about such a decision because of feelings of failure on their part and because of their negative attitudes toward old-age institutions. This may be especially true when institutionalization is done against an elderly person's wishes. Butler and Lewis (1977) point out that families who care often experience a grief reaction on admission, as though the

person had already died, and this death may be more traumatic than the actual death of the older person later on. Where possible, family members should be counseled about their own feelings of guilt and about the supportive things they can do to help the institutionalized patient.

When an aged family member is placed in a nursing home, many of the responsibilities for caring for that individual shift from the family to the institution. Still, many families continue to remain involved with that family member. Some literature suggests that when families remain involved with their relative in a nursing home, the quality of nursing-home care appears to improve.

What is the most effective way for a family to remain involved with an institutionalized relative so as to promote higher quality nursing-home care? What responsibilities do institutions have to provide support to families that want to stay involved? A first step in answering these questions and ultimately in providing optimal care is for both parties— families and nursing home staff—to understand and accept their respective responsibilities in providing services to the institutionalized individual.

Shuttlesworth and his colleagues (1982) have assessed the extent to which Texas nursing-home administrators and relatives of institutional residents have congruous attitudes about whether the nursing home or the family is responsible for performing an inventory of tasks that are essential in nursing-home care. Two findings are worthy of mention. First, both administrators and relatives assigned responsibility to the nursing home for the majority of tasks that they see as vital to care. These include technical tasks involving medical care, security, housekeeping, cooking and the like.

Second, in most cases of discrepancies, relatives were more likely than administrators to assign responsibility to families. For the most part, these discrepancies involved non-technical tasks such as room furnishings, leisure-time activities, clothing and special foods.

This study suggests that a problem in engaging families in the care of institutionalized relatives is not with the willingness of families to claim responsibility for non-technical aspects of care, but with administrators' insufficient recognition of family responsibility for non-technical tasks. As a result, administrators may fail to communicate sufficient support for family involvement in such tasks. They may overlook possible policy or procedural changes in institutional arrangements that could better facilitate family involvement in overseeing the non-technical aspects of care.

WHAT DO INSTITUTIONS DO TO THE OLD?

The gerontological literature is filled with descriptions of the institutionalized elderly as disorganized, disoriented and depressed. Tobin and Lieberman (1976) offer three sources of explanation for this portrait (these are not mutually exclusive): relocation, pre-admission effects and selection processes, and the totality of institutions.

Problems of Relocation

The relationship of environmental change to mortality and morbidity has been investigated in mental hospitals, nursing homes and homes for the aged. Moving the older person from a familiar setting into an institution, or even into surroundings similar to his own home, has been reported to cause psycho-logical disorganization and distress. Verwoerdt (1976) offers the following case:

A 74-year old man had lived alone for years in a dilapidated shack. . . . For years, the social service department had tried to improve the habitat of this recluse, but in vain. Finally, a solution seemed to present itself. A well-to-do farmer nearby had a cabin and offered it to our hermit. . . . The old man was persuaded to make the move, and a long-standing problem . . . appeared to have been solved in a humane fashion. A few days after the move, however, the social worker received an urgent call from the farmer in whose cabin the old man was now living. Upon her arrival, the social worker found the man in a state of acute confusion, he was lying in his bed, with the evidence of fecal incontinence all around him.

The significance of this episode, according to Verwoerdt, is that to the old man, home was the old shack where he had lived for decades. It was there that he felt he belonged, not in the nice new cabin. The social worker felt exactly the opposite. What she failed to realize was that the physical relocation became a psychological dislocation, with the old man losing his grip on the world.

Some investigators argue that examples such as the one given support the proposition that the disruption of life caused by relocating an elderly individual into new surroundings may create many of the effects formerly attributed to living in that new setting (Tobin and Lieberman, 1976). Further support for this proposition comes from studies on naturally occurring closings of institutions that required mass transfer of residents to new institutions. The residents showed higher than expected mortality and morbidity in the relocated populations.

Other researchers argue that it is not simply stress of relocation that may explain the effects observed after institutionalization, but also *environmental discontinuity,* the degree of change between a new and old environment. In fact, Lawton (1974) believes that the elderly, and particularly the newly institutionalized elderly, face double jeopardy in this regard. He argues that individuals with health-related incapacities are less capable of adapting to new environmental situations. Lawton states this in the *environmental docility hypothesis:* The less competent the individual in terms of personal disability or deprived status, the more susceptible is his or her behavior to the influence of immediate environmental situations.

How can the impact of environmental discontinuity be reduced for the institutional patient? Lawton (1974) suggests that one implication of the environmental docility hypothesis is that desirable behavior may be elicited, or even elevated in quality, by the provision of a favorable environment. This implies that there may be effective ways of altering an environment in order to increase the competence of an elderly individual. Carp (1966) and Lipman (1968a) have both reported on favorable changes experienced by elderly individuals during the year after a move into an age-segregated housing situation. Important in such settings are the physical proximity of age peers and the development of behavioral expectations appropriate to the level of competence of the average resident (Lawton, 1974).

Butler and Lewis (1977) recommend some practical programs that may be useful for attenuating institutional effects. Day programs, preliminary admissions for weekends, and provisions for family or friends to sleep in the institution may soften the transition to a new environment. Family and friends should be encouraged to visit regularly, and children and grandchildren should have access to the institutionalized person. These visits and the activities that accompany them may make the relationship between the institution and the community less distant.

Pre-admission Effects and Selection Processes

The older person anticipating entrance into a nursing home has arrived at this point after several steps. He or she has had to make the decision to seek care, has had to apply for admission, has waited to learn if the application has been accepted and perhaps has been placed on a waiting list. Going through these steps and anticipating moving into the institution can be very stressful. The effects of this stress on the older person before admission are often very similar to what have been described as institutional effects.

In their study of the institutionalization process, Tobin and Lieberman (1976) found that old people who were awaiting institutionalization were markedly different from those living in the community in terms of cognitive functioning, affective response, emotional state and self-perceptions. What is even more interesting is that the psychological status of the study sample awaiting institutionalization was not unlike the psychological status generally descriptive of aged persons in institutions: slight cognitive disorganization, constriction in affective response, less than optimal feelings of well-being, diminished self-esteem and depression (Tobin and Lieberman, 1976:55–56). This evidence supports the existence of an anticipatory psychosocialization process in which forces are set into motion so that the individual comes to approximate the institutionalized elderly in frame of mind even before entering the institutionalized environment.

Another explanation that has been offered in the literature is that selection biases account for the usual portrait of the institutionalized elderly. In this context, the term *selection bias* refers to the fact that people who are admitted to institutions may have characteristics that sensitize them to respond negatively to living in those institutions. In this view, it would be considered that differences found between older persons living in the community and those living in institutions are not a function of institutional life but of population differences (Tobin and Lieberman, 1976). If selection is playing a role, then, in Tobin and Lieberman's words, "the institutionalized aged share some characteristics because of who they are and not where they are."

The Total Institution

The most compelling answer to the question, "What do institutions do to the old?" has been offered by Erving Goffman (1961) in his characterization of the total institution. According to Goffman, a basic social arrangement in contemporary society is that the individual tends to sleep, play and work in different settings with different co-participants. A central feature of total institutions is the breakdown of the barriers that ordinarily separate these activities so that all three take place in the same setting with the same people. Four characteristics are necessary for the classification of an institution as total (Goffman, 1961:6): (1) all aspects of the resident's life are conducted in the same place and under the same authority; (2) each of the resident's daily activities is carried out in the immediate company of a large number of

others, all of whom are treated alike and are required to do the same thing; (3) all of the day's activities are tightly scheduled, with each leading at a prearranged time to the next, and with the sequence of events being imposed by officials at the top; (4) all activities are rationally planned and carried out for the sake of the institution.

Goffman classifies total institutions into five general categories. The first includes those places that care for persons who are perceived to be both incapable and harmless; included here are nursing homes, homes for the aged and homes for the poor and indigent. The second category includes those places that care for people who may be incapable of looking after themselves but who are perceived as possibly being a threat to the community, such as mental hospitals. The third category includes those total institutions that have been explicitly developed to protect the community against those seen as potentially dangerous, such as jails and prisons. The fourth category of total institutions includes places such as army barracks and boarding schools, which are established to allow the pursuit of work tasks of one kind or another. The final category includes institutions designed as retreats from the world; monasteries and convents are examples of total institutions that serve as training institutions for religious organizations and fit in this category.

Goffman argues that common to all total institutions is the fact that individuals in such institutions undergo a process of *self-mortification*. This process, which involves interacting with others in the institutional setting, strips the resident of his or her identity. It is also implied that this mortification of the self occurs regardless of how therapeutic or nontherapetuic the environment of the total institution happens to be. Goffman (1961:14–43) identifies the features of an institutional environment that he suggests contribute to the mortification process. These features are discussed here with particular emphasis on the old-age institution and the implications for its residents.

Admission procedures. Admission procedures typically bring loss. The individual is often stripped of personal possessions, issued institutional clothing and "shaped and coded" into an object that can be worked on smoothly by the institution. Such procedures are depersonalizing in that they serve to detach the individual from the social system at large. Jules Henry (1973) refers to this as "depersonalization through symbolic means," with a person even losing his or her name, or being addressed as "you" instead of as "Mrs. Jones."

Barriers. The total institution places barriers between the resident and the outside world that result in a loss of roles that are a part of the resident's self. Most institutionalized individuals are simply not able to play the roles of mother and father, grandmother and grandfather, aunt or uncle, and friend in the way these roles were played on the outside. The quantity of interaction is perhaps most obviously affected. Many facilities reduce or withhold the privilege of having visitors. Others do not allow residents to leave the premises for day or overnight trips. Some facilities bar minors from visiting. Telephones are often inaccessible. All institutional persons face the loss of a familiar way of living. Most describe it simply in terms of losing others and leaving their families' possessions at home. A resident of Murray Manor comments as follows:

And it wasn't easy, you know, living alone. It was hard breaking up a home that you've had, you know, and entertained a lot. And I had a lot of friends. They always felt free to come in. Well, of course, it's limited here. I miss the activity (at home), but I wouldn't be able to do. . . . I'm eighty years old. I'm gonna be eighty-one and I know I wouldn't be able to do what I did before. (Gubrium, 1975:85–86).

Deference obligations. Because total institutions deal with almost all the aspects of a resident's life, there is a special need to obtain the resident's cooperation. Thus, the resident may be required to show physical and verbal deference to the staff members or be subject to punishment. Such deference may be humiliating and result in loss of self-esteem. Often the individual is asked to engage in activity whose symbolic implications are incompatible with conceptions of self. Sharon Curtin (1972) describes the case of Miss Larson at shower time in the Montcliffe Convalescent Hospital:

I could hear Miss Larson. "No, no, I can bathe myself, just let me alone, I can do it" . . . Two aides, one on each side, would pick up the old carcasses, place them in a molded plastic shower chair, deftly remove the blanket, push them under the shower and rather haphazardly soap them down . . . The aides were quick, efficient, not at all brutal; they kept up a running conversation between themselves about food prices, the new shoes one had bought, California divorce laws. They might have been two sisters doing dishes. Lift, scrub, rinse, dry, put away. And did you hear that one about. . . .

Verbal or physical humiliation. Residents may have to beg or humbly ask for little things, such as a glass of water or permission to use the telephone. Staff or fellow residents may call the resident obscene names, curse him, publicly point out his negative attributes or talk about him as if he were not there. At the extreme there may be loss of a sense of personal safety—beatings, shock therapies or in some cases the understanding that one will be denied necessary treatment—that may lead residents to feel they are in an environment that does not guarantee their physical integrity.

Contaminative exposure. On the outside, the individual can hold his or her feelings about self, actions, thoughts and some possessions clear from others. In the total institution these areas of self are violated. Facts about the resident's social status and past behavior, including negative information, are collected upon admission and continually recorded and made available to staff. Physical contamination, such as unclean food, messy quarters, shoes and clothing soiled by previous users and interpersonal contamination such as forced social relationships and denial of privacy may occur as well.

Admission procedures, barriers, deference obligations, verbal or physical humiliation and contaminative exposure are the mortifying processes that patients are subject to in old-age and other institutions. These processes must also be adapted to by the patient. Goffman (1961) identifies four modes of adaptation to the processes of mortification that take place in an institution. The first, "situational withdrawal," occurs most frequently in old-age institutions and can be described in terms previously used to describe institutional effects. The patient withdraws from everything around him or her, and there is a drastic curtailment of interaction. "Regression" occurs and is often irreversible. A second mode of adaptation is what Goffman calls the "intransigent line":

The inmate intentionally challenges the institution by flagrantly refusing to cooperate with staff members. This mode of adaptation can lead to patient abuse. Stannard (1973) reports on an example of patient abuse in a nursing home. Two accounts of the events emerged. The incident took place as follows.

> That night the evening shift was also short of help; there were four people to do the work of nine . . . Early in the evening an orderly went to put a patient, Mr. Jones, to bed. The patient had soiled himself and his bed. According to the nurse, the orderly had the "good sense" to clean him and change his linen. . . . He undressed the patient and put him in the bath tub. After washing him, the orderly went to get a towel and clean linen, but there were none in the closet. . . . He went to the basement for some clean towels and linen. . . . The orderly returned to the floor at about the same time and found Mr. Jones sitting in a tub of hot water with the faucet on. . . . They picked the patient up, wrapped him in a clean sheet, and put him in bed . . . (and) did not tell the nurse what happened. . . . The evening nurse "happened" to look in on Mr. Jones. There, lying in bed, was Mr. Jones with the skin and tissue on his legs and lower trunk "coming off in hunks" . . . . The nurse called an ambulance, and he was taken to a local hospital.

In the official explanation, the nurses and the owners of the nursing home theorized that the patient, in his mental confusion, was attracted by the shininess of the faucet and reached out for it, accidentally turning on the hot water. He sat there while the tub filled with hot water until he was found. The patient died two weeks after the scalding.

Some time after the patient's death a second, unofficial account of the events surfaced. According to this version, the orderly put the patient into the tub of hot water in order to punish the patient for cursing him. This patient was one who rarely spoke to people except in anger or fear. He would often curse, usually calling someone a "son of a bitch." This patient had only one visitor, a wife, who rarely came to the home. The shortage of help that night gave the orderly the chance to use a form of punishment on the patient.

Two other modes of adaptation to the total institution, described by Goffman, are "colonization" and "conversion." Patients who take a colonization tack accept the sampling of the outside world provided by the institution and build a stable, contented existence by attempting to procure the maximum satisfaction available in the home. Such patients turn the institution into a home away from home and may find it difficult to leave. As Goffman (1961:63) points out, the staff who try to make life in total institutions more bearable must face the possibility that doing so may increase the likelihood of colonization. Patients who convert take on the staff view of the patient and often attempt to act out the role of perfect patient. A patient employing this mode of adaptation might adopt the manner and dress of the attendants while helping them to manage other patients.

THE QUALITY OF INSTITUTIONAL CARE

While Goffman implies that mortification of the self is characteristic of all total institutions (no matter how therapeutic the environment), it makes intuitive sense that some institutional settings are more or less mortifying than others.

How such evaluations are made is often difficult to determine. Health care practitioners and researchers find the issue of evaluating institutional care to be extraordinarily complex. Clearly, a dirty, crowded, understaffed nursing home in which old people live unhappily and die rapidly is a bad institution. But what is a good one? Should quality be measured in terms of resident satisfaction or professional nursing care? Given limited resources, is it more important to spend money on gardeners, interior design, janitorial services and food quality, or on an abundance of aides, orderlies and health professionals?

Obviously, no one type of facility will be best for all types of people. However, it is important to recognize the complexity of quality and to deal with its many aspects. Looking at federal and state regulations, we see that the emphasis has been almost exclusively on promoting higher standards of safety and health care. Still, this same regulatory power could be used to influence esthetic features of facility design, the incorporation of educational and recreational activities into facility programs, and other features related to "quality of life." Thoughtful persons in a position to influence the regulation and development of old-age institutions will be frustrated by the current state of research into quality.

Researchers have generally taken one of two approaches to the investigation of quality. One method is to devise a list of "probable indicators" of quality and to study what types of facilities rate high. For example, Anderson, Holmberg, Schneider, and Stone (1969) thought that the following would be important characteristics in the quality of nursing homes: the number of patients per room and bathroom; whether the facility had been originally designed as a nursing home; the number of staff hours per patient; patient participation in various activities; and the therapeutic orientation of the administration. They found higher quality in facilities that had fewer welfare patients, higher costs, rural location, and larger size; in those that were attached to hospitals; those with fewer ambulatory patients; and those that were accredited. One problem with this approach to the measurement of quality is that we often do not really know what difference it makes to the patient; for example, having more nurses available. Gottesman and Bourestom (1974) made detailed observation of 1,144 residents in 40 licensed nursing homes in Detroit. Less than one in four (23 percent) residents were observed receiving any nursing contacts at all; however, based on direct testing, one-half of the sample was either moderately or very confused and 40 percent were reported to need some assistance in activities of daily living.

A second approach has been to study a probable indicator, such as crowding or staffing patterns, in relation to various outcome measures—resident satisfaction, social participation, staff performance and the like (Dick and Friedsam, 1964; Lawton, 1974; Schooler, 1969). The problem with this type of investigation is that, as Alexander Pope put it, "we murder to dissect." In other words, if we know that residents are happiest in small homes, new homes, homes with many nurses and homes in rural areas, we still do not know much about small, new homes, with many nurses, in rural areas.

A third approach, rarely used, is that employed by Taietz (1953) in his admirable study of three homes for the aged, completed some 35 years ago. Taietz selected homes of high, medium and low quality as determined by professionals working in the area. He found that resident happiness was indeed highest in the home judged to be of the best quality by outside observers; however, he also found that the characteristics that made this home the best in professional eyes were not in many cases what made it the best environment for the residents.

A number of researchers have looked to the relationship between institutional characteristics and quality of care. For example, it is generally believed that non-profit facilities provide higher quality care than do proprietary facilities. Townsend (1962) devised a multiple-item index of quality of care and surveyed 173 British institutions for the aged. He reported that voluntary non-profit homes were the best, proprietary homes occupied a middle position and public homes were the worst. The National Health Survey's studies of old-age institutions report that residents in proprietary facilities are in the poorest health and have the shortest mean length of stay compared to residents in facilities under government or non-profit management (U.S. Department of Health, Education and Welfare, 1968, 1972, 1973).

Not all empirical studies support the above-described relationship between ownership and quality of care. In a study of 129 Massachusetts nursing homes in 1965 and 1969, Levey, Ruchlin, Stotsky, Kinloch and Oppenheim (1973) looked at the relationship between quality of care, ownership and cost. Three types of facility (non-corporate proprietary, corporate proprietary and corporate charitable) were rated on a nine-component aggregate quality-of-care scale. The researchers found no significant relationship between quality of care and facility ownership. In both 1965 and 1969, the highest per capita per diem costs were reported by corporate charitable homes, and the lowest by non-corporate proprietary homes.

When the authors employed a multiple-regression technique to explain variation in their 1969 quality-of-care rating, no significant relationship appeared between the dependent variable and ownership. Thus, while cost was not related to quality of care and ownership, ownership was not related to quality. Disaggregating the quality-of-care scale into its nine major components and analyzing each score by type of ownership also showed no significant differences among ownership types. The individual dimensions of quality included measures relating to the personal care of patients, the maintenance of patient records, patient activities, equipment and resources available, nursing personnel and services and the physical plant.

Institutional size is another characteristic believed to be related to quality care. Greenwald and Linn (1971) have suggested that as nursing homes get larger, activity and communication decline. Curry and Ratliff (1973) argue that a person's life satisfaction is likely to be influenced by certain aspects of his or her current environment. They contend that since smaller facilities generally have a more homelike atmosphere than larger facilities, smaller homes create fewer disruptions in accustomed living arrangements. They suggested that this ought to favor resident satisfaction.

Studying a sample of Ohio proprietary nursing homes, Curry and Ratliff (1973) found that the residents of the smaller facilities had more friends within the home, more monthly contacts with these friends, and more total monthly contacts, despite the fact that residents of the larger homes had more living relatives and more contacts with these relatives. This may suggest that increased sociability developed within the smaller homes as a result of the greater proximity of residents.

Three additional characteristics of facilities that have interested investigators concerned with quality are socioeconomic status, social integration and professionalism. These are discussed below.

Socioeconomic status. The socioeconomic status of an institution has several components, including the socioeconomic status of the residents and staff, the resources of the facility and possibly the price of care in the facility. Surprisingly little work has been done relative to the socioeconomic status of institutions and quality of care. The gerontological truism seems to be that upper-class identification implies greater resources, which in turn implies a higher quality of care. Empirical studies partially support this easy assumption.

In a survey conducted in 1969 of 126 Minnesota nursing homes, Anderson and her colleagues (1969) found that quality of care was inversely related to the percentage of welfare patients in a facility, and positively correlated with daily per capita facility expenditures. Levey and others (1973), studying Massachusetts facilities, report that quality of care was higher in those that spent more money.

Kosberg (1971, 1973) studied the relationship between organizational characteristics and treatment resources (e.g., professional personnel, equipment) in 214 Chicago area nursing homes. He found only a modest relationship between level of care offered and available resources. But availability of resources in the facilities was highly correlated with the characteristics of resident populations. It appears, for example, that the non-affluent and minority elderly are often institutionalized in homes lacking treatment resources. These populations are often further inconvenienced by being placed in facilities located farther from their families and previous homes than are the affluent elderly.

Social integration.   Very little is known about the attempts of old-age institutions to promote the development of new social relationships to replace other social relationships abandoned in the process of aging.

Jacobs (1969) has reported on the adjustment of a group of 46 women occupying one-half of a floor in a Jewish home for the aged. Using a conflict model, she views inter- and intra-group conflict as measures of integration and adjustment, respectively. In the institution she observed, conflict promoted interaction, which in turn led to a group cohesiveness and solidarity among the women. Suppression of conflict was seen as a barrier to adjustment for these women.

Lipman (1968b), using what he calls a socio-architectural approach, examined the relationship between seating patterns and social interaction in three homes for the aged in England. He found that while sustained verbal interaction was a factor in establishing friendships, the residents' practice of regularly occupying particular chairs and the fixed furniture arrangements seemed to limit the scope and range of possible friendships in the home. He proposed, from a disengagement perspective, that regular occupation of chairs in fixed arrangements may be a preferred manner of coming to terms with enforced proximity to others in institutions.

Bennett (1963) has argued that as institutions for the elderly become more "total," increased regimentation occurs. Administrators may foster a feeling of dependence and inactivity in residents by discouraging close relationships among residents and between them and the staff. The end result may be increased feelings of isolation and powerlessness on the part of the residents.

Gelfand (1968) tested the general hypothesis that social adjustment among the institutionalized aged is related to the totality of the institution; he also tested the more specific hypothesis that adjustment is related to the degree to which residents have access to the outside community. A sample of 32 women and men residing in a St. Louis old-age home was used. All members of the group were both ambulatory and in good mental health. High correlations were reported for the relationship between outside visiting and adjustment, sociability and adjustment, and sociability and outside visiting. The author's explanation of these findings reflected a fourth relationship, that between outside visiting and identification with the home. He argued that the ability of residents to visit outside the institution increases acceptance of the home and its goals and thus promotes greater social adjustment.

Grant (1970) discussed the relationship between age-segregated housing and the satisfaction of the elderly. From his review of the gerontological literature, it appears that age-homogeneous housing contributes to high morale and life satisfaction for the aged. However, we cannot generalize from this conclusion to the organization of all old-age institutions. Kahana and Kahana (1967), studying a psychiatric facility, found that placing newly admitted patients in an age-integrated rather than age-segregated ward had a stimulating effect on social interaction.

Professionalism.   Institutions vary in the degree of sophistication of management, the proportion of highly trained professionals on the staff and the manner in which formally prescribed procedures are carried out. These elements, among others, contribute to what might be called a professionalism factor. We know of no studies dealing specifically with this composite characteristic. However, the results of some related studies suggest that professionalism and some aspects of quality of patient care may be inversely related.

One study of Massachusetts nursing facilities reported a great increase between 1965 and 1969 in the proportion of facilities in compliance with regulatory standards for eight out of nine quality-of-care measures (Levey et al., 1973). However, a measure on which compliance declined from 1965 to 1969 related to personal care of the patients. In 1965, 90 percent of all facilities were in compliance on patient personal care (e.g., patient is clean, has clean clothes, is well-groomed); by 1969 this had fallen to 78 percent. Similarly, for care of the bedside unit, the percentage in compliance decreased from 60 to 55 percent. On facility-oriented items (e.g., personnel records, diet orders, medical records, and so on) compliance had improved dramatically.

A number of researchers have pointed out the difficulties involved in sorting old-age institutions into state licensure categories (for example, Manard, Kart and van Gils, 1975). Generally speaking, however, lower-level facilities are less professional than higher-level ones. Beattie and Bullock (1964) reported that St. Louis facilities licensed as homes for the aged received more favorable observer ratings of social milieu and administrator's attitudes than did facilities licensed for nursing care, practical nursing care or domiciliary care. In addition, the personnel of homes for the aged were reported to have more positive attitudes toward the residents than had the personnel of other facility types.

Someone looking for suggestions on how to choose a quality nursing facility for an aged friend or relative might, on the basis of a reading of the preceding literature, select an institution that is non-proprietary, relatively small in size, wealthy in resources, sociable and with a staff that has positive attitudes toward the residents. Unfortunately, such institutions are rare. Their scarcity directs us to a serious problem with the research literature—its inability to direct one toward answers to the question, "How can the quality of care in the remaining facilities be improved?" As many are aware, sufficient licensing procedures and operating regulations already exist, although some cynics suggest that even the inspectors and regulators themselves admit regulation is a poor tool for assuring quality institutional care.

A report by Senator Moss's Subcommittee on Long-Term Care (U.S. Senate Special Committee on Aging, 1974), in the chapter "Nursing Home Inspections: A National Farce," pointed out the following:

1. Few weapons exist other than the threat of license revocation to bring a facility into compliance with operating regulations.
2. Because of legal and administrative procedures required, license revocation is itself ineffective.
3. In many instances in which revocation is implemented, judges are reluctant to close a facility when an operator claims deficiencies are being corrected.
4. Inspections are geared to surveying the physical plant rather than evaluating the quality of care.

What is the answer, then? A principle that one hears discussed is accountability—but to whom and for what? Barney (1974) proposes that facilities be accountable to the community for the care they provide, with this accountability ensured by direct community involvement. Gaynes (1973) and Tobin (1974) also suggest "community-based-sponsored institutional facilities" as substitutes for the worst homes, which do not now provide needed services for the chronically ill elderly. Gottesman (1974) advises administrative changes to make all homes accountable for providing the kind of responsible high-quality care observed in many non-profit facilities.

The past record on administrative and regulatory changes, however, is not good. As Mendelson and Hapgood (1974) point out, personal connections between the industry and its regulators, occasional instances of blatant corruption and downright bureaucratic weariness have deterred attempts in this sphere before, and new approaches may be necessary. These same authors argue, however, that lack of continued effective public pressure is the most basic reason for the failure of nursing home regulation. It is just this lack of sustained public pressure that may prove problematic for proposals related to community involvement. Still, lack of public pressure itself may be symptomatic rather than causal. On the one hand, although the population of old persons continues to grow faster than any other age group, and the institutional population is increasing as well, only a small proportion of the general population is believed to have any experience with aged institutionalized individuals. Thus relatively few of the non-institutionalized have personal experience with old-age institutions. On the other hand, lack of public pressure may be symptomatic of an old bugaboo with which gerontologists are quite familiar—deep-rooted fears and attitudes toward aging and death.

SUMMARY

Currently, more than 1 million elderly individuals (about 5 percent of the aged population) reside in nursing homes in the United States. Typically, this population is white, female, widowed, over 75 and has lived in an institutional facility for more than two years. Over 80 percent of nursing-home residents were admitted primarily for physical reasons.

The great majority of nursing homes in the United States today are run for profit. The average number of beds in U.S. facilities is 76. Three-quarters of all homes are certified to participate in Medicare or Medicaid or both.

Nursing homes have an unfavorable reputation, and elderly individuals often have strong negative feelings toward being institutionalized, even when institutional care is absolutely necessary. In part, this results from the portrait the gerontological literature paints of the institutionalized elderly. This population is overwhelmingly characterized as disorganized, disoriented and depressed. Three explanations for this negative portrait are discussed. These include problems of relocation, pre-admission effects and selection processes and the totality of institutions.

A body of literature dealing with the quality of institutional care is reviewed, and it was determined that the "best" institutions are nonprofit, small in size, wealthy in resources, sociable and with staff that have positive attitudes toward the residents. Unfortunately, such institutions are quite rare.

KEY TERMS

environmental discontinuity
environmental docility hypothesis
extended-care facility (ECF)
intermediate nursing care

Medicaid
Medicare
proprietary nursing homes
selection bias
self-mortification
skilled nursing care
total institution

STUDY QUESTIONS

1. Explain the fallacy of assuming that the institutionalization rate for the elderly could be used as an estimation of their cumulative chances for institutionalization.
2. Describe the "typical" nursing-home resident. Explain the disproportionate number of women and the underrepresentation of non-whites in nursing homes.
3. Discuss the relative importance of Medicare and Medicaid in relation to coverage for nursing-home care.
4. List some major organizational dimensions along which nursing homes vary. How have nursing-home costs increased in relation to prices in general? How and why do charges vary between different nursing homes?
5. Explain the impact of environmental discontinuity on the nursing home resident. What steps can be taken to reduce the effects of institutionalization?
6. What is the process of "self-mortification" as defined by Goffman? List and explain the features of institutional environment that he suggests contribute to the mortification process.
7. Explain how the ownership, size, socioeconomic status, social integration and staff professionalism of an institution are related to the quality of institutional care.

BIBLIOGRAPHY

Anderson, N., Holmberg, R., Schneider, R., and Stone, L. 1969. *Policy Issues Regarding Nursing Homes, Findings from a Minnesota Study.* Minneapolis, Minn.: Institute for Interdisciplinary Studies, American Rehabilitation Foundation.

Barney, J. 1974. Community pressure as a key to quality of life in nursing homes. *American Journal of Public Health* 64: 265–268.

Beattie, W., and Bullock, J. 1964. Evaluating services and personnel in facilities for the aged. In M. Leeds, and H. Shore, eds., *Geriatric Institutional Management.* New York: G.P. Putnam.

Bennett, R. 1963. The meaning of institutional life. *Gerontologist* 3: 117–125.

Brody, S.J. 1984. Goals of geriatric care. In S. Brody and N. Persily, eds., *Hospitals and the Aged: The New Old Market.* Rockville, Md: Aspen Publishing.

Butler, R.N. 1975. *Why Survive? Being Old in America.* New York: Harper & Row.

———, and Lewis, M. 1977. *Aging and Mental Health,* 2nd ed. St. Louis, Mo.: Mosby.

Carp, F.M. 1966. *A Future for the Aged.* Austin, Tex.: University of Texas Press.

Curry, T., and Ratliff, B. W. 1973. The effects of nursing home size on resident isolation and life satisfaction. *Gerontologist* 13: 296–298.

Curtin, S. 1972. *Nobody Ever Died of Old Age.* Boston: Little, Brown.

Dick, H.R., and Friedsam, H. 1964. Adjustment of residents of two homes for the aged. *Social Problems.* 27: 282–290.

Fox, P.D., and Clauser, S.V. 1980. Trends in nursing home expenditures: Implications for aging policy. *Health Care Finance Review* 2(Fall): 65–70.

Gaynes, N.L. 1973. A logic to long-term care. *Gerontologist* 13: 277–281.

Gelfand, D.E. 1968. Visiting patterns and social adjustment in an old age home. *Gerontologist* 8: 272–275.

Goffman, E. 1961. *Asylums.* New York: Doubleday.

Gottesman, L. 1974. Nursing home performance as related to resident traits, ownership, size, and source of payment. *American Journal of Public Health* 64: 269–281.

———, and Bourestom, N. 1974. Why nursing homes do what they do. *Gerontologist* 14: 501–506.

Grant, D.P. 1970. Architect discovers the aged. *Gerontologist* 10: 275–281.

Greenwald, S. R., and Linn, M. W. 1971. Intercorrelations of data on nursing homes. *Gerontologist* 11: 337–340.

Gubrium, J. 1975. *Living and Dying at Murray Manor.* New York: St. Martin's Press.

Henry, J. 1973. Personality and aging—with special reference to hospitals for the aged poor. In J. Henry, ed., *On Shame, Vulnerability and Other Forms of Self-Destruction.* New York: Random House.

Hing, E. 1981. *Characteristics of Nursing Home Residents, Health Status and Care Received.* Vital and Health Statistics, Series 13, No. 51. Washington, D.C.: U.S. Government Printing Office.

Jacobs, R. 1969. One-way street: An intimate view of adjustment. *Gerontologist 9:* 268–275.

Kahana, E., and Kahana, B. 1967. The effects of age segregation on interaction patterns of elderly psychiatric patients. Paper presented at the annual meeting of the American Psychological Association, Washington, D.C.

Kart, C.S., and Beckham, B. 1976. Black–white differentials in the institutionalization of the elderly. *Social Forces 54:* 901–910.

Kastenbaum, R., and Candy, S. 1973. The 4 percent fallacy: A methodological and empirical critique of extended care facility population statistics. *International Journal of Aging and Human Development 4:* 15–21.

Koff, T.H. 1982. *Long Term Care: An Approach to Serving the Frail Elderly.* Boston: Little, Brown.

Kosberg, J. 1971. The relationship between organizational characteristics and treatment resources in nursing homes. Ph.D. dissertation, University of Chicago.

——————. 1973. Differences in proprietary institutions care for affluent and nonaffluent elderly. *Gerontologist 13:* 299–304.

Lawton, M.P. 1974. Social ecology and the health of older people. *American Journal of Public Health 64:* 257–260.

Levey, S., Ruchlin, H.S., Stotsky, B.A., Kinloch, D.R., and Oppenheim, W. 1973. An appraisal of nursing home care. *Journal of Gerontology 28:* 222–228.

Lieberman, M. 1969. Institutionalization of the aged: Effects of behavior. *Gerontology 24:* 330–340.

Lipman, A. 1968a. Public housing and attitudinal adjustment in old age: A comparative study. *Journal of Geriatric Psychiatry 2:* 88–101.

——————. 1968b. A socio-architectural view of life in three old peoples' homes. *Gerontology Clinician 10:* 88–101.

Manard, B., Kart, C.S., and van Gils, D. 1975. *Old Age Institutions.* Lexington, Mass.: D.C. Heath.

Mendelson, M.A. 1974. *Tender Loving Greed.* New York: Random House.

——————, and Hapgood, D. 1974. The political economy of nursing homes. *Annals of the American Academy of Political and Social Sciences 415:* 95–105.

National Center for Health Statistics. 1978. An overview of nursing home characteristics: Provisional data from the 1977 National Nursing Home Survey. *Advance Data from Vital and Health Statistics,* No. 35, Hyattsville, Md.: Public Health Service, Sept. 6, 1978.

Palmore, E. 1976. Total chance of institutionalization among the elderly. *Gerontologist 16:* 504–507.

Schooler, K. 1969. The relationship between social interaction and morale of the elderly as a function of environmental characteristics. *Gerontologist 9:* 25–29.

Shanas, E. 1962. *The Health of Older People: A Social Survey.* Cambridge, Mass.: Harvard University Press.

Shuttlesworth, G.E., Rubin, A., and Duffy, M. 1982. Families versus institutions: Incongruent role expectations in the nursing home. *Gerontologist 22*(2): 200–208.

Stannard, C. 1973. Old folks and dirty work: The social conditions for patient abuse in a nursing home. *Social Problems 20:* 329–342.

Taietz, P. 1953. Administrative practices and personal adjustment in homes for the aged. *Cornell Experiment Station Bulletin.*

Tobin, S. 1974. How nursing homes vary. *Gerontologist 14:* 516–519.

——————, and Lieberman, M. 1976. *The Last Home for the Aged.* San Francisco: Jossey-Bass.

Townsend, C. 1970. *Old Age: The Last Segregation.* New York: Grossman Publishers.

Townsend, P. 1962. *The Last Refuge.* London: Routledge & Kegan Paul.

Twente, E. 1970. *Never Too Old: The Aged in Community Life.* San Francisco: Jossey-Bass.

U.S. Bureau of the Census. 1985. *Statistical Abstract of the United States: 1986*. Washington, D.C.: U.S. Government Printing Office.

U.S. Department of Health, Education and Welfare. 1968. *Nursing and Personal Care Services, U.S., May–June, 1964*. Public Health Service. Hyattsville, Md.: U.S. Government Printing Office.

_____ . 1972. *Nursing Homes: Their Admission Policies, Admissions and Discharges, U.S., April–September, 1968*. Public Health Service. Hyattsville, Md.: U.S. Government Printing Office.

_____ . 1973. *Characteristics of Residents in Nursing and Personal Care Homes, U.S., June–August, 1969*. Public Health Service. Hyattsville, Md.: U.S. Government Printing Office.

_____ . 1977. *Characteristics, Social Contacts, and Activities of Nursing Home Residents. U. S. 1973 National Nursing Home Survey*. DHEW Pub. No (HRA) 77–1778. Public Health Service. Hyattsville, Md.: U.S. Government Printing Office.

_____ . 1978. Elderly people: The population 65 years and over. In *Health, United States, 1976–1977*. DHEW Pub. No (HRA) 77–1232. Public Health Service. Hyattsville, Md.: U.S. Government Printing Office.

U.S. Senate Special Committee on Aging. 1974. *Nursing Home Care in the U.S.: Failure in Public Policy*. Washington, D.C.: U.S. Government Printing Office.

_____ . 1982. *Developments in Aging*. Vol. 1. Report 97–314, 97th Congress, Second Session. Washington, D.C.: U. S. Government Printing Office.

Verwoerdt, A. 1976. *Clinical Geropsychiatry*. Baltimore, Md.: Williams and Wilkins.

CHAPTER **20**

Alternatives to Institutionalization

Ruth E. Dunkle, Ph.D.

This chapter focuses specifically on types of services that are alternatives to institutionalization and, more broadly, on how and why these services exist. Assessment of needs and issues involved in matching client to service will be explored as well as the policy and financing issues that shape these services.

ASSESSING NEEDS AND MATCHING SERVICES

Receiving needed long-term care services can be a complex task. It exceeds the ability to pay and involves, among other issues, the attitude of the patient as well as that of the care provider. Ageism, patient passivity, the time-income factor and Medicare (Libow, 1977) are just a few of the service delivery barriers for older persons.

In general, the elderly are reluctant to admit need or accept help and may even deny using services (Moen, 1978). When they do use services, it is most likely those that are perceived as earned, not services that are based on a means test with income the root of eligibility (Moen, 1978). The use of services requires geographical proximity to those services. Although models of service delivery to the aged are relatively scarce (Smith, 1971), urban areas have been able to provide a greater variety of services at a lower per capita cost (Williams, Youmans and Sorensen, 1975).

Service organization has been found also to affect utilization (McKinley, 1972), but little seems to be known about the decision-making process that leads to service utilization (Ward, 1977). Knowledge of variation in service use among different groups of the elderly is sparse. For instance, little is known about aged blacks or immigrants (Ward, 1977). One study on racial difference in help-seeking behavior noted that older whites seemed more likely than blacks to exaggerate their problems to justify seeking care (McCaslin and Calvert, 1975). Youmans (1974) indicates that there is a geographic difference in attitudes regarding health and dependency that may subsequently affect service receptivity. Income has little effect on service use (Ward, 1977), but people with health insurance seem to consume more services (Wan and Soifer, 1974; Kronenfeld, 1978). Transportation affects utilization among older patients but not younger ones (Garitz and Peth, 1974).

One major consideration in service utilization is access. In part, access depends on information about available services. As shown in a study of ambulatory elderly in New York City, there is a need to provide information about services that would be required in an emergency (Auerbach, Gordon, Ullman and Weisel, 1977). Access is also related to socioeconomic, cultural, psychological and organizational barriers, and not merely availability of service (Wan, 1982).

In summary, while knowledge regarding service use is incomplete, it is clear that service creation is not enough to insure use. As Ward indicates (1977:66), "Making services objectively available to older people is not sufficient—they must perceive a need, know about the service, view it as appropriate, etc." Little (1982) takes this perspective one step further to discuss the design of services for older people: The key issues are political or allocative—who delivers the service, where the service is delivered, when the service is delivered and who receives the service.

With the needs and desires for service for the older person changing over time, the issues in service delivery also change. Unfortunately, this is not always readily acknowledged by those providing the service, including family members and agency personnel (Kahana, 1974). Kahana (1974) concludes that there is a great deal of overlap in areas of need unmatched by available services that tend to be isolated bandaid offerings.

By and large, kin provide care to older relatives. The estimate of need by elderly persons who live in the community and require some kind of supportive services ranges from 12 to 40 percent (Brody, 1981). It is only when relatives are not available or cannot do more to help that formal organizations become involved in the caregiving process. Litwak (1965, 1978) argues that the dependency needs of the elderly are best met if there is a proper balance between formal and informal support, with each system performing the tasks for which it is best suited.

Litwak (1985) also predicts that the delivery of appropriate services to older people may ultimately require that three moves be made. First, when the older person's health is good, he or she is likely to benefit from living in an age-homogeneous community. Second, when disability occurs, the ideal living arrangement is an age-heterogeneous community near the older person's children. Finally, if disability progresses to the point that the person needs 24-hour care, the best environment is a nursing home.

Each of these moves involves an attempt to match the caregiving task with the most appropriate group structure. According to Litwak (1985), making this match requires completing five main tasks. These include (1) tasks requiring continual proximity or distance; (2) tasks requiring long- or short-term commitment; (3) tasks requiring large or small groups; (4) tasks requiring common or different life styles; and (5) tasks requiring internalized forms of motivation versus those requiring instrumental ones. Older people can optimize their goal achievement if they have a network consisting of friends, neighbors, spouses, kin and acquaintances (Litwak, 1985). Litwak believes that all groups are necessary and cannot easily substitute for one another in providing appropriate care.

Mismatch between service and need can occur for several reasons. Many times a false dichotomy is thought to exist between cure and care; long-term care is sometimes viewed as an alternative to cure. At times long-term care is not viewed in all its components (logistical, medical, psychological and social). Rather, it is viewed as either formal or informal and only provided in one type of setting. As a recent report of the Institute of Medicine (1985:23) states, "Long term care has been a chronic misfit in the United States health care and social services programs."

TYPES OF SERVICES

Unlike service provision to people in younger age groups, services that are considered alternatives to institutionalization are designed and delivered to the older person and his or her support network. Typically, institutionalization is the result of an older person's decline in health along with family members who are unavailable, unwilling or unable to provide care.

How older people choose which service they will use is determined by a complex set of interacting personal and environmental facts (McAuley and Blieszner, 1985). Personal, demographic, psychological, economic and health-related factors come into play. Environmental issues relate to the availability of informal support, and community and institutional services (Branch and Jette, 1982; Soldo, 1981). While several researchers have identified sets of predictors of institutional vs. home-based long-term care (Branch and Jette, 1982; Greenberg and Genn, 1979), few have examined how older people might select from various types of long-term care services. Indeed, many older community residents may not understand the services existing apart from the nursing home.

Stoller (1982) asked elderly persons living in the community what they would do if they were ill and needed constant care. Thirty percent could not name any strategy for obtaining care. For those who did, the nursing home was mentioned most frequently. In a study of hospitalized elders making long-term care arrangements, Dunkle and associates (1982) found that when these patients were asked about existing services in their own communities, the majority had no idea what was available. Lack of a strategy for providing long-term care services may result from avoidance as much as from ignorance. Furthermore, even if a selection is made, many elderly persons do not know in advance what long-term care arrangements they would find most acceptable (McAuley and Blieszner, 1985).

When arrangements require a change of residence, people most often identify a nursing home, not a relative's home, as the residence of preference. One study found the nursing home to be the long-term care arrangement of choice for non-whites and unmarried persons with higher incomes who felt they had no one to care for them for an extended period (McAuley and Blieszner, 1985). Adult day care was the choice of younger persons and non-whites in better health as well as those who had more emotional problems. Paid home care seemed more appealing for whites with emotional problems.

We really do not know enough about the views of various long-term care arrangements held by family members of elderly persons who are prospective consumers of such services. We do not know if the views of the elderly and their family members differ with regard to the perceived efficacy of these various arrangements (Neu, 1982), or even if congruence of view is related in any way to successful outcomes for the elderly person.

Informal Service

The main source of support for older persons is the family. Yet research findings indicate that residing with relatives is not the living arrangement of choice for most elderly persons. Kobrin (1981) and Troll and her colleagues (1979) found that when older people were physically and financially able to live independently, they did so. Living with relatives was typically a result of impaired health or low income. Certain living arrangements do, however, appear more satisfying than

others. Johnson (1983) found that dissatisfaction with caregiving arrangements is more likely when the caregiver is a child rather than a spouse. Johnson suggests that dissatisfaction may result from a change in the relationship between child and parent when the parent becomes ill. A norm of obligation can surface, resulting in ambivalence in both child and parent. For the parent, the end product of such ambivalence is dissatisfaction with care provided by the child. Implicit is the assumption that the elderly person receiving care does not feel this ambivalence toward the caregiving spouse. Presumably, this is because caregiving is considered part of the marital relationship.

Various family members seem to be used for caregiving, depending on the type of help required. For instance, the main source of support for the bedfast and homebound is the husband or wife of the invalid. Children, whether they live inside or outside the house, are a second important source of help. Not all older persons have children; about 13 percent of elderly Americans have no surviving children. Childless elders rely on other sources of informal support. Barbara Silverstone (1985: 156) describes this support system as, "a rich fabric of informal relationships which envelopes the majority of elders in our society along a number of dimensions. This fabric is bonded most strongly by marriage, and adjacent generational and peer relationships and for racial minorities, by expanded kin as well."

It is generally recognized that family and other informal supports cannot provide help on a long-term basis to elders who are impaired and disabled (Shanas, 1979; Litman, 1971). The informal network of friends and neighbors who provide help with nonpersonal tasks of daily living do so to supplement, not compete with or compensate for, other types of help.

Emotional, physical and financial strains appear to be associated with personal and situational characteristics of the caregiver, with emotional strain seemingly the hardest to bear (Cantor, 1981; Horowitz, 1981). Isolation of a caregiver, as well as a decrease in emotional resilience and morale (Archbold, 1980), may provoke many elderly persons and their families to turn to formal service providers for help.

Formal Services

For many older persons the need to consider long-term care confronts them first in a hospital. About 20 percent of all older people use inpatient facilities at least once a year. In fact, hospitals service more elderly persons than any other community agency (Brody and Persily, 1984). Older persons also have more long-lasting hospital stays than younger patients. Hospital stays are twice as common among older patients and average 50 percent longer, consuming a total of 38 percent of total hospital-bed days in the United States.

The inpatient hospitalization rate for older people is almost four times that of the entire population. The hospitalization of an elderly person often precipitates a series of decisions that have profound implications for the remainder of the individual's lifetime. When the hospitalization is associated with physical or mental impairment, plans must often be made for some type of long-term care. Presently many hospitals are actively involved in the provision of long-term care services (Brody and Persily, 1984). The decisions for use of these services are usually made under severe stress occasioned by injury or increasing impairment. All of the alternatives may entail difficulties or risks, furthering psychological stress. A sense of urgency typically accompanies discharge from the hospital,

and this may interfere with usual patterns of problem solving. Moreover, the extent to which the elderly patient participates in the decision may be limited by the circumstances under which the plans are made.

> After acute care, the demand is for services of a very different nature and with other objectives. The new needs are for long term, often continuous support services provided by a different cadre of personnel much of which may be provided outside the hospital. . . . The key requirements for continuity of care are to provide the right service at the right time and to assure the availability of that service. Many communities already have a substantial range of services. For the most part, however, no community has a complete set of services and few have an adequate amount of any single service. (Brody, 1984:26.34)

Studies identify the fact that many nursing home residents can perform activities of daily living without assistance, indicating that institutionalization would be unnecessary if alternative services were available in the community. Generally speaking, most elderly people prefer to live independently in the residential environment where they lived during their middle years. Although institutionalization provides physical security, it separates the elderly from a familiar world and diminishes the sense of privacy and individuality.

The array of services that are available to older people outside of institutions covers a broad range that includes health, housing and nutrition (see Figure 20.1). Perhaps no other group has received as much attention for such a broad array of social problems (i.e., nutrition, isolation, loneliness, etc.). Support services have been designed to aid the informal caregiving structure. How these services are organized and delivered result from policy and financing issues that will be

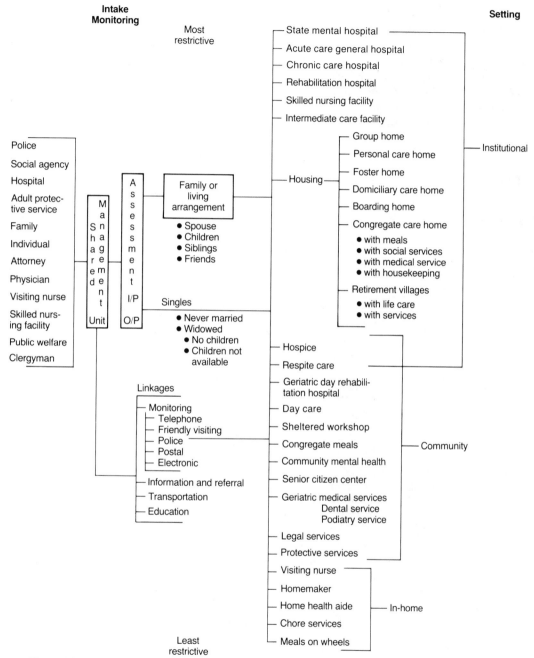

Figure 20.1 Inventory of recommended available services appropriate to a long-term care/support system. (From Brody, S.J. and Masciocchi, C. 1980. Data for long-term care planning by health systems agencies. *American Journal of Public Health* 70(11):1194–1198. Reprinted with permission.)

discussed later in this chapter. First, some existing formal services will be identified to help define the range of services available. By no means is the list all-inclusive. Only a limited number of the non-institutional services available to the elderly are presented. The service list goes from most to least restrictive.

ADULT DAY CARE

The term *day care* applies to any service provided during the day. Such services range from social to health-related care, from home care to hospital care, and include rehabilitation as well as physical and mental health care. Weiler and Rathbone-McCuan (1978) define day care as a unique service modality because it meets the long-term care needs of people while allowing for individual differences. These tailor-made services can have a therapeutic objective of prevention, rehabilitation or maintenance.

Table 20.1 depicts the services available under the rubric of day care. As can be seen, a wide range of services are offered to vari-

TABLE 20.1 Geriatric day services

Modality	Major service objective	Type of client	Service setting
Day hospital	To provide daily medical care and supervision to help the individual regain an optimal level of health following an acute illness	Individual is in active phase of recovery from an acute illness and no longer requires intense medical intervention on a periodic basis.	Extended-care facility or hospital
Social/health center	To provide health-care resources when needed by chronically impaired individuals	Individual has chronic physical illness or disabilities; condition does not require daily medical intervention but does require nursing and other health supports.	Long-term care institution of free-standing center
Psychosocial center	To provide a protective or transitional environment that assists the individual in dealing with multiple problems or daily coping	Individual has a history of psychiatric disorder; could reactivate or suffer from mental deterioration (organic or functional) that places him or her in danger if not closely supervised.	Psychiatric institution or free-standing center
Social center	To provide appropriate socialization services	Individual's social functioning has regressed to the point where overall capacity for independent functioning would not be possible without formal, organized social stimuli.	Specialized senior-citizen center

Source: Weiler, P. and Rathbone-McCuan, E. 1978. *Adult Day Care: Community Work With the Elderly*. New York: Springer Publishing Co. P.7. Reprinted with permission of the publisher.

ous types of clients in many different service settings. This type of service helps the older person placed in day care as well as those who provide care for that person by providing relief from the total responsibility for care.

HOME CARE

During the last 15 years, *home health care* has burgeoned, especially with the shortened length of hospital stays resulting from the prospective payment plan under Medicare. Home health care provides coordinated multidisciplinary services, including skilled nursing and therapeutic services as well as social casework, mental health, legal, financial and personal care, and household management assistance (Berg, Atlas and Zeiger, 1974; Bloom and Blenkner, 1970; Wahl, 1974). As Noelker and Harel (1978:37) state; "Its purpose is to aid the elderly person in the performance of activities of daily living which are essential for continued independence yet are problematic for many aged given their health problems and functional impairments."

Home health services include the in-home services of a homemaker or home health aide. Unfortunately, the eligibility requirements under Medicare limit access to this type of service. Home health care accounted for less than 1 percent of Medicare expenditures for fiscal year 1975. About 80 percent of home care patients are post-hospital referrals; the others are referred by a physician after an outpatient episode of illness or by family or friends who need help in providing care. Home health services are available from proprietary and private service organizations, although use of such organizations may be limited by availability and cost.

Historically, home health services were only available under voluntary or public auspices. Usually, this involved a visiting nurse service, public health or welfare department and, on rare occasions, an extension of hospital services. A recent study on home health care costs was conducted by the U.S. House of Representatives Subcommittee on Health and Long Term Care (Shannon, 1985). Findings showed that home health agencies were doing well financially; during 1980–1982, the average home-health-care agency's revenue increased by 52 percent. With the increased profitability of this sector of the health care market, there has been increased development of profit-making agencies that function as local franchises of national organizations.

Research findings support the fact that home health care reduces the amount of institutional care needed. Nielsen and associates (1972) report a study conducted by the Benjamin Rose Institute in which a group of elderly persons receiving home health services was compared with a group that did not receive these services. The group with home health services spent an average of eight days per person per year in institutional care; those without care spent an average of 53 days per person per year in institutional care. Generally, the provision of home health services is less costly than institutional care (Rozelle, 1980).

FOSTER CARE

Foster family care approximates the normal living environment, but with the added dimension of supervision. It allows the older person an element of privacy as well as freedom that is not possible in the larger, protected environment of the nursing home.

Adult foster care is considered among the least restrictive housing options available to help older persons stay in the community. It utilizes a private residence for the care of a non-related elderly person who is in need of supervision or assistance with the activities of daily living. Definitions of foster care vary by state. In Ohio, only homes that have SSI recipients are subject to licensing regulations that control foster care. A foster care facility in Ohio is defined as a personal residence or family home in which accommodations and personal assistance are provided to no more than five unrelated adults, at least one of whom receives SSI. It can also be a group home providing accommodations and assistance for six to 16 unrelated adults, at least one of whom receives SSI.

Although foster care offers an alternative living arrangement to elderly persons in need of care, there are certain inherent problems centering around the caregiving relationship per se, the older person's needs and the demands made on the care provider. Unlike foster care for children, where the child moves toward independence and gains the capacity to contribute to the foster family, the elderly person is viewed as only moving toward greater dependence. With this view of the older foster care recipient, many potential care providers are reluctant to offer their foster homes to the elderly. They typically view the older person's dependence as restrictive to their own family life, with the caregiving relationship ending only with the older person's death. The necessary 24-hour care provided in foster homes makes this residential service less popular than day care. Finding people who want to provide this degree of care can be difficult.

HOSPICE

Hospice is a model of care for the terminally ill that is gaining popularity in the United States. It is more than a program of medical health care for the terminally ill. The services are often directed by a physician with an interdisciplinary team to provide psychological, social and spiritual services when needed by the patient or family members 24-hours a day, seven days a week. These services can continue for family and friends after the patient's death.

PROTECTIVE SERVICES

Protective services have been defined by the U.S. Senate Special Committee on Aging (1977) as visits by the social worker with supplemental community services, such as visiting nurses, homemakers, clinical services, meals, telephone checks and transportation. A myriad of needs are addressed by protective services and include daily living, physical health, psychosocial problems, household management, housing, economic management, and legal protection (Hall and Mathiasen, 1973). These services are similar to those delivered through the social-service delivery system, although their effects may vary due to the potential for legal intervention in the form of guardianship, placement or commitment and emergency services.

Every older person who is incapacitated is not necessarily a candidate for protective services (Ferguson, 1978). The decisive factor appears to be the availability of a reliable person to help the needy individual. Thus protective services encompass a wider range of consideration than just the condition of the individual.

Characteristics of the Protective Client

A U.S. Department of Health, Education and Welfare report (1971) identifies the characteristics of protective-service clients. These clients can be found in rural as well as urban locations. Most are over 60 years of age, widowed, poor and living alone. Blenkner and colleagues (1964) further defined this group of older persons as predominantly female, white, over the age of 75 and having between 8 and 12 years of schooling. Sources of income are limited to Social Security benefits, Old Age Assistance, Aid to the Blind and aid to the permanently and totally disabled, or to a combination of Social Security and public assistance.

While older people with the above-mentioned characteristics tend to be vulnerable, they are not always receptive to institutionalization and may prefer continued residence in the midst of decay and danger. Some are homebound or bedfast, others antisocial to the point of reclusion. Still others demonstrate some memory loss or are paranoid to the degree of violence, thus presenting further danger of physical harm to themselves and others (U.S. Department of Health, Education and Welfare, 1971).

Goals of Service

There are three goals involved in the provision of protective services to older persons (Hall and Mathiasen, 1968). These are prevention, support and surrogate service.

Prevention.   Rather than merely meeting the needs of the client in crisis, protective services strive to maintain the well-being of the older person through reducing or remedying conditions that place the older person at risk, thus preventing unnecessary institutionalization.

Support.   Services provide the aid necessary for the impaired older person to maintain independence and self-direction to the maximum level possible.

Surrogate service.   This particular type of service is the dimension most frequently considered when the issue of protective services is raised. In providing surrogate services, the service provider is required to act in behalf of or assist someone to act in behalf of the impaired older persons. The task is to provide the necessary supportive services *with or without* the client's approval.

RESPITE CARE

Respite care, though not a new concept, is a recent entry in health-care options for frail older persons living in the community. It has become increasingly widespread because it provides support to family caregivers so that they can continue to provide care (Archbold, 1980; Blazer, 1978; Crossman, London and Barry, 1981; Howells, 1980). There is clear evidence that families express a need for respite care (Hagan, 1980; Upshur, 1978) and that it may prevent or delay institutionalization (Townsend and Flanagan, 1976). Even with these noted advantages, however, respite care is not widely available to families caring for disabled elders.

There are four models of respite care (Hagan, 1980; Upshur, 1978): (1) home-based; (2) group day care; (3) group residential care; and (4) residential programs providing respite care as an adjunct service (Upshur, 1983). These models are described in some detail in Table 20.2.

Home-based respite care uses trained sitters who provide the service in the client's home and are matched with the appropriate family. While it is the preferred service by most elders and their families, it is not always possible when more care is needed than a non-professional caregiver can give. Group day care has been described above. The

TABLE 20.2 Summary of major approaches to respite care

1. Home-based care	
a. Respite placement agency:	Community providers are recruited and trained to provide day or overnight care in their own home or in the client's home.
b. Funding conduit:	Agency reimburses families for respite care, which they arrange on their own.
c. Respite home or apartment:	Agency provides a homelike space for client and community provider to "live-in" while respite care is provided.
d. Individual provider:	Persons unaffiliated with an agency take clients into their own home for respite care.
2. Group day care	Groups of clients are provided daytime activities so family members are free to run errands, go to meetings, etc., for a few hours weekly.
3. Group residential care	Groups of clients are provided overnight care from one night to several weeks in a facility that provides only respite care.
4. Respite care as an adjunct service	
a. Community residences:	One or two beds are reserved for planned or emergency respite care in a home that primarily services long-term clients.
b. Residential treatment facilities:	Some beds are reserved for respite care in a program that primarily provides educational or therapeutic services to longer-term clients.
c. Nursing homes:	On a reserved or as-available basis, respite care is provided to clients with medical needs.
d. State institutions:	Respite-care clients are taken into groups of longer-term clients, or special respite beds are designated.

Source: Upshur, C. 1978. Developing respite care: A support service for families with disabled members. *Family Relations 31*: 13–20. P. 16. Copyrighted 1978 by the National Council on Family Relations, 1910 West County Road B, Suite 147, St. Paul, Minnesota 55113. Reprinted by permission.

advantage for the caregiver is the regularly scheduled relief periods.

Residential care involves a residential facility that is established to provide respite care to small groups of disabled persons (Upshur, 1983). More intensive care can be given in this setting to medically and behaviorally difficult clients. These services, while offered in a facility designed and staffed for short stays, can also be given on an adjunct basis. Group homes and nursing homes, for instance, maintain a few beds for emergency or respite care. It must be noted that these types of services can interfere with the long-term goals of the facility.

FINANCING SYSTEMS

Services that are delivered through the long-term care system are fragmented primarily due to the payment structure. The complexity of this structure is illustrated in Figure 20.2. In the United States, service eligibility is frequently determined by a means test. This can eliminate persons in need from the service-delivery system. As can be seen from Table 20.3, community-based long-term care programs comprise a heterogeneous collection of agencies, institutions and programs both private and public (Somers, 1985).

Federal Funding Source

**Service Needs of the
Chronically Impaired Elderly**

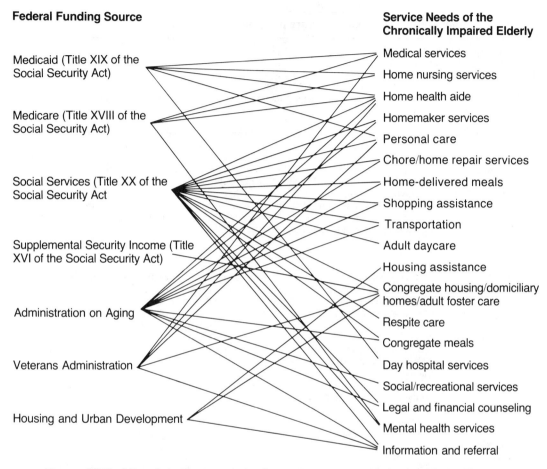

Medicaid (Title XIX of the
Social Security Act)

Medicare (Title XVIII of the
Social Security Act)

Social Services (Title XX of the
Social Security Act

Supplemental Security Income (Title
XVI of the Social Security Act)

Administration on Aging

Veterans Administration

Housing and Urban Development

Medical services

Home nursing services

Home health aide

Homemaker services

Personal care

Chore/home repair services

Home-delivered meals

Shopping assistance

Transportation

Adult daycare

Housing assistance

Congregate housing/domiciliary
homes/adult foster care

Respite care

Congregate meals

Day hospital services

Social/recreational services

Legal and financial counseling

Mental health services

Information and referral

Figure 20.2   Major federal programs funding community services for the elderly. (From U.S. General Accounting Office 1979. *Entering a Nursing Home—Costly Implications for Medicaid and the Elderly.* Report to Congress. Washington, D.C.: U.S. Government Printing Office. P. 74.)

Much of the health-related services are covered by Medicare and Medicaid dollars (see Figure 20.3). Medicare, and its recent amendments to home health care, has shown increased sensitivity in connecting acute-care services to long-term care services. This has been accomplished by having no prior hospitalization required for Part A coverage as well as having the 100 home-health-visits limit removed (Somers, 1983).

Medicaid benefits do attempt to meet the acute and long-term care needs of the elderly poor (Davis and Rowland, 1986). Most states provide optional services and offer intermediate nursing-care coverage as an alternative to skilled nursing care.

TABLE 20.3 Community-based long-term care programs

Protected living arrangements
Personal/domiciliary care facilities
Personal care facilities usually provide assistance with three or more activities of daily living (e.g., bathing, eating, toileting, transferring, ambulation), domiciliary facilities, only one or two. Must be licensed in most states. No Medicare or Medicaid reimbursements, but residents generally pay with Supplemental Security Income, supplemented by some states.
Foster homes
Private homes providing meals, housekeeping, minimum surveillance and personal care. States may use Social Security Act Title XX money for this purpose.
Congregate housing/retirement communities
Age-separated housing for the elderly, providing on-site meals and minimum surveillance. Assistance for construction available from the Department of Housing and Human Development.
Life-care (continuing-care) retirement communities
A special category of housing and retirement community that also provides lifetime nursing-home care if needed. Privately funded. Fairly expensive; generally considered beyond means of most elders but may be ideal for several millions of upper- and middle-class individuals or couples.

Home care
Home health care
Includes skilled nursing, physical, occupational and speech therapy, medical social services, home health aide assistance, and medical supplies and appliances. Generally provided or supervised by Visiting Nurse Association personnel. Medicare reimbursement limited to the "homebound" and those in need of skilled nursing care, i.e., generally post-hospital recuperation. Medicaid less restrictive in terms of physical condition but highly restrictive in terms of income eligibility. All Medicare/Medicaid services formally under physician supervision.
Personal care/homemaker/chore services
Assistance with activities of daily living intended to keep elderly at home and to avoid institutionalization. Limited reimbursement under Medicaid and Social Security Act Titles III and XX.
Home delivery/congregate meals
"Meals on wheels" or meals provided in communal locations (e.g., churches and senior-citizen centers). Funding primarily private, but some from Titles III and XX.
Adult day care
Community-based programs intended to help isolated individuals remain at home. Vary widely, although most provide lunch, social activities, dietary counseling and instruction in personal hygiene. Limited Medicaid and Titles III and XX funding.

Source: Adapted from U.S. Department of Health and Human Services. Health Care Financing Administration. 1981. *Long-Term Care: Background and Future Direction.* Washington, D.C.: U.S. Government Printing Office.

Benefits for Medicaid vary by state. Personal care services seem to be underutilized because of the problems of controlling costs. Chore services, homemaker aid and other types of social services are now covered by Medicaid under a waiver provision if the state can demonstrate that total expenditures are not increased by the use of this type of service. Unfortunately, a recent study by the U.S. General Accounting Office (1982) found that expanded home health services do not necessarily reduce nursing-home or hospital use or total service costs. Even with these changes in Medicare and Medicaid, public spending has reinforced the use of institutions for providing long-term care (Davis and Rowland, 1986).

Public expenditures for long-term care include nutritional and social services under the Older American's Act, Title XX of the Social Security Act and various long-term care programs of the Veteran's Administra-

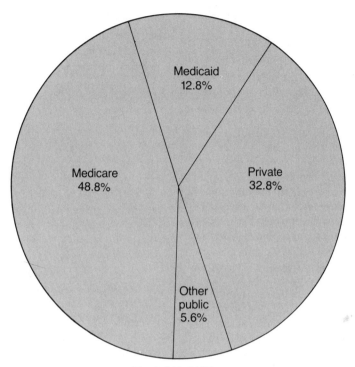

Total: $83.2 billion

Figure 20.3   Personal health care expenditures for persons 65 or older by source of payment, 1984. (Source: U.S. Senate Special Committee on Aging, 1985–1986. *Aging America: Trends and Projections.* Table 5-7A, p. 103.)

tion. Title XX of the Social Security Act provides federal block grants to the states for a broad range of social services to the poor. The Older American's Act of 1965 provides community health services.

Most people agree that reform is needed in the current system for financing health and long-term care services for the elderly. The conflict exists between the increasing need for acute and long-term health services and economic restraints (Davis and Rowland, 1986). Multiple solutions have been proposed to resolve this conflict: (1) The individual should be responsible for choosing from alternative services, (2) the service provider

should make the choice, (3) appropriate resources and financial support should be committed to meet the health-care needs of the aged population, and (4) the decision to allocate health-care resources should be shifted from the federal to the state government.

POLICY ISSUES

Policies provide the structural support for services to older people. Any change that the long-term care system will undergo will begin with those policies that shape and determine financing. This change is imminent due to rising costs, inappropriate use of nursing homes and increasing numbers of the very old (Arling and McAuley, 1984).

On policy issues and the elderly, the World Health Organization has stated,

> It is now more widely accepted that public policies should aim at maintaining elderly people at home with dignity and maximum independence and that admission to a nursing home or similar institution should be a consideration only when constant professional nursing supervision or other intensive levels of service are necessary. In this context, multidisciplinary geriatric assessment and disciplinary geriatric assessment and rehabilitation services are being seen as essential elements of any comprehensive system of service provision for frail and disabled people. It is also being recognized that these services need to be well supported by domiciliary services and institutional facilities which offer medico-social services of varying intensity (e.g. outpatient rehabilitation services, day hospital facilities, long term home nursing services and respite beds. [Nusberg, 1984])

Cost seems to be the crux of any proposal to provide long-term care services. It has been recommended that Medicare simply be extended to include the types of services described above in this chapter. Some suggest a completely separate program with different funding methods, standards of eligibility and administration. Somers (1983) has proposed a compromise of the two perspectives. She recommends that a schedule of benefits for institutional and home-based long-term care be included in Medicare. These new benefits would be paid for by transferring funds now budgeted for long-term care of the elderly and disabled under Medicaid and Title XX. All Medicare provid-

ers would be paid on a prospective rate basis with no deterrent patient-cost-sharing formulas developed by the federal government. Somers further proposes new federal-state community programs to coordinate long-term care for Medicare beneficiaries with administration at the community or county level.

Many policy proposals and initiatives contain latent functions that may be difficult to anticipate. One special concern involves the possibility that a new program or program change might act as a disincentive to continuation of family care or that a newly developed service would simply act as a substitute to family care (Gibson, 1984).

In many developed countries family resources are assessed in the decision to provide aid to an elder. In the United States, for example, SSI benefits are reduced for older persons when they live in another's home. According to Schorr (1980), this does not encourage household independence for the older person but instead makes it more difficult financially for parents and children who live together out of economic necessity.

Many countries have legal requirements that children provide care for their elderly parents. There appears to be no evidence that family solidarity is enhanced when this financial obligation occurs nor does it seem to save public monies that supposedly would have been spent on the care of the older person. Even with this evidence, Medicaid statutes have been interpreted under the Reagan administration as providing legal support to force adult relatives to pay for nursing-home care for elderly relatives.

There has been great concern that if long-term care services were increased to older people, families would not provide care or at least reduce the amount given. While there is no research to support this fear, no family policy for the aged has been developed in the United States (Kamerman, 1976). The future trend in family support of older people is somewhat unpredictable as a result of uncertain fertility rates. Changes in family composition may cause changes in the quantity and type of care that families can offer their elders.

Certain consumer incentives have been designed to aid with the payment for long-term care. Tapping home equity and employing private insurance are two approaches. Money accumulated in home equity can be released to the older person through reverse-annuity mortgages and sale-leaseback arrangements. Private insurance is being marketed to cover long-term care costs and to enable people who can afford to pay for services to have access to some sort of savings insurance mechanism (Brody and Magel, 1986); only 1 percent of the $27 billion spent on nursing-home care in the United States in 1982 was covered by private health insurance (Gibson, Waldo and Levit, 1983).

Is expansion of the long-term care component of the health-care market necessary? Perhaps an alternative strategy can be devised. Health care, whether acute or long-term, is a continuum. Resources could be dispensed more effectively along that continuum. Furthermore, the need for long-term care can be on two levels, permanent or extended care as well as temporary care. Many times the same client can require both.

"Short-term" long-term care is considered care that is offered for less than 90 days. "Stepdown" services can be used, ranging from outpatient rehabilitation to community outreach services. Brody and Magel (1986) recommend the use of stepdown services to cross traditional service lines where service settings are organized to respond to a hierarchy of patient care needs. When short-term care is used, case management is frequently called into play. According to Kemp (1981), "It is a method of providing comprehensive, unified, coordinated, and timely services to people in need of them through the efforts of a primary agent who, together with the client (and the client's family), takes responsibility for providing or procuring the services needed."

All too often, the aged person is unaware of the available services (Branch, 1978). Silverstein (1984) found that lack of knowledge about resources and services limits the search for information about what services exist. In addition, knowledge about services does not mean that people are able to see the connection to their own needs. In general, older people may not be inclined to use services or even know how to negotiate receiving services from agencies (Bild and Havighurst, 1976; Cantor, 1975; Comptroller General of the United States, 1977).

Public policy initiatives should be expanded to include: (1) Elimination of homebound requirements for Medicare and provision of additional services, such as homemakers; (2) expansion of Medicaid to a greater proportion of low-income elderly either by imposing federal standards of eligibility on states or by increasing the federal share of Medicaid payments; (3) offering of tax incentives to family members who care for impaired elders; (4) payment under public programs to family caregivers for their services; (5) public funding for supportive services; and (6) changes in Supplemental

Security Income and Food Stamp rules so that allocations under these programs would not be reduced if the elder moved in with a family member (Doty, 1986).

Other suggestions for policy changes have been taken from the results of federally supported demonstration projects that have emphasized new approaches to the provision of community care (Benjamin, 1985). Such suggestions include: (1) Coordinating and managing a mix of social services both to meet clients' needs and to reduce the rate of institutionalization; (2) providing Medicare and Medicaid coverage to pay for travel to medical services or changing the location of services to reduce costs; and (3) experimenting with reimbursement methods that test whether costs are reduced without adversely affecting patient outcomes (Hamm, Kickham and Cutler, 1983). It should be noted, however, that not all students of long-term care view federal demonstration projects in positive terms (Trager, 1981). Some argue that the money could be put to better use by funding additional services.

In some ways, fear has blocked legislation to expand non-institutional long-term care benefits along the lines described in this chapter. These fears are related to predictions about the increasing numbers of older people, the difficulty in assessing need for long-term care and the fear that with added services, families will abandon their elders.

SUMMARY

Assessing the needs of the elderly and matching services to those needs can be a difficult task. There are many service delivery barriers for older people. In general, the elderly are reluctant to admit that they have needs

and may even deny using services. Knowledge regarding service use is inconclusive. Just because services are made available to an elderly population does not mean that the services will be used. Mismatches between service and needs can occur.

A broad array of services is available to older people outside of institutions, including health, housing and nutrition. The main source of support for older persons is the family. A limited number of these non-institutional services available to the elderly are discussed in this chapter. These include adult day care, home care, foster care, hospice, protective services and respite care.

The payment structure contributes to the fragmenting of the long-term care system. Most health-related services are covered by Medicare and Medicaid dollars. And Medicaid varies from state to state. In general, these funding mechanisms reinforce the use of institutions when providing long-term care. Reform is required in the current system for financing health and long-term care services for the elderly.

Rising costs, inappropriate use of nursing homes and increasing numbers of the very old are factors likely to cause policy reform in the long-term care system. Proposals for change should avoid disincentives to continuation of family care. Substituting for family care will only increase system costs. Tapping home-equity funds and using private insurance carriers are two approaches currently under consideration.

KEY TERMS

day care
foster family care
home health care
hospice
protective services
respite care

STUDY QUESTIONS

1. Why is assessing the service needs of the elderly so difficult? List several factors that appear to be related to service use among the elderly.
2. Litwak predicts that the delivery of appropriate services to older people may require three moves. Describe these.
3. How do alternatives to institutionalization services that are delivered to the elderly differ from those that are delivered to the young? Distinguish informal from formal services.
4. Identify the following:
   a. Adult day care
   b. Home care
   c. Foster care
   d. Hospice
   e. Protective services
   f. Respite care
5. Why do many researchers argue that reform is needed in the current system of financing health and long-term care services for the elderly?
6. Why do new policy initiatives need to avoid disincentives to family caregiving? What role might home equity and private insurance play in financing long-term care?
7. List three possible policy initiatives to expand alternative long-term care services.

BIBLIOGRAPHY

Archbold, P.G. 1980. Impact of parent caring on middle-aged offspring. *Journal of Geriatric Nursing 6:* 2:78–85.

Arling, G., and McAuley, W. 1984. The family public policy of long term care. In W. Quinn and G. Hughston, eds.,*Independent Aging: Family and Social Systems Perspectives.* Rockville, Md.: Aspen Publishing.

Auerbach, M., Gordon, D., Ullman, A., and Weisel, M. 1977. Health care in a selected urban elderly population: Utilization patterns and perceived needs. *Gerontologist 17:* 341–346.

Benjamin, A. 1985. Community based long-term care. In C. Harrington, R. Newcomer, C. Estes and associates, eds., *Long Term Care of the Elderly: Public Policy Issues.* Beverly Hills, Calif.: Sage Publications.

Berg, W., Atlas, L., and Zeiger, J. 1974. Integrated homemaking services for the aged in urban neighborhoods. *Gerontologist 14:* 388–393.

Bild, B., and Havighurst, R. 1976. Senior citizens in great cities: The case of Chicago. *Gerontologist 16:* 4–88.

Blazer, D. 1978. Working with the elderly patient's family. *Geriatrics 33:* 117–118, 123.

Blenkner, M., Bloom, M., and Weber, R. 1964. *Protective services for older people: Final Report on the Planning Phase of a Research and Demonstration Project.* Cleveland, Ohio: The Benjamin Rose Institute.

Bloom, M., and Blenkner, M. 1970. Assessing functioning of older persons living in the community. *Gerontologist 10:* 31–37.

Branch, L.G., 1978. *Boston Elders.* Program Report. Boston: University of Massachusetts Center for Survey Research.

Branch, L.G., and Jette, A.M. 1982. A prospective study of long-term care institutionalization among the aged. *American Journal of Public Health 72:* 1373–1379.

Brody, E. 1981. "Women in the middle" and family help to older people. *Gerontologist 21(5):* 471–480.

Brody, S.J. 1984. Goals of geriatric care. In S. Brody and N. Persily, eds., *Hospitals and the Aged: The New Old Market.* Rockville, Md.: Aspen Publishing.

_____, and Magel, J. 1986. Long term care: The long and short of it. In C. Eisdorfer, ed., *Reforming Health Care for the Elderly: Recommendations for National Policy.* Baltimore, Md.: Johns Hopkins.

_____, and Persily, N., eds. 1984. *Hospitals and the Aged: The New Old Market.* Rockville, Md.: Aspen Publishing.

Cantor, M. 1975. Life space and the social support system of the inner city elderly of New York City. *Gerontologist 15:* 23–27.

_____. 1981. Factors associated with strain among family, friends and neighbors caring for the frail elderly. Paper presented at the Annual Scientific Meeting of the Gerontological Society of America, Toronto, Canada.

Comptroller General of the United States. 1977. *The Well-Being of Older People in Cleveland, Ohio.* Washington, D.C.: General Accounting Office.

Crossman, L., London, C., and Barry, C. 1981. Older women caring for disabled spouses: A model for supportive services. *Gerontologist* 21(5): 464–470.

Davis, K., and Rowland, D. 1986. *Medicare Policy.* Baltimore, Md.: Johns Hopkins.

Doty, P. 1986. Family care of the elderly: The role of public policy. *The Milbank Quarterly* 64(1): 34–75.

Dunkle, R., Coulton, C., Mackintosh, J., and Goode, R. 1982. The decision making process among the hospitalized elderly. *Journal of Gerontological Social Work* 4(3): 95–106.

Ferguson, E. 1978. *Protecting the Vulnerable Adult.* Ann Arbor, Mich.: Institute of Gerontology, University of Michigan.

Garitz, F., and Peth, P. 1974. An outreach program of medical care for aged highrise residents. *Gerontologist* 14: 404–407.

Gibson, M. 1984. Family support patterns, policies and programs. In C. Nusberg, ed., *Innovative Aging Programs Abroad.* Westport, Conn.: Greenwood Press.

Gibson, R., Waldo, D., and Levit, K. 1983. National health expenditures, 1982. *Health Care Financing Review* 5(1): 1–31.

Greenberg, J.N., and Genn, A. 1979. A multivariate analysis of the predictors of long-term care placement. *Home Health Care Services Quarterly* 1: 75–99.

Hagan, J. 1980. Report on respite care services in Indiana. South Bend, Ind.: Northern Indiana Health Systems Agency.

Hall, G., and Mathiasen, G. 1968. *Overcoming Barriers to Protective Services for the Aged: Report of the National Institute on Protective Services.* New York: National Council on Aging.

———. 1973. *Guide to the Development of Protective Services for Older People.* Springfield, Ill.: Charles C. Thomas.

Hamm, L.V., Kickham, T., and Cutler, D. 1983. Research, demonstrations and evaluations. In R. Vogel and H. Palmer, eds., *Long Term Care: Perspectives from Research and Demonstrations.* Washington, D.C.: Health Care Financing Administration.

Horowitz, A. 1981. Sons and daughters as caregivers to older parents: Differences in role performance and consequences. Paper pre-

sented at the Annual Scientific Meeting of the Gerontological Society of America, Toronto, Canada.

Howells, D. 1980. Reallocating institutional resources: Respite care as a supplement to family care of the elderly. Paper presented at the Annual Scientific Meeting of the Gerontological Society of America, San Diego, Calif.

Institute of Medicine. 1985. *America's Aging: Health in an Older Society.* Washington, D.C.: National Academy Press.

Johnson, C. 1983. Dyadic family relations and social supports. *Gerontologist* 23(4) 377–383.

Kahana, E. 1974. Service needs of urban aged. Paper presented at the 27th Annual Meeting of the U.S. Gerontological Society, Portland, Oregon.

Kamerman, S. 1976. Community services for the aged. *Gerontologist* 16(6): 13–18.

Kemp, B. 1981. The case management model of human service delivery. In E. Pan, T. Barker and C. Vash, eds., *Annual Review of Rehabilitation,* vol. 2. New York: Springer Publishing.

Kobrin, F. 1981. Family extension and the elderly: Economic, demographic and family cycle factors. *Journal of Gerontology* 36: 370–377.

Kronenfeld, J. 1978. Provider variables and the utlization of ambulatory care services. *Journal of Health and Social Behavior* 19: 68–76.

Libow, L. 1977. The issues in geriatric medical education and postgraduate training: Old problems in a new field. *Geriatrics* 32: 99–102.

Litman, T.J. 1971. Health care and the family: A three-generational analysis. *Medical Care 9:* 67–81.

Little, V. 1982. *Open Care for the Aging.* New York: Springer Publishing.

Litwak, E. 1965. Extended kin relations in an industrial democratic society. In E. Shanas and G. Streib, eds., *Social Structure and the Family.* Englewood Cliffs, N.J.: Prentice-Hall.

———. 1978. Agency and family linkages in providing services. In D. Thursz and J. Vigilante, eds., *Reaching People: The Structure of Neighborhood,* Vol. 3. Social Service Delivery Systems: An International Annual. Beverly Hills, Calif.: Sage.

_____ . 1985. *Helping the Elderly.* New York: Guilford Press.

McAuley, W., and Blieszner, R. 1985. Selection of long-term care arrangements by older community residents. *Gerontologist 25:* 188–193.

McCaslin, R., and Calvert, W.C. 1975. Social indicators in black and white: Some ethnic considerations in delivery of service to the elderly. *Journal of Gerontology 30:* 60–66.

McKinley, J. 1972. Some approaches and problems in the study and use of services. *Journal of Health and Social Behavior 13:* 115–152.

Moen, E. 1978. The reluctance of the elderly to accept help. *Social Problems 25:* 293–303.

Neu, C.R. 1982. Individual preferences for life and health: Misuses and possible uses. In R.L. Kane and R.A. Kane, eds., *Values and Long Term Care.* Lexington, Mass.: Lexington Books.

Nielsen, M., Blenkner, M., Bloom, M., Downs, T., and Beggs, H. 1972. Older persons after hospitalization: A controlled study of home aide service. *American Journal of Public Health 62:* 1094–1101.

Noelker, L., and Harel, Z. 1978. Aged excluded from home health care: An interorganizational solution. *Gerontologist 18:* 37–41.

Nusberg, C. 1984. *Innovative Aging Programs Abroad.* London: Greenwood Press.

Rozelle, G. 1980. If home care is effective, why is it underutilized? *Ohio Home Health Observer.*

Schorr, A. 1980. *Thy Father and Thy Mother: A Second Look at Filial Responsibility and Family Policy.* Washington, D.C.: U.S. Social Security Administration.

Shanas, E. 1979. The family as a social support system in old age. *Gerontologist 19:* 169–174.

Shannon, K. 1985. Home health care study paves way for fixed home care benefits. *Hospitals 59*(5): 12.

Silverstein, N. 1984. Informing the elderly about public services: The relationship between sources of knowledge and service utilization. *Gerontologist 24:* 37–40.

Silverstone, B. 1985. Informal social support systems for the frail elderly. In Institute of Medicine/National Research Council, ed., *America's Aging: Health in an Older Society.* Washington, D.C.: National Academy Press.

Smith, S. 1971. Reaction. In R. Atchley, ed., *Rural Environments in Aging.* Washington, D.C.: Gerontological Society.

Soldo, B.J. 1981. The living arrangements of the elderly in the near future. In S.B. Kiesler, J.N. Morgan and V.K. Oppenheimer, eds., *Aging: Social Change.* New York: Academic Press.

Somers, A.R. 1983. Medicare and long-term care. *Perspective on Aging* (March/April): 5–8.

_____ . 1985. Financing long-term care for the elderly: Institutions, incentives, issues. In Committee on an Aging Society, Institute of Medicine and the National Research Council, ed., *America's Aging: Health in an Older Society.* Washington, D.C.: National Academic Press.

Stoller, E.P. 1982. Sources of support for the elderly during illness. *Health and Social Work 7:* 111–122.

Townsend, P.W., and Flanagan, J.J. 1976. Experimental pre-admission program to encourage home care for severely and profoundly retarded children. *American Journal of Mental Deficiency 180:* 562–569.

Trager, B. 1981. In place of policy: Public adventures in non-institutional long-term care. Unpublished paper presented at the American Public Health Association Meeting, Los Angeles, November.

Troll, L., Miller, S., and Atchley, R. 1979. *Families in Later Life.* Belmont, Calif.: Wadsworth.

Upshur, C. 1978. *Final Report on Respite Care Policy Development Project.* Boston: Providers' Management, Inc.

_____ . 1983. Developing respite care: A support service for families with disabled members. *Family Relations 31:* 13–20.

U.S. Department of Health, Education and Welfare. 1971. *Report of the National Protective Services Project for Older Adults.* Washington, D.C.: U.S. Government Printing Office.

U.S. Department of Health and Human Services. Health Care Financing Administration. 1981. *Long Term Care: Background and Future Direction.* No. (HCFA) 81–20047. Washington, D.C.: U.S. Government Printing Office.

U.S. General Accounting Office. 1977. Report to the Congress on Home Health—The Need for a National Policy to Better Provide for the

Elderly. Washington, D.C.: U.S. Government Printing Office.

——————. 1982. The Elderly Should Benefit from Expanded Home Health Care but Increasing These Services Will Not Insure Cost Reductions. (Public No. GAO/IDE–83–1). Washington, D.C.: U.S. Government Printing Office.

U.S. Senate Special Committee on Aging. 1977. Protective services for the elderly: A working paper prepared for the Special Committee on Aging. Washington, D.C.: U.S. Government Printing Office.

——————. 1982. Developments in Aging, 1981, Vol. 1. Rept. 97–314, 97th Congress, 2nd Session. Washington, D.C.: U.S. Government Printing Office.

Wahl, D. 1974. Model for protective-advisory-legal service project for the elderly: A multidisciplinary approach. Paper presented at the 27th Annual Meeting of the U.S. Gerontological Society, Portland, Oregon.

Wan, T. 1982. Use of health services by the elderly in low-income communities. *Milbank Memorial Fund Quarterly 60:* 82–107.

——————, and Soifer, S. 1974. Determinants of physician utilization: A causal analysis. *Journal of Health and Social Behavior 18:* 61–70.

Ward, R. 1977. Services for older people: An integrated framework for research. *Journal of Health and Social Behavior 18:* 61–70.

Weiler, P., and Rathbone-McCuan, E. 1978. *Adult Day Care: Community Work with the Elderly.* New York: Springer Publishing.

Williams, A., Youmans, C., and Sorensen, D. 1975. *Providing Rural Public Services.* Corvallis, Ore.: Oregon State University Agricultural Experiment Station.

Youmans, E. 1974. Age group, health, and attitudes. *Gerontologist 14:* 210–214.

CHAPTER **21**

Death and Dying

Death is not a concern unique to the elderly. It is, however, an event they must inevitably face. The deaths of friends and loved ones occur more frequently for the older adult. For those of advanced old age, the loss of peers, siblings, spouse and even children may become a reality. Even when the deceased are not especially close friends or relatives, their successive demise serves as a reminder of one's own mortality. The accumulated losses, often in rapid succession, make the study of grief and bereavement a special concern for the gerontologist.

Age may be an important variable in the study of a wide array of issues related to death and dying. These issues include the relationship between age and the meaning of death, study of the grief and bereavement

process, characterizations of the dying process, decisions about where death should take place and who should decide about the access of older people to life-prolonging medical treatments. This chapter presents an overview of such issues as they pertain to the older adult.

AGING AND THE MEANING OF DEATH

The meanings that individuals give to death vary as a function of age. Nagy (1959) studied post-war Hungarian children and argued that the child's idea of death develops in three stages, each marked by a different view of death. She found that children under five did not recognize death as irreversible; they viewed it as a temporary "departure or sleep," a type of separation. Between the ages of five and nine, death was often personified and seen as a contingency. Although viewed as irreversible, it was not necessarily inevitable, at least as far as the child was concerned. Death existed but was remote. By nine or ten, the children understood death to be inevitable and final. Death was less remote, and conceived of as a part of the life cycle of all living organisms.

Some have questioned the universal application of Nagy's findings. McIntire and his colleagues (1972) found that unlike Hungarian children, American children are able to conceptualize "organic decomposition" as early as age five and in some cases as early as age three. The tendency to personify death as noted by Nagy during stage 2 is not a common finding in more recent studies (Kastenbaum, 1986). Kastenbaum considers that children since Nagy's research may have developed a "fashionably scientific look" in response to death. He notes one 7-year-old who likened death to when a computer is down. Perhaps these children's tendency to personify is masked by contemporary images and terms. Such work demonstrates the need to examine variations within cultural groups.

Bluebond-Langer (1977) summarizes research on the relationship between social class and children's views of death as follows: Children from lower socioeconomic groups are more likely to cite "violence as the general and specific cause of death," whereas middle-class children are more likely to cite "disease and old age" as the general cause, and the "arrest of vital functions" as the specific cause of death. These variations seem to reflect differences in the life experiences of the children.

Two meanings of death with particular significance for the elderly are suggested by a large body of literature: death as an organizer of time and death as loss. To both the elderly and the terminal patient, death is a clearly perceived constraint that limits the future (Kalish, 1976). Anticipating the end of one's life may bring a reorganization of time and priorities. In work done more than 20 years ago, Kastenbaum (1966) found that older persons projected themselves into a much more limited time frame than did younger persons when asked to report coming important events in their lives and the timing of these events.

Death also makes all possessions and experiences transient. For many elderly persons, the anticipation of death may generate feelings of meaninglessness. There is nothing meaningful to do because whatever is attempted will be short-lived or unfinished (Kalish, 1976). Kurt Back (1965) asked residents of rural communities in the West what they would do if they knew they were to die in 30 days. The elderly were less likely than younger respondents to indicate that their activities would change at all. A more recent study by Kalish and Reynolds (1976) supported Back's findings. Using respondents in three age groups and extending the duration to the time of death to six months instead of 30 days, more of the older group were found unwilling to change their lifestyle. Nearly three times as many older persons as younger reported that they would spend their remaining time in prayer, reading, contemplation or other activities that reflected inner life, spiritual needs or withdrawal.

Perception by the elderly of the finitude of life comes not only from within. Older persons receive many reminders of their impending death from other individuals and from social institutions. Society tends to perceive the older person as not having sufficient futurity to deserve a major investment of the resources of others.

GRIEF AND BEREAVEMENT

Bereavement refers to the state of having sustained a loss. For the elderly, losses accumulate and become very much a part of life. *Grief* is the reaction to loss. It is a necessary yet painful process that facilitates adjustment to the loss. Its course is quite variable; it may be short or long, taking months to years for the loss to be resolved and a normal life to resume. It may vary in its intensity. Reactions may include anger, guilt, anxiety and preoccupation with thoughts of the deceased, in addition to depression.

In his pioneering work, Lindemann (1944) described the physical symptoms of grief, which may include sensations of somatic distress lasting from 20 minutes to an hour. Stomach upset, shortness of breath, tightness in the throat, frequent sighing, an empty feeling in the abdomen, lack of muscular power and "subjective distress" were found to be common among the grieving. Confusion, disorganization, absentmindedness and insomnia were also expressed.

In part, the loss reaction is shaped by cultural norms and experiences. In less-developed societies with extended families, the trauma of death is only minimally disruptive. In pre-literate families, the primary relationships involving parents, children and spouses may be extended to other relatives. In this way, others may serve to "compensate" for a loss. For instance, among the Trobrianders the role of the father is assumed by the mother's brother. Such is not the case in the small, nuclear families that characterize industrialized societies. Nuclear family members are customarily left to their own resources to adjust to the psychological and social impact of loss.

In many societies, including our own, established rituals determine how life crises such as death are to be managed. Rituals have important social functions as well as utilitarian value to those who are grieving. They serve to channel and legitimize the normal expression of grief as well as to rally emotional support for the bereaved through the participation of friends and relatives. *Mourning,* the culturally patterned manner by which grief is managed, is quite variable from one society to another as well as among subcultures within our own society.

The elderly in our society are not always provided an outlet for the expression of grief. Goodstein (1984) asserts that because of their significant longevity, the elderly may be expected to "grin and bear" their losses rather than to grieve. Loss is expected with old age. When held by family, friends and practitioners, such an attitude may compel an older person to act strong, fearing that doing otherwise might label him or her as weak.

Various types of losses accumulate with age, underscoring the possibility of severe grief reactions after the loss of a spouse, relative, friend, home, employment, financial security or health as well as the loss of personal belongings such as a domestic pet (Keddie, 1977). Attachments to remaining people and objects may take on increasing value. Their loss may generate an intense response.

Symptoms of grief in the elderly may be mistaken for another set of conditions in what is referred to as a devious pattern of grief (Goodstein, 1984). The clinician may attribute these symptoms to another physical illness or to dementia. As the grief remains ignored, episodic exacerbation of the symptoms may result. Unresolved grief is one of the most frequently misdiagnosed "illnesses" in the elderly. Continued physical and emotional pain, if verbalized by the victim, may be dismissed as hypochondriasis.

Physical and emotional symptoms of grief usually subside in time, but some bereaved individuals are at increased risk for illness and possibly death (Osterweis, 1985). Existing illness may worsen and new ones may be precipitated. Frederick (1976; 1982–1983) has suggested a pathway by which illnesses might be triggered. A chain of hormonal responses to the stress of loss leads to depression of the body's immune system; if the response pattern continues, the immune suppression can lead to the development of infection and cancer. Up to about age 75, widowed men are one-and-one-half times more likely to die than are married men (Helsing and Szklo, 1981). Morbidity, hospitalization and mortality exceed expected rates in the two-year period following a loss of spouse (Greenblatt, 1978; Rowland, 1977).

A number of factors appear to exert significant influence on the resolution of grief (Lieberman, 1978; Osterweis, 1985; Osterweis, Solomon and Green, 1984). The nature of the lost relationship is important. Loss of spouse has received considerable attention. More research needs to be focused on the loss of friends, siblings and adult children. Gorer (1965) posits that the loss of a grown child would seem to be "the most distressing and long-lasting of all griefs." Besides exerting emotional trauma, the death of an adult child might leave the older person without a caregiver. Yet research on such losses is extremely limited (Levav, 1982). The intensity, duration and consequences of the grieving process can be influenced by how the death occurred, the availability of a social-support system, the occurrence of several deaths within a short period of time, the existence of illness prior to or at the time of loss and life changes necessitated by the loss.

Although it is almost always best to allow the bereaved to experience the grieving process, problems may arise if the grieving appears interminable. In old age the depression involved in bereavement may not be self-limiting (Brocklehurst and Hanley, 1976). Treatment may be necessary. Care may involve simple encouragement, personal warmth, understanding and compassion; or it may require antidepressant drug therapy or psychiatric management. Life decisions related to finances, living arrangements and personal care may have to be made by others. Counsel should be given carefully, lawfully and in cooperation with the physician and family members. No irrevocable decisions involving such important matters should be made until the main period of grieving has passed.

SUICIDE

Bereavement is a significant contributing factor to suicide, which is more frequent among the widowed. The resolution of grief goes hand in hand with the resumption and development of interpersonal relationships. The psychosocial environment of the aged widow or widower may not furnish the opportunity for the important reestablishment of old links or the building of important new ones (Bromberg and Cassel, 1983). Older persons who are married and who maintain contact with their children and other relatives are less likely to commit suicide (Robbins, West and Murphy, 1977).

The elderly are more likely than the young to complete a suicide effort (Maris, 1981). Perhaps the older person who attempts suicide is less ambivalent about doing so and more likely to use a more lethal technique.

THE DYING PROCESS

Death and the dying process itself are being looked upon more and more as the terminal phase of the life cycle. Professionals who work with the dying and those who study death and dying have attempted to understand this final stage. It is hoped that such understanding will help health-care professionals to enrich the lives of the dying and their families, and to provide personalized care for those who have been defined as terminal.

The Dying Trajectory

The Glaser-Strauss research team was the first to study and clarify the various sequences and distinctive characteristics of the terminal course. They observed the social process of dying in six medical facilities in the San Francisco area. The majority of their findings are published in two books, *Awareness of Dying* (1966) and *Time for Dying* (1968). While their research was not limited to older patients, the results of their work are relevant to the elderly dying patient.

According to Glaser and Strauss (1968), staff members working with the ill must answer two questions for themselves about every patient: Will he or she die? If so, when? These questions are important because the staff generates expectations about a patient's death and takes its treatment and other attitudinal cues from the answers that are developed.

Perceptions about the course of dying are referred to as *dying trajectories*. The nature of staff members' interactions with patients is closely related to the particular expectations they have formed about the patient's dying. This is the case regardless of whether the staff happens to be correct in its expectations. Patient expectations about their own dying trajectories are greatly affected by staff expectations as well.

In perceptions of a lingering trajectory, custodial care predominates. Aggressive treatment is rare. Health-care professionals tend not to find the support of such patients challenging or rewarding. Lower-paid staff workers may provide the majority of care for such patients (Friedman and DiMatteo, 1982).

When staff members perceive a patient as being in a lingering death trajectory, the patient may suffer a loss in his or her own perceived social worth and relinquish control over his or her care (Kastenbaum, 1986). The staff members may feel that they have done everything that is possible to care for the patient, and they may view a downhill course as inevitable. Death of one who has been on a lingering trajectory may seem appropriate to the staff workers, who rationalize that the patient's life held limited value. Intense emotional reactions at the death of such a patient may serve to confuse those who have made assumptions about the patient's limited social worth. Or stress may result when the lingering patient does not die "on schedule."

In contrast, the expected quick trajectory typically involves acute life-or-death crises. The patient's perceived social worth can influence the type of care delivered. The unexpected quick trajectory brings an unanticipated crisis that may challenge the professional caregiver's defenses regarding anxiety about death.

Dying: The Career Perspective

Julius Roth (1963:93) has written that "when people go through the same series of events, we speak of this as a career and of the sequence and timing of events as their career timetable." Roth used the institutionalized tuberculosis patient as his career model. He argued that individuals involved in a career try to define when certain salient things will happen to them, developing time norms against which to measure their individual progress. The benchmarks on this timetable are the significant events that occur in the average career (Gustafson, 1972).

Gustafson has applied Roth's notion of career timetables to the nursing-home setting. She views the last phase of life as a career that moves in a series of related and regressive stages toward death. These stages, she argues, are defined by a series of "benchmarks," which, for elderly patients, consist of the degree of deterioration indicated by their social activity, mobility and physical and mental functioning. A "successful" career in this sense consists of the slowest possible regression through one stage to another.

Gustafson identifies bargaining as an important aspect of the career timetable, although she identifies it in a way that contrasts with Roth's original model. Roth depicts the TB patient as bargaining with medical and hospital authorities to move as quickly as possible toward the goal of restored health. But Gustafson sees the elderly nursing-home patient as bargaining with God, the disease and the nursing-home staff in an attempt to slow down the movement toward death.

Using this perspective, the dying process is not conceptualized as an undifferentiated unbroken decline toward death. Rather, the dying career is viewed as consisting of a social stage and a terminal stage. In the social stage the elderly patient fights against the tendency of society (as represented by relatives, staff members, visitors and peers) to impose a premature social death. Such fighting (or bargaining) may involve holding onto status symbols that indicate the possibility of a future. An elderly woman may never read, but she indignantly demands a new pair of eyeglasses. An elderly man may not be able to walk yet demands a new walker or cane. In the terminal phase, when the signs of death are more dependable and its imminence cannot be avoided, the patient may begin bargaining directly with God or the disease in an effort to secure additional time.

According to Gustafson, a nursing-home patient's dying career can be made less difficult if the staff adopts a view of the dying process as consisting of a social stage and a terminal stage. A nursing staff with this view could try to extend the social stage as long as possible and be supportive during the terminal stage. Later in this chapter we will discuss some ways in which health professionals, family members and others can help terminal patients to achieve a successful dying career.

The Stages of Dying

The best-known conceptualization of the dying process is that proposed by Elizabeth Kubler-Ross (1969) in her landmark best seller *On Death and Dying*. In her view, various stages or emotional reactions mark an awareness of dying. The patient may experience denial, anger, bargaining, depression and acceptance. The applicability and universality of these five stages are still empirical questions. Kubler-Ross (1974:25–26) points out that patients may skip a stage, exhibit two or three simultaneously, or experience them out of order. Kalish (1976) contends that Kubler-Ross's stages are in danger of becoming self-fulfilling prophecies: "Some health caretakers have been observed trying to encourage, or even manipulate, their dying patients through Kubler-Ross's stages; patients occasionally become concerned if they are not progressing adequately" (p.38).

The first stage, denial, is most evident during the early period of awareness of impending death. It may be viewed as a coping mechanism to buffer the shock of such news; "No, not me, it cannot be true." Kubler-Ross (1969:38) offers the case of a patient who went through a long and expensive ritual to support her denial.

She was convinced that the xrays were "mixed up." She asked for reassurance that her pathology report could not possibly be back so soon and that another patient's report must be marked with her name. When none of this could be confirmed, she quickly asked to leave the hospital, looking for another physician in the vain hope "to get a better explanation for my troubles. . . ." She asked for examination and re-examination, partially knowing that the original diagnosis was correct, but also seeking further evaluations in the hope that the first conclusion was indeed in error.

When the first stage of denial cannot be maintained any longer, it is often replaced by feelings of anger or rage. The patient finally realizes that denial is fruitless, "It is me, it was not a mistake." The next question becomes, "Why me?" This stage is perhaps the most difficult for staff and family members to deal with. Anger may be displaced and projected on anyone and everyone who comes into

contact with the patient. Much of this anger is rational and should be expected. Place yourself in the terminal patient's position. You too would be angry if your life's activities had been interrupted and you could no longer enjoy life, especially if you had been kept too long in a hospital subject to unpleasant tests and treatments, and if you were constantly being reminded that you could no longer carry out your own affairs.

The third stage, bargaining, is really an attempt on the part of the patient to postpone the inevitable. As Kubler-Ross (1969:82) indicates, the terminal patient in this stage uses the same maneuvers as would a child; he or she asks to be rewarded "for good behavior." Most bargains are made with God and almost always include the wishes for removal of pain or discomfort and an extension of life. Kubler-Ross (1969:83) presents the case of a woman quite dependent on injections for painkillers. The woman had a son who was to be married, and she was sad at the prospect of being unable to attend the wedding. With great effort she was taught self-hypnosis and was able to be comfortable for several hours at a time.

She had made all sorts of promises if she could only live long enough to attend this marriage. The day preceding the wedding she left the hospital as an elegant lady. Nobody would have believed her real condition. She was "the happiest person in the whole world" and looked radiant.

Patients rarely hold up their end of the bargain. This same woman returned to the hospital and remarked, "Now don't forget, I have another son."

When the terminally ill person is unable to continue to deny the illness, when the rage and anger are dissipated, and when bargaining efforts are seen as hopeless, depression may begin. This fourth stage is characterized by feelings of loss, and two types of depression may be evident. *Reactive depression* is a result of the various other losses that accompany illness and dying. For instance, the patient may mourn the loss of a limb that has been amputated. The cancer patient may mourn the loss of her beautiful hair to radiation therapy. The second type of depression, *preparatory depression,* takes impending losses into account; that is, it prepares the individual for the loss of all love objects. It facilitates acceptance, the final stage.

Acceptance should not be mistaken for happiness or capitulation. The dying patient can accept his imminent death without joy and without giving up the life that remains for him. According to Kubler-Ross (1969:112–113), this is often a time when the dying individual will "contemplate his coming end with a certain degree of quiet expectation." This stage may represent "the final rest before the long journey."

Although many researchers and practitioners find Kubler-Ross's conceptualization of the dying process extremely valuable, others are critical (Feigenberg, 1977; Metzger, 1979; Schulz and Aderman, 1974; Shneidman, 1980). Weisman (1972), for example, rather than using the notion of "acceptance of death," encourages the concept of "appropriate death." Such a death means that the person has died in a fashion that resembles as much as possible the way that he or she wished to die. The totality of the person's life can be ignored in strict adherence to the stages of dying. The effects of age, gender, ethnic background and one's life experience have not been studied as they apply to Kubler-Ross's stage theory (Kastenbaum, 1986). Remember as well that the process of dying may be very strongly influenced by the behavior and attitudes of those persons in the dying individual's social milieu.

Kubler-Ross's work has been of tremendous value in sensitizing us to the needs and rights of the dying. Shortcomings in the application of her work or its uncritical acceptance by some should not lead to a discounting of her many useful insights or of the need for further research in this area (Kastenbaum, 1986). Kubler-Ross argued that the physician can help the patient reach a calm acceptance of death. Schulz (1978) summarizes a body of literature that finds physicians avoiding patients once they begin to die. The nature and impact of the doctor–dying patient relationship on the dying process would seem an area ripe for additional research.

THE WHERE OF DYING

Today most people die in health-care institutions of one kind or another. In hospitals, rest homes and nursing homes, the dying process has become bureaucratized and, to a great extent, depersonalized. Such institutions, while treating the terminally ill, also isolate them from the rest of society. These institutions have routinized the handling of death for their own benefit. This may reduce disturbance and disruption for the institution. Standardized procedures render death nearly invisible. Bodies may not be removed during visiting hours to protect relatives and other visitors. When death appears imminent, the patient may be moved to a private room to protect other patients.

Many people, health professionals and laypersons alike, are aware of the depersonalized treatment provided the terminally ill in our health facilities. On the basis of their study of individuals in four ethno-racial communities in Los Angeles, Kalish and Reynolds (1976) report that most people would prefer to die at home, particularly those under 40 and those over 59. Although many dying patients and their families wish for death at home, the wish is not often realized. One recent study clearly indicates that even when plans for home death have been made, they may be precluded by many factors, the most prominent of which appears to be the emotional and physical exhaustion of the family (Groth-Junker and McCusker, 1983).

New options for care of the dying are becoming available. One such option, called a *hospice,* combines the technical expertise for caring for the ill that is available in our health-care bureaucracies with the personalized attention of home care. The most widely known is St. Christopher's Hospice in London, founded by Dr. Cicily Saunders.

A hospice is not a place, but rather a concept of care that combines various elements. It emphasizes *palliative care* rather than cure. Control of pain and distressing symptoms is viewed as a treatment goal in its own right. If a patient's preoccupation with suffering is of such intensity that everything else in life is excluded, then self-control, independence, human dignity and interpersonal relations are sacrificed. Each patient is seen as a part of a family whose total well-being and life-style may be affected by the circumstance of having a terminally ill member. Caring does not stop when the patient dies but continues to help the family during bereavement. The hospice concept also views the home as a suitable domain for patient care. An interdisciplinary team involving physician, nursing staff, social worker, counselor and volunteer provides hospice care.

The first hospice in the United States became operative in 1974. Known as the Connecticut Hospice (originally Hospice,

Inc.), it provides both inpatient and home care services. Since the concept's inception, hospice programs have developed in every state in the nation. They now take several forms in their organization. Home care programs have been preferred in the United States. Connecticut Hospice began as a home-care program and later added an inpatient facility. Some hospitals are developing hospice units within their walls to deliver hospicelike care, and other separate or free-standing facilities are being developed.

In the United States, hospice has evolved from a radical alternative led by a group of idealistic professionals and volunteers to an accepted mainstream approach to terminal care (Tehan, 1985). Much of this change has been precipitated by legislation that allows terminally ill patients over the age of 65 to receive Medicare-reimbursable services from certified hospice programs.

The National Hospice Study conducted between 1980 and 1984 was spawned by a concern for the feasibility of a Medicare hospice benefit (Greer and Mor, 1985). Its results presently represent the largest collection of carefully controlled data on hospice care in the nation. In general, results of the study demonstrate that hospice care tends to be less expensive than traditional hospital care and that hospice patients spend more time at home during the course of their terminal illnesses.

Medical anthropologist Robert Buckingham and his colleagues (1976) have, through participant observation, compared the relative merits of standard hospital versus hospice care for the dying. Using an elaborate and deceptive scheme that was aided by physicians, Buckingham played the role of a cancer patient. He prepared himself in a number of ways before entering the hospital. He went on a severe six-month diet and lost

22 pounds from his already spare frame. Exposure to ultraviolet rays made it appear that he had undergone cancer radiation therapy. Puncture marks from intravenous needles on his hands and arms indicated that he had also had chemotherapy. A cooperative surgeon performed minor surgery on him in order to produce biopsy scars, indicating that exploratory surgery had been performed. Buckingham reviewed medical charts and maintained close contact with patients dying of cancer of the pancreas. He was thus able to imitate suitable behavior. A patchy beard and the results of several days of not washing completed the picture. He spent two days in the holding unit, four days on a surgical-care ward and four days on the hospice or palliative-care ward of Royal Victoria Hospital in Montreal.

Buckingham's findings lend empirical support to the assumption that the hospice system of care for the terminally ill is effective. He lists certain hospital-staff practices that were observed in the surgical-care ward that should be sources of concern in attempting to develop an optimal environment for the dying. These practices are as follows: (1) the tradition of physicians making their patient rounds in groups (this fostered social and medical discussion between the doctors but completely prevented doctor–patient communication on any but the most superficial level); (2) the lack of eye contact between staff members and patient (patients walked in the halls close to the walls, greetings were rare and staff members frequently crossed to the other side of the hall, walking by, heads averted); (3) reference to a patient by the name of his or her disease rather than by the name of the person; (4) the accentuation of negative aspects of a patient's condition; (5) the lack of affection given to the complacent patient; and (6) the discontinuity of communication among medical and nursing staff.

Staff–patient and staff–family relationships were qualitatively different on the hospice-care ward. Buckingham describes his arrival on this ward as follows:

> The initial nursing interview was conducted by a nurse who introduced herself by name, sat down so that her eyes were on a level with [the patient's] and proceeded to listen. There was no hurry, her questions flowed from [the patient's] previous answers, and there was acceptance of the expression of his concerns. She asked questions such as "What do you like to eat?" and "Is there anything special you like to do?"
>
> In the hospice care unit Buckingham observed relatives enquiring for the doctor five times. On each occasion the doctor was reached and either came or spoke to the family on the phone. . . . Families also spent much time at the bedside participating in the care of the patient. They changed the bed linen, washed and fed the patient, brought the urinal and plumped the pillows frequently. The staff encouraged the family to experience the meaning of death by allowing them to help in the care of the dying. [Buckingham, Lack, Mount, MacLean and Collins, 1976].

A greater effort is necessary to accomplish total care of the terminally ill. Four observations made by Buckingham that are often overlooked by health-care professionals may facilitate the total-care effort.

1. The sharing and help provided by other patients is a powerful social-support system for patients with terminal disease.
2. The need for the patient as a person to give and thus retain his or her individuality should be recognized.

3. The care given by families is a source of support for patients that must be recognized and emphasized.
4. The interest and care given by student nurses and volunteers is important, particularly in bringing the person out of the patient.

TERMINATION OF TREATMENT

Who Decides?

Central issues concerning who decides or exerts control in matters related to death and dying are exemplified in a series of recent court cases about the access of older people to life-prolonging medical treatments. One such case worthy of our attention here is that of Earle Spring (Kart, 1981).

Earle Spring was born in 1901. In his working years, he was a chemist and metallurgist at a tool-and-die plant in Greenfield, Massachusetts. He was an avid outdoorsman who retired in 1966. In November 1977, Mr. Spring hurt his foot, developed an infection and was hospitalized. He subsequently suffered pneumonia and then developed kidney failure and nearly died. Early in 1978 he was transferred to a hospital closer to his home, where hemodialysis treatments began. Within several weeks, Mr. Spring was returned to his home, where he received dialysis treatments three times a week on an outpatient basis at a private facility in the community.

According to the court record, Mr. Spring began to show signs of mental deterioration in conjunction with his progressive kidney failure. At home he became destructive and was unable to care for himself. After being diagnosed as having "chronic organic brain syndrome," he was admitted to a nursing home. By early 1979 his mental deterioration had continued to the point that he failed to recognize his wife and son. Yet he was ambulatory and, except for his kidney disease, in good physical condition.

On January 25, 1979, Mr. Spring's son and wife petitioned a local probate court for an order to terminate hemodialysis treatments. The medical consensus was that Mr. Spring might live for four or five weeks following the termination of these treatments. The probate judge appointed a guardian for Spring, who in this case opposed the petition. Yet in May 1979, the judge ordered the temporary guardian to "refrain from authorizing any further life-prolonging medical treatment." The guardian appealed, but after a stay of the order, the judge ruled that the attending physician, together with the wife and son, were to make the decision to continue or terminate the dialysis treatments.

The guardian appealed this decision to the Court of Appeals of Massachusetts, where it was affirmed. A further appeal was made to the Massachusetts Supreme Judicial Court, where, on May 13, 1980 (approximately one month after Earle Spring's death), it was reversed and remanded to the lower court. The Massachusetts Supreme Judicial Court acknowledged the substance of the lower court's decision yet opined that the ultimate decision-making responsibility should not have been shifted away from the probate court by delegating the decision to continue or terminate care to the physician and Mr. Spring's wife and son.

Who should decide in this matter? The court itself? The physicians? Spring's family members? What about Earle Spring himself? Let us look closely at some underlying issues in this case. A careful reading of the transcript of the probate court's hearing in the matter of

Earle Spring shows that the court found that Mr. Spring would, "if competent, choose not to receive the life-prolonging treatment." In so finding, the court followed a standard applied in another Massachusetts case, *Superintendent of Belchertown State School v. Saikewicz* (370 N.E.2d 417, 1977), and invoked the principle of *substitute judgment*.

Joseph Saikewicz was 67 years old, had a mental age of approximately three years, and had been a resident of the Belchertown State School for 48 years. He was well-nourished and ambulatory, could make his wishes known through gestures and grunts, but was suffering from leukemia. In April 1976, the superintendent of the school filed a petition in local probate court asking for the appointment of a guardian for purposes of making decisions about Saikewicz's care and treatment for the leukemia. The judge did so, and the guardian filed a report with the court stating that the illness was incurable, that the indicated treatment would cause adverse side effects and discomfort and that Saikewicz was incapable of understanding the treatment. In sum, it was the view of the guardian that the negative aspects of the treatment situation outweighed the uncertain and clearly limited extension of life that the treatment could bring; in the guardian's opinion, treating Saikewicz would not be in his "best interests."

In May 1976, the probate judge entered an order agreeing with the guardian; the Massachusetts Supreme Judicial Court concurred, and later that summer Joseph Saikewicz died without pain. It is noteworthy that in November of that year, the Supreme Judicial Court handed down a written decision in the Saikewicz case. In this the court argued that like competent persons, incompetents must also have the right to refuse medical treatment. In making this argument, the court recognized what may currently be a widely held view—that medical treatment does not always further the best interests of the patient. The central problem the court faced, however, was in deciding how to determine what is in the best interest of an incompetent person (Glantz and Swazey, 1979). The standard adopted was the substitute judgment test, which, according to the court, seeks "to determine with as much accuracy as possible the wants and needs of the individual involved."

In the case of Joseph Saikewicz, the use of the substitute judgment test would seem a "legal fiction" (Glantz and Swazey, 1979). How is it possible to know the wishes of a 67-year-old who has been severely retarded all his life? In effect the court substituted its own judgment for that of the incompetent person. Earle Spring's case is another matter, however. He was competent for the greater part of his adult life. Nevertheless how did the Spring court ascertain that "if competent, Spring would choose not to receive the life-sustaining treatment." Mr. Spring had never stated his preference regarding continuing or terminating life-sustaining medical treatment.

The probate court substituted the judgment of his wife, who indicated that on the basis of their long years of marriage, she believed "he wouldn't want to live." In doing so, the court employed a variant of the substitute judgment standard used by the Supreme Court of New Jersey in *In re Quinlan* (355 A.2d 647, 1976). Karen Quinlan was an adult woman in a persistent vegetative state from which her physicians felt she could not recover. Her father sought to be appointed her guardian so that he should have the power to authorize the discontinuance of all extraordinary medical procedures for sustaining his daughter's vital processes. The Quinlan court assumed that if Karen were competent and perceptive of her irreversible condition, "she could effectively decide upon discontinuance of the life-sustaining apparatus, even if it meant the prospect of natural death." Since the patient was not competent, the court concluded that her father and other family members, with the concurrence of a hospital ethics committee, could assert this decision for her.

This variant of the substitute-judgment test was applied by the probate court in the Spring case even though Spring's wife could offer no evidence to support her conclusion about his wishes. No evidence was put forth that might provide a basis for believing that Earle Spring would reject life-sustaining medical treatment. Nothing was made of the fact that when Spring first began hemodialysis treatments, before he was believed to be incompetent, he cooperated in taking these treatments. In fact, the court took testimony from family members that Earle Spring's activity level had fallen off considerably before the diagnosis of organic brain syndrome. He was no longer able to hunt and fish as in his younger years. This is precisely what some gerontologists argue is "supposed" to happen in old age. From this view, activity reduction in the later years is "natural," expected and even looked forward to by the aging.

The Massachusetts Supreme Judicial Court rejected the lower court's delegation of authority to withhold life-sustaining medical treatment to Earle Spring's wife, family and physicians. In effect, the higher court rejected the approach employed in the Quinlan case and reasserted the standard employed in the Saikewicz case: "When a court is properly presented with the legal question, whether treatment may be withheld, it must decide the question and not delegate it to some private person or group" (Mass., 405 N.E.2d 115, 122).

Does relevant literature provide a basis for rejecting the substitute judgment of family members for that of an incompetent OBS patient? Some would say "yes." Several recent papers suggest that great stress is felt by family members of OBS patients (Mace, Rabins and Lucas, 1980; Schneider and Garron, 1980). Mace and her colleagues report that more than 90 percent of the families they studied showed anger—at the situation, the patient, other family members or professionals—as a response to the presence of a dementia patient in the family. Other stress responses include depression, grief, conflict with family members and withdrawal from social activity. Such research suggests that family members may not be in the best position to substitute their judgment for that of an incompetent when deciding whether to continue life-sustaining medical treatment.

Some would argue that the decision whether to continue medical treatment in cases such as Spring, Saikewicz and Quinlan should be based on quality-of-life issues. Defining the issue in these terms may serve to exclude physicians, since there is nothing inherently medical about a quality-of-life decision. Rather it seems, as some have indicated, that cases that raise quality-of-life questions are the ones that need to be resolved by a court of law.

Traditionally, decisions about how long to maintain a hopeless patient have been made by the physician, sometimes in concert with family members, and less frequently with input from the dying person. Many dying patients, particularly those who are very old and extremely deteriorated, have no input whatsoever in decisions about their own death. However, there have been several recent attempts to represent the patient's wishes better in such a decision. *Living wills* are being used by some to specify the conditions under which they would prefer not to be subject to extraordinary measures to keep them alive. In September 1976, the state of California passed Assembly Bill 3060, the so-called Natural Death Act. The law authorized the withholding or withdrawal of life-sustaining procedures from adults who have a terminal condition and who have executed such a directive. Several other states have passed similar legislation.

> Death is as much a reality as birth, maturity, and old age. It is the one certainty of life. If time comes when I, _____ , can no longer take part in decisions for my own future, let this statement stand as an expression of my wishes while I am of sound mind."

These words begin the living will, a document first devised in 1969 by the Euthanasia Educational Council, now called Concern for Dying. In a majority of the states, living wills have legal standing. With one, a competent person can instruct a physician not to use heroic measures to prolong life when "there is no reasonable expectation of recovery from physical or mental disability."

Still, controversy exists over the meaning and application of the document. In particular, some argue, difficulties may arise out of uncertainties of clinical prognosis that allow for misinterpretation of the living will. Two safeguards are in order. First, discussion of the details of the living will with the physician when it is completed may lessen the chances of misinterpretation. If the physician refuses to carry out the patient's wishes, another

doctor can be found. Second, another person can be named in the will to interpret the patient's exact wishes if he or she is ever unable to express them. This provision, known as a *durable power of attorney*, is especially important should the person become incompetent. Such a designated person can then make decisions as to specific measures to be taken or not taken in the other's behalf.

Removal of Food and Fluids

As Steinbock (1983) indicates, a substantial body of legal opinion views the disconnection of all life-support apparatus from irreversibly comatose patients as morally and legally permissible. Nevertheless, many fear that such permissiveness leads to the "slippery slope" whereby the lives of all terminally ill and handicapped individuals are endangered. For example, Steinbock (1983) asks, "If it is permissible to remove a feeding tube from a permanently comatose patient, why not from a barely conscious, senile and terminal patient?"

In January, 1985, the Supreme Court of New Jersey ruled that artificial feeding, like other life-sustaining treatment, may be withheld or withdrawn from an incompetent patient if it represents a disproportionate burden and would have been refused by the patient under the circumstances. This decision was made in the case of Claire Conroy, an 84-year-old nursing-home resident who suffered irreversible physical and mental impairments. She could move to a minor extent, groan and sometimes smile in response to certain physical stimuli. She had no cognitive ability and was unaware of her surroundings.

She had been placed in a nursing home after having been declared incompetent. Eventually, she was transferred to a hospital for treatment of a gangrenous leg (a complication of her diabetes). Amputation was recommended, but Ms. Conroy's nephew and legal guardian refused consent. He maintained that she would have refused treatment. Surgery was not performed, but while she was in the hospital a nasogastric tube was inserted. Her nephew requested that its use be discontinued in the hospital and in the nursing home, where she eventually returned. On both requests, permission was denied by her attending physician.

Conroy's nephew filed suit to obtain court permission to remove her feeding tube. A lower court granted permission. The decision was appealed and reversed by the appellate court in a declaration that termination of feeding constituted homicide. Ms. Conroy died during the appeal with the nasogastric tube still in place. Her guardian carried the case to the state's supreme court.

The New Jersey supreme court ruling is consistent with that of the Barber case decided by the California Court of Appeals in 1983. In this case the cessation of intravenous feeding was equated with the removal of a respirator. The Conroy case represents the first time that a state supreme court has eliminated a distinction between artificial feeding and other artifical life supports (Nevins, 1986).

While recognizing the legal rights of all patients to self-determination, the New Jersey court imposed very strict requirements in providing previously competent patients the proxy right to refuse treatment. Through the application of a "best-interest test," the court must ascertain the patient's known or suspected personal attitude toward life-sustaining treatment and the burden of pain.

The New Jersey court feels a special duty to protect the rights of the now-incompetent nursing-home patient. It maintains that the patient's guardian, next-of-kin, the attending physician, two consulting physicians (unaffiliated with the nursing home) and the state Office of the Ombudsman for the Institutionalized Elderly must all concur in the decision to remove life-sustaining treatment. The procedural portion of the court decision has received considerable criticism on the basis that it fosters a climate of distrust, is difficult to implement and artificially distinguishes between nursing-home and hospital patients (Annas, 1985a; 1985b; Nevins, 1985; 1986; Olins, 1986).

The court does heavily involve the state *Ombudsman,* an office charged with guarding against and investigating allegations of elder abuse in conjunction with the state's Elder Abuse Statute. The Ombudsman must be notified before any such decision to terminate treatment is rendered and must consider *every* such decision as a possible case of abuse.

The court asserts that special precautions are necessary because elderly nursing-home patients present special problems; indeed, the court's holding is restricted to nursing-home patients. Reasons cited are the patient's average age, general lack of next-of-kin, the limited role of physicians in nursing homes, reports of inhuman treatment and understaffing in nursing homes, and the less urgent decisionmaking that occurs within these facilities allowing for more time to review options.

It has been held by others that nursing-home-based decisions can confound ethical considerations in a number of ways: (1) Personal autonomy may be lost because nursing-home admission might result in a new physician providing care rather than one who has previously treated the patient and is familiar with his or her wishes; (2) the patient may feel that life is diminished by virtue of entry into the nursing home; (3) the possibility of dementing illness does not allow for informed consent; and (4) the typical advanced age of the residents may influence decisions concerning the limitations of treatment (Besdine, 1983).

Annas (1985b) charges that the court's strict differentiation between nursing-home and hospital patients regarding life-sustaining treatment decisions is artificial. He states that almost all nursing-home patients will be transferred to hospitals when invasive treatment is required. He adds that if Ombudsman intervention is appropriate, it should apply in both settings. More appropriately, the Ombudsman should be available to investigate cases of "suspected" abuse. Otherwise, the Conroy approach requires that time be wasted on cases that do not need investigation. Annas also posits that the court decision may create confusion in its applicability to nursing-home residents who are temporarily hospitalized.

Changes in Medicare funding are moving patients from hospitals to nursing homes "sooner and sicker." Although differences exist, problems of the two patient populations promise to become more similar (Nevins, 1986). Nevins concludes:

> So although their rhythms may differ, the two populations and their problems are becoming more homogenous. No doubt differences exist, but to devise a totally new mechanism to resolve the same clinical issues depending on the locus of decision-making is unnecessary and unwise (Nevins, 1986:143).

The court's ruling is binding only in New Jersey. How it ultimately influences decision-making there rests largely with how the Ombudsman's office interprets and applies the court's rulings in Conroy. Although the mechanism set forth to allow incompetent patients to exercise the right to refuse treatment is cumbersome and restrictive, it stands as testimony to a sensitive concern for human dignity and patient autonomy for people of all ages.

SUMMARY

Death is not an event that is unique to the elderly, but it must inevitably be faced. The death of friends, relatives and others are more frequent occurrences for the older adult. Yet death may have different meanings for people of different ages. Two meanings with particular significance for the elderly are death as an organizer of time and death as loss.

Bereavement refers to the state of having sustained a loss, while grief is the reaction to loss. In part, the loss reaction is shaped by cultural norms and experiences. Mourning, the culturally prescribed manner in which grief is managed, is quite variable from group to group within a society as well as between societies. And a wide variety of factors appears to exert influence on the resolution of grief.

A number of conceptualizations of the dying process have been offered in attempting to understand this final stage of life. Dying has been described as a trajectory, a career and a five-stage process. It is hoped that added understanding of the dying process will allow health care professionals and family members to provide for personalized care to the dying.

Today most people die in health care institutions. One response to this practice is the development of the hospice—a new, caring community that provides medical and psychosocial care to the dying and their bereaved family members. The Earle Spring case involves the question of whether the decision to continue life-prolonging medical treatment should be in the hands of the individual, the family, the physicians or the courts. This is especially problematic in cases involving incompetent patients. The living will is a possible solution to such dilemmas in the future.

Recently the morality of withholding food and hydration in the case of severely demented or comatose elderly has been raised. Do such provisions constitute life-sustaining medical treatment? In the case of Claire Conroy, the Supreme Court of New Jersey ruled that artificial feeding, like other life-sustaining medical treatments may be withheld from an incompetent patient if it represents a disproportionate burden to others.

KEY TERMS

bereavement
durable power of attorney
dying trajectory
grief
hospice
living will
mourning
Ombudsman
palliative care
preparatory depression
reactive depression
substitute judgment

STUDY QUESTIONS

1. Explain how the meanings that individuals give to death vary as a function of age. Describe the two meanings of death found to have particular significance for the elderly.
2. Note some symptoms associated with the grieving process. Differentiate bereavement, grief and mourning.
3. Explain how the established rites and rituals of bereavement are functional to grieving individuals.
4. What factors might influence the expression of grief among the elderly? What is meant by a devious pattern of grief? Note various factors that might influence the resolution of grief.
5. Define the dying trajectory, noting its variations.
6. Discuss Gustafson's concept of dying as a career timetable. How is bargaining used to manipulate the timetable?
7. List and explain the five stages of the dying process as conceptualized by Elisabeth Kubler-Ross. What has been the reaction to the stage theory of dying?
8. Define hospice, tracing its development in the United States. Explain how a hospice provides care for the terminally ill patient and his or her family.
9. Discuss the conflicting private and public interests involved in decisions about the continuance of life-prolonging medical treatments; include the Spring and Saikewicz cases in your discussion.
10. Explain the purpose of a living will. What are the arguments against the use of these instruments?
11. Present an overview of the Claire Conroy case. What has been the reaction to the Supreme Court of New Jersey's ruling in this case?

BIBLIOGRAPHY

Annas, G. 1985a. Fashion and freedom: When artificial feeding should be withdrawn. *American Journal of Public Health 75:* 685.
————. 1985b. When procedures limit rights: From Quinlan to Conroy. *Hastings Center Report 15:* 24–26.
Back, K. 1965. Meaning of time in later life. *Journal of Genetic Psychology 109:* 9–25.
Besdine, R. 1983. Decisions to withhold treatment from nursing home residents. *Journal of the American Geriatrics Society 31:* 602.
Bluebond-Langer, M. 1977. Meanings of death to children. In H. Feifel, ed., *New Meanings of Death.* New York: McGraw-Hill.

Brocklehurst, J., and Hanley, T. 1976. *Geriatric Medicine for Students*. Edinburgh, U.K.: Churchill Livingston.

Bromberg, S., and Cassel, C. 1983. Suicide in the elderly: The limits of paternalism. *Journal of the American Geriatrics Society 31:* 698–703.

Buckingham, R., Lack, S., Mount, B., MacLean, L., and Collins, J. 1976. Living with the dying. *Canadian Medical Association Journal 115:* 1211–1215.

Feigenberg, L. 1977. *Terminalvård*. Lund, Sweden: Liber Läromedel.

Frederick, J. 1976. Grief as a disease process. *Omega 7:* 297–306.

——————. 1982–1983. The biochemistry of bereavement: Possible basis for chemotherapy. *Omega 13:* 295–304.

Friedman, H., and DiMatteo, M. 1982. Interpersonal issues in health care: Healing as an interpersonal process. In H. Friedman and M. DiMatteo, eds., *Interpersonal Issues in Health Care*. New, York: Academic Press.

Glantz, L., and Swazey, J. 1979. Decisions not to treat: The Saikewicz case and its aftermath. *Forum on Medicine 2* (January): 22–32.

Glaser, B., and Strauss, A. 1966. *Awareness of Dying*. Chicago: Aldine.

——————. 1968. *Time for Dying*. Chicago: Aldine.

Goodstein, R. 1984. Grief reactions and the elderly. *Carrier Letter 99:* 1–5.

Gorer, G. 1965. *Death, Grief and Mourning*. New York: Doubleday.

Greenblatt, J. 1978. The grieving spouse. *American Journal of Psychiatry 135:* 43–47.

Greer, D., and Mor, V. 1985. How Medicare is altering the hospice movement. *Hastings Center Report 15:* 5–9.

Groth-Junker, A., and McCusker, J. 1983. Where do elderly patients prefer to die? Place of death and patient characteristics of 100 elderly patients under the care of a home health care team. *Journal of the American Geriatrics Society 31:* 457–461.

Gustafson, E. 1972. Dying: The career of the nursing home patient. *Journal of Health and Social Behavior 13:* 226–235.

Helsing, G., and Szklo, M. 1981. Mortality after bereavement. *American Journal of Epidemiology 114:* 41–52.

Kalish, R. 1976. Death and dying in a social context. In R. Binstock and E. Shanas, eds., *Handbook of Aging and the Social Sciences*. New York: Van Nostrand Reinhold.

Kalish, R., and Reynolds, D. 1976. *Death and Ethnicity: A Psychocultural Study*. Los Angeles: University of Southern California Press.

Kart, C. 1981. In the matter of Earle Spring: Some thought on one court's approach to senility. *The Gerontologist 21:* 417–423.

Kastenbaum, R. 1966. On the meaning of time in later life. *Journal of Genetic Psychology 109:* 9–25.

——————. 1986. *Death, Society and Human Experience*. Columbus, Ohio: Charles E. Merrill.

Keddie, K. 1977. Pathological mourning after the death of a domestic pet. *British Journal of Psychiatry 139:* 21–25.

Kubler-Ross, E. 1969. *On Death and Dying*. New York: MacMillan.

——————. 1974. *Questions and Answers on Death and Dying*. New York: MacMillan.

Levav, I. 1982. Mortality and psychopathology following the death of an adult child: An epidemiological review. *Israel Journal of Psychiatry and Related Sciences 19:* 23–38.

Lieberman, S. 1978. Nineteen cases of morbid grief. *British Journal of Psychiatry 132:* 159–163.

Lindemann, E. 1944. Symptomatology and management of acute grief. *American Journal of Psychiatry 101:* 141–148.

Mace, N., Rabins, P., and Lucas, M. 1980. Areas of stress on families of dementia patients. Paper presented at the annual meeting of the Gerontological Society of America, San Diego, Calif.

Maris, R. 1981. *Pathways to Suicide*. Baltimore, Md.: Johns Hopkins.

McIntire, M., Angle, C., and Struempl, L. 1972. The concept of death in Midwestern children and youth. *American Journal of Diseases of Childhood 123:* 527–532.

Metzger, A. 1979. A Q-methodological study of the Kubler-Ross stage theory. *Omega 10:* 291–302.

Nagy, M. 1959. The child's theories concerning death. In H. Feifel, ed., *The Meaning of Death*. New York: McGraw-Hill.

Nevins, M. 1985. Big brother at the bedside. *New Jersey Medicine 82:* 950.

─────────. 1986. Analysis of the Supreme Court of New Jersey's decision in the Claire Conroy case. *Journal of the American Geriatrics Society 34:* 140–143.

Olins, N. 1986. Feeding decisions for incompetent patients. *Journal of the American Geriatrics Society 34:* 313–317.

Osterweis, M. 1985. Bereavement and the elderly. *Aging 348:* 8–13.

Osterweis, M., Solomon, F., and Green, M. 1984. *Bereavement: Reactions, Consequences and Care: A Report of the Institute of Medicine.* Washington, D.C.: National Academy Press.

Robbins, L., West, P., and Murphy, G. 1977. The high rate of suicide in older white men: A study testing ten hypotheses. *Social Psychiatry 12:* 1–20.

Roth, J. 1963. *Timetables.* Indianapolis, Ind.: Bobbs-Merrill.

Rowland, K. 1977. Environmental events predicting death for the elderly. *Psychology Bulletin 84:* 349–372.

Schneider, A., and Garron, D. 1980. Problems of families in recognizing and coping with dementing disease. Paper presented at the annual meeting of the Gerontological Society of America, San Diego, Calif.

Schulz, R. 1978. *The Psychology of Death, Dying and Bereavement.* Reading, Mass.: Addison-Wesley.

─────────, and Aderman, D. 1974. Clinical research and the stages of dying. *Omega 5:* 137–144.

Shneidman, E. 1980. *Voices of Death.* New York: Harper and Row.

Steinbock, B. 1983. The removal of Mr. Herbert's feeding tube. *Hastings Center Report 13:* 13–16.

Tehan, C. 1985. Has success spoiled hospice? *Hastings Center Report 15:* 10–13.

Weisman, A. 1972. *On Dying and Denying.* New York: Behavioral Publications.

Glossary

acetylcholine: a neurotransmitter

achalasia: failure to relax the smooth muscle of the GI tract at any juncture

achlorhydria: the absence of hydrochloric acid from the stomach juices

acoustic trauma: noise-induced hearing loss

actinic keratosis: horny growth of the skin due to exposure to the sun

activity limitations: limitations in activities of daily living, work outside the home and housekeeping

acute illness: a condition, disease or disorder that is temporary

adenomatous coli polyps: colon polyps that often become malignant

adipose: referring to fat

adverse drug reaction (ADR): any unintended or undesired effect of a drug (intentional overdose is not included in this definition)

aged families: family in which the head of household is age 65 or older

age-specific life expectancy: the average duration of life expected for an individual of a given stated age

age strata: categories used to classify people into different age groups

age stratification: a concept that divides society on the basis of age, with each age stratum having its own set of rights, obligations, and opportunities

alimentation: the process of ingesting food

aluminum hydroxide gel: a substance used in anti-acids

alveoli: the air sacs of the lungs

Alzheimer's disease: a progressively deteriorating form of senile dementia of unknown etiology involving a dimunition of intellectual capabilities, as well as memory loss, impaired judgment and personality change

amino acids: organic acids that contain an amine group (NH ^{2}) and are the hydrolysis products of proteins (e.g., lysine, tyrosine, glutamate)

amylase: an enzyme that digests starch

amyloid infiltration: an abnormal material, probably a glycoprotein, resembling starch that invades tissues during aging

amyloidosis: the accumulation of amyloid material in various body tissues

analgesics: drugs used as pain-relieving remedies (e.g., aspirin, ibuprofen, acetaminophen)

ancestry group: defined by individuals in terms of the nation or nations of family origin

anemia: a disorder in the oxygen-carrying capacity of the blood

angina pectoris: a syndrome characterized by constricting pain below the sternum

antediluvian theme: the belief that people lived much longer in the distant past

anticholinergic: a drug that blocks the passage of impulses through autonomic nerves

anticholinergic agents: drugs that antagonize the effects of parasympathetic or other cholinergic fibers (e.g., atropine, scopolamine, trihexyphenidyl)

anticoagulants: agents that prevent coagulation of the blood (e.g., warfarin, heparin)

anticonvulsants: drugs that inhibit convulsions

antidiuretic hormone: pituitary hormone that controls urine production

antihistamine: drug that counteracts the action of a histamine

antioxidant: substance that reduces the rate of cellular oxidation

antiperoxidative activities: activities that inhibit the oxidation of cell membranes

antipsychotic agents: drugs that antagonize the symptoms of psychosis—hallucinations, delusions and belligerent behavior (i.e., major tranquilizers)

antrum: cavity or chamber, especially within a bone

apatite: a series of minerals containing calcium

aphasia: the loss of the ability to express oneself by speech or writing or to comprehend spoken or written language due to injury or disease of the brain centers

appendicitis: inflammation of the appendix

argon laser photocoagulation therapy: a type of laser treatment that seeks to seal off abnormal vascular growth

arteriosclerosis: a generic term indicating a hardening or loss of elasticity of the arteries

arthritis: inflammation or degenerative joint change often characterized by stiffness, swelling and joint pain articular cartilage: cartilage that lines the joints

aspiration pneumonia: pneumonia related to the aspiration of foreign material into the lungs

asset income: income derived from money or other liquid assets

atheroma: lesion of atherosclerosis

atherosclerosis: a condition marked by lipid deposits and a thickening of the inner wall of an artery

atherosclerotic plaque: lesion of atherosclerosis

atrophic senile macular degeneration: a slowly progressing form of senile macular degeneration

atrophy: a diminution of the size of a cell, tissue or organ

attrition: wearing away

autoantibody: an antibody that attacks host tissue

average life expectancy at birth: defined as the average number of years a person born today can expect to live under current mortality conditions

bacterial deconjugation: process of breakdown of bile salts by bacteria

Bacteroides: a genus of bacteria

bacteriostatic: state of bacterial equilibrium

bacteriuria: the presence of bacteria in the urine

basal cell: the early keratinocyte present in the basal layer of the epidermis

basal cell carcinoma: the most common type of skin cancer, usually non-spreading; a pearly nodule that becomes encrusted and develops into a shallow ulcer

basal membrane: demarcates the border between the skin's epidermal and dermal layers

basal metabolism rate (BMR): energy required to maintain the body at rest

benefit periods: Hospital insurance benefits under Part A of Medicare are measured by periods of time known as benefit periods. Benefit periods begin when a patient enters the hospital and end when he or she has not been a hospital patient for 60 days

bereavement: state of having sustained a loss

beta-blockers: drugs used to counteract the effects of epinephrine (adrenaline) on the heart so as to treat symptoms of hypertension, angina or arrhythmia (e.g., propranolol, nadolol)

biochemical individuality: the concept that claims that individual biochemical requirements are very variable

biocultural: interaction between biological and cultural factors

bone formation: the addition of new bone

bone remodeling: the process by which bone material is built up and broken down

bone resorption: the dissolution of bone on the inside

Bouchard's nodes: nodules on the second joints of the fingers

calculi: stones that form in the kidney or gall bladder

cardiovascular agents: drugs that have their action on the heart or peripheral blood vessels and are used for the treatment of hypertension, angina, heart failure, cardiac arrhythmia (e.g., beta-blockers, nitroglycerin, digoxin)

carotid artery syndrome: a condition marked by transient occlusion of the major arteries supplying the brain

carpometacarpal joint: the place where the wrist bone meets the hand

cataract: an opacity of the normally transparent lens of the eye resulting in reduced visual acuity

catheter: a tube used to drain the bladder

centenarians: those who live 100 years or more

central vision: permits visual detection of detail via the function of cones within the macula or center of the retina

cerebral hemorrhage: an escape of blood from an artery into the cerebrum; a form of stroke

cerumen: ear wax

cholangitis: inflammation of the bile duct

cholecystitis: inflammation of the gallbladder

cholelithiasis: gallstones in the gallbladder

chronic bronchitis: a long-continued inflammation of the bronchial tubes characterized by a chronic cough and sputum production for a minimum of three consecutive months for at least two consecutive years

chronic illness: a condition, disease or disorder that is permanent or that will incapacitate an individual for a long period of time

cilia: hairlike cells

circuit training: a modified form of weight lifting that consists of 20 to 40 minutes of lifting relatively light weights with only short, 15-second rests between exercise sets

claudication: limping or lameness brought on by physical activity

clitoris: a small, sensitive projection at the front of the vulva that is sexually reactive

Clostridia: a genus of bacteria

cochlea: auditory receptor organ located in the inner ear housing the organ of Corti

cochlear implant: an electronic prosthetic device that utilizes a microsurgical implant to stimulate the auditory nerve

coenzyme: a small molecule that works with an enzyme to promote the enzyme's activity

cohort: term used for a group of persons born at approximately the same time; although defined broadly, no two birth cohorts can be expected to age in the same way; each has a particular history and arrives at old age with unique experiences

cohort-centric: describes the fact that people in the same place on the life-course dimension experience historical events similarly and as a result may come to see the world in a like fashion

coitus: sexual intercourse

collagen: structural protein of skin and connective tissue

collateral circulation: movement of blood by secondary vessels after obstruction of the principal vessel supplying an area

colles fracture: fracture of the distal end of the radius

colostomy: surgical removal of part of the colon

combined systolic-diastolic hypertension: elevated blood pressure equal to or greater than 160 mm Hg/ 95 mm Hg

complex carbohydrate: starch

complicated lesion: an advanced lesion of atherosclerosis associated with occlusive disease

conductive hearing loss: hearing loss resulting from the interrupted conduction of sound waves

congestive heart failure: a state of circulatory congestion produced by the impaired pumping action of the heart

coronary artery disease: occurs when arteries supplying the heart become narrowed, reducing blood flow to the heart

cor pulmonale: in pulmonary heart disease, the enlargement of the right side of the heart

cortical bone: the compact bone that makes up the shaft of the long bones giving them strength

cross-linkage: a process whereby proteins in the body bind to one another

cross-sectional research: studies based on observations representing a single point in time; studies using this research design are useful in emphasizing differences

crush fractures: fractures usually in the vertebra resulting from osteoporosis

cutaneous tumors: tumorous growth of the skin

cystitis: bacterial infection of the urinary bladder

day care: includes a wide range of services for older people who have some mental or physical impairments but can remain in the community if supportive services are provided

decub: lying down

decubitus ulcers: pressure or bed sores

degenerative joint disease: osteoarthritis

dementing illness: any disease that produces a decline in intellectual abilities of sufficient severity to interfere with social or occupational functioning (memory disorder is usually prominent)

demography: the study of the size, territorial distribution and composition of a population and the changes therein

depression: the most common functional psychiatric disorder among older people, varying in duration and degree and showing psychological as well as physiological manifestations

dermis: inner layer of the skin

detoxification process: breaking down and neutralizing toxic substances

diabetes insipidus: metabolic disorder accompanied by excess urine output without an excess of sugar

diabetes mellitus: a metabolic disorder of carbohydrate utilization

diabetic acidosis: the accumulation of ketones in the blood due to uncontrolled diabetes; can lead to coma

diabetic retinopathy: a complication of diabetes affecting the capillaries and arterioles of the retina

Diagnostic-Related Groups (DRGs): a categorization scheme for illnesses and injuries that form the basis for the prospective-payment system that fixes Medicare hospital-payment rates in advance

diastolic pressure: denotes arterial pressure while the heart is resting between beats

disengagement theory: developed by Cumming and Henry; postulates that aging involves a mutual withdrawal between the older person and society

diuretics: drugs used to promote the excretion of urine to treat symptoms of heart failure and hypertension (e.g., furosemide)

diverticula: outpouchings of the wall of an organ, especially the large intestine

dopamine: intermediate product in synthesis of norepinephrine; a neurotransmitter

dorsal kyphosis: increased curvature of the thoracic spine leading to hunchback

dorsal root ganglia: groups of spinal-nerve-cell bodies located outside the central nervous system

Dowager's hump: extreme kyphosis associated with osteoporosis

drug-drug interaction: adverse drug reaction produced when a second drug modifies the way the body handles or reacts to the first agent

duodenum: the first few inches of the small intestine

durable power of attorney: legal instrument that allows another to act on a person's behalf in light of his or her incompetence

dying trajectory: the perceived course of a patient's dying based on expectations regarding its certainty and timing

dyspareunia: painful sexual intercourse

dysuria: painful urination

edema: presence of excessive amounts of fluid in the intercellular tissue spaces

edentulism: lacking all teeth

ego integrity: key concept in Erikson's eighth age that describes a basic acceptance of one's life as appropriate and meaningful

eighth cranial nerve: auditory nerve

embolus: a clot or other foreign plug carried by the blood and blocking a vessel

emphysema: overinflation of air sacs resulting in destruction of capillary beds and shortness of breath

emulsification: the break-up of fat molecules

enabling factors: term used by Andersen to describe individual characteristics and circumstances (e.g., family income, accessibility of health service) that might hinder or accelerate use of health services

enculturation: the process of learning one's language and culture

endarterectomy: surgical removal of a thickened, atherosclerotic arterial lining

endogenously: produced internally

ensophagitis: inflammation of the esophagus

environmental discontinuity: degree of change between a new and old environment that may explain the effects observed after institutionalization

environmental docility hypothesis: "The less competent the individual, the greater the impact of environmental factors on the individual." (M. Lawton and B. Simon, 1968.)

epidermis: the outer layer of the skin

epilepsy: a chronic seizure-disorder condition characterized by paroxysmal attacks of brain dysfunction; usually associated with alteration of consciousness

erectile dysfunction: inability to maintain an erection capable of sexual activity

error catastrophe: maintains that aging results from mutations

erythrocyte sedimentation rate: test that measures abnormal concentrations of fibrinogen and serum globulins that may accompany pathology

essential hypertension: elevated blood pressure, the cause of which is unknown

estrogen-replacement therapy: medical treatment for post-menopausal osteoporosis

excessive effect: adverse drug reaction that is dose-related and predictable since symptoms are an exaggeration of the desired therapeutic effect (e.g., diarrhea with certain laxatives, hypoglycemia with antidiabetic agents, hypotension with beta-blockers)

exopthalmia: condition in which the eyeballs abnormally protrude

expressive aphasia: language deficit characterized by inability to express oneself via the spoken or written word due to damaged brain centers controlling such activity

extended care facility: long-term care facility equipped to provide skilled nursing care around the clock

exudative: pertaining to exudation, whereby fluid or debris escape from blood vessels to be deposited in or on tissues

family dependency ratio: defined in simple demographic terms (e.g., population 65–79/population 45/49), crude ratio that illustrates shifts in ratio of elderly parents to children who would support them

family life cycle: concept used by family sociologists to characterize the changes families undergo from their establishment through the post-parental stage

fat-soluble vitamins: those that are soluble in fat, such as A, D, E and K

fatty streak: earliest lesion of atherosclerosis

fertility rate: number of births that occur in a year per 1,000 women of childbearing age

fibroma: tumor consisting of connective tissue

fistula: abnormal canal, frequently in the anal region

food faddism: extreme pursuit of food-related activity

foster care: use of private residences for the care of a non-related elderly person who needs supervision or assistance with daily living activities

free radical: unstable molecules produced in the course of cellular oxidation

fund of sociability hypothesis: According to this idea, there is a certain quantity of interaction with others that people require and that they may achieve in a variety of ways, through one or two intense relationships or a larger number of less-intense relationships

gallstones: insoluble stones that form in the gallbladder

gastritis: inflammation or irritations of the stomach lining

gelling or gel phenomenon: stiffness associated with arthritis

gingivitis: inflammation of the gums

glaucoma: group of diseases characterized by increased intraocular pressure and auditory nerve damage

glomerulonephritis: inflammation of the renal glomeruli

glucose tolerance: the ability of the body to utilize sugar or carbohydrates

glycosuria: presence of sugar in the urine, often associated with diabetes

gout: painful condition associated with urate deposits in the joints

Grave's disease: diffuse hyperplasia with hypothyroidism

grief: the response to loss manifested by physical, emotional and psychological symptoms

gustatory: related to the sense of smell

hair cell: hairlike cells within the inner ear that are important in transmitting sound

heart failure: condition where the heart fails to pump blood efficiently; fluid accumulates in peripheral tissues and lungs, producing edema and shortness of breath

Heberden's nodes: small, hard nodules usually formed at the distal interphalangeal articulation of the fingers in osteoarthritis

hematuria: presence of blood in the urine

hemianopia: defective vision or blindness in half of the visual field

hemiplegia: paralysis of one side of the body

hemodialysis: the removal of waste products from the blood by mechanical means

hepatitis: inflammation of the liver

hepatobiliary: referring to the liver and gallbladder

herpes zoster: the clinical condition resulting from a recurrent episode of the varicella-zoster virus

hidden poor: those living in institutions or with relatives and not counted among the aged poor

high-density lipoprotein: transports cholesterol from cells to the liver; increased concentrations seem to protect against coronary heart disease

home health care: the provision of coordinated multidisciplinary services including skilled nursing and therapeutic services as well as social casework, mental health, legal, financial and personal care, and household management assistance

homeostasis: state of balance; a stable internal environment of the organism

hospice: program of palliative and supportive services for dying persons and their families

housing inadequacy: housing unit with deficient physical condition, overcrowding or an inability of the household to afford the unit

hyperborean theme: the belief that people live much longer in remote, faraway places

hypercalcemia: increased levels of calcium in the blood

hyperglycemia: increased blood sugar levels

hyperkinesis: abnormally increased mobility or motor function

hyperosmatic non-ketonic coma: often found in elderly diabetics, in the absence of ketosis; a result of rapid dehydration

hypertension: high arterial blood pressure

hyperthyroidism: overactivity of the thyroid gland

hypervitaminosis: excess of one or more vitamins in the body

hypochondriasis: overconcern for one's health, usually accompanied by delusions about physical dysfunction or disease

hypoglycemia: abnormally low concentration of sugar in the blood

hyponatremia: salt depletion or deficiency of sodium in the blood

hypotension: diminished blood pressure often related to postural changes from the supine to erect posture

hypothermia: low state of body temperature due to dysfunction of thermoregulation

hypothyroidism: underactivity of the thyroid gland

idiopathic: of unknown origins

idiopathic hypertension: elevated blood pressure of unknown causation

idiosynchratic reaction: adverse drug reaction that is neither dose-related nor predictable (e.g., lowered white-blood-cell count with chloramphenicol, malignant hyperthermia with anaesthetic agents)

ileum: distal portion of the small intestine

iliac crests: bony edge of the hips

immunocompetence: characterized by the ability to produce a proper immune response

in-kind income: income received indirectly or in the form of goods and services that are free or at reduced cost

insulin shock: acute hyperglycemia related to sudden lowering of blood glucose due to overdose of insulin or oral hypoglycemics

intercostal muscles: group of muscles of the thoracic cavity involved with inspiration and expiration

interiority of the personality: concept used by Neugarten (1968) to describe age-related increase in introspection, contemplation, reflection and self-evaluation as characteristic forms of mental life

interleukin-2: substance important in production and maintenance of appropriate immune reponse

intermediate nursing care: provision of health-related care and services (often in an institution) to those who need less than skilled nursing care but more than custodial care

intermittent claudication: characterized by pain, weakness and fatigue of the legs due to occlusive atherosclerotic disease

interphalangeal joints: where the finger bones meet each other

intima: innermost layer of an artery, specifically known as the tunica intima

intrinsic factor: factor present in the stomach that is necessary for the proper absorption of vitamin B12

introitus: penal entry into the vagina

in vitro: within a glass or test tube

ischemic heart disease: a functional constriction or actual obstruction of blood vessels, leading to a deficiency of blood flow to the heart muscle

islets of Langerhans: insulin-producing portion of the pancreas

isolated systolic hypertension: when systolic blood pressure is 160 + mm Hg and diastolic pressure is ≤ 90 mm Hg

jaundice: yellowing of the skin and eyes due to too much bile in the blood

keratin: insoluble protein that is the principle component of epidermis, nails, hair, bony tissues and the organic part of tooth enamel

ketones: condensation products of fat metabolism that accumulate in the blood and urine when carbohydrates are not available

ketonuria: excessive ketones in the urine

labia: outer folds of skin surrounding the vulva

lactose intolerance: inability to digest lactose due to absence of the enzyme lactase

lay-referral system: Freidson's term for describing an informal system in which medical advice and recommendations are communicated between and among individuals

L-Dopa: compound used to treat the symptoms of Parkinson's disease left ventricular hypertrophy: enlargement of the left pumping chamber of the heart

Leighton flexometer: mechanical device for measuring flexibility

lens: transparent structure of the eye through which light passes and the movement of which allows for visual focusing

leukoplakias: white thickened patches on the cheeks, gums or tongue

levodopa: drug used in the treatment of Parkinson's disease (also L-Dopa)

life review: postulated by Robert Butler to describe an almost universal tendency of older people toward self-reflection and reminiscence

lifespan: extreme limit of human longevity; age beyond which no one can expect to live

life table: shows the probability of surviving from any age to any subsequent age based on the death rates at a particular time and place

lipase: enzymes that digest fat

lipids: fats

lipofuscin: class of fatty pigments that accumulate with age

lipoprotein: fat and protein complexes that transport cholesterol via the blood

liquid assets: financial assets (e.g., stocks or bonds) easily convertible to goods, services or money

living will: instrument providing written instructions on behalf of an adult that directs the withholding or withdrawing of life-sustaining extraordinary procedures under circumstances of incurable or terminal illness

longitudinal research: studies designed to collect data at different points in time; emphasizes study of change

low-density lipoprotein: transports cholesterol from the blood stream to cells; elevated levels have been associated with increased risk of coronary heart disease

low-tension glaucoma: optic-nerve damage occurring in the absence of elevated intraocular pressure

L-Thyroxine: drug used to treat hypothyroidism

lumen: the channel within a tube or tubular organ

lymphokine: substance important in activation and maintenance of immune response

lymphomas: tumor of lymphoid tissue

macrocytic anemia: anemia characterized by abnormally large red cells

macronutrients: essential nutrients needed by the body in large amounts

macula: key focusing area of the retina

maladjustment: behavior that does not completely satisfy the individual and social needs of the person

mandible: lower jaw

mandibular dentures: lower plate of dentures

maxillary dentures: upper plate of dentures

maximum lifespan: hereditary capability of a species for survival or length of life

media: the middle layer of an artery, specifically known as the tunica media

Medicaid: a public-welfare program for indigent persons of all ages paid for with matching federal and state funds; has become the principal public mechanism for funding nursing-home care

Medicare: a federal-insurance program financing a portion of the health-care costs of persons 65 and older

megadoses: doses of a nutrient or chemical in great excess of normal requirement

melanin: pigment in the skin that determines darkness or lightness

melanocyte: cell that is responsible for the synthesis of melanin

melanoma: tumor made of melanin-pigmented cells; has a marked tendency to metastasis

menopause: cessation of menstruation between ages 40 and 55

mesenteric: referring to the fold of peritoneum that attaches the intestine to the posterior abdominal wall

metacarpophalangeal joint: place where the bones of the hand meet the fingers

metatarsophalangeal joints: place where the bones of the foot meet the toes

micronutrients: essential nutrients needed by the body in trace amounts

micturition: urination

migration: movement of populations from one geographical region to another

minimum adequate diet: lowest-cost food budget that could be devised to supply all essential nutrients using food readily purchasable in the U.S. market

moniliasis: infection of the mucous membranes caused by fungi of the genus Candida

monoamine-oxidase inhibitors: drugs that block the breakdown of monoamine neurotransmitters (dopamine and norepinephrine)

monoclonal hypothesis: theory maintaining that atherosclerotic plaque formation arises from a neoplastic transformation of arterial smooth-muscle cells

morbidity: condition of being ill; often used to refer to the rate of illness per some unit of population in a society

mortality rate: total number of deaths in a year per 1,000 individuals in the society

mourning: culturally patterned process by which grief is managed or resolved

multiple myeloma: malignant tumor of the bone marrow

multiple sclerosis: chronic disease characterized by central nervous system deterioration

mycobacterium tuberculosis: bacteria that causes tuberculosis mytotonia: a generalized muscle tension, which decreases with age

myxedema: hypothyroidism in adults

need factors: term used by Andersen to describe subjective perceptions and judgments about the seriousness of illness symptoms and the need for healthcare services

neovascular: formation of new blood vessels

nephropathy: kidney disease

nephrosclerosis: hardening and thickening of kidney tissues

neurotoxin: substance that is poisonous to nerve tissue

neurotransmitters: chemicals that promote the transmission of nerve impulses in the central and peripheral nervous systems by translating electrical to chemical energy and then back again

nocturia: the necessity to rise during the night to urinate

nodular hyperplasia: benign enlargement of the prostate

non-liquid assets: assets that are not easily convertible into cash

nucleic acids: the DNA and RNA of the cell nucleus

old-age dependency ratio: ratio of the population of those too old to work to the population of working age

old-old: those 75 years of age and older

Ombudsman: representative concerned with the maintenance and restoration of patients' rights and investigation of suspected violations thereof

organ of Corti: located within the inner ear; consists of the hair cells or hearing receptors

organic brain syndrome (OBS): constellation of psychological or behavioral signs and symptoms without reference to etiology

organic mental disorder (OMD): designates a particular organic brain syndrome that has a known or presumed cause

orgasmic phase: when muscle tension and engorgement of blood vessels peak during sexual activity

orgasmic platform: narrowing of the vaginal opening providing a tighter grip on the penis during sexual activity

ossicles: small bones

osteoarthritis: characterized by chronic breakdown of joint tissues; also known as degenerative joint disease

osteoblast: young bone-forming cell

osteoclast: cell that absorbs bone tissue

osteophyte: bony outgrowth

otitis media: inflammation or infection of the middle ear

otosclerosis: formation of spongy bone within the ear

ototoxic drugs: drugs that have a toxic effect on the eighth cranial nerve or upon hearing

overdosage: an adverse drug reaction manifested by symptoms of an excessive dose, even if that dose may be routinely prescribed and well-tolerated by many (e.g., tinnitus with aspirin, weakness with beta-blockers)

over-the-counter (OTC): medication that can be purchased in a pharmacy without a prescription (e.g., analgesics, laxatives, cold remedies)

oxalate: salt of oxalic acid

oxalic acid: chemical that tends to combine with some nutrients to produce indigestible oxalates

oxidation: the combination of substances with oxygen

Paget's disease: chronic localized bone disease of unknown origin that causes skeletal deformity, usually in those over 50

palliative: affording relief but not cure

palliative care: care directed at symptom control rather than cure

pancreatitis: inflammation of the pancreas

pancreozymin: intestinal hormone that stimulates the secretion activity of the pancreas

papillae: small nipple-shaped projections on elevations

paranoia: form of psychopathology that involves delusions, usually of a persecutory nature

parathyroid hormone: substance produced by the parathyroid glands that regulates calcium metabolism

parenteral: generally refers to medications given through a route other than the mouth

Parkinson's disease: central-nervous-system disorder characterized by muscular rigidity and rhythmic tremor

pectin: complex carbohydrate that is a component of dietary fiber

penile detumescence: subsiding of erection of penis after ejaculation

pepsinogen: substance in the stomach that is changed into pepsin by hydrochloric acid, acts in protein digestion

Peptic ulcer: ulceration of a mucous membrane caused by the action of gastric juice

periodontal disease: pathology of the gum tissue

periodontitis: inflammation of the gums

peripheral vascular disease: atherosclerotic disease of the extremities, especially the lower leg

peripheral vision: side vision

peritonitis: inflammation of the peritoneal membranes lining the abdominal cavity

pernicious anemia: megaloblastic anemia related to vitamin $B12$ deficiency or its lack of absorption

peroxidation: process of the transfer of oxidation out of the cell

pharmacodynamics: biochemical and physiological effects of drugs and their mechanisms of action

pharmacokinetics: study of the dynamics of drug absorption, transportation, metabolism and excretion

phenylbutazone: chemical used as an analgesic and antipyretic phytic acid: substance that tends to form insoluble products with nutrients

platelet: thrombocyte found in mammalian blood that is involved in the coagulation or clotting of blood

Plummer's disease: hyperthyroidism associated with simple adenoma

political economy: critical approach that allows for broadly viewing old age and the aging process within the economic and political context of the society

polyarticular: affecting many joints

polyps: tiny, fingerlike projections from a mucous surface

polyunsaturated fat: as a liquid, includes corn, soybean, safflower, sunflower and fish oils; has been associated with decreased levels of serum cholesterol

polyuria: increase in urine production

porphyria: defect in porphyrin metabolism

post-central gyrus: the convolution of the parietal lobe located between the central and post-central sulci

post-herpetic neuralgia: pain along the course of one or more nerves associated with herpes zoster

post-mitotic cells: cells that do not divide

poverty index: index developed by the Social Security Administration based on the amount of money needed to purchase a minimum adequate diet as determined by the Department of Agriculture; most frequently used measure of income adequacy

predisposing factors: term used by Andersen to describe social-structural variables (e.g., race, religion, ethnicity) as well as family attitudes and health beliefs that may affect the recognition that health services are needed

preparatory depression: depression associated with impending death

presbycusis: hearing loss that occurs with age

presbyopia: impaired vision due to farsightedness associated with aging

pressure sore: an ulceration caused by unrelieved pressure to an area

primary hypertension: elevated blood pressure with unknown cause

primary osteoarthritis: idiopathic or unknown cause

p.r.n.: abbreviation of the Latin, pro re nata, meaning to give a drug (or procedure) according to needs (e.g., sleeping pills p.r.n. insomnia; analgesics p.r.n pain)

prolongevity: the significant extension of the length of life by human action

proprietary nursing homes: old-age institutions operated for profit

prospective-payment system: Medicare-based reimbursement system that fixes in advance how much payment a hospital will receive for care provided

prostatitis: inflammation of the prostate

protective services: visits by the social worker with supplemental community services such as visiting nurses, homemakers, clinical services, meals, telephone checks and transportation

proteinuria: presence of protein in the urine

prothrombin: glycoprotein present in the plasma that is converted to thromboplastin as part of the clotting process

pruritus vulvae: itching of the vulva

ptyalin: enzyme produced by the salivary glands to digest starch

purine: colorless, crystalline substance not found in nature and important part of some uric acid compounds

pyelonephritis: bacterial infection of the kidney

pylorus: sphincter that controls the opening between the stomach and the small intestine

radioimmune assays: analysis of radioactivity

radioiodine: radioactivity of iodine

reaction time: measure of psychomotor performance affected by familiarity of task, practice at a task, task complexity and other factors

reactive depression: depression associated with the various losses that accompany illness and dying; i.e., loss of functional ability, employment, etc

receptive aphasia: language deficit characterized by an inability to understand the spoken or written word due to damage within the brain's speech center

refractory period: period after orgasm when returning to an unstimulated, deeply relaxed state

renal excretion: clearance of a drug via the kidneys

residual urine: urine retained in the bladder after urination

renal calculi: kidneystones

resorption: loss of substance through physiologic or pathologic means

respite care: temporary services that use trained sitters to provide relief for permanent caregivers of the frail elderly

response to injury hypothesis: theory that maintains that atherosclerosis is initiated as a result of injury to the inner layer of the artery

rheumatoid arthritis: a type of arthritis characterized by serious inflammation and joint destruction

rheumatoid factor: autoantibody found in the blood that might be indicative of rheumatoid arthritis.

right ventricular hypertrophy: enlargement of the right pumping chamber of the heart, characteristic of pulmonary heart disease

role loss: effect of life changes that involve loss of important social relationships and roles typical of adulthood

rugae: ridges, wrinkles or folds in mucous membranes

saturated fat: tends to be a hard fat at room temperature, found in butterfat, meat, coconut oil and certain shortenings; diets high in this substance tend to increase serum-cholesterol levels

schizophrenia: chronic psychiatric disorder manifested by psychotic thinking, withdrawal, apathy and impoverishment of human relationships

sclera: white of the eye

seborrheic keratosis: benign, non-invasive tumor of epidermal origin that appears as a thin, greasy scale

sebum: secretion of the sebaceous glands

secondary hypertension: elevated blood pressure related to a definable cause, such as previously existing kidney disease

secondary osteoarthritis: due to an injury or other stress

secondary side effect: adverse reaction that is an indirect consequence of a drug's action but is nevertheless predictable (e.g., lowered potassium with diuretics, nausea with digoxin, dry mouth with antidepressants)

selection bias: used in this context to describe those older people who may have characteristics that sensitize them to respond negatively to living in institutional settings

self-mortification: a process, associated by Erving Goffman with institutional settings, by which an individual is stripped of his or her identity

senescence: process of aging; the term used by biological gerontologists to describe all the post-maturational changes in an individual

senile macular degeneration: visual impairment as a result of damage to the macular area of the retina

senile osteopenia: loss of bone with age

senile pruritus: intense itching of the aged skin

sensorineural hearing loss: hearing loss related to disorders of the inner ear where conducted sound vibrations are transformed into electrical impulses

sensory deprivation: state of limited sensory contact and experiences

sex-ratio: the number of males for every 100 females ($\times$ 100)

shared household: two or more older people (relatives or non-family members) who share a residence

shingles: illness caused by herpes zoster virus; presents itself with intense burning pain in the dermatomes of the affected nerve roots

silent heart attack: heart attack unaccompanied by chest pain

skilled nursing care: typically offered in a specially qualified facility that has the staff and equipment necessary for providing high-level nursing care and rehabilitation services as well as other health services

skin cancer: malignant growth of skin

social security: colloquial term used to describe the Old Age Survivors, Disability, and Health Insurance (OASDHI) program administered by the federal government; best-known aspect of this program is the public-retirement-pension system, which provides income support to more than 90 percent of U.S. elderly people

Social Security Act of 1935: The original piece of legislation, put forth by an advisory committee created by President Franklin D. Roosevelt, that created the so-called social security system. It has been amended and expanded numerous times. For example, Medicare and Medicaid represent Titles XVIII and XIX of the Social Security Act

societal modernization: perspective that looks to changes in the role and status of older people as society modernizes (in general, with increasing modernization the status of older people declines)

sociocultural matrix: network of social and cultural factors

squamous cell cancer: warty nodules that ulcerate, forming an irregular ulcer with firm everted edges; found usually on exposed skin

statsis: stagnation or stoppage

status epilepticus: condition seen in epileptic patients in which one seizure closely follows another without an intervening period of alertness

status passage: process of negotiating a passage from one age-based status to another; may have both an objective and subjective reality

Streptococcus mutans: species of bacteria that may be related to dental decay

stress test: test that examines physiological reaction of an individual

stroke volume: amount of blood expelled from the heart during contraction

subcutaneous fat: fat layer beneath the skin

sublingual spider nevi: blood-vessel pattern on the underside of the tongue, weblike in appearance

substantia nigra: area of the brain that undergoes a loss of dopamine-producing cells in Parkinson's disease

substituted judgment: doctrine that seeks to protect the rights of the incompetent through the use of a surrogate decisionmaker

sunbelt: made up of those states in the South and Southwestern regions of the United States

sundowner syndrome: behavioral pattern often exhibited at night among those who have undergone a loss in sensory stimulation

superoxide dismutase: an enzyme that can scavenge free radicals

support system: system of relationships (friends, neighbors and family) in which health and social services are provided to the aged

symbolic interactionism: theoretical orientation based on the premise that people behave toward objects and others according to perceptions and meanings developed through social interaction

synovial membrane: lining of a joint cavity

systolic pressure: denotes the force exerted when the heart beats, sending blood into the arteries

tardive dyskinesia: abnormal involuntary-movement-disorder caused by chronic use of antipsychotic agents

thalamus: main relay center in the brain for sensory impulses to cerebral cortex

thermoregulation: heat regulation

thymus gland: endocrine gland located in the chest that plays an essential role in immunity; produces a hormone that directs the maturation of special immune cells

thrombus: clot that forms in and obstructs a blood vessel

thrombosis: the process of blood clot formation within the circulatory system

thyrotoxicosis: hyperactivity of the thyroid gland

tinnitus: ringing in the ears

total institution: institutional setting within which the barriers that ordinarily separate the activities of work, play, and sleep are broken down so that all these activities take place in the same setting with the same people

trabecular bone: spongy bone that makes up long-bone heads and vertebral bodies

transient ischemic shock (TIA): brief episode of circulatory deficiency to the cerebrum

trypsin: enzyme that digests protein

tympanic membrane: ear drum; separates the external and middle ear

Type I osteoporosis: early fractures characteristic of trabecular bone such as vertebrae

Type II osteoporosis: later fractures that affect cortical bone such as the hip

tyramine: organic acid contained in red wine, bleu cheese or pickled herring that can imitate the effects of monoamine neurotransmitters (dopamine and norepinephrine) in the brain; a "false neurotransmitter"

urea: the final product of the decomposition of protein in the body, and form in which nitrogen is given off

uremia: renal or kidney failure

ureolytic: pertaining to the decomposition of urea

uric acid: one of the products of protein metabolism found in the urine

urinalysis: microscopic or chemical analysis of the urine

vaginismus: involuntary spasm of the muscles surrounding the vagina that makes penetration painful or impossible

varicella-zoster virus: herpes virus that causes chickenpox and shingles

vasocongestive response: occurs when more blood flows into an organ than flows out

Veillonella: genus of bacteria

very-old: those 85 and older

vesical: small sac-like or bladderlike cavity filled with fluid

vital capacity: total inspiration capacity and expiration reserve of the lungs

vulva: external structures of the female genitalia.

water-soluble vitamins: those vitamins that are soluble in water, such as vitamin C and the B-complex

widowhood: stage of life, experienced more by aged women than aged men, defined by death of a spouse

xerosis: dry skin

young-old: those aged 55 to 74 years of age

Index